The firstwriter.com

Writers' Handbook

2023

The firstwriter.com

Writers' Handbook

2023

EDITOR

J. PAUL DYSON

Published in 2022 by JP&A Dyson
27 Old Gloucester Street, London WC1N 3AX, United Kingdom

https://www.jpandadyson.com
https://www.firstwriter.com

ISBN 978-1-909935-42-6

Foreword

The firstwriter.com Writers' Handbook returns for its 2023 edition with over 2,000 listings of literary agents, literary agencies, publishers, and magazines that have been updated in firstwriter.com's online databases between 2020 and 2022. This includes revised and updated listings from the previous edition and over 300 new entries.

Previous editions of this handbook have been bought by writers across the United States, Canada, and Europe; and ranked in the United Kingdom as the number one bestselling writing and publishing directory on Amazon. The 2023 edition continues this international outlook, giving writers all over the English-speaking world access to the global publishing markets.

Finding the information you need is made quick and easy with multiple tables, a detailed index, and unique paragraph numbers to help you get to the listings you're looking for.

The variety of tables helps you navigate the listings in different ways, and includes a Table of Authors, which lists over 4,000 authors and tells you who represents them, or who publishes them, or both.

The number of genres in the index has expanded to over 800. So, for example, while there was only one option for "Romance" in previous editions, you can now narrow this down to Historical Romance, Fantasy Romance, Supernatural / Paranormal Romance, Contemporary Romance, Diverse Romance, Erotic Romance, Feminist Romance, Christian Romance, or even Amish Romance.

The handbook also provides free online access to the entire current firstwriter.com databases, including 2,300 magazines, over 2,400 literary agents and agencies, over 2,700 book publishers that don't charge fees, and constantly updated listings of current writing competitions, with typically more than 50 added each month.

For details on how to claim your free access please see the end of this book.

Included in the subscription

A subscription to the full website is not only free with this book, but comes packed with all the following features:

Advanced search features

- Save searches and save time – set up to 15 search parameters specific to your work, save them, and then access the search results with a single click whenever you log in. You can even save multiple different searches if you have different types of work you are looking to place.
- Add personal notes to listings, visible only to you and fully searchable – helping you to organise your actions.
- Set reminders on listings to notify you when to submit your work, when to follow up, when to expect a reply, or any other custom action.
- Track which listings you've viewed and when, to help you organise your search – any listings which have changed since you last viewed them will be highlighted for your attention.

Daily email updates

As a subscriber you will be able to take advantage of our email alert service, meaning you can specify your particular interests and we'll send you automatic email updates when we change or add a listing that matches them. So if you're interested in agents dealing in romantic fiction in the United States you can have us send you emails with the latest updates about them – keeping you up to date without even having to log in.

User feedback

Our agent, publisher, and magazine databases all include a user feedback feature that allows our subscribers to leave feedback on each listing – giving you not only the chance to have your say about the markets you contact, but giving a unique authors' perspective on the listings.

Save on copyright protection fees

If you're sending your work away to publishers, competitions, or literary agents, it's vital that you first protect your copyright. As a subscriber to firstwriter.com you can do this through our site and save 10% on the copyright registration fees normally payable for protecting your work internationally through the Intellectual Property Rights Office (https://www.CopyrightRegistrationService.com).

Monthly newsletter

When you subscribe to firstwriter.com you also receive our monthly email newsletter – described by one publishing company as "the best in the business" – including articles, news, and interviews for writers. And the best part is that you can continue to receive the newsletter even after you stop your paid subscription – at no cost!

For details on how to claim your free access please see the back of this book.

Contents

Index

Free Access

Glossary of Terms

This section explains common terms used in this handbook, and in the publishing industry more generally.

Academic
Listings in this book will be marked as targeting the academic market only if they publish material of an academic nature; e.g. academic theses, scientific papers, etc. The term is not used to indicate publications that publish general material aimed at people who happen to be in academia, or who are described as academic by virtue of being educated.

Adult
In publishing, "adult" simply refers to books that are aimed at adults, as opposed to books that are aimed at children, or young adults, etc. It is not a euphemism for pornographic or erotic content. Nor does it necessarily refer to content which is unsuitable for children; it is just not targeted at them. In this book, most ordinary mainstream publishers will be described as "adult", unless their books are specifically targeted at other groups (such as children, professionals, etc.).

Advance
Advances are up-front payments made by traditional publishers to authors, which are off-set against future royalties.

Agented
An *agented* submission is one which is submitted by a literary agent. If a publisher accepts only *agented* submissions then you will need a literary agent to submit the work on your behalf.

Author bio
A brief description of you and your life – normally in relation to your writing activity, but if intended for publication (particularly in magazines) may be broader in scope. May be similar to *Curriculum Vitae* (CV) or résumé, depending on context.

Bio
See *Author bio*.

Curriculum Vitae
A brief description of you, your qualifications, and accomplishments – normally in this context in relation to writing (any previous publications, or awards, etc.), but in the case of nonfiction proposals may also include relevant experience that qualifies you to write on the subject. Commonly abbreviated to "CV". May also be referred to as a résumé. May be similar to *Author bio*, depending on context.

CV
See *Curriculum Vitae*.

International Reply Coupon
When submitting material overseas you may be required to enclose *International Reply Coupons*, which will enable the recipient to send a response and/or return your material at your cost. Not applicable/available in all countries, so check with your local Post Office for more information.

IRC
See *International Reply Coupon*.

Manuscript
Your complete piece of work – be it a novel, short story, or article, etc. – will be referred to as your manuscript. Commonly abbreviated to "ms" (singular) or "mss" (plural).

MS
See *Manuscript*.

MSS
See *Manuscript*.

Professional
Listings in this book will be marked as targeting the professional market if they publish material serving a particular profession: e.g. legal journals, medical journals, etc. The term is not used to indicate publications that publish general material aimed at a notional "professional class".

Proposal
A proposal is normally requested for nonfiction projects (where the book may not yet have been completed, or even begun). Proposals can consist of a number of components, such as an outline, table of contents, CV, marketing information, etc. but the exact requirements will vary from one publisher to another.

Query
Many agents and publishers will prefer to receive a query in the first instance, rather than your full *manuscript*. A query will typically consist of a cover letter accompanied by a *synopsis* and/or sample chapter(s). Specific requirements will vary, however, so always check on a case by case basis.

Recommendation
If an agent is only accepting approaches by recommendation this means that they will only consider your work if it comes with a recommendation from an established professional in the industry, or an existing client.

RoW
Rest of world.

SAE
See *Stamped Addressed Envelope*. Can also be referred to as SASE.

SASE
Self-Addressed Stamped Envelope. Variation of SAE. See *Stamped Addressed Envelope*.

Simultaneous submission
A simultaneous submission is one which is sent to more than one market at the same time. Normally you will be sending your work to numerous different magazines, agents, and publishers at the same time, but some demand the right to consider it exclusively – i.e. they don't accept simultaneous submissions.

Stamped Addressed Envelope
Commonly abbreviated to "SAE". Can also be referred to as Self-Addressed Stamped Envelope, or SASE. When supplying an SAE, ensure that the envelope and postage is adequate for a reply or the return of your material, as required. If you are submitting overseas, remember that postage from your own country will not be accepted, and you may need to provide an *International Reply Coupon*.

Synopsis
A short outline of your story. This should cover all the main characters and events, including the ending. It is not the kind of "teaser" found on a book's back cover. The length of synopsis required can vary, but is generally between one and three pages.

TOC

Table of Contents. These are often requested as part of nonfiction proposals.

Unagented

An unagented submission is one which is not submitted through a literary agent. If a publisher accepts unagented submissions then you can approach them directly.

Unsolicited mss

A manuscript which has not been requested. Many agents and publishers will not accept unsolicited mss, but this does not necessarily mean they are closed to approaches – many will prefer to receive a short *query* in the first instance. If they like the idea, they will request the full work, which will then be a solicited manuscript.

The Writer's Roadmap

With most objectives in life, people recognise that there is a path to follow. Whether it is career progression, developing a relationship, or chasing your dreams, we normally understand that there are foundations to lay and baby steps to take before we'll be ready for the main event.

But for some reason, with writing (perhaps because so much of the journey of a writer happens in private, behind closed doors), people often overlook the process involved. They often have a plan of action which runs something like this:

1. Write novel.
2. Get novel published.

This is a bit like having a plan for success in tennis which runs:

1. Buy tennis racket.
2. Win Wimbledon.

It misses out all the practice that is going to be required; the competing in the minor competitions and the learning of the craft that will be needed in order to succeed in the major events; the time that will need to be spent gaining reputation and experience.

In this roadmap we'll be laying out what we think is the best path to follow to try and give yourself the best shot of success in the world of writing. You don't necessarily have to jump through all the hoops, and there will always be people who, like Pop Idol or reality TV contestants, get a lucky break that propels them to stardom without laying any of the foundations laid out below, but the aim here is to limit your reliance on luck and maximise your ability to shape your destiny yourself.

1: Write short material

Writers will very often start off by writing a novel. We would advise strongly against this. It's like leaving school one day and applying for a job as a CEO of an international corporation the next. Novels are the big league. They are expensive to produce, market, and distribute. They require significant investment and pose a significant financial risk to publishers. They are not a good place for new writers to try and cut their teeth. If you've already written your novel that's great – it's great experience and you'll have learned a lot – but we'd recommend shelving it for now (you can always come back to it later) and getting stuck into writing some short form material, such as poetry and short fiction.

This is what novelist George R. R. Martin, author of *A Game of Thrones*, has to say on the subject:

> "I would also suggest that any aspiring writer begin with short stories. These days, I meet far too many young writers who try to start off with a novel right off, or a trilogy, or even a nine-book series. That's like starting in at rock climbing by tackling Mt Everest. Short stories help you learn your craft."

You will find that writing short material will improve your writing no end. Writing short fiction allows you to play with lots of different stories and characters very quickly. Because you will probably only spend a few days on any given story you will quickly gain a lot of experience with plotting stories and will learn a lot about what works, what doesn't work, and what you personally are good at. When you write a novel, by contrast, you may spend years on a single story and one set of characters, making this learning process much slower.

Your writing will also be improved by the need to stick to a word limit. Writers who start their career by writing a novel often produce huge epics, the word counts of which they wear as a badge of honour, as if they demonstrate their commitment to and enthusiasm for writing. What they actually demonstrate is a naivety about the realities of getting published. The odds are already stacked against new writers getting a novel published, because of the cost and financial risk of publishing a novel. The bigger the novel, the more it will cost to print, warehouse, and distribute. Publishers will not look at a large word count and be impressed – they will be terrified. The longer the novel, the less chance it has of getting published.

A lengthy first novel also suggests that the writer has yet to learn one of the most critical skills a writer must possess to succeed: brevity. By writing short stories that fit the limits imposed by competitions and magazines you will learn this critical skill. You will learn to remove unnecessary words and passages, and you will find that your writing becomes leaner, more engaging, and more exciting as a result. Lengthy first novels are often rambling and sometimes boring – but once you've been forced to learn how to "trim the fat" by writing short stories, the good habits you've got into will transfer across when you start writing long form works, allowing you to write novels that are pacier and better to read. They will stand a better chance of publication not just because they are shorter and cheaper to produce, but they are also likely to be better written.

2: Get a professional critique

It's a good idea to get some professional feedback on your work at some point, and it's probably better to do this sooner, rather than later. There's no point spending a long time doing something that doesn't quite work if a little advice early on could have got you on the right track sooner. It's also a lot cheaper to get a short story critiqued than a whole novel, and if you can learn the necessary lessons now it will both minimise the cost and maximise the benefit of the advice.

Should you protect the copyright of short works before showing them to anyone?

This is a matter of personal preference. We'd suggest that it certainly isn't as important to register short works as full novels, as your short works are unlikely to be of much financial value to you. Having said that, films do sometimes get made which are based on short stories, in which case you'd want to have all your rights in order. If you do choose to register your short works this can be done for a relatively small amount online at https://www.copyrightregistrationservice.com/register.

3: Submit to competitions and magazines, and build a list of writing credits

Once you have got some short works that you are happy with you can start submitting them to competitions and small magazines. You can search for competitions at https://www.firstwriter.com/competitions and magazines at https://www.firstwriter.com/magazines. Prize money may not be huge, and you probably won't be paid for having your work appear in the kind of small literary magazines you will probably be approaching at first, but the objective here is to build up a list of writing credits to give you more credibility when approaching agents and publishers. You'll be much more likely to grab their attention if you can reel off a list of places where you have already been published, or prizes you have won.

4: Finish your novel and protect your copyright

Okay – so you've built up a list of writing credits, and you've decided it's time to either write a novel, or go back to the one you had already started (in which case you'll probably find yourself cutting out large chunks and making it a lot shorter!). Once you've got your novel to the point where you're happy to start submitting it for publication you should get it registered for copyright. Unlike the registration of short works, which we think is a matter of personal preference, we'd definitely recommend registering a novel, and doing so before you show it to anybody. That *includes* family and friends. Don't worry that you might want to change it – as long as you don't rewrite it to the point where it's not recognisable it will still be protected – the important thing is to get it registered without delay. You can protect it online at https://www.copyrightregistrationservice.com/register.

If you've already shown it to other people then just register it as soon as you can. Proving a claim to copyright is all about proving you had a copy of the work before anyone else, so time is of the essence.

5: Editing

These days, agents and publishers increasingly seem to expect manuscripts to have been professionally edited before being submitted to them – and no, getting your husband / wife / friend / relative to do it doesn't count. Ideally, you should have the whole manuscript professionally edited, but this can be expensive. Since most agents and publishers aren't going to want to see the whole manuscript in the first instance you can probably get away with just having the first three chapters edited. It may also be worth having your query letter and synopsis edited at the same time.

6: Submit to literary agents

There will be many publishers out there who will accept your submission directly, and on the face of it that might seem like a good idea, since you won't have to pay an agent 15% of your earnings.

However, all the biggest publishers are generally closed to direct submissions from authors, meaning that if you want the chance of getting a top publisher you're going to need a literary agent. You'll also probably find that their 15% fee is more than offset by the higher earnings you'll be likely to achieve.

To search for literary agents go to https://www.firstwriter.com/Agents. Start by being as specific in your search as possible. So if you've written a historical romance select "Fiction", "Romance", and "Historical". Once you've approached all the agents that specifically mention all three elements broaden your search to just "Fiction" and "Romance". As long as the new results don't specifically say they don't handle historical romance, these are still valid markets to approach. Finally, search for just "Fiction", as there are many agents who are willing to consider all kinds of fiction but don't specifically mention romance or historical.

Don't limit your approaches to just agents in your own country. With more and more agents accepting electronic queries it's now as easy to approach agents in other countries as in your own, and if you're ignoring either London or New York (the two main centres of English language publishing) you're cutting your chances of success in two.

7: Submit directly to publishers

Once you're certain that you've exhausted all potential agents for your work, you can start looking for publishers to submit your work directly to. You can search for publishers at https://www.firstwriter.com/publishers. Apply the same filtering as when you were searching for agents: start specific and gradually broaden, until you've exhausted all possibilities.

8: Self-publishing

In the past, once you got to the point where you'd submitted to all the publishers and agents who might be interested in your book, it would be time to pack away the manuscript in the attic, chalk it up to experience, and start writing another. However, these days writers have the option to take their book directly to market by publishing it themselves.

Before you decide to switch to self-publishing you must be sure that you've exhausted all traditional publishing possibilities – because once you've self-published your book you're unlikely to be able to submit it to agents and publishers. It will probably take a few years of exploring the world of traditional publishing to reach this point, but if you do then you've nothing to lose by giving self-publishing a shot. See our guide to self-publishing for details on how to proceed.

Why Choose Traditional Publishing

When **firstwriter.com** first started, back in 2001, there were only two games in town when it came to getting your book published: traditional publishing, and vanity publishing – and which you should pick was a no-brainer. Vanity publishing was little more than a scam that would leave you with an empty bank account and a house full of unsold books. If you were serious about being a writer, you had to follow the traditional publishing path.

Since then, there has been a self-publishing revolution, with new technologies and new printing methods giving writers a genuine opportunity to get their books into the market by themselves. So, is there still a reason for writers to choose traditional publishing?

The benefits of traditional publishing

Despite the allure and apparent ease of self-publishing, the traditional path still offers you the best chance of making a success of being a writer. There are rare cases where self-published writers make staggering fortunes and become internationally renowned on the back of their self-published books, but these cases are few and far between, and a tiny drop in the rapidly expanding ocean of self-published works. The vast majority of successful books – and the vast majority of successful writers – have their homes firmly in the established publishing houses. Even those self-published authors who find success usually end up moving to a traditional publisher in the end.

This is because the traditional publishers have the systems, the market presence, and the financial clout to *make* a book a bestseller. While successful self-published authors often owe their success in no small part to a decent dose of luck (a social media comment that goes viral; the right mention on the right media outlet at the right time), traditional publishers are in the business of engineering that success. They might not always succeed, but they have the marketing budgets and the distribution channels in place to give themselves, and the book they are promoting, the best possible chance.

And it's not just the marketing and the distribution. Getting signed with a traditional publisher brings a whole team of people with a wealth of expertise that will all work towards the success of the book. It will provide you with an editor who may have experience of working on previous bestsellers, who will not only help you get rid of mistakes in your work but may also help you refine it into a better book. They will help make sure that the quality of your content is good enough to make it in the marketplace.

The publishers will source a professional cover designer who will make your book look the part on the shelves and on the pages of the bookselling websites. They will have accountants who will handle the technicalities of tax regimes both home and abroad. They will have overseas contacts for establishing foreign publishing rights; translations; etc. They may even have contacts in the film industry, should there be a prospect of a movie adaptation. They will have experts working on every aspect of your book, right down to the printing and the warehousing and the shipping of the physical products. They will have people to manage the ebook conversion and the electronic distribution. As an author, you don't need to worry about any of this.

This means you get more time to simply be a writer. You may have to go on book tours, but even these will be organised for you by PR experts, who will also be handling all the press releases, etc.

And then there's the advances. Advances are up-front payments made by traditional publishers to authors, which are off-set against future royalties. So, an author might receive a $5,000 advance before their book is published. When the royalties start coming in, the publisher keeps the first $5,000 to off-set the advance. The good news for the author is that if the book flops and doesn't make $5,000 in royalties they still get to keep the full advance. In an uncertain profession, the security of an advance can be invaluable for an author – and of course it's not something available to self-published authors.

The drawbacks of traditional publishing

The main downside of traditional publishing is just that it's so hard to get into. If you choose to self-publish then – provided you have enough perseverance, the right help and advice, and perhaps a little bit of money – you are guaranteed to succeed and see your book in print and for sale. With traditional publishing, the cold hard fact is that most people who try will not succeed.

And for many of those people who fail it may not even be their fault. That aspect of traditional publishing which can bring so many benefits as compared to self-publishing – that of being part of a team – can also be part of its biggest drawback. It means that you have to get other people to buy into your book. It means that you have to rely on other people being competent enough to spot a bestseller. Many failed to spot the potential of the Harry Potter books. How many potential bestsellers never make it into print just because none of the professionals at the publishers' gates manage to recognise their potential?

So if you choose traditional publishing your destiny is not in your own hands – and for some writers the lack of exclusive control can also be a problem. Sometimes writers get defensive when editors try to tinker with their work, or annoyed when cover artists don't realise their vision the way they expect. But this is hardly a fair criticism of traditional publishing, as most writers (particularly when they are starting out) will benefit from advice from experienced professionals in the field, and will often only be shooting themselves in the foot if they insist on ignoring it.

The final main drawback with traditional publishing is that less of the sale price of each copy makes it to the writer. A typical royalty contract will give the writer 15%. With a self-published book, the author can expect to receive much more. So, all other things being equal, the self-published route can be more profitable – but, of course, all things are not equal. If self-publishing means lower sales (as is likely), then you will probably make less money overall. Remember, it's better to have 15% of something than 50% of nothing.

Conclusion

In conclusion, our advice to writers would be to aim for traditional publishing first. It might be a long shot, but if it works then you stand a much better chance of being successful. If you don't manage to get signed by an agent or a publisher then you still have the option of self-publishing, but make sure you don't get tempted to resort to self-publishing too soon – most agents and publishers won't consider self-published works, so this is a one-way street. Once you've self-published your work, you probably won't be able to change your mind and go back to the traditional publishers with your book unless it becomes a huge hit without them. It's therefore important that you exhaust all your traditional publishing options before making the leap to self-publishing. Be prepared for this to take perhaps a few years (lots of agents and publishers can take six months just to respond), and make sure you've submitted to everyone you can on *both* sides of the Atlantic (publishing is a global game these days, and you need to concentrate on the two main centres of English-language publishing (New York and London) equally) before you make the decision to self-publish instead.

Formatting Your Manuscript

Before submitting a manuscript to an agent, magazine, or publisher, it's important that you get the formatting right. There are industry norms covering everything from the size of your margins to the font you choose – get them wrong and you'll be marking yourself out as an amateur. Get them right, and agents and editors will be far more likely to take you seriously.

Fonts

Don't be tempted to "make your book stand out" by using fancy fonts. It *will* stand out, but not for any reason you'd want. Your entire manuscript should be in a monospaced font like Courier (not a proportional font, like Times Roman) at 12 points. (A monospaced font is one where each character takes up the same amount of space; a proportional font is where the letter "i" takes up less space than the letter "m".)

This goes for your text, your headings, your title, your name – everything. Your objective is to produce a manuscript that looks like it has been produced on a simple typewriter.

Italics / bold

Your job as the author is to indicate words that require emphasis, not to pick particular styles of font. This will be determined by the house style of the publisher in question. You indicate emphasis by underlining text; the publisher will decide whether they will use bold or italic to achieve this emphasis – you shouldn't use either in your text.

Margins

You should have a one inch (2.5 centimetre) margin around your entire page: top, bottom, left, and right.

Spacing

In terms of line spacing, your entire manuscript should be double spaced. Your word processor should provide an option for this, so you don't have to insert blank lines manually.

While line spacing should be double, spaces after punctuation should be single. If you're in the habit of putting two spaces after full stops this is the time to get out of that habit, and remove them from your manuscript. You're just creating extra work for the editor who will have to strip them all out.

Do not put blank lines between paragraphs. Start every paragraph (even those at the start of chapters) with an indent equivalent to five spaces. If you want a scene break then create a line with the "#" character centred in the middle. You don't need blank lines above or below this line.

Word count

You will need to provide an estimated word count on the front page of your manuscript. Tempting as it will be to simply use the word processor's word counting function to tell you exactly how many words there are in your manuscript, this is not what you should do. Instead, you should work out the maximum number of characters on a line, divide this number by six, and then multiply by the total number of lines in your manuscript.

Once you have got your estimated word count you need to round it to an approximate value. How you round will depend on the overall length of your manuscript:

- up to 1,500 words: round to the nearest 100;
- 1,500–10,000 words: round to the nearest 500;
- 10,000–25,000 words: round to the nearest 1,000;
- Over 25,000 words: round to the nearest 5,000.

The reason an agent or editor will need to know your word count is so that they can estimate how many pages it will make. Since actual pages include varying amounts of white space due to breaks in paragraphs, sections of speech, etc. the formula above will actually provide a better idea of how many pages will be required than an exact word count would.

And – perhaps more importantly – providing an exact word count will highlight you immediately as an amateur.

Layout of the front page

On the first page of the manuscript, place your name, address, and any other relevant contact details (such as phone number, email address, etc.) in the top left-hand corner. In the top right-hand corner write your approximate word count.

If you have registered your work for copyright protection, place the reference number two single lines (one double line) beneath your contact details. Since your manuscript will only be seen by agents or editors, not the public, this should be done as discreetly as possible, and you should refrain from using any official seal you may have been granted permissions to use. (For information on registering for copyright protection see "Protecting Your Copyright", below.)

Place your title halfway down the front page. Your title should be centred and would normally be in capital letters. You can make it bold or underlined if you want, but it should be the same size as the rest of the text.

From your title, go down two single lines (or one double line) and insert your byline. This should be centred and start with the word "By", followed by the name you are writing under. This can be your name or a pen name, but should be the name you want the work published under. However, make sure that the name in the top left-hand corner is your real, legal name.

From your byline, go down four single lines (or two double lines) and begin your manuscript.

Layout of the text

Print on only one side of the paper, even if your printer can print on both sides.

In the top right-hand corner of all pages except the first should be your running head. This should be comprised of the surname used in your byline; a keyword from your title, and the page number, e.g. "Myname / Mynovel Page 5".

Text should be left-aligned, *not* justified. This means that you should have a ragged right-hand edge to the text, with lines ending at different points. Make sure you don't have any sort of hyphenation function switched on in your word processor: if a word is too long to fit on a line it should be taken over to the next.

Start each new chapter a third of the way down the page with the centred chapter number / title, underlined. Drop down four single lines (two double lines) to the main text.

At the end of the manuscript you do not need to indicate the ending in any way: you don't need to write "The End", or "Ends", etc. The only exception to this is if your manuscript happens to end at the bottom of a page, in which case you can handwrite the word "End" at the bottom of the last page, after you have printed it out.

Protecting Your Copyright

Protecting your copyright is by no means a requirement before submitting your work, but you may feel that it is a prudent step that you would like to take before allowing strangers to see your material.

These days, you can register your work for copyright protection quickly and easily online. The Intellectual Property Rights Office operates a website called the "Copyright Registration Service" which allows you to do this:

- *https://www.CopyrightRegistrationService.com*

This website can be used for material created in any nation signed up to the Berne Convention. This includes the United States, United Kingdom, Canada, Australia, Ireland, New Zealand, and most other countries. There are around 180 countries in the world, and over 160 of them are part of the Berne Convention.

Provided you created your work in one of the Berne Convention nations, your work should be protected by copyright in all other Berne Convention nations. You can therefore protect your copyright around most of the world with a single registration, and because the process is entirely online you can have your work protected in a matter of minutes, without having to print and post a copy of your manuscript.

What is copyright?

Copyright is a form of intellectual property (often referred to as "IP"). Other forms of intellectual property include trade marks, designs, and patents. These categories refer to different kinds of ideas which may not exist in a physical form that can be owned as property in the traditional sense, but may nonetheless have value to the people who created them. These forms of intellectual property can be owned in the same way that physical property is owned, but – as with physical property – they can be subject to dispute and proper documentation is required to prove ownership.

The different types of intellectual property divide into these categories as follows:

- **Copyright:** copyright protects creative output such as books, poems, pictures, drawings, music, films, etc. Any work which can be recorded in some way can be protected by copyright, as long as it is original and of sufficient length. Copyright does not cover short phrases or names.
- **Trade marks:** trade marks cover words and/or images which distinguish the goods or services of one trader from another. Unlike copyright, trade marks can cover names and short phrases.
- **Designs:** designs cover the overall visual appearance of a product, such as its shape, etc.
- **Patents:** patents protect the technical or functional aspects of designs or inventions.

The specifics of the legal protection surrounding these various forms of intellectual property will vary from nation to nation, but there are also generally international conventions to which a lot if not most of the nations of the world subscribe. The information provided below outlines the common situation in many countries but you should be aware that this may not reflect the exact situation in every territory.

The two types of intellectual property most relevant to writers are copyright and trade marks. If a writer has written a novel, a short story, a poem, a script, or any other piece of writing then the contents themselves can be protected by copyright. The title, however, cannot be protected by copyright as it is a name. An author may therefore feel that they wish to consider protecting the title of their work by registering it as a trade mark, if they feel that it is particularly important and/or more valuable in itself than the cost of registering a trade mark.

If a writer wants to register the copyright for their work, or register the title of their work as a trade mark, there are generally registration fees to be paid. Despite the fact that copyright covers long works that could be hundreds of thousands of words long, while trade marks cover single words and short phrases, the cost for registering a trade mark is likely to be many times higher than that for registering a work for copyright protection. This is because trade marks must be unique and are checked against existing trade marks for potential conflicts. While works to be registered for copyright must also not infringe existing works, it is not practical to check the huge volume of new works to be registered for copyright against the even larger volume of all previously copyrighted works. Copyright registration therefore tends to simply archive the work in question as proof of the date at which the person registering the work was in possession of it.

In the case of both copyright and trade marks the law generally provides some protection even without any kind of registration, but registration provides the owner of the intellectual property with greater and more enforceable protection. In the case of copyright, the creator of a work usually automatically owns the copyright as soon as the work is recorded in some way (i.e. by writing it down or recording it electronically, etc.), however these rights can be difficult to prove if disputed, and therefore many countries (such as the United States) also offer an internal country-specific means of registering works. Some countries, like the United Kingdom, do not offer any such means of registration, however an international registration is available through the Intellectual Property Rights Office's Copyright Registration Service, and can be used regardless of any country-specific provisions. This can help protect copyright in all of the nations which are signatories of the Berne Convention.

In the case of trade marks, the symbol "™" can be applied to any mark which is being used as a trade mark, however greater protection is provided if this mark is registered, in which case the symbol "®" can be applied to the mark. It is often illegal to apply the "®" symbol to a trade mark which has not been registered. There are also options for international registrations of trade marks, which are administered by the World Intellectual Property Organization, however applications cannot be made to the WIPO directly – applications must be made through the relevant office of the applicant's country.

Copyright law and its history

The modern concept of copyright can be traced back to 1710 and the "Statute of Anne", which applied to England, Scotland, and Wales. Prior to this Act, governments had granted monopoly rights to publishers to produce works, but the 1710 Act was the first time that a right of ownership was acknowledged for the actual creator of a work.

From the outset, the attempt to protect the creator's rights was beset with problems due to the local nature of the laws, which applied in Britain only. This meant that lots of copyrighted works were reproduced without the permission of the author in Ireland, America, and in European countries. This not only hindered the ability of the London publishers to sell their legitimate copies of their books in these territories, but the unauthorised reproductions would also find their way into Britain, harming the home market as well.

A natural progression for copyright law was therefore its internationalisation, beginning in 1846 with a reciprocal agreement between Britain and Prussia, and culminating in a series of international treaties, the principal of which is the Berne Convention, which applies to over 160 countries.

Traditionally in the United Kingdom and the United States there has been a requirement to register a work with an official body in order to be able to claim copyright over it (Stationers Hall and the US Library of Congress respectively), however this has been changed by the Berne Convention, which requires signatory countries to grant copyright as an automatic right: i.e. the creator of a work immediately owns its copyright by virtue of creating it and recording it in some physical way (for instance by writing it down or making a recording of it, etc.). The United Kingdom and the United States have both been slow to fully adopt this approach. Though the United Kingdom signed the Berne Convention in 1887, it took 100 years for it to be fully implemented by the Copyright Designs and Patents Act 1988. The United States did not even sign the convention until 1989.

In the United States the US Library of Congress continues to provide archiving services for the purposes of copyright protection, but these are now optional. US citizens no longer need to register their work in order to be able to claim copyright over it. It is necessary, however, to be able to prove when the person who created it did so, and this is essentially the purpose of the registration today. In the United Kingdom, Stationers Hall has ceased to exist, and there is no longer any state-run means of registering the copyright to unpublished works, leaving the only available options as independent and/or international solutions such as the copyright registration service provided by the IP Rights Office.

Registering your work for copyright protection

Registering your work for copyright protection can help you protect your rights in relation to your work. Generally (particularly if you live in a Berne Convention country, as most people do) registration will not be compulsory in order to have rights over your work. Any time you create a unique original work you will in theory own the copyright over it, however you will need to be able to prove when you created it, which is the purpose of registering your work for copyright protection. There are other ways in which you might attempt to prove this, but registration provides better evidence than most other forms.

There are a range of different options for protecting your copyright that vary depending on where you live and the kind of coverage you want. Some countries, like the United States, provide internal means of registering the copyright of unpublished works, however the scope of these will tend to be restricted to the country in question. Other countries, like the United Kingdom, do not offer any specific government-sponsored system for registering the copyright of unpublished works. An international option is provided by the Intellectual Property Rights Office, which is not affiliated to any particular government or country. As long as you live in a Berne Convention country you should be able to benefit from using their Copyright Registration Service. You can register your work with the Intellectual Property Rights Office regardless of whether or not there are any specific arrangements in your home country (you may even choose to register with both to offer your work greater protection). Registration with the Intellectual Property Rights Office should provide you with protection throughout the area covered by the Berne Convention, which is most of the world.

Registering your work for copyright protection through the Intellectual Property Rights Office is an online process that can be completed in a few minutes, provided you have your file in an accepted format and your file isn't too large (if your file is too large and cannot be reduced you may have to split it and take out two or more registrations covering it). There is a registration fee to pay ($45 / £25 / €40 at the time of writing) per file for registration, however if you are a subscriber to **firstwriter.com** you can benefit from a 10% discount when you start the registration process on our site.

When registering your work, you will need to give some consideration to what your work actually consists of. This is a straightforward question if your work is a novel, or a screenplay, but if it is a collection of poetry or short stories then the issue is more difficult. Should you register your collection as one file, or register each poem separately, which would be more expensive? Usually, you can answer this question by asking yourself what you propose to do with your collection. Do you intend to submit it to publishers as a collection only? Or do you intend to send the constituent parts separately to individual magazines? If the former is the case, then register the collection as a single work under the title of the collection. If the latter is the case then this could be unwise, as your copyright registration certificate will give the name of the collection only – which will not match the names of the individual poems or stories. If you can afford to, you should therefore register them separately. If you have so many poems and / or stories to register that you cannot afford to register them all separately, then registering them as a collection will be better than nothing.

Proper use of the copyright symbol

The first thing to note is that for copyright there is only one form of the symbol (©), unlike trade marks, where there is a symbol for registered trade marks (®) and a symbol for unregistered trade marks (™).

To qualify for use of the registered trade mark symbol (®) you must register your trade mark with the appropriate authority in your country, whereas the trade mark symbol (™) can be applied to any symbol you are using as a trade mark. Use of the copyright symbol is more similar to use of the trade mark symbol, as work does not need to be registered in order to use it.

You can place the copyright symbol on any original piece of work you have created. The normal format would be to include alongside the copyright symbol the year of first publication and the name of the copyright holder, however there are no particular legal requirements regarding this. While it has historically been a requirement in some jurisdictions to include a copyright notice on a work in order to be able to claim copyright over it, the Berne Convention does not allow such restrictions, and so any country signed up to the convention no longer has this requirement. However, in some jurisdictions failure to include such a notice can affect the damages you may be able to claim if anyone infringes your copyright.

A similar situation exists in relation to the phrase "All Rights Reserved". This phrase was a requirement in order to claim international copyright protection in countries signed up to the 1910 Buenos Aires Convention. However, since all countries signed up to the Buenos Aires Convention are now also signed up to the Berne Convention (which grants automatic copyright) this phrase has become superfluous. The phrase continues to be used frequently but is unlikely to have any legal consequences.

The Berne Convention

The Berne Convention covers 162 of the approximately 190 countries in the world, including most major nations. Countries which are signed up to the convention are compelled to offer the same protection to works created in other signatory nations as they would to works created in their own. Nations not signed up to the Berne Convention may have their own arrangements regarding copyright protection.

You can check if your country is signed up to the Berne Convention at the following website:

- *https://www.CopyrightRegistrationService.com*

The status of your country should be shown automatically on the right side of the screen. If not, you can select your country manually from the drop-down menu near the top right of the page.

Should You Self-Publish

Over recent years there has been an explosion in self-published books, as it has become easier and easier to publish your book yourself. This poses writers with a new quandary: continue to pursue publication through the traditional means, or jump into the world of self-publishing? As the rejections from traditional publishers pile up it can be tempting to reach for the control and certainty of self-publishing. Should you give into the temptation, or stick to your guns?

Isn't it just vanity publishing?

Modern self-publishing is quite different from the vanity publishing of times gone by. A vanity publisher would often pose or at least seek to appear to be a traditional publisher, inviting submissions and issuing congratulatory letters of acceptance to everyone who submitted – only slowly revealing the large fees the author would have to pay to cover the cost of printing the books.

Once the books were printed, the vanity publisher would deliver them to the author then cut and run. The author would be left with a big hole in their pocket and a mountain of boxes of books that they would be unlikely to ever sell a fraction of.

Modern self-publishing, on the other hand, is provided not by shady dealers but by some of the biggest companies involved in the publishing industry, including Penguin and Amazon. It doesn't have the large fees that vanity publishing did (depending on the path you choose and your own knowledge and technical ability it can cost almost nothing to get your book published); it *does* offer a viable means of selling your books (they can appear on the biggest bookselling websites around the world); and it *doesn't* leave you with a house full of unwanted books, because modern technology means that a copy of your book only gets printed when it's actually ordered.

That isn't to say that there aren't still shady characters out there trying to take advantage of authors' vanity by charging them enormous fees for publishing a book that stands very little chance of success, but it does mean that self-publishing – done right – can be a viable and cost effective way of an author taking their book to market.

The benefits of self-publishing

The main benefit of self-publishing, of course, is that the author gets control of whether their book is published or not. There is no need to spend years submitting to countless agents and publishers, building up countless heartbreaking rejection letters, and possibly accepting in the end that your dreams of publication will never come true – you can make them come true.

And this need not be pure vanity on the author's part. Almost every successful book – even such massive hits as *Harry Potter* – usually build up a string of rejections before someone finally accepts them. The professionals that authors rely on when going through the traditional publishing process – the literary agents and the editors – are often, it seems, just not that good at spotting what the public are going to buy. How many potential bestsellers might languish forever in the slush pile, just because agents and editors fail to spot them? What if your book is one of them? The traditional publishing process forces you to rely on the good judgment of others, but the self-publishing process enables you to sidestep that barrier and take your book directly to the public, so that readers can decide for themselves.

Self-publishing also allows you to keep control in other areas. You won't have an editor trying to change your text, and you'll have complete control over what kind of cover your book receives.

Finally, with no publisher or team of editors and accountants taking their slice, you'll probably get to keep a lot more of the retail price of every book you sell. So if you can sell the same amount of books as if you were traditionally published, you'll stand to make a lot more money.

The drawbacks of self-publishing

While self-publishing can guarantee that your book will be available for sale, it cannot guarantee that it will actually sell. Your self-published book will probably have a much lower chance of achieving significant sales than if it had been published traditionally, because it will lack the support that a mainstream publisher could bring. You will have no marketing support, no established position in the marketplace, and no PR – unless you do it yourself. You will have to arrange your own book tours; you will have to do your own sales pitches; you will have to set your own pricing structure; and you will have to manage your own accounts and tax affairs. If you're selling through Amazon or Smashwords or Apple (and if you're not, then why did you bother self-publishing in the first place?) you're going to need to fill in the relevant forms with the IRS (the US tax office) – whether you're a US citizen or not. If you're not a US citizen then you'll have to register with the IRS and complete the necessary tax forms, and potentially other forms for claiming treaty benefits so that you don't get taxed twice (in the US and your home country). And then of course you'll also have to register for tax purposes in your home nation and complete your own tax return there (though you would also have to do this as a traditionally published author).

It can all get very complicated, very confusing, and very lonely. Instead of being able to just be a writer you can find yourself writing less and less and becoming more and more embroiled in the business of publishing a book.

And while it's great to have control over your text and your cover, you'd be ill advised to ignore the value that professionals such as editors and cover designers can bring. It's tempting to think that you don't need an editor – that you've checked the book and had a friend or family member check it too, so it's probably fine – but a professional editor brings a totally different mindset to the process and will check things that won't have even occurred to you and your reader. Without a professional editor, you will almost certainly end up publishing a book which is full of embarrassing mistakes, and trust me – there is no feeling quite as deflating as opening up the first copy of your freshly printed book to see an obvious error jump out – or, even worse, to have it pointed out in an Amazon review, for all to see.

The cover is also incredibly important. Whether for sale on the shelf or on a website, the cover is normally the first point of contact your potential reader has with your book, and will cause them to form immediate opinions about it. A good cover can help a book sell well, but a bad one can kill its chances – and all too often self-published books have amateurish covers that will have readers flicking past them without a second glance.

Finally, the financial benefits of self-publishing can often be illusory. For starters, getting a higher proportion of the retail price is pretty irrelevant if you don't sell any copies. Fifty per cent of nothing is still nothing. Far better to have 15% of something. And then there's the advances. Advances are up-front payments made by traditional publishers to authors, which are off-set against future royalties. So, an author might receive a $5,000 advance before their book is published. When the royalties start coming in, the publisher keeps the first $5,000 to off-set the advance. The good news for the author is that if the book flops and doesn't make $5,000 in royalties they still get to keep the full advance. In an uncertain profession, the security of an advance can be invaluable for an author – and of course it's not something available to self-published authors.

Conclusion

Self-publishing can seem like a tempting shortcut to publication, but in reality it has its own challenges and difficulties. For the moment at least, traditional publishing still offers you the best shot of not only financial success, but also quality of life as a writer. With other people to handle all the other elements of publishing, you get to concentrate on doing what you love.

So we think that writers should always aim for traditional publishing first. It might be a long shot, but if it works then you stand a much better chance of being successful. If you don't manage to get signed by an agent or a publisher then you still have the option of self-publishing, but make sure you don't get tempted to resort to self-publishing too soon – most agents and publishers won't consider self-published works, so this is a one-way street. Once you've self-published your work, you probably won't be able to change your mind and go back to the traditional publishers with your book unless it becomes a huge hit without them. It's therefore important that you exhaust all your traditional publishing options before making the leap to self-publishing. Be prepared for this to take perhaps a few years (lots of agents and publishers can take six months just to respond), and make sure you've submitted to everyone you can on *both* sides of the Atlantic (publishing is a global game these days, and you need to concentrate on the two main centres of English-language publishing (New York and London) equally) before you make the decision to self-publish instead.

However, once you have exhausted all options for traditional publishing, modern self-publishing does offer a genuine alternative path to success, and there are a growing number of self-published authors who have managed to sell millions of copies of their books. If you don't think traditional publishing is going to be an option, we definitely think you should give self-publishing a shot.

For directions on your path through the traditional publishing process see our Writers' Roadmap, above.

If you're sure you've already exhausted all your options for traditional publishing then see below for our quick guide to the self-publishing process.

The Self Publishing Process

Thinking about self-publishing your book? Make sure you go through all these steps first – and in the right order! Do them the wrong way round and you could find yourself wasting time and/or money.

1. Be sure you want to self-publish

You need to be 100% sure that you want to self-publish, because after you've done it there is no going back. Publishers and literary agents will not normally consider books that have been self-published, so if you wanted to get your book to print the old fashioned way you should stop now and rethink. Make absolutely sure that you've exhausted every possible opportunity for traditional publishing before you head down the self-publishing path.

For more information, see "Why choose traditional publishing?" and "Should you self-publish?", above.

2. Protect your copyright

Authors often wonder about what stage in the process they should protect their copyright – often thinking that it's best to leave it till the end so that there are no more changes to make to the book after it is registered.

However, this isn't the case. The key thing is to protect your work before you let other people see it – or, if you've already let other people see it, as soon as possible thereafter.

Don't worry about making small changes to your work after registering it – as long as the work is still recognisable as the same piece of work it will still be protected. Obviously, if you completely change everything you've written then you're going to need another registration, as it will effectively be a different book, but if you've just edited it and made minor alterations this won't affect your protection.

You can register you copyright online at https://www.copyrightregistrationservice.com.

3. Get your work edited

Editing is a vital step often overlooked by authors who self-publish. The result can often be an amateurish book littered with embarrassing mistakes. Any professionally published book will go through an editing process, and it's important that the same applies to your self-published book. It's also important to complete the editing process before beginning the layout, or you could find yourself having to start the layout again from scratch.

4. Choose your self-publishing path

Before you can go any further you are going to need to choose a size for your book, and in order to do that you are going to need to choose a self-publishing path.

There are various different ways of getting self-published, but in general these range from the expensive hands off approach, where you pay a company to do the hard work for you, to the cheap DIY approach, where you do as much as you can yourself.

At the top end, the hands off approach can cost you thousands. At the bottom end, the DIY approach allows you to publish your book for almost nothing.

5. Finalise your layout / typesetting

Before you can finalise your layout (often referred to in the industry as "typesetting") you need to be sure that you've finalised your content – which means having your full work professionally edited and all the necessary changes made. If you decide to make changes after this point it will be difficult and potentially costly, and will require you to go through many of the following steps all over again.

You also need to have selected your path to publication, so that you know what page sizes are available to you, and what page margins you are going to need to apply. If you create a layout that doesn't meet printing requirements (for instance, includes text too close to the edge of the page) then you will have to start the typesetting process all over again.

6. Organise your ISBN

Your book needs to have an ISBN. If you are using a self-publishing service then they may provide you with one of their own, but it is likely to come with restrictions, and the international record for your book will show your self-publishing service as the publisher.

You can acquire your own ISBNs directly from the ISBN issuer, but they do not sell them individually, so you will end up spending quite a lot of money buying more ISBNs than you need. You will, however, have control of the ISBN, and you will be shown as the publisher.

Alternatively, you can purchase a single ISBN at a lower price from an ISBN retailer. This should give you control over the ISBN, however the record for the book will show the ISBN retailer as the publisher, which you may not consider to be ideal.

Whatever you choose, you need to arrange your ISBN no later than this point, because it needs to appear in the preliminary pages (prelims) of your book.

7. Compile your prelims

Your prelims may include a variety of pages, but should always include a title page, a half title page, and an imprint/copyright page. You might then also include other elements, such as a foreword, table of contents, etc. You can only compile your table of contents at this stage, because you need to know your ISBN (this will be included on the copyright/imprint page) and the page numbers for your table of contents. You therefore need to make sure that you are happy with the typesetting and have no further changes to make before compiling your prelims.

8. Create your final press proof

Depending on the self-publishing path you have chosen, you may be able to use a Word file as your final document. However, you need to be careful. In order to print your book it will have to be converted into a press-ready PDF at some point. If a self-publishing service is doing this for you then you will probably find that they own the PDF file that is created, meaning you don't have control over your own press files. Some services will impose hefty charges (hundreds or even more than a thousand dollars) to release these press files.

It might also be the case that you won't get to see the final PDF, and therefore won't get chance to check it for any errors introduced by the conversion process. If it's an automated system, it may also be difficult to control the output you get from it.

We'd suggest that it's best to produce your own PDF files if possible. To do this you will need a copy of Adobe Acrobat Professional, and you will need to be familiar with the correct settings for creating print ready PDFs. Be careful to embed all fonts and make sure that all images are at 300 DPI.

9. Create your cover

Only once your press proof is finalised can you complete your cover design. That's because your cover includes not only the front cover and the back cover, but also (critically) the spine – and the width of the spine will vary according to the number of pages in your final press proof. In order to complete your cover design you therefore need to know your page size, your page count (including all prelims), and your ISBN, as this will appear on the back cover. You also need to get a barcode for your ISBN.

10. Produce your book

Once your cover and press proof are ready you can go through whichever self-publishing path you have chosen to create your book. With some pathways the production of a print proof can be an optional extra that is only available at an extra cost – but we'd recommend standing that cost and getting a print version of your book to check. You never know exactly how it's going to come out until you have a physical copy in your hand.

If you're happy with the proof you can clear your book for release. You don't need to do anything to get it on online retailers like Amazon – they will automatically pick up the ISBN and add your book to their websites themselves.

11. Create an ebook version

In the modern day, having an ebook version of your book is imperative. Ebooks account for a significant proportion of all book sales and are a particularly effective vehicle for unknown and self-published authors.

There are various different file formats used by the different platforms, but .epub is emerging as a standard, and having your book in .epub format should enable you to access all the platforms with a single file.

12. Distribute your ebook

Unlike with print books, you will need to act yourself to get your ebooks into sales channels. At a minimum, you need to ensure that you get your ebook available for sale through Amazon, Apple, and Google Play.

Table of US Literary Agencies

Table of UK Literary Agencies

Table of US Literary Agents

Table of UK Literary Agents

Table of Canadian Literary Agents

Table of US Magazines

Table of UK Magazines

Table of Canadian Magazines

Table of US Book Publishers

Table of UK Book Publishers

Table of Canadian Book Publishers

Table of Authors

Literary Agents and Agencies

For the most up-to-date listings of these and hundreds of other literary agents and agencies, visit https://www.firstwriter.com/Agents

To claim your free access to the site, please see the back of this book.

L001 3 Seas Literary Agency

Literary Agency
PO Box 444, Sun Prairie, WI 53590
United States
Tel: +1 (608) 834-9317

threeseaslit@aol.com

https://www.threeseasagency.com
https://www.facebook.com/3-Seas-Literary-Agency-75205869856/
https://twitter.com/threeseaslit?lang=en

ADULT > **Fiction** > *Novels*
Fantasy; Romance; Science Fiction; Thrillers; Women's Fiction

CHILDREN'S > **Fiction** > *Middle Grade*

YOUNG ADULT > **Fiction** > *Novels*

How to send: Query Manager
How not to send: Email

Accepts queries through online submission system only. See website for full guidelines.

Literary Agents: Cori Deyoe (**L171**); Stacey Graham (**L279**); Michelle Grajkowski (**L281**)

L002 42 Management and Production

Literary Agency
Palladium House, 7th Floor, 1-4 Argyll Street, London, W1F 7TA
United Kingdom
Tel: +44 (0) 20 7292 0554

https://www.42mp.com

Professional Body: The Association of Authors' Agents (AAA)

A fully integrated management and production company, producing film, television and content, representing actors, writers, directors, producers, casting directors and media book rights; with offices in London and Los Angeles.

Literary Agents: Eugenie Furniss (**L243**); Emily MacDonald (**L455**); Marilia Savvides (**L621**)

L003 A.M. Heath & Company Limited, Author's Agents

Literary Agency
6 Warwick Court, Holborn
London, WC1R 5DJ
United Kingdom
Tel: +44 (0) 20 7242 2811

enquiries@amheath.com

https://amheath.com
https://twitter.com/AMHeathLtd
https://www.instagram.com/a.m.heath

Professional Body: The Association of Authors' Agents (AAA)

Fiction > *Novels*

Nonfiction > *Nonfiction Books*

Send: Query; Synopsis; Writing sample
How to send: Online submission system
How not to send: Post; Email

Handles general commercial and literary fiction and nonfiction. Submit work with cover letter, synopsis, and writing sample up to 10,000 words, via online submission system only. No paper submissions or submissions by email. Aims to respond within six weeks.

Agency Assistant: Jessica Lee

Agency Assistant / Associate Agent: Florence Rees

Literary Agents: Julia Churchill; Bill Hamilton; Victoria Hobbs (**L325**); Zoe King; Oli Munson; Rebecca Ritchie (**L591**); Euan Thorneycroft

L004 A3 Artists Agency

Literary Agency
The Empire State Building, 350 Fifth Ave. 38th Floor, New York, NY 10118, 750 North San Vicente Blvd., East Tower, 11th Floor, Los Angeles, CA 90069
United States
Tel: +1 (646) 486-4600

contactla@a3artistsagency.com
contactny@a3artistsagency.com

https://www.a3artistsagency.com/

Scripts
Film Scripts; *TV Scripts*

Closed to approaches.

L005 Kwaku Acheampong

Literary Agent
United States

kwaku@carolynjenksagency.com

https://www.carolynjenksagency.com/agent/Kwaku-Acheampong

Literary Agency: Carolyn Jenks Agency (**L106**)

ADULT
Fiction > *Novels*
Nonfiction > *Nonfiction Books*

NEW ADULT
Fiction > *Novels*
Nonfiction > *Nonfiction Books*

Send: Query; Writing sample
How to send: In the body of an email

Looking for fiction and nonfiction across most genres, though he has a special passion for new adult.

L006 Seren Adams

Associate Agent
United Kingdom

SAdams@unitedagents.co.uk

https://www.unitedagents.co.uk/sadamsunitedagentscouk
https://twitter.com/serenadams

Literary Agency: United Agents (**L704**)
Literary Agent: Anna Webber (**L725**)

Fiction > *Novels*: Literary

Nonfiction > *Nonfiction Books*: Narrative Nonfiction

Send: Query; Synopsis; Pitch; Market info
How to send: Email

Her list focuses on literary fiction and narrative non-fiction, and she has a particular passion for precise prose and unconventional storytelling.

Authors: Kim Adrian; Jen Calleja; Sean Patrick Cooper; Al Crow; Lauren Aimee Curtis; Sam Diamond; Lucie Elven; Rakaya Fetuga; Ronan Fitzgerald; Amaryllis Gacioppo; Maria Giron; Lili Hamlyn; Catherine Humble; Blair James; Liza St. James; Ana Kinsella; Sonal Kohli; Aileen Maguire; Laura Maw; Sinéad Mooney; Caleb Azumah Nelson; Timothy Ogene; Joanna Pocock; Issa Quincy; Karina Lickorish Quinn; Gemma Reeves; Laura Robertson; Olivia Rosenthall; Alan Rossi; Taylor-Dior Rumble; Michael Salu; Lina Scheynius; Laura

Southgate; Olivia Spring; Sean Stoker; Jordan Sullivan; Georgina Terry; Zakia Uddin; Kenechi Uzor; Lauren Wallach; Eva Warrick

L007 Phil Adie

Literary Agent
United Kingdom

http://nickturnermanagement.com/about-us/

Literary Agency: Nick Turner Management Ltd (**L526**)

Represents writers and directors for film and television, and is currently building his client list.

L008 Aevitas Creative Management (ACM) UK

Literary Agency
49 Greek Street, London, W1D 4EG
United Kingdom

ukenquiries@aevitascreative.com

https://aevitascreative.com/home/acm-uk/
https://twitter.com/AevitasCreative
https://www.facebook.com/AevitasCreative/

Literary Agency: Aevitas

UK branch of a US agency, founded in 2019, representing writers and brands throughout the world.

Chief Executive Officer / Literary Agent: Toby Mundy (**L514**)

Literary Agents: Trevor Dolby (**L175**); Max Edwards (**L192**); Natalie Jerome; Sara O' Keeffe (**L381**); Simon Targett (**L689**)

L009 The Agency (London) Ltd

Literary Agency
24 Pottery Lane, Holland Park, London, W11 4LZ
United Kingdom

submissions@theagency.co.uk

http://www.theagency.co.uk

Professional Body: The Association of Authors' Agents (AAA)

ADULT > **Scripts**
Film Scripts; *TV Scripts*; *Theatre Scripts*
CHILDREN'S > **Fiction**
Middle Grade; *Novels*; *Picture Books*
TEEN > **Fiction** > *Novels*

YOUNG ADULT > **Fiction** > *Novels*

Send: Query; Synopsis; Writing sample
How to send: Email

Represents writers and authors for film, television, radio and the theatre. Also represents directors, producers, composers, and film and television rights in books, as well as authors of children's books from picture books to teen fiction. For script writers, only considers unsolicited material if it has been recommended by a producer, development executive or course tutor. If this is the case send CV, covering letter and details of your referee by email. Do not email more than one agent at a time. For directors, send CV, showreel and cover letter by email. For children's authors, send query by email with synopsis and first three chapters (middle grade, teen, or Young Adult) or complete ms (picture books) to address given on website.

Literary Agents: Gina Andrews (**L023**); Ian Benson; Nicola Biltoo; Simon Blakey; Hannah Boulton; Hilary Delamere; Stephen Durbridge; Bethan Evans; Katie Haines; Jessica Hare (**L304**); Emily Hickman; Jonathan Kinnersley; Julia Kreitman; Norman North; Nick Quinn; Leah Schmidt; Emily Smith; Tanya Tillett

L010 AHA Talent Ltd

Literary Agency
2 Percy Street, London, W1T 1DD
United Kingdom
Tel: +44 (0) 20 7250 1760

mail@ahacreatives.co.uk

https://www.ahatalent.co.uk
https://twitter.com/AHAcreatives

Scripts
Film Scripts; *Radio Scripts*; *TV Scripts*; *Theatre Scripts*

Send: Query; Author bio; Writing sample

Handles actors and creatives. Send query with CV/bio, and examples of your work.

Literary Agent: Amanda Fitzalan Howard (*L333*)

L011 The Ahearn Agency, Inc

Literary Agency
3436 Magazine St., #615, New Orleans, LA 70115
United States
Tel: +1 (504) 589-4200
Fax: +1 (504) 589-4200

pahearn@aol.com

http://www.ahearnagency.com

Fiction > *Novels*
Suspense; Women's Fiction

Send: Query; Market info; Self-Addressed Stamped Envelope (SASE)
How to send: Email; Post
How not to send: Email attachment

Send one page query with SASE, description, length, market info, and any writing credits. Accepts email queries without attachments. Response in 2-3 months.

Specialises in women's fiction and suspense. No nonfiction, poetry, juvenile material or science fiction.

Authors: Michele Albert; Rexanne Becnel; Wendy Hilton; Sabrina Jeffries; Connie Koslow; Sandra Landry; Deb Marlowe; Meagan McKinney; Kate Moore; Gerri Russell; Susan Sipal

Literary Agent: Pamela G. Ahearn

L012 Clementine Ahearne

Literary Agent; Company Director
United Kingdom

clementine.ahearne@ila-agency.co.uk

Literary Agency: ILA (Intercontinental Literary Agency) (**L339**)

Closed to approaches.

L013 Jamilah Ahmed

Associate Agent
United Kingdom

Literary Agency: Barbara Levy Literary Agency (**L044**)

Fiction > *Novels*

Nonfiction > *Nonfiction Books*

Briefed with developing new writers in fiction and nonfiction.

L014 Alan Brodie Representation

Literary Agency
Paddock Suite, The Courtyard, 55 Charterhouse Street, London, EC1M 6HA
United Kingdom
Tel: +44 (0) 20 7253 6226

ABR@alanbrodie.com

https://www.alanbrodie.com
https://www.facebook.com/Alan-Brodie-Representation-Ltd-407206926050145/
https://twitter.com/abragency
https://www.instagram.com/abragency/?hl=en

Scripts
Film Scripts; *Radio Scripts*; *TV Scripts*; *Theatre Scripts*

Send: Query; Author bio
Don't send: Writing sample; Full text
How to send: By referral

Handles scripts only. No books. Approach with preliminary letter, recommendation from industry professional, and CV. Do not send a sample of work unless requested. No fiction, nonfiction, or poetry.

Literary Agents: Alan Brodie; Kara Fitzpatrick; Victoria Williams

L015 Alice Williams Literary

Literary Agency
United Kingdom
Tel: +44 (0) 20 7385 2118

submissions@alicewilliamsliterary.co.uk

https://www.alicewilliamsliterary.co.uk
https://twitter.com/alicelovesbooks
http://instagram.com/agentalicewilliams

Professional Body: The Association of Authors' Agents (AAA)

CHILDREN'S
Fiction
Middle Grade; *Novels*; *Picture Books*
Nonfiction > *Nonfiction Books*

YOUNG ADULT
Fiction > *Novels*
Nonfiction > *Nonfiction Books*

How to send: Email

A specialist literary agency proudly representing writers and illustrators of picture books, young fiction, middle-grade, YA and non-fiction.

Literary Agent: Alice Williams (**L736**)

L016 Alive Literary Agency

Literary Agency
5001 Centennial Blvd #50742, Colorado Springs, CO 80908
United States

https://aliveliterary.com

Nonfiction > *Nonfiction Books*
Lifestyle; Personal Development; Religion

How to send: By referral

Accepts queries from referred authors only. Works primarily with well-established, best-selling, and career authors.

Authors: Jamie Blaine; Michael Hyatt; Karen Kingsbury

Literary Agents: Andrea Heinecke; Lisa Jackson; Rachel Jacobson (**L347**); Kathleen Kerr (*L384*); Bryan Norman

L017 The Ampersand Agency Ltd

Literary Agency
Ryman's Cottages, Little Tew, Chipping Norton, Oxfordshire, OX7 4JJ
United Kingdom
Tel: +44 (0) 1608 683677 / 683898
Fax: +44 (0) 1608 683449

submissions@theampersandagency.co.uk

http://www.theampersandagency.co.uk

Professional Body: The Association of Authors' Agents (AAA)

Fiction > *Novels*
Contemporary; Crime; Fantasy; Historical Fiction; Literary; Science Fiction; Thrillers

Nonfiction > *Nonfiction Books*
Biography; Current Affairs; History; Popular Science

Send: Query; Synopsis; Author bio; Writing sample
How to send: Email; Post

Costs: Author covers sundry admin costs.

We handle contemporary and historical novels, literary, crime, thrillers, fantasy, science fiction; non-fiction: current affairs, history, biography, popular science. Send query by post or email with brief bio, outline, and first three chapters. If emailing material, send as attachments rather than pasted into the body of the email. Also accepts science fiction, fantasy, horror, and Young Adult material to separate email address listed on website. No scripts except those by existing clients, no poetry, self-help or illustrated children's books. No unpublished American writers, because in our experience British and European publishers aren't interested unless there is an American publisher on board. And we'd like to make it clear that American stamps are no use outside America!

Authors: Quentin Bates; Will Davis; Phillip Hunter; Vikas Swarup

Literary Agents: Peter Buckman; Jamie Cowen; Anne-Marie Doulton

L018 Darley Anderson

Literary Agent
United Kingdom

https://www.darleyanderson.com/our-team

Literary Agency: The Darley Anderson Agency

ADULT > **Fiction** > *Novels*
Noir; Romance; Thrillers

CHILDREN'S > **Fiction** > *Novels*: Animals

How to send: Email; Post

Looking specifically for thrillers and Scandi-Noir with a strong central character set in America or Ireland or other internationally appealing locations and tear-jerking love stories. He is looking specifically for children's books featuring an original series character and animal stories. Email submissions should be sent to the agent's assistant.

Agency Assistant / Literary Agent: Rebeka Finch (**L226**)

Authors: Constance Briscoe; Chris Carter; Cathy Cassidy; Lee Child; Martina Cole; Liza Costello; Margaret Dickinson; Clare Dowling; Jack Ford; Tana French; Paul Hauck; Joan Jonker; Annie Murray; Abi Oliver; Adrian Plass; Hazel Prior; David Rhodes; Jacqui Rose; Stephen Spotswood; Erik Storey; Anna-Lou Weatherley; Lee Weeks

L019 Hannah Andrade

Literary Agent
United States

https://bradfordlit.com/hannah-andrade-agent/
https://twitter.com/hhandrade93
https://querymanager.com/hannahandrade

Literary Agency: Bradford Literary Agency (**L077**)

ADULT
Fiction > *Novels*: Mystery

Nonfiction > *Nonfiction Books*
Commercial; Crime; Investigative Journalism; Narrative Nonfiction

CHILDREN'S > **Fiction**
Graphic Novels: General
Middle Grade: General, and in particular: Dark Humour; Folklore, Myths, and Legends; Ghost Stories; Historical Fiction

YOUNG ADULT > **Fiction**
Graphic Novels: General
Novels: General, and in particular: Dark Fantasy; Folklore, Myths, and Legends; Historical Fiction; Mystery

Send: Query; Synopsis; Writing sample
How to send: Query Manager

Likes to think of herself as an editorial-focused agent and is particularly eager to acquire BIPOC/underrepresented voices. She is prioritizing stories of joy where identity isn't the focus and is especially excited about stories rooted in history, mythology, and legends, particularly those that are lesser-known or underrepresented in traditional publishing.

Very interested in stories that explore the intricacies of multicultural identities. She loves stories of immigration (not relegated to America) and of first/second generation Americans who struggle balancing the values of their country with the culture and heritage of their parents (as in the tv shows Ramy or Gentefied). As a Mexican-American, she would particularly love to see the stories that she grew up with showcased in new and creative ways.

L020 Andrew Lownie Literary Agency Ltd

Literary Agency
36 Great Smith Street, London, SW1P 3BU
United Kingdom
Tel: +44 (0) 20 7222 7574
Fax: +44 (0) 20 7222 7576

lownie@globalnet.co.uk

http://www.andrewlownie.co.uk
https://twitter.com/andrewlownie

Nonfiction > *Nonfiction Books*

Send: Query; Synopsis; Author bio; Market info; Writing sample
How to send: Email

This agency, founded in 1988, is now one of the UK's leading literary agencies with some two hundred nonfiction and fiction authors. It prides itself on its personal attention to its clients and specialises both in launching new writers and taking established writers to a new level of recognition.

Authors: Daniel Cowling; James Davies; Andy Donaldson; Angela Findlay; Katreen Hardt;

Catherine Hewitt; Christian Jennings; David McClure; Danny Orbach; Linda Porter; Louise Ramsay; Dan Smith; Nicola Stow; Tim Tate; Ian Williams; Chris Woodford

Literary Agent: Andrew Lownie (*L443*)

L021 Andrew Nurnberg Associates, Ltd

Literary Agency
3-11 Eyre St Hill, London, EC1R 5ET
United Kingdom
Tel: +44 (0) 20 3327 0400

info@nurnberg.co.uk
submissions@nurnberg.co.uk

http://www.andrewnurnberg.com
https://twitter.com/nurnberg_agency
https://www.instagram.com/andrewnurnbergassociates/?hl=en

Professional Body: The Association of Authors' Agents (AAA)

ADULT
Fiction > *Novels*
Nonfiction > *Nonfiction Books*

CHILDREN'S > **Fiction** > *Novels*

Does not want:

ADULT > **Scripts**
Film Scripts; Radio Scripts; TV Scripts; Theatre Scripts
CHILDREN'S > **Fiction** > *Picture Books*

Send: Query; Synopsis; Writing sample
How to send: Email

Handles adult fiction and nonfiction, and children's fiction. No poetry, children's picture books, or scripts for film, TV, radio or theatre. Send query by email with one-page synopsis and first three chapters or 50 pages as attachments.

Literary Agency: The Wallace Literary Agency (**L717**)

Literary Agents: Sarah Nundy; Andrew Nurnberg

L022 Nelle Andrew

Literary Agent
United Kingdom

nelle@rmliterary.co.uk

Literary Agency: Rachel Mills Literary (**L578**)

Fiction > *Novels*
Book Club Fiction; Commercial Women's Fiction; Crime; Feminism; Historical Fiction; Literary; Suspense; Thrillers

Nonfiction > *Nonfiction Books*: Narrative Nonfiction

Closed to approaches.

Looking for fiction and nonfiction. Loves historical, literary, commercial female fiction, reading group, suspense and thrillers and intelligent crime. Particularly interested in books that shine a light on new ideas or little known histories, diverse backgrounds, and emotionally moving narratives that resonate with modern complexities.

L023 Gina Andrews

Literary Agent
United Kingdom

gandrews@theagency.co.uk

https://theagency.co.uk/the-agents/gina-andrews/

Literary Agency: The Agency (London) Ltd (**L009**)

L024 Anne Clark Literary Agency

Literary Agency
United Kingdom

submissions@anneclarkliteraryagency.co.uk

https://www.anneclarkliteraryagency.co.uk

Professional Body: The Association of Authors' Agents (AAA)

CHILDREN'S
Fiction
Middle Grade; Picture Books
Nonfiction > *Nonfiction Books*

YOUNG ADULT
Fiction > *Novels*
Nonfiction > *Nonfiction Books*

Send: Synopsis; Writing sample; Full text; Proposal
How to send: Email

Handles fiction and picture books for children and young adults. Send query by email only with the following pasted into the body of the email (not as an attachment): for fiction, include brief synopsis and first 3,000 words; for picture books, send complete ms; for nonfiction, send short proposal and the text of three sample pages. No submissions by post. See website for full guidelines.

Literary Agent: Anne Clark

L025 Anne Edelstein Literary Agency

Literary Agency
258 Riverside Drive #8D, New York, NY 10025
United States
Tel: +1 (212) 414-4923

information@aeliterary.com

https://aeliterary.com

Professional Body: Association of American Literary Agents (AALA)

Fiction > *Novels*
Commercial; Literary

Nonfiction > *Nonfiction Books*
Memoir; Narrative History; Psychology; Religion

Closed to approaches.

Send query letter with SASE and for fiction a summary of your novel plus the first 25 pages, or for nonfiction an outline of your book and one or two sample chapters. No queries by email.

Authors: Roderick Anscombe; Stephen Batchelor; Sophy Burnham; Mark Epstein; Kathleen Finneran; James Goodman; Patricia Hersch; His Holiness the Dalai Lama with Jeffrey Hopkins; Peter Levitt; Josip Novakovich; Natasha Rodijcic-Kane; James Shapiro; Jody Shields; Russell Shorto; Rachel Simon; Sasha Troyan; Phyllis Vane

Literary Agent: Anne Edelstein

L026 Annette Green Authors' Agency

Literary Agency
5 Henwoods Mount, Pembury, Kent, TN2 4BH
United Kingdom

annette@annettegreenagency.co.uk
david@annettegreenagency.co.uk

http://www.annettegreenagency.co.uk

Types: Fiction; Nonfiction
Formats: Film Scripts; TV Scripts
Subjects: Autobiography; Comedy / Humour; Commercial; Culture; Current Affairs; History; Horror; Literary; Music; Politics; Science; Sport; Thrillers
Markets: Adult; Children's; Young Adult

Send: Query
Don't send: Full text
How to send: Email

Costs: Offers services that writers have to pay for.

Send query by email with a brief synopsis (fiction) or overview (nonfiction), and the opening few chapters (up to about 10,000 words). No poetry, scripts, science fiction, or fantasy. Send Word documents rather than PDFs.

L027 Jason Anthony

Literary Agent
United States

Literary Agency: Massie & McQuilkin

Closed to approaches.

L028 Zoe Apostolides

Literary Agent
United Kingdom

https://cmm.agency/about-us.php

Literary Agency: Coombs Moylett & Maclean Literary Agency (**L139**)

ADULT
Fiction > *Novels*
Coming of Age; Crime; Historical Fiction; Horror; Mystery

Nonfiction > *Nonfiction Books*

CHILDREN'S > **Fiction** > *Novels*

YOUNG ADULT > **Fiction** > *Novels*

Send: Synopsis; Writing sample
How to send: Online submission system

Manages a list of crime, historical, young adult and children's authors and is also looking to build a nonfiction list. She is especially interested in original horror novels, coming-of-age stories and any sort of whodunnit.

L029 Sophieclaire Armitage

Literary Agent
United Kingdom

Literary Agency: Noel Gay (**L528**)

L030 Victoria Wells Arms

Literary Agent
United States

submissions@wellsarms.com

https://www.hgliterary.com/victoria
https://twitter.com/VWArms
https://querymanager.com/query/VictoriaWellsArms

Literary Agencies: Wells Arms Literary; HG Literary
Professional Bodies: Association of American Literary Agents (AALA); Society of Children's Book Writers and Illustrators (SCBWI)

ADULT
Fiction > *Novels*

Nonfiction > *Nonfiction Books*: Food

CHILDREN'S > **Fiction**
Middle Grade; *Picture Books*
YOUNG ADULT > **Fiction** > *Novels*

How to send: Query Manager

Represents authors of children's books of all ages, select adult authors, food authors, and many talented picture book illustrators. Always open to queries, but not actively looking for new clients.

L031 Arthur B Pulitzer Agency

Literary Agency
236 Moreland Street, Worcester, MA 01609
United States
Tel: +1 (646) 279-3118

arthur@pulitzer.biz

http://www.pulitzer.biz
http://www.pulitzer.biz/other-opportunities.html

ADULT
Nonfiction > *Nonfiction Books*: Crime

Scripts
Film Scripts: Crime
TV Scripts: Crime

CHILDREN'S > **Fiction** > *Middle Grade*

PROFESSIONAL > **Nonfiction** > *Nonfiction Books*: Education

Send: Query
How to send: Email

Costs: Offers services that writers have to pay for.

True Crime Manuscripts, Screenplays, Poems based on real people.

As their literary agent, I am in personal contact with each of these authors Since 2009 I have been corresponding with inmates by mail, email, telephone. I have corresponded via letters, email, and phone calls to inmates and some of their relatives. I have thoroughly read all manuscripts, correspondence and taken notes during direct phone calls and researched the court documents (including appeals) of each inmate. Each story, manuscript as written by the inmate, includes such injustices as: wrongful conviction, ineffective counsel, racially biased juries, police wrongdoing, evidence withheld, prosecutorial misconduct, racism in the courtroom, and constitutional rights' violations. Inmate backgrounds include horrific conditions such as: incest, parental abuse, domestic violence, poverty, drugs, and sexual abuse. All original screenplays, manuscripts were sourced by me directly from men and women inmates. Most are still in prison.

Literary Agent: Arthur B. Pulitzer (*L576*)

L032 Wayne Arthurson

Associate Agent
Canada

https://www.therightsfactory.com/Agents/Wayne-Arthurson

Literary Agency: The Rights Factory

ADULT
Fiction > *Novels*
Crime; Fantasy; Literary; Science Fiction

Nonfiction > *Nonfiction Books*
Memoir; Narrative Nonfiction

YOUNG ADULT
Fiction > *Novels*
Crime; Fantasy; Literary; Science Fiction

Nonfiction > *Nonfiction Books*
Memoir; Narrative Nonfiction

Currently building his list of talent, looking specifically for YA or adult literary, crime and SFF and narrative nonfiction and memoir. He's actively seeking works by Indigenous writers.

Authors: Greg Bechtel; Eric Beetner; Deryn Collier; Candas Jane Dorsey; Brittlestar aka Stewart Reynolds; Steven Sandor; Coltrane Seesequasis

L033 ASH Literary

Literary Agency
United Kingdom

info@ashliterary.com
submissions@ashliterary.com

https://www.ashliterary.com/
https://twitter.com/ashliterary
https://instagram.com/aliceisagenting
https://querymanager.com/query/ASH_Literary

Professional Body: The Association of Authors' Agents (AAA)

CHILDREN'S > **Fiction**
Chapter Books: General
Graphic Novels: Contemporary; Fantasy; Magical Realism; Surreal
Middle Grade: Contemporary; Magical Realism
YOUNG ADULT > **Fiction**
Graphic Novels: Contemporary; Fantasy; Magical Realism; Surreal
Novels: General

Send: Synopsis; Writing sample
How to send: Query Manager

Looking for extraordinary stories for children that reflect and celebrate the diversity of our world. As of July 2021, our focus is on Middle Grade, particularly illustrated Middle Grade, and graphic novels across all ages.

Authors: Dina Al-Sabawi; HF Brownfield; Ryan Crawford; Alex Falase-Koya; Kereen Getten; Gina Gonzales; Sarah Guillory; Ravena Guron; Radiya Hafiza; Anika Hussain; Jennifer Iacopelli; Nansubuga Isdahl; Samantha Joyce; Amy Leow; Richard Mercado; Yasmine Naghdi; Samuel Pollen; Ryan Robinson; Elizabeth Rounding; Kelly Sharpe; Cynthia So; Chitra Soundar; Claire Tomasi; Adelle Yeung

Literary Agent: Alice Sutherland-Hawes (**L680**)

L034 Charlotte Atyeo

Literary Agent
United Kingdom

charlotte@greyhoundliterary.co.uk

https://greyhoundliterary.co.uk/agent/charlotte-atyeo/
https://twitter.com/EverSoBookish

Literary Agency: Greyhound Literary (**L288**)

ADULT
Fiction > *Novels*: Literary

Nonfiction > *Nonfiction Books*
General, and in particular: Biography; Equality; Feminism; Gender Issues; Memoir; Music; Nature; Sport

CHILDREN'S > **Fiction** > *Novels*

Send: Query; Synopsis; Writing sample; Outline
How to send: Email
How not to send: Post

Represents non-fiction authors as well as a select number of children's and fiction authors. Primarily looking for original and brilliantly written general non-fiction, biography and memoir, sport, music, nature writing, and feminism, gender and equality issues. On the fiction side, she is taking on a small number of literary novels.

Authors: Saskia Gwinn; Ed Hawkins; Michael Holding; Michael Hutchinson; Jennifer Lane; Michelle Lovric; Susan Richardson; Sarah Shephard; Tatton Spiller; Jen Wight

L035 AVAnti Productions & Management

Literary Agency
7 Parkside Mews, Hurst Road, Horsham, West Sussex, RH12 2SA
United Kingdom

avantiproductions@live.co.uk

https://www.avantiproductions.co.uk

Scripts > *Film Scripts*

Send: Full text
How to send: Email
How not to send: Post

Costs: Author covers sundry admin costs.

Talent and literary representation. Open to screenplay submissions for short films and feature films, but no theatre scripts.

Literary Agent: Veronica Lazar (**L415**)

L036 Ayesha Pande Literary

Literary Agency
128 West 132 Street, New York, NY 10027
United States
Tel: +1 (212) 283-5825

queries@pandeliterary.com

http://pandeliterary.com

A New York based boutique literary agency with a small and eclectic roster of clients. Submit queries via form on website. No poetry, business books, cookbooks, screenplays or illustrated children's books.

Literary Agents: Jake Allgeier; Madison Smartt Bell (**L053**); Stephany Evans (**L211**); Serene Hakim (**L297**); Annie Hwang (**L338**); Kayla Lightner (**L426**); Luba Ostashevsky (**L542**); Ayesha Pande (**L546**); Anjali Singh (**L646**)

L037 Azantian Literary Agency

Literary Agency
United States

http://www.azantianlitagency.com
https://www.facebook.com/azantianlitagency/
https://twitter.com/jenazantian
https://www.instagram.com/azantianbooknerd/

Fiction > *Novels*

Nonfiction > *Nonfiction Books*

Committed to guiding the careers of both new and established voices in fiction and nonfiction, particularly those who have been historically underrepresented.

Associate Agents: Masha Gunic (**L293**); Renae Moore (**L505**); Amanda Rutter (**L614**); Andrea Walker; Alexandra Weiss (**L727**)

Literary Agents: Jennifer Azantian (**L038**); Ben Baxter; T.S. Ferguson (**L222**)

L038 Jennifer Azantian

Literary Agent
United States

http://www.azantianlitagency.com/pages/team-ja.html

Literary Agency: Azantian Literary Agency (**L037**)

ADULT > **Fiction** > *Novels*
General, and in particular: Fantasy; Psychological Horror; Science Fiction

CHILDREN'S > **Fiction**
Graphic Novels: Contemporary; Fantasy; Magical Realism
Middle Grade: General

YOUNG ADULT > **Fiction**
Graphic Novels: Contemporary; Fantasy; Magical Realism
Novels: General, and in particular: Mystery; Psychological Thrillers; Speculative

How to send: Query Manager

Focuses primarily on fiction across genres for mg, YA, and adult readers. Currently accepting submissions of graphic novels only.

L039 Oliver Azis

Literary Agent
United Kingdom

Literary Agency: Independent Talent Group Ltd (**L340**)

L040 Becky Bagnell

Literary Agent
United Kingdom

Literary Agency: Lindsay Literary Agency (**L430**)

L041 Emma Bal

Literary Agent
United Kingdom

https://madeleinemilburn.co.uk/looking-for/emma-bal-what-im-looking-for/

Literary Agency: Madeleine Milburn Literary, TV & Film Agency (**L464**)

Nonfiction > *Nonfiction Books*
Anthropology; Arts; Cookery; Culture; Economics; Food; Geography; History; Literature; Memoir; Narrative Nonfiction; Nature; Philosophy; Politics; Psychology; Science; Travel

Actively looking for: new perspectives in history, arts & culture, politics, economics, philosophy, psychology, and science; original approaches to travel and nature writing; unusual illustrated projects; thoughtful and dynamic cookery and food writing; and atypical narrative non-fiction and memoir. See agency listing for submission guidelines.

L042 Natalie Ball

Literary Agent
United Kingdom

Literary Agency: Noel Gay (**L528**)

L043 Sarah Ballard

Literary Agent
United Kingdom

sballard@unitedagents.co.uk

https://www.unitedagents.co.uk/sballardunitedagentscouk

Literary Agency: United Agents (**L704**)

Fiction > *Novels*

Nonfiction > *Nonfiction Books*
Feminism; History; Memoir

Does not want:

Fiction > *Novels*
Saga; Science Fiction

Closed to approaches.

I have extremely broad taste in fiction and non-fiction, but the underlying quality of the work that I'm interested in is a sense of urgency, and an attempt to make a change in the world, whether that is fiction with a compelling plot or structure overlaying a set of big ideas; memoir-ish non fiction flavoured with obsession and unfolding a hidden agenda; or meticulously researched history which changes our world view. I have a particular interest in feminism and feminist approaches – but exploring ideas or angles which are completely new to me is one of the great joys of my job. I prefer to work with writers who are more-or-less based in the UK, and are aiming to deliver a book every one or two years, and for whom I can add something to every area of their creative lives.

Associate Agent: Eli Keren (**L383**)

L044 Barbara Levy Literary Agency

Literary Agency
64 Greenhill, Hampstead High Street, London, NW3 5TZ

United Kingdom
Tel: +44 (0) 20 7435 9046

submissions@barbaralevyagency.com

http://barbaralevyagency.com
https://twitter.com/BLLA_NW3

Professional Body: The Association of Authors' Agents (AAA)

Types: Fiction; Nonfiction
Markets: Adult

Send: Query; Synopsis; Author bio; Writing sample
How to send: Email; Post

Send query with synopsis and first three chapters (approximately 50 pages) by email or by post with SAE. No poetry, plays, original screenplays, scripts or picture books for children.

Associate Agent: Jamilah Ahmed (**L013**)

Literary Agents: Barbara Levy (*L424*); Vicki Salter (*L615*)

L045 Baror International, Inc.

Literary Agency
P.O. Box 868, Armonk, NY 10504-0868
United States

Heather@Barorint.com

http://www.barorint.com

ADULT
Fiction > *Novels*
Commercial; Fantasy; Literary; Science Fiction

Nonfiction > *Nonfiction Books*

YOUNG ADULT > **Fiction** > *Novels*

Closed to approaches.

Specialises in the international and domestic representation of literary works in both fiction and nonfiction, including commercial fiction, literary, science fiction, fantasy, young adult and more.

Literary Agents: Danny Baror; Heather Baror-Shapiro

L046 Jason Bartholomew

Literary Agent
United Kingdom

https://www.thebksagency.com/submissions

Literary Agency: The BKS Agency (**L065**)

Fiction > *Novels*
Crime; Thrillers

Nonfiction > *Nonfiction Books*
Biography; Current Affairs; History; Memoir; Narrative Nonfiction; Politics

Send: Query; Outline; Author bio
How to send: Online submission system

Originally from America. Spent ten years working in New York publishing, primarily for Hachette Book Group USA. He moved to Hachette UK in 2008 where he was the Rights Director across Hodder & Stoughton, Headline Publishing Group, Quercus Books, and John Murray Press.

L047 Bath Literary Agency

Literary Agency
5 Gloucester Road, Bath, BA1 7BH
United Kingdom

submissions@bathliteraryagency.com

https://www.bathliteraryagency.com
https://twitter.com/BathLitAgency
http://instagram.com/bathlitagency

Professional Body: The Association of Authors' Agents (AAA)

CHILDREN'S
Fiction
Middle Grade; *Picture Books*
Poetry > *Picture Books*

YOUNG ADULT
Fiction > *Novels*
Nonfiction > *Nonfiction Books*

Send: Query; Synopsis; Writing sample; Full text; Self-Addressed Stamped Envelope (SASE)
How to send: Email; Post

Handles fiction and nonfiction for children, from picture books to Young Adult. Send query by email or by post with SAE for reply and return of materials if required, along with the first three chapters (fiction) or the full manuscript (picture books). See website for full details.

Literary Agent: Gill McLay

L048 Erica Bauman

Literary Agent
United States

https://aevitascreative.com/agents/
https://querymanager.com/query/EricaBauman

Literary Agency: Aevitas

ADULT > **Fiction**
Graphic Novels: General
Novels: Commercial; Folklore, Myths, and Legends; Magic; Romantic Comedy; Speculative
CHILDREN'S > **Fiction** > *Graphic Novels*

YOUNG ADULT > **Fiction** > *Graphic Novels*

Closed to approaches.

Most interested in commercial novels that feature an exciting premise and lyrical, atmospheric writing; imaginative, genre-blending tales; speculative worlds filled with haunting, quietly wondrous magic; fresh retellings of mythology, ballet, opera, and classic literature; sharply funny rom-coms; graphic novels for all ages; fearless storytellers that tackle big ideas and contemporary issues; and working with and supporting marginalized authors and stories that represent the wide range of humanity.

L049 Jan Baumer

Literary Agent
United States

jan@foliolitmanagement.com

https://www.foliolit.com/agents-1/jan-baumer

Literary Agency: Folio Literary Management, LLC

Fiction > *Novels*
Allegory; Literary

Nonfiction > *Nonfiction Books*
Business; Comedy / Humour; Cookery; Health; Memoir; Narrative Nonfiction; Parenting; Prescriptive Nonfiction; Religion; Self Help; Spirituality; Wellbeing

Closed to approaches.

Interests as an agent are largely nonfiction, specifically spirituality, religion, self-help, health and wellness, parenting, memoir, and business with a spirituality or self-help angle. Also open to allegorical fiction, but it must have a literary voice and an author with the writing credentials to pull it off.

L050 Veronique Baxter

Literary Agent; Company Director
United Kingdom

veroniquemanuscripts@davidhigham.co.uk

https://www.davidhigham.co.uk/agents-dh/veronique-baxter/

Literary Agency: David Higham Associates Ltd (**L161**)

ADULT
Fiction > *Novels*
Historical Fiction; Literary; Speculative; Upmarket Crime; Upmarket Thrillers

Nonfiction > *Nonfiction Books*
Current Affairs; Feminism; History; Memoir; Narrative Nonfiction

CHILDREN'S > **Fiction** > *Middle Grade*: Adventure

YOUNG ADULT > **Fiction** > *Novels*: Adventure

Agency Assistant: Sara Langham

Assistant Agent: Becca Challis (*L113*)

Authors: Richard Adams; Naomi Alderman; Hannah Begbie; Carys Bray; Kevin Brockmeier; Glen Brown; Nick Butterworth; Nick Crumpton; Nicola Davies; Jonathan Dimbleby; Berlie Doherty; Ellie Eaton; David Edmonds; Maz Evans; Jamila Gavin; Guinevere Glasfurd; Candy Guard; Saleem Haddad; Oliver Harris; Lisa Heathfield; Neil Hegarty; Emma Henderson; Edward Hogan; Phil Hogan; Ian Holding; Lucy Hounsom; Tristan Hughes; William Hussey; Will Iredale;

Diana Wynne Jones; Claire King; Saci Lloyd; Kesia Lupo; Patrick Marnham; Geraldine McCaughrean; Jean McNeil

L051 Diana Beaumont

Literary Agent
United Kingdom

diana@marjacq.com

http://www.marjacq.com/diana-beaumont.html

Literary Agency: Marjacq Scripts Ltd (**L469**)

Fiction > *Novels*
Book Club Fiction; Commercial; Contemporary; Crime; High Concept; Historical Fiction; Literary; Saga; Thrillers; Upmarket Women's Fiction

Nonfiction > *Nonfiction Books*
Cookery; Feminism; Lifestyle; Memoir; Social Justice

Closed to approaches.

Looking for upmarket women's commercial fiction with depth and heart, including reading group, historical, saga, uplit and contemporary stories that are irreverent and make her laugh; accessible literary fiction, high-concept crime fiction and thrillers. On the non-fiction side: memoir, smart, funny feminists, lifestyle, cookery and social justice, and open to anything with a strong, original voice. She also encourages submissions from writers who have been traditionally under-represented.

Authors: Tanya Atapattu; Holly Baxter; Alexandra K Benedict; Daisy Buchanan; Cecil Cameron; James Campbell; Angela Clarke; Mathew Clayton; Fiona Collins; Caroline Corcoran; Isabel Costello; Hannah Dolby; Francesca Dorricott; Lilly Ebert; Dov Forman; Eve Harris; Louise Hulland; Catriona Innes; Harriet Johnson; Amy Jones; Eve Makis; Andrea Mara; Francesca May; Claire McGowan; Adam Pearson; Alice Peterson; Das Petrou; Rachel Phipps; Carmen Reid; Samantha Renke; Lee Ridley; Diana Rosie; Frances Ryan; Jennifer Savin; Hema Sukumar; Lucy Vine; James Wallman; Roz Watkins; Eva Woods

L052 Rachel Beck

Literary Agent
United States

queryrachel@lizadawson.com

https://www.lizadawsonassociates.com/team/rachel-beck/

Literary Agency: Liza Dawson Associates (**L436**)

ADULT
Fiction > *Novels*
Book Club Women's Fiction; Contemporary Romance; Domestic Suspense; Millennial Fiction; Upmarket Women's Fiction

Nonfiction > *Nonfiction Books*
Career Development; Feminism; Personal Development

YOUNG ADULT > **Fiction** > *Novels*
Contemporary; Cyberpunk; Post-Apocalyptic

Send: Query; Writing sample
How to send: In the body of an email

Believes that the right book can change or heal a life, and she wants to find those. But she's also interested in lighter fiction that helps you escape or simply makes you laugh after a tough day. Or nonfiction that teaches you something about an obscure topic, thus opening up a new world.

L053 Madison Smartt Bell

Literary Agent
United States

https://www.pandeliterary.com/about-pandeliterary

Literary Agency: Ayesha Pande Literary (**L036**)

Fiction > *Novels*
Literary; Noir; Police Procedural

L054 Maria Bell

Associate Agent
United States

Literary Agency: Sterling Lord Literistic, Inc. (**L662**)
Literary Agent / Vice President: Douglas Stewart (**L665**)
Senior Agent: Neeti Madan (**L463**)

ADULT
Fiction > *Novels*
Baseball; LGBTQIA; Literary; Nature

Nonfiction > *Nonfiction Books*
Baseball; LGBTQIA; Nature

YOUNG ADULT > **Fiction** > *Novels*
Baseball; LGBTQIA; Nature

Send: Query; Synopsis; Proposal; Writing sample
How to send: Online submission system

Drawn to adult literary fiction and YA that break conventions in form, voice and character. In both fiction and nonfiction, she's partial to stories involving the natural world, queer identities, baseball, and all those that grapple with conflicts and truths from which most of us instinctively distance ourselves.

L055 Maddy Belton

Literary Agent
United Kingdom

submissions@grahammawchristie.com

http://www.grahammawchristie.com/about1.html

Literary Agency: Graham Maw Christie Literary Agency (**L278**)

Nonfiction > *Nonfiction Books*
General, and in particular: Memoir; Narrative Nonfiction; Psychology

Send: Outline; Author bio; Market info; Marketing Plan; Writing sample
How to send: Email

Interests are broad but she is particularly interested in memoir, psychology and narrative non-fiction She is also interested in hearing from marginalised voices including, but not limited to, those in the LGBTQ+ community and BIPOC.

L056 Laura Bennett

Associate Agent; Editor
United Kingdom

https://www.liverpool-literary.agency/about

Literary Agency: The Liverpool Literary Agency (**L435**)

ADULT > **Fiction** > *Novels*
Dystopian Fiction; Fantasy; Post-Apocalyptic; Science Fiction; Steampunk; Urban Fantasy

YOUNG ADULT > **Fiction** > *Novels*
Dystopian Fiction; Fantasy; Post-Apocalyptic; Science Fiction; Steampunk; Urban Fantasy

L057 The Bent Agency (UK)

Literary Agency
17 Kelsall Mews, Richmond, TW9 4BP
United Kingdom

info@thebentagency.com

https://www.thebentagency.com
https://www.instagram.com/thebentagency/

Professional Body: The Association of Authors' Agents (AAA)
Literary Agency: The Bent Agency (**L058**)

ADULT
Fiction
Graphic Novels; *Novels*
Nonfiction > *Nonfiction Books*

CHILDREN'S > **Fiction**
Chapter Books; *Graphic Novels*; *Middle Grade*

YOUNG ADULT
Fiction
Graphic Novels; *Novels*
Nonfiction > *Nonfiction Books*

Send: Query
How to send: Email; Query Manager

UK office of established US agency. See website for individual agent interests and contact details and approach appropriate agent. Do not send submissions to general agency email address. See website for full submission guidelines.

Assistant Agent: Martha Perotto-Wills (**L556**)

Literary Agents: Molly Ker Hawn (**L314**); Sarah Hornsley

L058 The Bent Agency

Literary Agency
529 W 42nd St, Suite 3P, New York, NY 10036
United States

info@thebentagency.com

https://www.thebentagency.com
https://www.instagram.com/thebentagency/

ADULT
Fiction
Graphic Novels; *Novels*
Nonfiction > *Nonfiction Books*

CHILDREN'S > **Fiction**
Chapter Books; *Graphic Novels*; *Middle Grade*
YOUNG ADULT
Fiction
Graphic Novels; *Novels*
Nonfiction > *Nonfiction Books*

Send: Query
How to send: Email; Query Manager

Accepts email or Query Manager queries only. See website for agent bios and specific interests and email addresses, then query one agent only. See website for full submission guidelines.

Literary Agency: The Bent Agency (UK) (**L057**)

Literary Agents: Nicola Barr; Jenny Bent; Victoria Cappello; Gemma Cooper (**L140**); Claire Draper; Louise Fury (*L244*); James Mustelier (**L518**); Zoe Plant (**L566**); John Silbersack; Laurel Symonds (**L685**); Desiree Wilson (**L740**)

L059 John Berlyne

Literary Agent
United Kingdom

http://zenoagency.com/about-us/

Literary Agency: Zeno Agency Ltd (**L759**)

ADULT > **Fiction** > *Novels*
Crime; Fantasy; Historical Fiction; Horror; Science Fiction; Space Opera; Thrillers; Urban Fantasy

YOUNG ADULT > **Fiction** > *Novels*

Closed to approaches.

L060 Betsy Amster Literary Enterprises

Literary Agency
607 Foothill Blvd #1061, La Canada Flintridge, CA 91012
United States

b.amster.assistant@gmail.com
b.amster.kidsbooks@gmail.com

http://amsterlit.com

Fiction > *Novels*
Literary; Mystery; Thrillers; Upmarket Commercial Fiction; Upmarket Women's Fiction

Nonfiction
Gift Books: General
Nonfiction Books: Biography; Career Development; Cookery; Gardening; Health; History; Lifestyle; Medicine; Narrative Nonfiction; Nutrition; Parenting; Popular Culture; Psychology; Self Help; Social Issues; Travel; Women's Issues

How to send: Email
How not to send: Post

A full-service literary agency based in Los Angeles, California. No romances, screenplays, poetry, westerns, fantasy, horror, science fiction, techno thrillers, spy capers, apocalyptic scenarios, political or religious arguments, or self-published books. See website for full guidelines.

Authors: Amy Alkon; Dwight Allen; Will Allen; Jess J. Araujo; Elaine N. Aron; Sandi Ault; Lois Barr; Ariel Bernstein; Kim Boyce; Helene Brenner; Karen Briner; Catheryn J. Brockett; Karen Burns; Mónica Bustamante; Joe P. Carr; Steven Carter; Lillian Castillo-Speed; Robin Chotzinoff; Frank Clifford; Rob Cohen; David Cundy; Leela Cyd; Margaret Leslie Davis; Jan DeBlieu; David J. Diamond; Martha O. Diamond; Phil Doran; Suzanne Dunaway; Nick Dyer; J. Theron Elkins; Ruth Andrew Ellenson; Loretta Ellsworth; James P. Emswiler; Mary Ann Emswiler; Naomi Epel; Alex Epstein; Karin Esterhammer; Jeannette Faurot; Tom Fields-Meyer; Joline Godfrey; Tanya Ward Goodman; Michael I. Goran; Hindi Greenberg; Ellen Hawley; Marian Henley; Charney Herst; Leigh Ann Hirschman; Ariel Horn; Lisa Hunter; Jackie; Melissa Jacobs; Janet Jaffe; Emily Katz; E. Barrie Kavasch; Joy Keller; Eileen Kennedy-Moore; Rachel Tawil Kenyon; Camille Landau; Carol Lay; Anna Lefler; Margaret Lobenstine; Mark Lowenthal; Paul Mandelbaum; Ivy Manning; Melissa Martin; Domenico Minchilli; Elizabeth Helman Minchilli; Wendy Mogel; Sharon Montrose; Bonnie Frumkin Morales; Yolanda Nava; Joy Nicholson; Judith Nies; Susie Norris; Christopher Noxon; Lynette Padwa; Neela Paniz; Kishani Perera; Cash Peters; Barry Prizant; Winifred Reilly; Andrea Richards; Eileen Roth; Adam Sappington; Marjorie Barton Savage; Anthony Schmitz; M.D. Edward Schneider; Kyle Schuneman; George Shannon; Nancy Spiller; Allison Mia Starcher; Louise Steinman; Bill Stern; Terry Theise; Christina Baglivi Tinglof; Linda Venis; MPH Emily Ventura; Marisel Vera; Elizabeth Verdick; John Vorhaus; Hannah Voskuil; Diana Wells; Tiare White; Chris Witt; Karen Witynski; Steve D. Wolf; David Wollock; Dawn Young

Literary Agent: Betsy Amster

L061 Tina Betts

Literary Agent; Company Director
United Kingdom

https://www.andrewmann.co.uk/agents

Literary Agency: Andrew Mann Ltd

ADULT
Fiction > *Novels*: Commercial

Nonfiction > *Nonfiction Books*

Scripts
Radio Scripts; *TV Scripts*
CHILDREN'S > **Fiction** > *Novels*

Closed to approaches.

List includes quality commercial fiction, as well as some non-fiction and children's titles.

Also represents a small list of dramatists for television and radio.

L062 Beverley Slopen Literary Agency

Literary Agency
131 Bloor St. W., Suite 711, Toronto, M5S 1S3
Canada
Tel: +1 (416) 964-9598

beverley@slopenagency.ca

https://slopenagency.com

Fiction > *Novels*
Commercial; Literary

Nonfiction > *Nonfiction Books*

One of Canada's leading literary agents. Based in Toronto, her list includes serious non-fiction and literary and commercial fiction.

Literary Agent: Beverley Slopen

L063 Elizabeth Bewley

Literary Agent
United States

ebewley@sll.com

https://www.sll.com/our-team

Literary Agency: Sterling Lord Literistic, Inc. (**L662**)

ADULT
Fiction > *Novels*
High Concept; Romance; Upmarket Commercial Fiction

Nonfiction > *Nonfiction Books*: Narrative Nonfiction

CHILDREN'S > **Fiction**
Middle Grade; *Picture Books*
YOUNG ADULT > **Fiction** > *Novels*
High Concept; Romance

Send: Query; Synopsis; Writing sample
How to send: Online submission system; Email

On the children's side of her list, she represents young adult and middle grade fiction, and the occasional picture book. On the adult side, she is eager to represent more upmarket commercial fiction and narrative nonfiction. Current submission wish list includes high-concept young adult novels, especially from underrepresented voices, accessible middle grade novels that will foster a love of reading (think: fun, funny, or both!), young adult romance, high-concept adult love stories, and any upmarket commercial fiction with a witty voice and eye for detail.

L064 Victoria Birkett

Literary Agent
United Kingdom

https://milesstottagency.co.uk/representatives/victoria-birkett/

Literary Agency: Miles Stott Children's Literary Agency (**L498**)

Author: Gill Lewis

L065 The BKS Agency

Literary Agency
Pennine Place, 2A Charing Cross Road, London, WC2H 0FH
United Kingdom

https://www.thebksagency.com
https://www.facebook.com/thebksagency
https://twitter.com/ThebksAgency

A literary management agency based in London. Founded in 2018 by three friends, each of whom has spent over two decades working across the biggest publishing houses in London and New York.

Literary Agents: Jason Bartholomew (**L046**); Joanna Kaliszewska (**L367**); Jessica Killingley (**L387**); James Spackman (**L655**)

L066 The Blair Partnership

Literary Agency
PO Box, 7828, London, W1A 4GE
United Kingdom
Tel: +44 (0) 20 7504 2520

info@theblairpartnership.com

https://www.theblairpartnership.com

Professional Body: The Association of Authors' Agents (AAA)

ADULT

Fiction > *Novels*
Book Club Fiction; Commercial; Crime; Detective Fiction; Dystopian Fiction; High Concept; Historical Fiction; Literary; Speculative; Thrillers; Upmarket; Women's Fiction

Nonfiction > *Nonfiction Books*
Crime; Lifestyle; Personal Development

CHILDREN'S

Fiction
Middle Grade: Adventure
Novels: General, and in particular: Commercial

Nonfiction > *Nonfiction Books*

TEEN > **Fiction** > *Novels*

YOUNG ADULT > **Fiction** > *Novels*

Send: Query; Synopsis; Proposal; Writing sample
How to send: Word file email attachment; PDF file email attachment

We welcome all submissions and consider everything that is sent to the agency, though we are not currently accepting submissions for screenplays, short stories or poetry.

We welcome approaches from both debut writers and established authors. We're very happy to receive submissions from overseas, as long as they're written in English.

Associate Agent: Jordan Lees (**L420**)

Authors: Marina Abramović; Bana Alabed; Matt Allen; JJ Arcanjo; Jane Asher; Rafael Behr; Gary Bell; Ronen Bergman; David Bolchover; YolanDa Brown; Michael Byrne; Michael Calvin; Tom Carlisle; Sir Ronald Cohen; Dawn Coulter-Cruttenden; Susanna H Cunningham; Helena Duggan; Owen Eastwood; Emma Farrarons; Henry Fraser; William Friend; Paris Fury; Tyson Fury; Marina Gerner; Erica Gomez; Pippa Grange; Catherine Green; Toby Gutteridge; Maria Hatzistefanis; Amelia Henley; Leigh Hosy-Pickett; Chris Hoy; Oli Hyatt; James Inverne; Louise Jensen; Ruth Kelly; Scott Kershaw; Joanne Lake; Frank Lampard; Kieran Larwood; Elspeth Latimer; Liz Lawler; Lee Lawrence; The Urban Legend; Rose Lihou; John Lutz; Dan Malakin; Aseem Malhotra; Joe Marler; Luna McNamara; Major Scotty Mills; Markus Motum; Mercy Muroki; Shabnam Nasimi; Maajid Nawaz; Michal Oshman; Justine Pattison; Rogba Payne; Daisy Pearce; Adam Peaty; Trevor Phillips; Nirmal Purja; Duncan Roe; Terry Ronald; Stephen Ronson; J.K. Rowling; Dan Saunders; Babita Sharma; Jon Smith; Jon Sopel; Tom Spencer; P. A. Staff; Dean Stott; Jessica Taylor; Nicki Thornton; Pete Townshend; John Volanthen; Tom Watson; Brian Wood

Company Director / Literary Agent: Rory Scarfe (**L624**)

Literary Agents: Hattie Grunewald (**L291**); Josephine Hayes; Rachel Petty (**L562**)

L067 Blake Friedmann Literary Agency Ltd

Literary Agency
15 Highbury Place, London, N5 1QP
United Kingdom
Tel: +44 (0) 20 7387 0842

info@blakefriedmann.co.uk

http://www.blakefriedmann.co.uk
https://twitter.com/BlakeFriedmann
https://www.instagram.com/blakefriedmannliteraryagency/

Professional Body: The Association of Authors' Agents (AAA)

Fiction > *Novels*

Nonfiction > *Nonfiction Books*

Send: Query; Synopsis; Writing sample
How to send: Word file email attachment

Always on the lookout for exciting new work and welcomes submissions from both published and debut authors, across many genres, and from any background.

Associate Agent: Sian Ellis-Martin (**L202**)

Authors: Diane Abbott; Gilbert Adair; Tatamkhulu Afrika; Mary Akers; Shani Akilah; Kasim Ali; Ted Allbeury; Dima Alzayat; Graeme Armstrong; Paul Ashton; MiMi Aye; Trezza Azzopardi; Bolu Babalola; Jendella Benson; Meliz Berg; Ian Birch; Rachel Blackmore; Nora Anne Brown; Erin Bunting; Ailsa Caine; Natasha Carthew; Norie Clarke; Julia Cole; Sue Cook; Sara Crowe; Tuyen Do; Michael Donkor; Jo Facer; Alix Fox; Sarah Franklin; Roxy Freeman; Janice Galloway; Gabriella Griffith; Sarah Hartley; Emma Forsyth Haslett; Kate Hodges; Michael Hogan; Kerry Hudson; Leah Hyslop; Alexandra Jellicoe; Benjamin Johncock; Konditor; Kat Lister; Richard Littler; Clayton Littlewood; Anneliese Mackintosh; Ailbhe Malone; Lucy Mangan; Amy Mason; Nina-Sophia Miralles; Emma Mitchell; Sue Moorcroft; Grace Mortimer; Emer O'Toole; Sara Ochs; Rosalind Powell; Annie Robertson; Elliot Ryan; Lora Stimson; Jack Urwin; Pippa Vosper; Helen Walmsley-Johnson; Andrew Wong

Literary Agent / Managing Director: Isobel Dixon (**L174**)

Literary Agents: Samuel Hodder (**L327**); Juliet Pickering (**L565**); Tom Witcomb

Senior Agent: Kate Burke (**L095**)

L068 Felicity Blunt

Literary Agent
United Kingdom

http://submissions.curtisbrown.co.uk/agents/

Literary Agency: Curtis Brown

Fiction > *Novels*
Domestic Suspense; Historical Fiction; Literary Thrillers; Psychological Suspense; Speculative

Nonfiction > *Nonfiction Books*
Cookery; Food

Send: Full text; Synopsis; Author bio
How to send: Email

"Most simply put I am looking for good stories, compellingly told. The books on my list have one thing in common, the combination of a distinctive voice and a great narrative."

L069 Camilla Bolton

Senior Agent
United Kingdom

camilla@darleyanderson.com

https://www.darleyanderson.com/our-team
https://twitter.com/CamillaJBolton

Literary Agency: The Darley Anderson Agency

Fiction > *Novels*
Book Club Fiction; Crime; Mystery; Suspense; Thrillers; Women's Fiction

How to send: Email attachment

Looking for accessible and commercial crime, thrillers, mysteries, suspense and women's fiction.

Assistant Agent: Jade Kavanagh (**L376**)

Authors: Emma Bamford; Vicki Bradley; James Carol; Gloria Cook; A J Cross; Jason Dean; Hayley Doyle; C. M. Ewan; G.R. Halliday; Egan Hughes; Emma Kavanagh; T M Logan; Imran Mahmood; L V Matthews; Phoebe Morgan; B.A. Paris; Jo Platt; Meera Shah; Rebecca Shaw; KL Slater; Kim Slater; Sean Slater; Catherine Steadman; G X Todd; Tim Weaver

L070 Luigi Bonomi

Literary Agent
United Kingdom

http://www.lbabooks.com/agent/luigi-bonomi/

Literary Agency: LBA Books Ltd (**L417**)

Fiction > *Novels*: Commercial

Nonfiction > *Nonfiction Books*: Commercial

Closed to approaches.

I love commercial fiction across all genres, as well as intelligent non-fiction written for a commercial audience, and am always on the lookout for authors who aspire to hit the bestseller list.

Authors: Will Adams; Lizzy Barber; James Becker; Jason Bray; Fern Britton; James Cheshire; Rosemary Conley; Gennaro Contaldo; Josephine Cox; Mason Cross; Louise Curtis; A.M. Dean; Georgia Fancett; Dan Farnworth; Liz Fenwick; Judy Finnigan; Nick Foulkes; Mark Frary; Daniel Freeman; Susan Gee; David Gibbins; Jane Gordon; Tom Grass; Mark Griffin; Michael Gustafson; Rachel Hamilton; Richard Hammond; Duncan Harding; Matt Hilton; John Humphrys; Jessica Jarlvi; Sarah Johnson; Annabel Kantaria; Catherine Kirwan; Guy Leschziner; Susan Lewis; Amy Lloyd; Richard Madeley; Tom Marcus; Ben Miller; Michael Morley; Louise Morrish; Anthony Mosawi; Karen Osman; S.A. Patrick; Andrew Pepper; Gervase Phinn; Richard Porter; Esther Rantzen; Madeleine Reiss; Alice Roberts; Simon Scarrow; Colin Shindler; Lucy Strange; Rachel de Thame; Alan Titchmarsh; Oliver Uberti; Phil Vickery; Tamsin Winter

L071 The Book Group

Literary Agency
20 West 20th Street, Suite 601, New York, NY 10011
United States
Tel: +1 (212) 803-3360

submissions@thebookgroup.com
info@thebookgroup.com

http://www.thebookgroup.com
https://www.facebook.com/thebookgrp
https://twitter.com/thebookgrp
https://www.instagram.com/thebookgrp/

Fiction > *Novels*

Nonfiction > *Nonfiction Books*

Send: Query; Writing sample
How to send: In the body of an email
How not to send: Email attachment; Post; Phone

Represents a broad range of fiction and nonfiction. No poetry or screenplays. Send query by email only with ten sample pages and the first and last name of the agent you are querying in the subject line (see website for individual agent interests). No attachments. Include all material in the body of the email. See website for full guidelines. Response only if interested.

Authors: Nishant Batsha; Suhaly Bautista-Carolina; Rachel Broderick; Wendy Chin-Tanner; Tiana Clark; Tracy Clark-Flory; Chloe Cole; Ella Dawson; Kimberly Drew; Susie Dumond; Taylor Hahn; Alex Hoopes; Mike Lala; Melissa Larsen; Ashton Lattimore; Esther Levy-Chehebar; Vanessa Lillie; Kristen Martin; Laura McKowen; Abi Morgan; Victoria Savanh; Sophia Shalmiyev; Rainesford Stauffer; Elissa Strauss; Sara Sutter; Noor Tagouri; Rachel Zarrow

Literary Agents: Julie Barer; Faye Bender; Brettne Bloom; Jamie Carr (**L107**); Dana Murphy; Elisabeth Weed

L072 Bookseeker Agency

Literary Agency
PO Box 7535, Perth, PH2 1AF
United Kingdom
Tel: +44 (0) 1738 620688

bookseeker@blueyonder.co.uk

https://bookseekeragency.com
https://twitter.com/BookseekerAgent

Fiction > *Novels*

Poetry > *Any Poetic Form*

Send: Query; Synopsis; Writing sample
How to send: Email; Post

Handles fiction and (under some circumstances) poetry. No nonfiction. Send query by post or email outlining what you have written and your current projects, along with synopsis and sample chapter (novels).

Literary Agent: Paul Thompson (*L696*)

L073 BookStop Literary Agency, LLC

Literary Agency
P.O. Box 626, Lafayette, CA 94549
United States
Tel: +1 (925) 254-2664

info@bookstopliterary.com

http://www.bookstopliterary.com
https://www.facebook.com/bookstopliterary/
https://www.instagram.com/bookstopliterary/

CHILDREN'S
Fiction
Chapter Books; *Graphic Novels*; *Middle Grade*; *Novels*; *Picture Books*
Nonfiction > *Nonfiction Books*

YOUNG ADULT > **Fiction** > *Novels*

Handles fiction and nonfiction for children and young adults.

Literary Agents: Minju Chang (**L118**); Karyn Fischer (**L228**); Kendra Marcus (**L468**)

L074 Stefanie Sanchez Von Borstel

Literary Agent
United States

https://www.fullcircleliterary.com/our-agents/stefanie-von-borstel/

Literary Agency: Full Circle Literary, LLC
Professional Bodies: Society of Children's Book Writers and Illustrators (SCBWI); Association of American Literary Agents (AALA)

CHILDREN'S
Fiction > *Middle Grade*
Contemporary; Historical Fiction

Poetry > *Novels in Verse*
Contemporary; History

Looking for middle grade fiction and novels-in-verse (contemporary or historical) with memorable characters and voice.

L075 Sarah Bowlin

Literary Agent
Los Angeles
United States

https://aevitascreative.com/agents/

Literary Agency: Aevitas

Fiction > *Novels*
General, and in particular: Literary

Nonfiction > *Nonfiction Books*
General, and in particular: Comedy / Humour; Dance; Food History; History; Narrative Nonfiction; Popular Culture; Wine

Send: Query; Market info; Author bio; Writing sample
How to send: Online submission system

Focused on bold, diverse voices in fiction and nonfiction. She's especially interested in stories of strong or difficult women and unexpected narratives of place, of identity, and of the shifting ways we see ourselves and each other. She's also interested in food history, wine, and dance.

L076 Katherine Boyle

Literary Agent
United States

katherine@veritasliterary.com

http://www.veritasliterary.com

Literary Agency: Veritas Literary Agency (**L712**)

ADULT
Fiction > *Novels*
Historical Fiction; Literary

Nonfiction > *Nonfiction Books*
Culture; History; Memoir; Narrative Nonfiction; Nature; Popular Culture; Women's Studies

CHILDREN'S > **Fiction**
Middle Grade; *Picture Books*
YOUNG ADULT > **Fiction** > *Novels*

L077 Bradford Literary Agency

Literary Agency
5694 Mission Center Road # 347, San Diego, CA 92108
United States
Tel: +1 (619) 521-1201

hannah@bradfordlit.com

https://bradfordlit.com

ADULT
Fiction > *Novels*
Contemporary Romance; Erotic Romance; Historical Romance; Literary; Mystery; Romance; Romantic Suspense; Supernatural / Paranormal Romance; Thrillers; Upmarket Commercial Fiction; Urban Fantasy; Women's Fiction

Nonfiction > *Nonfiction Books*
Biography; Business; Comedy / Humour; Cookery; Food; History; Memoir; Parenting; Popular Culture; Relationships; Self Help; Social Issues

CHILDREN'S > **Fiction**
Novels; *Picture Books*

How to send: Query Manager

Represents a wide range of fiction and nonfiction. Select a particular agent at the agency to submit to, and submit to only one agent at a time.

Literary Agents: Hannah Andrade (**L019**); Laura Bradford (**L078**); Sarah LaPolla; Kari Sutherland; Jennifer Chen Tran; Katherine Wessbecher (**L730**)

L078 Laura Bradford

Literary Agent
United States

https://bradfordlit.com/about/laura-bradford/
https://querymanager.com/query/laurabradford
http://www.twitter.com/bradfordlit

Literary Agency: Bradford Literary Agency (**L077**)
Professional Bodies: Association of American Literary Agents (AALA); Romance Writers of America (RWA); Society of Children's Book Writers and Illustrators (SCBWI)

ADULT
Fiction
Graphic Novels: General
Novels: Contemporary Romance; Erotic Romance; Historical Fiction; Historical Romance; Mystery; Romance; Romantic Suspense; Speculative; Thrillers; Women's Fiction
Nonfiction > *Nonfiction Books*

CHILDREN'S > **Fiction** > *Middle Grade*

YOUNG ADULT > **Fiction** > *Novels*

How to send: Query Manager

Interested in romance (historical, romantic suspense, category, contemporary, erotic), speculative fiction, women's fiction, mystery, thrillers, young adult, upper middle grade, illustration as well as some select non-fiction.

L079 Brandt & Hochman Literary Agents, Inc.

Literary Agency
1501 Broadway, Suite 2605, New York, NY 10036
United States
Tel: +1 (212) 840-5760

http://brandthochman.com

See website for full submission guidelines and for details of individual agents' interests and direct contact details, then approach one agent specifically.

Literary Agents: Emily Forland; Gail Hochman (**L326**); Jody Kahn (**L366**); Marianne Merola; Emma Patterson; Henry Thayer; Mitchell Waters

L080 Hannah Brattesani

Literary Agent
United States

http://www.friedrichagency.com/about-alternate-2/

Literary Agency: The Friedrich Agency LLC

Fiction > *Novels*: Literary

Nonfiction > *Nonfiction Books*
Culture; Lifestyle; Narrative Nonfiction; Popular Science

Send: Query
How to send: In the body of an email

L081 The Brattle Agency LLC

Literary Agency
PO Box 380537, Cambridge, MA 02238
United States

submissions@thebrattleagency.com

https://thebrattleagency.com

Fiction
Graphic Novels: General
Novels: Literary

Nonfiction > *Nonfiction Books*
American History; Art History; Culture; European History; Music; Politics; Sport

Closed to approaches.

Accepts submissions only during one-month reading periods. See website for details.

L082 The Bravo Blue Agency

Literary Agency
United Kingdom

charlotte@bravoblue.co.uk

https://www.bravoblue.co.uk

Literary Agency: Tibor Jones & Associates

ADULT
Fiction > *Novels*
Commercial; Historical Fiction; Literary

Nonfiction > *Nonfiction Books*
Lifestyle; Narrative Nonfiction; Nature; Popular History; Science; Wellbeing

CHILDREN'S > **Fiction**
Early Readers; *Middle Grade*; *Picture Books*
YOUNG ADULT > **Fiction** > *Novels*

Send: Query; Author bio; Synopsis; Writing sample
How to send: Email

Literary Agent: Charlotte Colwill

L083 Helen Breitwieser

Literary Agent
United States

https://twitter.com/HelenBreit
http://aaronline.org/Sys/PublicProfile/2176619/417813

Professional Body: Association of American Literary Agents (AALA)
Literary Agency: Cornerstone Literary Agency (**L142**)

Authors: Jackie Ashenden; Anne Barton; Anna Bennett; Bethany Blake; Marnee Blake; Maya Blake; Katherine Center; Zara Cox; Robert Evans; Beth Fantaskey; Jane Goodger; Sherilee Gray; C.S. Harris; Nicole Helm; Lisa Hendrix; Kate Hewitt; Rachael Johns; Diane Kelly; Rachel Lee; Fiona Lowe; Mary McKinley;

Annabel Monaghan; Trish Morey; Kerry O'Connor; Mary-Anne O'Connor; Michael Paraskevas; Kayla Perrin; Candice Proctor; Kay Thomas; Christine Trent; Ursula Vernon; Tracy Anne Warren; Michelle Willingham; Maisey Yates

L084 Amy Brewer

Senior Agent
United States

https://www.metamorphosisliteraryagency.com/about
https://querymanager.com/query/1379

Literary Agency: Metamorphosis Literary Agency (**L487**)

Fiction > *Novels*
General, and in particular: Book Club Fiction; Comedy / Humour; LGBTQIA; Romance; Women's Fiction

Closed to approaches.

For the last few years, she has been learning all she can about social media optimization and platform building in the publishing industry. Her experience in the mental health field and yoga training help her guide and assist clients with stress and anxiety in this highly competitive industry.

L085 The Bright Agency

Literary Agency
103-105 St John's Hill, London, SW11 1SY
United Kingdom
Tel: +44 (0) 20 7326 9140

mail@thebrightagency.com

https://thebrightagency.com
https://thebrightagency.com/uk/submissions/new

Media Company: The Bright Group International Limited

ADULT > **Fiction**
Graphic Novels; *Novels*
CHILDREN'S > **Fiction**
Chapter Books; *Middle Grade*; *Picture Books*
YOUNG ADULT > **Fiction** > *Novels*

Send: Outline; Synopsis; Writing sample
How to send: Online contact form

Welcomes submissions from illustrators and authors who are looking for representation. Interested in children's picture book texts, chapter books, middle grade fiction, YA, adult and graphic novels. Provide an outline with a synopsis and the first three chapters.

Literary Agent: Vicki Willden-Lebrecht

L086 Bright Group US Inc.

Literary Agency
50 West Street, C12, New York, NY 10006
United States
Tel: +1 (646) 578 6542

mail@thebrightagency.com

https://thebrightagency.com
https://thebrightagency.com/us/submissions/new

Media Company: The Bright Group International Limited

CHILDREN'S > **Fiction**
Chapter Books; *Middle Grade*; *Picture Books*

Send: Outline; Synopsis; Writing sample
How to send: Online contact form

Welcomes submissions from illustrators and authors who are looking for representation. Interested in children's picture book texts, chapter books and middle grade fiction. Provide an outline with a synopsis and the first three chapters.

L087 Philippa Brophy

Literary Agent; President
United States

https://www.sll.com/our-team
http://aaronline.org/Sys/PublicProfile/4090020/417813

Literary Agency: Sterling Lord Literistic, Inc. (**L662**)
Professional Body: Association of American Literary Agents (AALA)

Fiction > *Novels*

Nonfiction > *Nonfiction Books*
General, and in particular: Journalism

Closed to approaches.

L088 Brotherstone Creative Management

Literary Agency
Mortimer House, 37-41 Mortimer Street, London, W1T 3JH
United Kingdom
Tel: +44 (0) 7908 542886

submissions@bcm-agency.com
info@bcm-agency.com

http://bcm-agency.com

Professional Body: The Association of Authors' Agents (AAA)

Types: Fiction; Nonfiction
Subjects: Commercial; Literary
Markets: Adult

Send: Query; Writing sample; Synopsis
How to send: Email

Always on the search for talented new writers. Send query by email. For fiction, include the first three chapters or 50 pages and 2-page synopsis. For nonfiction, include detailed outline and sample chapter. No children's and young adult fiction, sci-fi and fantasy novels or unsolicited short story and poetry collections, or scripts.

Literary Agent: Charlie Brotherstone

L089 Justin Brouckaert

Literary Agent
New York
United States

https://aevitascreative.com/agents/

Literary Agency: Aevitas

Fiction
Novels: Literary
Short Fiction: Literary

Nonfiction > *Nonfiction Books*
Current Affairs; History; Journalism; Memoir; Narrative Nonfiction; Parenting; Politics; Sport; Travel

Closed to approaches.

Actively seeking character-driven and formally inventive literary fiction and memoir, as well as narrative nonfiction in the areas of sports, internet culture, politics and current affairs, parenting, travel, and history. Regardless of genre, he is most passionate about projects that shine a light on underserved and overlooked communities and/or highlight unique relationships between people and places. He is especially interested in pairing with debut authors and helping them grow their careers.

Authors: Lauren Aguirre; Matthew H. Birkhold; Greg Bluestein; Diane Cardwell; Jesselyn Cook; Susan Crawford; R.S. Deeren; Benoit Denizet-Lewis; William Deverell; Rebekah Diamond; Ali Drucker; Brian Dumaine; Ken Ellingwood; Marisa Franco; Sarah Gearhart; Jeffrey Gettleman; Wade Graham; Gabrielle Hartley; Jesse Horwitz; Jacqueline Lewis; Joe Milan; Luma Mufleh; Pamela Pavliscak; Lindsay Powers; Julian Sancton; Amber Share; Meg Vondriska; Evan Waite; Bryan Walsh; Ali Marie Watkins

L090 Michelle Brower

Literary Agent; Partner
United States

https://aevitascreative.com/agents/

Literary Agency: Aevitas

ADULT
Fiction > *Novels*
Book Club Fiction; Commercial; Literary; Suspense; Upmarket; Women's Fiction

Nonfiction > *Nonfiction Books*
Memoir; Narrative Nonfiction

CHILDREN'S > **Fiction** > *Middle Grade*

YOUNG ADULT > **Fiction** > *Novels*

Send: Pitch; Market info; Writing sample
How to send: Online submission system

Represents fiction and narrative nonfiction. Her interests include book club fiction (a commercial concept with a literary execution), literary fiction (including with an element of genre), and smart women's fiction. She also represents select young adult, middle grade, and memoir projects.

L091 Andrea Brown

President; Literary Agent
United States

andrea@andreabrownlit.com

https://www.andreabrownlit.com/Team/Andrea-Brown

Literary Agency: Andrea Brown Literary Agency, Inc.
Professional Body: Association of American Literary Agents (AALA)

Closed to approaches.

L092 Browne & Miller Literary Associates

Literary Agency
United States

mail@browneandmiller.com

https://www.browneandmiller.com
https://www.facebook.com/browneandmiller
https://twitter.com/BrowneandMiller

Fiction > *Novels*: Commercial

Nonfiction > *Nonfiction Books*: Commercial

Closed to approaches.

Handles books for the adult commercial book markets. No children's, young adult, science fiction, fantasy, horror, short stories, poetry, screenplays, or academic works. Send query only by email. No attachments.

Literary Agent: Danielle Egan-Miller

L093 Chris Bucci

Literary Agent
New York
United States

https://aevitascreative.com/agents/

Literary Agency: Aevitas

Fiction > *Novels*
Commercial; Historical Fiction; History; Literary; Mystery; Popular Culture; Popular Science; Thrillers

Nonfiction > *Nonfiction Books*
Narrative Nonfiction; Politics; Sport

Send: Author bio; Outline; Market info; Writing sample
How to send: Online submission system

Based in the New York Metropolitan area. Represents a broad range of fiction and nonfiction.

L094 Danielle Bukowski

Literary Agent
United States

https://www.sll.com/our-team

Literary Agency: Sterling Lord Literistic, Inc. (**L662**)

Fiction > *Novels*
Book Club Fiction; Literary

Nonfiction > *Nonfiction Books*

Send: Query; Synopsis; Writing sample
How to send: Online submission system

Represents fiction for adults, from smart bookclub to literary, and select nonfiction, Particularly looking for narratives from writers traditionally excluded from the publishing industry. For fiction, she likes books that balance plot with voice, have a strong sense of place, a unique hook, and are stylistically bold; for nonfiction, she's looking for work grounded in the author's personal interest, rigorously reported and researched, and will expand the reader's view of the world.

L095 Kate Burke

Senior Agent
United Kingdom

kate@blakefriedmann.co.uk

http://blakefriedmann.co.uk/kate-burke
https://twitter.com/kbbooks

Literary Agency: Blake Friedmann Literary Agency Ltd (**L067**)

Fiction > *Novels*
Book Club Women's Fiction; Commercial; Contemporary; Crime; High Concept Thrillers; Historical Fiction; Literary; Romance; Speculative; Thrillers; Women's Fiction

Send: Query; Synopsis; Writing sample
How to send: Word file email attachment

My list is made up of everything I like to read – gripping fiction featuring characters you can't get enough of and whom you don't want to part with at the end of a novel. I love dark stories but also uplifting love stories, too, and I'm keen to work with authors from all over the world. I'm fortunate to represent a list of bestselling crime and thriller writers, and authors of contemporary and historical women's fiction. I'm always open to submissions of commercial and literary fiction.

In terms of what I'm looking for: on the crime side, I love dark thrillers (literary or commercial) that keep me turning the page long into the night and that surprise me with plot twists and interesting narrative structures, crime series featuring new and fresh lead investigators, and high-concept thrillers (contemporary, historical or speculative) that have a 'what if?' plot structure and say something about our society now or then. On the women's fiction side, I love historical fiction that appeals to a reading group market (anything set during or post-WW2 is a particular interest of mine) and contemporary love stories that sweep you away with romance and/or heartbreak. Anything that has a discussable issue at its heart, that sucks you in as a reader and takes you on a rollercoaster emotional journey (tears and laughter!), is what I'm interested in.

Author: Sara Ochs

L096 Megan Burkhart

Junior Agent
United States

megan@cyleyoung.com

https://cyleyoung.com/literary-agent/my-team/
https://meganlynneauthor.weebly.com/
https://www.facebook.com/meganlynne.13/
https://twitter.com/writemeganlynne
https://www.youtube.com/channel/UCv23mXzg0-9PuXBnGDAuqmg
https://www.linkedin.com/in/megan-burkhart-93858814a/
https://www.instagram.com/authormeganlynne

Literary Agency: Cyle Young Literary Elite (**L152**)

YOUNG ADULT > **Fiction** > *Novels*: Fantasy

Send: Query; Synopsis; Writing sample
How to send: Email

Costs: Offers services that writers have to pay for. Also offers editorial services.

Looks for YA fantasy and children's picture books, especially those with a strong narrative voice. Closed to picture book submissions as at June 2020.

L097 Emelie Burl

Associate Agent
United States

emelie@schulmanagency.com

https://twitter.com/BigKidBookworm
https://www.facebook.com/emelie.s.samuelson
https://www.publishersmarketplace.com/members/Schulman/

Literary Agency: Susan Schulman Literary Agency (**L678**)

ADULT > **Nonfiction** > *Nonfiction Books*: Popular Culture

CHILDREN'S > **Fiction** > *Middle Grade*
Comedy / Humour; Magic

YOUNG ADULT > **Fiction** > *Novels*
Comedy / Humour; Magic; Romantic Comedy

Focuses on children's, young adult, and pop culture nonfiction. Likes stories of hope and humor, rom-coms, strong female leads, and magic of all sorts. Also interested in LGBT+ and BIPOC. Not keen on murder.

L098 Kate Bussert

Literary Agent

Literary Agency: Bret Adams Ltd

L099 Ellie Cahill-Nicholls
Literary Agent
United Kingdom

Literary Agency: Noel Gay (**L528**)

L100 Linda Camacho
Literary Agent
United States

linda@galltzacker.com
QueryLinda@galltzacker.com

Literary Agency: Gallt & Zacker Literary Agency

Fiction > *Novels*
Romance; Women's Fiction

Closed to approaches.

L101 Charlie Campbell
Literary Agent
United Kingdom

charlie@greyhoundliterary.co.uk

https://greyhoundliterary.co.uk/agent/charlie-campbell/
https://twitter.com/ScapegoatCC

Literary Agency: Greyhound Literary (**L288**)

ADULT
Fiction > *Novels*
Commercial; Crime; Historical Fiction; Literary; Thrillers

Nonfiction > *Nonfiction Books*
Comedy / Humour; Commercial; History; Literary; Popular Science; Sport

CHILDREN'S > **Fiction** > *Novels*

Send: Query; Synopsis; Writing sample
How to send: Email

Primarily looking for crime and thrillers, as well as literary and historical fiction. In non-fiction, his interests include sport, popular science, history, humour and business.

Authors: Guy Adams; SJ Bennett; Edward Brooke-Hitching; Theodore Brun; Andy Bull; Jen Campbell; Bonnie Chung; David Collins; Zoë Colville; Duncan Crowe; Iain Dey; Chris Dodd; Adam Fergusson; Jamie Fewery; Rebecca Front; Tom Gabbay; Julian Gough; David Higgins; Will Hill; Thomas W. Hodgkinson; Nicholas Hogg; Andrew Hosken; Simon Jones; Paul Levy; Shingi Mararike; Hugh Matheson; Neil McCormick; Anthony McGowan; Barry McKinley; Moin Mir; Anton Mosimann; Rebecca Myers; James Peak; Edvard Radzinsky; Amy Raphael; Andrea Stuart; Tom Tivnan; Hana Videen; Wendy Wason; Sioned Wiliam; Hywel Williams; Mike Woodhouse

L102 Elise Capron
Literary Agent
United States

https://dijkstraagency.com/agent-page.php?agent_id=Capron
https://querymanager.com/query/DijkstraCapron

Literary Agency: Sandra Dijkstra Literary Agency

Fiction > *Novels*: Literary

Nonfiction > *Nonfiction Books*
Culture; History; Memoir; Narrative Nonfiction; Science

How to send: Query Manager; By referral

Most interested in well-written narrative non-fiction (particularly trade-friendly history, cultural studies, and science) as well as character-driven literary fiction. While she will consider memoir, please note that she is very selective in this genre.

L103 Amber J. Caravéo
Literary Agent
United Kingdom

Literary Agency: Skylark Literary (**L647**)

L104 Carol Mann Agency
Literary Agency
55 Fifth Avenue, New York, NY 10003
United States
Tel: +1 (212) 206-5635

submissions@carolmannagency.com

https://www.carolmannagency.com

Send: Query; Author bio; Writing sample
How to send: In the body of an email
How not to send: Email attachment; Post; Phone

Send query by email only, including synopsis, brief bio, and first 25 pages, all pasted into the body of your email. No attachments. No submissions by post, or phone calls. Allow 3-4 weeks for response.

Authors: Jane Alexander; Clifton Hoodl Maria Goodavage; Rachel Kelly

Literary Agents: Maile Beal; Agnes Carlowicz; Gareth Esersky (**L206**); Iris Blasi; Carol Mann (**L466**); Dani Segelbaum (**L633**); Myrsini Stephanides; Joanne Wyckoff (**L749**); Laura Yorke

L105 Caroline Sheldon Literary Agency
Literary Agency
71 Hillgate Place, London, W8 7SS
United Kingdom
Tel: +44 (0) 20 7727 9102

info@carolinesheldon.co.uk

http://www.carolinesheldon.co.uk

Professional Body: The Association of Authors' Agents (AAA)

ADULT > **Fiction** > *Novels*

CHILDREN'S > **Fiction**
Board Books; *Chapter Books*; *Early Readers*; *Middle Grade*; *Novels*; *Picture Books*

Closed to approaches.

Interested in fiction and all types of children's books. Send query by email only, addressed to appropriate agent. Do not send submissions to their individual email addresses.

Literary Agents: Caroline Sheldon; Felicity Trew

L106 Carolyn Jenks Agency
Literary Agency
30 Cambridge Park Drive, #3140, Cambridge, MA 02140
United States

https://www.carolynjenksagency.com
https://www.facebook.com/carolynjenksagency
https://twitter.com/TheJenksAgency

Company Director / Literary Agent: Carolyn Jenks (**L351**)

Literary Agents: Kwaku Acheampong (**L005**); Becca Crandall (**L146**); Brenna Girard (**L263**); Molly McQuade

L107 Jamie Carr
Literary Agent
United States

http://www.thebookgroup.com/jamie-carr

Literary Agency: The Book Group (**L071**)

Fiction > *Novels*
Literary; Upmarket Commercial Fiction

Nonfiction > *Nonfiction Books*
Culture; Food; Journalism; Narrative Nonfiction

Send: Query; Writing sample
How to send: In the body of an email

Represents novelists, short story writers, journalists, activists, and food and culture writers. Most interested in adult literary and upmarket commercial fiction and narrative nonfiction, she is drawn to writing that is voice-driven, highly transporting, from unique perspectives and marginalized voices, and that seeks to disrupt or reframe what appears to be known.

Authors: Nishant Batsha; Suhaly Bautista-Carolina; Rachel Broderick; Wendy Chin-Tanner; Tiana Clark; Tracy Clark-Flory; Chloe Cole; Ella Dawson; Kimberly Drew; Susie Dumond; Taylor Hahn; Alex Hoopes; Mike Lala; Melissa Larsen; Ashton Lattimore; Esther Levy-Chehebar; Vanessa Lillie; Kristen Martin; Laura McKowen; Abi Morgan; Victoria Savanh; Sophia Shalmiyev; Rainesford Stauffer; Elissa Strauss; Sara Sutter; Noor Tagouri; Rachel Zarrow

L108 Michael Carr

Literary Agent
United States

http://www.veritasliterary.com

Literary Agency: Veritas Literary Agency (**L712**)

Fiction > *Novels*
Fantasy; Historical Fiction; Science Fiction; Women's Fiction

Nonfiction > *Nonfiction Books*

L109 Megan Carroll

Literary Agent
United Kingdom

Literary Agency: Watson, Little Ltd

Closed to approaches.

L110 Rebecca Carter

Literary Agent
United Kingdom

http://www.janklowandnesbit.co.uk/node/404
https://rebeccacarterliteraryagent.wordpress.com/
https://twitter.com/RebeccasBooks

Literary Agency: Janklow & Nesbit UK Ltd (**L349**)

ADULT
Fiction > *Novels*
Crime; Experimental

Nonfiction > *Nonfiction Books*
Biography; Creative Nonfiction; Cultural Commentary; Design; Environment; History; Memoir; Politics; Social Commentary; Technology; Travel

CHILDREN'S
Fiction > *Novels*
Nonfiction > *Nonfiction Books*

Send: Query; Synopsis; Writing sample
How to send: Email

L111 Robert Caskie

Literary Agent
United Kingdom

robert@robertcaskie.com
submissions@robertcaskie.com

https://www.robertcaskie.com
https://twitter.com/rcaskie1

Literary Agency: Robert Caskie Ltd (**L593**)

Fiction > *Novels*
Book Club Fiction; Commercial; Literary

Nonfiction > *Nonfiction Books*
Memoir; Narrative Nonfiction; Nature; Politics; Social Issues

Closed to approaches.

Keen to receive fiction and nonfiction writing that stimulates debate, comments on the world around us, and invokes an emotional response.

L112 Cecily Ware Literary Agents

Literary Agency
30 Elsiedene Road, London, N21 2RP
United Kingdom
Tel: +44 (0) 20 7359 3787

info@cecilyware.com

http://www.cecilyware.com

Scripts
Radio Scripts; *TV Scripts*

Send: Full text; Author bio
How to send: Word file email attachment; PDF file email attachment; Final Draft email attachment

Handles television and radio writers and producers. No books or theatre scripts.

Literary Agents: Carol Reyes; Gilly Schuster; Warren Sherman

L113 Becca Challis

Assistant Agent
United Kingdom

Literary Agency: David Higham Associates Ltd (**L161**)
Literary Agent: Caroline Walsh (**L719**)
Literary Agent / Company Director: Veronique Baxter (**L050**)

L114 Jemiscoe Chambers-Black

Associate Agent
Los Angeles
United States

jemiscoe@andreabrownlit.com

https://www.andreabrownlit.com/agents.html
https://twitter.com/Jemiscoe
https://querymanager.com/query/Jemiscoe

Literary Agency: Andrea Brown Literary Agency, Inc.

ADULT > **Fiction** > *Novels*
Comedy / Humour; Cozy Mysteries; Crime; LGBTQIA; Literary; Low Fantasy; Psychological Thrillers; Romance; Urban Fantasy

CHILDREN'S > **Fiction**
Graphic Novels: General
Middle Grade: Adventure; Comedy / Humour; Contemporary; Culture; Fantasy; Folklore, Myths, and Legends; Ghost Stories; Horror; LGBTQIA; Magical Realism; Mystery; Supernatural / Paranormal
YOUNG ADULT > **Fiction** > *Novels*
Contemporary; Fantasy; Ghost Stories; Horror; LGBTQIA; Mystery; Romance; Romantic Comedy; Supernatural / Paranormal

Send: Author bio; Query; Synopsis; Writing sample; Pitch; Market info
How to send: Query Manager

Currently building her client list in the middle grade, YA, and adult categories. She is also interested in considering illustrators and author-illustrators.

L115 Jamie Chambliss

Literary Agent
United States

jamie@foliolitmanagement.com

https://www.foliolit.com/agents-1/jamie-chambliss
https://twitter.com/JChambliss1

Literary Agency: Folio Literary Management, LLC

Fiction > *Novels*
Book Club Fiction; Literary; Upmarket

Nonfiction > *Nonfiction Books*
Food; History; Memoir; Narrative Nonfiction; Popular Culture; Prescriptive Nonfiction; Science; Sport

Closed to approaches.

L116 Sonali Chanchani

Literary Agent
United States

sonali@foliolit.com

https://www.foliolit.com/agents-1/sonali-chanchani

Literary Agency: Folio Literary Management, LLC
Professional Body: Association of American Literary Agents (AALA)

Fiction > *Novels*
Book Club Fiction; Comedy / Humour; Coming of Age; Disabilities; Ethnic Groups; Family; Folklore, Myths, and Legends; Friends; Historical Fiction; LGBTQIA; Literary; Magical Realism; Mental Health; Psychological Suspense; Thrillers; Upmarket Women's Fiction; Women's Fiction

Nonfiction > *Nonfiction Books*
Culture; Disabilities; Ethnic Groups; Gender; LGBTQIA; Mental Health; Narrative Nonfiction; Politics; Social Justice; Society

Send: Query; Writing sample
How to send: In the body of an email

In fiction, I'm looking for literary fiction and upmarket women's fiction with a strong, distinctive voice. I'm particularly interested in smart, funny novels about identity and coming of age; braided narratives of friendship and/or family; and elevated psychological suspense. I love novels that speak in some way to our current conversations and blend emotional depth with sharp, witty insights. I also gravitate towards lyrical, atmospheric stories with a speculative or fabulist twist. In general, I have a soft spot for small towns, quirky characters, magical realism, and elements of folklore or mythology.

In nonfiction, I'm looking for narratives and collections that illuminate some aspect of our society or culture with an eye towards social justice. I'm especially interested in reported narratives that advance our current conversations about race, class, gender, and/or politics.

L117 Anish Chandy

Literary Agent
India

Literary Agency: The Labyrinth Literary Agency (**L402**)

L118 Minju Chang

Literary Agent
United States

Literary Agency: BookStop Literary Agency, LLC (**L073**)

CHILDREN'S
Fiction
Chapter Books; *Graphic Novels*; *Middle Grade*; *Picture Books*
Nonfiction > *Nonfiction Books*

YOUNG ADULT > **Fiction** > *Novels*

How to send: By referral

Represents both fiction and nonfiction in all children's book categories: picture books, chapter books, middle-grade, graphic novels and YA. She also represents illustrators and is on the hunt for author-illustrators.

L119 Nicola Chang

Literary Agent
United Kingdom

nicolasubmissions@davidhigham.co.uk

https://www.davidhigham.co.uk/agents-dh/nicola-chang/

Literary Agency: David Higham Associates Ltd (**L161**)

Fiction > *Novels*

Nonfiction > *Nonfiction Books*
Cookery; Cultural Criticism; Culture; Food; Memoir; Narrative Nonfiction; Philosophy; Politics; Psychology; Revisionist History; Society

Poetry > *Any Poetic Form*

Send: Query; Writing sample
How to send: Email

Represents writers of fiction and non-fiction as well as a small list of poets. She is an editorially-focused agent and is passionate about working with writers closely to develop their proposals and manuscripts for submission to publishers.

Authors: Arenike Adebajo; Ore Agbaje-Williams; Sara Ahmed; Rosanna Amaka; Iman Amrani; Raymond Antrobus; Yemisí Aríbisálà; Gina María Balibrera; Amman Brar; Symeon Brown; Judith Bryan; Stephen Buoro; Vanessa Chan; Jacqueline Crooks; Tsitsi Dangarembga; Subhadra Das; Olivia Dunnett; Mila Franklin; Orit Gat; Nikita Gill; Emma Glass; Helen Goh; Will Harris; Alex Holder; Angela Hui; Sara Jafari; Keith Jarrett; Bhanu Kapil; Lara Lee; Huw Lemmey; Momtaza Mehri; Anna Metcalfe; Emma-Lee Moss; Mark Mukasa; Sri Owen; James Conor Patterson; Riaz Phillips; Alake Pilgrim; Leone Ross; Saba Sams; Lisa Smith; Varaidzo; Christian Weaver; Mandy Yin

L120 Mic Cheetham

Literary Agent
United Kingdom

Mic@miccheetham.co.uk

Literary Agency: Mic Cheetham Literary Agency (**L488**)

L121 Elyse Cheney

Literary Agent
United States

https://www.cheneyagency.com/elyse-cheney

Literary Agency: The Cheney Agency

L122 Anwar Chentoufi

Literary Agent
United Kingdom

Literary Agency: Independent Talent Group Ltd (**L340**)

L123 Jennifer Chevais

Assistant Agent
Canada

https://www.therightsfactory.com/Agents/Jennifer-Chevais/
https://querymanager.com/query/JChevais
https://twitter.com/jchevais

Literary Agency: The Rights Factory

Fiction > *Graphic Novels*

Nonfiction > *Nonfiction Books*
General, and in particular: Memoir

How to send: Query Manager

Currently building her list of authors specialising in fantasy, science fiction, and horror, but she also has a soft spot for thrillers, upmarket fiction, memoir, graphic novels, and many more.

Authors: Tal Cohen; Eleanor Cooney; Drew Dotson; Richard A. Kirk; A. A. Livingston; Art Ruben; Emma Sachsse; Mark David Smith

L124 Patrick Child

Literary Agent
United Kingdom

Literary Agency: Independent Talent Group Ltd (**L340**)

L125 Jamie Weiss Chilton

Senior Agent
United States

jamie@andreabrownlit.com

https://www.andreabrownlit.com/Team/Jamie-Weiss-Chilton
http://twitter.com/jwchilton

Literary Agency: Andrea Brown Literary Agency, Inc.

CHILDREN'S > **Fiction**
Middle Grade: Realistic; Science Fiction; Speculative; Thrillers
Picture Books: General

YOUNG ADULT > **Fiction** > *Novels*
Realistic; Science Fiction; Speculative; Thrillers

Closed to approaches.

Represents children's books in all categories, with a focus on preschool, picture books, novelty, and real-world-based middle grade and YA. Genre interests include thrillers, science fiction, and speculative fiction.

L126 Danielle Chiotti

Literary Agent
United States

danielle.submission@gmail.com

https://www.upstartcrowliterary.com/agents/danielle-chiotti

Literary Agency: Upstart Crow Literary (**L707**)

ADULT
Fiction > *Novels*: Upmarket Commercial Fiction

Nonfiction > *Nonfiction Books*
Comedy / Humour; Cookery; Current Affairs; Food; Lifestyle; Memoir; Narrative Nonfiction; Relationships; Wine

CHILDREN'S > **Fiction** > *Middle Grade*

YOUNG ADULT > **Fiction** > *Novels*

How to send: Email

Specializes in upmarket and literary fiction, young adult and middle grade fiction, as well as cookbooks and select nonfiction. Thanks to her extensive editorial background, she enjoys working closely with authors to develop projects. She welcomes first-time authors with a unique voice and point of view.

L127 Catherine Cho

Literary Agent
United Kingdom

https://www.paperliterary.com/submissions-catherine/
https://twitter.com/catkcho

Literary Agency: Paper Literary (**L547**)

ADULT
Fiction > *Novels*

Book Club Fiction; Family; Folklore, Myths, and Legends; High Concept; Literary; Magical Realism; Psychological Suspense; Relationships; Speculative

Nonfiction > *Nonfiction Books*
Crime; Entrepreneurship; History; Memoir; Narrative Nonfiction; Psychology; Science

YOUNG ADULT > **Fiction** > *Novels*: Fantasy

Send: Query; Synopsis; Writing sample

Originally from Kentucky. After a background in law and public affairs, she began her publishing career in New York at Folio Literary Management before moving to London.

L128 Erica Christensen

Senior Agent
United States

https://www.metamorphosisliteraryagency.com/about
https://querymanager.com/query/ericachristensen
https://twitter.com/literaryerica

Literary Agency: Metamorphosis Literary Agency (**L487**)

ADULT > **Fiction** > *Novels*
Romance; Thrillers

YOUNG ADULT > **Fiction** > *Novels*
Contemporary; Romance

Does not want:

ADULT > **Fiction** > *Novels*
Historical Romance; Supernatural / Paranormal Romance

YOUNG ADULT > **Fiction** > *Novels*
Historical Romance; Supernatural / Paranormal Romance

How to send: Query Manager

Only open to SUBSIDIARY RIGHTS queries for established Romance and Thriller authors (Self-Published/Indie and Traditional) who retain the subsidiary rights (audio, foreign, gaming, film/tv) for their book(s). The book(s) must have a minimum of 50 reviews. Please include your Amazon author page and Goodreads page in the Bio section.

L129 Jennifer Christie

Literary Agent
United Kingdom

http://www.grahammawchristie.com/about1.html

Literary Agency: Graham Maw Christie Literary Agency (**L278**)

Nonfiction > *Nonfiction Books*
Business; Comedy / Humour; Memoir; Philosophy; Popular Science

Send: Outline; Author bio; Market info; Writing sample
How to send: Email

Interests are wide ranging, from popular science, philosophy and humour to business and memoir.

L130 The Chudney Agency

Literary Agency
72 North State Road, Suite 501, Briarcliff Manor, NY 10510
United States
Tel: +1 (201) 758-8739
Fax: +1 (201) 758-8739

steven@thechudneyagency.com

http://www.thechudneyagency.com

ADULT
Fiction > *Novels*
General, and in particular: Gender; Historical Fiction; LGBTQIA; Middle East; Mystery; Sexuality; Thrillers; Women's Fiction

Nonfiction
Gift Books: General
Illustrated Books: General
Nonfiction Books: Comedy / Humour

CHILDREN'S > **Fiction**
Chapter Books: General, and in particular: Comedy / Humour; Coming of Age; Contemporary; Culture; Gender; Historical Fiction; Literary; Mystery; Spirituality
Middle Grade: General, and in particular: Comedy / Humour; Coming of Age; Contemporary; Culture; Gender; Historical Fiction; Literary; Mystery; Spirituality
Picture Books: General

TEEN > **Fiction** > *Novels*
General, and in particular: Comedy / Humour; Coming of Age; Contemporary; Culture; Gender; Historical Fiction; Literary; Mystery; Spirituality

Send: Query
How to send: Email
How not to send: Post

Specialises in children's and teen books, but will also consider adult fiction. Send query only in first instance. Happy to accept queries by email. Submit material upon invitation only. No fantasy, science fiction, early readers, or scripts. See website for full guidelines.

Authors: Jessica Alexander; Mary Jane Beaufrand; Tess Hilmo; Kristen Landon

Literary Agent: Steven Chudney

L131 Kayla Cichello

Literary Agent
United States

kayla.submission@gmail.com

https://www.upstartcrowliterary.com/agents/kayla-cichelloa
https://twitter.com/SeriousKayla

Literary Agency: Upstart Crow Literary (**L707**)

CHILDREN'S > **Fiction**
Middle Grade: General
Picture Books: Comedy / Humour

YOUNG ADULT > **Fiction** > *Novels*
Commercial; Dark Humour; Literary; Magical Realism; Mystery; Romance; Romantic Comedy; Suspense

How to send: Email
How not to send: Post

Seeking everything from heartfelt or humorous picture books (she has a soft spot for animal protagonists) to dynamic, unpredictable YA (she loves a good murder mystery or a clever rom-com).

L132 Clare Hulton Literary Agency

Literary Agency
United Kingdom

info@clarehulton.co.uk

https://www.clarehulton.com

Professional Body: The Association of Authors' Agents (AAA)

Fiction > *Novels*

Nonfiction > *Nonfiction Books*
General, and in particular: Business; Cookery; Health; History; Lifestyle; Parenting; Philosophy; Pregnancy; Self Help

Send: Query
How to send: In the body of an email

Specialises in nonfiction, but also has a small commercial fiction list. Finds most authors through recommendation, but open to brief queries by email, explaining what your book is about. No attachments. If no response within two weeks, assume rejection.

Literary Agent: Clare Hulton (*L334*)

L133 Ginger Clark

Literary Agent
United States

submissions@GingerClarkLiterary.com

https://gingerclarkliterary.com/About
https://gingerclarkliterary.com/Submissions

Literary Agency: Ginger Clark Literary (**L262**)

ADULT > **Fiction** > *Novels*
Fantasy; Horror; Romance; Science Fiction; Women's Fiction

CHILDREN'S
Fiction > *Middle Grade*
Nonfiction > *Middle Grade*

YOUNG ADULT
Fiction > *Novels*

Nonfiction > *Nonfiction Books*

Send: Query
How to send: Email

Has a special focus on science fiction, fantasy, horror, romance, and women's fiction. For children's works, she represents young adult and middle grade fiction and nonfiction in all genres. Emailed queries are strongly preferred.

L134 Therese Coen

Literary Agent
United Kingdom

therese@hardmanswainson.com
submissions@hardmanswainson.com

https://www.hardmanswainson.com/agent/therese-coen/
https://twitter.com/theresecoen

Literary Agency: Hardman & Swainson (**L302**)

ADULT > **Fiction** > *Novels*
Coming of Age; Crime; High Concept Romance; Historical Fiction

CHILDREN'S > **Fiction** > *Novels*
Adventure; Comedy / Humour; Fantasy; Space

Send: Query; Synopsis; Full text
How to send: Email

In terms of adult fiction, I have a soft spot for historical fiction, having read Early Modern History at university, but am also very much on the hunt for crime, coming-of-age stories and high-concept love stories. I love strong female characters, especially when they go through an evolution as the story progresses and gradually find that inner strength.

On the children's fiction front, I love all things fantasy and adventure – across lands, time and space, and involving strong friendships and strong lead characters. I want to be transported straight away when I start reading a manuscript. Right this moment, I would love to see something involving an Orient Express-style train, or maybe an Agatha Christie-type cruise boat (perhaps without the gruesome murder). I like very vivid, well-crafted and imaginative worlds, for example stories set in a toy factory or in an underwater world. I'd love some more adventures set in space, à la Star Trek and Wall-E. I want mysteries, quirky characters, explorers and imaginary friends.

Send submissions by email to the submissions email address only.

L135 Chris Combemale

Associate Agent
United States

https://www.sll.com/our-team

Literary Agency: Sterling Lord Literistic, Inc. (**L662**)

Fiction > *Novels*
Literary; Upmarket Commercial Fiction

Nonfiction
Essays: Economics; Food; Popular Science; Technology
Nonfiction Books: Economics; Food; Memoir; Popular Science; Technology

Send: Query; Synopsis; Proposal; Writing sample
How to send: Online submission system

Looking for a broad range of literary fiction and commercial fiction with an unexpected hook, from psychological suspense to speculative and fantasy. In non-fiction he is interested in memoir, essay, and expert-driven projects across subject areas with special attention to technology, food, pop-science, economics, and any book that asks big questions about forces of change.

L136 Concord Theatricals

Literary Agency; Book Publisher
250 W. 57th Street, 6th Floor, New York, NY 10107-0102
United States
Tel: +1 (866) 979-0447

info@concordtheatricals.com

https://www.concordtheatricals.com/

Scripts > *Theatre Scripts*

Closed to approaches.

Publishes plays and represents writers of plays. Deals in well-known plays from Broadway and London's West End.

L137 Claire Paterson Conrad

Literary Agent
United Kingdom

http://www.janklowandnesbit.co.uk/node/671

Literary Agency: Janklow & Nesbit UK Ltd (**L349**)

Fiction > *Novels*

Nonfiction > *Nonfiction Books*
Biology; Creative Nonfiction; Environment; Nature; Popular Science

Send: Query; Synopsis; Writing sample; Outline
How to send: Email
How not to send: Post

Keen to represent more books about the natural world and our co-existence with it (whether that be popular science, biology, ecology or nature writing); books that celebrate women in science; books that help us understand the world and bring change; and creative nonfiction that blends genres. In fiction, gravitates towards atmospheric, character-driven novels that are rooted to a strong sense of place.

L138 Clare Coombes

Literary Agent
United Kingdom

https://www.liverpool-literary.agency/about

Literary Agency: The Liverpool Literary Agency (**L435**)

Fiction > *Novels*
General, and in particular: Crime; Historical Fiction; Psychological Thrillers; Women's Fiction

Would love to see historical fiction, crime fiction, psychological thrillers and women's fiction, but as a new agent, she is open to all great writing with a strong hook in any area (excluding non-fiction, children's and YA).

L139 Coombs Moylett & Maclean Literary Agency

Literary Agency
120 New Kings Road, London, SW6 4LZ
United Kingdom

info@cmm.agency

https://cmm.agency
https://www.instagram.com/cmmlitagency/
https://www.facebook.com/cmmlitagency/

Professional Body: The Association of Authors' Agents (AAA)

ADULT
Fiction > *Novels*
Chick Lit; Commercial; Contemporary; Crime; Historical Fiction; Horror; Literary; Mystery; Suspense; Thrillers; Women's Fiction

Nonfiction > *Nonfiction Books*
General, and in particular: Biography; Crime; Current Affairs; Environment; Food; History; How To; Lifestyle; Narrative Nonfiction; Politics; Popular Science; Self Help

YOUNG ADULT > **Fiction** > *Novels*

Send: Synopsis; Writing sample; Query; Author bio
How to send: Online submission system
How not to send: Email; Post

Send query with synopsis and first three chapters via online form. No submissions by email, fax or by post. No poetry, plays or scripts for film and TV. Whole books and postal submissions will not be read.

Editor / Literary Agent: Jamie Maclean (**L460**)

Literary Agents: Zoe Apostolides (**L028**); Elena Langtry (**L410**); Lisa Moylett (**L513**)

L140 Gemma Cooper

Literary Agent
United States

http://www.thebentagency.com/gemma-cooper

Literary Agency: The Bent Agency (**L058**)

CHILDREN'S
Fiction
Chapter Books; *Graphic Novels*; *Illustrated Books*; *Middle Grade*

Nonfiction > *Nonfiction Books*
History; Science

YOUNG ADULT
Fiction > *Novels*
Comedy / Humour; Contemporary; Family; Fantasy; Friends; High Concept; Romance; Supernatural / Paranormal

Nonfiction > *Nonfiction Books*

Does not want:

YOUNG ADULT > **Fiction** > *Novels*: High / Epic Fantasy

Represents authors and author / illustrators who write chapter books, middle-grade, and young adult fiction and nonfiction, as well as select webcomic adaptations. No adult fiction or nonfiction, or children's picture books, other than by existing clients.

L141 Maggie Cooper

Literary Agent
Boston, MA
United States

https://aevitascreative.com/agents/
https://querymanager.com/query/cooper

Literary Agency: Aevitas

Fiction > *Novels*
Feminist Romance; Historical Fiction; LGBTQIA; Literary

Nonfiction > *Nonfiction Books*
Cookery; Food

Closed to approaches.

Represents imaginative, genre-bending literary fiction; capacious historical novels; beautifully told queer stories; and smart, feminist romance. Her other loves include unclassifiable book projects, food and cookbooks, and work by writers traditionally underrepresented in mainstream publishing.

Authors: Emma Ahlqvist; Will Betke-Brunswick; Rita Zoey Chin; Marisa Crane; Carla Fernandez; JR Ford; Vanessa Ford; Andrew J. Graff; Rebecca Kling; Rue Mapp; Jessica Martin; Carolyn Prusa; Nina Sharma; Jack Shoulder; Mark Small; Julia Ridley Smith; June Thomas

L142 Cornerstone Literary Agency

Literary Agency
United States

info@cornerstoneliterary.com

http://www.cornerstoneliterary.com

Fiction > *Novels*
Commercial; Literary

Nonfiction > *Nonfiction Books*: Narrative Nonfiction

Send: Query; Author bio; Writing sample; Self-Addressed Stamped Envelope (SASE)
How to send: Post; Email

Send query by post or by email. No business, how-to, photography books, poetry, screenplays, self-help or Westerns.

Literary Agent: Helen Breitwieser (**L083**)

L143 The Cowles Agency

Literary Agency
United States

katherine@cowlesagency.com

http://www.cowlesagency.com
https://twitter.com/cowlesagency
https://www.instagram.com/cowlesagency/

Nonfiction > *Nonfiction Books*
Business; Cookery; Design; Health; Memoir; Narrative Nonfiction; Photography

Authors: Bryant Austin; Catherine Bailey; Andy Baraghani; Nils Bernstein; Taylor Boetticher; Jon Bonne; Carrie Brown; Chris Burkard; Courtney Burns; Gabriela Camara; Henry Carroll; Josef Centeno; Baylor Chapman; Andrew Chau; Bin Chen; Mark Cushing; Sohla El-Waylly; Renee Erickson; Susan Fisher; Camille Fourmont; Andrea Gentl; Monica Khemsurov; Eric Kim; George King; Jessica Koslow; Lauri Krantz; Jeff Krasno; Chris Kronner; Jonathan Kung; Travis Lett; Peter Liem; Kermit Lynch; Rick Martinez; Ignacio Mattos; Margarita Matzke; Emeran Mayer; Amy Merrick; Toponia Miller; Serena Mitnik-Miller; Sam Mogannam; Carla Lalli Music; Marie-Pierre St. Onge; Ivan Orkin; Rafael Pelayo; Robin Petravic; Charles Phan; Natasha Pickowicz; Elisabeth Prueitt; Christian Puglisi; Chad Robertson; Sharon Robinson; Besha Rodell; Julia Sherman; Sheldon Simeon; Jill Singer; Garrett Snyder; David Tanis; Erica Tanov; Andrew Tarlow; Pierre Thaim; Thaddeus Vogler; Eric Werner; Kris Yenbamroong; Chris Ying; Maria Zizka

Literary Agent: Katherine Cowles (**L144**)

L144 Katherine Cowles

Literary Agent
United States

katherine@cowlesagency.com

Literary Agency: The Cowles Agency (**L143**)
Professional Bodies: Association of American Literary Agents (AALA); The Authors Guild

L145 Peter Cox

Literary Agent
United Kingdom

Literary Agency: Redhammer (**L580**)

L146 Becca Crandall

Literary Agent
United States

becca@carolynjenksagency.com

https://www.carolynjenksagency.com/agent/BECCA-CRANDALL

Literary Agency: Carolyn Jenks Agency (**L106**)

ADULT
Fiction
Graphic Novels; *Novels*
Nonfiction > *Nonfiction Books*

CHILDREN'S > **Fiction**
Middle Grade; *Picture Books*
YOUNG ADULT > **Fiction** > *Novels*

Send: Query; Writing sample
How to send: In the body of an email

L147 The Creative Rights Agency

Literary Agency
United Kingdom
Tel: +44 (0) 20 3371 7673

info@creativerightsagency.co.uk

http://www.creativerightsagency.co.uk

Fiction > *Novels*

Nonfiction > *Nonfiction Books*

Publishing, Licensing, Film/TV. Based in London.

Literary Agent: Richard Scrivener

L148 Cull & Co. Ltd

Literary Agency
United Kingdom

tom@cullandco.com

https://cullandco.com
https://www.facebook.com/cullandco/
https://www.youtube.com/channel/UCp8AcbMXQ7UenhgFxX4XM6g

Professional Body: The Association of Authors' Agents (AAA)

Nonfiction > *Nonfiction Books*
Biography; Crime; Memoir; Military; Narrative Nonfiction; Politics; Sport; Travel

Send: Synopsis; Writing sample; Author bio
How to send: Email

Handles full-length fiction and nonfiction for adults only. No children's picture books, poetry, plays or musical theatre. Primarily looking for authors from the UK and Ireland writing in English. Occasionally considers international writers but you must make it clear when submitting why you are looking for a literary agent in the UK.

L149 Mary Cummings

Literary Agent
United States

Literary Agency: Great River Literary (**L284**)
Professional Bodies: Association of American

Literary Agents (AALA); Society of Children's Book Writers and Illustrators (SCBWI)

L150 Curtis Brown (Australia) Pty Ltd

Literary Agency
Australia

submission@curtisbrown.com.au

https://www.curtisbrown.com.au

Professional Body: Australian Literary Agents' Association (ALAA)

Fiction > *Novels*

Nonfiction > *Nonfiction Books*

How to send: Email
How not to send: Post

Accepts submission from within Australia and New Zealand only, during February, June, and October. No fantasy, sci-fi, stage/screenplays, poetry, self-help books, children's picture books, early reader books, young adult books, comic books, short stories, cookbooks, educational, corporate books or translations. Send query by email with synopsis up to two pages and first three chapters. See website for full guidelines.

Literary Agents: Clare Forster; Grace Heifetz; Fiona Inglis; Pippa Masson; Tara Wynne

L151 John Cusick

Literary Agent; Vice President
United States

https://www.publishersmarketplace.com/members/JohnC/
https://twitter.com/johnmcusick

Literary Agencies: Folio Literary Management, LLC; Folio Jr.

ADULT > **Fiction** > *Novels*
Fantasy; Horror; Science Fiction; Suspense; Thrillers

CHILDREN'S > **Fiction** > *Middle Grade*
Comedy / Humour; Contemporary; Fantasy; Science Fiction; Speculative

YOUNG ADULT > **Fiction** > *Novels*
Comedy / Humour; Contemporary; Fantasy; Science Fiction; Speculative

Closed to approaches.

Authors: Courtney Alameda; Kayla Cagan; Josephine Cameron; Anna Carey; Marina Cohen; Paula Garner; Joan He; Christian McKay Heidicker; Sailor J; Jeramey Kraatz; Kristen Lippert-Martin; Julie Murphy; Abdi Nazemian; Jordan Reeves; Laura Sebastian; Quinn Sosna-Spear; Sharon Biggs Waller; Don Zolidis

L152 Cyle Young Literary Elite

Literary Agency
United States

https://cyleyoung.com
https://www.facebook.com/cyle61?fref=ts
https://twitter.com/cyleyoung

Associate Agents: Hope Bolinger; Caroline George; Alyssa Roat

Author / Junior Agent: Del Duduit (**L183**)

Author / Literary Agent: Cyle Young (**L754**)

Junior Agents: Megan Burkhart (**L096**); Jori Hanna; Chrysa Keenon; Kenzi Nevins

Literary Agent: Tessa Emily Hall (*L298*)

L153 Cynthia Cannell Literary Agency

Literary Agency
54 West 40th Street, New York, NY 10018
United States
Tel: +1 (212) 396-9595

info@cannellagency.com

http://cannellagency.com

Professional Body: Association of American Literary Agents (AALA)

Types: Fiction; Nonfiction
Subjects: Autobiography; Contemporary; Current Affairs; Health; Literary; Personal Development; Religion
Markets: Adult

Closed to approaches.

Full-service literary agency based in New York. Represents fiction, memoir, biography, self-improvement, spirituality, and nonfiction on contemporary issues. No screenplays, children's books, illustrated books, cookbooks, romance, category mystery, or science fiction. Send query by email only, including brief description of the project, relevant biographical information, and any publishing credits. No attachments or submissions by post. Response not guaranteed.

Literary Agent: Cynthia Cannell

L154 Laura Dail

Literary Agent; President
United States

http://www.ldlainc.com/about
http://twitter.com/ledail
http://aaronline.org/Sys/PublicProfile/2176649/417813

Literary Agency: Laura Dail Literary Agency (**L413**)
Professional Body: Association of American Literary Agents (AALA)

Closed to approaches.

L155 Melissa Danaczko

Literary Agent
United States

Literary Agency: Stuart Krichevsky Literary Agency, Inc. (**L675**)

Closed to approaches.

L156 Margaret Danko

Literary Agent
United States

submissions@paperoverboard.com

https://www.irenegoodman.com/margaret-danko

Literary Agency: Irene Goodman Literary Agency (IGLA)

ADULT

Fiction > *Novels*
Contemporary; Historical Fiction; Literary; Magical Realism; Romantic Comedy; Suspense; Upmarket

Nonfiction > *Nonfiction Books*
Comedy / Humour; Cookery; Crime; Environment; Health; Lifestyle; Mental Health; New Age; Popular Science; Spirituality; Wellbeing

YOUNG ADULT > **Fiction** > *Novels*: Fantasy

Closed to approaches.

Actively looking for attention-grabbing voices especially historical fiction with a dash of magical realism, literary and upmarket suspense and horror, spooky contemporary and fantasy YA, narratives with a deep sense of place and history, quirky and heartwarming family stories, and rom-coms full of charm and whimsy. She is also interested in nonfiction in the areas of humor, lifestyle, new age and general spirituality, popular science especially in environmental and human sciences, mental health/wellness, true crime that challenges established conventions, and select cooking projects with an emphasis on new takes on tradition, especially within the Latine diaspora. She does not represent Middle Grade or picture books.

L157 Jon Michael Darga

Literary Agent
New York
United States

https://aevitascreative.com/agents/

Literary Agency: Aevitas

ADULT

Fiction > *Novels*: Commercial

Nonfiction > *Nonfiction Books*
Biography; Cookery; History; Photography; Popular Culture

YOUNG ADULT > **Fiction** > *Novels*: Commercial

Closed to approaches.

Represents both nonfiction and fiction. He is most interested in voice-driven pop culture writing and histories that re-cast the narrative by emphasizing unexpected or unheard voices.

Authors: Matt Abdoo; Zac Bissonnette; Sydney Bucksbaum; Tony Chin-Quee; Angel Luis Colón; Melissa Croce; Sarah Horowitz; Patty Lin; Violet Lumani; Hugo Huerta Marin; Ann Marks; Shane McBride; Tarek El Moussa; James Park; Erik Piepenburg; Lynette Rice; Geena Rocero; Ashley Spencer; Jason Sperling; Jesse Szewczyk; Amy Watson; Rusty Williams; Angel Di Zhang

L158 Darhansoff & Verrill Literary Agents

Literary Agency
275 Fair Street, Suite 17D, Kingston NY, 12401
United States
Tel: +1 (917) 305-1300

submissions@dvagency.com
info@dvagency.com

https://www.dvagency.com

ADULT
Fiction > *Novels*
Nonfiction > *Nonfiction Books*

YOUNG ADULT > **Fiction** > *Novels*

Send: Query; Writing sample
How to send: In the body of an email
How not to send: Post

Response only if interested. If no response within eight weeks, assume rejection.

Literary Agents: Liz Darhansoff; Michele Mortimer (**L511**); Charles Verrill

L159 Darley Anderson Children's

Literary Agency
Unit 19, Matrix Studios, 91 Peterborough Road, London, SW6 3BU
United Kingdom
Tel: +44 (0) 20 7386 2674

childrens@darleyanderson.com

http://www.darleyandersonchildrens.com
http://twitter.com/DA_Childrens

Professional Body: The Association of Authors' Agents (AAA)

CHILDREN'S
Fiction
Chapter Books; *Middle Grade*; *Picture Books*
Nonfiction > *Nonfiction Books*

YOUNG ADULT > **Fiction** > *Novels*

Send: Query; Synopsis; Writing sample; Author bio; Pitch
How to send: Word file email attachment; PDF file email attachment
How not to send: Post

Always on the look out for exciting, inspiring and original novels for both Young Adult and Middle-Grade readers, chapter books, picture books, and nonfiction.

Literary Agent: Clare Wallace (**L718**)

L160 David Godwin Associates

Literary Agency
2nd Floor, 40 Rosebery Avenue, Clerkenwell, London, EC1R 4RX
United Kingdom
Tel: +44 (0) 20 7240 9992

submissions@davidgodwinassociates.co.uk

http://www.davidgodwinassociates.com

Fiction > *Novels*

Nonfiction > *Nonfiction Books*

Send: Query; Synopsis; Writing sample
How to send: Email

Handles a range of nonfiction and fiction. Send query by email with synopsis and first 30 pages. No poetry. No picture books, except for existing clients.

Literary Agent: David Godwin

L161 David Higham Associates Ltd

Literary Agency
6th Floor, Waverley House, 7-12 Noel Street, London, W1F 8GQ
United Kingdom
Tel: +44 (0) 20 7434 5900
Fax: +44 (0) 20 7437 1072

reception@davidhigham.co.uk
submissions@davidhigham.co.uk
childrenssubmissions@davidhigham.co.uk

http://www.davidhigham.co.uk

Professional Body: The Association of Authors' Agents (AAA)

Agency Assistant: Sara Langham

Assistant Agents: Becca Challis (*L113*); David Evans (**L210**)

Authors: Rachel Abbott; J. R. Ackerley; Richard Adams; Arenike Adebajo; Ore Agbaje-Williams; Katie Agnew; Sara Ahmed; Kat Ailes; Naomi Alderman; Tracy Alexander; Elizabeth Alker; Rachael Allen; Jason Allen-Paisant; Alan Allport; Nuar Alsadir; Geraint Anderson; Kelly Andrew; Abi Andrews; Carol Anshaw; Michael Arditti; Edward Ardizzone; Noga Arikha; Michael Arlen; Thomas Asbridge; Jenn Ashworth; Jennifer Atkins; Julian Baggini; Harriet Baker; Gina María Balibrera; Katy Balls; Antonia Barber; Lindsey Bareham; Nigel Barley; Suzanne Barton; Kaushik Basu; Felix Bazalgette; Ella Beech; Laura Beers; Hannah Begbie; Annie Bell; Aimee Bender; Joe Berger; Sarah Bernstein; Elizabeth Berridge; Tessa Bickers; Rebecca Birrell; James Bloodworth; Edmund Blunden; Margaret Boden; Jonathan Boff; Tim Bowler; E. R. Braithwaite; Mikki Brammer; Lauren Bravo; Carys Bray; Neville Braybrooke; Kevin Brazil; Theresa Breslin; Kevin Brockmeier; Glen Brown; Martin Brown; Hester Browne; Janet Browne; Mike Brownlow; Jessica Bruder; Arthur Bryant; Ella Bucknall; Anthony Burgess; Mark Burnell; Rob Burnett; Nick Butterworth; Eliza Barry Callahan; John Carey; John Dickson Carr; Jess Cartner-Morley; Anne-Marie Casey; Barbara Castle; Charles Causley; Kathryn Cave; Aditya Chakrabortty; Vanessa Chan; Jason Chapman; Eve Chase; James Hadley Chase; Seerut K. Chawla; Emma Chichester Clark; Arthur C. Clarke; Lady Mary Clive; Michael Cockerell; J. M. Coetzee; Kathleen Collins; Sophie Collins; Charlie Connelly; Alan Connor; Peter Cook; Trish Cooke; Emily S. Cooper; Bernard Cornwell; Chris Cove-Smith; Cressida Cowell; Jason Cowley; Nick Crumpton; John Cunliffe; James Curtis; Roald Dahl; David Daiches; Alex Danchev; Tsitsi Dangarembga; Nicola Davies; Susie Day; Tish Delaney; R. F. Delderfield; Kady MacDonald Denton; Lucy Diamond; Lucy Dillamore; Lucy Dillon; Jonathan Dimbleby; Berlie Doherty; Naoise Dolan; Sareeta Domingo; Alicia Drake; Bobby Duffy; Sarah Duguid; Ruth Eastham; Mark Easton; Ellie Eaton; David Edmonds; Eve Edwards; Kerry Egan; Jonathan Emmett; Gavin Esler; Maz Evans; Seb Falk; Eleanor Farjeon; J. Jefferson Farjeon; Ben Faulks; Felipe Fernández-Armesto; Elizabeth Ferrars; Ophelia Field; Anne Fine; Cordelia Fine; Nicholas Fisk; Pauline Fisk; Theodora Fitzgibbon; Corina Fletcher; Margot Fonteyn; Ford Madox Ford; Alex Foulkes; Karen Joy Fowler; Catherine Fox; Matthew Frank; Mila Franklin; P. M. Freestone; Tom de Freston; Stephen Fry; Mavis Gallant; Jane Gardam; Susan Gates; Jonathan Gathorne-Hardy; Ryan Gattis; Jamila Gavin; Alex George; Jessica George; Adèle Geras; Susannah Gibson; Andrew Gimson; Guinevere Glasfurd; Ralph Glasser; Victoria Glendinning; Julia Golding; Anthony Good; Elizabeth Goudge; Caroline Graham; Marlowe Granados; Ryan Graudin; Saska Graville; Dominic Green; Linda Green; Peter Green; Graham Greene; Richard Greene; John Gribbin; Geoffrey Grigson; Jane Grigson; Dennis Grube; Candy Guard; Saleem Haddad; Araminta Hall; Jo Hamya; Isabel Hardman; Sophie Harman; Candida Harper; Ali Harris; Oliver Harris; Sarah J. Harris; Alice Hattrick; Paula Hawkins; Lottie Hazell; Oli Hazzard; Claire Marie Healy; Lisa Heathfield; Neil Hegarty; Emma Henderson; James Herbert; Deborah Hewitt; Rosie Hewlett; Chris Hirst; Russell Hoban; Eric Hobsbawm; Gavanndra Hodge; Leigh Hodgkinson; Jesse Hodgson; Paul Hoffman; Dianne Hofmeyr; Edward Hogan; Phil Hogan; Anna Hoghton; Ian Holding; Euny Hong; Meredith Hooper; Simon Hopkinson; Trevor Horn; Tansy Hoskins; Lucy Hounsom; Yuji Huang; Suzanna Hubbard; Tristan Hughes; William Hussey; Alex Hutchinson; Will Iredale; Julian Jackson; Julia Jarman; Milly Johnson; Rebecca May Johnson; Diana Wynne Jones; Owen Jones; Alan Judd;

Amie Kaufman; Anna Keay; John Keay; Anna Kemp; Laura Kemp; Paul Kennedy; Sulmaan Wasif Khan; Rachel Khoo; Claire King; Clive King; Binnie Kirshenbaum; Jay Kristoff; Fifi Kuo; Emily LaBarge; Stephen Lacey; David Lammy; Hugh Laurie; Eleanor Lavender; Natalie Lawrence; Elisabeth Leake; Jeremy Lee; Beth Lewis; Penelope Lively; Saci Lloyd; Jo Lodge; Joanna Lumley; Richard Lumsden; Kesia Lupo; Dame Vera Lynn; Sophie Mackintosh; Kathryn Mannix; Sarfraz Manzoor; Greil Marcus; Kathryn Maris; Jan Mark; Ellie Marney; Patrick Marnham; David Marquand; Helen Marten; Simon Mason; Sadie Matthews; Evan Mawdsley; Peter May; Helen McCarthy; Michael McCarthy; Geraldine McCaughrean; Elizabeth McCracken; Iain McGilchrist; Elizabeth McKenzie; Tom McLaughlin; Thomas McMullan; Jean McNeil; Rosanna Mclaughlin; Anna Metcalfe; Ed Miliband; Louise Millar; Kei Miller; Gwen Millward; Myfanwy Millward; Kate Milner; Alex Milway; Tony Mitton; Victoria Moore; Kate Morton; Emma-Lee Moss; Laura Mucha; Fraser Nelson; Jenny Nimmo; Megan Nolan; Johan Norberg; David Nott; Sigrid Nunez; Peter Oborne; Laurie Owens; Susan Owens; Deborah O'Donoghue; Ellie Mae O'Hagan; C. S. Pacat; Helen Parr; James Conor Patterson; Harry Pearson; Eleanor Penny; Alison Percival; Gilles Peterson; Kate Reed Petty; Liz Pichon; Tamora Pierce; John Pilger; Alake Pilgrim; Courtney Pine; Christina Pishiris; Anna Politkovskaya; Anthony Powell; Shannon Pufahl; Sadiah Qureshi; Amol Rajan; Madhvi Ramani; Catherine Rayner; Jacqui Rayner; Gwyneth Rees; Katy Regan; Hannah Regel; Chris Renwick; Jasmine Richards; Steve Richards; Fiona Roberton; Lucy Robinson; Helen Roche; Claudia Roden; Jane Rogoyska; Rachel Rooney; Leone Ross; Rupert Russell; Saba Sams; Jane Sanderson; Kathryn Scanlan; Izabella Scott; Alice Sebold; Antonia Senior; Miranda Seymour; Nick Sharratt; Penelope Shuttle; Jake Wallis Simons; Sujit Sivasundaram; Alexander McCall Smith; Lisa Smith; Mark B. Smith; Peter Snowdon; Mary South; Kristina Spohr; Hilary Spurling; Devi Sridhar; Jessica Stanley; Joss Stirling; Peter Stott; Hew Strachan; Jeremy Strong; Tasha Sylva; Sally Symes; Vanessa Tait; Dizz Tate; Lulu Taylor; Sureka Thanenthiran-Dharuman; Dylan Thomas; Frances Thomas; Simon Thurley; Phil Tinline; Theresa Tomlinson; Lynne Truss; Ann Turnbull; Simon Tyler; Jack Underwood; Rosamund Urwin; Varaidzo; Yanis Varoufakis; Sarah Vaughan; Brian Viner; Martin Waddell; Lucy Wadham; Alice Walker; Joanna Walsh; Melanie Walsh; Rosie Walsh; Stephen Walsh; Vanessa Walters; Miranda Ward; Bernard Wasserstein; Holly Watt; Christian Weaver; Sam Wetherell; Phil Whitaker; Elizabeth Wilhide; Gina Wilson; Jacqueline Wilson; Jon Wilson; David Wojtowycz; Hope Wolf; Carolyn Woods; Mandy Yin; Kate Zambreno; Adam Zmith

Chair / Literary Agent: Anthony Goff (**L273**)

Company Director / Literary Agent: Veronique Baxter (**L050**)

Literary Agents: Olivia Barber; Nicola Chang (**L119**); Elise Dillsworth (**L173**); Jemima Forrester (**L232**); Georgia Glover (**L271**); Andrew Gordon (**L277**); Lizzy Kremer (**L397**); Harriet Moore (**L503**); Caroline Walsh (**L719**); Laura West; Jessica Woollard (**L747**)

L162 David Luxton Associates

Literary Agency
United Kingdom

admin@davidluxtonassociates.co.uk

https://www.davidluxtonassociates.co.uk
https://twitter.com/DLuxAssociates
https://www.instagram.com/davidluxtonassociates/

Professional Body: The Association of Authors' Agents (AAA)

Nonfiction > *Nonfiction Books*
Food; Investigative Journalism; Lifestyle; Music; Nature; Photography; Sport

Send: Query; Synopsis; Writing sample; Author bio
How to send: Email
How not to send: Post

Specialises in nonfiction, including sport, celebrity biography, business & leadership, food-writing, nature-writing and lifestyle. No scripts or screenplays.

Literary Agents: David Luxton (**L451**); Nick Walters (**L721**); Rebecca Winfield (**L742**)

L163 Bonnie Davis

Literary Agent

Literary Agency: Bret Adams Ltd

L164 Chloe Davis

Assistant Agent
United Kingdom

http://www.darleyanderson.com/our-team

Literary Agent: Clare Wallace (**L718**)
Literary Agency: The Darley Anderson Agency

CHILDREN'S > **Fiction** > *Middle Grade*: Adventure

YOUNG ADULT > **Fiction** > *Novels*: Contemporary Romance

Particularly enjoys reading submissions, especially middle grade adventures and contemporary YA love stories.

Author: Addy Farmer

L165 Meg Davis

Literary Agent
United Kingdom

meg@ki-agency.co.uk

https://ki-agency.co.uk/contact

Literary Agency: Ki Agency Ltd (**L385**)

Fiction > *Novels*

Scripts
Film Scripts; *TV Scripts*; *Theatre Scripts*

Happy to consider scripts in all genres, and books in some genres, especially genre fiction. Not a good bet for fiction that might be considered to be wearing a cardigan, or which is narrated by an animal.

L166 Caroline Dawnay

Literary Agent
United Kingdom
Tel: +44 (0) 20 3214 0931

kaitken@unitedagents.co.uk

https://www.unitedagents.co.uk/cdawnayunitedagentscouk

Literary Agency: United Agents (**L704**)

Fiction > *Novels*: Literary

Nonfiction > *Nonfiction Books*

Send: Query; Author bio; Writing sample
How to send: Email

Interested in serious nonfiction and literary fiction. For submissions please email a short cover letter, biographical note and the first 10,000 words of your text.

Authors: Rennie Airth; Laura Beatty; Stephen Bernard; Alain de Botton; Susie Boyt; Christopher Brookmyre; James Buchan; Eleanor Catton; Charles Chadwick; Catherine Chidgey; Rupert Christiansen; Charles Clover; Peter Conrad; Jill Dawson; Guy Deutscher; Minoo Dinshaw; Gaston Dorren; Philip Eade; James Le Fanu; Tim Finch; Tom Fort; Richard Francis; John Fuller; James Grant; Thomas Grant; Tessa Hadley; James Hall; Christopher de Hamel; Lynsey Hanley; Alexandra Harris; Jane Hasell-McCosh; David Hendy; Richard Holloway; Sheena Joughin; Adam Forrest Kay; Martin Kemp; Nick Lane; Richard Layard; Hermione Lee; Margaret MacMillan; Jan Morris; Chris Mullin; James Mylet; Jeremy Mynott; Virginia Nicholson; Constantine Phipps; Edward Platt; Jennifer Potter; Matthew Rice; Jane Ridley; Posy Simmonds; Helen Smith; Dan Snow; Donald Sturrock; Sasha Swire; Stephen Taylor; Tony Thompson; Francesca Wade; Nadia Wassef; Philip Ziegler; Sofka Zinovieff

L167 Liza DeBlock

Literary Agent
United Kingdom

submissions@mushens-entertainment.com

https://www.mushens-entertainment.com/liza-deblock

Literary Agency: Mushens Entertainment (**L516**)

Fiction > *Novels*
Grounded Fantasy; Historical Fiction; Literary; Romantic Comedy; Thrillers; Upmarket

Nonfiction > *Nonfiction Books*
Cookery; Popular Science; Social History

Send: Query; Synopsis; Writing sample
How to send: Email

Looking for both fiction and non fiction. For fiction, she is interested in adult and YA only. She is looking for historical fiction, commercial fantasy, romcom, saga, uplit, and thriller.

On the nonfiction side, she is looking for books that teach her something new or reframe a topic from an alternative point of view. This can include cookery, pop science, social history, and current events.

Authors: Sally Abe; Natalie Chandler; Eleanor Houghton; Hayley Nolan; Stacey Thomas; Pim Wangtechawat

L168 The Dench Arnold Agency

Literary Agency
United Kingdom
Tel: +44 (0) 20 7437 4551
Fax: +44 (0) 20 7437 4551

fiona@dencharnold.com

https://www.dencharnold.com
https://www.instagram.com/dencharnold_agency/
https://twitter.com/DenchArnold

Scripts
Film Scripts; *TV Scripts*

Send: Query; Author bio; Synopsis
How to send: Email

Send query with CV and synopsis by email only. Represents writers, directors and heads of department (directors of photography, production designers, costume designers, editors and make-up designers).

Authors: Joe Ainsworth; Maurice Bessman; Giles Borg; William Borthwick; Peter Briggs; Karen Brown; Peter Chelsom; Rob Churchill; David Conolly; Hannah Davies; Jim Davies; Eric Deacon; Adrian Dunbar; Chris Fallon; Susanne Farrell; Matthew Faulk; Lucy Flannery; Ellis Freeman; Liam Gavin; Nicholas Gibbs; Steve Gough; Robert Hammond; James Handel; Michael Harvey; Jo Ho; David Lg Hughes; Julian Kemp; Malcolm Kohll; Anna Kythreotis; Sarah Lambert; Dominic Macdonald; Steve Mcateer; Alan Mcdonald; Kevin Molony; Courttia Newland; Matthew Newman; Omid Nooshin; Paul Parkes; Junior Rhone; Dave Simpson; Mark Skeet; Mark Stay; Francesca Tatini; Stewart Thomson; Alan Whiting; Terry Winsor; Kate Wood

Literary Agents: Michelle Arnold; Elizabeth Dench; Matthew Dench

L169 Francesca Devas

Literary Agent
United Kingdom

Literary Agency: Independent Talent Group Ltd (**L340**)

L170 Allison Devereux

Literary Agent
United States

https://www.cheneyagency.com/allison-devereux

Literary Agency: The Cheney Agency

L171 Cori Deyoe

Literary Agent
United States

cori@threeseaslit.com

https://www.threeseasagency.com/cori-deyoe
https://querymanager.com/query/Cori3Seas

Literary Agency: 3 Seas Literary Agency (**L001**)

ADULT > **Fiction** > *Novels*
Mystery; Romance; Thrillers; Women's Fiction

CHILDREN'S > **Fiction**
Middle Grade; *Picture Books*
YOUNG ADULT > **Fiction** > *Novels*

Send: Query; Synopsis; Writing sample; Pitch; Market info
How to send: Query Manager

Actively looking to expand her list of clients. She represents all sub-genres of romance, women's fiction, young adult, middle grade, picture books, thrillers, mysteries and select non-fiction.

L172 DHH Literary Agency Ltd

Literary Agency
23-27 Cecil Court, London, WC2N 4EZ
United Kingdom
Tel: +44 (0) 20 3990 2452

enquiries@dhhliteraryagency.com

http://www.dhhliteraryagency.com

Professional Body: The Association of Authors' Agents (AAA)

ADULT
Fiction > *Novels*
Nonfiction > *Nonfiction Books*

CHILDREN'S > **Fiction** > *Novels*

YOUNG ADULT > **Fiction** > *Novels*

Send: Query
Don't send: Full text

Accepts submissions by email only. No postal submissions. See website for specific agent interests and email addresses and approach one agent only. Do not send submissions to generic "enquiries" email address.

Associate Agent: Tom Drake Lee (**L419**)

Authors: Kishan Devani BEM; Graham Bartlett; Louise Beech; R.C. Bridgestock; Caraline Brown; Paul Burston; Paul Fraser Collard; Howard Colyer; M.W. Craven; John Curran; Libby Cutts; Heather Darwent; Becca Day; Michael Delahaye; Suzie Edge; Stephen Edger; Emma Ellis; Rachael Featherstone; David Fennell; Fishlove; Essie Fox; Anita Frank; Erin Green; Lisa Hilton; Dixie Innes; Valerie Jack; Ragnar Jonasson; Carys Jones; Katrín Júlíusdóttir; Diana Kessler; Caroline Lamond; Robin Laurance; S.V. Leonard; Jean Levy; Sean Lusk; Jo Lyons; Adrian Magson; Brian McGilloway; Rachel Meller; Janie Millman; Noel O'Reilly; Valerie O'Riordan; Vikki Patis; Reagan Lee Ray; Iain Rowan; Talia Samuels; Robert Scragg; Victoria Selman; Richard Stirling; Eleanor Tattersfield; Annie May Taylor; Jo Thomas; Rebecca Thorne; Bar Tozino; Amanda Tuke; Ola Tundun; Ronnie Turner; L.C. Tyler; Stephen Walker; A. J. West; Clare Whitfield; Kathleen Whyman; Eva Björg Ægisdottir

Literary Agent / Managing Director: David H. Headley (**L316**)

Literary Agents: Broo Doherty; Emily Glenister (**L269**); Harry Illingworth; Hannah Sheppard

L173 Elise Dillsworth

Literary Agent
United Kingdom

elise@elisedillsworthagency.com

https://www.davidhigham.co.uk/agents-dh/elise-dillsworth/

Literary Agencies: Elise Dillsworth Agency (EDA); David Higham Associates Ltd (**L161**)

Fiction > *Novels*
Commercial; International; Literary

Nonfiction > *Nonfiction Books*
Commercial; International; Literary

Represents literary and commercial fiction and nonfiction, with a keen aim to reflect writing that is international.

Author: Courtney Pine

L174 Isobel Dixon

Literary Agent; Managing Director
United Kingdom

isobeldixon@blakefriedmann.co.uk

http://blakefriedmann.co.uk/isobel-dixon
https://twitter.com/isobeldixon

Literary Agency: Blake Friedmann Literary Agency Ltd (**L067**)

Fiction > *Novels*
Contemporary; Crime; Historical Fiction; Literary; Thrillers

Nonfiction > *Nonfiction Books*
Biography; Memoir; Narrative History

Closed to approaches.

Interests are wide-ranging and her clients' work includes contemporary, historical and literary fiction, crime and thrillers, memoir, biography and narrative history.

L175 Trevor Dolby

Literary Agent
United Kingdom

https://aevitascreative.com/agents/#agent-7410

Literary Agency: Aevitas Creative Management (ACM) UK (**L008**)

Nonfiction > *Nonfiction Books*
Biography; Comedy / Humour; Memoir; Military History; Narrative History; Nature; Popular Culture; Popular Science

Send: Query; Writing sample
How to send: Online submission system

Looking for popular science with a clear relevance to everyday life, narrative history, military history, humour, biography, popular culture, natural history and great memoirs by passionate people whose lives have been well lived.

L176 Adriana Dominguez

Senior Agent
United States

https://aevitascreative.com/agents/
https://querymanager.com/query/2243

Literary Agency: Aevitas

ADULT > **Nonfiction** > *Nonfiction Books*: Narrative Nonfiction

CHILDREN'S
Fiction
Middle Grade; *Picture Books*
Nonfiction > *Nonfiction Books*

How to send: Query Manager

Interested in illustrators with fresh, unmistakable styles, platform-driven narrative nonfiction from children to adult, and select children's fiction from picture books to middle grade.

Authors: Jacqueline Alcántara; Emma Otheguy; Katheryn Russell-Brown; Janelle Washington

L177 Don Buchwald and Associates

Literary Agency
United States

info@buchwald.com

https://www.buchwald.com
https://twitter.com/buchwaldtalent
https://www.facebook.com/buchwaldtalent
https://www.instagram.com/buchwaldtalent

Professional Body: Writers Guild of America (WGA)

Scripts
Film Scripts; *TV Scripts*; *Theatre Scripts*

Closed to approaches.

Does not accept unsolicited submissions of any kind.

L178 Don Congdon Associates, Inc.

Literary Agency
88 Pine Street, Suite 730, New York, NY 10005
United States
Tel: +1 (212) 645-1229

dca@doncongdon.com

http://doncongdon.com

Professional Body: Association of American Literary Agents (AALA)

Fiction > *Novels*

Nonfiction > *Nonfiction Books*

Send: Query; Synopsis; Writing sample
How to send: Email

Send query by email (no attachments) only. Include one-page synopsis, relevant background info, and first chapter, all within the body of the email if submitting by email. Include the word "Query" in the subject line. See website for full guidelines. No unsolicited MSS.

Literary Agents: Cristina Concepcion; Michael Congdon; Katie Grimm (*L289*); Katie Kotchman; Maura Kye-Casella; Susan Ramer (*L579*)

L179 Donaghy Literary Group

Literary Agency
United States

stacey@donaghyliterary.com

http://www.donaghyliterary.com

ADULT > **Fiction** > *Novels*
Fantasy; Historical Fantasy; Historical Fiction; Mystery; Romance; Science Fiction; Suspense; Thrillers; Women's Fiction

YOUNG ADULT > **Fiction** > *Novels*
Fantasy; Historical Fantasy; Historical Fiction; Mystery; Romance; Science Fiction; Suspense; Thrillers; Women's Fiction

Send: Query
How to send: Online submission system

See website for individual agent interests, and submit using online submission system.

Literary Agents: Amanda Ayers Barnett; Stacey Donaghy; Liis McKinstry; Sue Miller; Valerie Noble; Susan Spann

L180 Priya Doraswamy

Literary Agent
United States

Literary Agency: Lotus Lane Literary (**L441**)

L181 Dorie Simmonds Agency

Literary Agency
United Kingdom

info@doriesimmonds.com

https://doriesimmonds.com/

Professional Body: The Association of Authors' Agents (AAA)

ADULT
Fiction > *Novels*: Commercial

Nonfiction > *Nonfiction Books*

CHILDREN'S > **Fiction** > *Novels*

Send: Query; Writing sample; Author bio
How to send: PDF file email attachment; Word file email attachment

Send query by email as Word or PDF attachments. Include details on your background and relevant writing experience, and first three chapters or fifty pages. See website for full details.

Literary Agents: Pearl Baxter; Dorie Simmonds (**L644**)

L182 Alec Drysdale

Literary Agent
United Kingdom

Literary Agency: Independent Talent Group Ltd (**L340**)

L183 Del Duduit

Junior Agent; Author
United States

https://cyleyoung.com/literary-agent/my-team/

Literary Agency: Cyle Young Literary Elite (**L152**)
Literary Agent / Author: Cyle Young (**L754**)

Nonfiction > *Nonfiction Books*
Christian Living; Cookery; Health; Inspirational; Leadership; Leisure; Lifestyle; Motivational Self-Help; Sport; Travel

L184 Dunham Literary, Inc.

Literary Agency
United States

query@dunhamlit.com

https://www.dunhamlit.com

ADULT
Fiction > *Novels*

Nonfiction > *Nonfiction Books*: Narrative Nonfiction

CHILDREN'S > **Fiction**
Novels; *Picture Books*

Send: Query; Writing sample
Don't send: Full text
How to send: In the body of an email
How not to send: Post; Fax; Phone; Email attachment

Handles quality fiction and nonfiction for adults and children. Send query by email only. See website for full guidelines. No approaches by post, phone or fax. No email attachments.

Literary Agents: Jennie Dunham (**L185**); Bridget Smith; Leslie Zampetti (**L758**)

L185 Jennie Dunham

Literary Agent
United States

https://www.dunhamlit.com/jennie-dunham.html
http://aaronline.org/Sys/PublicProfile/2176658/417813

Literary Agency: Dunham Literary, Inc. (**L184**)
Professional Bodies: Association of American Literary Agents (AALA); Society of Children's Book Writers and Illustrators (SCBWI)

ADULT
Fiction
Graphic Novels: General
Novels: Comedy / Humour; Historical Fiction; LGBTQIA; Literary; Mystery; Thrillers; Women's Fiction
Nonfiction > *Nonfiction Books*
Biography; Current Affairs; Family; History; Memoir; Narrative Nonfiction; Parenting; Politics; Relationships; Science; Technology

CHILDREN'S > **Fiction**
Middle Grade; *Picture Books*
NEW ADULT
Fiction > *Novels*
Nonfiction > *Nonfiction Books*

YOUNG ADULT > **Fiction** > *Novels*

Send: Query; Writing sample
Don't send: Full text
How to send: In the body of an email
How not to send: Post; Fax; Phone; Email attachment

Represents literary fiction and non-fiction for adults and children.

L186 Neil Dunnicliffe

Literary Agent
United Kingdom

neil@springliterary.com

https://www.springliterary.com/about

Literary Agency: Spring Literary (**L656**)

L187 E. J. McCarthy Agency

Literary Agency
United States

ejmagency@gmail.com

https://twitter.com/ejmccarthy

Nonfiction > *Nonfiction Books*
Biography; History; Memoir; Military History; Sport

Send: Query
How to send: Email

Literary agency from former executive editor with experience at some of the world's largest publishing houses, specialising in military history, politics, history, biography, memoir, media, public policy, and sports.

Literary Agent: E. J. McCarthy

L188 Adam Eaglin

Literary Agent
United States

https://www.cheneyagency.com/adameaglin

Literary Agency: The Cheney Agency

L189 Chelsea Eberly

Literary Agent; Company Director
United States

https://www.greenhouseliterary.com/the-team/chelsea-eberly/
https://twitter.com/chelseberly
https://www.publishersmarketplace.com/members/ChelseaEberly/
https://querymanager.com/query/ChelseaEberly

Literary Agency: The Greenhouse Literary Agency (**L286**)

ADULT > **Fiction** > *Novels*
Book Club Women's Fiction; Upmarket Women's Fiction

CHILDREN'S
Fiction
Graphic Novels: General
Middle Grade: Adventure; Comedy / Humour; Fantasy; Folklore, Myths, and Legends; Magical Realism; Mystery
Picture Books: General

Nonfiction
Nonfiction Books; *Picture Books*
YOUNG ADULT
Fiction
Graphic Novels: Comedy / Humour; Contemporary; Fantasy; Magical Realism; Romance
Novels: Commercial; Fantasy; Feminism; Literary; Mystery; Romance; Social Justice; Thrillers
Nonfiction > *Graphic Nonfiction*
General, and in particular: History

Does not want:

CHILDREN'S > **Fiction** > *Middle Grade*: Horror

YOUNG ADULT > **Fiction** > *Novels*: Horror

Send: Query; Author bio; Writing sample; Proposal
How to send: By referral

Represents authors of middle grade, young adult, graphic novels, and women's fiction, as well as illustrators who write picture books.

L190 Eddison Pearson Ltd

Literary Agency
West Hill House, 6 Swains Lane, London, N6 6QS
United Kingdom
Tel: +44 (0) 20 7700 7763

enquiries@eddisonpearson.com

https://www.eddisonpearson.com
https://linktr.ee/ClarePearson
https://eddisonpearson.tumblr.com/
https://www.linkedin.com/in/clare-pearson-epla
https://twitter.com/ClarePearson_EP

Professional Body: The Association of Authors' Agents (AAA)

CHILDREN'S
Fiction
Novels: Contemporary; Historical Fiction
Picture Books: General

Poetry > *Any Poetic Form*

YOUNG ADULT > **Fiction** > *Novels*

Send: Query; Writing sample
How to send: Email
How not to send: Social Media; Post

A London-based literary agency providing a personal service to a small stable of talented authors, mainly of books for children and young adults. Send query by email only for auto-response containing up-to-date submission guidelines and email address for submissions. No submissions or enquiries by post.

Authors: Valerie Bloom; Michael Catchpool; Sue Heap; Caroline Lawrence; Robert Muchamore; Mary Murphy; Megan Rix

Literary Agent: Clare Pearson (*L553*)

L191 Sam Edenborough

Literary Agent; Foreign Rights Director
United Kingdom

sam@greyhoundliterary.co.uk

https://greyhoundliterary.co.uk/agent/sam-edenborough/
https://twitter.com/SamEdenborough

Literary Agency: Greyhound Literary (**L288**)

Fiction > *Novels*
Fantasy; Romance; Science Fiction; Thrillers

Nonfiction > *Nonfiction Books*
Classical Music; History; Jazz; Science

Send: Synopsis; Outline; Writing sample
How to send: Email

Would like to see: a stylishly-crafted thriller; a funny, feel-good romance with a great hook; most kinds of science fiction and fantasy (particularly hard SF that explores the biggest questions about what it means to be human); fiction and non-fiction which engages with landscape or the sea in a profound and original way; books about jazz and classical music and musicians; historians and novelists who challenge us to rethink comfortable assumptions about an era or a culture; and scientists working in complex fields of study who are able to communicate ideas to a wide readership with verve.

L192 Max Edwards

Literary Agent
United Kingdom

max@appletreeliterary.co.uk

https://aevitascreative.com/agents/#agent-7412
http://appletreeliterary.co.uk/about/

Literary Agency: Aevitas Creative Management (ACM) UK (**L008**)

Fiction > *Novels*
Commercial; Crime; Fantasy; High Concept; Science Fiction

Nonfiction > *Nonfiction Books*
Arts; Football / Soccer; Journalism; Science; Sport

Send: Author bio; Query; Writing sample; Synopsis
How to send: Email; Online submission system

Looking for commercial and genre novels, and is a fan of novels that mix genres in a unique way. Keen on high concepts, smart plots and unique characters – twists and turns, good (and bad) guys with depth and life. Also looking for great stories that can be told through nonfiction; either unique or surprising takes on a subject, or something wildly original. Would like to hear from academics mixing the arts and science in a new way, journalists wanting to take their writing beyond the article, sports writers with a new way of exploring what we play (particularly football/soccer), or writers with an untold history to tell.

L193 Silé Edwards

Literary Agent
United Kingdom

submissions@mushens-entertainment.com

https://www.mushens-entertainment.com/submissions
https://twitter.com/sileloquies

Literary Agency: Mushens Entertainment (**L516**)

Fiction > *Novels*
Book Club Fiction; Commercial; Psychological Thrillers; Upmarket

Nonfiction
Illustrated Books: Lifestyle
Nonfiction Books: Autobiography; Biography; Cookery; Narrative Nonfiction; Society

Send: Query; Proposal; Writing sample; Synopsis
How to send: Email

Looking for authors, personalities and brands who will create engaging books for every kind of reader. Is interested in a range of Non-Fiction, from emotive life writing and topical essay-like writing on the things that affect us as a society to illustrated lifestyle and cookery. She is particularly keen on finding experts in their field who want to write about what they know in a way that everyone can understand, appreciate and enjoy.

Also accepts fiction submissions. She is looking for psychological thriller, reading group fiction and uplifting novels. She is especially interested in character and voice driven upmarket, commercial and book club fiction with strong discussion points and thought-provoking themes.

Authors: Yewande Biala; Anna Bogutskaya; Laura Jane Clark; Sally El-Arifi; Naomi Evans; Natalie Evans; Claire Frances; Angie Greaves; Della Hicks-Wilson; Thom Insley; Kuchenga; Caroline Magennis; Liberty Mendez; Denai Moore; Illiyin Morrison; Lauren Rae; Victoria Sanusi; Joe Talbot; Hope Whitmore

L194 Einstein Literary Management

Literary Agency
United States
Tel: +1 (212) 221-8797

submissions@einsteinliterary.com

https://www.einsteinliterary.com
https://twitter.com/Einstein_Lit

ADULT

Fiction > *Novels*
Commercial; Literary

Nonfiction > *Nonfiction Books*
Cookery; Memoir; Narrative Nonfiction

CHILDREN'S > **Fiction** > *Novels*

YOUNG ADULT > **Fiction** > *Novels*

Send: Query; Writing sample
How to send: In the body of an email

Send query by email with first ten double-spaced pages pasted into the body of the email. No attachments. See website for details of individual agents and their interests and include the name of specific agent you are submitting to in the subject line. No poetry, textbooks, or screenplays. No queries by post or by phone. Response only if interested.

Associate Agent: Paloma Hernando (**L321**)

Literary Agents: Susanna Einstein (**L195**); Susan Graham (**L280**); Shana Kelly

L195 Susanna Einstein

Literary Agent
United States

https://www.einsteinliterary.com/staff/
http://aaronline.org/Sys/PublicProfile/4557347/417813

Literary Agency: Einstein Literary Management (**L194**)
Professional Body: Association of American Literary Agents (AALA)

ADULT

Fiction > *Novels*
Commercial Women's Fiction; Crime; Upmarket Women's Fiction

Nonfiction > *Nonfiction Books*: Narrative Nonfiction

CHILDREN'S > **Fiction** > *Middle Grade*

YOUNG ADULT > **Fiction** > *Novels*

Closed to approaches.

Has a particular fondness for crime fiction, upmarket commercial women's fiction, MG and YA fiction, and narrative non-fiction. She likes a good story well told.

L196 Nicole Eisenbraun

Literary Agent
United States

nme@gingerclarkliterary (dot) com

https://gingerclarkliterary.com/About
https://gingerclarkliterary.com/Submissions
http://aaronline.org/Sys/PublicProfile/51483163/417813

Literary Agency: Ginger Clark Literary (**L262**)
Professional Body: Association of American Literary Agents (AALA)

CHILDREN'S

Fiction > *Middle Grade*
General, and in particular: Fairy Tales

Nonfiction > *Middle Grade*
History; Popular Culture; Science

YOUNG ADULT

Fiction > *Novels*
General, and in particular: Fairy Tales

Nonfiction > *Nonfiction Books*
History; Popular Culture; Science

Send: Query
How to send: Email

Looking for middle grade and young adult in all genres, fiction and nonfiction. For fiction, she is particularly interested in great fairytale retellings with colorful twists and stories that tackle difficult subjects in unexpected ways. For nonfiction, she is looking for books focusing on science, history, and popular culture.

L197 Caroline Eisenmann

Senior Agent
United States

ce@goldinlit.com

https://goldinlit.com/agents/

Literary Agency: Frances Goldin Literary Agency, Inc.
Professional Body: Association of American Literary Agents (AALA)

Fiction > *Novels*
Literary; Social Issues; Upmarket

Nonfiction
Essays: General
Nonfiction Books: Biography; Cultural Criticism; History; Literary Memoir; Sub-Culture

How to send: Email

Particularly drawn to novels that engage with social issues, stories about obsession, and work that centers around intimacy and its discontents. Her nonfiction interests include deeply reported narratives (especially those that take the reader into the heart of a subculture), literary memoir, cultural criticism, essay collections, and history and biography with a surprising point of view.

Authors: Kyle Chayka; Ye Chun; Linda Rui Feng; Amanda Goldblatt; James Gregor; Peter Kispert; Theresa Levitt; Micah Nemerever; Jenny Odell; Kate Wagner; Michelle Webster-Hein

L198 The Ekus Group

Literary Agency
57 North Street, Hatfield, MA 01038
United States
Tel: +1 (413) 247-9325

info@lisaekus.com

https://ekusgroup.com

Nonfiction > *Nonfiction Books*: Cookery

How to send: Online submission system

Handles cookery books only. Submit proposal through submission system on website.

Literary Agent: Lisa Ekus

L199 Elaine Markson Literary Agency

Literary Agency
116 West 23rd Street, 5th flr, New York, NY 10011
United States

https://www.marksonagency.com

Fiction > *Novels*

Nonfiction > *Nonfiction Books*

Literary Agent: Jeff Gerecke (**L256**)

L200 Elaine Steel

Literary Agency
49 Greek Street, London, W1D 4EG
United Kingdom
Tel: +44 (0) 1273 739022

es@elainesteel.com

https://www.elainesteel.com

Professional Body: The Association of Authors' Agents (AAA)

Fiction > *Novels*

Nonfiction > *Nonfiction Books*

Scripts
Film Scripts; *Radio Scripts*; *TV Scripts*; *Theatre Scripts*

Send: Query; Author bio; Outline
Don't send: Full text
How to send: Email

Represents writers and directors in film, television, stage and radio as well as book writers. Send query by email with CV and outline, along with details of experience. No unsolicited mss.

Authors: Gwyneth Hughes; James Lovelock; Ben Steiner

L201 Humphrey Elles-Hill

Literary Agent
United Kingdom

Literary Agency: Independent Talent Group Ltd (**L340**)

L202 Sian Ellis-Martin

Associate Agent
United Kingdom

sian@blakefriedmann.co.uk

http://blakefriedmann.co.uk/sianellis-martin
https://twitter.com/sianellismartin

Literary Agency: Blake Friedmann Literary Agency Ltd (**L067**)

Fiction > *Novels*
Book Club Fiction; Coming of Age; Contemporary; Ethnic Groups; Gender; Mental Health; Romance; Sexuality; Social Class; Upmarket

Nonfiction
Illustrated Books: General
Nonfiction Books: Cookery; Food; Memoir; Narrative Nonfiction; Recipes

Send: Query; Synopsis; Writing sample
How to send: Email attachment

In fiction, I'm looking for contemporary book club and upmarket novels, particularly from authors who are currently underrepresented in literature. I'm especially passionate about LGBTQIA+ representation. I'm also looking for illustrated and narrative non-fiction and memoir. I'm keen on books that make complicated or niche ideas more accessible. I'd love to find cookery and food books too, and am open to lots of ideas there, and am especially drawn to simple recipes suitable for those on a budget, those who are time starved and those who just can't be bothered with cooking half the time!

Author: Shani Akilah

L203 Zabé Ellor

Literary Agent
United States

https://www.jdlit.com/zabe-ellor
https://querymanager.com/query/ZabeEllor
https://twitter.com/ZREllor

Literary Agency: The Jennifer DeChiara Literary Agency

ADULT
Fiction
Graphic Novels: General
Novels: Commercial; Fantasy; Mystery; Science Fiction; Thrillers; Upmarket Contemporary Fiction
Nonfiction > *Nonfiction Books*
History; Science

CHILDREN'S > **Fiction**
Graphic Novels: General
Middle Grade: Adventure; Comedy / Humour; Speculative
YOUNG ADULT > **Fiction**
Graphic Novels: General
Novels: General, and in particular: Contemporary; Fantasy; Mystery; Romance; Science Fiction; Thrillers

Closed to approaches.

For fiction, send a query, a 1-2 page synopsis, and the first 25 pages of your project. For nonfiction, send a query and a sample chapter. For graphic novels, send a query with a link to your portfolio website. I strive to respond to all queries in 12-14 weeks.

L204 Emily Sweet Associates

Literary Agency
United Kingdom

http://www.emilysweetassociates.com

Professional Body: The Association of Authors' Agents (AAA)

Types: Fiction; Nonfiction
Subjects: Biography; Commercial; Cookery; Current Affairs; History; Literary
Markets: Adult

Send: Query
Don't send: Full text

No Young Adult or children's. Query through form on website in first instance.

Literary Agent: Emily Sweet

L205 Jessica Errera

Literary Agent
United States

https://www.janerotrosen.com/agents
https://www.janerotrosen.com/contact-jessica-errera

Literary Agency: Jane Rotrosen Agency

ADULT > **Fiction** > *Novels*
Commercial Women's Fiction; Contemporary Romance; Historical Fiction; Suspense; Thrillers

YOUNG ADULT > **Fiction** > *Novels*

Looking for commercial women's fiction with a fresh and fun hook, all genres of YA (especially diverse stories), contemporary romance, thrillers and suspense, the occasional historical fiction, and anything that might be read in a day on the beach.

L206 Gareth Esersky

Literary Agent
United States

gesersky@verizon.net

https://www.carolmannagency.com/gareth-esersky

Literary Agency: Carol Mann Agency (**L104**)

Nonfiction > *Nonfiction Books*
Health; Jewish Culture; Literary; Memoir; Narrative Nonfiction; Nutrition; Parenting; Psychology; Spirituality

Send: Query; Author bio; Writing sample
How to send: In the body of an email

Represents nonfiction authors whose work falls into the following categories: health, nutrition, psychology, parenting, spirituality, Judaica, and literary and narrative nonfiction and memoir.

L207 Ethan Ellenberg Literary Agency

Literary Agency
United States

agent@ethanellenberg.com

https://ethanellenberg.com

Professional Bodies: Science Fiction and Fantasy Writers of America (SFWA); Society of Children's Book Writers and Illustrators (SCBWI); Romance Writers of America (RWA); Mystery Writers of America (MWA)

ADULT
Fiction > *Novels*
General, and in particular: Commercial; Ethnic; Fantasy; Literary; Mystery; Romance; Science Fiction; Thrillers; Women's Fiction

Nonfiction > *Nonfiction Books*
General, and in particular: Adventure; Biography; Cookery; Crime; Current Affairs; Health; History; Memoir; New Age; Popular Culture; Psychology; Science; Spirituality

CHILDREN'S > **Fiction** > *Novels*

Send: Query; Synopsis; Writing sample; Proposal
How to send: In the body of an email

Send query by email (no attachments; paste material into the body of the email). For fiction send synopsis and first 50 pages. For nonfiction send proposal, author bio, and sample chapters. For picture books send complete MS. No poetry, short stories, or scripts.

We have been in business for over 17 years. We are a member of the AAR. We accept unsolicited submissions and, of course, do not charge reading fees.

Author Estates: The Estate of Bertrice Small; The Estate of Johnny Quarles

Authors: G.A. Aiken; Jay Allan; Carac Allison; Amanda Ashley; Claire Avery; Madeline Baker; Sarah Banks; Jon Bergeron; Patty Blount; Pat Bowne; Robin Bridges; Leah Marie Brown; James Cambias; Elaine Coffman; MaryJanice Davidson; Delilah Devlin; John Domagalski; Ian Douglas; Bill Ferris; Candace Fleming; Whitney Gaskell; Susan Grant; James Hider; Ben Hillman; Marthe Jocelyn; Aer-ki Jyr; William H. Keith; Kay Kenyon; Marko Kloos; Travis Langley; Shelly Laurenston; Georgie Lee; Michael Livingston; Kevin Luthardt; Gail Z. Martin; Lt. Col. Matt Martin; Thersa Matsuura; John McCormack; Karen Miller; Lucy Monroe; Helen Myers; J. Madison Newsome; Andre Norton; Christopher Nuttall; Mel Odoam; Melissa F. Olson; Tim Owens; Cindy Spencer Pape; Thomas Philpott; Steven Popkes; Paladin Press; Riptide Publishing; Clay Reynolds; Matthew Rivett; Eric Rohmann; Peter Sasgen; Charles Sasser; John Scalzi; Eric Schnabel; Sharon Shinn; Susan Sizemore; Oz Spies; Ferret Steinmetz; James Tabor; Dennis E. Taylor; Kimberly Kaye Terry; Kate Tietje; Judd Trichter; Margaret Vellez; Wendy Wagner; Christine Warren; Jennifer Wilde; Edward Willett; Robert Wolke; Rebecca York

Literary Agent / President: Ethan Ellenberg

Literary Agents: Evan Gregory; Bibi Lewis

L208 Nicole Etherington

Assistant Agent
United Kingdom

nicole@hardmanswainson.com
submissions@hardmanswainson.com
https://www.hardmanswainson.com/agent/nicole-etherington/
https://twitter.com/thewelshnicole

Literary Agency: Hardman & Swainson (**L302**)

Fiction > *Novels*
Book Club Fiction; Contemporary; Literary

Nonfiction > *Nonfiction Books*

Send: Query; Synopsis; Full text
How to send: Email

Tastes lean towards literary and bookclub fiction. In terms of nonfiction, drawn to books that make readers think or explore familiar topics in interesting ways. No submissions to personal email address.

L209 Eunice McMullen Children's Literary Agent Ltd

Literary Agency
Low Ibbotsholme Cottage, Off Bridge Lane, Troutbeck Bridge, Windermere, Cumbria, LA23 1HU
United Kingdom
Tel: +44 (0) 1539 448551

eunice@eunicemcmullen.co.uk

http://www.eunicemcmullen.co.uk

CHILDREN'S > **Fiction**
Middle Grade; *Novels*; *Picture Books*
TEEN > **Fiction** > *Novels*

Send: Query; Synopsis; Writing sample; Full text
How to send: Email

Enquire by email, including details about yourself, the opening chapters and synopsis, or two or three full texts for picture books. All types of material for children, particularly for those 9 and over. Strong list of authors and illustrators of picture books.

Literary Agent: Eunice McMullen (*L482*)

L210 David Evans

Assistant Agent
United Kingdom

davidevans@davidhigham.co.uk

https://www.davidhigham.co.uk/agents-dh/david-evans/

Literary Agency: David Higham Associates Ltd (**L161**)
Literary Agent: Andrew Gordon (**L277**)

ACADEMIC > **Nonfiction** > *Nonfiction Books*

ADULT
Fiction
Novels: Literary
Short Fiction: Literary

Nonfiction > *Nonfiction Books*
Culture; History; Journalism; Nature; Philosophy; Politics; Science

How to send: Email

Looking for literary fiction of style and ambition. He admires novelists who create memorable and unsettling voices, and short story writers with a keen sense of the poetic and absurd. In non-fiction, he enjoys projects of rigour, clarity and passion that can make small ideas radiate and big ideas graspable. He is particularly looking for works of academic research or journalistic investigation written for a wide readership, across areas such as culture, philosophy, politics, history, science, nature.

L211 Stephany Evans

Literary Agent
United States

https://www.pandeliterary.com/about-pandeliterary
https://twitter.com/fireroster
http://aaronline.org/Sys/PublicProfile/2176670/417813

Literary Agency: Ayesha Pande Literary **(L036)**
Professional Bodies: Association of American Literary Agents (AALA); Romance Writers of America (RWA); Mystery Writers of America (MWA); The Agents Round Table (ART)

Fiction > *Novels*
Commercial; Crime; Literary; Mystery; Romance; Thrillers; Upmarket Women's Fiction; Women's Fiction

Nonfiction > *Nonfiction Books*
Fitness; Food and Drink; Health; Lifestyle; Memoir; Narrative Nonfiction; Running; Spirituality; Sustainable Living; Wellbeing

Closed to approaches.

L212 Samantha Fabien

Literary Agent
United States

http://twitter.com/samanthashnh
http://aaronline.org/Sys/PublicProfile/48927898/417813
https://querymanager.com/query/samanthafabien

Professional Body: Association of American Literary Agents (AALA)

ADULT > **Fiction**
Graphic Novels: General
Novels: Book Club Fiction; Commercial; Fantasy; High Concept; Historical Fiction; Horror; Mystery; Psychological Thrillers; Romantic Comedy; Speculative; Suspense; Thrillers; Upmarket Women's Fiction

CHILDREN'S > **Fiction**
Graphic Novels: General
Middle Grade: Contemporary; Grounded Fantasy; Horror; Mystery; Romance; Romantic Comedy; Speculative; Suspense; Thrillers

YOUNG ADULT > **Fiction**
Graphic Novels: General
Novels: Contemporary; Grounded Fantasy; Horror; Mystery; Romance; Romantic Comedy; Speculative; Suspense; Thrillers

Send: Query; Synopsis; Writing sample
How to send: Query Manager

Across genres, I'm looking for high-concept, commercial fiction for adults and children that feature diverse, marginalized, and/or underrepresented voices with all-or-nothing stakes.

L213 Fairbank Literary Representation

Literary Agency
21 Lyman Street, Waltham, MA 02452
United States
Tel: +1 (617) 576-0030

queries@fairbankliterary.com

https://fairbankliterary.com
https://www.publishersmarketplace.com/members/SorcheFairbank/
http://www.twitter.com/FairbankLit

ADULT
Fiction > *Novels*
International; Literary

Nonfiction
Gift Books: General
Nonfiction Books: Comedy / Humour; Crafts; Design; Food; Lifestyle; Memoir; Narrative Nonfiction; Popular Culture; Wine

CHILDREN'S > **Fiction**
Middle Grade; *Picture Books*

Send: Query; Writing sample
How to send: In the body of an email; Online contact form; Post
How not to send: Email attachment; Phone

Clients range from first-time authors to international best-sellers, prize winning-journalists to professionals at the top of their fields. Tastes tend toward literary and international fiction; voice-y novels with a strong sense of place; big memoir that goes beyond the me-moir; topical or narrative nonfiction with a strong interest in women's voices, global perspectives, and class and race issues; children's picture books & middle grade from illustrator/artists only; quality lifestyle books (food, wine, and design); pop culture; craft; and gift and humor books. Most likely to pick up works that are of social or cultural significance, newsworthy

Literary Agent: Sorche Elizabeth Fairbank

L214 Delia Berrigan Fakis

Literary Agent
United States

Delia@MartinLit.com

http://www.martinliterarymanagement.com
https://twitter.com/PrimarilyProse

Literary Agency: Martin Literary Management

ADULT
Fiction > *Novels*
Commercial; Literary; Mystery

Nonfiction > *Nonfiction Books*
Business; Crime; Current Affairs; History; Leadership; Memoir; Narrative Nonfiction; Religion; Spirituality

CHILDREN'S > **Fiction** > *Picture Books*

Send: Query
How to send: Email

Most interested in representing adult nonfiction, but will also consider select fiction and children's picture books.

L215 Holly Faulks

Literary Agent
United Kingdom

http://greeneheaton.co.uk/agents/holly-faulks/
https://twitter.com/hollycfaulks

Literary Agency: Greene & Heaton Ltd **(L285)**

Fiction > *Novels*
Literary; Upmarket Commercial Fiction

Nonfiction > *Nonfiction Books*
Current Affairs; Language; Lifestyle; Memoir; Popular Science

Send: Synopsis; Writing sample
How to send: Email

Authors: Emily Bootle; Zoe Burgess; Joseph Coward; Emma Garland; Lily Hackett; Jake Hall; Kit Heyam; Juliet Jacques; Iggy LDN; Carina Maggar; Anna Sulan Masing; Sara-Ella Ozbek; Jyoti Patel; Julie Reverb; Ella Frances Sanders

L216 Ariella Feiner

Literary Agent
United Kingdom

afeiner@unitedagents.co.uk

https://www.unitedagents.co.uk/afeinerunitedagentscouk
https://twitter.com/ariellafeiner

Literary Agency: United Agents **(L704)**

Fiction > *Novels*
Book Club Fiction; Crime; High Concept; Historical Fiction; Thrillers

Nonfiction > *Nonfiction Books*
Cookery; Memoir

Send: Synopsis; Writing sample; Proposal
How to send: Email

Always open to submissions. In fiction, would like to see crime and thrillers, issue-led books, plot-driven stories, reading group books, high-concept tales, a great elevator pitch, novels with strong female characters, and historical fiction with a twist. In nonfiction, is interested in topics which feel untouched before now or are inspiring, expert-led ideas, mouth-watering cook books, narrative memoir, and empowering female tales.

Authors: Francesca Armour-Chelu; Holly Bell; Nargisse Benkabbou; Vicky Bennison; Mark Bostridge; Robert Bryndza; Beth Cartwright; Jane Casey; Alice Clark-Platts; John Coldstream; Elle Croft; Laura Dockrill; Mike Gayle; Paul Grzegorzek; Olia Hercules; Mina Holland; Laura Jarratt; Lora Jones; Dean Lomax; Emily Midorikawa; Robert Nicholls; Selina Periampillai; Sarah Peverley; Natasha Preston; Jane Riley; Nick Spalding; Danny Wallace; Lucy Watson; Julie Welch; Kate Williams; Louisa Young

L217 The Feldstein Agency

Literary Agency; Editorial Service; Consultancy
54 Abbey Street, Bangor, Northern Ireland, BT20 4JB
United Kingdom
Tel: +44 (0) 2891 312485

submissions@thefeldsteinagency.co.uk

https://www.thefeldsteinagency.co.uk
https://twitter.com/feldsteinagency

Fiction > *Novels*

Nonfiction > *Nonfiction Books*

Does not want:

Fiction > *Novels*
Fantasy; Historical Fiction; Romance; Science Fiction

Send: Query; Synopsis; Author bio
How to send: Word file email attachment; PDF file email attachment

Costs: Offers services that writers have to pay for. Offers editing, ghostwriting, and consultancy services.

Handles adult fiction and nonfiction only. No children's, young adult, romance, science fiction, fantasy, poetry, scripts, or short stories. Send query by email with 1-2 pages synopsis. No reading fees or evaluation fees. The only instance in which an author would be charged a fee is for ghost-writing.

Consultant / Literary Agent: Paul Feldstein (**L218**)

Editor / Literary Agent: Susan Feldstein (**L219**)

L218 Paul Feldstein

Literary Agent; Consultant
United Kingdom

paul@thefeldsteinagency.co.uk

Literary Agency / Editorial Service / Consultancy: The Feldstein Agency (**L217**)

L219 Susan Feldstein

Literary Agent; Editor
United Kingdom

susan@thefeldsteinagency.co.uk

http://www.susanfeldstein.co.uk

Literary Agency / Editorial Service / Consultancy: The Feldstein Agency (**L217**)

L220 Felicity Bryan Associates

Literary Agency
2a North Parade Avenue, Banbury Road, Oxford, OX2 6LX
United Kingdom
Tel: +44 (0) 1865 513816

submissions@felicitybryan.com

https://felicitybryan.com

Professional Body: The Association of Authors' Agents (AAA)

Fiction > *Novels*
Book Club Fiction; Literary

Nonfiction > *Nonfiction Books*: Upmarket

Send: Query; Synopsis; Proposal; Writing sample
How to send: Online submission system

Looking for accessible, upmarket non-fiction, written by an author with clear and demonstrable expertise (in practice, this means many years of professional work or PhD level study within the topic), and exciting, original 'bookclub' and literary debut fiction, particularly from underrepresented writers.

Author: Amy Key

Literary Agent: Angelique Tran Van Sang (**L618**)

L221 Hannah Ferguson

Literary Agent
United Kingdom

hannah@hardmanswainson.com
submissions@hardmanswainson.com

https://www.hardmanswainson.com/agent/hannah-ferguson/
https://twitter.com/AgentFergie

Literary Agency: Hardman & Swainson (**L302**)

Fiction > *Novels*
General, and in particular: Book Club Fiction; Commercial; Crime; Literary; Thrillers; Women's Fiction

Nonfiction > *Nonfiction Books*: Narrative Nonfiction

Closed to approaches.

Represents women's fiction, from the more literary to the very commercial. Likes book club reads that really capture a reader's attention or heart. Always on the lookout for great crime and thrillers and interesting non-fiction.

L222 T.S. Ferguson

Literary Agent
United States

http://www.azantianlitagency.com/pages/team-tf.html
https://querymanager.com/query/TSFerguson

Literary Agency: Azantian Literary Agency (**L037**)

CHILDREN'S > **Fiction**
Graphic Novels: General
Middle Grade: General, and in particular: Adventure; Dark; Fairy Tales; Folklore, Myths, and Legends; High Concept; Horror; LGBTQIA

YOUNG ADULT > **Fiction**
Graphic Novels: General
Novels: General, and in particular: Adventure; Dark; Fairy Tales; Folklore, Myths, and Legends; High Concept; Horror; LGBTQIA

Does not want:

CHILDREN'S > **Fiction** > *Middle Grade*
Hard Science Fiction; Sport

YOUNG ADULT > **Fiction** > *Novels*
Hard Science Fiction; Sport

How to send: Query Manager

Looking for young adult and middle grade fiction across all genres that combines high-concept, hooky stories with writing and voice that feel standout. An addicting, page-turning quality is always a plus! He has a special place in his heart for dark and edgy stories (including but not limited to horror), fairy tales, mythology, action-adventure, LGBTQ stories, graphic novels, and stories by and about under-represented voices. He is not the best fit for sports-centric stories, high sci-fi, or non-fiction.

L223 Julie Fergusson

Literary Agent
United Kingdom

http://thenorthlitagency.com/our-friends-in-the-north/
https://twitter.com/julie_fergusson

Literary Agency: The North Literary Agency (**L530**)

Fiction > *Novels*
Book Club Fiction; Domestic Suspense; Literary; Psychological Thrillers; Romantic Comedy; Speculative

Nonfiction > *Nonfiction Books*
Popular Science; Social Justice

Closed to approaches.

Looking for fiction across a range of genres, particularly psychological thrillers, domestic suspense, near-future speculative, romcoms, reading group and literary fiction. She is interested in nonfiction that explores big ideas in the areas of popular science and social justice.

L224 Fillingham Weston Associates

Literary Agency
20 Mortlake High Street, London, SW14 8JN
United Kingdom
Tel: +44 (0) 20 8748 5594

info@fillinghamweston.com
submissions@fillinghamweston.com

https://www.fillinghamweston.com
https://www.facebook.com/Fillingham-Weston-Associates-117304691662209
https://twitter.com/fwa_litagency
https://www.instagram.com/fillinghamwestonassociates/

ADULT > **Scripts**
Film Scripts; *TV Scripts*; *Theatre Scripts*
CHILDREN'S > **Scripts**
Film Scripts; *TV Scripts*; *Theatre Scripts*
YOUNG ADULT > **Scripts**
Film Scripts; *TV Scripts*; *Theatre Scripts*

Send: Query; Author bio
Don't send: Full text; Writing sample
How to send: Email

Represents writers and directors for stage, film and TV, as well as librettists, lyricists and composers in musical theatre. Does not represent books. See website for full submission guidelines.

Literary Agents: Janet Fillingham; Kate Weston

L225 Alison Finch

Literary Agent
United Kingdom

Literary Agency: JFL Agency (**L353**)

L226 Rebeka Finch

Agency Assistant; Literary Agent
United Kingdom

rebeka@darleyanderson.com

https://www.darleyanderson.com/our-team
https://www.instagram.com/rebeka.finch/

Literary Agency: The Darley Anderson Agency
Literary Agent: Darley Anderson (**L018**)

ADULT > **Fiction** > *Novels*: Contemporary Romance

NEW
ADULT > **Fiction** > *Novels*: Contemporary Romance

How to send: Email attachment

Looking for character driven contemporary romances. and contemporary new adult romance that bridges the gap between YA and adult fiction, for the 20 something lover of modern romantic novels.

L227 Stevie Finegan

Literary Agent
United Kingdom

finegan@zenoagency.com

http://zenoagency.com/news/stevie-finegan/
https://twitter.com/StevieFinegan

Literary Agency: Zeno Agency Ltd (**L759**)

ADULT
Fiction
Graphic Novels: Feminism; LGBTQIA
Novels: High / Epic Fantasy; Soft Science Fiction
Nonfiction > *Nonfiction Books*
Feminism; Mental Health; Politics; Social Issues

CHILDREN'S > **Fiction**
Early Readers; *Middle Grade*; *Picture Books*

Authors: Travis Baldree; Alice Bell; Andrew Cartmel; Mário Coelho; Craig Laurance Gidney; J.T. Greathouse; Anna McNuff; Adam Oyebanji; Farrah Riaz; Katherine Toran; R.R. Virdi; Angus Watson; Gary Wigglesworth; Jasmine Wigham; Yudhanjaya Wijeratne

L228 Karyn Fischer

Literary Agent
United States

http://www.bookstopliterary.com/submission.html
https://querymanager.com/query/KarynFischer

Literary Agency: BookStop Literary Agency, LLC (**L073**)

CHILDREN'S > **Fiction** > *Middle Grade*
General, and in particular: Contemporary; Dark; Fantasy; Gothic; Historical Fiction; Literary Thrillers

YOUNG ADULT > **Fiction** > *Novels*
General, and in particular: Contemporary; Dark; Fantasy; Gothic; Historical Fiction; Literary Thrillers

Closed to approaches.

Particularly drawn to young adult and middle grade novels. Her favorite genres include gothic novels with twisty narratives and dark secrets, historical fiction, literary thrillers, well-drawn fantasy, and heart-tugging contemporary stories. She's looking for anything with memorable characters, an engaging voice, and a tightrope- taut plot.

L229 Flannery Literary

Literary Agency
United States

jennifer@flanneryliterary.com

https://flanneryliterary.com

CHILDREN'S
Fiction > *Middle Grade*
Nonfiction > *Nonfiction Books*

YOUNG ADULT > **Fiction** > *Novels*

Send: Query; Writing sample; Full text
How to send: Email
How not to send: Email attachment

Send query by email, with the word "Query" in the subject line. Include first 5-10 pages of your novel or full picture book text. Deals exclusively in children's and young adults' fiction and nonfiction, including picture books. See website for full guidelines.

Literary Agent: Jennifer Flannery

L230 Diana Flegal

Literary Agent; Editor
United States

https://www.hartlineagency.com/agents-and-authors

Literary Agency: Hartline Literary Agency (**L311**)

Fiction > *Novels*
General, and in particular: Christianity

Nonfiction > *Nonfiction Books*
General, and in particular: Christianity

A freelance editor and literary coach. Has successfully sold both fiction and nonfiction titles to the Christian and General markets.

Authors: DeAngelo Burse; Nicole Faye Golden; Michael Richard

L231 A for Authors

Literary Agency
73 Hurlingham Road, Bexleyheath, Kent, DA7 5PE
United Kingdom
Tel: +44 (0) 1322 463479

enquiries@aforauthors.co.uk

http://aforauthors.co.uk

Fiction > *Novels*
Commercial; Literary

Closed to approaches.

Query by email only. Include synopsis and first three chapters (or up to 50 pages) and short author bio. All attachments must be Word format documents. No poetry, fantasy, SF, horror, erotica, or short stories. No submissions by post or by downloadable link.

Literary Agents: Annette Crossland; Bill Goodall

L232 Jemima Forrester

Literary Agent
United Kingdom

jemimaforrester@davidhigham.co.uk

https://www.davidhigham.co.uk/agents-dh/jemima-forrester/

Literary Agency: David Higham Associates Ltd (**L161**)

Fiction > *Novels*
Commercial; Crime; Feminism; High Concept; Historical Fiction; Literary; Psychological Suspense; Speculative; Thrillers; Upmarket; Women's Fiction

Nonfiction > *Nonfiction Books*
Comedy / Humour; Cookery; Feminism; Lifestyle; Popular Culture

Send: Query; Synopsis; Writing sample
How to send: Email

Looking for commercial and upmarket fiction, including accessible literary fiction, crime and thrillers, historical, psychological suspense, women's fiction and speculative/high-concept novels. Loves distinctive narrative voices, well-paced plots with a great hook, and complex female characters. In non-fiction, she is looking for innovative lifestyle, cookery and popular-culture projects, unique personal stories and humour.

Authors: Kat Ailes; Tessa Bickers; Mikki Brammer; Lauren Bravo; Rob Burnett; Seerut K. Chawla; Lizzie Daykin; Sarah Daykin; Jessica George; Sarah J. Harris; Deborah Hewitt; Rosie Hewlett; Alex Hutchinson; Beth Lewis; Richard Lumsden; Deborah O'Donoghue; Alison Percival; Christina Pishiris; Tasha Sylva; Sureka Thanenthiran-Dharuman; Vanessa Walters; Adam Zmith

L233 Gráinne Fox

Literary Agent
United States

Literary Agency: Fletcher & Company

L234 FRA (Futerman, Rose, & Associates)

Literary Agency
91 St Leonards Road, London, SW14 7BL
United Kingdom
Tel: +44 (0) 20 8255 7755

guy@futermanrose.co.uk

http://www.futermanrose.co.uk

Professional Body: The Association of Authors' Agents (AAA)

Nonfiction > *Nonfiction Books*
General, and in particular: Entertainment; Media; Music; Politics; Sports Celebrity

Scripts
Film Scripts; *TV Scripts*

Send: Query
Don't send: Full text
How to send: Email

Handles nonfiction on practically any subject, but particularly interested in politics, sport, show business and the music industry. Also handles scripts for film and television. No educational textbooks.

For nonfiction, send proposal including chapter breakdown, two or three sample chapters, and any relevant biographical detail.

For scripts, send sample episode or section of the script.

Accepts submissions by post (include SAE of return of work required) or by email with attachments.

See website for full guidelines.

Not currently accepting film and TV scripts.

Authors: Jill Anderson; Larry Barker; Nick Battle; Christian Piers Betley; Tracey Cheetham; Chengde Chen; Kevin Clarke; Lesley Crewe; Richard Digance; Peter Dobbie; Bobby Elliott; Paul Ferris; John French; Susan George; Keith Gillespie; Stephen Griffin; Paul Hendy; Terry Ilott; Sara Khan; Jerry Leider; Sue Lenier; Keith R. Lindsay; Stephen Lowe; Eric MacInnes; Paul Marsden; Paul Marx; Tony McAndrew; Tony McMahon; Sir Vartan Melkonian; Michael Misick; Max Morgan-Witts; Sir Derek Morris; Peter Murphy; Judge Chris Nicholson; Antonia Owen; Tom Owen; Mary O'Hara; Ciarán O'Keeffe; Miriam O'Reilly; Zoe Paphitis; Liz Rettig; Kenneth G. Ross; Robin Callender Smith; Rt. Hon Iain Duncan Smith; Paul Stinchcombe; Felicity Fair Thompson; Bill Tidy; Mark White; Toyah Willcox; Simon Woodham; Tappy Wright; Allen Zeleski

Literary Agents: James Jacob; Guy Rose

L235 Frances Collin Literary Agent

Literary Agency
PO Box 33, Wayne, PA 19087-0033
United States
Tel: +1 (610) 254-0555
Fax: +1 (610) 254-5029

queries@francescollin.com

http://www.francescollin.com
https://aaronline.wildapricot.org/Sys/PublicProfile/2176642/417813

Professional Body: Association of American Literary Agents (AALA)

Fiction > *Novels*
Fantasy; Historical Fiction; Literary; Science Fiction; Women's Fiction

Nonfiction > *Nonfiction Books*
Biography; Culture; History; Memoir; Narrative Nonfiction; Nature; Travel

Send: Query
How to send: Email
How not to send: Email attachment; Phone; Fax

Prefers queries by email (no attachments). No queries by phone or fax.

Literary Agent: Frances Collin

L236 Frances Kelly Agency

Literary Agency
111 Clifton Road, Kingston upon Thames, Surrey, KT2 6PL
United Kingdom
Tel: +44 (0) 20 8549 7830

Professional Body: The Association of Authors' Agents (AAA)

ACADEMIC > **Nonfiction**
Nonfiction Books; *Reference*
ADULT > **Nonfiction**
Nonfiction Books; *Reference*
PROFESSIONAL > **Nonfiction**
Nonfiction Books; *Reference*

Send: Query; Synopsis; Author bio; Self-Addressed Stamped Envelope (SASE)
Don't send: Full text
How to send: Post

Send query with SAE, CV, and synopsis or brief description of work. Scripts handled for existing clients only. No unsolicited MSS.

Literary Agent: Frances Kelly (*L382*)

L237 Robert Freedman

Literary Agent; President
United States

https://aaronline.wildapricot.org/Sys/PublicProfile/2176681/417813

Literary Agency: Robert A. Freedman Dramatic Agency, Inc. (**L592**)
Professional Body: Association of American Literary Agents (AALA)

Scripts > *Theatre Scripts*

L238 Sarah Jane Freymann

Literary Agent
United States

sarah@sarahjanefreymann.com

http://www.sarahjanefreymann.com/?page_id=3872

Literary Agency: Sarah Jane Freymann Literary Agency (**L619**)

ADULT
Fiction > *Novels*
Literary; Mainstream

Nonfiction > *Nonfiction Books*
Alternative Health; Cookery; Health; Journalism; Lifestyle; Memoir; Men's Issues; Multicultural; Narrative Nonfiction; Nature; Parenting; Psychology; Science; Self Help; Spirituality; Travel; Women's Issues

YOUNG ADULT > **Fiction** > *Novels*

Send: Query; Writing sample
How to send: In the body of an email; Post
How not to send: Email attachment

In nonfiction, interested in spiritual, psychology, self-help, women/men's issues, books by health experts (conventional and alternative), cookbooks, narrative non-fiction, natural science, nature, memoirs, cutting-edge journalism, travel, multicultural issues, parenting, lifestyle. In fiction, interested in sophisticated mainstream and literary fiction with a distinctive voice. Also looking for edgy Young Adult fiction.

L239 Claire Friedman

Literary Agent
United States

http://www.inkwellmanagement.com/staff/claire-friedman

Literary Agency: InkWell Management

ADULT
Fiction > *Novels*: Commercial

Nonfiction > *Nonfiction Books*: Narrative Nonfiction

CHILDREN'S > **Fiction** > *Novels*

YOUNG ADULT > **Fiction** > *Novels*

Send: Query; Writing sample
How to send: In the body of an email

L240 Fredrica Friedman

Literary Agent

Professional Body: The Agents Round Table (ART)
Literary Agency: Fredrica S. Friedman and Co. Inc.

L241 Jessica Friedman

Literary Agent
United States

https://www.sll.com/our-team

Literary Agency: Sterling Lord Literistic, Inc. (**L662**)

Fiction > *Novels*: Literary

Nonfiction > *Nonfiction Books*

Represents literary fiction and nonfiction. Interested in distinctive voices and writing that challenges the expected -- stylistically, formally, or otherwise. Particularly drawn to incisive, voice-driven writing and underrepresented narratives.

L242 Sarah Fuentes

Literary Agent
United States

https://www.fletcherandco.com/team/sarah-fuentes/

Literary Agency: Fletcher & Company

Fiction > *Novels*
Comedy / Humour; Dark; Literary; Relationships; Speculative; Upmarket

Nonfiction > *Nonfiction Books*
Cultural Criticism; Economics; History; Literary Memoir; Literary; Memoir; Narrative Nonfiction; Nature; Politics; Popular Culture; Popular Science; Science; Social Justice; Technology; Upmarket

Send: Query; Synopsis; Writing sample
How to send: In the body of an email

Represents a range of literary and upmarket fiction and nonfiction, including narrative nonfiction, memoir, cultural criticism, history, and popular science writing.

L243 Eugenie Furniss

Literary Agent

eugeniefurniss@42mp.com

https://www.42mp.com/agents
https://twitter.com/Furniss

Literary Agency: 42 Management and Production (**L002**)

Fiction > *Novels*
Comedy / Humour; Crime; Historical Fiction

Nonfiction > *Nonfiction Books*
Biography; Finance; Memoir; Politics; Popular History

How to send: Email

Drawn to crime in all its guises and historical fiction. On the nonfiction front seeks biography and popular history, and politics.

L244 Louise Fury

Literary Agent
United States

Literary Agency: The Bent Agency (**L058**)

Closed to approaches.

L245 The G Agency, LLC

Literary Agency
116 West 23rd Street, 5th floor, New York, NY 10011
United States
Tel: +1 (718) 664-4505

Literary Agent: Jeff Gerecke (**L256**)

L246 Nancy Gallt

Literary Agent
United States

nancy@galltzacker.com

Literary Agency: Gallt & Zacker Literary Agency

CHILDREN'S > **Fiction**
Middle Grade; *Picture Books*
YOUNG ADULT
Fiction > *Novels*
Nonfiction > *Nonfiction Books*

Closed to approaches.

L247 Natalie Galustian

Literary Agent
United Kingdom

natalie@greyhoundliterary.co.uk

https://greyhoundliterary.co.uk/agent/natalie-galustian/
https://twitter.com/natgalustian

Literary Agency: Greyhound Literary (**L288**)

Fiction
Novels: Literary
Short Fiction: Literary

Nonfiction
Essays: General
Nonfiction Books: Arts; Biography; Comedy / Humour; Commercial; Cookery; Drama; History; Memoir; Music; Narrative Nonfiction

Send: Query; Synopsis; Writing sample; Outline
How to send: Email
How not to send: Post

Represents narrative and commercial non-fiction as well as literary fiction. She is primarily looking for strong new voices in non-fiction across musical, visual, dramatic and culinary arts, history, memoir, biography, essays and humour, along with some select fiction and short stories of literary quality.

Author Estates: The Estate of Alan Rickman; The Estate of Alfred H. Mendes

Authors: Jennifer Lucy Allan; Jeremy Allen; Lulah Ellender; Stephen Mallinder; Charlotte Mitchell; David Moats; Holly Norman; Andrew Perry; Hamilton Richardson; Lias Saoudi; Matthew Shaw; Michael Smith; Harry Sword; James Thomas; Luke Turner; Robin Turner; Michael Volpe; Liam Patrick Young

L248 Lori Galvin

Literary Agent
Boston
United States

https://aevitascreative.com/agents/
https://querymanager.com/query/QueryLoriGalvin

Literary Agency: Aevitas

Fiction > *Novels*
General, and in particular: Crime; Women's Fiction

Nonfiction > *Nonfiction Books*
Cookery; Food; Memoir

Closed to approaches.

Represents both adult fiction (especially women's fiction and thrillers) and nonfiction (personal development and cookbooks).

L249 Anna Gamble

Assistant Agent; Editor
United Kingdom

https://www.liverpool-literary.agency/about

Literary Agency: The Liverpool Literary Agency (**L435**)

CHILDREN'S > **Fiction**
Chapter Books: High Concept
Middle Grade: Adventure
Picture Books: General

Closed to approaches.

Would love to see warm, funny and engaging picture books, high concept chapter books with a strong hook and middle grade fiction that really knows its audience and offers a sense of adventure.

L250 The Garamond Agency, Inc.

Literary Agency
United States

query@garamondagency.com

https://garamondagency.com
http://www.facebook.com/garamondagency/
https://twitter.com/@garamondagency

Nonfiction > *Nonfiction Books*
General, and in particular: Business; History; Narrative Nonfiction; Politics; Psychology; Science; Sociology

Does not want:

Nonfiction > *Nonfiction Books*: Memoir

Send: Query
Don't send: Proposal
How to send: Email
How not to send: Email attachment

Represents only adult, nonfiction projects.

Do not send proposals for children's books, young adult, fiction, poetry, or memoirs.

Query first if you have any questions about whether this is the right agency for your work.

Send email containing a short description of your project before forwarding your proposal. Please send brief queries only. No attachments. Unsolicited attachments will be deleted unread.

Literary Agent: Lisa Adams

L251 Sulamita Garbuz

Associate Agent
United States

sg@goldinlit.com

https://goldinlit.com/agents/

Literary Agency: Frances Goldin Literary Agency, Inc.

Fiction > *Novels*
Literary; Speculative

Nonfiction > *Nonfiction Books*
Journalism; Memoir; Narrative Nonfiction; Psychology; Science; Social Justice

How to send: Email

Gravitates primarily towards nonfiction, with an emphasis on books with a social justice bent. Her areas of specialty include narrative nonfiction, memoir, psychology, science, and journalism. She is also looking for character driven literary fiction, and is especially excited by novels that use speculative or dreamlike elements to explore current social dynamics, stories of obsession and women misbehaving, and narratives about immigration and the 2nd generation experience.

L252 Jennifer Gates

Senior Partner; Literary Agent
United States

https://aevitascreative.com/agents/

Literary Agency: Aevitas

ADULT
Fiction > *Novels*: Literary

Nonfiction > *Nonfiction Books*
Current Affairs; Memoir; Narrative Nonfiction; Popular Culture

CHILDREN'S > **Fiction** > *Novels*

Send: Author bio; Pitch; Market info; Writing sample
How to send: Online submission system

Represents a range of nonfiction, including narrative and expert-driven works, memoir, current affairs, pop culture, as well as literary fiction and children's books.

Authors: Lesley Alderman; Dale Archer; Andrew Auseon; Jimmy Santiago Baca; Ed Bacon; April Balascio; Thomas P. M. Barnett; Mira Bartók; Jared Brock; Lily Brooks-Dalton; Mariann Edgar Budde; David L. Carroll; Neko Case; Andy Corren; Wayne Curtis; Kevin Davies; Kenneth J. Doka; Ilana Edelstein; Owen Elliot-Kugell; Melissa Falcon Field; Aria Finger; Maureen Foley; Arun Gandhi; Mayte Garcia; Chris Gardner; Peter Guralnick; Jorge Hachumak; Meredith Hall; Jacqueline Holland; Robby Krieger; Neil Lane; Morgan Levine; Eva Longoria; Ndaba Mandela; Patricia McConnell; Jillian Medoff; Rhett Miller; Robert Tate Miller; John Moe; Earl "The Pearl" Monroe; Colten Moore; Tracy Moore; Catherine Newman; Alice Ozma; Liz Phair; SQuire Rushnell; Maya Soetoro-Ng; Kevin Sorbo; Elizabeth Stein; Darryl and Tracy Strawberry; Quincy Troupe; Deborah Tuerkheimer; Donna VanLiere; Lynx Vilden; Tony Weaver; Tess Wilkinson-Ryan; Mary Ann Winkowski; Jung Yun; Anya Yurchyshyn

L253 Ellen Geiger

Senior Agent; Vice President
United States

https://goldinlit.com/agents/

Literary Agency: Frances Goldin Literary Agency, Inc.

Fiction > *Novels*
Culture; Historical Fiction; Literary Thrillers; Multicultural

Nonfiction > *Nonfiction Books*
Biography; History; Investigative Journalism; Multicultural; Politics; Psychology; Religion; Social Issues; Women's Issues

Closed to approaches.

Represents a broad range of fiction and non-fiction. She has a lifelong interest in multicultural and social issues embracing change. History, biography, progressive politics, psychology, women's issues, religion and serious investigative journalism are special interests.

In fiction, she loves a good literary thriller, and novels in general that provoke and challenge the status quo, as well as historical and multicultural works. She is drawn to big themes which make a larger point about the culture and times we live in, such as Barbara Kingsolver's Poisonwood Bible. She is not the right agent for New Age, romance, how-to or right-wing politics.

L254 Nicole Geiger

Literary Agent
United States

https://www.fullcircleliterary.com/submissions/
https://querymanager.com/query/NicoleFCL

Literary Agency: Full Circle Literary, LLC

CHILDREN'S > **Fiction** > *Graphic Novels*

Closed to approaches.

Represents graphic novels for middle grade and younger only.

L255 Jonny Geller

Literary Agent
United Kingdom

http://submissions.curtisbrown.co.uk/agents/

Literary Agency: Curtis Brown

Fiction > *Novels*
Commercial Women's Fiction; Literary; Thrillers

Nonfiction > *Nonfiction Books*: Journalism

Send: Query; Synopsis; Writing sample
How to send: Online submission system

"I am lucky enough to work with a fantastic range of writers – from authors of first class literary fiction to best selling thriller writers, from ground-breaking journalists to the very best writers in the field of women's commercial fiction – my focus is original fiction from writers who have a distinctive voice."

Associate Agent: Viola Hayden (**L315**)

L256 Jeff Gerecke

Literary Agent
United States

gagencyquery@gmail.com
jeff@gagencylit.com
jeff@marksonagency.com

https://www.publishersmarketplace.com/members/jeffg/
http://aaronline.org/Sys/PublicProfile/2176689/417813

Professional Body: Association of American Literary Agents (AALA)
Literary Agencies: The G Agency, LLC (**L245**); Elaine Markson Literary Agency (**L199**)

Fiction > *Novels*
General, and in particular: Commercial; Literary; Mystery

Nonfiction > *Nonfiction Books*
Biography; Business; Computers; Finance; History; Military History; Popular Culture; Sport; Technology

Send: Query; Writing sample
How to send: Email attachment

I am interested in commercial and literary fiction, as well as serious non-fiction and pop culture. My focus as an agent has always been on working with writers to shape their work for its greatest commercial potential. I provide lots of editorial advice in sharpening manuscripts and proposals before submission.

L257 Josh Getzler

Literary Agent; Partner
United States

josh@hgliterary.com

https://www.hgliterary.com/josh
https://twitter.com/jgetzler
http://www.publishersmarketplace.com/members/jgetzler/
http://aaronline.org/Sys/PublicProfile/2902758/417813
http://queryme.online/Getzler

Literary Agency: HG Literary
Professional Body: Association of American Literary Agents (AALA)

ADULT
Fiction > *Novels*
Historical Fiction; Mystery; Thrillers; Women's Fiction

Nonfiction > *Nonfiction Books*
Business; History; Politics

CHILDREN'S > **Fiction** > *Middle Grade*
Comedy / Humour; Contemporary

Closed to approaches.

L258 Lilly Ghahremani

Literary Agent
United States

https://www.fullcircleliterary.com/our-agents/lilly-ghahremani/
https://twitter.com/Wonderlilly

Literary Agency: Full Circle Literary, LLC

Closed to approaches.

L259 Jim Gill

Literary Agent
United Kingdom

jgill@unitedagents.co.uk

https://www.unitedagents.co.uk

Literary Agency: United Agents (**L704**)

Fiction > *Novels*

Nonfiction > *Nonfiction Books*

Acts for a broad range of both fiction and non-fiction authors writing for the general-trade market, and is always on the look-out for the original and the excellent.

Authors: Ishbel Addyman; Dr Elizabeth Archibald; Joe Bennett; Mark Binelli; Jonathan Blyth; Lawrence Booth; Pete Brown; Christopher Bryant; Barnabas Calder; Justin Cartwright; Tom Chatfield; John Henry Clay; Sean Conway; Nicholas Crane; Emma Dibdin; Dominick Donald; Margaret Drabble; David Hart Dyke; Giles Foden; Tom Gregory; Sudhir Hazareesingh; Eleanor Henderson; Patrick Hennessey; Mark Keating; Yasmin Khan; Jamie Kornegay; Robert Lautner; Thomas Leveritt; Joshua Levine; Matt Lewis; Rebecca Loncraine; Robert Low; Kevin Maher; Liam McIlvanney; Ciarán McMenamin; Steven Merritt Miner; Jonny Owen; Justin Pollard; Tony Pollard; Oliver Poole; James Rebanks; Jasper Rees; Harry Sidebottom; Ian Thomson; Joanna Trollope; Teddy Wayne; James Yorkston

L260 Claire Gillespie

Associate Agent
United States

submissions@cheneyagency.com

http://cheneyassoc.com/#scrollto-agents

Fiction > *Novels*
Literary; Upmarket

Nonfiction > *Nonfiction Books*
Cultural Criticism; Memoir

Send: Query; Author bio; Writing sample; Self-Addressed Stamped Envelope (SASE)
How to send: Post; Email

Focuses on literary fiction, memoir, cultural criticism, upmarket fiction, and audio.

L261 Amy Gilroy

Trainee Agent
United Kingdom

https://katenashlit.co.uk/people/
https://twitter.com/amygilroy_

Literary Agency: Kate Nash Literary Agency (**L375**)

Fiction > *Novels*
General, and in particular: Crime; Romance

Send: Query; Pitch; Author bio; Synopsis; Writing sample
How to send: In the body of an email

Reads a wide range of genres, from romance to crime. She enjoys books that feature strong and diverse characters with powerful voices and reading books set in distant places with rich cultures.

L262 Ginger Clark Literary

Literary Agency
176 Amity Road, Suite 132, Woodbridge, CT 06525
United States
Tel: +1 (646) 396-0903

info@GingerClarkLiterary.com

https://gingerclarkliterary.com
https://www.instagram.com/clarkliterary/
https://twitter.com/ClarkLiterary

Literary Agents: Ginger Clark (**L133**); Nicole Eisenbraun (**L196**)

L263 Brenna Girard

Literary Agent
United States

brenna@carolynjenksagency.com

https://www.carolynjenksagency.com/agent/BRENNA-GIRARD

Literary Agency: Carolyn Jenks Agency (**L106**)

Nonfiction > *Nonfiction Books*
General, and in particular: Business; Cookery

L264 The Gislason Agency

Literary Agency
7362 University Avenue NE Ste 120, Fridley, MN 55432
United States
Tel: +1 (763) 220-2983
Fax: +1 (763) 571-1576

http://www.thegislasonagency.com

Fiction > *Novels*

Closed to approaches.

Costs: Offers services that writers have to pay for.

Represented fiction writers, including a mystery author who received critical acclaim in Publishers Weekly. Currently, she will only consider solicited authors. In some instances, she is willing to give people feedback on a writing project for a fee.

Authors: Linda Cook; Terence Faherty; Deborah Woodworth

Literary Agent: Barbara J. Gislason (*L265*)

L265 Barbara J. Gislason

Literary Agent
United States

Literary Agency: The Gislason Agency (**L264**)

L266 Linda S. Glaz

Author; Literary Agent; Editor; Proofreader
United States

linda@hartlineliterary.com

https://www.hartlineagency.com/agents-and-authors
https://www.facebook.com/linda.glaz
https://twitter.com/LindaGlaz

Literary Agency: Hartline Literary Agency (**L311**)
Professional Body: Advanced Writers and Speakers Association (AWSA)

Fiction > *Novels*
General, and in particular: Contemporary Romance; Historical Romance; Romance; Romantic Suspense

Nonfiction > *Nonfiction Books*

Looking for nonfiction by experts in their field. In fiction, will consider anything well written, particularly romance, either contemporary, suspense, or historic. No children's or works that include graphic sexuality or profanity.

Authors: Karla Akins; Rick Barry; Kate Breslin; Lance Brown; Raquel Byrnes; J'nell Ciesielski; Ben Conlon; Angela Couch; Susan F. Craft; Rhonda Dragomir; Barbara Ellin Fox; Linda Gilden; Samantha Gomolka; Janet Grunst; Hilary Hamblin; Hilary Hamblin Voni Harris; Voni Harris; Julie Hatch; K Denise Holmberg; Dennis Lambert; A. D. Lawrence; Delores Liesner; Ashley Ludwig; Jessica Manfre; Merliyn Howton Marriott; Cheryl Linn Martin; Joy Massenburge; Dale McElhinney; Donna Mumma; Naomi Musch; Luke Negron; Jessica Nelson Tiffany Nicole; Candice Patterson; Carmen Peone; Karen Prough; DeBora Rachelle; Maria Reed; Cindy Regnier; Kathleen Rouser; Susan Browning Schulz; Colleen Scott; Laura Smith; Donnie Steven; Donnie Stevens; Patti Stockdale; Beth Summitt; Ken Swarner; Tiffany Tajiri; Donn Taylor; Donn Taylor Evelyn Taylor; Evelyn Taylor; Pegg Thomas; Tom Threadgill; Kari Trumbo; Susan L. Tuttle; Jennifer Uhlarik; Hannah Vanderpool; Denise Weimer; Karen Wingate; Maureen Wise; Frank Yates

L267 Gleam Futures

Literary Agency
10 Triton Street, London, NW1 3BF
United Kingdom
Tel: +44 (0) 20 3772 2940

info@gleamfutures.com

https://www.gleamfutures.com
https://www.gleamfutures.com/gleamtitles
https://twitter.com/gleamfutures
https://www.linkedin.com/company/1330612/admin/
https://www.instagram.com/gleamfutures

Fiction > *Novels*

Nonfiction > *Nonfiction Books*

Send: Query; Proposal; Author bio; Writing sample; Synopsis
How to send: Email; Online contact form

We represent a wide range of fiction and non-fiction writers and are extremely proud to have launched nearly 40 Sunday Times bestselling books to date.

Always on the lookout for original, brave, and exciting new voices who are looking to build and nurture an authentic connection with their audiences across social media and drive long-term value in their books across multiple media platforms.

Authors: Emmanuel Asuquo; Ellie Austin-Williams; Yasmin Benoit; Grace Beverley; Grant Brydon; Kat Farmer; Amber Fossey; Marvyn Harrison; Omari McQueen; Tiwalola Ogunlesi; Tom Parker; Adele Roberts; Becky Smethurst; Sam Stern; Grace Victory; Hana Walker-Brown; Harriet De Winton

Literary Agency: Gleam Futures (US)

L268 Kerry Glencorse

Literary Agent
United Kingdom

https://www.susannalea.com/team-member/kerry-glencorse/

Literary Agency: Susanna Lea Associates (UK) (**L679**)

Fiction > *Novels*
Crime; Historical Fiction; Literary; Thrillers; Upmarket Commercial Fiction; Women's Fiction

Nonfiction > *Nonfiction Books*
Cultural History; Memoir; Narrative Nonfiction; Nature; Popular Science; Social History

Send: Query; Synopsis; Writing sample
How to send: Email

Always on the lookout for new talent, especially in the areas of literary and upmarket commercial fiction; well-written genre fiction, including crime, thrillers, women's fiction, and historical. And on the non-fiction side: memoir, narrative non-fiction, popular science, natural science, social and cultural history.

L269 Emily Glenister

Literary Agent
United Kingdom

eg.submission@dhhliteraryagency.com

http://www.dhhliteraryagency.com/emily-glenister.html
http://www.twitter.com/emily_glenister

Literary Agency: DHH Literary Agency Ltd (**L172**)

Fiction > *Novels*
Book Club Fiction; Commercial; Crime; Folklore, Myths, and Legends; Ghost Stories; Historical Fiction; Horror; Mystery; Psychological Thrillers; Romance; Romantic Comedy; Urban Fantasy

Nonfiction > *Nonfiction Books*
Autobiography; Biography; Crime; History; Medicine; Memoir; Popular Culture; Women

Send: Synopsis; Writing sample
How to send: Email

Looking for female-led commercial and book club fiction, with an emphasis on diverse / own voices. A gripping psychological thriller or a twisty crime book will always grab the attention (though she takes on very little police procedural); as will a witty and observant rom-com, an epic love story, historical fiction with a strong focus on women, modern retellings of classics / myths / legends (again, with women at the centre). She's also partial to a little urban fantasy. Concept-led mysteries – whether historical or contemporary – are also very high on the wish list and if an original horror novel / ghost story landed in her inbox, she would be delighted. In non-fiction, she is keen to expand her list and is looking in the areas of history (specifically the monarchy, medicine and women), pop culture, biographies / autobiographies / memoir and true crime.

Authors: Louise Beech; Libby Cutts; Heather Darwent; Becca Day; Suzie Edge; Stephen Edger; Emma Ellis; Carys Jones; Caroline Lamond; S.V. Leonard; Vikki Patis; Reagan Lee Ray; Reagan Lee Ray; Talia Samuels; Annie May Taylor; Rebecca Thorne; Ola Tundun; Ronnie Turner; Kathleen Whyman

L270 Global Lion Intellectual Property Management, Inc.

Literary Agency
PO BOX 669238, Pompano Beach, FL 33066
United States

peter@globallionmgt.com

https://globallionmanagement.com
https://www.facebook.com/GlobalLionMgt/
https://twitter.com/globallionmgt
https://www.instagram.com/globallionmgt/

Fiction > *Novels*
Commercial; Fantasy; Science Fiction

Nonfiction > *Nonfiction Books*
Arts; Business; Commercial; Education; Film Industry; Self Help; TV; Technology

Send: Query
How to send: Online submission system

Currently looking for commercial fiction, fantasy, science fiction, and intriguing studies of interesting subjects, art, and "making of" books on the film and television industry. Will not turn down anything with sharp prose, modern takes on classic concepts, a great mystery to solve or intriguing characters.

L271 Georgia Glover

Literary Agent
United Kingdom

https://www.davidhigham.co.uk/agents-dh/georgia-glover/

Literary Agency: David Higham Associates Ltd (**L161**)

Fiction > *Novels*

Nonfiction > *Nonfiction Books*

Looks after an eclectic list of clients, including a large stable of literary estates, working to ensure that the work of these classic writers remains available for new generations to discover and seeking new opportunities to bring back into print those works that are perhaps less well known but no less deserving of attention.

Authors: J. R. Ackerley; Edward Ardizzone; Michael Arlen; Elizabeth Berridge; Edmund Blunden; E. R. Braithwaite; Neville Braybrooke; Arthur Bryant; Anthony Burgess; John Dickson Carr; Barbara Castle; Charles Causley; James Hadley Chase; Arthur C. Clarke; Lady Mary Clive; Peter Cook; Chris Cove-Smith; James Curtis; David Daiches; R. F. Delderfield; Eleanor Farjeon; J. Jefferson Farjeon; Elizabeth Ferrars; Nicholas Fisk; Pauline Fisk; Theodora Fitzgibbon; Margot Fonteyn; Ford Madox Ford; Mavis Gallant; Jonathan Gathorne-Hardy; Ralph Glasser; Elizabeth Goudge; Peter Green; Geoffrey Grigson; Jane Grigson

L272 Susannah Godman

Literary Agent
United Kingdom

Literary Agency: Lutyens and Rubinstein (**L448**)

L273 Anthony Goff

Literary Agent; Chair
United Kingdom

submissions@davidhigham.co.uk

https://www.davidhigham.co.uk/agents-dh/anthony-goff/

Literary Agency: David Higham Associates Ltd (**L161**)

ADULT
Fiction > *Novels*
Commercial; Literary

Nonfiction > *Nonfiction Books*
Commercial; Literary

CHILDREN'S > **Fiction** > *Novels*

Send: Query; Synopsis; Writing sample

Represents many high-profile and successful authors of literary and commercial fiction and non-fiction, and also several children's writers.

Authors: Carol Anshaw; Jenn Ashworth; Nigel Barley; Aimee Bender; Margaret Boden; Janet Browne; Jessica Bruder; Mark Burnell; J. M. Coetzee; Bernard Cornwell; John Cunliffe; Roald Dahl; Anne Fine; Karen Joy Fowler; Catherine Fox; Stephen Fry; Caroline Graham; Linda Green; Graham Greene; James Herbert; Paul Hoffman; Simon Hopkinson; Alan Judd; Binnie Kirshenbaum; Stephen Lacey; Hugh Laurie; Joanna Lumley; Greil Marcus; David Marquand; Simon Mason; Evan Mawdsley; Peter May; Elizabeth McCracken; Iain McGilchrist; Elizabeth McKenzie; Sigrid Nunez; Kate Reed Petty; Anthony Powell; Shannon Pufahl; Alice Sebold; Miranda Seymour; Nick Sharratt; Hilary Spurling; Hew Strachan; Jeremy Strong; Lynne Truss; Lucy Wadham; Alice Walker; Stephen Walsh; Elizabeth Wilhide

L274 Ellen Goff

Associate Agent
United States

ellen@hgliterary.com

https://www.hgliterary.com/ellen

Literary Agency: HG Literary

CHILDREN'S > **Fiction**
Middle Grade; *Picture Books*
YOUNG ADULT > **Fiction**
Graphic Novels: General
Novels: General, and in particular: Ghost Stories; Gothic; Historical Fiction

List consists of YA writers and illustrators, as well as middle grade and picture book writers. Interested in all genres and formats of YA, especially anything spooky, historical fiction, martial arts, graphic novels, and novels-in-verse. She has a soft spot for Shakespeare as well as southern gothic stories that remind her of her home state of Kentucky.

L275 Veronica Goldstein

Literary Agent
United States

https://www.fletcherandco.com/team/veronica-goldstein/

Literary Agency: Fletcher & Company

Fiction > *Novels*
Autofiction; Contemporary; Culture; Experimental; Literary; Politics; Speculative

Nonfiction in Translation > *Nonfiction Books*
Climate Science; Culture; Economics; Memoir; Narrative Nonfiction; Politics; Social Issues; Technology

Nonfiction > *Nonfiction Books*
Climate Science; Culture; Economics; Memoir; Narrative Nonfiction; Politics; Social Issues; Technology

Send: Query; Synopsis; Writing sample
How to send: In the body of an email

Her list includes contemporary literary fiction and voice-driven narrative nonfiction that probes important social issues.

L276 The Good Literary Agency

Literary Agency
United Kingdom

info@thegoodliteraryagency.org

https://www.thegoodliteraryagency.org
https://twitter.com/thegoodagencyuk

Professional Body: The Association of Authors' Agents (AAA)

ADULT
Fiction > *Novels*
General, and in particular: Romance

Nonfiction > *Nonfiction Books*
General, and in particular: Health; Lifestyle

CHILDREN'S
Fiction > *Novels*
General, and in particular: Adventure

Nonfiction > *Nonfiction Books*
General, and in particular: Lifestyle

YOUNG ADULT
Fiction > *Novels*
General, and in particular: Adventure

Nonfiction > *Nonfiction Books*
General, and in particular: Lifestyle

Send: Query
Don't send: Full text

Focused on discovering, developing and launching the careers of writers of colour, disability, working class, LGBTQ+ and anyone who feels their story is not being told in the mainstream. Writers must be born or resident in Britain. No poetry, plays, or screenplays. Accepts submissions from the 1st to the 21st of each month only. See website for full guidelines and to submit via online form.

L277 Andrew Gordon

Literary Agent
United Kingdom

andrewgordon@davidhigham.co.uk

https://www.davidhigham.co.uk/agents-dh/andrew-gordon/

Literary Agency: David Higham Associates Ltd (**L161**)

ACADEMIC > **Nonfiction** > *Nonfiction Books*: History

ADULT
Fiction > *Novels*
Commercial; Literary

Nonfiction > *Nonfiction Books*
Adventure; Biography; Business; Current Affairs; Economics; Films; History;

Memoir; Music; Narrative Nonfiction; Politics; Popular Culture; Popular Science; Psychology; Sport

List is primarily non-fiction. Open to new projects in most genres, especially history, current affairs, biography and memoir, narrative non-fiction, sport, popular culture, popular science and psychology, smart thinking and business books with a strong story. In fiction, likes novels that grab the attention, whether literary or commercial. No YA authors, or science fiction/fantasy.

Assistant Agent: David Evans (**L210**)

Authors: Elizabeth Alker; Alan Allport; Noga Arikha; Thomas Asbridge; Katy Balls; Lindsey Bareham; Kaushik Basu; Laura Beers; James Bloodworth; Jonathan Boff; John Carey; Aditya Chakrabortty; Michael Cockerell; Alan Connor; Jason Cowley; Alex Danchev; Bobby Duffy; Mark Easton; Gavin Esler; Seb Falk; Felipe Fernández-Armesto; Cordelia Fine; Matthew Frank; Alex George; Susannah Gibson; Andrew Gimson; Victoria Glendinning; Anthony Good; Richard Greene; John Gribbin; Dennis Grube; Isabel Hardman; Sophie Harman; Chris Hirst; Russell Hoban; Eric Hobsbawm; Trevor Horn; Tansy Hoskins; Julian Jackson; Owen Jones; Anna Keay; John Keay; Paul Kennedy; Sulmaan Wasif Khan; David Lammy; Elisabeth Leake; Dame Vera Lynn; Kathryn Mannix; Sarfraz Manzoor; Helen McCarthy; Michael McCarthy; Ed Miliband; Fraser Nelson; Johan Norberg; David Nott; Peter Oborne; Susan Owens; Ellie Mae O'Hagan; Helen Parr; Harry Pearson; Gilles Peterson; John Pilger; Anna Politkovskaya; Sadiah Qureshi; Amol Rajan; Chris Renwick; Steve Richards; Helen Roche; Jane Rogoyska; Rupert Russell; Jane Sanderson; Antonia Senior; Jake Wallis Simons; Sujit Sivasundaram; Mark B. Smith; Peter Snowdon; Kristina Spohr; Devi Sridhar; Peter Stott; Dylan Thomas; Simon Thurley; Phil Tinline; Simon Tyler; Rosamund Urwin; Yanis Varoufakis; Brian Viner; Bernard Wasserstein; Holly Watt; Sam Wetherell; Phil Whitaker; Jon Wilson; Hope Wolf; Carolyn Woods

L278 Graham Maw Christie Literary Agency

Literary Agency
37 Highbury Place, London, N5 1QP
United Kingdom
Tel: +44 (0) 7971 268342

submissions@grahammawchristie.com

http://www.grahammawchristie.com
https://twitter.com/litagencygmc
https://www.instagram.com/litagencygmc/

Professional Body: The Association of Authors' Agents (AAA)

Nonfiction > *Nonfiction Books*
Memoir; Music; Narrative Nonfiction; Politics; Popular Culture; Popular Science; Psychology; Sport

Send: Query; Outline; Author bio; Market info; Marketing Plan; Writing sample
How to send: Email

No fiction, poetry, or scripts. Send query with one-page summary, a paragraph on the contents of each chapter, your qualifications for writing it, details of your online presence, market analysis, what you could do to help promote your book, and a sample chapter or two.

Literary Agents: Maddy Belton (**L055**); Jennifer Christie (**L129**); Jane Graham Maw (**L478**)

L279 Stacey Graham

Literary Agent
United States

stacey@threeseaslit.com

https://www.threeseasagency.com/copy-of-michelle-grajkowski
http://querymanager.com/Stacey3Seas

Literary Agency: 3 Seas Literary Agency (**L001**)

ADULT
Fiction > *Novels*: Romantic Comedy

Nonfiction > *Nonfiction Books*

CHILDREN'S > **Fiction** > *Middle Grade*
Comedy / Humour; Ghost Stories

How to send: Query Manager

Currently looking to expand her list with snappy Rom-Coms, hilarious/spooky middle grade, and weird nonfiction.

L280 Susan Graham

Literary Agent
United States

https://www.einsteinliterary.com/staff/
http://aaronline.org/Sys/PublicProfile/52451502/417813

Literary Agency: Einstein Literary Management (**L194**)
Professional Body: Association of American Literary Agents (AALA)

ADULT > **Fiction** > *Novels*
General, and in particular: Fantasy; LGBTQIA; Science Fiction

CHILDREN'S > **Fiction** > *Novels*
General, and in particular: Fantasy; LGBTQIA; Science Fiction

YOUNG ADULT
Fiction > *Novels*
General, and in particular: Fantasy; LGBTQIA; Science Fiction

Nonfiction > *Nonfiction Books*

Looking for children's and young adult fiction in all genres, but their favorite books are often science fiction and fantasy, especially written with a queer lens. They also enjoy picture books and represent graphic novels in all age categories and in all genres. They're particularly interested in friendships and sibling narratives, and monster protagonists are always a plus. They're looking for a good non-fiction or two for children or teens but don't know about what. For adult prose, they prefer genre fiction, and monster protagonists are still a plus. Works by and about marginalized voices are welcome and encouraged.

L281 Michelle Grajkowski

Literary Agent
United States

michelle@threeseaslit.com

https://www.threeseasagency.com/michelle-grajkowski
http://querymanager.com/Michelle3Seas
http://aaronline.org/Sys/PublicProfile/2176701/417813

Literary Agency: 3 Seas Literary Agency (**L001**)
Professional Body: Association of American Literary Agents (AALA)

ADULT
Fiction > *Novels*
Romance; Women's Fiction

Nonfiction > *Nonfiction Books*

CHILDREN'S > **Fiction** > *Middle Grade*

How to send: Query Manager

Primarily represents romance, women's fiction, young adult and middle grade fiction along with select nonfiction projects with a terrific message. She is currently looking for fantastic writers with a voice of their own.

Authors: Katie MacAlister; Cathy McDavid; Kerrelyn Sparks; C.L. Wilson

L282 David Granger

Literary Agent
New York
United States

https://aevitascreative.com/agents/

Literary Agency: Aevitas

Nonfiction > *Nonfiction Books*
Celebrity; Culture; Design; Food; Politics; Science; Technology

Closed to approaches.

Represents primarily non-fiction and is obsessed with topics across an extremely wide spectrum – politics; food culture; actual innovation in design, tech and science; fame. What binds these things is a yen for intensely original ideas and writing that pushes boundaries.

L283 Olivia Gray

Literary Agent
United Kingdom

Literary Agency: Independent Talent Group Ltd (**L340**)

L284 Great River Literary

Literary Agency
United States

greatriverliterary@gmail.com

https://www.greatriverliterary.com

CHILDREN'S
Fiction
Board Books; *Chapter Books*; *Middle Grade*; *Picture Books*
Nonfiction > *Nonfiction Books*: Literary

Poetry > *Any Poetic Form*

YOUNG ADULT > **Fiction** > *Novels*

How to send: Email
How not to send: Email attachment; Phone; Post

An agency devoted exclusively to representing authors and author/illustrators of books for children and teens.

Literary Agent: Mary Cummings (*L149*)

L285 Greene & Heaton Ltd

Literary Agency
T18, West Wing, Somerset House, Strand, London, WC2R 1LA
United Kingdom

submissions@greeneheaton.co.uk
info@greeneheaton.co.uk

http://www.greeneheaton.co.uk
https://twitter.com/greeneandheaton

Professional Body: The Association of Authors' Agents (AAA)

Fiction > *Novels*

Nonfiction > *Nonfiction Books*

Does not want:

CHILDREN'S > **Fiction** > *Picture Books*

Send: Query; Synopsis; Writing sample
Don't send: Full text
How to send: Email
How not to send: Post

Send query by email only, including synopsis and three chapters or approximately 50 pages. No submissions by post. No response unless interested. Handles all types of fiction and nonfiction, but no scripts or children's picture books.

Author Estates: The Estate of Julia Darling; The Estate of Sarah Gainham

Authors: Juliana Adelman; Amen Alonge; Anthony Anaxagorou; Lucy Ashe; Louise Atkinson; Raffaella Barker; Charlotte Bauer; Laurie Bolger; Emily Bootle; Lucy Brazier; Bridget; Lynne Bryan; Zoe Burgess; Jason Byrne; Tom Campbell; Emma Chapman; Charles Cockell; Pam Corbin; Andrew Davidson; Russell Davies; Anna Davis; Rachel Dawson; Patrick Drake; Nikki Duffy; Kim Duke; Lily Dunn; Suzannah Dunn; Jeremy Duns; Jonn Elledge; Olaf Falafel; Hugh Fearnley-Whittingstall; Jane Fearnley-Whittingstall; Christopher Fitz-Simon; Felix Flicker; Christophe Galfard; Helen Giltrow; Francis Gimblett; Molly Greeley; Jake Hall; Stuart Heritage; Kit Heyam; Kat Hill; Julian Hitch; Beatrice Hitchman; Wayne Holloway-Smith; Andrew Holmes; Alex Hourston; David Howard; Daisy J. Hung; Charles Jennings; Joan; D.B. John; Sam Johnson-Schlee; Keith Kahn-Harris; Fiona Keating; Gabrielle Kimm; Esme King; Max Kinnings; David Kirk; Rikke Schmidt Kjærgaard; Rebecca Dinerstein Knight; Joseph Knox; Sonya Kudei; William Leith; Dan Lepard; Robert Lewis; Eric Lindstrom; Kieran Long; Dorian Lynskey; L. A. MacRae; Carina Maggar; Anna Sulan Masing; Jolyon Maugham; James McGee; Gill Meller; Thomasina Miers; Lottie Moggach; Cathy Newman; Mary-Ann Ochota; Ciara Ohartghaile; Christopher Osborn; Iain Overton; John O'Connell; Pete Paphides; Anna Parker; Jyoti Patel; Neel Patel; Tom Phillips; Shivi Ramoutar; Richard Reed; Sam Rice; C. J. Sansom; Marcus du Sautoy; Indyana Schneider; Eddie Scott; Rebecca Seal; Paul Keers: Sediment; Laura Shepherd-Robinson; Mimi Spencer; Count Arthur Strong; Jacqueline Sutherland; Andrew Taylor; Ian Vince; John Vincent; Adam Wagner; Jennie Walker; Sarai Walker; Andrew Webb; Mark Wernham; Robyn Wilder; Will Wiles; Jason Wilson; Susie Yang; Erin Young; Robyn Young; Andrew Ziminski

Literary Agents: Holly Faulks (**L215**); Carol Heaton (**L319**); Imogen Morrell (**L508**); Judith Murray; Antony Topping; Laura Williams; Claudia Young (**L753**)

L286 The Greenhouse Literary Agency

Literary Agency

https://www.greenhouseliterary.com
https://www.facebook.com/The-Greenhouse-Literary-Agency-359292813053/?ref=nf

CHILDREN'S > **Fiction**
Chapter Books; *Graphic Novels*; *Middle Grade*; *Picture Books*
YOUNG ADULT > **Fiction** > *Novels*

How to send: Query Manager

Transatlantic literary agency with agents in the US and UK. See individual agent details for more info.

Company Director / Literary Agent: Chelsea Eberly (**L189**)

Literary Agents: Sarah Davies; Polly Nolan; Kristin Ostby (**L543**)

L287 Katie Greenstreet

Literary Agent
United Kingdom

submissions@paperliterary.com

Literary Agency: Paper Literary (**L547**)

Fiction > *Novels*
Book Club Fiction; Commercial; Family; Historical Fiction; Literary Suspense; Psychological Suspense; Romance; Upmarket

Nonfiction > *Nonfiction Books*: Memoir

I'm building a list of quality commercial and upmarket/book club fiction, with a select number of memoirs and non-fiction projects also in the mix.

L288 Greyhound Literary

Literary Agency
United Kingdom

info@cclagents.com

https://greyhoundliterary.co.uk

Professional Body: The Association of Authors' Agents (AAA)

ADULT
Fiction > *Novels*
Commercial; Literary

Nonfiction > *Nonfiction Books*
General, and in particular: Biography; Comedy / Humour; Cookery; History; Lifestyle; Memoir; Music; Politics; Sport; Wellbeing

CHILDREN'S
Fiction > *Novels*
Nonfiction > *Nonfiction Books*

Send: Query; Synopsis; Writing sample
How to send: Email

Author Estates: The Estate of Alan Rickman; The Estate of Alfred H. Mendes

Authors: Guy Adams; Poppy Alexander; Jennifer Lucy Allan; Jeremy Allen; SJ Bennett; Leona Nichole Black; Owen Booth; Luce Brett; Edward Brooke-Hitching; Theodore Brun; Andy Bull; Jen Campbell; Bonnie Chung; David Collins; Zoë Colville; Duncan Crowe; Iain Dey; Chris Dodd; Lulah Ellender; Adam Fergusson; Jamie Fewery; Liz Fraser; Rebecca Front; Tom Gabbay; Julian Gough; Janet Gover; Sarah Graham; Karen Gurney; Saskia Gwinn; Ed Hawkins; David Higgins; Maisie Hill; Will Hill; Thomas W. Hodgkinson; Nicholas Hogg; Michael Holding; Andrew Hosken; Michael Hutchinson; Jo Iozzi; Heidi James; Simon Jones; Jennifer Lane; Carlie Lee; Paul Levy; Fiona Longmuir; Michelle Lovric; Stephen Mallinder; Shingi Mararike; Amanda Mason; Hugh Matheson; Alison May; Neil McCormick; Anthony McGowan; Barry McKinley; Moin Mir; Charlotte Mitchell; David Moats; Anton Mosimann; Rebecca

Myers; Holly Norman; James Peak; Andrew Perry; Charlotte Philby; Edvard Radzinsky; Amy Ransom; Amy Raphael; Hamilton Richardson; Susan Richardson; Lias Saoudi; Rebecca Schiller; Clare Seal; Matthew Shaw; Sarah Shephard; Michael Smith; Tatton Spiller; Andrea Stuart; Emma Svanberg; Harry Sword; James Thomas; Tom Tivnan; Luke Turner; Robin Turner; Hana Videen; Michael Volpe; Wendy Wason; Jen Wight; Sioned Wiliam; Hywel Williams; Mike Woodhouse; Liam Patrick Young

Chair: Patrick Janson-Smith

Foreign Rights Director / Literary Agent: Sam Edenborough (**L191**)

Literary Agents: Charlotte Atyeo (**L034**); Charlie Campbell (**L101**); Natalie Galustian (**L247**); Julia Silk (**L641**)

L289 Katie Grimm

Literary Agent
United States

Literary Agency: Don Congdon Associates, Inc. (**L178**)

Closed to approaches.

L290 Pam Gruber

Literary Agent
United States

pam.queries@irenegoodman.com

https://www.irenegoodman.com/pam-gruber
https://www.instagram.com/pjgruber/
https://twitter.com/Pamlet606

Literary Agency: Irene Goodman Literary Agency (IGLA)

ADULT
Fiction > *Novels*
Coming of Age; Commercial; Fantasy; Literary; Magical Realism; Romantic Comedy; Speculative

Nonfiction > *Nonfiction Books*

CHILDREN'S > **Fiction**
Graphic Novels: General
Middle Grade: Coming of Age; Commercial; Fantasy; Literary; Magical Realism; Romantic Comedy; Speculative
YOUNG ADULT > **Fiction**
Graphic Novels: General
Novels: Coming of Age; Commercial; Fantasy; Literary; Magical Realism; Romantic Comedy; Speculative

How to send: Email

Looking for adult, young adult, and middle grade fiction with literary voices and commercial hooks. She is particularly interested in layered fantasy, speculative fiction, fantastical realism, rom-coms, and coming-of-age stories with a twist. She is also open to middle grade and YA graphic novels, as well as select narrative non-fiction on lesser-known subjects. She would not be the best fit for prescriptive non-fiction, anthologies, potty humor, paranormal, or erotica.

L291 Hattie Grunewald

Literary Agent
United Kingdom

hattiesubmissions@theblairpartnership.com

https://www.theblairpartnership.com/literary-agents/hattie-grunewald/
https://twitter.com/hatteatime

Literary Agency: The Blair Partnership (**L066**)

Fiction > *Novels*
Book Club Fiction; Commercial; Crime; Historical Fiction; Thrillers; Upmarket

Nonfiction > *Nonfiction Books*
Lifestyle; Mental Health; Personal Development

Send: Pitch; Market info; Synopsis; Writing sample
How to send: Email

Represents commercial and upmarket fiction, including women's fiction, crime and thriller, historical and book club fiction. Also represents some non-fiction in the areas of lifestyle and personal development.

Authors: Marina Gerner; Luna McNamara

L292 Robert Guinsler

Senior Agent
United States

https://www.sll.com/our-team

Literary Agency: Sterling Lord Literistic, Inc. (**L662**)

Nonfiction > *Nonfiction Books*

Send: Query; Synopsis; Writing sample
How to send: Online submission system

L293 Masha Gunic

Associate Agent
United States

http://www.azantianlitagency.com/pages/team-mg.html
https://querymanager.com/query/MashaGunic

Literary Agency: Azantian Literary Agency (**L037**)

CHILDREN'S > **Fiction** > *Middle Grade*
Adventure; Comedy / Humour; Contemporary; Fantasy; Historical Fiction; Horror

YOUNG ADULT > **Fiction** > *Novels*
Commercial; Contemporary; Fantasy; High Concept; Historical Fiction; Literary; Magical Realism; Mystery; Science Fiction; Space Opera; Thrillers

How to send: Query Manager

Represents middle grade and young adult novels.

L294 Gurman Agency, LLC

Literary Agency
United States
Tel: +1 (212) 749-4618

assistant@gurmanagency.com

http://www.gurmanagency.com

Professional Body: Writers Guild of America (WGA)

Scripts > *Theatre Scripts*

How to send: By referral

Represents playwrights, directors, choreographers, composers and lyricists. New clients by referral only, so prospective clients should seek a referral rather than querying. No queries accepted.

Literary Agent: Susan Gurman (*L295*)

L295 Susan Gurman

Literary Agent
United States

Literary Agency: Gurman Agency, LLC (**L294**)

L296 Allan Guthrie

Literary Agent
United Kingdom

http://thenorthlitagency.com/our-friends-in-the-north/

Literary Agency: The North Literary Agency (**L530**)

Fiction > *Novels*: Crime

Send: Query; Synopsis; Writing sample; Proposal
How to send: Email

Has worked in the book trade since 1996 and has been a literary agent since 2005. He is also an award-winning novelist, freelance editor and former publisher. His main area of interest is crime fiction.

L297 Serene Hakim

Literary Agent
United States

https://www.pandeliterary.com/about-pandeliterary
https://twitter.com/serenemaria
http://aaronline.org/Sys/PublicProfile/52119398/417813

Literary Agency: Ayesha Pande Literary (**L036**)
Professional Body: Association of American Literary Agents (AALA)

ADULT
Fiction > *Novels*
Feminism; International; LGBTQIA; Literary; Middle East

Nonfiction > *Nonfiction Books*
Feminism; International; LGBTQIA; Middle East; Narrative Nonfiction

CHILDREN'S > **Fiction** > *Middle Grade*

YOUNG ADULT
Fiction > *Novels*
Fantasy; Feminism; International; LGBTQIA; Middle East; Realistic; Science Fiction

Nonfiction > *Nonfiction Books*
Feminism; International; LGBTQIA; Middle East

Send: Pitch; Author bio; Synopsis; Writing sample
How to send: Online submission system

L298 Tessa Emily Hall
Literary Agent
United States

Literary Agency: Cyle Young Literary Elite (**L152**)

L299 Carrie Hannigan
Literary Agent; Partner
United States

carrie@hgliterary.com

https://www.hgliterary.com/carrie
http://queryme.online/Hannigan

Literary Agency: HG Literary
Professional Body: Association of American Literary Agents (AALA)

ADULT > **Nonfiction** > *Nonfiction Books*

CHILDREN'S
Fiction
Graphic Novels: General
Novels: Comedy / Humour; Contemporary; Fantasy
Nonfiction > *Nonfiction Books*

How to send: Query Manager

L300 Stephanie Hansen
Senior Agent
United States

https://www.metamorphosisliteraryagency.com/about
https://querymanager.com/query/Query_Metamorphosis

Literary Agency: Metamorphosis Literary Agency (**L487**)

ADULT
Fiction > *Novels*: Thrillers

Nonfiction > *Nonfiction Books*

YOUNG ADULT > **Fiction** > *Novels*
Contemporary; Thrillers

Closed to approaches.

Represents authors with their debut novels and New York Times-bestsellers and has brokered deals with small presses, mid-size publishers, major publishing houses, foreign publishers, audio producers, gaming app companies, reading app companies, and film producers. Looks for Thrillers (YA & Adult); YA contemporary with unexpected antagonists; Prose that flows as smoothly as poetry; Unforgettable plot twists; Well-rounded characters; and Non-fiction with heart.

L301 Jana Hanson
Senior Agent
United States

https://www.metamorphosisliteraryagency.com/about
https://querymanager.com/query/agentjana18
https://twitter.com/agentjana18

Literary Agency: Metamorphosis Literary Agency (**L487**)

ADULT > **Fiction** > *Novels*
Cozy Mysteries; Romance; Suspense; Thrillers; Women's Fiction

CHILDREN'S > **Fiction** > *Middle Grade*

YOUNG ADULT > **Fiction** > *Novels*

Closed to approaches.

Seeking: romance (any pairing, any subgenre), YA, middle grade, cozy mysteries, women's fiction, suspense, and thrillers.

L302 Hardman & Swainson
Literary Agency
S106, New Wing, Somerset House, Strand, London, WC2R 1LA
United Kingdom
Tel: +44 (0) 20 3701 7449

submissions@hardmanswainson.com

http://www.hardmanswainson.com
https://twitter.com/HardmanSwainson

Professional Body: The Association of Authors' Agents (AAA)

Send: Full text; Synopsis
How to send: Email
How not to send: Post

Agency launched June 2012 by former colleagues at an established agency. Welcomes submissions of fiction and nonfiction, but no submissions by post. See website for full submission guidelines.

Assistant Agent: Nicole Etherington (**L208**)

Authors: Jennifer Barclay; Lilly Bartlett; Jackie Bateman; Alex Bell; Anna Bell; Jon Bounds; Oggy Boytchev; Paul Braddon; Cathy Bramley; Elizabeth Brooks; Isabelle Broom; Mark Broomfield; Tracy Buchanan; Meg Cabot; Elisabeth Carpenter; Simon Cheshire; Adrienne Chinn; Abby Clements; Helen Cox; Jeremy Craddock; Sara Crowe; Joshua Cunningham; Emma Darwin; Stuart David; Daniel M. Davis; Caroline Davison; Lisa Dickenson; Miranda Dickinson; Sarah Ditum; Carol Donaldson; Charlotte Duckworth; Simon David Eden; Rachel Edwards; Miranda Emmerson; Miguel Farias; Helen Fields; Rosie Fiore; Carrie Hope Fletcher; Giovanna Fletcher; Nicola Ford; Harry Freedman; Michele Gorman; James Gould-Bourn; Vanessa Greene; Kirsty Greenwood; Alastair Gunn; Tom Higham; Michael Jecks; Dinah Jefferies; Oskar Cox Jensen; Stuart Johnstone; Ishani Kar-Purkayastha; Elaine Kasket; Beth Kempton; Holly Kingston; Lucy Lawrie; Peter Laws; Christine Lehnen; Malinda Lo; Alice Loxton; Kevin Macneil; Katie Marsh; S R Masters; Cressida Mclaughlin; Ali Mcnamara; Susy Mcphee; Siobhan Miller; Kr Moorhead; Martina Murphy; Julien Musolino; Helen Naylor; Nigel Packer; Lauren Price; Philip C Quaintrell; Martina Reilly; Charlotte Rixon; Caroline Roberts; Patrick Roberts; Nick Russell-Pavier; Nikola Scott; Catherine Simpson; Emma Slade; Danny Smith; Karen Ingala Smith; Victoria Smith; Gareth Southwell; Elisabeth Spencer; Hollie Starling; Fiona Sussman; Eliska Tanzer; Sarah Tierney; Liz Trenow; Sarah Turner; Rebecca Wait; B P Walter; Louise Walters; Victoria Walters; Sue Watson; Alison White; Catherine Wikholm; Samantha Wilson; Laura Ziepe

Literary Agents: Therese Coen (**L134**); Hannah Ferguson (**L221**); Caroline Hardman (**L303**); Joanna Swainson (**L681**)

L303 Caroline Hardman
Literary Agent
United Kingdom

submissions@hardmanswainson.com
caroline@hardmanswainson.com

http://www.hardmanswainson.com/agents/caroline-hardman/

Literary Agency: Hardman & Swainson (**L302**)

Fiction > *Novels*
Book Club Fiction; Crime; Historical Fiction; Literary; Thrillers; Upmarket Commercial Fiction

Nonfiction > *Nonfiction Books*
Current Affairs; Feminism; Food; Health; Human Biology; Lifestyle; Medicine; Memoir; Narrative Nonfiction; Nutrition; Popular Science; Psychology; Wellbeing

Closed to approaches.

Direct submissions to the agent, but send to the submissions email address, not her individual email address.

Authors: Katie Allen; Jennifer Barclay; Lilly Bartlett; Tracy Buchanan; Elisabeth Carpenter; HS Chandler; Emma Christie; Daniel M. Davis; Sarah Ditum; Andrew Doig; Charlotte Duckworth; Miranda Emmerson; Miguel Farias; Louise Fein; Helen Fields; Eliese Colette Goldbach; Michele Gorman; Paula Greenlees; Alastair Gunn; Dinah Jefferies; Helen Joyce; Ishani Kar-Purkayastha; Elaine Kasket; Beth Kempton; Alice Loxton; Martina

Murphy; Helen Naylor; Jenni Nuttall; Julia Parry; Laura Pashby; Vanessa Potter; Martina Reilly; Charlotte Rixon; Nikola Scott; Joanne Sefton; Karen Ingala Smith; Victoria Smith; Miss South; Elisabeth Spencer; Kathleen Stock; John Tregoning; Liz Trenow; Rebecca Wait; Alison White; Catherine Wikholm; Ryan Wilson; Eleanor Wood

L304 Jessica Hare

Literary Agent
United Kingdom

jhare@theagency.co.uk

https://theagency.co.uk/the-agents/jessica-hare/
https://twitter.com/jcehare
https://instagram.com/jcehare

Literary Agency: The Agency (London) Ltd (**L009**)

L305 Esmond Harmsworth

Literary Agent; President
United States

https://aevitascreative.com/agents/

Literary Agency: Aevitas

Fiction > *Novels*
Crime; Historical Fiction; Horror; Literary; Mystery; Suspense; Thrillers

Nonfiction > *Nonfiction Books*
Business; Culture; History; Politics; Psychology; Science

How to send: Online submission system

Represents serious nonfiction books on topics such as politics, psychology, culture, business, history and science. For fiction, he represents literary fiction, mystery and crime, thriller, suspense and horror, and historical novels.

Authors: Ron Adner; Aaron Ahuvia; Devery Anderson; Erin Arvedlund; Dave Balter; Justin L. Barrett; Jean-Louis Barsoux; Christian Bason; Ann Bauer; David Benjamin; Jedediah Berry; Lucy Blake; Didier Bonnet; Giacomo Bono; Lisa Borders; Cyril Bouquet; Carolyn S. Briggs; Debra Bruno; Majka Burhardt; Tara Button; Jonathan Byrnes; Shawn Casemore; Paola Cecchi-Dimegli; Ulrik Christensen; Joshua Cohen; Nan Cuba; James Cullen; David Dabscheck; Niraj Dawar; Sandeep Dayal; Jeremy DeSilva; Brian Deer; Dan DiMicco; Barry C. Dorn; Ilana Edelstein; Elisabeth Elo; Robert Emmons; Mark Esposito; David Farbman; Keith Ferrazzi; Noah Fleming; Chad E. Foster; Rebecca Frankel; Seth Freeman; Jeffrey Froh; Samuel W. Gailey; Jeff Gothelf; Ronnie Greene; Olaf Groth; Sunetra Gupta; Lise Haines; Chris Hamby; George Harrar; Joseph M. Henderson; Michelle Hoover; John Horn; Erich Joachimsthaler; Jon Katzenbach; Fred Kiel; Kim Kleman; David Komlos; Andrew Lam; Adam Lashinsky; Junheng Li; Josh Linkner; Barbara K. Lipska; Tim Lomas; Courtney Lynch; Sean Lynch; Dario Maestripieri; David Magee; Leonard J. Marcus; Robert Martin; Grace Dane Mazur; Elaine McArdle; Jeffrey D. McCausland; Claire McDougall; Keith McFarland; Eric J. McNulty; Christopher Michaelson; Nathaniel Miller; Paddy Miller; Angie Morgan; Nick Morgan; Jim Morris; Mark Nitzberg; Howard Nusbaum; Barry O'Reilly; Nikolaus Obwegeser; Angela V. Paccione; Patricia Park; Deborah Plummer; Dan Pope; Sebastian Purcell; Anne Raeff; Amanda Ripley; Sara Roahen; Barbara Roberts; Victoria L. Roberts; Craig Ross; John J. Ross; David Rothkopf; Paul Rudnick; Laurie Ruettimann; Craig Russell; SHRM; Scott Sampson; R. Keith Sawyer; Bradley Schurman; Josh Seiden; Jens Martin Skibsted; Marc Solomon; Nick Sonnenberg; Mathew Sweezey; Sarah Stewart Taylor; Jennifer Tosti-Kharas; Terence Tse; Michael Veltri; Marga Vicedo; Tom Vossler; Michael Wade; Tony Wagner; John Wass; Luc Wathieu; Holly Watt; Thomas Wedell-Wedellsborg; Dan Willingham; Everett Worthington; Tomoko Yokoi; Hester Young; Sergey Young; Howard Yu; Dan Zehr

L306 Logan Harper

Literary Agent
United States

https://www.janerotrosen.com/agents

Literary Agency: Jane Rotrosen Agency

Fiction > *Novels*
Book Club Fiction; Crime; Domestic Suspense; Horror; Literary; Mystery; Psychological Thrillers; Upmarket; Women's Fiction

Send: Query
How to send: Online contact form

Seeking a variety of character-driven fiction and is particularly drawn to women's fiction, book club fiction, psychological thrillers, domestic suspense, horror, mystery/crime, upmarket and literary fiction. She is always eager to read and champion underrepresented voices and perspectives.

L307 Erin Harris

Literary Agent; Vice President
United States

eharris@foliolitmanagement.com

https://www.publishersmarketplace.com/members/eharris/
https://twitter.com/ErinHarrisFolio

Literary Agency: Folio Literary Management, LLC
Professional Body: Association of American Literary Agents (AALA)

ADULT
Fiction
Novels: Book Club Fiction; Family Saga; Folklore, Myths, and Legends; Historical Fiction; Literary Mystery; Suspense
Short Fiction: General
Nonfiction
Essays: General
Nonfiction Books: High Concept; Memoir; Narrative Nonfiction; Social Issues
YOUNG ADULT > **Fiction** > *Novels*
Contemporary; Fantasy; Speculative; Suspense

Send: Query; Writing sample
How to send: In the body of an email

L308 Samara Harris

Literary Agent
United States

Literary Agency: Robert A. Freedman Dramatic Agency, Inc. (**L592**)

L309 Jim Hart

Literary Agent
United States

jim@hartlineliterary.com

https://www.hartlineagency.com/agents-and-authors

Literary Agency: Hartline Literary Agency (**L311**)

Fiction > *Novels*
Amish Romance; Contemporary Romance; Historical Romance; Romance; Romantic Suspense; Science Fiction; Speculative; Suspense; Thrillers; Women's Fiction

Nonfiction > *Nonfiction Books*
Business; Christian Living; Leadership; Parenting; Self Help; Social Issues

Send: Query; Proposal
How to send: Email attachment

Serves both Christian and general markets. Currently most interested in non-fiction on the topics of Christian living, church growth, leadership, business, social issues, parenting, and some self-help. Non-fiction writers will need to show a strong platform in their area of expertise. He is not looking at memoirs or devotionals at this time.

Also looking at select fiction in these categories: suspense/thrillers, romance (contemporary, historical, suspense, Amish), women's fiction, and some speculative and sci-fi. Fiction writers should possess a strong and growing platform. He is not looking at children's or middle-grade fiction at this time.

Not looking at proposals for books that have been previously self-published. Please do not send proposals for books that include graphic language and sex.

Authors: Mark Baker; Chaim Bentorah; Robin Bertram; Shanna Brickell; Terri Clark; Jacqueline Gillam Fairchild; William P. Farley; Malinda Fuller; Heidi Gaul; PJ Gover; John Gray; Brandy Heineman; Chaka Heinz; Kim Taylor Henry; Bill Higgs; Dena Hobbs;

Jason Hobbs; Vivian Hyatt; Dalton Jantzen; Vicki Jantzen; Gary Keel; Troy Kennedy; Anita Knight Kuhnley; R.J. Larson; Joseph Max Lewis; Kathi Macias; Vicki McCollum; Stephenia McGee; Jairo de Oliveira; Kevin Ott; Ava Pennington; R.K. Pillai; Leigh Powers; Daniel Rhee; Penny Richards; Mary Selzer; Laurel Shaler; Marc Sikma; Adam Smith; Richard Spillman; John Stange; Buck Storm; Leah Weber; Hope Welborn; Susan Kimmel Wright; Beth Ann Ziarnik

L310 Joyce A. Hart

Literary Agent; President
United States

joyce@hartlineliterary.com

http://hartlineliteraryagency.blogspot.com

Literary Agency: Hartline Literary Agency (**L311**)

Fiction > *Novels*: Inspirational

Closed to approaches.

Over 35 years of experience marketing and promoting books. A pioneer of selling high quality fiction to the inspirational market.

Authors: Christy Barritt; Lorraine Beatty; Molly Noble Bull; Peggy Byers; Daniel Carl; Michael Carl; Dorothy Clark; Ace Collins; Dawn Crandall; Lena Nelson Dooley; Birdie Etchison; Suzanne Woods Fisher; Lisa Godfrees; Jeenie Gordon; Anne Greene; Pamela Griffin; Eleanor Gustafson; Ann Guyer; Lisa Harris; Sandra M. Hart; Rebecca Jepson; Melanie M. Jeschke; Mary Johnson; Jane Kirkpatrick; Zoe M. McCarthy; Rebekah Montgomery; Pola Marie Muzyka; Darrel Nelson; Melissa Ohden; Susan Titus Osborne; Carrie Fancett Pagels; Sam D. Pakan; Susan J. Reinhardt; Rita A. Schulte; Stacie Ruth Stoelting; Ward Tanneberg; Diana Taylor; Margorie Vawter; Jacqueline Wheelock; Nancy Willich; Courtney Young

L311 Hartline Literary Agency

Literary Agency
United States
Tel: +1 (412) 829-2483

http://www.hartlineliterary.com

Fiction > *Novels*

Nonfiction > *Nonfiction Books*

Costs: Offers services that writers have to pay for.

Specialises in Christian bookseller market, and particularly interested in adult fiction, nutritional, business, devotional, and self-help. No short fiction, screenplays, scripts, poetry, magazine articles, science fiction, fantasy, extraordinary violence, unnecessary profanity, gratuitous sexuality, or material that conflicts with the Christian worldview. Probably not the right agency for literary fiction, either. See website for detailed submission guidelines.

Note that this agency also offers literary services, which may be considered a conflict of interests.

Author / Editor / Literary Agent: Patricia Riddle-Gaddis (**L590**)

Author / Editor / Literary Agent / Proofreader: Linda S. Glaz (**L266**)

Author / Literary Agent: Cyle Young (**L754**)

Authors: Karla Akins; Mark Baker; Rick Barry; Chaim Bentorah; Robin Bertram; Kate Breslin; Shanna Brickell; Lance Brown; DeAngelo Burse; Raquel Byrnes; J'nell Ciesielski; Terri Clark; David E. Clarke; Karen Condit; Ben Conlon; Angela Couch; Susan F. Craft; Rhonda Dragomir; Jacqueline Gillam Fairchild; William P. Farley; Barbara Ellin Fox; Malinda Fuller; Heidi Gaul; Linda Gilden; Nicole Faye Golden; Samantha Gomolka; PJ Gover; John Gray; Janet Grunst; Hilary Hamblin Voni Harris; Julie Hatch; Brandy Heineman; Chaka Heinz; Kim Taylor Henry; Bill Higgs; Dena Hobbs; Jason Hobbs; K Denise Holmberg; Vivian Hyatt; Dalton Jantzen; Vicki Jantzen; Gary Keel; Troy Kennedy; Anita Knight Kuhnley; Dennis Lambert; R.J. Larson; Julie Lavender; A. D. Lawrence; Joseph Max Lewis; Delores Liesner; Ashley Ludwig; Kathi Macias; Jessica Manfre; Merliyn Howton Marriott; Cheryl Linn Martin; Joy Massenburge; Vicki McCollum; Dale McElhinney; Stephenia McGee; Donna Mumma; Naomi Musch; Luke Negron; Jessica Nelson Tiffany Nicole; Jairo de Oliveira; Kevin Ott; Candice Patterson; Ava Pennington; Carmen Peone; R.K. Pillai; Leigh Powers; Karen Prough; DeBora Rachelle; Maria Reed; Cindy Regnier; Daniel Rhee; Michael Richard; Penny Richards; Kathleen Rouser; Susan Browning Schulz; Colleen Scott; Mary Selzer; Laurel Shaler; Marc Sikma; Adam Smith; Laura Smith; Richard Spillman; Debbie Sprinkle; John Stange; Donnie Steven; Donnie Stevens; Patti Stockdale; Buck Storm; Beth Summitt; Ken Swarner; Tiffany Tajiri; Donn Taylor Evelyn Taylor; Pegg Thomas; Tom Threadgill; Kari Trumbo; Susan L. Tuttle; Jennifer Uhlarik; Hannah Vanderpool; Leah Weber; Denise Weimer; Karen Wingate; Maureen Wise; Susan Kimmel Wright; Frank Yates

Editor / Literary Agent: Diana Flegal (**L230**)

Literary Agent: Jim Hart (**L309**)

Literary Agent / President: Joyce A. Hart (**L310**)

L312 Jack Haug

Associate Agent
United States

Literary Agency: Aevitas

L313 Susan Hawk

Literary Agent
United States

susanhawk.submission@gmail.com

http://www.upstartcrowliterary.com/agent/susan-hawk/
https://twitter.com/@susanhawk

Literary Agency: Upstart Crow Literary (**L707**)

CHILDREN'S
Fiction
Chapter Books; *Middle Grade*; *Picture Books*
Nonfiction > *Nonfiction Books*

TEEN > **Fiction** > *Novels*

YOUNG ADULT > **Fiction** > *Novels*

Closed to approaches.

Represents work for children and teens only: picture books, chapter books, middle grade, and young adult, along with some non-fiction for young readers. She doesn't represent adult projects.

L314 Molly Ker Hawn

Literary Agent
United Kingdom

hawnqueries@thebentagency.com

http://www.thebentagency.com/molly-ker-hawn
http://www.twitter.com/mollykh
https://www.publishersmarketplace.com/members/mkhawn

Literary Agency: The Bent Agency (UK) (**L057**)

CHILDREN'S
Fiction
Graphic Novels; *Middle Grade*
Nonfiction > *Nonfiction Books*

YOUNG ADULT > **Fiction**
Graphic Novels; *Novels*

How to send: Email

I'm looking for middle grade and young adult fiction and graphic novels that are inventive, well-crafted, and rich with emotion. I'm also interested in non-fiction for readers ages 8–18. I like wit, but not snark; I prefer books that lean more toward literary than commercial, but of course, my perfect book neatly bridges the two. The fiction on my list all has a strong sense of authentic place, whether real or imaginary; I'm not the right agent for books with animal protagonists. Except maybe cats.

Assistant Agent: Martha Perotto-Wills (**L556**)

L315 Viola Hayden

Associate Agent
United Kingdom

http://submissions.curtisbrown.co.uk/agents/

Literary Agency: Curtis Brown
Literary Agent: Jonny Geller (**L255**)

Fiction > *Novels*

Nonfiction > *Nonfiction Books*

Send: Query; Synopsis; Writing sample
How to send: Online submission system

I am looking for confident writing that puts me at ease from the first page; a captivating voice or character, an exciting style, an unusual structure, an original premise or fresh take. A book that can't be replicated. If you have written a book like that – fiction or non-fiction – then it's on my wish list.

L316 David H. Headley

Literary Agent; Managing Director
United Kingdom

submission@dhhliteraryagency.com

http://www.dhhliteraryagency.com/david-h-headley.html
https://twitter.com/davidhheadley

Literary Agency: DHH Literary Agency Ltd (**L172**)

Fiction > *Novels*
General, and in particular: Crime; High Concept; Suspense; Thrillers

Nonfiction > *Nonfiction Books*
Biography; Food; History; Memoir; Politics; Popular Culture; Science

Closed to approaches.

Actively looking for: character-driven debuts and epic sweeping stories with big universal themes. Issue-driven crime and thrillers, high concepts and fear-inducing suspense. Thought-provoking stories, original narrative voices, uplifting fiction and emotional journeys – "stories that I don't want to end". Also accepts non-fiction submissions, from memoir, biography and history to politics, science, popular culture and food.

Authors: Kishan Devani BEM; Graham Bartlett; R.C. Bridgestock; Caraline Brown; Paul Burston; Paul Fraser Collard; M.W. Craven; John Curran; Rachael Featherstone; David Fennell; Fishlove; Essie Fox; Anita Frank; Erin Green; Lisa Hilton; Dixie Innes; Ragnar Jonasson; Katrín Júlíusdóttir; Jean Levy; Sean Lusk; Jo Lyons; Adrian Magson; Brian McGilloway; Janie Millman; Noel O'Reilly; Robert Scragg; Victoria Selman; Eleanor Tattersfield; Jo Thomas; Bar Tozino; L.C. Tyler; Stephen Walker; A. J. West; Clare Whitfield; Eva Björg Ægisdottir

L317 Duncan Heath

Literary Agent
United Kingdom

Literary Agency: Independent Talent Group Ltd (**L340**)

L318 Rupert Heath

Literary Agent
United Kingdom

Literary Agency: Rupert Heath Literary Agency (**L610**)

L319 Carol Heaton

Literary Agent
United Kingdom

http://greeneheaton.co.uk/agents/carol-heaton/

Literary Agency: Greene & Heaton Ltd (**L285**)

Fiction > *Novels*

Nonfiction > *Nonfiction Books*
Biography; Current Affairs; Gardening; Health; History; Travel

Closed to approaches.

Author Estate: The Estate of P.D. James

Authors: Stephen Anderton; Lewis Chester; Helen Craig; Charles Elliott; Michael Frayn; Richard Jenkyns

L320 Saritza Hernandez

Literary Agent
United States

Literary Agency: Corvisiero Literary Agency

Closed to approaches.

L321 Paloma Hernando

Associate Agent
United States

submissions@einsteinliterary.com

https://www.einsteinliterary.com/staff/
https://twitter.com/AgentPaloma

Literary Agency: Einstein Literary Management (**L194**)

ADULT
Fiction
Graphic Novels: High / Epic Fantasy; LGBTQIA; Magic; Romance; Science Fiction
Novels: High / Epic Fantasy; LGBTQIA; Magic; Romance; Science Fiction
Nonfiction > *Nonfiction Books*
General, and in particular: History; Media

CHILDREN'S
Fiction > *Middle Grade*: Comedy / Humour

Nonfiction > *Nonfiction Books*
General, and in particular: History; Media

YOUNG ADULT > **Fiction**
Graphic Novels: High / Epic Fantasy; LGBTQIA; Magic; Romance; Science Fiction
Novels: High / Epic Fantasy; LGBTQIA; Magic; Romance; Science Fiction

Send: Query; Writing sample
How to send: In the body of an email
How not to send: Email attachment

Her favorite books often have a bit of magic in them, and she loves being able to dive into any world, real or invented, presented on the page. She is looking for both graphic novels and prose fiction for YA or adult, including more mature stories, particularly ones that deal with difficult emotions and nuanced characters. She loves romance, particularly queer romance, science fiction that feels fresh, high fantasy, and middle grade with a good sense of humor. She is interested in non-fiction for all ages, especially anything that digs into media analysis or an event in history. She loves a story with a strong voice and solid construction.

L322 Danny Hertz

Literary Agent
United States

Literary Agency: The Cheney Agency

L323 Lane Heymont

President; Literary Agent
United States

https://www.thetobiasagency.com/lane-heymont
https://querymanager.com/query/1291
http://aaronline.org/Sys/PublicProfile/27203936/417813

Literary Agency: The Tobias Literary Agency (**L699**)
Professional Body: Association of American Literary Agents (AALA)

ADULT
Fiction > *Novels*
Commercial; Horror; Speculative; Women's Fiction

Nonfiction > *Nonfiction Books*
Celebrity; Culture; History; Popular Culture; Science

YOUNG ADULT > **Fiction** > *Novels*

Send: Author bio; Query; Market info; Writing sample
How to send: Query Manager

Represents a broad range of commercial fiction and serious nonfiction. In fiction, he is open to projects broadly defined as speculative fiction. He is most interested in horror defined however one defines it. This includes select young adult projects. He prefers contemporary settings and is always looking for own voices projects by BIPOC, LGBTQIA+, and other underrepresented cultures/identities in both fiction and nonfiction. In nonfiction, Lane acquires celebrity projects, science, cultural studies, history, and pop-culture.

L324 Sam Hiyate

Literary Agent; President; Chief Executive Officer
Canada

Literary Agency: The Rights Factory

Associate Agent / Author: Cecilia Lyra

Authors: Oscar Allueva; Ho Che Anderson; Michel Basilières; Margot Berwin; Charles Bongers; Alex Brueckmann; Varda Burstyn; Dave Butler; Timothy Christian; Elaine Dewar; Oonagh Duncan; Norine Dworkin-McDaniel; Benjamin Errett; Saad T. Farooqi; Bronwyn Fischer; Sara Flemington; Debbie Fox; Patricia Fulton; Rupinder Gill; Jesse Gilmour; Peter Goddard; Lee Matthew Goldberg; Shinan Govani; Lee Gowan; Alexandra Grigorescu; Karen Grose; Nadia Guo; Kamal Gupta; Nicole Hackett; Wes Hall; Denise Hearn; Alex Huntley; Chris Johns; Sam Juric; Andrew Kaufman; Michelle Kim; Sohan Koonar; Arkadi Kuhlmann; David Layton; David Leach; Barbra Leslie; Claire Letemendia; Emily Lipinski; Anneke Lucas; Natalie MacLean; Kiirsten May; Maureen Medved; Mark Milke; Elana Millman; Nathaniel G Moore; Sally Moore; Hal Niedzviecki; Rebecca Nison; Ell Orion; Brad Orsted; Kathryn Paulsen; Nick Pengelley; Katie Peyton; Bruce Philp; Barbara Radecki; Greg Rhyno; Alexandra Risen; John Semley; Leslie Shimotakahara; David Skuy; Michael Soussan; Robert Earl Stewart; Stephen Stohn; Jonathan Tepper; Diane Terrana; Chris Turner; Joanne Vannicola; Alex Varricchio; Maurice Vellekoop; Willow Verkerk; Cory Vitiello; Andy Walker; Kay Walker; Imogen Lloyd Webber; Emily Weedon; Jessica Westhead; Molly Roden Winter; Showey Yazdanian; E. Paul Zehr; Yvette d'Entremont

L325 Victoria Hobbs

Literary Agent
United Kingdom

https://amheath.com/agents/victoria-hobbs/
http://twitter.com/victoriajhobbs

Literary Agency: A.M. Heath & Company Limited, Author's Agents (**L003**)

Fiction > *Novels*
General, and in particular: Crime; Thrillers

Nonfiction > *Nonfiction Books*
General, and in particular: Cookery; Food; Health; Narrative Nonfiction; Nature; Politics

Agency Assistant: Jessica Lee

L326 Gail Hochman

Literary Agent
Brandt & Hochman Literary Agents, Inc., 1501 Broadway, Suite 2310, New York, NY 10036
United States

ghochman@bromasite.com

Literary Agency: Brandt & Hochman Literary Agents, Inc. (**L079**)
Professional Body: Association of American Literary Agents (AALA)

ADULT
Fiction > *Novels*: Literary

Nonfiction > *Nonfiction Books*
General, and in particular: Literary Memoir

CHILDREN'S > **Fiction** > *Novels*

Send: Query
How to send: Email

L327 Samuel Hodder

Literary Agent
United Kingdom

samuel@blakefriedmann.co.uk

http://blakefriedmann.co.uk/samuel-hodder
https://linktr.ee/samuelhodder

Literary Agency: Blake Friedmann Literary Agency Ltd (**L067**)

Fiction > *Novels*
Coming of Age; Contemporary; Crime Thrilllers; Fantasy; Historical Fiction; LGBTQIA; Literary; Psychological Suspense; Science Fiction; Speculative; Supernatural / Paranormal

Nonfiction > *Nonfiction Books*
Classics / Ancient World; Crime; Current Affairs; LGBTQIA; Narrative History; Nature; Personal Development; Political History; Politics; Popular Culture; Popular Science; Psychology; Social History; Visual Culture

Send: Query; Synopsis; Writing sample
How to send: Email

Keen to see a wide range of fiction and non-fiction books. In literary and contemporary fiction, loves distinctive voices, dark themes, and complex characters, coming-of-age novels, and novels that explore the loss of innocence, desire, deceit, class, or the world of work. Passionate about LGBTQIA+ stories and enjoys pitch-black or offbeat sense of humour.

L328 Jodie Hodges

Literary Agent
United Kingdom
Tel: +44 (0) 20 3214 0891

jhodges@unitedagents.co.uk

https://www.unitedagents.co.uk/jhodgesunitedagentscouk
http://twitter.com/jodiehodges31

Literary Agency: United Agents (**L704**)

CHILDREN'S > **Fiction**
Middle Grade; Picture Books
TEEN > **Fiction** > *Novels*

YOUNG ADULT > **Fiction** > *Novels*

Send: Query; Synopsis; Writing sample; Full text
How to send: Email attachment
How not to send: Post

"I enjoy strong, original storytelling and a unique voice. I have a passion for funny writing for 7-12s and also a penchant for the realisms of teenage life – be that gritty or hilarious – in writing for that age group. That said, I also love classic, epic adventure stories and a sprinkling of the fantastic."

"Additionally, I'm always searching for children's book illustrators or writer/illustrators with a contemporary, quirky style. A kind word of advice, though, please ensure your portfolio is ready for children's books. Make sure you're showing the best of yourself by showcasing the sort of illustration found in children's picture books in the UK."

Submit by email to the agent's assistant.

Agency Assistant: Molly Jamieson

Associate Agent: Emily Talbot (**L687**)

L329 Scott Hoffman

Literary Agent; Partner
United States

shoffman@foliolitmanagement.com

https://www.foliolit.com/agents-1/scott-hoffman

Literary Agency: Folio Literary Management, LLC

Nonfiction > *Nonfiction Books*
Business; Fitness; Health; History; Psychology; Social Issues; Wellbeing

Closed to approaches.

Send query by email with first ten pages. Assume rejection if no response within six weeks.

L330 Vanessa Holt

Literary Agent
United Kingdom

v.holt791@btinternet.com

Literary Agency: Vanessa Holt Ltd (**L709**)

L331 Millie Hoskins

Associate Agent
United Kingdom

https://www.unitedagents.co.uk/mhoskinsunitedagentscouk

Literary Agency: United Agents (**L704**)

Fiction > *Novels*
Commercial; Historical Fiction; Literary; Thrillers; Upmarket; Women's Fiction

Nonfiction > *Nonfiction Books*
Memoir; Narrative Nonfiction

Send: Synopsis; Writing sample; Proposal
How to send: Email

On the lookout for exciting debut authors of both commercial and literary upmarket fiction of any genre (excluding SFF), with a particular focus on women's fiction, thrillers and historical fiction. Especially interested in finding more great zeitgeist novels for our generation and discovering new experiences and places through people's writing. With regards to non-fiction, largely drawn to memoirs and narrative non-fiction with a distinct writing style, an incredible story, or an underrepresented voice or topic.

Authors: Amrou Al-Kadhi; Hina Belitz; LMK Berry; Sophie Ellis Bextor; Quentin Blake; Maggie Brookes; Emma Campbell; Brian Catling; Jessie Cave; Leah Cowan; JP Delaney; Rebecca Gibb; Susannah Hoffman; Alison Irvine; Lenka Janiurek; Katie Kirby; James McNicholas; Coco Mellors; Michelle Morgan; Bobby Palmer; Philip Pullman; Talulah Riley; LJ Ross; Kate Saunders; Mika Simmons

L332 Valerie Hoskins

Literary Agent
United Kingdom

Literary Agency: Valerie Hoskins Associates

L333 Amanda Fitzalan Howard

Literary Agent
United Kingdom

Literary Agency: AHA Talent Ltd (**L010**)

L334 Clare Hulton

Literary Agent
United Kingdom

Literary Agency: Clare Hulton Literary Agency (**L132**)

L335 Greg Hunt

Literary Agent
United Kingdom

Literary Agency: Independent Talent Group Ltd (**L340**)

L336 Hunter Profiles

Literary Agency
London
United Kingdom

info@hunterprofiles.com

http://www.hunterprofiles.com

Fiction > *Novels*: Commercial

Nonfiction > *Nonfiction Books*: Commercial

Send: Query; Author bio; Synopsis; Writing sample
How to send: Email
How not to send: Post

We specialise in commercial and narrative fiction and nonfiction. We only accept proposals by email. See website for submission guidelines.

Author / Literary Agent / Publisher: Humfrey Hunter (**L337**)

L337 Humfrey Hunter

Literary Agent; Publisher; Author
United Kingdom

https://www.silvertailbooks.com/author/humfrey-hunter/

Literary Agency: Hunter Profiles (**L336**)
Book Publisher: Silvertail Books (**P708**)

A former journalist and public relations consultant who is now a publisher and literary agent.

L338 Annie Hwang

Literary Agent
United States

https://twitter.com/AnnieAHwang
https://www.publishersmarketplace.com/members/hwangan/

Literary Agency: Ayesha Pande Literary (**L036**)

Fiction > *Novels*
General, and in particular: Literary

Nonfiction > *Nonfiction Books*
Memoir; Narrative Nonfiction

Closed to approaches.

Represents voice-driven literary fiction and select nonfiction. In particular, she gravitates toward subversive, genre-inflected literary fiction and impactful mission-driven narrative nonfiction that explores and grapples with the complex, fundamental truths of our world.

L339 ILA (Intercontinental Literary Agency)

Literary Agency
10 Waterloo Court, Theed Street, London, SE1 8ST
United Kingdom
Tel: +44 (0) 20 7379 6611

ila@ila-agency.co.uk

http://www.ila-agency.co.uk

Professional Body: The Association of Authors' Agents (AAA)

ADULT
Fiction in Translation > *Novels*
Nonfiction in Translation > *Nonfiction Books*

CHILDREN'S > **Fiction in Translation** > *Novels*

Closed to approaches.

Handles translation rights only for, among others, the authors of LAW Ltd, London; Harold Matson Co. Inc., New York; PFD, London. Submissions accepted via client agencies and publishers only – no submissions from writers seeking agents.

Company Director / Literary Agent: Clementine Ahearne (**L012**)

Literary Agents: Nicki Kennedy; Jenny Robson; Katherine West

L340 Independent Talent Group Ltd

Literary Agency
40 Whitfield Street, London, W1T 2RH
United Kingdom
Tel: +44 (0) 20 7636 6565

writersubmissions@independenttalent.com

http://www.independenttalent.com

Scripts
Film Scripts; *Radio Scripts*; *TV Scripts*; *Theatre Scripts*

Send: Author bio
How to send: By referral

Specialises in scripts and works in association with agencies in Los Angeles and New York.

Literary Agents: Oliver Azis (*L039*); Anwar Chentoufi (*L122*); Patrick Child (*L124*); Francesca Devas (*L169*); Alec Drysdale (*L182*); Humphrey Elles-Hill (*L201*); Olivia Gray (*L283*); Duncan Heath (*L317*); Greg Hunt (*L335*); Jago Irwin (*L346*); Georgia Kanner (*L369*); Paul Lyon-Maris (*L452*); Michael McCoy (*L480*); Jennie Miller (*L500*); Ikenna Obiekwe (*L538*); Will Peterson (*L561*); Lyndsey Posner (*L569*); Sue Rodgers (*L597*); Laura Rourke (*L608*); Alex Rusher (*L611*); Paul Stevens (*L664*); Jessica Stewart (*L666*); Jessica Sykes (*L683*); Jack Thomas (*L695*); Sarah Williams (*L738*); Hugo Young (*L755*)

L341 Ink and Colors Ltd

Literary Agency
Casella postale 10947, Cpd Milano Isola, 20110 Milano
Italy
Tel: +44 (0) 20 7558 8374

http://www.inkandcolors.com

ADULT
Fiction > *Novels*
General, and in particular: Commercial; Ethnic; Fantasy; Mystery; Romance; Science Fiction; Thrillers; Women's Fiction

Nonfiction > *Nonfiction Books*
General, and in particular: Adventure; Biography; Cookery; Crime; Current Affairs; Health; Memoir; New Age; Popular Culture; Psychology; Science; Spirituality

CHILDREN'S > **Fiction**
Novels; *Picture Books*

Send: Query; Full text; Self-Addressed Stamped Envelope (SASE)
How to send: Post; Email
How not to send: Email attachment

Costs: Offers services that writers have to pay for.

International agency with offices in UK and Italy, representing Publishing Houses, Authors and Illustrators all over the world. On our website you'll find the submission guide and all information.

Accepts submissions by post with SASE or queries by email (no attachments).

firstwriter.com note: This agency submitted their details for inclusion in our database in January 2007. Upon receiving a negative feedback comment in June 2007 they have made demands that we remove the negative comment and have also made threats of legal action. We have offered to post their response to the negative comment, but this has only been met by further threats of legal action.

Literary Agent: Andrea Sabbadini

L342 Amy Ireson

Literary Agent
United Kingdom

Literary Agency: The Narrow Road Company (**L520**)

L343 Dan Ireson

Literary Agent
United Kingdom

Literary Agency: The Narrow Road Company (**L520**)

L344 James Ireson

Literary Agent
United Kingdom

Literary Agency: The Narrow Road Company (**L520**)

L345 Richard Ireson

Literary Agent
United Kingdom

richardireson@narrowroad.co.uk

Literary Agency: The Narrow Road Company (**L520**)

Closed to approaches.

Do not approach directly. Approaches should be sent to the agency rather than individual agents.

L346 Jago Irwin

Literary Agent
United Kingdom

Literary Agency: Independent Talent Group Ltd (**L340**)

L347 Rachel Jacobson

Literary Agent
United States

https://aliveliterary.com/about/

Literary Agency: Alive Literary Agency (**L016**)

Nonfiction > *Nonfiction Books*

How to send: By referral

Enjoys helping authors hone their ideas, tap into their generative creativity, and share their message—because she wholeheartedly believes books can be a positive force for good in the world.

L348 The James Fitzgerald Agency

Literary Agency
PO Box 940, 70 Irish Road, Ranchos de Taos, NM 87557
United States
Tel: +1 (575) 758-2687

submissions@jfitzagency.com

https://jfitzagency.com

ADULT
Fiction > *Novels*
Crime; Popular Culture

Nonfiction
Illustrated Books: Popular Culture
Nonfiction Books: Adventure; Biography; Crime; Films; Food; History; Memoir; Music; Popular Culture; Religion; Socio-Political; Spirituality; Sport; TV

CHILDREN'S > **Fiction** > *Novels*

YOUNG ADULT > **Fiction** > *Novels*

Send: Full text; Synopsis; Author bio; Market info
How to send: Email attachment

Primarily represents books reflecting the popular culture of the day, in fiction, nonfiction, graphic and packaged books. No poetry or screenplays. All information must be submitted in English, even if the manuscript is in another language. See website for detailed submission guidelines.

Editorial Assistant: Anna Tatelman

Literary Agent: Dylan Lowy

Literary Agent / President: James Fitzgerald

L349 Janklow & Nesbit UK Ltd

Literary Agency
66-67 Newman Street, Fitzrovia, London, W1T 3EQ
United Kingdom
Tel: +44 (0) 20 7243 2975

submissions@janklow.co.uk

http://www.janklowandnesbit.co.uk
https://twitter.com/JanklowUK

Professional Body: The Association of Authors' Agents (AAA)

ADULT
Fiction > *Novels*
General, and in particular: Commercial; Literary

Nonfiction > *Nonfiction Books*

CHILDREN'S > **Fiction** > *Novels*

YOUNG ADULT > **Fiction** > *Novels*

Send: Query; Synopsis; Writing sample
How to send: Email

Send query by email, including informative covering letter providing background about yourself and your writing; first three chapters / approx. 50 pages; a brief synopsis for fiction, or a full outline for nonfiction.

Literary Agents: Rebecca Carter (**L110**); Claire Paterson Conrad (**L137**); Will Francis; Hellie Ogden (**L539**)

L350 The Jeff Herman Agency, LLC

Literary Agency
PO Box 1522, Stockbridge, MA 01262
United States
Tel: +1 (413) 298-0077

https://jeffherman.com

Nonfiction
Nonfiction Books: Business; Crime; Health; History; How To; Memoir; Multicultural; Narrative Nonfiction; Parenting; Psychology; Self Help; Spirituality
Reference: General

Send: Query; Pitch
Don't send: Proposal; Full text
How to send: Post

Send query by post with SASE. With few exceptions, handles nonfiction only, with particular interest in the genres given above. No scripts or unsolicited MSS.

Literary Agents: Deborah Levine Herman; Jeff Herman

L351 Carolyn Jenks

Literary Agent; Company Director
United States

carolyn@carolynjenksagency.com

https://www.carolynjenksagency.com/agent/CAROLYN-JENKS

Literary Agency: Carolyn Jenks Agency (**L106**)

Fiction > *Novels*

Nonfiction > *Nonfiction Books*

Send: Author bio; Writing sample; Pitch
How to send: In the body of an email

L352 JetReid Literary Agency

Literary Agency
151 1st Ave #257, New York, NY 10003
United States

http://www.jetreidliterary.com

Authors: Robin Becker; Bill Cameron; Gary Corby; Phillip DePoy; Stephanie Evans; Kennedy Foster; Lee Goodman; Dana Haynes; Patrick Lee; Thomas Lippman; Jeff Marks;

Warren Richey; Terry Shames; Jeff Somers; Robert Stubblefield; Deb Vlock

Literary Agent: Janet Reid (**L582**)

L353 JFL Agency

Literary Agency
48 Charlotte Street, London, W1T 2NS
United Kingdom
Tel: +44 (0) 20 3137 8182

representation@jflagency.com
agents@jflagency.com

http://www.jflagency.com

Scripts
Film Scripts; *Radio Scripts*; *TV Scripts*; *Theatre Scripts*

Send: Query
How to send: Email

Handles scripts only (for television, film, theatre and radio). Considers approaches from established writers with broadcast experience, but only accepts submissions from new writers during specific periods – consult website for details.

Authors: Humphrey Barclay; Liam Beirne; Adam Bostock-Smith; Tim Brooke-Taylor; Ian Brown; Grant Cathro; Paul Charlton; Gabby Hutchinson Crouch; Bill Dare; Tim Dawson; Martin Day; Ed Dyson; Polly Eden; Jan Etherington; Sinéad Fagan; Anji Loman Field; Phil Ford; Patrick Gallagher; Ted Gannon; Lisa Gifford; Rob Gittins; Ben Harris; James Hendrie; Wayne Jackman; Tony Lee; Richard Leslie Lewis; Jane Marlow; Jonathan Morris; Cardy O'Donnell; Jim Pullin; Jackie Robb; Graeme Rooney; Gary Russell; David Semple; James Serafinowicz; Pete Sinclair; Paul Smith; Fraser Steele

Literary Agents: Alison Finch (*L225*); Dominic Lord (*L440*); Gary Wild (*L735*)

L354 Jo Unwin Literary Agency

Literary Agency
West Wing, Somerset House, London, WC2R 1LA
United Kingdom
Tel: +44 (0) 20 7257 9599

submissions@jounwin.co.uk

http://www.jounwin.co.uk

Professional Body: The Association of Authors' Agents (AAA)

ADULT
Fiction > *Novels*
Nonfiction > *Nonfiction Books*

CHILDREN'S > **Fiction** > *Novels*

YOUNG ADULT > **Fiction** > *Novels*

Closed to approaches.

Handles literary fiction, commercial women's fiction, comic writing, narrative nonfiction, Young Adult fiction and fiction for children aged 9+. No poetry, picture books, or screenplays, except for existing clients. Accepts submissions by email. Mainly represents authors from the UK and Ireland, and sometimes Australia and New Zealand. Only represents US authors in very exceptional circumstances. See website for full guidelines.

Literary Agents: Donna Greaves; Rachel Mann (**L467**); Milly Reilly (*L583*); Jo Unwin (*L706*)

L355 Joelle Delbourgo Associates, Inc.

Literary Agency
101 Park St., Montclair, Montclair, NJ 07042
United States
Tel: +1 (973) 773-0836

joelle@delbourgo.com

https://www.delbourgo.com

ADULT
Fiction > *Novels*
Commercial; Fantasy; Literary; Mystery; Science Fiction; Thrillers; Women's Fiction

Nonfiction
Nonfiction Books: Biography; Business; Cookery; Crafts; Current Affairs; Food; Gardening; Health; History; Memoir; Mind, Body, Spirit; Narrative Nonfiction; Parenting; Popular Culture; Psychology; Science
Reference: Popular

CHILDREN'S
Fiction
Middle Grade; *Picture Books*
Nonfiction > *Middle Grade*

YOUNG ADULT
Fiction > *Novels*
Nonfiction > *Nonfiction Books*

Send: Query; Writing sample
How to send: Email
How not to send: Phone

Costs: Author covers sundry admin costs.

A boutique literary agency based in the greater New York City area. We represent a wide range of authors writing for the adult trade market, from creative nonfiction to expert-driven nonfiction, commercial fiction to literary fiction, as well as new adult, young adult and middle grade fiction and nonfiction.

Authors: Tanya Acker; Jennifer Lynn Alvarez; Heather Anastasiu; Lisa Anselmo; Thomas Armstrong; Sara Au; Frances Bartkowski; Suzanne Bohan; Lynn Kiele Bonasia; Michele Borba; Robert Bornstein; Elizabeth Reid Boyd; Nora Bradbury-Haehl; Anne Greenwood Brown; Gay Browne; Ariel Burger; Craig Carlson; Debbie Cenziper; Rachael Cerrotti; Marj Charlier; John Christianson; Tara L. Clark; Gay Courter; Nancy Cowan; Michelle Dempsey-Multack; Karla Dougherty; Nancy Dreyfus; Charity Elder; Chris Farrell; Marilyn Fedewa; Michael Feuer; Laura Berman Fortgang; Susan Forward; Philip Freeman; Terry Gaspard; John Gaudet; Susan Gilbert-Collins; Ann E. Grant; Jonathon Grayson; Brenda Greene; Beth A. Grosshans; Julie L. Hall; Kate Harding; Laura Hartema; Kristi Hedges; Holly Herrick; Roy Hoffman; Helaina Hovitz; Erik Forrest Jackson; Theresa Kaminski; Rachelle Katz; Joseph Kelly; Stephen Kelly; Brynne S. Kennedy; Nancy Kennedy; Sean Kingsley; Willem Kuyken; Mary Languirand; Missy Chase Lapine; Claire Lerner; Irene S. Levine; Alexandra Levitt; Lisa L. Lewis; Geralyn Lucas; Lauren Mackler; Juliet Madison; Kerstin March; David J. Marsh; Chuck Martin; Lama Marut; Carol Masciola; Emily J. O'Dell; Colleen O'Grady; Jim Obergefell; Elaine Neil Orr; Lindsey J. Palmer; Theresa Payton; Michelle Pearce; Scott Peeples; Julia Pimsleur; Gleb Raygorodetsky; Eliza Redgold; Michael Reichert; Ashley Rhodes-Courter; Paige Rien; Alexandra Rimer; Jillian Roberts; Tatsha Robertson; Lisa Romeo; Marilyn Simon Rothstein; Dale Russakoff; Michael Sadowski; Karla Salinari; Roberta Sandenbergh; Sue Scheff; Elisa A. Schmitz; Melissa Schorr; Ellen E. Schultz; Robert Sher; Heather Shumaker; Alexandra Silber; Pamela Slim; Laura Sobiech; Julie M. Stamm; Peter L. Stavinoha; Maryon Stewart; Nancy Rubin Stuart; Rachel Sulivan; Deborah J. Swiss; Jeff Sypeck; Ericka Sóuter; John Temple; Christopher Van Tilburg; M.D. Usher; Julie Valerie; Michael Volpatt; Caroline Welch; Susan Wels; Kristin M. White; Barrie Wilson; Ben H. Winters; Jon Wuebben; Gabra Zackman; Peter Zheutlin; Gabe Zichermann

Literary Agents: Carrie Cantor; Joelle Delbourgo; Jacqueline Flynn

L356 Johnson & Alcock

Literary Agency
Bloomsbury House, 74-77 Great Russell Street, London, WC1B 3DA
United Kingdom
Tel: +44 (0) 20 7251 0125

http://www.johnsonandalcock.co.uk

Professional Body: The Association of Authors' Agents (AAA)

Send: Query; Synopsis; Writing sample
How to send: Email attachment
How not to send: Post

Send query by email to specific agent. Response only if interested. Include synopsis and first three chapters (approximately 50 pages).

Chair / Literary Agent: Michael Alcock

Company Director / Literary Agent: Andrew Hewson

Literary Agent / Managing Director: Anna Power (**L571**)

Literary Agents: Liz Dennis; Charlotte Seymour (**L635**); Becky Thomas; Ed Wilson (**L741**)

L357 Jonathan Clowes Ltd

Literary Agency
10 Iron Bridge House, Bridge Approach,
London, NW1 8BD
United Kingdom
Tel: +44 (0) 20 7722 7674

admin@jonathanclowes.co.uk

https://www.jonathanclowes.co.uk

Professional Body: The Association of Authors' Agents (AAA)

Fiction > *Novels*

Nonfiction > *Nonfiction Books*

Send: Query; Synopsis; Writing sample
How to send: Email

Send query with synopsis and three chapters (or equivalent sample) by email.

Authors: Michael Baigent; David Bellamy; Oscar Brodkin; Angela Chadwick; Simon Critchley; Len Deighton; Maureen Duffy; Brian Freemantle; Miles Gibson; Victoria Glass; Rana Haddad; Francesca Hornak; Elizabeth Jane Howard; Ruqaya Izzidien; Richard Leigh; Doris Lessing; Mario Matassa; Clive McAlpin; Claire Miles; Teresa Forcades i Vila

Literary Agents: Ann Evans; Nemonie Craven Roderick; Cara Lee Simpson

L358 Jonathan Pegg Literary Agency

Literary Agency
c/o Workshop, 47 Southgate Street,
Winchester, SO23 7EH
United Kingdom
Tel: +44 (0) 1962 656101

submissions@jonathanpegg.com
info@jonathanpegg.com

https://jonathanpegg.com

Professional Body: The Association of Authors' Agents (AAA)

Fiction > *Novels*
Historical Fiction; Literary; Suspense; Thrillers; Upmarket

Nonfiction
Gift Books: Comedy / Humour
Nonfiction Books: Biography; Business; Comedy / Humour; Current Affairs; History; Lifestyle; Memoir; Nature; Popular Psychology; Popular Science

Send: Query; Synopsis; Author bio; Market info; Writing sample
How to send: Email

Aims to read every submission and respond within a month, but cannot guarantee to do so in all cases.

Literary Agent: Jonathan Pegg

L359 Jonathan Williams Literary Agency

Literary Agency
1 Urban Villas, Tivoli Terrace North, Dun Laoghaire, County Dublin, A96 YC95
Ireland
Tel: +353 (0) 1-280-3482
Fax: +353 (0) 1-280-3482

Types: Fiction; Nonfiction
Subjects: Literary
Markets: Adult

Costs: Offers services that writers have to pay for.

Agency also has agents in Holland, Italy, France, Spain, and Japan. Send SASE with IRCs if outside of Ireland. Charges a reading fee if a very fast decision is required.

Literary Agent: Rosney Mews

L360 Barbara Jones

Literary Agent
United States

bjquery@skagency.com

http://skagency.com/submission-guidelines/

Literary Agency: Stuart Krichevsky Literary Agency, Inc. (**L675**)

How to send: Email

L361 Joy Harris Literary Agency, Inc.

Literary Agency
1501 Broadway, Suite 2605, New York, NY 10036
United States
Tel: +1 (212) 924-6269
Fax: +1 (212) 840-5776

submissions@joyharrisliterary.com

http://www.joyharrisliterary.com

Professional Body: Association of American Literary Agents (AALA)

Types: Fiction; Nonfiction; Translations
Formats: Short Fiction
Subjects: Autobiography; Comedy / Humour; Commercial; Culture; Experimental; History; Literary; Media; Mystery; Satire; Spirituality; Suspense; Women's Interests
Markets: Adult; Young Adult

Closed to approaches.

Costs: Author covers sundry admin costs.

Closed to submissions as at October 2019. Check website for current status.

Send query by email, including sample chapter or outline. No poetry, screenplays, genre fiction, self-help, or unsolicited mss. See website for full guidelines.

Literary Agents: Joy Harris; Adam Reed

L362 Julie Crisp Literary Agency

Literary Agency; Editorial Service
United Kingdom

julieacrisp@gmail.com

http://www.juliecrisp.co.uk
https://querymanager.com/query/2079

Professional Body: The Association of Authors' Agents (AAA)

Fiction > *Novels*
Book Club Fiction; Crime; Fantasy; Historical Fiction; Science Fiction; Thrillers

Closed to approaches.

Costs: Offers services that writers have to pay for.

Open to submissions and looking forward to considering any fantasy, science fiction, historical, bookclub, crime/thrillers. Would be particularly pleased to consider diverse and own voices novels.

Authors: E. J. Beaton; Heather Child; John Gwynne; Sam Hawke; Lucy Kissick; Devin Madson; Den Patrick; C. T. Rwizi; Nick Setchfield

L363 Ria Julien

Literary Agent
United States

rj@goldinlit.com

https://francesgoldinliteraryagency.submittable.com/submit

Literary Agency: Frances Goldin Literary Agency, Inc.

How to send: Submittable

L364 K2 Literary

Literary Agency
Canada

https://k2literary.com
https://www.facebook.com/k2literary/
https://twitter.com/k2literary
https://instagram.com/k2literary

ADULT > **Fiction** > *Novels*

CHILDREN'S > **Fiction** > *Novels*

Closed to approaches.

Literary Agent: Kelvin Kong

L365 Ella Diamond Kahn

Literary Agent
United Kingdom

http://dkwlitagency.co.uk/agents/
https://twitter.com/elladkahn

Literary Agency: Diamond Kahn and Woods (DKW) Literary Agency Ltd

Closed to approaches.

L366 Jody Kahn

Literary Agent
United States

jkahn@bromasite.com

http://brandthochman.com/agents
http://aaronline.org/Sys/PublicProfile/7225167/417813

Literary Agency: Brandt & Hochman Literary Agents, Inc. (**L079**)
Professional Body: Association of American Literary Agents (AALA)

Fiction > *Novels*
Comedy / Humour; Culture; Literary; Upmarket

Nonfiction > *Nonfiction Books*
Culture; Food; History; Journalism; Literary Memoir; Narrative Nonfiction; Social Justice; Sport

Send: Query
How to send: Email

L367 Joanna Kaliszewska

Literary Agent
United Kingdom

https://www.thebksagency.com/about
https://www.thebksagency.com/submissions

Literary Agency: The BKS Agency (**L065**)

Fiction > *Novels*
General, and in particular: Book Club Fiction; Crime; Literary; Thrillers; Upmarket Commercial Fiction

Looking for all types of fiction but particularly interested in reading group, upmarket commercial, literary, crime and thriller.

L368 Kane Literary Agency

Literary Agency
United Kingdom

submissions@kaneliteraryagency.com
getintouch@kaneliteraryagency.com

https://www.kaneliteraryagency.com
https://www.facebook.com/kaneliteraryagency/
https://twitter.com/YasminKane3
https://www.instagram.com/YasminKane3/

Professional Body: The Association of Authors' Agents (AAA)

Fiction > *Novels*
Crime; Domestic Thriller; Noir; Police Procedural; Psychological Thrillers; Thrillers

Closed to approaches.

Currently only looking for: crime fiction, thrillers, police procedurals, psychological thrillers, and domestic thrillers. Bring on the noir!

Authors: Simon Arrowsmith; J Y Bee; Isabelle Brizec; Louise Cliffe-Minns; Sarah Harris; Vicki Howie; Zoe Marriott; Andrew Murray; Emily Nagle; Marisa Noelle

Literary Agent: Yasmin Standen

L369 Georgia Kanner

Literary Agent
United Kingdom

Literary Agency: Independent Talent Group Ltd (**L340**)

L370 Julia Kardon

Literary Agent
United States

julia@hgliterary.com

https://www.hgliterary.com/julia
https://twitter.com/jlkardon
https://querymanager.com/query/JuliaKardon

Literary Agency: HG Literary

Fiction > *Novels*
Literary; Upmarket

Nonfiction > *Nonfiction Books*
History; Journalism; Memoir; Narrative Nonfiction

How to send: Query Manager

L371 Maryann Karinch

Literary Agent
United States

mak@rudyagency.com

http://rudyagency.com

Literary Agency: The Rudy Agency (**L609**)

Fiction > *Novels*
Adventure; Crime; Historical Fiction; Mystery; Thrillers

Nonfiction > *Nonfiction Books*
General, and in particular: Business; Health; History; Investigative Journalism; Medicine; Sport

Send: Query
Don't send: Proposal; Full text
How to send: Email

Wants to see non-fiction projects from authors who are experts in their field, and that could be any field—business, investigative journalism, sports, history, health and medicine. Genre fiction is preferred. Grab her with your storytelling on the first page.

L372 Michelle Kass

Literary Agent
United Kingdom

Literary Agency: Michelle Kass Associates (**L493**)

L373 Kiran Kataria

Literary Agent
United Kingdom

https://www.keanekataria.co.uk/agents/

Literary Agency: Keane Kataria Literary Agency (**L379**)

L374 Kate Barker Literary, TV, & Film Agency

Literary Agency
London,
United Kingdom
Tel: +44 (0) 20 7688 1638

kate@katebarker.net

https://www.katebarker.net

Professional Body: The Association of Authors' Agents (AAA)

Fiction > *Novels*
Book Club Fiction; Commercial; Contemporary; High Concept; Historical Fiction; Literary

Nonfiction > *Nonfiction Books*
History; Lifestyle; Memoir; Nature; Popular Psychology; Science; Wellbeing

Closed to approaches.

I'm looking for commercial, literary and reading group novels: my taste in fiction is broad. I like strong stories, interesting settings (contemporary or historical) and high concept novels. I especially love books that make me cry. Please note that I do not represent science fiction, fantasy or books for children. Work in those genres will not be read. Non-fiction: I'm looking for smart thinking, history, memoir, popular psychology and science, nature writing, lifestyle and wellbeing. Big ideas and subjects that get people talking. I particularly enjoy helping experts translate their work for a general audience.

Literary Agent: Kate Barker

L375 Kate Nash Literary Agency

Literary Agency
United Kingdom

submissions@katenashlit.co.uk

https://katenashlit.co.uk
https://www.facebook.com/KateNashLiteraryAgency/
https://twitter.com/katenashagent
https://www.youtube.com/channel/UCAugaYbUoZXD7wldntZ8DwQ

Professional Body: The Association of Authors' Agents (AAA)

ADULT
Fiction > *Novels*

Nonfiction > *Nonfiction Books*: Commercial

CHILDREN'S > **Fiction** > *Middle Grade*

YOUNG ADULT > **Fiction** > *Novels*

Send: Query; Synopsis; Writing sample; Pitch; Author bio
How to send: In the body of an email
How not to send: Email attachment

Open to approaches from both new and established authors. Represents general and genre fiction and popular nonfiction. No poetry, drama, or genre SFF. Send query by email with synopsis and first chapter (fiction) or up to three chapters (nonfiction) pasted into the body of the email (no attachments).

Assistant Agent: Saskia Leach (**L418**)

Editor / Junior Agent / Proofreader: Robbie Guillory

Literary Agent: Kate Nash

Literary Agent / Managing Director: Justin Nash (**L521**)

Trainee Agents: Amy Gilroy (**L261**); Bethany Lucas (**L444**)

L376 Jade Kavanagh

Assistant Agent
United Kingdom

https://www.darleyanderson.com/our-team

Literary Agency: The Darley Anderson Agency
Senior Agent: Camilla Bolton (**L069**)

Author: Holly Craig

L377 Simon Kavanagh

Literary Agent
United Kingdom

Simon@miccheetham.co.uk

Literary Agency: Mic Cheetham Literary Agency (**L488**)

L378 Kay Peddle Literary

Literary Agency
London
United Kingdom

https://kaypeddleliterary.co.uk/
https://www.instagram.com/kaypeddlebooks
http://twitter.com/kaypeddle

Professional Body: The Association of Authors' Agents (AAA)

Literary Agent: Kay Peddle (**L554**)

L379 Keane Kataria Literary Agency

Literary Agency
United Kingdom

info@keanekataria.co.uk

https://www.keanekataria.co.uk/submissions/

Fiction > *Novels*
Book Club Fiction; Commercial Women's Fiction; Contemporary; Cozy Mysteries; Historical Fiction; Romance; Saga

Send: Query; Synopsis; Writing sample
How to send: PDF file email attachment

Currently accepting submissions in the crime, domestic noir and commercial women's fiction genres. No thrillers, science fiction, fantasy or children's books. Send query by email only with synopsis and first three chapters. Attachments in PDF format only.

Literary Agents: Kiran Kataria (**L373**); Sara Keane (**L380**)

L380 Sara Keane

Literary Agent
United Kingdom

https://www.keanekataria.co.uk/agents/

Literary Agency: Keane Kataria Literary Agency (**L379**)

L381 Sara O' Keeffe

Literary Agent
United Kingdom

submissions@saraokeeffe.co.uk

https://www.saraokeeffe.co.uk
https://aevitascreative.com/agents/#agent-7942
https://www.instagram.com/sarabookcrazy/
https://twitter.com/okeeffe05

Literary Agency: Aevitas Creative Management (ACM) UK (**L008**)

Fiction > *Novels*
Crime; Ireland; Science Fiction; Women's Fiction

Send: Writing sample; Query
How to send: Email

Has worked with major brand names in crime, science fiction and has a passion for Irish writing.

L382 Frances Kelly

Literary Agent
United Kingdom

Literary Agency: Frances Kelly Agency (**L236**)

L383 Eli Keren

Associate Agent
United Kingdom
Tel: +44 (0) 20 3214 0775

ekeren@unitedagents.co.uk

https://www.unitedagents.co.uk/ekerenunitedagentscouk
https://twitter.com/EliArich

Literary Agency: United Agents (**L704**)
Literary Agent: Sarah Ballard (**L043**)

Fiction > *Novels*
Commercial; LGBTQIA; Literary; Magical Realism; Speculative

Nonfiction > *Nonfiction Books*
General, and in particular: LGBTQIA; Popular Science

Send: Query; Synopsis; Writing sample
How to send: Email

In non-fiction, I am particularly interested in smart and engaging popular science. My own background is in chemistry, but I'm fairly omnivorous and happy to look at any non-fiction that grips me, be that science, history or something else. I enjoy books by writers completely obsessed with a niche subject who are skilled enough communicators to make the rest of the world fall in love with their passion too, whatever that passion might be. I am interested in any book that will change the world for the better.

In fiction, I'm happy to look at commercial, literary and anything in between across genres. I don't tend to work with science-fiction or high fantasy, but am open to grounded speculative fiction and magical realism.

I do not represent authors for children's and YA literature.

Authors: Marieke Bigg; Sarah Burton; Huho Greenhalgh; Ioan Marc Jones; Johanna Lukate; David Miles; Jem Poster; Claire Seeber; Sam White

L384 Kathleen Kerr

Literary Agent
United States

Literary Agency: Alive Literary Agency (**L016**)

L385 Ki Agency Ltd

Literary Agency
Studio 105, Screenworks, 22 Highbury Grove, London, N5 2ER
United Kingdom
Tel: +44 (0) 20 3214 8287

https://ki-agency.co.uk

Professional Bodies: The Association of Authors' Agents (AAA); Personal Managers' Association (PMA); Writers' Guild of Great Britain (WGGB)

Fiction > *Novels*

Nonfiction > *Nonfiction Books*
Coaching; Leadership; Personal Development

Scripts
Film Scripts; TV Scripts; Theatre Scripts

Send: Synopsis; Writing sample
How to send: Email attachment

Represents novelists and scriptwriters in all media. No children's or poetry, or submissions from writers in the US or Canada. Send synopsis and first three chapters / first 50 pages by email. See website for individual agent interests.

Authors: John Allison; Ahmed Baba; Fiona Barnett; Simon Bestwick; Linda Carey; Louise Carey; Mike Carey; Lucy Chalice; Jenny

Chamarette; Kate Charlesworth; Amber Chen; Daniel Church; Helena Coggan; Daniel Depp; Joanne Drayton; Diane Duane; Matthew Feldman; Kitty Ferguson; Marianne Gordon; Meredith Hart; Shaun Hutson; Luke Kondor; Paula Lennon; Ryan Love; Samantha MacLeod; Annie Machon; Sarah McManus; Robin Norwood; Anne Perry; Alex Ries; Adam Roberts; Phoenicia Rogerson; Angela Slatter; Gillian Spraggs; Jesse Stuart; Nicole Swengley; Catherine Webb

Literary Agents: Meg Davis (**L165**); Roz Kidd (**L386**); Ruth Needham; Anne C. Perry (**L558**)

L386 Roz Kidd

Literary Agent
United Kingdom

roz@ki-agency.co.uk

https://ki-agency.co.uk/contact

Literary Agency: Ki Agency Ltd (**L385**)

Scripts
Film Scripts; *TV Scripts*; *Theatre Scripts*

Accepts submissions of scripts for film, TV or theatre in any genre.

L387 Jessica Killingley

Literary Agent
United Kingdom

https://www.thebksagency.com/about
https://www.thebksagency.com/submissions

Literary Agency: The BKS Agency (**L065**)

Nonfiction > *Nonfiction Books*
Business; Personal Development; Self Help

Send: Query; Outline; Author bio
How to send: Online submission system

Looking for self help, personal development and business books from tomorrow's Thought Leaders. A strong personal brand, a great platform and a clear vision for the future a must!

L388 Natalie Kimber

Literary Agent
Canada

Literary Agency: The Rights Factory

ADULT
Fiction
Graphic Novels: General
Novels: Adventure; Commercial; Cookery; Historical Fiction; Literary; Science Fiction
Nonfiction > *Nonfiction Books*
Creative Nonfiction; Memoir; Popular Culture; Science; Spirituality; Sustainable Living

YOUNG ADULT > **Fiction** > *Novels*: Boy Books

Send: Query; Author bio; Writing sample
How to send: Email

L389 Robert Kirby

Literary Agent
United Kingdom

https://www.unitedagents.co.uk/rkirbyunitedagentscouk

Literary Agency: United Agents (**L704**)

Fiction > *Novels*
Adventure; Commercial; Speculative

Nonfiction > *Nonfiction Books*
Cultural History; Environment; Psychology; Science

Send: Synopsis; Writing sample
How to send: Email
How not to send: Post

I have an interest in science, psychology, cultural history and environmental issues. I enjoy gripping adventure fiction, speculative fiction and emotionally driven commercial fiction. Submissions should be sent to my assistant by via email, with a synopsis and first three chapters. Please do not send submissions via the post.

Associate Agent: Kate Walsh (**L720**)

L390 Kelly Knatchbull

Literary Agent; Company Director
United Kingdom

Literary Agency: Sayle Screen Ltd

L391 Knight Features

Literary Agency
Trident Business Centre, 89 Bickersteth Road, London, SW17 9SH
United Kingdom
Tel: +44 (0) 20 7622 1467

http://www.knightfeatures.com

Nonfiction > *Nonfiction Books*
Business; Military

Send: Proposal; Query; Self-Addressed Stamped Envelope (SASE)
How to send: Phone; Post; Online submission system

Make initial contact by phone or proposal through online submission system. If sending work by post, include SAE. Main areas of interest are: Motorsports, Graphic Novels, Business, History, Factual and Biographical/Autobiographical. Closed to fiction submissions as at February 2020.

Company Directors: Samantha Ferris; Gaby Martin

Managing Director: Andrew Knight

L392 Knight Hall Agency

Literary Agency
Lower Ground Floor, 7 Mallow Street, London, EC1Y 8RQ
United Kingdom
Tel: +44 (0) 20 3397 2901

office@knighthallagency.com

http://www.knighthallagency.com

Types: Scripts
Formats: Film Scripts; TV Scripts; Theatre Scripts
Subjects: Drama
Markets: Adult

Closed to approaches.

Note: Closed to submissions as at February 2020. Check website for current status.

Send query by post or email (no attachments). Only send sample if requested. Represents playwrights, screenwriters and writer-directors. Handles adaptation rights for novels, but does not handle books directly.

Authors: Simon Beaufoy; Jeremy Brock; Liz Lochhead; Martin McDonagh; Simon Nye

Literary Agents: Charlotte Knight (**L393**); Martin Knight (*L394*); Katie Langridge (*L406*)

L393 Charlotte Knight

Literary Agent
United Kingdom

http://www.knighthallagency.com/about-us/who-we-are/

Literary Agency: Knight Hall Agency (**L392**)

L394 Martin Knight

Literary Agent
United Kingdom

Literary Agency: Knight Hall Agency (**L392**)

L395 Kohner Agency

Literary Agency
9300 Wilshire Boulevard, Suite 555, Beverly Hills, CA 90212
United States
Tel: +1 (310) 550-1060

http://paulkohner.com

Closed to approaches.

The second oldest talent agency in Los Angeles, with a literary department boasting representation of 24 major publishing houses. No unsolicited submissions, ideas, or suggestions.

Literary Agents: Stephen Moore; Deborah Obad; Pearl Wexler

L396 Stacey Kondla

Literary Agent
Canada

Literary Agency: The Rights Factory

L397 Lizzy Kremer

Literary Agent
United Kingdom

lizzymanuscripts@davidhigham.co.uk

https://www.davidhigham.co.uk/agents-dh/lizzy-kremer/
https://publishingforhumans.com/
https://twitter.com/lizzykremer

Literary Agency: David Higham Associates Ltd (**L161**)

Fiction > *Novels*
Commercial; Literary

Nonfiction > *Nonfiction Books*

Send: Query; Synopsis; Writing sample
How to send: Email

Represents commercial and literary fiction and non-fiction. She was President of the Association of Authors' Agents from January 2018-2020 and was named the British Book Industry Awards 2016 Agent of the Year in May 2016. Always keen to discover compelling new voices in commercial and literary fiction.

Authors: Rachel Abbott; Julian Baggini; Annie Bell; Hester Browne; Jess Cartner-Morley; Anne-Marie Casey; Eve Chase; Charlie Connelly; Tish Delaney; Lucy Diamond; Lucy Dillon; Sareeta Domingo; Alicia Drake; Sarah Duguid; Kerry Egan; Ophelia Field; Ryan Gattis; Saska Graville; Dominic Green; Araminta Hall; Ali Harris; Paula Hawkins; Gavanndra Hodge; Euny Hong; Yuji Huang; Milly Johnson; Laura Kemp; Rachel Khoo; Jeremy Lee; Penelope Lively; Sadie Matthews; Louise Millar; Victoria Moore; Kate Morton; Laurie Owens; Katy Regan; Lucy Robinson; Claudia Roden; Jessica Stanley; Lulu Taylor; Sarah Vaughan; Rosie Walsh

L398 Mary Krienke

Literary Agent
United States

https://www.sll.com/our-team

Literary Agency: Sterling Lord Literistic, Inc. (**L662**)

Fiction > *Novels*
Literary; Upmarket

Nonfiction > *Nonfiction Books*
Culture; Health; Sexuality

Send: Query; Synopsis; Writing sample
How to send: Online submission system

Represents literary and upmarket fiction, voice-driven nonfiction, and memoir. She is particularly drawn to nonfiction that speaks to something essential and of-the-moment, especially work that engages with themes of culture, identity, sexuality, and health.

L399 Kruger Cowne

Literary Agency
Unit 7C, Chelsea Wharf, 15 Lots Road, London, SW10 0QJ
United Kingdom
Tel: +44 (0) 20 3124 1860

hello@krugercowne.com

https://www.krugercowne.com
https://twitter.com/krugercowne
https://www.instagram.com/krugercowne/
https://www.facebook.com/krugercowne
https://www.linkedin.com/company/kruger-cowne
https://www.youtube.com/user/KrugerCowneTalent

Professional Body: The Association of Authors' Agents (AAA)

Nonfiction > *Nonfiction Books*
General, and in particular: Celebrity; Entrepreneurship; Futurism; Journalism

How to send: Email

A talent management agency, with an extremely strong literary arm.

The majority of the works handled by the agency fall into the category of celebrity nonfiction. However, also regularly work with journalists, entrepreneurs and influencers on projects, with a speciality in polemics, and speculative works on the future.

Authors: Akala; Steven Bartlett; Boris Becker; Kelly Holmes; Lia Leendertz; Selene Nelson; John Simpson; Dave Stewart

L400 David Kuhn

Literary Agent; Chief Executive Officer
United States

https://aevitascreative.com/agents/

Literary Agency: Aevitas

Nonfiction > *Nonfiction Books*
Culture; Current Affairs; Entertainment; Food; History; Memoir; Music; Politics

Closed to approaches.

Represents nonfiction books that will educate, entertain, and enlighten in the areas of memoir, current events, history, politics, culture, style, food, music, and entertainment.

Authors: Hawa Abdi; Marina Abramović; Liaquat Ahamed; Shawn Amos; Pamela Anderson; Carl Sferrazza Anthony; Gustavo Arellano; Steven M. L. Aronson; Joana Avillez; Mark Bailey; Laura Ballance; Neil Barofsky; Luke Barr; Samara Bay; Elizabeth Beller; Joshua Bennett; Leslie Bennetts; Kate Betts; Zac Bissonnette; Kate Black; Charles Blow; Mark Boal; Scotty Bowers; Hamish Bowles; Steven Brill; Amanda Brooks; Holly Brubach; Jim Carrey; Pat Cleveland; Pan Cooke; Robyn Crawford; Kimberlé Crenshaw; Rudy Crew; Ted Danson; John Derian; Matthew Diffee; Liza Donnelly; Karen Duffy; Emily Eakin; Hugh Eakin; America Ferrera; Patricia Field; Lionel Friedberg; John Gapper; Gina Gershon; John Giorno; Robin Givhan; Lee Grant; Mark Green; Karl Taro Greenfeld; Joel Grey; Sam Gross; Michael Grynbaum; David Hallberg; Nick Haramis; David Haskell; Allegra Hicks; Linda Hirshman; Charlayne Hunter-Gault; Steve Israel; Jessica Kerwin Jenkins; Betsey Johnson; Bong Joon-ho; Elise Jordan; Henry Louis Gates Jr.; Sam Kashner; Kerry Kennedy; Ro Khanna; Jessi Klein; Yael Kohen; William Kuhn; Laetitia Ky; Jessica Lange; Amy Larocca; John Lithgow; Glamour Magazine; New York Magazine; Rookie Magazine; Ellen Malcolm; Bob Mankoff; Michael Maslin; Andrew McCarthy; Mac McCaughan; Duff McDonald; Lisa Miller; Janice Min; Isaac Mizrahi; Julianne Moore; Susan Morrison; Adam Moss; Kurt Newman; Jessye Norman; Mary Norris; Mark Oppenheimer; Tatum O'Neal; Rosie Perez; Jeremy W. Peters; Holly Peterson; Lindsay Pollock; Zac Posen; Parker Posey; Gerald Posner; Alice Quinn; Peter Rader; June Diane Raphael; Emily Ratajkowski; Evan Ratliff; James Reginato; Andrea Reusing; Michael Riedel; Michael Roberts; Nile Rodgers; Karin Roffman; James Romm; Paul Rudnick; David Salle; Felix Salmon; Elizabeth Samet; Kate Schelter; Paul Schneider; Nancy Schoenberger; Michael Schulman; Amy Schumer; Erich Schwartzel; Ramin Setoodeh; Elizabeth Shackelford; Sam Sheridan; Gabourey Sidibe; Colin Spoelman; David Steinberg; Greg Steinmetz; Sarah Thornton; Craig Unger; Dana Vachon; Jack Viertel; Jesse Wegman; Genevieve West; Kevin West; Senator Sheldon Whitehouse; Elettra Wiedemann; Casey Wilson; Elizabeth Winder

L401 Danya Kukafka

Literary Agent
United States

https://aevitascreative.com/agents/

Literary Agency: Aevitas

Fiction > *Novels*
Experimental; Literary; Speculative; Suspense; Thrillers; Upmarket

Nonfiction > *Nonfiction Books*
Crime; Culture

Send: Query; Writing sample
How to send: Online submission system

She is interested literary fiction with particularly propulsive storylines. She is seeking literary suspense, sophisticated thrillers, speculative fiction, and experimental fiction—she also loves true crime that feels attuned to today's cultural conversations, as well as upmarket literary fiction you can read in one gulp.

L402 The Labyrinth Literary Agency

Literary Agency
India

ac@labyrinthagency.com

http://www.labyrinthagency.com
https://www.instagram.com/labyrinthagency/

https://twitter.com/LabyrinthAgency
https://twitter.com/LabyrinthAgency

Fiction > *Novels*

Nonfiction > *Nonfiction Books*

Send: Synopsis; Writing sample; Author bio
How to send: Email

Costs: Offers services that writers have to pay for. Offers editorial and advice services to authors with whom they do not have a business relationship.

Literary Agent: Anish Chandy (*L117*)

L403 Natalie Lakosil

Literary Agent
United States

https://www.adventuresinagentland.com
https://www.irenegoodman.com/natalie-lakosil
https://twitter.com/Natalie_Lakosil
http://www.manuscriptwishlist.com/mswl-post/natalie-lakosil/
https://querymanager.com/query/natlak

Literary Agency: Irene Goodman Literary Agency (IGLA)

ADULT
Fiction > *Novels*
Cozy Mysteries; Crime; Thrillers; Upmarket Women's Fiction; Upmarket

Nonfiction > *Nonfiction Books*
Business; Parenting; Psychology; Science; Self Help

CHILDREN'S
Fiction
Chapter Books; *Middle Grade*; *Picture Books*
Nonfiction
Gift Books: General
Nonfiction Books: Biography; Comedy / Humour; Feminism; New Age; Social Issues
YOUNG ADULT > **Fiction** > *Novels*

How to send: By referral

Represents adult nonfiction, adult cozy mystery/crime, female-driven thrillers, upmarket women's/general fiction, illustrators, and all ages (picture book, chapter book, MG, YA) of children's literature, both fiction and nonfiction.

Assistant Agent / Junior Agent: Antoinette Van Sluytman (**L648**)

L404 Sarah Landis

Literary Agent
United States

https://www.sll.com/our-team

Literary Agency: Sterling Lord Literistic, Inc. (**L662**)

CHILDREN'S > **Fiction** > *Middle Grade*
Comedy / Humour; Contemporary; Fantasy

YOUNG ADULT > **Fiction** > *Novels*
Contemporary; Fantasy; High Concept; Historical Fiction; Mystery; Science Fiction; Thrillers

Send: Query; Synopsis; Writing sample
How to send: Online submission system

This agent is looking for middle grade and young adult books across all genres. She is particularly drawn to middle grade fantasy and contemporary with heart, humor, and magic. In the young adult space, she has an affinity for southern voices, high-concept plots, grounded sci-fi/fantasy, historical, mysteries and thrillers, and emotionally compelling contemporary.

L405 Lina Langlee

Literary Agent
United Kingdom

http://thenorthlitagency.com/our-friends-in-the-north/
https://twitter.com/LinaLanglee

Literary Agency: The North Literary Agency (**L530**)

ADULT
Fiction > *Novels*
Commercial; Crime; High Concept; Literary; Speculative; Thrillers

Nonfiction > *Nonfiction Books*

CHILDREN'S > **Fiction** > *Middle Grade*

YOUNG ADULT > **Fiction** > *Novels*

Closed to approaches.

Looking for books across genres: commercial fiction with a great hook, accessible literary fiction, speculative or high concept books that remain very readable, crime fiction that stands out, fun and moving Middle Grade, and 'big emotion' Young Adult. Across genres/age ranges, she prefers books that are fun and uplifting. In terms of non-fiction, she is interested either in 'the small made big' or 'the big made small': specialists that can make really niche subjects accessible and interesting to a wider market, or deeply personal accounts of the big issues we might all one day tackle. In general, does not offer representation to US-based authors.

L406 Katie Langridge

Literary Agent
United Kingdom

Literary Agency: Knight Hall Agency (**L392**)

L407 Becca Langton

Literary Agent
United Kingdom

https://www.darleyanderson.com/our-team

Literary Agency: The Darley Anderson Agency

CHILDREN'S > **Fiction**
Graphic Novels: General
Middle Grade: General, and in particular: Adventure
TEEN > **Fiction** > *Novels*

YOUNG ADULT > **Fiction** > *Novels*
General, and in particular: Contemporary; Fantasy; LGBTQIA; Romantic Comedy

Send: Query; Synopsis; Writing sample; Self-Addressed Stamped Envelope (SASE)
How to send: Word file email attachment; PDF file email attachment; Post

Looking for new stories in all shapes and sizes, from middle grade and graphic novel to teen and YA fiction. Reads widely but loves books with compelling voices, twists and brave new ideas. In YA she would love to see some Queer fantasy, rom-coms with plenty of 'com' and contemporary stories told from a new perspective. For younger readers she love/hates the books that make her cry and is on the search for characters that stay with her long after the final page. High-stakes adventure stories are welcome as are graphic novels and books that make you want to read just one more chapter…

L408 Linda Langton

Literary Agent
United States

https://langtonsinternational.com/langtons-international/about-us/
https://www.linkedin.com/in/lindalangton

Literary Agency: Langtons International (**L409**)

L409 Langtons International

Literary Agency
United States

llangton@earthlink.net
langtonsinternational@gmail.com

https://langtonsinternational.com
https://www.facebook.com/LangtonsInternationalAgency

Fiction > *Novels*
Literary; Mystery; Thrillers; Women's Fiction

Nonfiction > *Nonfiction Books*
Business; Crime; Memoir; Self Help

Literary agency based in New York, specializing in business, self-help, memoir, and true crime, as well as mystery, thrillers, women's and literary fiction.

Literary Agent: Linda Langton (**L408**)

L410 Elena Langtry

Literary Agent
United Kingdom

https://cmm.agency/about-us.php

Literary Agency: Coombs Moylett & Maclean Literary Agency (**L139**)

Fiction > *Novels*
Commercial Women's Fiction; Psychological Thrillers

Nonfiction > *Nonfiction Books*
Crime; Popular Science

How to send: Online submission system

L411 Katherine Latshaw

Literary Agent; Vice President
United States

klatshaw@foliolitmanagement.com

https://www.foliolit.com/agents-1/katherine-latshaw

Literary Agency: Folio Literary Management, LLC

ADULT

Fiction > *Novels*

Nonfiction
Essays: General
Illustrated Books: General
Nonfiction Books: Commercial; Cookery; Feminism; Health; Lifestyle; Memoir; Narrative Nonfiction; Popular Culture; Prescriptive Nonfiction; Wellbeing

CHILDREN'S > **Fiction** > *Middle Grade*

YOUNG ADULT > **Fiction** > *Novels*

How to send: Email

L412 Jennifer Laughran

Senior Agent
United States

jennL@andreabrownlit.com

https://www.jenniferlaughran.com
https://www.andreabrownlit.com/Team/Jennifer-Laughran
http://twitter.com/literaticat
http://www.instagram.com/literaticat
https://querymanager.com/JenniferLaughran
https://www.publishersmarketplace.com/members/jennla/
https://www.manuscriptwishlist.com/mswl-post/jennifer-laughran/

Literary Agency: Andrea Brown Literary Agency, Inc.
Professional Body: Association of American Literary Agents (AALA)

CHILDREN'S > **Fiction** > *Middle Grade*

YOUNG ADULT > **Fiction** > *Novels*

Send: Query; Author bio; Writing sample
How to send: Query Manager

Always on the lookout for sparkling YA and middle grade fiction with unusual and unforgettable characters and vivid settings, she is drawn to nearly all kinds of books, whether realistic comedies or richly imagined magical adventures. However, the common thread in her favorite stories is an offbeat world-view.

L413 Laura Dail Literary Agency

Literary Agency
121 West 27th Street, Suite 1201, New York, NY 10001
United States
Tel: +1 (212) 239-7477

queries@ldlainc.com

http://www.ldlainc.com
https://twitter.com/LDLiterary
https://www.instagram.com/lauradaillit/

How to send: Query Manager

Send query through online submission system only. Query one agent at a time with one project at a time.

Literary Agent / President: Laura Dail (**L154**)

Literary Agents: Elana Roth Parker (**L550**); Carrie Pestritto (**L559**)

L414 Laxfield Literary Associates

Literary Agency
United Kingdom

submissions@laxfieldliterary.com

https://laxfieldliterary.com

Professional Body: The Association of Authors' Agents (AAA)

Fiction > *Novels*
Commercial; Literary

Nonfiction > *Nonfiction Books*
Creative Nonfiction; Memoir; Nature; Travel

Send: Query; Synopsis; Writing sample; Author bio; Outline
How to send: Word file email attachment

We are looking for fiction and non-fiction of the highest quality. We are keen to receive literary and commercial fiction. We are also looking for non-fiction, particularly creative non-fiction, travel writing, memoir and nature writing. We do not represent poetry, plays, children's books or YA.

L415 Veronica Lazar

Literary Agent
United Kingdom

https://www.imdb.com/name/nm4400468/

Literary Agency: AVAnti Productions & Management (**L035**)

L416 Sarah Lazin

Literary Agent
United States

https://aevitascreative.com/agents/
http://lazinbooks.com/about-us/
https://aaronline.wildapricot.org/Sys/PublicProfile/1715266/417813

Literary Agencies: Sarah Lazin Books (**L620**); Aevitas
Professional Body: Association of American Literary Agents (AALA)

Nonfiction
Nonfiction Books: Biography; Current Affairs; Health; History; Journalism; Memoir; Parenting; Politics; Popular Culture; Social Issues
Reference: General

How to send: By referral

Represents a range of nonfiction writers working in fields such as popular culture, biography, history, politics, journalism, memoir, parenting, health, practical nonfiction, contemporary affairs, social issues, and general reference. She also handles fiction from literary works and short stories to commercial novels, and represents some photographers and illustrators and several estates. She accepts submissions through referral only.

L417 LBA Books Ltd

Literary Agency
91 Great Russell Street, London, WC1B 3PS
United Kingdom
Tel: +44 (0) 20 7637 1234

info@lbabooks.com

http://www.lbabooks.com

Professional Body: The Association of Authors' Agents (AAA)

Send query with synopsis and first three chapters to specific agent by email only. See website for specific agents' interests and email addresses. No scripts, short stories, or poetry.

Authors: Will Adams; Emily Adlam; Jaimie Admans; Emad Ahmed; Sarah Alderson; Dominique Antiglio; Helen Arney; Lizzy Barber; Kerry Barrett; James Becker; A.L. Bird; Darcie Boleyn; Christina Bradley; Jason Bray; Fern Britton; Amanda Brooke; Catherine Brookes; Julie Brunelle; Charlotte Butterfield; Anna Carey; Jo Carnegie; Lucie Cave; Rebecca Chance; Catherine Chang; James Cheshire; George Clarke; Rosemary Conley; Erin Connor; Gennaro Contaldo; Emma Cooper; Josephine Cox; Mason Cross; Louise Curtis; A.M. Dean; Susie Donkin; Kim Donovan; Hannah Doyle; Elizabeth Drummond; Chloe Duckworth; Katherine Dyson; Georgia Fancett; Dan Farnworth; Liz Fenwick; Judy Finnigan; Bea Fitzgerald; Nick Foulkes; Mark Frary; Daniel Freeman; Susan Gee; David Gibbins; Lucy Goacher; Jane Gordon; Tom Grass; Mark Griffin; Michael Gustafson; Kate Hackworthy; Rachel Hamilton; Richard Hammond; Isabella Harcourt; Duncan Harding; Fiona Harper; Natalie Heaton; Matt Hilton; John Humphrys; Anam Iqbal; Holly Jade; Jessica Jarlvi; Sarah Johnson; Annabel Kantaria; Lesley Kara; Eva Katzler; Jenni Keer; Simon Kernick; Emily Kerr; Ella King; Margaret Kirk; Catherine

Kirwan; Victoria Lamb; Amy Lavelle; Georgina Lees; Guy Leschziner; Susan Lewis; Lauren Libbert; Agnes Light; Freda Lightfoot; Jane Linfoot; Amy Lloyd; Rachael Lucas; Dee MacDonald; Richard Madeley; Ian Marber; Tom Marcus; Sam Masters; James May; Julie Mayhew; Marina McCarron; Colin McDowell; Lisa Medved; David Meikle; Gavin Menzies; Ben Miller; Nicole Mones; Michael Morley; Louise Morrish; Anthony Mosawi; Elizabeth Moss; Steve Mould; Andrea Mullaney; Faya Nilsson; Jen Offord; Karen Osman; Sue Palmer; Angelique Panagos; S.A. Patrick; Seth Patrick; Andrew Pepper; Ivor Peters; Melanie Phillips; Gervase Phinn; Catherine Piddington; Ande Pliego; Kate Poels; Anna Pointer; Richard Porter; Esther Rantzen; Louisa Reid; Madeleine Reiss; Gillian Richmond; Alice Roberts; Bernadette Robinson; Amber Rose; Mike Rossiter; Simon Scarrow; Super Scrimpers; Heidi Shertok; Colin Shindler; Celia Silvani; N J Simmonds; Fleur Sinclair; Jane Monckton Smith; Jack Steel; Zara Stoneley; Lucy Strange; Heidi Swain; Karen Swan; Joe Swift; Sophie Tanner; Rachel de Thame; Alan Titchmarsh; Andy Torbet; Jon Trace; Jonathan Trigell; David Turner; Anna Turns; Oliver Uberti; Phil Vickery; Ria Voros; Claire Wade; Jennifer Wells; Kate Winter; Tamsin Winter; Terry Wogan; Dalton Wong; Peter Wood; Katherine Woodfine; Fiona Woodifield; Sally Worboyes; Emma Yarlett

Literary Agents: Luigi Bonomi (**L070**); Louise Lamont; Amanda Preston (**L575**); Hannah Schofield (**L626**)

L418 Saskia Leach

Assistant Agent
United Kingdom

https://katenashlit.co.uk/people/
https://twitter.com/saskialeach_

Literary Agency: Kate Nash Literary Agency (**L375**)

Fiction > *Novels*

Send: Query; Pitch; Author bio; Synopsis; Writing sample
How to send: In the body of an email

Enjoys reading a wide range of genres and is fascinated by stories written from multiple perspectives. She also loves books which feature complex and dynamic characters.

L419 Tom Drake Lee

Associate Agent
United Kingdom

tdl.submission@dhhliteraryagency.com

http://www.dhhliteraryagency.com/tom-drake-lee.html
http://twitter.com/tomdrakelee

Literary Agency: DHH Literary Agency Ltd (**L172**)

Fiction > *Novels*
Commercial; Literary

Nonfiction > *Nonfiction Books*
History; Memoir; Nature; Popular Science

Closed to approaches.

Looking for commercial literary and genre fiction which tells stories and illuminates the human condition; fiction which has compelling plot, narrative and characters.

Also looking for non-fiction which tells us more about the world around us; nature writing, popular science, history and memoir.

No screenplays, short story / novellas, children's books / YA or Sci-Fi/Fantasy.

Authors: Howard Colyer; Michael Delahaye; Valerie Jack; Diana Kessler; Robin Laurance; Rachel Meller; Valerie O'Riordan; Iain Rowan; Richard Stirling; Amanda Tuke

L420 Jordan Lees

Associate Agent
United Kingdom

jordansubmissions@theblairpartnership.com

https://www.theblairpartnership.com/literary-agents/jordan-lees/

Literary Agency: The Blair Partnership (**L066**)

Fiction > *Novels*
Book Club Fiction; Commercial; Crime; Dark; High Concept; Historical Fiction; Literary; Thrillers; Upmarket

Nonfiction > *Nonfiction Books*
General, and in particular: Crime

Does not want:

Fiction > *Novels*: Spy Thrilllers

Send: Synopsis; Writing sample; Pitch; Market info
How to send: Email

Represents crime and thrillers, book club fiction, historical fiction and literary fiction, as well as true crime and non-fiction written by journalists and experts in their respective fields. Typically drawn to writing with a darker and/or upmarket edge, and open to anything high-concept or speculative.

Authors: Bana Alabed; JJ Arcanjo; YolanDa Brown; Tom Carlisle; Dawn Coulter-Cruttenden; Helena Duggan; Emma Farrarons; William Friend; Toby Gutteridge; Oli Hyatt; Ruth Kelly; Scott Kershaw; Kieran Larwood; Elspeth Latimer; The Urban Legend; John Lutz; Dan Malakin; Major Scotty Mills; Markus Motum; Rogba Payne; Daisy Pearce; Stephen Ronson; Babita Sharma; Tom Spencer; P. A. Staff; Nicki Thornton

L421 Lindsay Leggett

Associate Agent
Canada

Literary Agency: The Rights Factory

ADULT > **Fiction**
Graphic Novels: General
Novels: Horror; LGBTQIA; Romance; Thrillers

CHILDREN'S > **Fiction** > *Middle Grade*

YOUNG ADULT > **Fiction** > *Novels*

Closed to approaches.

L422 Paul S. Levine

Literary Agent
United States

paul@paulslevinelit.com

Literary Agency: Paul S. Levine Literary Agency (**L552**)

L423 Sarah Levitt

Literary Agent
New York
United States

https://aevitascreative.com/agents/

Literary Agency: Aevitas

Fiction > *Novels*: Literary

Nonfiction > *Nonfiction Books*
Comedy / Humour; History; Journalism; Memoir; Narrative Nonfiction; Popular Culture; Popular Science

Send: Author bio; Outline; Market info; Writing sample
How to send: Online submission system

Most interested in narrative nonfiction in the areas of popular science, big ideas, history, humor, pop culture, memoir, and reportage, in addition to voice-driven literary fiction with a bold plot and fresh, imaginative characters. She's excited by strong female and underrepresented voices, the strange and speculative, and projects that ignite cultural conversation.

Authors: Ruha Benjamin; Laura Bliss; Marc Bojanowski; Elizabeth Brooks; Adam Chandler; Bloomberg CityLab; Daniel M. Davis; Sarah Ditum; Baz Dreisinger; Sarah Duenwald; Mieke Eerkens; Claire Evans; Marion Gibson; Annette Giesecke; Eliese Colette Goldbach; Elyse Graham; Wade Graham; Ayanna Howard; Tung-Hui Hu; Saru Jayaraman; Nancy McSharry Jensen; Doma Mahmoud; Sara Majka; Antonia Malchik; Maggie Mertens; Ann Morgan; Laine Nooney; Jenni Nuttall; Abigail Pogrebin; Letty Cottin Pogrebin; Amelia Possanza; Steve Ramirez; Charlotte Rixon; Anjali Sachdeva; Suzanne Scanlon; Kathleen Sheppard; Lauren Shields; Ly Ky Tran; Phuc Tran; Sarah Turner; Sarah Vallance; Lizzie Wade; Peter von Ziegesar

L424 Barbara Levy

Literary Agent
United Kingdom

Literary Agency: Barbara Levy Literary Agency (**L044**)

L425 Alison Lewis

Literary Agent
United States

atl@goldinlit.com

https://www.goldinlit.com/alison-lewis
https://twitter.com/atatelewis

Literary Agency: Frances Goldin Literary Agency, Inc.

Fiction > *Novels*: Literary

Nonfiction > *Nonfiction Books*
Cultural Criticism; History; Journalism; Literary Memoir; Science

Send: Query; Writing sample; Proposal
How to send: Email

Represents a wide range of nonfiction, spanning journalism, cultural criticism, history, science, literary memoir, and essays, as well as select literary fiction. She is particularly drawn to writers with a distinctive voice and perspective, a sense of social or political imagination and responsibility, scholars and researchers who can translate their expertise for a wide readership, and writers pushing the boundaries of form, preconceived ideas, and histories of representation in literature.

L426 Kayla Lightner

Literary Agent
United States

https://www.pandeliterary.com/our-agents-pandeliterary
https://twitter.com/LightnerKayla

Literary Agency: Ayesha Pande Literary (**L036**)
Professional Body: Association of American Literary Agents (AALA)

Fiction
Graphic Novels: General
Novels: Comedy / Humour; Contemporary; Crime; Domestic Suspense; Dystopian Fiction; Fantasy; Gothic; Historical Fiction; Horror; Literary; Magical Realism; Psychological Horror; Science Fiction; Thrillers; Upmarket
Nonfiction > *Nonfiction Books*
Comedy / Humour; Crime; Family Saga; Journalism; Memoir; Narrative Nonfiction; Sport

Closed to approaches.

I love discovering diverse and fresh new perspectives across commercial fiction, literary + upmarket fiction, non-fiction, and graphic novels. I'm particularly a fan of authors with singular voices that masterfully straddle the line between story-telling and teaching readers something new (about themselves, their communities, or the world we live in).

L427 Limelight Management

Literary Agency
10 Filmer Mews, 75 Filmer Road, London, SW6 7BZ
United Kingdom
Tel: +44 (0) 20 7384 9950

mail@limelightmanagement.com

https://www.limelightmanagement.com
https://www.facebook.com/pages/Limelight-Celebrity-Management-Ltd/399328580099859?fref=ts
https://twitter.com/Fionalimelight
https://www.youtube.com/channel/UCCmxquRk_blKqjR8jKRryFA
https://instagram.com/limelightcelebritymanagement/
https://www.linkedin.com/company-beta/11219861/

Professional Body: The Association of Authors' Agents (AAA)

Fiction > *Novels*
Commercial Women's Fiction; Crime; Historical Fiction; Mystery; Suspense; Thrillers

Nonfiction > *Nonfiction Books*
Arts; Autobiography; Biography; Business; Cookery; Crafts; Health; Nature; Popular Science; Sport; Travel

Send: Query; Synopsis; Writing sample; Author bio
How to send: Email

Always looking for exciting new authors. Send query by email with the word "Submission" in the subject line and synopsis and first three chapters as Word or Open Document attachments. Also include market info, and details of your professional life and writing ambitions. Film and TV scripts for existing clients only. See website for full guidelines.

Literary Agent / Managing Director: Fiona Lindsay (*L431*)

L428 Linda Konner Literary Agency

Literary Agency
10 West 15 Street, Suite 1918, New York, NY 10011
United States

ldkonner@cs.com

http://www.lindakonnerliteraryagency.com

Types: Nonfiction
Formats: Reference
Subjects: Biography; Business; Cookery; Culture; Entertainment; Finance; Health; How To; Lifestyle; Personal Development; Psychology; Science; Women's Interests
Markets: Adult

Send: Query
Don't send: Full text
How to send: Email

Costs: Author covers sundry admin costs.

Send one to two page query by email only. Attachments from unknown senders will be deleted unread. Nonfiction only. Books must be written by or with established experts in their field. No Fiction, Memoir, Religion, Spiritual/Christian, Children's/young adult, Games/puzzles, Humour, History, Politics, or unsolicited MSS. See website for full guidelines.

Literary Agent: Linda Konner

L429 Linda Seifert Management

Literary Agency
United Kingdom
Tel: +44 (0) 20 3327 1180

contact@lindaseifert.com

http://www.lindaseifert.com

Professional Body: Personal Managers' Association (PMA)

ADULT > **Scripts**
Film Scripts; *TV Scripts*
CHILDREN'S > **Scripts**
Film Scripts; *TV Scripts*

Closed to approaches.

Costs: Author covers sundry admin costs.

A London-based management company representing screenwriters and directors for film and television. Our outstanding client list ranges from the highly established to the new and exciting emerging talent of tomorrow. Represents UK-based writers and directors only.

Literary Agent: Edward Hughes

L430 Lindsay Literary Agency

Literary Agency
United Kingdom
Tel: +44 (0) 1420 831430

info@lindsayliteraryagency.co.uk

http://www.lindsayliteraryagency.co.uk
https://twitter.com/lindsaylit

Professional Body: The Association of Authors' Agents (AAA)

CHILDREN'S > **Fiction**
Middle Grade; *Picture Books*
YOUNG ADULT > **Fiction** > *Novels*

Send: Query; Author bio; Pitch; Synopsis; Writing sample
How to send: Email

Send query by email only, including single-page synopsis and first three chapters. For picture books send complete ms. No submissions by post.

Authors: Helen Brandom; Pamela Butchart; Sital Gorasia Chapman; Christina Collins; Jim Daly; Donna David; Rachel Emily; Louise Finch; Sam Gayton; Ruth Hatfield; Larry Hayes; Sharon Hopwood; Peter Jones; Jay Joseph; Titania Krimpas; Mike Lancaster; Giles Paley-Phillips; Kate Peridot; Josh Silver; Sharon Tregenza; Rachel Valentine; Sue Wallman; Jacqueline Whitehart; Joe Wilson

Literary Agent: Becky Bagnell (*L040*)

L431 Fiona Lindsay

Literary Agent; Managing Director
United Kingdom

Literary Agency: Limelight Management (**L427**)

L432 Will Lippincott

Literary Agent
Los Angeles
United States

https://aevitascreative.com/agents/

Literary Agency: Aevitas

Nonfiction > *Nonfiction Books*
Current Affairs; Health; History; Journalism; Memoir; Narrative Nonfiction; Politics; Popular Culture; Science; Technology

Send: Query; Pitch; Market info; Writing sample
How to send: Online submission system

Agent based in Los Angeles. Interested in politics, journalistic narratives, history, health, technology, and memoir, with a special focus on multi-media storytelling.

Authors: William Lee Adams; Chris Babits; Catherine Bliss; Michael Brodeur; Will Bunch; Terri Cheney; Ken Duckworth; Ken Dychtwald; Chris Hayes; Thomas R. Insel; Scott C. Johnson; Mark Landler; Derek Leebaert; Emily Lordi; Michelle Miller; Simon Morrison; Jeremy Nobel; Paul Pringle; Ari Rabin-Havt; Anne-Marie Slaughter; Raphael Warnock

L433 Laurie Liss

Literary Agent; Executive Vice President
United States

https://www.sll.com/our-team
http://aaronline.org/Sys/PublicProfile/2176754/417813

Literary Agency: Sterling Lord Literistic, Inc. (**L662**)
Professional Body: Association of American Literary Agents (AALA)

Fiction > *Novels*
Commercial; Literary

Nonfiction > *Nonfiction Books*: Commercial

Send: Query; Synopsis; Writing sample
How to send: Online submission system

L434 Literary Management Group, Inc.

Literary Agency
150 Young Way, Richmond Hill, GA 31324
United States
Tel: +1 (615) 812-4445

BruceBarbour@LiteraryManagementGroup.com

https://literarymanagementgroup.com/

Nonfiction > *Nonfiction Books*
Biography; Business; Lifestyle; Religion

Send: Query; Writing sample
How to send: Word file email attachment
How not to send: PDF file email attachment

Handles Christian books (defined as books which are consistent with the historical, orthodox teachings of the Christian fathers). Handles adult nonfiction only. No children's or illustrated books, poetry, memoirs, YA Fiction or text/academic books. Download proposal from website then complete and send with sample chapters.

Literary Agent: Bruce R. Barbour

L435 The Liverpool Literary Agency

Literary Agency
Liverpool
United Kingdom

submissions@liverpool-literary.agency

https://www.liverpool-literary.agency/
https://twitter.com/LiverpoolLit
https://www.instagram.com/liverpool_literary_agency/

Professional Body: The Association of Authors' Agents (AAA)

ADULT > **Fiction** > *Novels*

YOUNG ADULT > **Fiction** > *Novels*
Dystopian Fiction; Fantasy; Post-Apocalyptic; Science Fiction; Steampunk; Urban Fantasy

Send: Query; Author bio; Market info; Synopsis; Writing sample
How to send: Email
How not to send: Post

Costs: Offers services that writers have to pay for. Also offers editorial services.

Literary agency based in Liverpool, focusing on helping writers from Northern England break into the publishing industry.

Assistant Agent / Editor: Anna Gamble (**L249**)

Associate Agent / Editor: Laura Bennett (**L056**)

Literary Agent: Clare Coombes (**L138**)

L436 Liza Dawson Associates

Literary Agency
121 West 27th Street, Suite 1201, New York, NY 10001
United States
Tel: +1 (973) 743-2535

queryliza@LizaDawsonAssociates.com

http://www.lizadawsonassociates.com

Professional Body: Association of American Literary Agents (AALA)

Types: Fiction; Nonfiction
Formats: Theatre Scripts
Subjects: Autobiography; Business; Comedy / Humour; Commercial; Culture; Current Affairs; Fantasy; History; Lifestyle; Literary; Medicine; Mystery; Personal Development; Politics; Psychology; Religion; Romance; Science; Science Fiction; Society; Suspense; Thrillers; Warfare; Women's Interests
Markets: Academic; Adult; Children's; Young Adult

See website for specific agent interests and query appropriate agent directly. Specific agent submission guidelines and contact details are available on website.

Authors: Marie Bostwick; Robyn Carr; Scott Hawkins; Marybeth Whalen

Literary Agents: Rachel Beck (**L052**); Caitlin Blasdell; Hannah Bowman; Liza Dawson; Caitie Flum; Tom Miller

L437 The LKG Agency

Literary Agency
134 West 83rd Street, 3rd Floor, New York, NY 10024
United States

mgya@lkgagency.com
query@lkgagency.com

http://lkgagency.com

CHILDREN'S
Fiction > *Middle Grade*
General, and in particular: Contemporary; High / Epic Fantasy; Magical Realism; Science Fiction; Thrillers

Nonfiction > *Nonfiction Books*

YOUNG ADULT > **Fiction** > *Novels*

Does not want:

CHILDREN'S > **Fiction** > *Middle Grade*: Horror

Send: Query; Synopsis; Writing sample
How to send: Email

Specializes in middle grade and young adult fiction. Within children's, is primarily drawn to contemporary and magical realism but is open to high fantasy, sci-fi, thriller, almost everything except maybe horror.

Literary Agents: Lauren Galit; Caitlen Rubino-Bradway

L438 Jonathan Lloyd

Literary Agent; President
United Kingdom

Literary Agency: Curtis Brown

Fiction > *Novels*

Nonfiction > *Nonfiction Books*

Send: Query; Synopsis; Writing sample
How to send: Online submission system

Represents a number of best-selling fiction authors who feature in the Guardian Top 100 annual list and he also has a wide range of non-fiction clients and well known autobiographers, from politicians to celebrities.

L439 Rozzy Lloyd

Literary Agent
United Kingdom

Literary Agency: The Narrow Road Company (**L520**)

L440 Dominic Lord

Literary Agent
United Kingdom

Literary Agency: JFL Agency (**L353**)

L441 Lotus Lane Literary

Literary Agency
United States

contact@lotuslit.com

https://lotuslit.com

Fiction > *Novels*

Nonfiction > *Nonfiction Books*

Send: Query; Author bio; Synopsis; Writing sample
How to send: Email

Independent literary agency based in New Jersey, representing a diverse list of debut and seasoned authors. Handles adult fiction and nonfiction, and sells rights to the US, UK, Europe, and India.

Literary Agent: Priya Doraswamy (*L180*)

L442 Amberley Lowis

Literary Agent
15 Lyne Crescent, London, E17 5HY
United Kingdom

amberley@thevineyagency.com

http://thevineyagency.com/about.html

Literary Agency: The Viney Agency (**L715**)

ADULT
Fiction > *Novels*
Book Club Fiction; Commercial; Literary

Nonfiction > *Nonfiction Books*
General, and in particular: Biography; Cookery; Memoir; Narrative Nonfiction

CHILDREN'S > **Fiction** > *Novels*

YOUNG ADULT > **Fiction** > *Novels*

Send: Query; Synopsis; Writing sample
How to send: Post

Actively building a diverse list, across a wide range of fiction and non-fiction titles. Looking for commercial and reading group fiction, literary fiction and a broad range of non-fiction. Interested in lively and original non-fiction, particularly in the areas of narrative non-fiction, biography, memoir and cookery. Also looking to represent children's and young adult fiction.

L443 Andrew Lownie

Literary Agent
United Kingdom

Literary Agency: Andrew Lownie Literary Agency Ltd (**L020**)

L444 Bethany Lucas

Trainee Agent
United Kingdom

https://katenashlit.co.uk/people/
https://twitter.com/bethanylucas_

Literary Agency: Kate Nash Literary Agency (**L375**)

Fiction > *Novels*

Send: Query; Pitch; Author bio; Synopsis; Writing sample
How to send: In the body of an email

Enjoys reading a wide range of genres and is interested in stories that put new spins on old ideas. She especially loves books with fully fleshed out characters, vibrant worlds, and endings that pack an emotional punch.

L445 Luithlen Agency

Literary Agency
United Kingdom

penny@luithlenagency.co.uk

http://www.luithlenagency.com

CHILDREN'S > **Fiction**
Early Readers; *Middle Grade*; *Novels*
YOUNG ADULT > **Fiction** > *Novels*

Closed to approaches.

Closed to submissions as at March 2020. Check website for current status.

Authors: David Belbin; Jennifer Bell; Caroline Clough; Harry Edge; John Hickman; Stuart Hill; Pete Johnson; Maxine Linnell; Clive Mantle; Gary Morecombe; Alison Prince; Bali Rai; James Riordan; Jamie Scallion; Joe Standerline; Robert Swindells; Gareth Thompson; John Townsend; Dan Tunstall

Literary Agent: Jennifer Luithlen (*L446*)

L446 Jennifer Luithlen

Literary Agent
United Kingdom

Literary Agency: Luithlen Agency (**L445**)

L447 Eric Lupfer

Literary Agent
United States

Literary Agency: Fletcher & Company

L448 Lutyens and Rubinstein

Literary Agency
21 Kensington Park Road, London, W11 2EU
United Kingdom
Tel: +44 (0) 20 7792 4855

submissions@lutyensrubinstein.co.uk

https://www.lutyensrubinstein.co.uk
https://twitter.com/LandRAgency
https://instagram.com/LandRAgency

Professional Body: The Association of Authors' Agents (AAA)

Fiction > *Novels*
Commercial; Literary

Nonfiction > *Nonfiction Books*

Send: Query; Synopsis; Writing sample
How to send: Email
How not to send: Post

Send up to 5,000 words or first three chapters by email with covering letter and short synopsis. No film or TV scripts, or unsolicited submissions by hand or by post.

Literary Agent: Susannah Godman (*L272*)

L449 Alice Lutyens

Literary Agent
United Kingdom

Literary Agency: Curtis Brown

L450 Reggie Lutz

Literary Agent
United States

Literary Agency: Prentis Literary (**L574**)

L451 David Luxton

Literary Agent
United Kingdom

https://www.davidluxtonassociates.co.uk/the-agency/

Literary Agency: David Luxton Associates (**L162**)

Nonfiction > *Nonfiction Books*
Food; Music; Politics; Sport

Principal interests are in the fields of sport, music, food-writing and politics and he represents a diverse range of authors including countless high-profile sports personalities.

L452 Paul Lyon-Maris

Literary Agent
United Kingdom

Literary Agency: Independent Talent Group Ltd (**L340**)

L453 Jennifer Lyons

Literary Agent; President
United States

jenniferlyonsagency@gmail.com

https://www.jenniferlyonsliteraryagency.com/who-we-are/

Literary Agency: The Jennifer Lyons Literary Agency, LLC

ADULT
Fiction > *Novels*
Commercial Women's Fiction; Literary; Upmarket

Nonfiction > *Nonfiction Books*: Narrative Nonfiction

CHILDREN'S > **Fiction** > *Middle Grade*

YOUNG ADULT > **Fiction** > *Novels*

Send: Query
How to send: Post; Email

Seeking: Literary fiction and upmarket, commercial women's fiction. Narrative nonfiction. Children's books, especially middle grade and young adult. Prefers hard copy queries, but can also be queried by email.

L454 Rhea Lyons

Literary Agent
United States

rhea@hgliterary.com

https://www.hgliterary.com/rhea

Literary Agency: HG Literary

ADULT
Fiction
Graphic Novels: General
Novels: Commercial; Fantasy; Horror; Literary; Science Fiction
Nonfiction > *Nonfiction Books*
Journalism; Narrative Nonfiction

CHILDREN'S > **Nonfiction** > *Nonfiction Books*

Closed to approaches.

Looking to represent writers of fiction, nonfiction, and graphic novelists who want to confront and destroy the status quo. For fiction, she is looking for anything that could be deemed literary/commercial crossover with a speculative bend, as well as science fiction and fantasy -- both true to the genre as well as genre-busting -- told in an accessible, entertaining voice. She likes horror but more on the cerebral end, less on the gory end (slashers are a no). For nonfiction, she is looking for narrative nonfiction and journalistic deep-dives into a single subject, particular location, or that examines a moment in history from an underrepresented, international, or little-known point of view. For children's books, she is especially interested in nonfiction that inspires learning and creativity for all ages.

L455 Emily MacDonald

Literary Agent
United Kingdom

emilymacdonald@42mp.com

https://www.42mp.com/agents
https://twitter.com/Ebh_mac

Literary Agency: 42 Management and Production (**L002**)

Fiction > *Novels*
Literary; Upmarket

Nonfiction > *Nonfiction Books*
History; Memoir; Narrative Nonfiction; Nature; Regional; Scotland; Social Commentary

How to send: Email

Looking for literary fiction, narrative nonfiction with an investigative twist, and untold true stories, either personal or historical. Also interested in Scottish and regional voices with stories to tell.

L456 Laura Macdougall

Literary Agent
United Kingdom

LMacdougall@unitedagents.co.uk

https://www.unitedagents.co.uk/lmacdougallunitedagentscouk
https://twitter.com/L_Macdougall
https://www.instagram.com/lmac_84/?hl=en
https://www.pinterest.co.uk/lmvmacdougall/

Literary Agency: United Agents (**L704**)

Fiction > *Novels*
Book Club Fiction; Commercial; Historical Fiction; LGBTQIA; Literary; Romance; Saga

Nonfiction
Illustrated Books: General
Nonfiction Books: Gardening; LGBTQIA; Narrative Nonfiction; Philosophy; Sociology

I represent a diverse range of commercial fiction – saga, romance, book club and 'up-lit' – and literary fiction, ranging from the quirky to the daring and experimental. I've always been a fan of historical fiction and also have a soft spot for novels that explore the complexities of relationships and family life.

My non-fiction list is equally diverse, from illustrated books to social science, popular philosophy and gardening, as well as narrative non-fiction on death, hormones, sexual desire and what it's like to live on a remote Scottish island. A writer who can successfully communicate their passion, whether that's about something niche or obscure or a global phenomenon, will always be of interest to me.

As a queer woman, I represent a large number of LGBTQ writers and I'm particularly keen to hear from those who also identify as LGBTQ and who are exploring the full spectrum of LGBTQ lives in their writing.

L457 MacGregor & Luedeke

Literary Agency
PO Box 1316, Manzanita, OR 97130
United States
Tel: +1 (503) 389-4803

submissions@macgregorliterary.com

http://www.macgregorandluedeke.com
https://twitter.com/MacGregorLit

Fiction > *Novels*
Christianity; Literary; Romance

Nonfiction > *Nonfiction Books*
Crime; Memoir; Self Help; Spirituality

Send: Query; Market info; Author bio; Writing sample
Don't send: Full text
How to send: Email

Costs: Author covers sundry admin costs.

The company has focused on specific niche markets — memoir, spirituality, self-help books, Christian and literary fiction, true crime, romance, as well as some specialty projects.

Authors: Don Brown; Davis Bunn; Rashawn Copeland; Sheila Gregoire; Rachel Hauck; James Byron Huggins; Steve Jackson; Jessica Kate; Rachel Linden; Holly Lorincz; Evelyn Lozada; Scott Parazynski; Jay Payleitner; Tom Satterly; Kimberly Stuart; David Thomas; Vincent Zandri

Literary Agent / President: Chip MacGregor (**L458**)

Literary Agent / Vice President: Amanda Luedeke

L458 Chip MacGregor

Literary Agent; President
United States

http://www.macgregorandluedeke.com/about/agents/chip-macgregor/
http://aaronline.org/Sys/PublicProfile/2176764/417813

Literary Agency: MacGregor & Luedeke (**L457**)
Professional Body: Association of American Literary Agents (AALA)

L459 Joanna MacKenzie

Literary Agent
United States

https://nelsonagency.com/joanna-mackenzie/
https://www.publishersmarketplace.com/

members/JoannaMacKenzie/
https://twitter.com/joannamackenzie
https://www.facebook.com/joanna.topor.mackenzie

Literary Agency: Nelson Literary Agency, LLC (**L524**)

Fiction > *Novels*
Commercial; Family; Friends; Mystery; Speculative; Thrillers; Women's Fiction

Closed to approaches.

Interested in high-concept, twisty, unputdownable stories with a strong voice in the areas of women's fiction, thriller, and speculative; timely commercial fiction in which the personal intersects with the world at large, and/or that explores toxic friendships and complex, challenging family dynamics; Heartfelt and timeless stories that you want to re-read about identity, unlikely friendships, reinvention, second acts, and women finding their voices and power, especially with touches of magic or speculative; Voicey, confident, atmospheric mysteries set in close-knit communities; creepy islands and Midwest-set are a plus. Always looking for stories about the immigrant experience.

Authors: Brooke Abrams; Kate Baer; Lina Chern; Shana Galen; John Galligan; Jill Grunenwald; Alison Hammer; Sarah Zachrich Jeng; Sierra Kincade; Karen Koh; Gillian Libby; Amanda Marbais; Jonathan Messinger; Meghan Scott Molin; Katrina Monroe; Kristen Simmons; Jennifer Springsteen; Stacy Stokes; Chrysler Szarlan; Ben Tanzer; Kathleen West

L460 Jamie Maclean

Literary Agent; Editor
United Kingdom

https://cmm.agency/about-us.php

Literary Agency: Coombs Moylett & Maclean Literary Agency (**L139**)
Online Magazine: Erotic Review (**M184**)

Fiction > *Novels*
Erotic; Historical Crime; Mystery; Thrillers

Nonfiction > *Nonfiction Books*
Gender Politics; How To; Lifestyle; Relationships

Send: Synopsis; Writing sample
How to send: Online submission system

Specialises in both fiction and nonfiction and is particularly interested in sexual politics, relationship, lifestyle how-to's, erotica, thrillers, whodunit and historical crime.

L461 Lauren MacLeod

Literary Agent
United States

https://www.strothmanagency.com/about
https://querymanager.com/query/LMacLeod
https://twitter.com/Lauren_MacLeod
http://aaronline.org/Sys/PublicProfile/12259463/417813

Literary Agency: The Strothman Agency (**L672**)
Professional Body: Association of American Literary Agents (AALA)

ADULT
Fiction > *Novels*: Literary

Nonfiction > *Nonfiction Books*
Crime; Feminism; Food; History; Narrative Nonfiction; Popular Culture; Science

CHILDREN'S > **Fiction** > *Middle Grade*

YOUNG ADULT
Fiction > *Novels*
General, and in particular: Environment; Politics; Social Issues

Nonfiction > *Nonfiction Books*
General, and in particular: Environment; Politics; Social Issues

Send: Query
How to send: Email; Query Manager
How not to send: Email attachment; Post; Fax; Phone; Social Media

Accepts young adult and middle grade fiction by referral only: contact directly by email. Accepts nonfiction without a referral through Query Manager only.

L462 Eve MacSweeney

Literary Agent
United States

https://www.fletcherandco.com/team/eve-macsweeney/

Literary Agency: Fletcher & Company

Fiction > *Novels*: Literary

Nonfiction > *Nonfiction Books*: Narrative Nonfiction

Developing narrative non-fiction and literary fiction titles that speak to her interest in emotionally driven stories, singular voices, and compelling social issues, particularly as they concern the lives of women.

L463 Neeti Madan

Senior Agent
United States

https://www.sll.com/our-team

Literary Agency: Sterling Lord Literistic, Inc. (**L662**)

Fiction > *Novels*

Nonfiction > *Nonfiction Books*
Journalism; Lifestyle; Memoir; Popular Culture

Send: Query; Synopsis; Writing sample
How to send: Online submission system

Her books run the gamut from the commercial to the cerebral. A true generalist, she is drawn to thoughtful writing on intriguing and important subjects, including memoir, journalism, popular culture, lifestyle, and the occasional novel. She is on the lookout for the types of books she loves as a reader—writing that breaks through barriers and elevates underrepresented voices, page-turners that keep her up until 3 AM, and irreverent books that makes her laugh.

Associate Agent: Maria Bell (**L054**)

L464 Madeleine Milburn Literary, TV & Film Agency

Literary Agency
The Factory, 1 Park Hill, London, SW4 9NS
United Kingdom
Tel: +44 (0) 20 7499 7550

submissions@madeleinemilburn.com
childrens@madeleinemilburn.com
info@madeleinemilburn.com

https://madeleinemilburn.co.uk
https://twitter.com/MMLitAgency
https://www.instagram.com/madeleinemilburn/?hl=en
https://www.facebook.com/MadeleineMilburnLiteraryAgency

Professional Body: The Association of Authors' Agents (AAA)

ADULT
Fiction > *Novels*
Nonfiction > *Nonfiction Books*

CHILDREN'S
Fiction > *Novels*
Nonfiction > *Nonfiction Books*

NEW ADULT
Fiction > *Novels*
Nonfiction > *Nonfiction Books*

TEEN
Fiction > *Novels*
Nonfiction > *Nonfiction Books*

YOUNG ADULT
Fiction > *Novels*
Nonfiction > *Nonfiction Books*

Send: Query; Synopsis; Pitch; Market info; Writing sample
How to send: Online submission system
How not to send: Post

Represents award-winning and bestselling authors of adult and children's fiction and non-fiction. Submit via online submissions system. No submissions by post.

Associate Agents: Vanessa Browne; Rachel Yeoh (**L751**)

Company Director / Literary Agent: Madeleine Milburn (**L496**)

Literary Agents: Emma Bal (**L041**); Olivia Maidment (**L465**); Chloe Seager (**L630**); Hayley Steed (**L658**); Hannah Todd (**L700**)

Managing Director: Giles Milburn

L465 Olivia Maidment

Literary Agent
United Kingdom

submissions@madeleinemilburn.com

https://www.madeleinemilburn.co.uk/agents/olivia-maidment/
https://twitter.com/liv_maidment

Literary Agency: Madeleine Milburn Literary, TV & Film Agency (**L464**)

Fiction > *Novels*
Book Club Fiction; Contemporary; High Concept; Historical Fiction; Literary; Magical Realism; Socio-Political; Speculative; Upmarket

Nonfiction > *Nonfiction Books*
Literary; Narrative Nonfiction

Send: Synopsis; Writing sample
How to send: Email
How not to send: Post

Looking for literary, upmarket, and book club fiction; narrative non-fiction; identity driven narratives; social, cultural, political themes; global voices; speculative fiction; magical realism; historical fiction; multi-generational; high concept stories; thought provoking narratives.

L466 Carol Mann

Literary Agent
United States

https://www.carolmannagency.com/our-team

Literary Agency: Carol Mann Agency (**L104**)
Professional Body: Association of American Literary Agents (AALA)

Fiction > *Novels*

Nonfiction > *Nonfiction Books*
Current Affairs; Health; History; Medicine; Narrative Nonfiction; Parenting; Religion; Self Help; Spirituality

Send: Query; Author bio; Writing sample
How to send: In the body of an email

Specialises in nonfiction (health/medical, religion, spirituality, self-help, parenting, current affairs, history, narrative non-fiction) while also taking on the occasional fiction writer.

L467 Rachel Mann

Literary Agent
United Kingdom

http://www.jounwin.co.uk/rachel-mann/

Literary Agency: Jo Unwin Literary Agency (**L354**)

ADULT
Fiction > *Novels*

Nonfiction > *Nonfiction Books*
Comedy / Humour; Lifestyle

CHILDREN'S
Fiction > *Middle Grade*
Comedy / Humour; Commercial; High Concept

Nonfiction > *Nonfiction Books*
Comedy / Humour; Lifestyle

Does not want:

CHILDREN'S > **Fiction** > *Picture Books*

Closed to approaches.

In all cases I want compelling voices, unpatronizing writing and vivid, complex characters. International settings and traditions, unconventional narratives, and progressive and/or radical social commentary will always get my attention. I'm particularly interested in writers from underrepresented backgrounds, especially if those stories are genre fiction, lifestyle or comic non-fiction, for both adults and children.

At the moment, I'm particularly on the look-out for funny, commercial and high-concept middle-grade series. I'd love to see strong hooks and rich worldbuilding, often with both humour and darkness.

I'm also looking for bold, voice-driven and emotionally engaging non-fiction across both adults' and children's.

L468 Kendra Marcus

Literary Agent
United States

http://www.bookstopliterary.com/submission.html

Literary Agency: BookStop Literary Agency, LLC (**L073**)

CHILDREN'S
Fiction
Novels: General
Picture Books: Comedy / Humour

Nonfiction > *Nonfiction Books*
General, and in particular: History; Science

How to send: By referral

Gravitates toward quirky and funny picture books, fiction with unforgettable characters and stories that will bring her to tears. Unusual non-fiction, especially science presented in new ways and little gems of history are also her cup of tea. Stories with Hispanic or Latino characters are always welcome, and she is thrilled to find accomplished illustrators with a fresh style who can tell a strong story in pictures to accompany a text.

L469 Marjacq Scripts Ltd

Literary Agency
The Space, 235 High Holborn, London, WC1V 7DN
United Kingdom
Tel: +44 (0) 20 7935 9499

enquiries@marjacq.com

http://www.marjacq.com
https://twitter.com/marjacqscripts

Professional Body: The Association of Authors' Agents (AAA)

ADULT
Fiction > *Novels*

Nonfiction > *Nonfiction Books*

Scripts
Film Scripts; *TV Scripts*

CHILDREN'S
Fiction > *Novels*
Nonfiction > *Nonfiction Books*

Send: Query
Don't send: Full text
How to send: Email
How not to send: Post

Accepts submissions by email only. For books, send query with synopsis and first 50 pages. For scripts, send short treatment and entire screenplay. Send only Word or PDF documents less than 2MB. Do not paste work into the body of the email. See website for full details. No children's picture books, poetry, plays or musical theatre.

Authors: Tanya Atapattu; Holly Baxter; Alexandra K Benedict; Daisy Buchanan; Cecil Cameron; James Campbell; Angela Clarke; Mathew Clayton; Fiona Collins; Caroline Corcoran; Isabel Costello; Hannah Dolby; Francesca Dorricott; Lilly Ebert; Dov Forman; Eve Harris; Louise Hulland; Catriona Innes; Harriet Johnson; Amy Jones; Eve Makis; Andrea Mara; Francesca May; Claire McGowan; Adam Pearson; Alice Peterson; Das Petrou; Rachel Phipps; Carmen Reid; Samantha Renke; Lee Ridley; Diana Rosie; Frances Ryan; Jennifer Savin; Hema Sukumar; Lucy Vine; James Wallman; Roz Watkins; Eva Woods

Literary Agents: Diana Beaumont (**L051**); Leah Middleton (**L494**); Philip Patterson; Imogen Pelham; Catherine Pellegrino; Sandra Sawicka (*L622*)

L470 Mildred Marmur

Literary Agent
United States

Literary Agency: Mildred Marmur Associates, Ltd. (**L497**)
Professional Body: Association of American Literary Agents (AALA)

L471 Jill Marr

Literary Agent
United States

https://www.dijkstraagency.com/agent-page.php?agent_id=Marr
https://querymanager.com/query/JillMarr

Literary Agency: Sandra Dijkstra Literary Agency

Fiction > *Novels*
Book Club Fiction; Commercial; Historical Fiction; Horror; Mystery; Thrillers

Nonfiction > *Nonfiction Books*
Comedy / Humour; Current Affairs; Health; History; Memoir; Music; Narrative Nonfiction; Nutrition; Politics; Popular Culture; Science; Sport

How to send: Query Manager

Looking for fiction and non-fiction by BIPOC and Latinx writers, disabled persons, and people identifying as LGBTQ+, among others. She is interested in commercial fiction, with an emphasis on mysteries, thrillers, and horror, book club, and historical fiction. She is also looking for non-fiction by authors with a big, timely, smart message as well as historical projects that look at big picture issues. Jill is looking for non-fiction projects in the areas of current events, science, history, narrative non-fiction, sports, politics, health & nutrition, pop culture, humor, music, and very select memoir.

L472 Jen Marshall

Literary Agent
New York
United States

https://aevitascreative.com/agents/

Literary Agency: Aevitas

ADULT
Fiction
Graphic Novels: General
Novels: Adventure; Commercial; Crime; Drama; Horror; Literary; Popular Culture; Romance; Thrillers
Nonfiction > *Nonfiction Books*
Arts; Health; History; Mathematics; Narrative Nonfiction; Science

CHILDREN'S > **Fiction** > *Novels*

Send: Author bio; Outline; Pitch; Market info; Writing sample
How to send: Online submission system

Represents a range of fiction and nonfiction. She is most interested in: literary fiction, commercial fiction, crime, thrillers, style, pop culture, and compelling narrative nonfiction.

Authors: Natasha S. Barrett; Elena Brower; Maggie Bullock; Windy Chien; Hopwood DePree; Danielle Dreilinger; Neil Gross; Ericka Hart; Gabrielle Hartley; Katherine Sharp Landdeck; Marisa Meltzer; Jenny Minton; Vanessa O'Brien; Joe Pompeo; Paul Pringle; Nancy Jo Sales; Kate Schapira; Chris Smalls; Keziah Weir

L473 Maria Massie

Literary Agent
United States

Literary Agency: Massie & McQuilkin

Fiction > *Novels*: Literary

Nonfiction > *Nonfiction Books*
Memoir; Narrative Nonfiction

Send: Query; Author bio; Writing sample
How to send: In the body of an email

Brings over two decades' worth of experience in representing authors and helping to make sure that they can be read around the world.

L474 Peter Matson

Literary Agent; Chair
United States

https://www.sll.com/our-team

Literary Agency: Sterling Lord Literistic, Inc. (**L662**)

Fiction > *Novels*

Nonfiction > *Nonfiction Books*
History; Science

Send: Query; Synopsis; Writing sample
How to send: Online submission system

L475 Jennifer Mattson

Literary Agent
United States

jmatt@andreabrownlit.com

https://www.andreabrownlit.com/Team/Jennifer-Mattson
http://twitter.com/jannmatt
http://instagram.com/jennmattson
https://www.publishersmarketplace.com/members/JenMatt/
https://www.manuscriptwishlist.com/mswl-post/jennifer-mattson/
https://querymanager.com/query/JenniferMattson

Literary Agency: Andrea Brown Literary Agency, Inc.

CHILDREN'S > **Fiction** > *Middle Grade*

YOUNG ADULT > **Fiction** > *Novels*

How to send: Query Manager

Represents authors, illustrators, and author-illustrators who bring a distinct point of view to their work, and who tell stories with multiple layers. In middle grade and YA both, her heart beats faster for stories that cascade from a mind-expanding premise. She also loves survival stories and losing herself in Dickensian sagas (WOLVES OF WILLOUGHBY CHASE!), and enjoys watching characters puzzle their way through problems. She has a special soft spot for middle grade about resilient kids sorting out the messiness of life.

L476 Bridget Wagner Matzie

Literary Agent; Partner
United States

https://aevitascreative.com/agents/

Literary Agency: Aevitas

Fiction > *Novels*: Commercial

Nonfiction > *Nonfiction Books*

Closed to approaches.

Represents nonfiction and commercial fiction.

L477 Shari Maurer

Literary Agent
United States

https://querymanager.com/query/1434

Literary Agency: The Stringer Literary Agency LLC (**L669**)

ADULT
Fiction > *Novels*
Crime; Fantasy; Suspense; Thrillers; Upmarket Women's Fiction

Nonfiction > *Nonfiction Books*
Memoir; Narrative Nonfiction; Parenting; Popular Science

CHILDREN'S
Fiction
Middle Grade: Contemporary; Historical Fiction; Literary; Mystery
Picture Books: General

Nonfiction > *Middle Grade*

YOUNG ADULT
Fiction > *Novels*
Contemporary; Historical Fiction; Literary; Mystery

Nonfiction > *Nonfiction Books*

Does not want:

ADULT > **Fiction** > *Novels*: Erotic Romance

CHILDREN'S > **Fiction** > *Middle Grade*: Fantasy

Send: Query; Synopsis; Writing sample; Pitch
How to send: Query Manager

L478 Jane Graham Maw

Literary Agent
United Kingdom

http://www.grahammawchristie.com/about1.html

Literary Agency: Graham Maw Christie Literary Agency (**L278**)

Nonfiction > *Nonfiction Books*
Activism; Environment; Inspirational Memoir; Nature; Spirituality; Wellbeing

Send: Outline; Author bio; Market info; Writing sample
How to send: Email

Particularly interested in inspirational memoir, nature writing, activism, green issues, spirituality, self-care and wellness titles.

L479 Juliana McBride

Literary Agent
United States

https://rfliterary.com/about/

Literary Agency: Rebecca Friedman Literary Agency

ADULT > **Fiction** > *Novels*
Commercial; Fantasy; Literary

YOUNG ADULT > **Fiction** > *Novels*

Send: Query; Writing sample
How to send: Email
How not to send: Email attachment

Loves commercial and literary fiction, young adult novels, and fantasy. Is looking for transcendent stories that linger.

L480 Michael McCoy

Literary Agent
United Kingdom

Literary Agency: Independent Talent Group Ltd (**L340**)

L481 Matt McGowan

Senior Agent; Vice President
United States

mm@goldinlit.com

Literary Agency: Frances Goldin Literary Agency, Inc.

Fiction > *Novels*: Literary

Nonfiction
Essays: General
Nonfiction Books: Biography; Crime; Culture; Food; Football / Soccer; History; Journalism; Memoir; Narrative Nonfiction; Politics; Popular Culture; Popular Science; Sport; Sub-Culture; Travel

How to send: Email

Looking for emotionally, intellectually, and formally adventurous work of all kinds and is particularly interested in writers who believe nonfiction can be as artful as fiction. Queries for essays; literary fiction (strong but difficult characters, examinations of place, sub-cultures, and/or recent history or time periods); researched narrative nonfiction; journalism; politics; history; memoir; biography; cultural studies; popular culture & science; sports (particularly soccer); travel, crime, food, literary graphic work (especially NF), are all welcome.

L482 Eunice McMullen

Literary Agent
United Kingdom

Literary Agency: Eunice McMullen Children's Literary Agent Ltd (**L209**)

L483 Jane von Mehren

Literary Agent; Partner
United States

https://aevitascreative.com/agents/

Literary Agency: Aevitas

Fiction > *Novels*
Book Club Fiction; Historical Fiction; Literary

Nonfiction > *Nonfiction Books*
Business; History; Memoir; Popular Culture; Science

Send: Query; Author bio; Market info; Writing sample
How to send: Online submission system

Interested in narratives in the areas of business, history, memoir, popular culture and science, books that help us live our best lives, literary, book club, and historical fiction.

L484 Isabel Mendia

Associate Agent
United States

https://www.cheneyagency.com/isabel-mendia

Literary Agency: The Cheney Agency

Nonfiction > *Nonfiction Books*
Cultural Criticism; History; Narrative Journalism; Politics

Send: Query; Self-Addressed Stamped Envelope (SASE)
How to send: Post; Email

Interested in representing a range of nonfiction, including cultural criticism, narrative reportage, politics, and history.

L485 Adam Mendlesohn

Literary Agent
United Kingdom

Literary Agency: The Narrow Road Company (**L520**)

L486 Meridian Artists

Literary Agency
349 Carlaw Ave, Suite 303, Toronto, Ontario M4M 2T1
Canada
Tel: +1 (416) 961-2777

info@meridianartists.com

https://www.meridianartists.com

Fiction > *Novels*

Nonfiction > *Nonfiction Books*

Scripts
Film Scripts; *TV Scripts*

Send: Synopsis; Author bio; Writing sample
How to send: Online submission system

Offers premier full-service entertainment industry representation with principal offices in Toronto and Los Angeles. An established leader in the representation and management of Talent, Screenwriters, Directors, Authors, and Key Creatives.

L487 Metamorphosis Literary Agency

Literary Agency
United States

info@metamorphosisliteraryagency.com

https://www.metamorphosisliteraryagency.com
https://www.facebook.com/metamorphosislitagent
https://twitter.com/MetamorphLitAg
https://www.linkedin.com/company/metamorphosis-literary-agency
https://www.instagram.com/metamorphosis_literary_agency/

ADULT
Fiction > *Novels*
Nonfiction > *Nonfiction Books*

CHILDREN'S > **Fiction** > *Middle Grade*

YOUNG ADULT > **Fiction** > *Novels*

Send: Query; Author bio; Writing sample; Synopsis
How to send: Query Manager

Costs: Author covers sundry admin costs.

Our mission is to help authors become traditionally published. We represent well-crafted commercial fiction and nonfiction. We work with authors to ensure that every book is in the best presentable form. Our publishing connections come from experience, numerous conferences, hard work, and genuine care.

Authors: Suleena Bibra; Kelly Cain; Natalie Cammaratta; Ashley M. Coleman; Stephanie Eding; Caroline Flynn; Charlee James; Karen Lynch; LaRonda Gardner Middlemiss; Janice Milusich; Anitra Rowe Schulte; Samara Shanker; Angela Shanté; Bruce Smith; Laura Snider; Heather Grace Stewart; Shannon Stults

Senior Agents: Amy Brewer (**L084**); Erica Christensen (**L128**); Stephanie Hansen (**L300**); Jana Hanson (**L301**); Jessica Reino (**L584**); Katie Salvo (**L616**)

L488 Mic Cheetham Literary Agency

Literary Agency
62 Grafton Way, London, W1T 5DW
United Kingdom
Tel: +44 (0) 20 3976 7713

submissions@miccheetham.co.uk

https://miccheetham.com

Fiction > *Novels*

Nonfiction > *Nonfiction Books*

Send: Query; Outline; Writing sample; Author bio
How to send: Email

Agency with a deliberately small list. Only takes on two or three new writers each year. New writers are advised to acquaint themselves with the work of the writers currently represented by the agency before submitting their own work.

Authors: Carol Birch; Nm Browne; Pat Cadigan; Alan Campbell; Gregory Doran; Barbara Ewing; Ian Green; M John Harrison; Alice James; Ken MacLeod; Paul Mcauley; China Miéville; Sharon Penman; Antony Sher; Adrian Tchaikovsky

Literary Agents: Mic Cheetham (**L120**); Simon Kavanagh (**L377**)

L489 The Michael Greer Literary Agency

Literary Agency
United Kingdom

melanie@michaelgreerliteraryagency.co.uk

http://www.michaelgreerliteraryagency.co.uk
https://twitter.com/SportLitAgent

ADULT
Fiction > *Novels*: Urban

Nonfiction > *Nonfiction Books*: Sport

YOUNG ADULT > **Fiction** > *Novels*

Send: Synopsis; Writing sample
How to send: Email

Costs: Author covers sundry admin costs.

Handles books in three areas: sport; City Fiction; and Young Adult. Send synopsis and three chapters by email.

Literary Agent: Melanie Michael-Greer (*L490*)

L490 Melanie Michael-Greer

Literary Agent
United Kingdom

Literary Agency: The Michael Greer Literary Agency (**L489**)

L491 Caroline Michel

Literary Agent; Chief Executive Officer
United Kingdom
Tel: +44 (0) 20 7344 1000

cmichelsubmissions@pfd.co.uk

https://petersfraserdunlop.com/agent/caroline-michel/

Literary Agency: Peters Fraser + Dunlop (**L560**)

Fiction > *Novels*

Nonfiction > *Nonfiction Books*
Biography; History; Science

Send: Query; Synopsis; Writing sample; Proposal; Author bio
How to send: Email
How not to send: Post

Loves everything and anything. She is endlessly curious about people's ideas, what's going on in the world and how to understand it, whether it's through history, fiction, biography, science. She is an eternal optimist and loves working with people who believe that everything is possible.

Authors: Jamie Bartlett; Camila Batmanghelidjh; Elaine Bedell; Simon Booker; Peter Bowles; Rosie Boycott; Pattie Boyd; Melvyn Bragg; Jonathan Bryan; Michael Caine; Emma Calder; Tamsin Calidas; Mark Carney; Augustus Casely-Hayford; Mavis Cheek; Rita Clifton; Sebastian Coe; Georgia Coleridge; Natalia Conroy; Susannah Constantine

L492 Micheline Steinberg Associates

Literary Agency
Suite 315, ScreenWorks, 22 Highbury Grove, London, N5 2ER
United Kingdom

info@steinplays.com

http://www.steinplays.com
https://twitter.com/steinbergassocs

Scripts
Film Scripts; *Radio Scripts*; *TV Scripts*; *Theatre Scripts*

Send: Query
How to send: By referral

We're a mid-size agency in which all the agents have background in theatre and related media. We work closely with writers and the industry, developing writers work, managing their careers, and negotiating all rights. We also have affiliations with book agents and agents overseas including in the USA. Please note that we do not accept unsolicited submissions without a letter of recommendation from an industry professional. All unsolicited material will be deleted unread. Does not consider books.

Literary Agents: Jazz Adamson; Micheline Steinberg

L493 Michelle Kass Associates

Literary Agency
85 Charing Cross Road, London, WC2H 0AA
United Kingdom
Tel: +44 (0) 20 7439 1624

office@michellekass.co.uk

http://www.michellekass.co.uk

Professional Body: The Association of Authors' Agents (AAA)

Fiction > *Novels*
Commercial; Literary

Scripts
Film Scripts; *TV Scripts*

How to send: Phone

Represents authors, dramatists/screenwriters, and screenwriters based in the UK and Ireland. Call before submitting.

Literary Agent: Michelle Kass (*L372*)

L494 Leah Middleton

Literary Agent
United Kingdom

leah@marjacq.com

http://www.marjacq.com/leah-middleton.html

Literary Agency: Marjacq Scripts Ltd (**L469**)

Scripts
Film Scripts: General, and in particular: Comedy / Humour
TV Scripts: General, and in particular: Comedy / Humour

Send: Full text; Synopsis; Author bio
How to send: Email

Represents book to screen and screenwriters.

L495 Natasha Mihell

Assistant Agent
Canada

https://www.therightsfactory.com/Agents/Natasha-Mihell
https://querymanager.com/query/natashatrf

Literary Agency: The Rights Factory

ADULT
Fiction > *Novels*
Fantasy; Historical Fiction; Literary; Science Fiction

Nonfiction
Graphic Nonfiction: History
Nonfiction Books: Memoir

CHILDREN'S
Fiction
Middle Grade: Allegory; Cyberpunk; Fantasy; Historical Fiction; Horror
Picture Books: Magic

Nonfiction > *Picture Books*

YOUNG ADULT
Fiction > *Novels*
Fantasy; Historical Fiction; Literary; Science Fiction

Nonfiction
Graphic Nonfiction: History
Nonfiction Books: Memoir

Closed to approaches.

Loves stories that sing, move, and shimmer, and most especially, those that are fearless in speaking their truths. She is a great fan of conceptual depth and courage (in characters and in writing), and will consider any story (Adult, YA, MG, and PB; fiction and nonfiction) that has clear heart and vision. She is always keen to support voices from the

2SLGBTQQIA+, BIPOC, #ownvoices, disabled and neurodiverse communities.

Authors: Sylvie Cathrall; Emily M. Dietrich; Taryn Herlich; Nicholas Pullen; Ana Toumine

L496 Madeleine Milburn

Literary Agent; Company Director
United Kingdom

https://madeleinemilburn.co.uk/team-member/madeleine-milburn/

Literary Agency: Madeleine Milburn Literary, TV & Film Agency (**L464**)

Fiction > *Novels*
General, and in particular: Book Club Fiction; Crime; Literary; Mystery; Romantic Comedy; Thrillers

Send: Query; Pitch; Market info; Author bio; Synopsis; Writing sample
How to send: Email
How not to send: Post

Reads across all areas of fiction but is immediately drawn to powerful, voice-led book club fiction with memorable characters and themes that will spark up conversation. She loves a literary voice that lingers on long after reading, an exciting concept that can be pitched in one sentence, and themes that resonate with readers on a universal level.

L497 Mildred Marmur Associates, Ltd.

Literary Agency
2005 Palmer Avenue, Suite 127, Larchmont, NY 10538
United States

https://aaronline.wildapricot.org/Sys/PublicProfile/2176773/417813

Fiction > *Novels*

Nonfiction > *Nonfiction Books*

Literary agent based in Larchmont, New York.

Literary Agent: Mildred Marmur (*L470*)

L498 Miles Stott Children's Literary Agency

Literary Agency
East Hook Farm, Lower Quay Road, Hook, Haverfordwest, Pembrokeshire, SA62 4LR
United Kingdom
Tel: +44 (0) 7855 252043

fictionsubs@milesstottagency.co.uk
picturebooksubs@milesstottagency.co.uk

https://www.milesstottagency.co.uk
https://www.facebook.com/pages/Miles-Stott-Childrens-Literary-Agency/311096870669
https://twitter.com/MilesStott
https://www.instagram.com/milesstottagency/

Professional Body: The Association of Authors' Agents (AAA)

CHILDREN'S
Fiction
Middle Grade; *Novels*; *Picture Books*
Nonfiction > *Nonfiction Books*

YOUNG ADULT > **Fiction** > *Novels*

Closed to approaches.

Handles Board books, Picture books, Novelty Books, Young fiction, Middle grade fiction, YA fiction, and Non-fiction. No poetry, musical works, or educational texts. For fiction send query with synopsis and first three chapters. For picture book submissions, send query by email only, with short covering letter, details about you and your background, and up to three stories. See website for full guidelines.

Authors: Kate Alizadeh; Kirsty Applebaum; Atinuke; Dominic Barker; Helen Baugh; Adam Beer; Rachel Bright; Mark Burgess; Ruth Doyle; Catherine Emmett; Jan Fearnley; Lu Fraser; Anneliese Gray; Stacy Gregg; Frances Hardinge; Caryl Hart; Sophie Kirtley; Gill Lewis; Zoë Marriott; Julia Miranda; Tom Percival; Gareth Peter; Tom Pollock; Mark Sperring; Amber Stewart; Leisa Stewart-Sharpe; Daniel Whelan

Literary Agents: Victoria Birkett (**L064**); Caroline Hill-Trevor; Nancy Miles (**L499**); Mandy Suhr (**L676**)

L499 Nancy Miles

Literary Agent
United Kingdom

nancy@milesstottagency.co.uk

https://www.milesstottagency.co.uk/about-nancy-miles.php

Literary Agency: Miles Stott Children's Literary Agency (**L498**)

CHILDREN'S > **Fiction** > *Novels*
Comedy / Humour; Contemporary; Fantasy; Historical Fiction; Science Fiction

YOUNG ADULT > **Fiction** > *Novels*
Comedy / Humour; Contemporary; Fantasy; Historical Fiction; Science Fiction

"Whatever the book – funny, fantasy, sci-fi, contemporary, historical – and for whichever age, a strong voice, great characters and an engaging plot will be the first things to reel me in."

L500 Jennie Miller

Literary Agent
United Kingdom

Literary Agency: Independent Talent Group Ltd (**L340**)

L501 Rachel Mills

Literary Agent; Company Director
United Kingdom

rachel@rmliterary.co.uk

https://twitter.com/bookishyogini

Literary Agency: Rachel Mills Literary (**L578**)

Nonfiction > *Nonfiction Books*
Biography; Commercial; Food; Narrative Nonfiction; Popular Science; Psychology; Upmarket; Wellbeing

Send: Query; Writing sample
How to send: Email

Very selectively looking for new clients writing commercial and upmarket non-fiction and wishing to develop their work into major global publishing and media brands. Areas of interest include psychology, popular science, well-being, narrative non-fiction, biography, food, sustainability, health, social media and platform led projects. She looks for projects which are international and will work on screen as well as in print.

L502 MMB Creative

Literary Agency
The Old Truman Brewery, 91 Brick Lane, London, E1 6QL
United Kingdom
Tel: +44 (0) 20 3582 9370
Fax: +44 (0) 20 3582 9377

Nonfiction@mmbcreative.com
Childrenswriter@mmbcreative.com
Childrensillustrator@mmbcreative.com
irelandgenrefiction@mmbcreative.com
irelandliteraryfiction@mmbcreative.com
ukgenrefiction@mmbcreative.com
ukliteraryfiction@mmbcreative.com

https://mmbcreative.com

Professional Body: The Association of Authors' Agents (AAA)

ADULT
Fiction > *Novels*
Adventure; Commercial Women's Fiction; Crime; Horror; Ireland; Literary; Mystery; Thrillers

Nonfiction > *Nonfiction Books*
General, and in particular: Autobiography; Current Affairs; Food and Drink; History; Memoir; Popular Culture

YOUNG ADULT
Fiction > *Novels*
Nonfiction > *Nonfiction Books*

Send: Query; Synopsis; Author bio; Writing sample
How to send: Email

Send submissions as a single document including a synopsis, author biography, writing sample, and a brief statement on why you are interested in being represented by this agency. See website for full guidelines.

Literary Agents: Ivan Mulcahy; Sallyanne Sweeney

L503 Harriet Moore

Literary Agent
United Kingdom

harrietmoore@davidhigham.co.uk

https://www.davidhigham.co.uk/agents-dh/harriet-moore/

Literary Agency: David Higham Associates Ltd (**L161**)

Fiction > *Novels*: Literary

Nonfiction > *Nonfiction Books*
Biography; History; Narrative Nonfiction

Poetry > *Poetry Collections*

How to send: Email

Represents literary fiction, narrative non-fiction, and poetry. In fiction, she admires clarity, energy, emotional candour, intense interior portraits, close observation, texture, craft and compression. In non-fiction she is interested in creative scholarship; intellectual and artistic endeavour; books which vibrantly engage with archival work, biography, history, criticism and private experience. In all forms she is interested in how writing and visual art correspond, and a scholarly attention to the ordinary and everyday.

Authors: Rachael Allen; Jason Allen-Paisant; Nuar Alsadir; Abi Andrews; Jennifer Atkins; Harriet Baker; Felix Bazalgette; Sarah Bernstein; Rebecca Birrell; Kevin Brazil; Ella Bucknall; Eliza Barry Callahan; Kathleen Collins; Sophie Collins; Emily S. Cooper; Naoise Dolan; Alicia Drake; Tom de Freston; Marlowe Granados; Jo Hamya; Alice Hattrick; Lottie Hazell; Oli Hazzard; Claire Marie Healy; Rebecca May Johnson; Emily LaBarge; Sophie Mackintosh; Kathryn Maris; Helen Marten; Thomas McMullan; Rosanna Mclaughlin; Kei Miller; Megan Nolan; Eleanor Penny; Hannah Regel; Kathryn Scanlan; Izabella Scott; Penelope Shuttle; Mary South; Dizz Tate; Jack Underwood; Joanna Walsh; Miranda Ward; Kate Zambreno

L504 Penny Moore

Literary Agent
United States

https://aevitascreative.com/agents/
https://querymanager.com/query/LiteraryPenny

Literary Agency: Aevitas

CHILDREN'S
Fiction
Middle Grade; *Picture Books*
Nonfiction > *Nonfiction Books*

YOUNG ADULT
Fiction > *Novels*
Nonfiction > *Nonfiction Books*

Send: Author bio; Query; Writing sample; Market info
How to send: Query Manager

Mainly represents children's literature, including picture books, middle grade, and young adult. She also has an interest in select platform nonfiction projects that speak to younger audiences. Though she's interested in all genres, she's specifically seeking inventive works featuring breakout voices and compelling plot lines that will make young readers feel seen and heard for the first time.

Authors: Shawn Amos; Akemi Dawn Bowman; Waka Brown; Auriane Desombre; Lyla Lee; Sangu Mandanna; Maya Prasad; Nicki Pau Preto; Rona Wang; Jenna Yoon; Katie Zhao

L505 Renae Moore

Associate Agent
United States

http://www.azantianlitagency.com/pages/team-rm.html
https://querymanager.com/query/renae

Literary Agency: Azantian Literary Agency (**L037**)

ADULT > **Fiction** > *Novels*
Literary Mystery; Literary; Speculative

YOUNG ADULT > **Fiction**
Graphic Novels: Adventure; Coming of Age; Mystery; Speculative
Novels: Adventure; Fantasy; Mystery; Romance; Science Fiction; Speculative

How to send: Query Manager

Gravitates to stories that have a balance of heart, mystery, magic, and adventure.

L506 Tim Moore

Associate Agent

https://www.therightsfactory.com/Agents/Tim-Moore
https://querymanager.com/query/2396

Literary Agency: The Rights Factory

Fiction > *Novels*
Commercial; Literary

Nonfiction > *Nonfiction Books*
Biography; Business; Comedy / Humour; Food and Drink; Health; Memoir; Personal Development; Photography; Self Help; Wellbeing

How to send: Query Manager

Represents adult non-fiction and fiction. He is interested in non-fiction which has a clear platform and fiction which has a distinctive voice.

L507 Max Moorhead

Junior Agent
United States

http://www.mmqlit.com/about/

Literary Agency: Massie & McQuilkin

L508 Imogen Morrell

Literary Agent
United Kingdom

http://greeneheaton.co.uk/agents/imogen-morrell/
https://twitter.com/imogen_morrell

Literary Agency: Greene & Heaton Ltd (**L285**)

Fiction > *Novels*
Book Club Fiction; Crime; Historical Fiction; Literary; Politics; Romance; Society; Thrillers

Nonfiction > *Nonfiction Books*
Cookery; Food; History; Nature; Politics

Send: Query; Synopsis; Writing sample
How to send: Email attachment

Looking for reading group and accessible literary fiction. Interested in brilliantly plotted social thrillers, unconventional love stories, crime novels with a difference, reimagined historical fiction. Always looking for a strong voice or a vivid main character that catches your attention from the very first page. Enjoys socially or politically informed fiction, set both now and in the past. In non-fiction, looks for proposals about food, nature, politics, history and identity, usually with a strong narrative or personal element, from academics who are writing their specialist subject for trade publication.

Authors: Juliana Adelman; Rachel Dawson; Kat Hill; Daisy J. Hung; Sam Johnson-Schlee; Fiona Keating; Anna Parker; Eddie Scott

L509 Lucy Morris

Literary Agent
United Kingdom

Literary Agency: Curtis Brown

L510 Natascha Morris

Senior Agent
United States

https://www.thetobiasagency.com/natascha-morris
https://querymanager.com/query/natascha

Literary Agency: The Tobias Literary Agency (**L699**)

CHILDREN'S > **Fiction**
Graphic Novels; *Picture Books*
YOUNG ADULT > **Fiction**
Graphic Novels; *Novels*

How to send: Query Manager

Primarily looking for picture books, middle grade graphic novels and young adult across most genres, including graphic novels. She is also open to illustrator submissions.

L511 Michele Mortimer

Literary Agent
United States

submissions@dvagency.com

https://www.dvagency.com/aboutus

Literary Agency: Darhansoff & Verrill Literary Agents (**L158**)

ADULT

Fiction > *Novels*
Crime; Historical Fiction; Literary; Mystery

Nonfiction > *Nonfiction Books*
Animals; Crime; Culture; Feminism; Memoir; Music; Narrative Nonfiction; Popular Culture; Sociology; Sport; Wellbeing

YOUNG ADULT > **Fiction** > *Novels*: Realistic

Send: Query; Writing sample
How to send: In the body of an email

Currently considers literary fiction, historical fiction, sophisticated crime and mystery, realism-based young adult fiction, and narrative nonfiction. Nonfiction interests include music, sports, wellness, animal welfare, feminism, true crime, sociology, culture both pop and serious, and memoir.

L512 Tasneem Motala

Assistant Agent
Canada

https://www.therightsfactory.com/submissions
https://querymanager.com/query/2005

Literary Agency: The Rights Factory

CHILDREN'S > **Fiction**
Graphic Novels; *Middle Grade*; *Picture Books*
YOUNG ADULT > **Fiction** > *Novels*

Closed to approaches.

Not currently accepting submissions from white people.

L513 Lisa Moylett

Literary Agent
United Kingdom

https://cmm.agency/about-us.php
http://twitter.com/MoylettLisa

Literary Agency: Coombs Moylett & Maclean Literary Agency (**L139**)

Fiction > *Novels*
Commercial Women's Fiction; Crime; Ireland; Northern Ireland; Psychological Thrillers

Nonfiction > *Nonfiction Books*
Politics; Popular Science

Send: Synopsis; Writing sample
How to send: Online submission system
How not to send: Email

Represents an eclectic list of authors and writers and is currently looking for well-written, commercial women's fiction.

L514 Toby Mundy

Literary Agent; Chief Executive Officer
United Kingdom

https://aevitascreative.com/agents/#agent-7413

Literary Agency: Aevitas Creative Management (ACM) UK (**L008**)

Fiction > *Novels*
Literary; Thrillers

Nonfiction > *Nonfiction Books*
Biography; Current Affairs; History; Memoir; Narrative Nonfiction; Popular Culture; Popular Science; Sport

Send: Query; Writing sample
How to send: Online submission system

Looking for gripping narrative nonfiction, and well written, mind-expanding works in the areas of history, biography, memoir, current affairs, sport, popular culture and popular science. Also represents a small number of thriller writers and literary novelists.

Authors: James Aldred; Michael Dine; Armand D'Angour; Jonathan Hillman; Graham Lawton; Mark Leonard; Isabel Losada; Kenan Malik; Peter Mead; Christopher Miller; Richard V. Reeves; Peter Ricketts; Donald Sassoon; Mark Sedgwick; Jeevan Vasagar; Owen Walker; Justin Webb; Christian Wolmar

L515 Nate Muscato

Literary Agent
New York
United States

https://aevitascreative.com/agents/

Literary Agency: Aevitas

Fiction > *Novels*

Nonfiction > *Nonfiction Books*
Arts; Culture; Current Affairs; History

Send: Author bio; Outline; Pitch; Market info; Writing sample
How to send: Online submission system

Interested in fiction that plays with conventions of narrative and genre, and in nonfiction that contemplates and critiques the arts, culture, history, current events, and the future.

L516 Mushens Entertainment

Literary Agency
London
United Kingdom

https://www.mushens-entertainment.com
https://twitter.com/MushensEnt

Professional Body: The Association of Authors' Agents (AAA)

London literary agency with a boutique feel. Represents a diverse range of Sunday Times and New York Times bestsellers, authors, actors, brands, and more.

Authors: Sally Abe; Yewande Biala; Anna Bogutskaya; Natalie Chandler; Laura Jane Clark; Clara Doran; Sally El-Arifi; Naomi Evans; Natalie Evans; Claire Frances; Kate Gray; Angie Greaves; Della Hicks-Wilson; Eleanor Houghton; Thom Insley; Hannah Kaner; Kuchenga; Caroline Magennis; Liberty Mendez; Denai Moore; Illiyin Morrison; Hayley Nolan; Lauren Pope; Lauren Rae; Victoria Sanusi; Joe Talbot; Stacey Thomas; Pim Wangtechawat; Hope Whitmore

Literary Agents: Liza DeBlock (**L167**); Silé Edwards (**L193**); Juliet Mushens (**L517**); Rachel Neely (**L523**)

L517 Juliet Mushens

Literary Agent
United Kingdom

submissions@mushens-entertainment.com

https://www.mushens-entertainment.com/juliet-mushens
https://twitter.com/mushenska

Literary Agency: Mushens Entertainment (**L516**)

Fiction > *Novels*
Book Club Fiction; Crime; Fantasy; Gothic; High Concept; Historical Fiction; Psychology; Science Fiction; Thrillers

Send: Query; Synopsis; Writing sample
How to send: Email

Looking for: crime, thriller, reading group fiction, gothic novels, historical fiction, and SFF. Do not send her: picture-books, MG, non-fiction, novellas, short stories/short story collections, screenplays, poetry collections or erotica. Please do not send her unfinished books. Unless she has specifically asked to see it, do not send her revised versions of earlier manuscripts she has rejected. Do not send her novels which her colleagues have rejected.

Authors: Kate Gray; Hannah Kaner

L518 James Mustelier

Literary Agent
United States

http://www.thebentagency.com/james-mustelier
https://querymanager.com/query/1908

Literary Agency: The Bent Agency (**L058**)

ADULT

Fiction > *Novels*
Alternative History; Commercial; Dark Humour; Fantasy; Horror; Literary; Mystery; Science Fiction; Speculative

Nonfiction > *Nonfiction Books*
Commercial; Literary

CHILDREN'S > **Fiction** > *Middle Grade*
Fairy Tales; Folklore, Myths, and Legends; High / Epic Fantasy; Historical Fiction; Science Fiction

YOUNG ADULT > **Fiction** > *Novels*
Fairy Tales; Folklore, Myths, and Legends; High / Epic Fantasy; Historical Fiction; Science Fiction

Does not want:

Fiction > *Novels*
High / Epic Fantasy; Space Opera

Closed to approaches.

L519 Jen Nadol

Associate Agent
United States

Jen.Nadol@theunteragency.com

http://theunteragency.com

Literary Agency: The Unter Agency (**L705**)

Send: Pitch
How to send: Email

L520 The Narrow Road Company

Literary Agency
1st Floor, 37 Great Queen Street, Covent Garden, London, WC2B 5AA
United Kingdom
Tel: +44 (0) 20 7831 4450

creatives@narrowroad.co.uk

https://narrowroad.co.uk/

Scripts
Film Scripts: General
Radio Scripts: General
TV Scripts: General
Theatre Scripts: Theatre

Send: Query
Don't send: Full text
How to send: Email
How not to send: Email attachment

Send query by email. Seeks writers with some experience and original ideas. Handles scripts only. No novels, poetry, unsolicited MSS, or email attachments.

Authors: Joe Graham; Richard Groves; Lincoln Hudson; Simon Macallum

Literary Agents: Amy Ireson (*L342*); Dan Ireson (*L343*); James Ireson (*L344*); Richard Ireson (**L345**); Rozzy Lloyd (*L439*); Adam Mendlesohn (*L485*); Sarah Veecock (*L711*)

L521 Justin Nash

Literary Agent; Managing Director
United Kingdom

https://katenashlit.co.uk/people/
https://twitter.com/JustinNashLit

Literary Agency: Kate Nash Literary Agency (**L375**)

Fiction > *Novels*
Book Club Fiction; Crime; Fantasy; Folklore, Myths, and Legends; Historical Fiction; Science Fiction; Thrillers

Nonfiction > *Nonfiction Books*
General, and in particular: Classics / Ancient World; History; Medieval; Military; Travel

Looking for thrillers and crime fiction of all types; book club and historical fiction that moves me and makes me think (including novels featuring fantasy/mythology) and SF. In non-fiction, books which open up the conversation and take me on a journey.

L522 Natasha Kern Literary Agency

Literary Agency
United States

http://natashakernliterary.com

Fiction > *Novels*

Closed to approaches.

Closed to queries from unpublished writers. Focusses on developing the careers of established writers. Will continue to accept referrals through current clients or editors, and through conferences.

Authors: Tamera Alexander; Nikki Arana; Nina Bangs; Angela Benson; Cheryl Bolen; Maggie Brendan

Literary Agent: Natasha Kern

L523 Rachel Neely

Literary Agent
United Kingdom

submissions@mushens-entertainment.com

https://www.mushens-entertainment.com/rachel-neely

Literary Agency: Mushens Entertainment (**L516**)

Fiction > *Novels*
Book Club Fiction; Crime; Historical Fiction; Literary; Thrillers; Upmarket Women's Fiction

Send: Query; Synopsis; Writing sample
How to send: Email

I'm looking for unforgettable and thought-provoking fiction, the kind that leaves your mind racing uncontrollably, hours after turning the last page. Whether commercial or literary, or something in between, I want authors who can match a distinctive voice with an equally compelling plot. I generally prefer darker stories; my favourite books often centre characters with tragic fates, dark pasts or buried trauma. I would also particularly like to find authors from underrepresented groups, who often bring a fresh perspective to well-worn story arcs or reflect experiences that are shared by many but, as of yet, underexplored in fiction.

L524 Nelson Literary Agency, LLC

Literary Agency
1732 Wazee Street, Suite 207, Denver, CO 80202
United States
Tel: +1 (303) 292-2805

info@nelsonagency.com

https://nelsonagency.com

Professional Body: Association of American Literary Agents (AALA)

ADULT > **Fiction** > *Novels*

CHILDREN'S > **Fiction**
Middle Grade; *Picture Books*
YOUNG ADULT > **Fiction** > *Novels*

Send: Query; Author bio; Writing sample
How to send: Query Manager

View individual agent interests and submit to one agent only.

Authors: Brooke Abrams; Kate Baer; L. Biehler; Jillian Boehme; Lina Chern; Kristen Ciccarelli; Jessi Cole; Lisa Duffy; Doug Engstrom; Reese Eschmann; Shana Galen; John Galligan; Florence Gonsalves; Jill Grunenwald; Alison Hammer; Sarah Zachrich Jeng; Becca Jones; Chloe Jory; Ausma Zehanat Khan; Sierra Kincade; Karen Koh; Gillian Libby; Maryann Jacob Macias; Amanda Marbais; Jonathan Messinger; Meghan Scott Molin; Katrina Monroe; Vanessa Montalban; Rosaria Munda; Jennifer Nissley; Lynette Noni; James Persichetti; Celesta Rimington; Laura Brooke Robson; Ehsaneh Sadr; Jeff Seymour; Kristen Simmons; Lisa Springer; Jennifer Springsteen; Stacy Stokes; Chrysler Szarlan; Ben Tanzer; Jordyn Taylor; Kathleen West

Literary Agents: Danielle Burby; Joanna MacKenzie (**L459**); Kristin Nelson (**L525**); Quressa Robinson

L525 Kristin Nelson

Literary Agent
United States

https://nelsonagency.com/kristin-nelson/
https://twitter.com/agentkristinNLA
https://querymanager.com/query/1350

Literary Agency: Nelson Literary Agency, LLC (**L524**)
Professional Body: Association of American Literary Agents (AALA)

ADULT > **Fiction** > *Novels*
Commercial; Fantasy; High Concept; Historical Fiction; Literary; Science Fiction; Speculative; Thrillers

YOUNG ADULT > **Fiction** > *Novels*

Send: Author bio; Query; Writing sample
How to send: Query Manager

My goal as an agent is simple: I want every client of mine to make a living solely from writing and 90% of my authors do without help from any other source of income.

L526 Nick Turner Management Ltd

Literary Agency
United Kingdom
Tel: +44 (0) 20 3723 8833

nick@nickturnermanagement.com

http://nickturnermanagement.com
https://uk.linkedin.com/in/nicolas-turner-2a84a1103
https://twitter.com/NickTurnerMgmt

ADULT > **Scripts**
Film Scripts; *Radio Scripts*; *TV Scripts*
CHILDREN'S > **Scripts** > *TV Scripts*

How to send: By referral

Creative talent agency representing a broad mix of writers, directors and producers working across feature-film, television drama, comedy, children's, continuing-drama and radio. No unsolicited submissions. New clients come through producer or personal recommendations only.

Literary Agents: Phil Adie (**L007**); Nick Turner (*L701*)

L527 Erin Niumata

Literary Agent; Senior Vice President
United States
Tel: +1 (212) 400-1494

erin@foliolit.com

https://www.foliolit.com/agents-1/erin-niumata
https://www.instagram.com/eeniumata/?hl=en
https://twitter.com/eeniumata?ref_src=twsrc%5Egoogle%7Ctwcamp%5Eserp%7Ctwgr%5Eauthor

Literary Agency: Folio Literary Management, LLC

Fiction > *Novels*
Book Club Fiction; Commercial Women's Fiction; Commercial; Historical Fiction; Mystery; Romance; Romantic Comedy; Thrillers; Women's Fiction

Nonfiction > *Nonfiction Books*
Commercial; Cookery; Memoir; Narrative Nonfiction; Prescriptive Nonfiction

Closed to approaches.

Looking for commercial nonfiction, from prescriptive and practical to narrative and memoir, as well as a select list of fiction including mysteries, rom-coms, and commercial women's fiction.

L528 Noel Gay

Literary Agency
1st Floor, 2 Stephen Street, Fitzrovia, London, W1T 1AN
United Kingdom
Tel: +44 (0) 20 7836 3941

info@noelgay.com

https://www.noelgay.com
https://twitter.com/NoelGay19

Scripts
Film Scripts; *Radio Scripts*; *TV Scripts*; *Theatre Scripts*

Agency representing writers, directors, performers, presenters, comedians, etc.

Literary Agents: Sophieclaire Armitage (*L029*); Natalie Ball (*L042*); Philip Bell; Ellie Cahill-Nicholls (*L099*)

L529 Laura Nolan

Literary Agent; Senior Partner
United States

https://aevitascreative.com/agents/

Literary Agency: Aevitas
Professional Body: Association of American Literary Agents (AALA)

Fiction > *Novels*: Upmarket Commercial Fiction

Nonfiction > *Nonfiction Books*
Alternative Health; Celebrity; Cookery; Food; Investigative Journalism; Lifestyle; Music; Politics; Science; Women's Issues

Send: Query; Writing sample
How to send: Online submission system

Represents platform-driven narrative nonfiction in the areas of celebrity, music, investigative journalism, women's issues, alternative health, and lifestyle. She is passionate about cookbooks and food narrative informed by politics or science. She is seeking challenging ideas, incisive writing that asks "big" questions, and artists who are successful in one medium but whose talents and passion translate into narrative.

L530 The North Literary Agency

Literary Agency
The Chapel, Market Place, Corbridge, Northumberland, NE45 5AW
United Kingdom

hello@thenorthlitagency.com

http://thenorthlitagency.com

Fiction > *Novels*

Nonfiction > *Nonfiction Books*: Narrative Nonfiction

Send: Query; Synopsis; Proposal; Writing sample
How to send: Email

Looking for all types of fiction and narrative nonfiction. No academic writing, poetry, self-help, picture books or screenplays. No submissions by post.

Literary Agents: Julie Fergusson (**L223**); Allan Guthrie (**L296**); Lina Langlee (**L405**); Kevin Pocklington (**L567**); Mark "Stan" Stanton (**L657**)

L531 Northbank Talent Management

Literary Agency
United Kingdom
Tel: +44 (0) 20 3973 0835

info@northbanktalent.com
fiction@northbanktalent.com
nonfiction@northbanktalent.com
childrens@northbanktalent.com

https://www.northbanktalent.com
https://twitter.com/NorthbankTalent
https://www.facebook.com/northbanktalent/
https://www.instagram.com/northbanktalent
https://www.linkedin.com/company/northbank-talent-management/
https://www.youtube.com/channel/UCKEAHOg6Y2G3NOy146k9y4A?view_as=subscriber

Professional Body: The Association of Authors' Agents (AAA)

ADULT
Fiction > *Novels*
Nonfiction > *Nonfiction Books*

CHILDREN'S
Fiction > *Middle Grade*: Commercial

Nonfiction > *Nonfiction Books*

YOUNG ADULT > **Fiction** > *Novels*

Send: Query; Synopsis; Writing sample
How to send: Email

Literary and talent agency based in central London. Actively seeking new clients. Send query by email with synopsis and first three chapters as Word or Open Document attachments to appropriate email address.

Literary Agents: Martin Redfern; Hannah Weatherill

L532 Trodayne Northern

Literary Agent; President
United States

Literary Agency: Prentis Literary (**L574**)

L533 Haskell Nussbaum

Associate Agent
Canada

Literary Agency: The Rights Factory

L534 NY Creative Management

Literary Agency
United States

http://www.nycreative.com

Types: Fiction; Nonfiction
Markets: Children's

Send: Synopsis

Send one-page synopsis by email, giving a brief, informative paragraph about your novel, non-fiction book, screenplay or magazine-length article, giving the main idea and basic structure of your project.

Literary Agent: Jeff Schmidt (**L625**)

L535 Lee O'Brien

Literary Agent
United States

Lee.queries@irenegoodman.com

https://www.irenegoodman.com/lee-obrien

Literary Agency: Irene Goodman Literary Agency (IGLA)

Fiction > *Novels*
LGBTQIA; Magic; Romance

Closed to approaches.

Across all age categories, they're looking for books with clear stakes and an immersive world, as well as anything with lots of atmosphere, magic, monsters, intrigue, or a plot full of twists and turns. They're actively seeking underrepresented voices, and they have a particular soft spot for queer romance (whether it's an epic love story or a first crush), ace rep, and trans kids with swords.

L536 Faith O'Grady

Literary Agent
108 Upper Leeson Street, Dublin 4
Ireland
Tel: + 353 1 637 5000
Fax: + 353 1 667 1256

info@lisarichards.ie

http://lisarichards.ie/writers#.YAgtljlxdaS

Literary Agency: The Lisa Richards Agency

ADULT
Fiction > *Novels*

Nonfiction > *Nonfiction Books*
Biography; Comedy / Humour; History; Lifestyle; Memoir; Motorsports; Narrative Nonfiction; Popular Culture; Self Help

CHILDREN'S > **Fiction**
Chapter Books; *Middle Grade*

Does not want:

ADULT
Fiction > *Novels*
Horror; Science Fiction

Scripts
Film Scripts; *TV Scripts*
CHILDREN'S > **Fiction** > *Picture Books*

Send: Query; Writing sample; Self-Addressed Stamped Envelope (SASE); Proposal
How to send: Email

If sending fiction, please limit your submission to the first three or four chapters. If sending non-fiction, please send a detailed proposal about your book, a sample chapter and a cover letter. Every effort will be made to respond to submissions within 3 months of receipt.

L537 Niamh O'Grady

Associate Agent
United Kingdom

https://www.thesohoagency.co.uk/agent/niamh-ogrady

Literary Agency: The Soho Agency

Fiction > *Novels*
Book Club Fiction; Comedy / Humour; Family; Literary; Relationships

Nonfiction > *Nonfiction Books*
Comedy / Humour; Narrative Nonfiction

Send: Query; Synopsis; Writing sample
How to send: Email attachment

Actively looking for accessible literary and reading-group fiction, and narrative non-fiction. She is drawn to books with heart and humour, thought-provoking writing and distinctive, compelling voices. She particularly loves novels that explore family and relationships and wants to read stories that leave an emotional impact, with characters that stay with her long after the final page. She is keen to find new Irish and Northern writing talent.

L538 Ikenna Obiekwe

Literary Agent
United Kingdom

Literary Agency: Independent Talent Group Ltd (**L340**)

L539 Hellie Ogden

Literary Agent
United Kingdom

submissions@janklow.co.uk

http://www.janklowandnesbit.co.uk/node/483
https://twitter.com/HellieOgden

Literary Agency: Janklow & Nesbit UK Ltd (**L349**)

ADULT
Fiction > *Novels*
Book Club Fiction; Commercial; Crime; High Concept Thrillers; Historical Fiction; Literary; Psychological Thrillers; Romance; Upmarket

Nonfiction > *Nonfiction Books*
Cookery; Lifestyle; Memoir; Narrative Nonfiction; Nature

CHILDREN'S > **Fiction** > *Middle Grade*
General, and in particular: Adventure; Magic

YOUNG ADULT > **Fiction** > *Novels*

How to send: Email

Represents fiction, children's books and non-fiction and enjoys novels with bold storytelling, moving prose and vivid, thought-provoking characters. In non-fiction she is looking for unique personal stories, campaigners, memoir and nature writing, cookery, lifestyle, and work that has a social following with cross-media potential. As an editorially focused agent, she has a keen interest in helping to develop and nurture debut writers.

L540 Kristin van Ogtrop

Literary Agent
United States

https://inkwellmanagement.com/staff/kristin-van-ogtrop

Literary Agency: InkWell Management

Fiction > *Novels*: Literary

Nonfiction
Illustrated Books: General
Nonfiction Books: Lifestyle; Memoir; Prescriptive Nonfiction

Represents lifestyle, illustrated books, prescriptive nonfiction, literary fiction and memoir.

L541 Mark Orsini

Literary Agent; Partner
United States

Literary Agency: Bret Adams Ltd

L542 Luba Ostashevsky

Literary Agent
United States

https://www.pandeliterary.com/about-pandeliterary

Literary Agency: Ayesha Pande Literary (**L036**)

Nonfiction > *Nonfiction Books*
Health; History; Popular Science

Send: Pitch; Author bio; Synopsis; Writing sample
How to send: Online submission system

Interested in nonfiction popular science projects, written by either research scientists, medical or mental health professionals, or journalists. Not comfortable representing fiction, cookbooks, YA, self help, nor business or politics (unless directly about science).

L543 Kristin Ostby

Literary Agent
United States

https://www.greenhouseliterary.com/the-team/kristin-ostby/
https://querymanager.com/query/kristinostby

Literary Agency: The Greenhouse Literary Agency (**L286**)

CHILDREN'S > **Fiction**
Graphic Novels: General
Middle Grade: Comedy / Humour; Commercial; Literary; Social Issues
YOUNG ADULT > **Fiction** > *Novels*
Contemporary; Literary; Mystery; Romantic Comedy; Thrillers

How to send: Query Manager

Represents authors of middle grade and young adult fiction, as well as picture book author/illustrators. She is primarily seeking voicey, character-driven middle-grade as well as literary and contemporary young adult fiction. In particular, she is looking for stories with unabashedly intersectional overtones.

L544 Bruce Ostler

Literary Agent; Partner
United States

Literary Agency: Bret Adams Ltd

L545 Anne Marie O'Farrell

Literary Agent

Professional Body: The Agents Round Table (ART)

L546 Ayesha Pande

Literary Agent
United States

https://www.pandeliterary.com/about-pandeliterary
https://twitter.com/agent_ayesha
http://aaronline.org/Sys/PublicProfile/2455085/417813

Literary Agency: Ayesha Pande Literary (**L036**)
Professional Bodies: Association of American Literary Agents (AALA); The Agents Round Table (ART)

ADULT
Fiction > *Novels*: Literary

Nonfiction > *Nonfiction Books*
Biography; Cultural Commentary; History; Memoir; Narrative Nonfiction

YOUNG ADULT > **Fiction** > *Novels*

Closed to approaches.

While her interests are wide-ranging and eclectic, she works mostly with literary fiction, narrative nonfiction across a broad range of topics including history and cultural commentary, memoir and biography, and the occasional work of young adult fiction. She is drawn to distinctive voices with a compelling point of view and memorable characters.

L547 Paper Literary

Literary Agency
United Kingdom

submissions@paperliterary.com

https://www.paperliterary.com
https://twitter.com/paperliterary
https://www.instagram.com/PaperLiterary/?hl=en

Professional Body: The Association of Authors' Agents (AAA)

Founded in 2021, with a vision of building author careers. Approach is built on a commitment to storytelling and maximizing every opportunity for our clients.

Literary Agents: Catherine Cho (**L127**); Katie Greenstreet (**L287**)

L548 Paradigm Talent and Literary Agency

Literary Agency
140 Broadway, 46th Floor, New York, NY 10005
United States
Tel: +1 (212) 897-6400
Fax: +1 (310) 288-2000

books@paradigmagency.com

https://www.paradigmagency.com

Fiction > *Novels*

Nonfiction > *Nonfiction Books*

Scripts
Film Scripts; *TV Scripts*; *Theatre Scripts*

Send: Query; Writing sample
How to send: In the body of an email

Talent and literary agency with offices in Los Angeles, New York, and London. Represents books in all areas and genres, as well as scriptwriters for film, TV, and theatre.

L549 Sandra Pareja

Literary Agent
United States

sandra@mmqlit.com

http://www.mmqlit.com/about/

Literary Agency: Massie & McQuilkin

Fiction > *Novels*: Literary

Nonfiction > *Nonfiction Books*: Narrative Nonfiction

Poetry > *Poetry Collections*

How to send: Email

Looking for authentic, unconventional literary voices in fiction, nonfiction and sometimes poetry. Query by email.

L550 Elana Roth Parker

Literary Agent
United States

http://www.ldlainc.com/submissions/
http://www.manuscriptwishlist.com/mswl-post/elana-roth-parker/
https://querymanager.com/query/queryelana
http://aaronline.org/Sys/PublicProfile/43775067/417813

Literary Agency: Laura Dail Literary Agency (**L413**)
Professional Body: Association of American Literary Agents (AALA)

CHILDREN'S > **Fiction** > *Middle Grade*
Adventure; Comedy / Humour; High / Epic Fantasy; High Concept

YOUNG ADULT > **Fiction** > *Novels*
Adventure; Comedy / Humour; Commercial; High Concept; Romance

Send: Query; Pitch; Synopsis; Author bio
How to send: Query Manager

Handles middle grade and young adult fiction. Closed to picture book submissions.

L551 Marina De Pass

Associate Agent
United Kingdom

https://www.thesohoagency.co.uk/agent/marina-de-pass
https://twitter.com/marinadepass

Literary Agency: The Soho Agency

Fiction > *Novels*
General, and in particular: Book Club Fiction; Comedy / Humour; Cookery; Folklore, Myths, and Legends; Food; Literary; Mystery; Romance; Upmarket Commercial Fiction; Upmarket Thrillers

Nonfiction > *Nonfiction Books*: Narrative Nonfiction

Does not want:

Fiction > *Novels*: Science Fiction

Send: Query; Synopsis; Writing sample
How to send: Email attachment

Building a list of upmarket commercial, reading group and accessible literary fiction – and is actively looking to take on clients in this area. She is looking for strong hooks, compelling writing and unforgettable characters. Among other things, she is drawn to books that feature: mysteries; heatwaves and/or raging storms; plot twists; hotels; secrets simmering under the surface; dramatic landscapes, a vivid sense of place; an unusual structure; characters who are not what they seem; cults; against-the-odds survival; dry humour; a light dusting of myths and folklore; chemistry that leaps off the page; love triangles, family tensions, heady affairs and forbidden romances – relationships under pressure, essentially.

L552 Paul S. Levine Literary Agency

Literary Agency
1054 Superba Avenue, Venice, CA 90291-3940
United States
Tel: +1 (310) 450-6711

http://www.paulslevinelit.com

ADULT

Fiction

Graphic Novels: General
Novels: Adventure; Legal; Mainstream; Mystery; Politics; Romance; Thrillers; Women's Fiction

Nonfiction > *Nonfiction Books*
Archaeology; Architecture; Arts; Autobiography; Business; Contemporary; Education; Gardening; Genealogy; Health; How To; Legal; Medicine; Mind, Body, Spirit; Politics; Popular Culture; Relationships; Science; Self Help; Sociology; Sport; Technology

CHILDREN'S

Fiction

Graphic Novels; *Novels*

Nonfiction > *Nonfiction Books*

YOUNG ADULT

Fiction

Graphic Novels; *Novels*

Nonfiction > *Nonfiction Books*

Send: Query
How to send: Email; Post
How not to send: Phone

Send query by email, or by post with SASE. No phone calls.

Literary Agent: Paul S. Levine (**L422**)

L553 Clare Pearson

Literary Agent
United Kingdom

Literary Agency: Eddison Pearson Ltd (**L190**)

L554 Kay Peddle

Literary Agent
United Kingdom

kay@kaypeddleliterary.co.uk

https://kaypeddleliterary.co.uk/about-us
http://instagram.com/kaypeddlebooks
http://twitter.com/kaypeddle

Literary Agency: Kay Peddle Literary (**L378**)

Nonfiction > *Nonfiction Books*
Cookery; Current Affairs; Food; History; Journalism; Literary Memoir; Narrative Nonfiction; Nature; Politics; Popular Science; Social Justice; Travel

Send: Query; Pitch; Proposal; Author bio; Market info; Writing sample; Outline
How to send: Word file email attachment

Looking for books that spark discussion, that have the potential to change opinions and reveal hidden aspects of a familiar story. Interested in narrative nonfiction; literary memoir; cookery and food writing; travel writing; nature writing; journalism with a social justice angle; politics; current affairs; history and popular science.

L555 Kristina Perez

Associate Agent
United Kingdom

perez@zenoagency.com

http://zenoagency.com/agents/kristina-perez/
https://twitter.com/kperezagent

Literary Agency: Zeno Agency Ltd (**L759**)

ADULT

Fiction > *Novels*
Dystopian Fiction; Fantasy; Feminism; Historical Fantasy; Historical Romance; Magical Realism; Retellings; Romance; Science Fiction; Space Opera; Supernatural / Paranormal Romance; Witches

Nonfiction > *Nonfiction Books*

CHILDREN'S

Fiction > *Middle Grade*
Fantasy; Historical Fiction

Poetry > *Novels in Verse*

YOUNG ADULT

Fiction > *Novels*
Coming of Age; Contemporary; Fantasy; Folklore, Myths, and Legends; Ghost Stories; Historical Fiction; LGBTQIA; Retellings; Romantic Comedy; Soft Science Fiction; Theatre; Vampires

Nonfiction > *Nonfiction Books*

Poetry > *Novels in Verse*

Does not want:

Fiction > *Novels*
Contemporary Romance; Hard Science Fiction

Closed to approaches.

Accepts submissions only from BAME and other marginalised creators.

Authors: Alexia Casale; Sharon Emmerichs; Marina Evans; Jennifer Wolf Kam; Erin Rose Kim; Martin Purbrick; Troy Tassier; Vincent Tirado; Amy True / Amy Trueblood; Khadija L. VanBrakle; Johanna van Veen; Stephen Vines; Cristin Williams; Josh Winning

L556 Martha Perotto-Wills

Assistant Agent
United Kingdom

http://www.thebentagency.com/martha-perotto-wills

Literary Agent: Molly Ker Hawn (**L314**)
Literary Agency: The Bent Agency (UK) (**L057**)

Fiction > *Novels*
General, and in particular: Literary; Speculative

Closed to approaches.

I read pretty omnivorously (though my sweet spot is the intersection of speculative and literary fiction), but across all genres I particularly enjoy unexpected narrative voices; good, stylish sentences; and transportive writing that immerses me in a fully-formed world, whether literal or emotional.

L557 Perry Literary

Literary Agency
211 South Ridge Street, Suite 2, Rye Brook, NY 10573
United States

jperry@perryliterary.com

https://www.perryliterary.com

Nonfiction > *Nonfiction Books*
Business; Cookery; Crime; Journalism; Memoir; Narrative Nonfiction; Parenting; Popular Culture; Psychology; Science; Self Help; Sociology; Sport; Technology

How to send: Email

Send query by email with first ten pages in the body of the email (or full manuscript for picture books). No attachments. See website for full guidelines.

Literary Agent: Joseph Perry

L558 Anne C. Perry

Literary Agent
United Kingdom

anne@ki-agency.co.uk

https://ki-agency.co.uk/contact

Literary Agency: Ki Agency Ltd (**L385**)

ADULT

Fiction > *Novels*

Nonfiction > *Nonfiction Books*
Adventure; Dinosaurs; Dorset; Memoir; Nature; Popular History; Popular Science; Robots; Romance

YOUNG ADULT > **Fiction** > *Novels*

Closed to approaches.

Happy to accept fiction submissions in all genres. In non-fiction, she is looking for popular science, natural history, popular history and memoirs. She loves dinosaurs, robots, the Dorset coast, and Oxford commas.

L559 Carrie Pestritto

Literary Agent
United States

http://www.ldlainc.com/about
http://aaronline.org/Sys/PublicProfile/53765008/417813
http://twitter.com/literarycarrie
https://literarycarrie.wixsite.com/blog
http://www.manuscriptwishlist.com/mswl-post/carrie-pestritto/

Literary Agency: Laura Dail Literary Agency (**L413**)
Professional Body: Association of American Literary Agents (AALA)

ADULT
Fiction > *Novels*
Chick Lit; Commercial; Cozy Mysteries; Historical Fiction; Literary; Mystery; Romance; Thrillers; Upmarket Women's Fiction

Nonfiction > *Nonfiction Books*
Biography; Memoir; Narrative Nonfiction

CHILDREN'S > **Fiction** > *Middle Grade*
Commercial; High Concept

YOUNG ADULT > **Fiction** > *Novels*
Contemporary; Fantasy; Historical Fiction; Horror; Mystery; Thrillers

Closed to approaches.

Loves the thrill of finding new authors with strong, unique voices and working closely with her clients. Always strives to help create books that will introduce readers to new worlds and is drawn in by relatable characters, meticulous world-building, and unusual, compelling premises.

L560 Peters Fraser + Dunlop

Literary Agency
55 New Oxford Street, London, WC1A 1BS
United Kingdom
Tel: +44 (0) 20 7344 1000
Fax: +44 (0) 20 7836 9539

info@pfd.co.uk

https://petersfraserdunlop.com
https://twitter.com/pfdagents
https://www.instagram.com/pfdagents/

Professional Body: The Association of Authors' Agents (AAA)

Fiction > *Novels*

Nonfiction > *Nonfiction Books*

Scripts
Film Scripts; *Radio Scripts*; *TV Scripts*

Send: Query; Synopsis; Writing sample
How to send: Email

One of the longest-established literary and talent agencies in London. We develop industry-leading work in the fields of literature, film, television, radio, audio, public speaking, digital platforms and journalism.

Authors: Jamie Bartlett; Camila Batmanghelidjh; Elaine Bedell; Simon Booker; Peter Bowles; Rosie Boycott; Pattie Boyd; Melvyn Bragg; Jonathan Bryan; Michael Caine; Emma Calder; Tamsin Calidas; Mark Carney; Augustus Casely-Hayford; Mavis Cheek; Rita Clifton; Sebastian Coe; Georgia Coleridge; Natalia Conroy; Susannah Constantine

Book Publisher: Agora Books (**P026**)

Chief Executive Officer / Literary Agent: Caroline Michel (**L491**)

Literary Agents: Alexandra Cliff; Tessa David; Kate Evans; Jon Fowler; Adam Gauntlett; Dan Herron; Laura McNeill; Annabel Merullo; Silvia Molteni; Michael Sissons and Fiona Petheram; Elizabeth Sheinkman; Camilla Shestopal; Jonathan Sissons; Rebecca Wearmouth

L561 Will Peterson

Literary Agent
United Kingdom

Literary Agency: Independent Talent Group Ltd (**L340**)

L562 Rachel Petty

Literary Agent
United Kingdom

rachelsubmissions@theblairpartnership.com

https://www.theblairpartnership.com/literary-agents/rachel-petty/
https://twitter.com/Rachel_petty_

Literary Agency: The Blair Partnership (**L066**)

CHILDREN'S
Fiction
Chapter Books; *Early Readers*; *Middle Grade*; *Picture Books*
Nonfiction > *Nonfiction Books*

YOUNG ADULT
Fiction > *Novels*
Fantasy; Horror; Romance; Thrillers

Nonfiction > *Nonfiction Books*

How to send: Email

Represents children's fiction and non-fiction, from picture books up to YA and crossover. Looking for ambitious storytelling, a bold approach to structure and voice and a fresh take on genre. Particularly interested in submissions from author/illustrators and people from underrepresented and marginalised communities. Likes YA romance, horror and thrillers (or a combination of all three, especially with a twist), hooky sweeping fantasy (wants excellent world building with a simple, clever pitch), hilarious middle grade, bold graphic picture books, and anything that has the potential to jump off the page and onto the screen.

Authors: Susanna H Cunningham; Erica Gomez; Rose Lihou

L563 Beth Phelan

Literary Agent
United States

QueryBeth@galltzacker.com
beth@galltzacker.com

https://www.galltzacker.com/submissions.html
https://querymanager.com/query/querybeth

Literary Agency: Gallt & Zacker Literary Agency

CHILDREN'S
Fiction > *Middle Grade*
Contemporary; Fantasy

Nonfiction > *Middle Grade*

YOUNG ADULT
Fiction > *Novels*
Contemporary; Fantasy

Nonfiction > *Nonfiction Books*

Closed to approaches.

Gravitates toward stories and characters that inspire, and anything with a touch of humor and the bittersweet. She is very interested in powerful and unique storytelling, offbeat contemporary fiction, immersive fantasy, and profoundly resonant voices.

L564 Ariana Philips

Literary Agent
United States

https://www.jvnla.com/our-team.php
https://twitter.com/ArianaPhilips

Literary Agency: The Jean V. Naggar Literary Agency

ADULT
Fiction > *Novels*
Commercial; Family Saga; Historical Fiction; Literary; Romantic Comedy; Upmarket Women's Fiction

Nonfiction
Gift Books: General
Illustrated Books: General
Nonfiction Books: Comedy / Humour; Cookery; Crime; Food; Lifestyle; Literary Memoir; Narrative Nonfiction; Popular Culture; Popular History; Prescriptive Nonfiction; Science; Social Issues; Sport; Travel

CHILDREN'S > **Fiction** > *Middle Grade*
Adventure; Magic; Mystery

YOUNG ADULT > **Fiction** > *Novels*
Contemporary; Romantic Comedy

Send: Query; Author bio
How to send: Online submission system

Loves to find new talent and work with her clients to develop strong proposals and manuscripts. She enjoys being the author's advocate, often being their first editor, business manager, and trusted confidante. Her personal agenting philosophy is to take on an author for the duration of their career and help guide them through the ever-changing publishing landscape. She is actively building her client list while also handling audio, permissions, and electronic rights for the agency.

L565 Juliet Pickering

Literary Agent
United Kingdom

juliet@blakefriedmann.co.uk

http://blakefriedmann.co.uk/juliet-pickering
https://twitter.com/julietpickering

Literary Agency: Blake Friedmann Literary Agency Ltd (**L067**)

Fiction > *Novels*
Book Club Fiction; Commercial; Literary

Nonfiction > *Nonfiction Books*
Cookery; Ethnic Groups; Food; Gender; Memoir; Popular Culture; Social Class; Social History

Closed to approaches.

Alongside literary, book club and commercial fiction, I represent non-fiction writers across the board, including memoir, pop culture, social history, writing on issues of race, gender and class, and cookery and food.

Authors: Diane Abbott; Kasim Ali; Dima Alzayat; Graeme Armstrong; MiMi Aye; Trezza Azzopardi; Bolu Babalola; Jendella Benson; Meliz Berg; Ian Birch; Rachel Blackmore; Nora Anne Brown; Erin Bunting; Ailsa Caine; Natasha Carthew; Norie Clarke; Julia Cole; Sue Cook; Sara Crowe; Tuyen Do; Michael Donkor; Jo Facer; Alix Fox; Sarah Franklin; Roxy Freeman; Janice Galloway; Gabriella Griffith; Sarah Hartley; Emma Forsyth Haslett; Kate Hodges; Michael Hogan; Kerry Hudson; Leah Hyslop; Alexandra Jellicoe; Benjamin Johncock; Konditor; Kat Lister; Richard Littler; Clayton Littlewood; Anneliese Mackintosh; Ailbhe Malone; Lucy Mangan; Amy Mason; Nina-Sophia Miralles; Emma Mitchell; Sue Moorcroft; Grace Mortimer; Emer O'Toole; Rosalind Powell; Annie Robertson; Elliot Ryan; Lora Stimson; Jack Urwin; Pippa Vosper; Helen Walmsley-Johnson; Andrew Wong

L566 Zoe Plant

Literary Agent
United States

plantqueries@thebentagency.com

http://www.thebentagency.com/zoe-plant
https://www.twitter.com/zoeplant89

Literary Agency: The Bent Agency (**L058**)

ADULT > **Fiction** > *Novels*
Commercial; Fantasy; Gothic; High Concept; Horror; Mystery; Science Fiction; Speculative

CHILDREN'S > **Fiction** > *Middle Grade*
General, and in particular: Commercial

YOUNG ADULT > **Fiction** > *Novels*
General, and in particular: Commercial; Horror; Magic; Science Fiction; Speculative; Thrillers

Closed to approaches.

I am looking for middle-grade and young adult fiction across all genres, as well as adult science fiction, fantasy, horror and speculative fiction. Across the board, my tastes lean towards commercial, entertaining, accessible books that also have something to say about the world. I am particularly interested in seeing submissions from writers from traditionally underrepresented backgrounds.

L567 Kevin Pocklington

Literary Agent
United Kingdom

http://thenorthlitagency.com/our-friends-in-the-north/

Literary Agency: The North Literary Agency (**L530**)

Fiction > *Novels*
Crime; Literary

Nonfiction > *Nonfiction Books*

Send: Query; Synopsis; Writing sample; Proposal
How to send: Email

Looking for a wide range of nonfiction submissions and would like to develop a fiction list with new authors, including accessible literary fiction and crime titles.

L568 Pontas Copyright Agency, S.L.

Literary Agency
P.O. Box / Apartat postal # 11, E-08183 Castellterçol (Barcelona)
Spain
Tel: (+34) 93 218 22 12

info@pontas-agency.com

http://www.pontas-agency.com

Fiction > *Novels*

Send: Author bio; Writing sample
How to send: Email

International literary and film agency accepting submissions of adult fiction in English and French by email only. Include at least the first five chapters and the author's biography.

L569 Lyndsey Posner

Literary Agent
United Kingdom

Literary Agency: Independent Talent Group Ltd (**L340**)

L570 Marcy Posner

Literary Agent; Senior Vice President
United States

marcy@foliolit.com

https://www.foliolit.com/agents-1/marcy-posner
https://querymanager.com/query/marcyposner

Literary Agency: Folio Literary Management, LLC

ADULT
Fiction > *Novels*
Historical Fiction; Mystery; Psychological Suspense; Thrillers; Women's Fiction

Nonfiction > *Nonfiction Books*
Culture; Environment; Journalism; Narrative Nonfiction; Nature; Psychology; Social Issues; Women's Issues

CHILDREN'S > **Fiction** > *Middle Grade*
Contemporary; Fantasy; Historical Fiction; Mystery; Science Fiction

YOUNG ADULT > **Fiction** > *Novels*
Contemporary; Historical Fiction; Mystery; Romance

How to send: Query Manager
How not to send: Email

Looking for Thrillers, Psychological suspense, Historical fiction, Women's fiction, Mystery, YA (contemporary, historical, romance, mystery), Middle grade (contemporary, SFF, historical, mystery, Narrative non-fiction, Cultural/social issues, Journalism, Nature and ecology, Psychology and Women's issues. No longer accepts queries through email. Submit through online submission system only.

Authors: Christi Clancy; Lexie Elliott; Jacqueline Kelly; Sheri Reynolds; Christine Sneed

L571 Anna Power

Literary Agent; Managing Director
Bloomsbury House, 74-77 Great Russell Street, London, WC1B 3DA
United Kingdom

anna@johnsonandalcock.co.uk

http://www.johnsonandalcock.co.uk/anna-power
https://twitter.com/APowerAgent

Literary Agency: Johnson & Alcock (**L356**)

Fiction
Graphic Novels: General
Novels: Book Club Fiction; Crime; Historical Fiction; Literary; Psychological Suspense

Nonfiction > *Nonfiction Books*
Cultural Criticism; Current Affairs; Food; History; Memoir; Popular Science; Psychology

Send: Query; Synopsis; Writing sample
How to send: Email attachment
How not to send: Post

In fiction, she is looking for voice-driven literary novels, book club and historical fiction, and psychological suspense and crime. Whatever the genre, she enjoys distinctive and compelling writing and worldbuilding that transports the reader. She is drawn especially to a moral dilemma, warm, human stories about families and relationships, and contemporary fiction with strong talking points, and which may be dark and funny. She is also keen to see graphic novels which appeal to a crossover readership.

In non-fiction, she invites submissions of history, memoir, current affairs, cultural criticism, popular science, psychology and food writing; anything that communicates an author's passion in an inventive and inspiring way. She particularly enjoys books by experts with new and surprising takes on subjects that change the way we think about the world.

L572 Marta Praeger

Literary Agent
United States

https://aaronline.wildapricot.org/Sys/PublicProfile/1715282/417813

Literary Agency: Robert A. Freedman Dramatic Agency, Inc. (**L592**)
Professional Body: Association of American Literary Agents (AALA)

Scripts > *Theatre Scripts*

L573 Tanusri Prasanna

Literary Agent
United States

tpsubmissions@defliterary.com

https://www.defliterary.com/agent/tanusri-prasanna/

Literary Agency: DeFiore and Company

ADULT
Fiction > *Novels*: Diversity

Nonfiction > *Nonfiction Books*
Memoir; Narrative Nonfiction; Social Justice

CHILDREN'S
Fiction
Middle Grade: Coming of Age; Contemporary; School; Suspense
Picture Books: General

Nonfiction
Middle Grade; *Picture Books*

YOUNG ADULT
Fiction > *Novels*
Coming of Age; Contemporary; School; Suspense

Nonfiction > *Nonfiction Books*

Send: Pitch; Author bio; Synopsis; Full text
How to send: Email

Looks for accessible and wide-reaching, narrative nonfiction set against themes in social justice and representation, as well as memoirs and select fiction featuring diverse perspectives, contexts, and even storytelling styles. In the YA and middle-grade spaces, Drawn to contemporary coming-of-age stories, charming and relatable romances, ambitious world-building fantasies, and well-plotted, voice-driven suspense. She's also a big fan of stories set in schools or interesting neighborhoods told from fresh viewpoints. For picture books, her list includes both meaningful, lyrical, stories as well as ones that bring alive the wonder and complexity of our world with humor and heart. She's also interested in nonfiction that excites the imagination and curiosity of young readers.

Send a concise pitch, short bio, and a two-page synopsis if querying YA/MG fiction. For picture books, include the entire text in the body of your email. If querying an illustrated project, provide sample illustrations and links to your website / Instagram page.

L574 Prentis Literary

Literary Agency
PMB 496, 6830 NE Bothell Way, Suite C, Kenmore, WA 98028
United States

info@prentisliterary.com

https://www.prentisliterary.com

ADULT
Fiction > *Novels*
Fantasy; Horror; LGBTQIA; Literary; Mystery; Romance; Science Fiction; Suspense; Thrillers; Women's Fiction

Nonfiction > *Nonfiction Books*: Memoir

CHILDREN'S > **Fiction**
Chapter Books; *Early Readers*; *Middle Grade*; *Picture Books*

YOUNG ADULT > **Fiction** > *Novels*

Closed to approaches.

Agency with a historic focus on science fiction and fantasy, but now working with well crafted stories in a variety of genres.

Literary Agents: Autumn Frisse; Reggie Lutz (*L450*)

Literary Agents / Presidents: Trodayne Northern (*L532*); Leslie Varney (*L710*)

L575 Amanda Preston

Literary Agent
United Kingdom

amandasubmissions@lbabooks.com

http://www.lbabooks.com/agent/amanda-preston/

Literary Agency: LBA Books Ltd (**L417**)

Fiction > *Novels*
Book Club Fiction; Commercial; Crime; High Concept Thrillers; Romance

Nonfiction > *Nonfiction Books*
Contemporary; Crime; Environment; History; Memoir; Narrative Nonfiction; Nature; Psychology; Science; Wellbeing

Represents a wide range of best-selling and award-winning authors across fiction and non-fiction. On the hunt for a high-concept thriller which is character and plot driven, but also has a discussable issue at its heart. Would also love a novel where the location is as integral to the plot as the crime. Would love a new crime series. On the hunt for a glorious book club love story that is doing something a bit different and special. For nonfiction, would love more true crime. It can be contemporary or historical, an unsolved case or a different perspective on a well known case. Not looking for any child-related crime stories. Looking for narrative non-fiction predominately in science, the environment, psychology, nature writing, well-being and memoir.

Authors: Emily Adlam; Jaimie Admans; Sarah Alderson; Dominique Antiglio; Kerry Barrett; A.L. Bird; Darcie Boleyn; Christina Bradley; Catherine Brookes; Jo Carnegie; Lucie Cave; Rebecca Chance; Emma Cooper; Susie Donkin; Hannah Doyle; Katherine Dyson; Kate Hackworthy; Fiona Harper; Natalie Heaton; Holly Jade; Lesley Kara; Simon Kernick; Emily Kerr; Ella King; Amy Lavelle; Georgina Lees; Freda Lightfoot; Jane Linfoot; Rachael Lucas; Dee MacDonald; Ian Marber; Colin McDowell; Lisa Medved; Angelique Panagos; Catherine Piddington; Kate Poels; Anna Pointer; Gillian Richmond; N J Simmonds; Zara Stoneley; Heidi Swain; Karen Swan; Sophie Tanner; Jonathan Trigell; Anna Turns; Claire Wade; Kate Winter; Dalton Wong; Fiona Woodifield

L576 Arthur B. Pulitzer

Literary Agent
United States

Literary Agency: Arthur B Pulitzer Agency (**L031**)

L577 Rufus Purdy

Literary Agent
United Kingdom

Literary Agency: The Two Piers Literary Agency (**L702**)

L578 Rachel Mills Literary

Literary Agency
M27, South Wing, Somerset House, Strand, London, WC2R 1LA
United Kingdom

submissions@rmliterary.co.uk

https://www.rachelmillsliterary.co.uk
https://twitter.com/bookishyogini
https://www.instagram.com/rachelmillsliterary/

Professional Body: The Association of Authors' Agents (AAA)

How to send: Email

As an agency we are particularly interested in female voices, and in showcasing talent which deserves to be heard, regardless of age or background. We seek to work with authors whose careers we can help build over the long term, across multiple projects.

Company Director / Literary Agent: Rachel Mills (**L501**)

Literary Agent: Nelle Andrew (**L022**)

L579 Susan Ramer

Literary Agent
United States

Literary Agency: Don Congdon Associates, Inc. (**L178**)

Closed to approaches.

L580 Redhammer

Literary Agency
United Kingdom

https://redhammer.info
https://www.facebook.com/RealLitopia
https://twitter.com/Litopia
https://www.linkedin.com/in/petecox/
https://studio.youtube.com/channel/UCmbrM2ciaxb4hHQFfnSeOpg

Fiction > *Novels*

Nonfiction > *Nonfiction Books*

Send: Pitch; Writing sample
How to send: Online submission system

Runs weekly pop-up submission sessions where you can watch your submission being discussed.

Literary Agent: Peter Cox (*L145*)

L581 Regina Ryan Publishing Enterprises

Literary Agency
251 Central Park West, #7D, New York, NY 10024
United States
Tel: +1 (212) 787-5589

queries@reginaryanbooks.com

http://www.reginaryanbooks.com

Professional Body: Association of American Literary Agents (AALA)

Types: Nonfiction
Formats: Reference
Subjects: Adventure; Architecture; Autobiography; Business; Cookery; Gardening; Health; History; Legal; Leisure; Lifestyle; Nature; Politics; Psychology; Science; Spirituality; Sport; Travel; Women's Interests
Markets: Adult

Send: Full text
How to send: Email

Costs: Author covers sundry admin costs.

Send submissions through email. See website for full guidelines.

Authors: Ben Austro; Randi Minetor; Doug Whynott

Literary Agent: Regina Ryan

L582 Janet Reid

Literary Agent
United States

Janet@JetReidLiterary.com

http://www.jetreidliterary.com
http://jetreidliterary.blogspot.com/
https://queryshark.blogspot.com/
http://aaronline.org/Sys/PublicProfile/2176820/417813
https://www.publishersmarketplace.com/members/JanetReid/

Literary Agency: JetReid Literary Agency (**L352**)
Professional Bodies: Association of American Literary Agents (AALA); Mystery Writers of America (MWA); Society of Children's Book Writers and Illustrators (SCBWI)

ADULT
Fiction > *Novels*
Commercial; Crime; Domestic Suspense; Literary; Mystery; Thrillers

Nonfiction > *Nonfiction Books*
Biography; History; Memoir; Narrative Nonfiction; Science

CHILDREN'S > **Nonfiction**
Middle Grade: Biography; History
Picture Books: Biography; History

Send: Query; Writing sample; Author bio; Proposal
How to send: In the body of an email
How not to send: Email attachment

New York literary agent with a list consisting mainly of crime novels and thrillers, and narrative nonfiction in history and biography.

Authors: Robin Becker; Bill Cameron; Gary Corby; Phillip DePoy; Stephanie Evans; Kennedy Foster; Lee Goodman; Dana Haynes; Patrick Lee; Thomas Lippman; Jeff Marks; Warren Richey; Terry Shames; Jeff Somers; Robert Stubblefield; Deb Vlock

L583 Milly Reilly

Literary Agent
United Kingdom

Literary Agency: Jo Unwin Literary Agency (**L354**)

L584 Jessica Reino

Senior Agent
United States

https://www.metamorphosisliteraryagency.com/about
https://querymanager.com/query/JessicaReino
https://twitter.com/jnrlitauthor

Literary Agency: Metamorphosis Literary Agency (**L487**)

ADULT
Fiction > *Novels*
General, and in particular: Contemporary Romance; Fantasy; Legal Thrillers; Mystery; Psychological Thrillers; Suspense; Women's Fiction

Nonfiction > *Nonfiction Books*
Comedy / Humour; Health; Parenting; Popular Culture; Sport

CHILDREN'S > **Fiction** > *Middle Grade*
General, and in particular: Horror

YOUNG ADULT > **Fiction** > *Novels*
Contemporary; Fantasy; Horror; Magical Realism; Romance; Science Fiction; Supernatural / Paranormal

Closed to approaches.

Looking for manuscripts that are well-written with a strong voice in order to make that emotional connection. Seeking MG, YA, Adult and nonfiction projects.

L585 Laura Rennert

Executive Agent
United States

ljrennert@mac.com

http://www.litagentlaurarennert.com
https://www.andreabrownlit.com/Team/Laura-Rennert
https://www.publishersmarketplace.com/members/LauraRennert/
https://www.manuscriptwishlist.com/mswl-post/laura-rennert/
https://querymanager.com/query/LauraRennert

Literary Agency: Andrea Brown Literary Agency, Inc.

ADULT > **Fiction**
Graphic Novels: General
Novels: Commercial; Fantasy; Folklore, Myths, and Legends; Gothic; Historical Fiction; Horror; Literary; Police Procedural; Science Fiction; Social Issues; Speculative; Thrillers
CHILDREN'S > **Fiction**
Chapter Books; *Middle Grade*; *Picture Books*
YOUNG ADULT > **Fiction** > *Novels*

Send: Query; Author bio; Writing sample
How to send: Email

Specializes in all categories of children's books, from picture books to young adult. On the adult side, she represents literary-commercial fiction, thrillers, horror, sci-fi/fantasy, speculative fiction, and select historical fiction. Her sweet spot in the market is literary voice and commercial conception.

L586 Richard Curtis Associates, Inc.

Literary Agency
United States

curtisagency@haroldober.com

https://www.haroldober.com/richard-curtis

Literary Agency: Harold Ober Associates, Inc.
Professional Body: Association of American Literary Agents (AALA)

Fiction > *Novels*

Nonfiction > *Nonfiction Books*

Closed to approaches.

Acquired in January 2022. Continues to administer advance, royalty and other payments for the thousands of backlist titles brought to readers since the agency was founded in 1979.

Literary Agent: Richard Curtis

L587 Nicki Richesin

Literary Agent
United States

https://www.dclagency.com

Literary Agency: Dunow, Carlson & Lerner Agency

ADULT > **Fiction** > *Novels*
Literary; Upmarket

YOUNG ADULT
Fiction > *Novels*

Nonfiction > *Nonfiction Books*
Biography; Cookery; Diversity; Feminism; Films; Investigative Journalism; Memoir; Music; Popular Culture; TV

Represents literary and upmarket fiction, and young adult fiction. She also focuses on nonfiction including investigative journalism, pop culture (especially film/TV and music), biography, cooking, and memoir that makes an impact and becomes part of a larger cultural conversation. She is particularly interested in discovering underrepresented voices from around the world exploring identity, feminism, and social diversity.

L588 Richford Becklow Literary Agency

Literary Agency
United Kingdom
Tel: +44 (0) 1728 660879 / + 44 (0) 7510 023823

lisa.eveleigh@richfordbecklow.co.uk

https://www.richfordbecklow.com
https://www.facebook.com/RichfordBecklowLiteraryAgency/
https://twitter.com/richfordbecklow

Fiction > *Novels*
Crime; Fantasy; Historical Fiction; Literary; Romance; Saga

Nonfiction > *Nonfiction Books*
Biography; Memoir

Closed to approaches.

Company founded in 2012 by an experienced agent, previously at the longest established literary agency in the world. Interested in fiction and nonfiction. See website for full submission guidelines.

Author Estate: The Estate of Leila Berg

Authors: Caroline Ashton; Amanda Austen; Hugo Barnacle; Stephen Buck; Anne Corlett; Iestyn Edwards; Ralph Fevre; Gray Freeman; Sam Giles; Jane Gordon-Cumming; R P Marshall; Carol McGrath; Sophie Parkin; Robert Ross; Lakshmi Raj Sharma; Tony Slattery; Jonathan Socrates; Adrienne Vaughan; Grace Wynne-Jones

Literary Agent: Lisa Eveleigh

L589 Rick Richter

Literary Agent; Partner
United States

https://aevitascreative.com/agents/

Literary Agency: Aevitas

ADULT
Fiction > *Novels*: Thrillers

Nonfiction > *Nonfiction Books*
Celebrity Memoir; Crime; Food; History; Memoir; Music; Narrative Nonfiction; Politics; Popular Culture; Religion; Self Help; Social Issues; Sports Celebrity

CHILDREN'S > **Fiction**
Middle Grade; *Picture Books*
YOUNG ADULT > **Fiction** > *Novels*

Send: Author bio; Market info; Writing sample
How to send: Online submission system

Areas of interest include self-help, pop culture, memoir, history, thriller, true crime, political and social issues, narrative food writing, and faith. He has deep experience and interest in children's books.

Authors: John Bainbridge; Rob Barnett; Mary Jane Begin; Sheryl Berk; Tom Booth; Marcus Brotherton; Kyle Buchanan; Marc and Angel Chernoff; Pan Cooke; Amanda Craig; Geoff Edgers; Michael Emberley; JR and Vanessa Ford; Michael and Ava Gardner; Dan Goldman; Margaret Greanais; Andy Greene; Peter Guralnick; Michael Hendrix; James Hibberd; Barry Jackson; Jeffrey H. Jackson; Alan Katz; Erin Kimmerle; Rebecca Kling; William J. Kole; Neil Lane; Kim Mager; Aaron Mahnke; Amanda Marrone; SSG Travis Mills; Malcolm Mitchell; Real Sports Entertainment Network; Chris and Emily Norton; Panos Panay; Shawn Peters; Greg Presto; Jessica Radloff; Michael Relth; David Ricciardi; Tim Sommer; Isaiah Stephens; Melanie Sumrow; Leah Tinari; Neil Tomba; Allison Varnes; Molly Webster; Paige Wetzel; Sean Fay Wolfe

L590 Patricia Riddle-Gaddis

Author; Literary Agent; Editor
United States

patricia@hartlineliterary.com

https://www.hartlineagency.com/agents-and-authors

Literary Agency: Hartline Literary Agency (**L311**)

ADULT
Fiction > *Novels*
Cozy Mysteries; Romance

Nonfiction > *Nonfiction Books*

YOUNG ADULT > **Fiction** > *Novels*

Interested in obtaining sweet romance, cozy mysteries, and young adult categories. (think Princess Diaries and a modern Nancy Drew.) She will also consider a range of nonfiction.

Authors: Marlys Johnson; Karl A. Schultz; Norma F. Swanson

L591 Rebecca Ritchie

Literary Agent
United Kingdom

https://amheath.com/agents/rebecca-ritchie/
https://twitter.com/Becky_Ritchie1

Literary Agency: A.M. Heath & Company Limited, Author's Agents (**L003**)

Fiction > *Novels*
Book Club Fiction; Comedy / Humour; Commercial; Contemporary Women's Fiction; Crime; High Concept; Historical Fiction; Police Procedural; Psychological Suspense; Romance; Saga; Thrillers

Nonfiction > *Nonfiction Books*
Cookery; Health; Travel; Wellbeing

L592 Robert A. Freedman Dramatic Agency, Inc.

Literary Agency
1501 Broadway, Suite 2310, New York, NY 10036
United States
Tel: +1 (212) 840-5760

info@robertfreedmanagency.com
mprfda@gmail.com
mp@bromasite.com

https://www.robertfreedmanagency.com
https://www.facebook.com/RAFagency/
https://twitter.com/RFreedmanAgency
https://www.linkedin.com/company/robert-a-freedman-dramatic-agency-inc/

Professional Body: Writers Guild of America (WGA)

Scripts
Film Scripts; *TV Scripts*; *Theatre Scripts*

Dramatic literary agency based in New York City representing playwrights and film and television writers.

Literary Agent / President: Robert Freedman (**L237**)

Literary Agents: Samara Harris (*L308*); Marta Praeger (**L572**)

L593 Robert Caskie Ltd

Literary Agency
United Kingdom

submissions@robertcaskie.com

https://www.robertcaskie.com/
https://twitter.com/rcaskie1

Literary Agent: Robert Caskie (**L111**)

L594 Robert Smith Literary Agency Ltd

Literary Agency
12 Bridge Wharf, 156 Caledonian Road, London, N1 9UU
United Kingdom
Tel: +44 (0) 20 8504 0024
Fax: +44 (0) 20 7833 5680

robert@robertsmithliteraryagency.com

https://www.robertsmithliteraryagency.com

Professional Body: The Association of Authors' Agents (AAA)

Nonfiction > *Nonfiction Books*
Autobiography; Biography; Comedy / Humour; Crime; Current Affairs; Fitness; Health; History; Inspirational; Language; Military; Personal Development; Popular Culture; Real Life Stories; Warfare

Send: Query; Outline; Author bio; Synopsis; Writing sample; Market info; Self-Addressed Stamped Envelope (SASE)
How to send: Post; Email

Email or post a covering letter, briefly describing the book you want to write and why you are well qualified to be its author. Do not submit proposals for novels, academic books, poetry, children's books, religious books or film / TV scripts.

Authors: Arthur Aldridge; Sarbjit Kaur Athwal; Richard Anthony Baker; Delia Balmer; Juliet Barnes; Amanda Barrie; John Baxter; William Beadle; Robert Beasley; Peta Bee; Paul Begg; John Bennett; Kevin Booth; Ralph Bulger; James Carnac; John Casson; Gary Chapman; Shirley Charters; John Clarke; Robert Clarke; Carol Clerk; Martyn Compton; Michelle Compton; Judy Cook; Les Cummings; Clive Driscoll; Rosie Dunn; Georgie Edwards; Russell Edwards; Kate Elysia; Stewart P. Evans; Penny Farmer; Martin Fido; Sarah Flower; Freddie Foreman; Helen Foster; Becci Fox; Astrid Franse; Stephen Fulcher; Alison Goldie; Charlotte Green; Christopher Green; Allan Grice; Christine Hamilton; Andrew Hansford; James Haspiel; Chris Hutchins; Rosalinda Hutton; Albert Jack; Naomi Jacobs; Muriel Jakubait; Nikola James; Sarah Jones; Christine Keeler; Anita Kelsey; Siobhan Kennedy-McGuinness; Heidi Kingstone; Brian Kirby; Tim Kirby; John Knight; Ronnie Knight; Reg Kray; Roberta Kray; Tony Lambrianou; Carol Ann Lee; John Lee; Angela Levin; Chris Lightbown; Seth Linder; David R. L. Litchfield; Mary Long; Tony Long; Jean MacColl; Gretel Mahoney; Maurice Mayne; Lenny McLean; Ann Ming; Paddy Monaghan; James Moore; Michelle Morgan; Caroline Morris; Zana Morris; Rochelle Morton; Alan Moss; Bobbie Neate; Paul Nero; Kim Noble; Laurie O'Leary; Marnie Palmer; Theo Paphitas; Gordon Rayner; Mike Reid; Frances Reilly; Lyn Rigby; William D. Rubinstein; Mark Ryan; Sarah Schenker; Nathan Shapow; Alexander Sinclair; Keith Skinner; David Slattery-Christy; Len Smith; Rita Smith; Allan Starkie; Jayne Sterne; Cameron Stewart; Neil R. Storey; Claudia Strachan; Bob Taylor; Christopher Warwick; Monica Weller; Natalie Welsh; Wynne Weston-Davies; Karl Williams; Peter Wilton; Robert Winnett; Joanne Zorian-Lynn

Literary Agents: Anne Smith; Robert Smith

L595 Soumeya Bendimerad Roberts

Literary Agent; Vice President
United States

soumeya@hgliterary.com

https://www.hgliterary.com/soumeya
https://querymanager.com/query/SBR
https://www.publishersmarketplace.com/members/SoumeyaRoberts/

Literary Agency: HG Literary
Professional Body: Association of American Literary Agents (AALA)

ADULT
Fiction
Novels: Literary; Postcolonialism; Upmarket
Short Fiction Collections: Literary

Nonfiction
Essays: Personal Essays
Nonfiction Books: Crafts; Design; How To; Lifestyle; Memoir; Narrative Nonfiction; Prescriptive Nonfiction

CHILDREN'S > **Fiction** > *Middle Grade*: Realistic

YOUNG ADULT > **Fiction** > *Novels*: Realistic

Closed to approaches.

Represents literary novels and collections, upmarket fiction, and non-fiction, both narrative and prescriptive. Though she is primarily seeking Adult genres, she also represents select, realistic middle-grade and YA. She is particularly, but not exclusively, interested in fiction that reflects on the post-colonial world, marginalized and liminal spaces, and narratives by people of color. In non-fiction, she is primarily looking for idea-driven or voice-forward memoirs, personal essay collections, and narrative non-fiction of all stripes. She also represents a curated list of practical and how-to books by makers across creative fields including design, craft, and lifestyle.

L596 Rochelle Stevens & Co.

Literary Agency
2 Terretts Place, Upper Street, London, N1 1QZ
United Kingdom
Tel: +44 (0) 20 7359 3900

info@rochellestevens.com

http://www.rochellestevens.com
http://twitter.com/TerrettsPlace
http://www.rochellestevens.com/submissions/#

Scripts
Film Scripts; *Radio Scripts*; *TV Scripts*; *Theatre Scripts*

Send: Query; Author bio; Synopsis; Writing sample
How to send: Email

Handles script writers for film, television, theatre, and radio. No longer handles writers of fiction, nonfiction, or children's books. See website for full submission guidelines.

Literary Agents: Frances Arnold; Rochelle Stevens

L597 Sue Rodgers

Literary Agent
United Kingdom

Literary Agency: Independent Talent Group Ltd (**L340**)

L598 Jennifer Rofe

Senior Agent
United States

jennifer@andreabrownlit.com

https://www.andreabrownlit.com/Team/Jennifer-Rof%C3%A9
http://twitter.com/jenrofe
http://instagram.com/jenrofe
https://www.publishersmarketplace.com/members/jenrofe/
https://www.manuscriptwishlist.com/mswl-post/jennifer-rofe/
http://queryme.online/jenrofe

Literary Agency: Andrea Brown Literary Agency, Inc.

CHILDREN'S > **Fiction**
Chapter Books: General
Middle Grade: General, and in particular: Commercial; Contemporary; Fantasy; Historical Fiction; Literary; Magic
Picture Books: General

Send: Query; Author bio; Writing sample
How to send: Query Manager

Always seeking distinct voices and richly developed characters. Middle grade has long been her soft spot and she's open to all genres in this category—literary, commercial, contemporary, magical, fantastical, historical, and everything in between. She especially appreciates stories that make her both laugh and cry, and that offer an unexpected view into the pre-teen experience. In picture books, she likes funny, character-driven projects; beautifully imagined and written stories; and milestone moments with a twist.

L599 Roger Hancock Ltd

Literary Agency
4th Floor, 7-10 Chandos Street, Cavendish Square, London, W1G 9DQ
United Kingdom
Tel: +44 (0) 20 8341 7243

enquiries@rogerhancock.com

http://www.rogerhancock.com

Types: Scripts
Subjects: Comedy / Humour; Drama; Entertainment
Markets: Adult

Handles scripts only. Interested in comedy dramas and light entertainment. No books or unsolicited MSS.

L600 Maria Rogers

Associate Agent
United States

https://www.thetobiasagency.com/maria-rogers
https://querymanager.com/query/MRogers

Literary Agency: The Tobias Literary Agency (**L699**)

ADULT > **Nonfiction** > *Nonfiction Books*
Cultural Criticism; Journalism; Science

CHILDREN'S > **Nonfiction** > *Nonfiction Books*
Classics / Ancient World; Contemporary

Send: Query; Synopsis; Writing sample; Pitch; Market info
How to send: Query Manager

Currently looking for non-fiction that explores big events from new angles, whip-smart cultural criticism, as well as original and urgent journalism and science writing. She's also on the lookout for books to engage kids in non-fiction topics, from ancient history to contemporary issues. She is not currently considering poetry, picture books, romance, science fiction, or fantasy at this time.

L601 The Rosenberg Group

Literary Agency
United States

http://www.rosenberggroup.com
https://querymanager.com/query/QueryManagerRosenbergGroup

Professional Body: Association of American Literary Agents (AALA)

ACADEMIC > **Nonfiction** > *Nonfiction Books*

ADULT

Fiction > *Novels*
Romance; Women's Fiction

Nonfiction > *Nonfiction Books*
General, and in particular: Apiculture (Beekeeping); History; Psychology; Wine

How to send: Query Manager

Represents romance and women's fiction for an adult audience, nonfiction, and college textbooks.

Literary Agent: Barbara Collins Rosenberg (*L602*)

L602 Barbara Collins Rosenberg

Literary Agent
United States

Literary Agency: The Rosenberg Group (**L601**)

L603 Whitney Ross

Literary Agent
United States

Literary Agency: Irene Goodman Literary Agency (IGLA)

L604 Zoe Ross

Literary Agent
United Kingdom

zross@unitedagents.co.uk

https://www.unitedagents.co.uk/zrossunitedagentscouk

Literary Agency: United Agents (**L704**)

Fiction > *Novels*: Literary

Nonfiction > *Nonfiction Books*
Food; Narrative Nonfiction

Works with a list of writers ranging from exciting new voices in literary fiction and narrative non-fiction, to award-winning food writers and academics. With a background in modern languages and psychoanalysis, she has a particular taste for stylish prose, sly humour and complex characterisation in fiction, and for challenging ideas and questions of identity across all genres.

L605 Stefanie Rossitto

Literary Agent
United States

https://www.thetobiasagency.com/stefanie-rossitto
https://querymanager.com/query/1927

Literary Agency: The Tobias Literary Agency (**L699**)

Fiction > *Novels*
Historical Fiction; Historical Romance; Medieval; Romance

How to send: Query Manager

Currently looking for historical fiction, and funny, witty, modern romances. She also enjoys anything and everything medieval as well as exciting historical romances and/or fiction based on real characters.

L606 Eliza Rothstein

Literary Agent
United States

http://www.inkwellmanagement.com/staff/eliza-rothstein
https://twitter.com/elizaloren

Literary Agency: InkWell Management

Fiction > *Novels*
Commercial; Literary

Nonfiction > *Nonfiction Books*
Business; Comedy / Humour; Food; Journalism; Medicine; Memoir; Narrative Nonfiction; Popular Culture; Psychology; Science; Technology

Send: Query; Writing sample
How to send: In the body of an email

Represents memoir, literary and commercial fiction, and a wide range of journalists and nonfiction authors who seek to generate deep conversations, inspire social and systemic change, or advance our understanding of our minds and bodies. In addition to finding publishers for their books, she helps writers expand their reach by placing essays and journalism in publications ranging from The New York Times and The Atlantic to National Geographic and Sports Illustrated. She is particularly interested in the intersection of narrative writing with topics of psychology, medicine, science, food, technology, business, humor and pop culture. She is also drawn to literary fiction that explores diverse communities or intergenerational stories, commercial fiction that crosses genre borders, and fiction from Latinx and Spanish-speaking writers.

L607 Steph Roundsmith

Literary Agent; Editor
United Kingdom

Literary Agency / Editorial Service: Steph Roundsmith Agent and Editor (**L659**)

L608 Laura Rourke

Literary Agent
United Kingdom

Literary Agency: Independent Talent Group Ltd (**L340**)

L609 The Rudy Agency

Literary Agency
United States
Tel: +1 (970) 577-8500

https://www.rudyagency.com

ADULT
Fiction > *Novels*

Nonfiction > *Nonfiction Books*
Business; Health; History; Investigative Journalism; Legal; Medicine; Politics; Science; Sport

CHILDREN'S
Fiction > *Picture Books*
Nonfiction > *Illustrated Books*

YOUNG ADULT > **Fiction** > *Novels*

Send: Query
Don't send: Proposal; Full text
How to send: Email

Agency representing both fiction and nonfiction. Send query before sending proposal or manuscript. Approach only one agent.

Literary Agents: Hilary Claggett; Maryann Karinch (**L371**); Vincent dePaul Lupiano; Lauren Manoy; Kimberly Peticolas; Geoffrey Stone (**L668**)

L610 Rupert Heath Literary Agency

Literary Agency
United Kingdom

emailagency@rupertheath.com

http://www.rupertheath.com
https://twitter.com/RupertHeathLit
https://www.facebook.com/RupertHeathLit/
https://www.pinterest.com/rupertheathlit/
https://www.youtube.com/user/RupertHeathLit
http://www.linkedin.com/company/rupert-heath-literary-agency

Professional Body: The Association of Authors' Agents (AAA)

Fiction > *Novels*
Commercial; Crime; Historical Fiction; Literary; Science Fiction; Thrillers

Nonfiction > *Nonfiction Books*
Arts; Autobiography; Biography; Comedy / Humour; Current Affairs; History; Nature; Politics; Popular Culture; Popular Science

Send: Query; Author bio; Outline
How to send: Email

Send query giving some information about yourself and the work you would like to submit by email. Response only if interested.

Authors: Michael Arnold; Mark Blake; Paddy Docherty; Peter Doggett; Nina Lyon; Lorna Martin; Christopher Moore

Literary Agent: Rupert Heath (*L318*)

L611 Alex Rusher

Literary Agent
United Kingdom

Literary Agency: Independent Talent Group Ltd (**L340**)

L612 Laetitia Rutherford

Literary Agent
United Kingdom

https://www.watsonlittle.com/agent/laetitia-rutherford/
http://www.twitter.com/laetitialit

Literary Agency: Watson, Little Ltd

Fiction > *Novels*
Africa; Crime; High Concept; Legal Thrillers; Literary; Upmarket

Nonfiction > *Nonfiction Books*
Contemporary; Culture; Environment; Gender; Nature; Parenting; Sexuality

Send: Query; Synopsis; Writing sample
How to send: Email

I represent a broad and diverse list of authors, ranging across Fiction and contemporary Non Fiction, and including literary prizewinners and commercial bestsellers. In Fiction, my special areas are Literary, Upmarket Fiction and Crime.

Author Estate: The Estate of Christine Evans

Authors: R.G. Adams; Lucy Ayrton; Jenny Blackhurst; Andrew Brown; Clare Brown; Ursula Brunetti; Emile Chabal; Ajay Chowdhury; Cynthia Clark; Vivianne Crowley; Jeremy Daldry; Rebecca Elliott; JM Hewitt; Samson Kambalu; Holan Liang; Lindiwe Maqhubela; Alex Marwood; Diana McCaulay; Thabi Moeketsi; Tamsin Omond; Matt Rendell; Richard Owain Roberts; Anika Scott; Hannah Silva; Zoe Somerville; Shane Spall; Akemi Tanaka; Geeta Vara; Vincent Vincent; Jeremy Williams

L613 Jim Rutman

Senior Agent
United States

https://www.sll.com/our-team
http://aaronline.org/Sys/PublicProfile/4090054/417813

Literary Agency: Sterling Lord Literistic, Inc. (**L662**)
Professional Body: Association of American Literary Agents (AALA)

Fiction > *Novels*

Nonfiction > *Nonfiction Books*
Culture; History

Send: Query; Synopsis; Writing sample
How to send: Online submission system

Represents formally adventurous and stylistically diverse authors of fiction as well as a variety of journalists and critics whose non-fiction work examines an array of cultural and historical subjects.

L614 Amanda Rutter

Associate Agent
United States

http://www.azantianlitagency.com/pages/team-ar.html

Literary Agency: Azantian Literary Agency (**L037**)

ADULT > **Fiction** > *Novels*
Fantasy; Science Fiction

CHILDREN'S > **Fiction** > *Middle Grade*
Fantasy; Science Fiction

YOUNG ADULT > **Fiction** > *Novels*
Fantasy; Science Fiction

Closed to approaches.

Looking for adult, YA and MG fantasy and science fiction. She is particularly keen to find hopeful science fiction, political fantasy and fresh takes on familiar tropes. Stories that definitely agree with her include: enemy to friend dynamics, women in STEM environments, antagonists with realistic motivations, and characters that overcome challenges in surprising ways. Stories that don't appeal include steampunk and zombie fiction! She would like to see witty dialogue, strong world building, and tales about characters from diverse backgrounds that don't concentrate on issues, but explore all facets of life.

L615 Vicki Salter

Literary Agent
United Kingdom

Literary Agency: Barbara Levy Literary Agency (**L044**)

L616 Katie Salvo

Senior Agent
United States

https://www.metamorphosisliteraryagency.com/about
https://querymanager.com/query/KatieSalvo
https://www.metamorphosisliteraryagency.com/submissions

Literary Agency: Metamorphosis Literary Agency (**L487**)

ADULT
Fiction > *Novels*
LGBTQIA; Romance; Women's Fiction

Nonfiction > *Nonfiction Books*
Biography; History; LGBTQIA

CHILDREN'S > **Fiction** > *Middle Grade*

YOUNG ADULT > **Fiction** > *Novels*

How to send: Query Manager

Has a background in literary criticism, philosophy, political theory, and history. She is particularly interested in representing women's fiction, romance, children's books, middle grade, young adult, LGBTQ+, and historical biography.

L617 Rayhane Sanders

Literary Agent
United States

http://www.mmqlit.com/about/

Literary Agency: Massie & McQuilkin
Professional Body: Association of American Literary Agents (AALA)

Fiction
Graphic Novels: General
Novels: Book Club Fiction; Historical Fiction; Literary; Upmarket
Short Fiction Collections: General

Nonfiction
Essays: General
Nonfiction Books: Memoir; Narrative Nonfiction

Does not want:

YOUNG ADULT > **Fiction** > *Novels*: Speculative

Represents and is on the lookout for literary and historical fiction, upmarket book-club fiction, comic novels, short story collections, propulsive narrative nonfiction, essay collections, and memoir. She likes projects that are voice-centered and site-specific, whether that be a place, profession, culture, or subculture. Though quality of writing is the most important factor, she is particularly interested in fresh voices telling fresh stories we haven't heard before and is fond of immigrant stories and stories concerned with race, sexuality, cross-cultural themes, and notions of identity.

L618 Angelique Tran Van Sang

Literary Agent
United Kingdom

Literary Agency: Felicity Bryan Associates (**L220**)

Fiction > *Novels*: Literary

Nonfiction > *Nonfiction Books*
Arts; History; Literature; Memoir; Narrative Nonfiction; Philosophy; Politics

Send: Query; Synopsis; Writing sample
How to send: Online submission system

Actively building a list of authors of literary fiction and narrative non-fiction. Interested in essays and longform narratives that have a distinctive voice. Also partial to an exquisitely written memoir, ideally one that weaves in art, literature, history, politics or philosophy.

Author: Amy Key

L619 Sarah Jane Freymann Literary Agency

Literary Agency
United States

Submissions@SarahJaneFreymann.com

http://www.sarahjanefreymann.com

ADULT
Fiction > *Novels*
Commercial; Literary

Nonfiction > *Nonfiction Books*
Cookery; Design; Journalism; Lifestyle; Memoir; Narrative Nonfiction; Self Help; Spirituality

YOUNG ADULT > **Fiction** > *Novels*

Send: Query; Writing sample
How to send: In the body of an email; Post

Strongly prefers to receive queries by email. Include pitch letter and first ten pages pasted into the body of the email (no attachments). If approaching by post, include SASE or email address for response.

Literary Agents: Sarah Jane Freymann (**L238**); Steve Schwartz (**L627**)

L620 Sarah Lazin Books

Literary Agency
19 West 21st Street, Suite 501, New York, NY 10001
United States
Tel: +1 (212) 765-6900

http://lazinbooks.com

Literary Agency: Aevitas

A full-service boutique agency founded in 1983. The agency is active in licensing first serial, audio, and e-book rights.

As of June 1st, 2018, Sarah Lazin Books has joined Aevitas Creative Management.

Authors: Marcus Baram; Patricia Romanowski Bashe; Michael Benson; Jenny Blake; Ianthe Brautigan; Richard Brautigan; Bill Brewster; Frank Broughton; Kate Brown; E. Jean Carroll; Ted Chapin; Robert Christgau; Julie Clow; Broughton Coburn; Charles R. Cross; Stephen DeAngelo; Anthony DeCurtis; Jim Dickinson; Banning Eyre; Jim Farber; Ben Fong-Torres; Georgia Freedman; Elysa Gardner; Richard Gehr; Nelson George; Holly George-Warren; Richard Goldstein; Jane Gottesman; Shirley Halperin; John Harris; Elizabeth Hess; Janet Hopson; Bill Ivey; Laura Joplin; Jason King; Michael Lang; Bernie Lierow; Diane Lierow; Alan Light; Kurt Loder; Kim MacQuarrie; Hans J. Massaquoi; Ed McCormack; Evelyn McDonnell; Kembrew McLeod; Dennis McNally; Paula Mejia; Joan Morgan; Robert K. Oermann; Robert Palmer; Sheri Parks; Patricia Pearson; Bruce Porter; Ann Powers; Parke Puterbaugh; Amy Rigby; Suze Rotolo; Chris Salewicz; Ben Sandmel; Sylvie Simmons; Ed Stafford; Robin Stone; Dominic Streatfeild; Ned Sublette; John Swenson; John Szwed; Paul Trynka; Jessica Vitkus; Elijah Wald; David Wild; Frank Wildman; Sue Williamson; Chris Willman; Douglas Wolk; Emily Zemler

Literary Agent: Sarah Lazin (**L416**)

L621 Marilia Savvides

Literary Agent
United Kingdom

mariliasavvides@42mp.com

https://www.42mp.com/agents
https://twitter.com/MariliaSavvides

Literary Agency: 42 Management and Production (**L002**)

Fiction > *Novels*
Book Club Fiction; Crime; Dark; High Concept Thrillers; Horror; Legal Thrillers; Psychological Suspense; Speculative

Nonfiction > *Nonfiction Books*
Crime; Investigative Journalism; Memoir; Narrative History; Popular Psychology; Popular Science

How to send: Email

On the hunt for high-concept thrillers, crime, psychological suspense, horror and speculative, genre-bending fiction, reading group fiction in the vein of Jodi Picoult or Liane Moriarty; pop science / psychology, narrative history, true crime and investigative journalism.

L622 Sandra Sawicka

Literary Agent
United Kingdom

Literary Agency: Marjacq Scripts Ltd (**L469**)

Closed to approaches.

L623 Sophie Scard

Literary Agent
United Kingdom

SScard@unitedagents.co.uk

https://www.unitedagents.co.uk/sscardunitedagentscouk

Literary Agency: United Agents (**L704**)

Fiction > *Novels*

Nonfiction > *Nonfiction Books*

Send: Query; Author bio; Writing sample
How to send: Email

Actively building her client list, and is looking for excellent writing of all types, fiction or nonfiction. For submissions please email a brief cover letter along with a biographical note and the first 10,000 words of your text.

Authors: Oana Aristide; Joan Bakewell; Stephen Bernard; Christopher Brookmyre; Robin Bunce; Alex Alvina Chamberland; Clare Chambers; Tom Chivers; Jill Dawson; Susannah Dickey; Minoo Dinshaw; Tim Finch; Ysenda Maxtone Graham; Charlotte Grimshaw; Camilla Grudova; Tessa Hadley; Lynsey Hanley; Jack Hartnell; Richard Holloway; Annaleese Jochems; Tobias Kelly; Clement Knox; Laura Kounine; Nakul Krishna; Samara Linton; Jan Morris; Anna Neima; Ambrose Parry; Ruth Pavey; Juno Roche; Saumya Roy; Tracey Slaughter; Emily Thomas; Ryan Turner; James Vincent; Francesca Wade; Stephen Walsh

L624 Rory Scarfe

Literary Agent; Company Director
United Kingdom

rorysubmissions@theblairpartnership.com

https://www.theblairpartnership.com/literary-agents/rory-scarfe/

Literary Agency: The Blair Partnership (**L066**)

ADULT
Fiction > *Novels*: Commercial

Nonfiction > *Nonfiction Books*: Commercial

Scripts
Film Scripts; *TV Scripts*
CHILDREN'S
Fiction > *Novels*
Nonfiction > *Nonfiction Books*

Closed to approaches.

Represents clients across commercial fiction, children's fiction and non-fiction, as well as screenwriters and brands.

Authors: Marina Abramović; Matt Allen; Jane Asher; Rafael Behr; Gary Bell; Ronen Bergman; David Bolchover; Michael Calvin; Sir Ronald Cohen; Owen Eastwood; Henry Fraser; Paris Fury; Tyson Fury; Pippa Grange; Catherine Green; Maria Hatzistefanis; Amelia Henley; Leigh Hosy-Pickett; Chris Hoy; James Inverne; Louise Jensen; Joanne Lake; Frank Lampard; Liz Lawler; Lee Lawrence; Aseem Malhotra; Joe Marler; Mercy Muroki; Shabnam Nasimi; Maajid Nawaz; Michal Oshman; Justine Pattison; Adam Peaty; Trevor Phillips; Nirmal Purja; Duncan Roe; Terry Ronald; Dan Saunders; Babita Sharma; Jon Smith; Jon Sopel; Dean Stott; Jessica Taylor; Pete Townshend; John Volanthen; Tom Watson; Brian Wood

L625 Jeff Schmidt

Literary Agent

jschmidt@nycreative.com

http://www.nycreative.com/contact.html

Literary Agency: NY Creative Management (**L534**)

L626 Hannah Schofield

Literary Agent
United Kingdom

hannahsubmissions@lbabooks.com

http://www.lbabooks.com/agent/hannah-schofield/

Literary Agency: LBA Books Ltd (**L417**)

ADULT
Fiction > *Novels*
Book Club Fiction; Commercial; Historical Fiction; Romantic Comedy; Suspense; Thrillers; Women's Fiction

Nonfiction > *Nonfiction Books*
Comedy / Humour; Crime; History; Memoir; Narrative Nonfiction; Personal Development; Social History

YOUNG ADULT > **Fiction** > *Novels*

How to send: Email

Currently building a list of commercial and reading-group fiction, and select nonfiction.

Authors: Emad Ahmed; Amanda Brooke; Charlotte Butterfield; Catherine Chang; Erin Connor; Kim Donovan; Elizabeth Drummond; Chloe Duckworth; Bea Fitzgerald; Lucy Goacher; Isabella Harcourt; Anam Iqbal; Jenni Keer; Amy Lavelle; Marina McCarron; Ande Pliego; Heidi Shertok; Celia Silvani; David Turner

L627 Steve Schwartz

Literary Agent
United States

http://www.sarahjanefreymann.com/?page_id=3872

Literary Agency: Sarah Jane Freymann Literary Agency (**L619**)

Fiction > *Novels*
Crime; Historical Fiction; Popular; Thrillers

Nonfiction > *Nonfiction Books*
Business; Comedy / Humour; Current Affairs; Psychology; Self Help; Sport; Travel

Send: Query; Writing sample
How to send: In the body of an email

Interested in popular fiction (crime, thrillers, and historical novels), world and national affairs, business books, self-help, psychology, humor, sports and travel.

L628 The Science Factory

Literary Agency
Scheideweg 34C, Hamburg, 20253
Germany
Tel: + 49 40 4327 4959; +44 (0) 20 7193 7296 (Skype)

info@sciencefactory.co.uk

https://www.sciencefactory.co.uk

Types: Fiction; Nonfiction
Subjects: Autobiography; Current Affairs; History; Medicine; Music; Politics; Science; Technology; Travel
Markets: Adult

Send: Query; Writing sample
Don't send: Full text
How to send: Email

Specialises in science, technology, medicine, and natural history, but will also consider other areas of nonfiction. Novelists handled only occasionally, and if there is some special relevance to the agency (e.g. a thriller about scientists, or a novel of ideas). See website for full submission guidelines.

Literary Agents: Jeff Shreve; Tisse Takagi; Peter Tallack

L629 Rosemary Scoular

Literary Agent
United Kingdom

https://www.unitedagents.co.uk/rscoularunitedagentscouk

Literary Agency: United Agents (**L704**)

Nonfiction > *Nonfiction Books*
Adventure; Arts; Food; History; Investigative Journalism; Memoir; Nature; Politics; Popular Science; Travel

Focuses on nonfiction, from food writing to history, popular science and nature, travel and adventure, politics and investigative journalism, the arts and memoir of all kinds.

L630 Chloe Seager

Literary Agent
United Kingdom

https://madeleinemilburn.co.uk/team-member/19023/

Literary Agency: Madeleine Milburn Literary, TV & Film Agency (**L464**)

CHILDREN'S
Fiction > *Middle Grade*
Nonfiction > *Middle Grade*

TEEN > **Fiction** > *Novels*

YOUNG ADULT
Fiction > *Novels*
Nonfiction > *Nonfiction Books*

Send: Query; Pitch; Market info; Author bio; Synopsis; Writing sample
How to send: Email
How not to send: Post

Actively looking for: Middle Grade age 7 and up; clean teen; young adult; non-fiction MG and YA.

Associate Agent: Vanessa Browne

L631 Sean McCarthy Literary Agency

Literary Agency
United States

submissions@mccarthylit.com

https://www.mccarthylit.com

CHILDREN'S > **Fiction**
Board Books; *Chapter Books*; *Early Readers*; *Middle Grade*; *Picture Books*

Send: Query; Synopsis; Author bio; Writing sample
How to send: Email

Accepts submissions across all genres and age ranges in children's books. Send query by email with a description of your book, author bio, and literary or relevant professional credits, and first three chapters (or roughly 25 pages) for novels, or complete ms if your work is a picture book. No picture books over 1,000 words. Response in 6-8 weeks.

Literary Agent: Sean McCarthy

L632 Sebes & Bisseling

Literary Agency
United Kingdom

https://sebesbisseling.co.uk

Fiction > *Novels*

Nonfiction > *Nonfiction Books*

Send: Query; Synopsis; Writing sample

London branch of a literary agency with offices in Amsterdam and Stockholm. Represents authors in the US, UK and in translation, for their book, digital and screen adaptation rights. Welcomes submissions from authors writing in English across all genres.

L633 Dani Segelbaum

Literary Agent
United States

dani@carolmannagency.com

https://www.carolmannagency.com/dani-segelbaum
https://www.instagram.com/danisegelbaum/
https://twitter.com/DaniSegelbaum

Literary Agency: Carol Mann Agency (**L104**)

Fiction > *Novels*
Historical Fiction; Literary; Mystery; Romantic Comedy; Upmarket; Women's Fiction

Nonfiction > *Nonfiction Books*
Cookery; Current Affairs; Lifestyle; Memoir; Narrative Nonfiction; Politics; Popular Culture; Women's Issues

Send: Query; Author bio; Writing sample; Synopsis; Proposal
How to send: In the body of an email
How not to send: Email attachment; Post

Interested in both fiction and non-fiction. Is seeking non-fiction titles with an emphasis on politics, women's issues, popular culture, and current events. Also loves memoir, narrative non-fiction, lifestyle, and cookbooks. In fiction, she is looking for literary and upmarket adult fiction including debut, historical, rom-coms, mysteries, and women's fiction. In both fiction and non-fiction, she hopes to work with authors from diverse backgrounds to tell stories that are important to them. She loves compelling narrators and is drawn to writing that is voice-driven, highly transporting, and features unique perspectives and marginalized voices.

L634 Selectric Artists

Literary Agency
9 Union Square #123, Southbury, CT 06488
United States
Tel: +1 (347) 668-5426

query@selectricartists.com

https://www.selectricartists.com

ADULT
Fiction
Graphic Novels: General
Novels: Commercial; Science Fiction; Thrillers
Nonfiction
Graphic Nonfiction: General
Nonfiction Books: Memoir; Narrative Nonfiction
YOUNG ADULT > **Fiction** > *Novels*
Fantasy; Science Fiction

Send: Query; Full text
How to send: Email

Send query by email with your manuscript attached as a .doc, .pdf, or .pages file. Put the word "query" in the subject line. No queries by phone. Response only if interested.

Literary Agent: Christopher Schelling

L635 Charlotte Seymour

Literary Agent
United Kingdom

charlotte@johnsonandalcock.co.uk

http://www.johnsonandalcock.co.uk/charlotte-seymour

Literary Agency: Johnson & Alcock (**L356**)

Fiction > *Novels*
Book Club Fiction; Crime; Literary; Suspense; Thrillers

Nonfiction > *Nonfiction Books*
Arts; Cookery; Cultural History; Food; Journalism; Nature; Popular Science; Social History

Send: Query; Synopsis; Writing sample
How to send: Email

In fiction, looks for book club and literary fiction as well as outstanding character – and voice-driven crime, thriller and suspense. She loves writing that crosses boundaries, whether geographic or linguistic or in bringing a twist to a genre.

In non-fiction, she is interested in accessible, engaging writing on a range of subjects including popular science, social and cultural history, reportage, nature, the arts, food and cookery. She especially loves hybrid books, for example, when in a memoir, the personal is interwoven with a bigger story or subject.

L636 Lauren Sharp

Literary Agent
United States

https://aevitascreative.com/agents/

Literary Agency: Aevitas

Nonfiction > *Nonfiction Books*
Current Affairs; History; Narrative Nonfiction; Politics; Science

Represents nonfiction in the areas of politics, history, current affairs, narrative nonfiction, and science.

L637 The Shaw Agency

Literary Agency
United Kingdom

https://www.theshawagency.co.uk

ADULT
Fiction > *Novels*
Commercial; Literary

Nonfiction > *Nonfiction Books*
Lifestyle; Narrative Nonfiction; Wellbeing

CHILDREN'S
Fiction > *Novels*
Nonfiction > *Nonfiction Books*

TEEN > **Fiction** > *Novels*

Send: Query; Pitch; Synopsis; Writing sample
Don't send: Full text
How to send: Online contact form

Handles literary and commercial fiction, fact and fiction books for children (6+) and teenagers/young adults, and narrative non-fiction. Send query through online form with one-page synopsis, first 10 pages, and email address for response. See website for full guidelines.

Literary Agent: Kate Shaw

L638 Todd Shuster

Literary Agent; Chief Executive Officer
United States

Literary Agency: Aevitas

Fiction > *Novels*
Commercial; Literary; Mystery; Thrillers

Nonfiction > *Nonfiction Books*
Business; Current Affairs; Health; History; Memoir; Politics; Wellbeing

Closed to approaches.

Represents both fiction and nonfiction. His nonfiction list primarily focuses on current affairs, politics and civil rights, health and wellness, memoir, business, and history. His fiction list includes both literary and commercial novels, including mysteries and thrillers.

L639 Signature Literary Agency

Literary Agency
4200 Wisconsin Ave, NW #106-233,
Washington, DC 20016
United States

gary@signaturelit.com

http://www.signaturelit.com

ADULT
Fiction
Graphic Novels: General
Novels: Commercial; Historical Fiction; Literary; Mystery; Thrillers
Nonfiction > *Nonfiction Books*
Biography; Comedy / Humour; Current Affairs; Entertainment; History; How To; Memoir; Narrative Nonfiction; Popular Culture; Science

YOUNG ADULT > **Fiction** > *Novels*

Send: Query
How to send: Email

Costs: Author covers sundry admin costs.

Agency with agents based in Washington DC and North Carolina. Send all queries by email only.

Literary Agents: Gary Heidt; Ellen Pepus; Amy Tipton

L640 Michael Signorelli

Literary Agent
United States

https://aevitascreative.com/agents/

Literary Agency: Aevitas

Fiction > *Novels*
Commercial; Literary; Thrillers

Nonfiction > *Nonfiction Books*
Adventure; Culture; Current Affairs; History; Narrative Nonfiction; Nature; Science; Sport

Send: Pitch; Market info; Writing sample
How to send: Online submission system

Oversees a list of literary and commercial fiction as well as nonfiction spanning nature, science, adventure, current affairs, sports, and cultural history.

Authors: Mark Arsenault; Brandi Collins-Dexter; Matthew Davis; Joan Donovan; Emily Dreyfuss; Abby Ellin; Morgan Falconer; Alex Cody Foster; Meryl Frank; Brian Friedberg; Nancy Kress; Robert Lanza; Oksana Masters; Kelly Richmond Pope; Benjamin Reeves; Kevin Sites; Adam Philip Stern; Deanne Stillman; Michelle Theall

L641 Julia Silk

Literary Agent
United Kingdom

julia@greyhoundliterary.co.uk

https://greyhoundliterary.co.uk/agent/julia-silk/
https://twitter.com/juliasreading
https://www.instagram.com/juliasreading/
https://www.pinterest.co.uk/juliasreadingbo/my-favourite-books/

Literary Agency: Greyhound Literary (**L288**)

Fiction > *Novels*
Commercial; Crime; Historical Fiction; Literary; Upmarket Thrillers

Nonfiction > *Nonfiction Books*
Health; Journalism; Wellbeing

Send: Query; Writing sample
How to send: Email

Particularly looking for crime with a series character, upmarket thrillers, and a compelling historical novel with a strong voice. In non-fiction she is also keen to hear from journalists and experts illuminating new stories and previously unexplored subjects, and on the practical side she represents a number of writers in health and wellbeing and is interested in original evidence-based proposals in this area from experts with a strong platform.

Authors: Poppy Alexander; Leona Nichole Black; Owen Booth; Luce Brett; Liz Fraser; Janet Gover; Sarah Graham; Karen Gurney; Maisie Hill; Jo Iozzi; Heidi James; Carlie Lee; Fiona Longmuir; Amanda Mason; Alison May; Charlotte Philby; Amy Ransom; Rebecca Schiller; Clare Seal; Emma Svanberg

L642 Janet Silver

Literary Agent; Senior Partner
United States

https://aevitascreative.com/agents/

Literary Agency: Aevitas

Fiction > *Novels*: Literary

Nonfiction > *Nonfiction Books*: Creative Nonfiction

Poetry > *Poetry Collections*

Closed to approaches.

Represents a roster of bestselling and award-winning authors of literary fiction, creative nonfiction, and poetry.

L643 Lydia Silver

Literary Agent
United Kingdom

https://www.darleyanderson.com/our-team
https://twitter.com/LydiaRSilver

Literary Agency: The Darley Anderson Agency

CHILDREN'S
Fiction
Chapter Books; *Middle Grade*; *Picture Books*
Nonfiction
Chapter Books; *Middle Grade*; *Picture Books*
TEEN
Fiction > *Novels*
Nonfiction > *Nonfiction Books*

YOUNG ADULT
Fiction > *Novels*
Nonfiction > *Nonfiction Books*

Send: Query; Synopsis; Writing sample
How to send: Word file email attachment; PDF file email attachment; Post

Represents clients across all age groups, including picture book, chapter book, middle grade and YA, and has a particular focus on non-fiction. Reads and considers widely, and among other things she is looking for snort-inducing stories for younger readers, clever and contemporary teenage and YA fiction, and non-fiction projects that take big ideas and make them easily navigable, accessible and fun. She loves working editorially with writers and is always on the lookout for new talent.

Authors: Maria Motunrayo Adebisi; Dominic Beesley; Gina Blaxill; Danielle Brown; Lanisha Butterfield; Ryan Hammond; Alice Harman; Joyce Efia Harmer; Catherine Jacob; Amie Jordan; Rachel Morrisroe; Eva Wong Nava; Nick Sheridan; Rashmi Sirdeshpande; Mimi Thebo

L644 Dorie Simmonds

Literary Agent
United Kingdom

https://doriesimmonds.com/about-us/
https://twitter.com/Dorie_Simmonds

Literary Agency: Dorie Simmonds Agency (**L181**)

Will consider material from any genre except reference books and children's picture books.

L645 Tanera Simons

Literary Agent
United Kingdom

tanera@darleyanderson.com

https://www.darleyanderson.com/our-team
https://twitter.com/tanera_simons

Literary Agency: The Darley Anderson Agency

Fiction > *Novels*
Book Club Fiction; Commercial; Historical Fiction; Romance; Romantic Comedy

How to send: Email attachment
How not to send: Post

Looking for romantic comedies, sweeping love stories, accessible book club fiction, historical/timeslip, and general commercial fiction.

Authors: Mandy Baggot; Sara Bragg; Laura Carter; Claire Frost; Nicola Gill; Mary Hargreaves; Sandie Jones; Lauren North; Beth O'Leary; Sally Page; Nancy Peach; Kate G. Smith; Sophie White; Ally Zetterberg

L646 Anjali Singh

Literary Agent
United States

https://www.pandeliterary.com/about-pandeliterary
https://twitter.com/agent_anjali
http://aaronline.org/Sys/PublicProfile/52119428/417813

Literary Agency: Ayesha Pande Literary (**L036**)
Professional Body: Association of American Literary Agents (AALA)

ADULT
Fiction
Graphic Novels: General
Novels: Literary

Nonfiction > *Nonfiction Books*: Narrative Nonfiction

CHILDREN'S > **Fiction** > *Graphic Novels*

YOUNG ADULT > **Fiction** > *Graphic Novels*

Closed to approaches.

Looking for new voices, character-driven fiction or nonfiction works that reflect an engagement with the world around us, literary thrillers, memoirs, YA literature and graphic novels.

L647 Skylark Literary

Literary Agency
19 Parkway, Weybridge, Surrey, KT13 9HD
United Kingdom
Tel: +44 (0) 20 8144 7440

submissions@skylark-literary.com
info@skylark-literary.com

http://www.skylark-literary.com
https://twitter.com/SkylarkLit
http://www.facebook.com/skylarkliteraryltd

Professional Body: The Association of Authors' Agents (AAA)

CHILDREN'S > **Fiction**
Chapter Books; *Early Readers*; *Middle Grade*
YOUNG ADULT > **Fiction** > *Novels*

Send: Full text; Synopsis
How to send: Word file email attachment

Handles fiction for children, from chapter books for emerging readers up to young adult / crossover titles. No picture books. Send query by email with one-page synopsis and full ms. No postal submissions.

Literary Agents: Amber J. Caravéo (*L103*); Joanna Moult

L648 Antoinette Van Sluytman

Junior Agent; Assistant Agent
United States

https://www.irenegoodman.com/antoinette-van-sluytman
https://twitter.com/antoinight
https://www.instagram.com/toni_vansluy

Literary Agency: Irene Goodman Literary Agency (IGLA)
Literary Agent: Natalie Lakosil (**L403**)

ADULT > **Fiction**
Graphic Novels: General
Novels: Adventure; Dark Fantasy; High / Epic Fantasy; Historical Fiction; Horror; Science Fiction; Speculative
YOUNG ADULT > **Fiction**
Graphic Novels; *Novels*

Interested in all genres of speculative fiction, specifically cosmic horror, dark fantasy, epic fantasy, sci-fi, in addition to historical fiction. Antoinette maintains special interest in adult projects but is also open to select YA and graphic novels. In general she loves lyrical prose that challenges narrative conventions, ambitiously immersive worlds inspired by different cultures, morally gray and dysfunctional lovable characters with fun dynamics, and new takes on old tropes. She is drawn to unique and bold prose that isn't afraid to challenge narrative conventions and complex philosophical/psychological themes across all genres. Overall she's looking for mind blowing stories that come with emotional damage. Some general themes she enjoys are adventures, antiheroines, creatures, dark fantasy, and anything outrageously quirky.

L649 Solow Literary Enterprises, Inc.

Literary Agency
United States

info@solowliterary.com

http://www.solowliterary.com
https://www.facebook.com/SolowLiterary
https://twitter.com/SolowLiterary

Nonfiction > *Nonfiction Books*
Business; Culture; Education; Health; Memoir; Narrative Nonfiction; Nature; Psychology; Science; Wellbeing

Send: Query
Don't send: Full text
How to send: Email

Handles nonfiction in the stated areas only. Send single-page query by email, providing information on what your book is about; why you think it has to be written; and why you are the best person to write it. Response only if interested.

Foreign Rights Manager: Taryn Fagerness

Literary Agent: Bonnie Solow (*L650*)

L650 Bonnie Solow

Literary Agent
United States

Literary Agency: Solow Literary Enterprises, Inc. (**L649**)
Professional Bodies: Association of American Literary Agents (AALA); The Authors Guild

L651 Jennifer March Soloway

Literary Agent
United States

soloway@andreabrownlit.com

https://querymanager.com/query/JenniferMarchSoloway
https://twitter.com/marchsoloway

Literary Agency: Andrea Brown Literary Agency, Inc.

ADULT > **Fiction** > *Novels*
Commercial; Crime; Literary; Psychological Suspense

CHILDREN'S > **Fiction**
Middle Grade: Adventure; Comedy / Humour; Contemporary; Fantasy; Ghost Stories; Mystery; Realistic
Picture Books: General, and in particular: Comedy / Humour
YOUNG ADULT > **Fiction** > *Novels*
Family; Literary; Mental Health; Psychological Horror; Relationships; Romance; Sexuality; Suspense; Thrillers

Send: Query
How to send: Email; By referral

Represents authors and illustrators of picture book, middle grade, and YA stories, and is actively building her list. Although she specializes in children's literature, she also represents adult fiction, both literary and commercial, particularly crime and psychological suspense projects.

Currently accepting queries by referral only.

L652 Kelly Sonnack

Senior Agent
United States

https://www.andreabrownlit.com/agents.html
https://twitter.com/KSonnack

Literary Agency: Andrea Brown Literary Agency, Inc.

CHILDREN'S > **Fiction** > *Picture Books*

YOUNG ADULT > **Fiction**
Graphic Novels; *Novels*

How to send: By referral

L653 Kaitlin Sooklal

Assistant Agent
Canada

https://www.therightsfactory.com/Agents/kaitlin-sooklal/

ADULT > **Fiction** > *Novels*
Fantasy; Historical Fiction; Science Fiction

YOUNG ADULT > **Fiction** > *Novels*

Authors: Karen Grose; Rebecca Jane

L654 Sophie Hicks Agency

Literary Agency
60 Gray's Inn Road, London, WC1X 8LU
United Kingdom
Tel: +44 (0) 20 3735 8870

info@sophiehicksagency.com

http://www.sophiehicksagency.com
https://twitter.com/SophieHicksAg
https://www.instagram.com/sophiehicksagency/

Professional Body: The Association of Authors' Agents (AAA)

ADULT
Fiction > *Novels*
Nonfiction > *Nonfiction Books*

CHILDREN'S > **Fiction** > *Novels*

Send: Query; Writing sample; Synopsis
How to send: Email

Welcomes submissions. Send query by email with sample pages attached as Word or PDF documents. See website for full guidelines and specific submissions email addresses. No poetry or scripts for theatre, film or television, and not currently accepting illustrated books for children.

Literary Agents: Sophie Hicks; Sarah Williams

L655 James Spackman

Literary Agent
United Kingdom

https://www.thebksagency.com/about
https://www.thebksagency.com/submissions

Literary Agency: The BKS Agency (**L065**)

Nonfiction > *Nonfiction Books*
Culture; Music; Sport

Send: Query; Outline; Author bio
How to send: Online submission system

Looking for sport, music, culture and smart thinking.

L656 Spring Literary

Literary Agency
United Kingdom

submissions@springliterary.com

https://www.springliterary.com
https://twitter.com/springliterary
https://www.instagram.com/springliterary

CHILDREN'S > **Fiction** > *Picture Books*

YOUNG ADULT
Fiction > *Novels*
Nonfiction > *Nonfiction Books*

Send: Query; Synopsis; Writing sample; Author bio; Full text
How to send: Email

Specialises in children's and YA writing and illustration. Works with all the major publishing houses, plus entertainment companies, to ensure the best match for each book, author and illustrator.

Literary Agent: Neil Dunnicliffe (**L186**)

L657 Mark "Stan" Stanton

Literary Agent
United Kingdom

http://thenorthlitagency.com/our-friends-in-the-north/
https://twitter.com/litagent007

Literary Agency: The North Literary Agency (**L530**)

Fiction > *Novels*
Book Club Fiction; Crime; High Concept; Historical Fiction; Politics; Romantic Comedy; Satire; Thrillers

Nonfiction > *Nonfiction Books*
Biography; Politics; Popular Culture; Popular Science; Sport

Send: Query; Synopsis; Writing sample; Proposal
How to send: Email

Actively searching for new novelists and nonfiction projects, particularly in the areas of sport, culture and politics.

L658 Hayley Steed

Literary Agent
United Kingdom

https://madeleinemilburn.co.uk/looking-for/hayley-steed-im-looking/

Literary Agency: Madeleine Milburn Literary, TV & Film Agency (**L464**)

Fiction > *Novels*
Book Club Fiction; Commercial; High Concept; Mystery; Romance; Suspense; Thrillers; Upmarket Women's Fiction

Send: Query; Pitch; Market info; Author bio; Synopsis; Writing sample
How to send: Email
How not to send: Post

Actively looking for: commercial and book-club fiction across all genres including women's fiction; uplifting love stories; suspense and mystery; upmarket general fiction; high concept novels; original crime; character-driven thrillers; emotional epics; complex characters; magical realism and cross-genre books.

L659 Steph Roundsmith Agent and Editor

Literary Agency; Editorial Service
United Kingdom

agent@stephroundsmith.co.uk

http://www.stephroundsmith.co.uk
https://twitter.com/StephRoundsmith

CHILDREN'S
Fiction > *Novels*
Nonfiction > *Nonfiction Books*

Closed to approaches.

Costs: Offers services that writers have to pay for.

Interested in any genre for children under 12. Also offers proofreading and editorial services.

Authors: Paul Adshead; Greg Dobbins; Jen Dodds; Sara Fellows; Julian Green; Diana Shaw

Editor / Literary Agent: Steph Roundsmith (*L607*)

L660 Stephanie Tade Literary Agency

Literary Agency
United States

https://www.stephanietadeagency.com

Nonfiction > *Nonfiction Books*: Mind, Body, Spirit

Send: Query
How to send: Online contact form

A full service literary agency with a focus on nonfiction, particularly in the categories of physical, psychological, and spiritual well-being.

Literary Agent: Stephanie Tade

L661 Jenny Stephens

Literary Agent
United States

https://www.sll.com/our-team

Literary Agency: Sterling Lord Literistic, Inc. (**L662**)

Nonfiction > *Nonfiction Books*
Cookery; Cultural Criticism; Economics; Environment; Food; History; Lifestyle; Nature; Science; Social Justice

Send: Query; Synopsis; Writing sample
How to send: Online submission system

L662 Sterling Lord Literistic, Inc.

Literary Agency
594 Broadway, New York, NY 10012
United States
Tel: +1 (212) 780-6050
Fax: +1 (212) 780-6095

info@sll.com

https://www.sll.com

Send: Query; Synopsis; Writing sample
How to send: Online submission system

Select one agent to query and approach via online form on website.

Associate Agents: Maria Bell (**L054**); Chris Combemale (**L135**); Nell Pierce

Chair / Literary Agent: Peter Matson (**L474**)

Executive Vice President / Literary Agent: Laurie Liss (**L433**)

Foreign Rights Director: Szilvia Molnar

Literary Agent / President: Philippa Brophy (**L087**)

Literary Agent / Vice President: Douglas Stewart (**L665**)

Literary Agents: Elizabeth Bewley (**L063**); Danielle Bukowski (**L094**); Brian Egan; Celeste Fine; Jessica Friedman (**L241**); Mary Krienke (**L398**); Sarah Landis (**L404**); Sterling Lord; John Maas; Alison MacKeen; Martha Millard; George Nicholson; Sarah Passick; Jenny Stephens (**L661**)

Senior Agents: Robert Guinsler (**L292**); Neeti Madan (**L463**); Jim Rutman (**L613**)

L663 Sternig & Byrne Literary Agency

Literary Agency
2370 S. 107th Street, Apt 4, Milwaukee, Wisconsin 53227-2036
United States
Tel: +1 (414) 328-8034

jackbyrne@hotmail.com

https://sternig-byrne-agency.com

Professional Bodies: Science Fiction and Fantasy Writers of America (SFWA); Mystery Writers of America (MWA)

Fiction > *Novels*
Fantasy; Mystery; Science Fiction

Send: Query; Self-Addressed Stamped Envelope (SASE)
How to send: Email; Post
How not to send: Email attachment; Links to material online

Send brief query by post or email in first instance (if sending by email send in the body of the mail, do not send attachments). Will request further materials if interested. Currently only considering science fiction, fantasy, and mysteries. Preference given to writers with a publishing history.

Authors: Katherine Addison; John Haefele; Lael Littke; Kelly McCullough; Sarah Monette; Moira Moore; Jo Walton; David Michael Williams; John C. Wright

Literary Agent: Jack Byrne

L664 Paul Stevens

Literary Agent
United Kingdom

Literary Agency: Independent Talent Group Ltd (**L340**)

L665 Douglas Stewart

Literary Agent; Vice President
United States

https://www.sll.com/our-team

Literary Agency: Sterling Lord Literistic, Inc. (**L662**)

ADULT
Fiction > *Novels*
Commercial; Literary

Nonfiction > *Nonfiction Books*: Narrative Nonfiction

CHILDREN'S
Fiction > *Novels*

Nonfiction > *Nonfiction Books*: Narrative Nonfiction

YOUNG ADULT
Fiction > *Novels*

Nonfiction > *Nonfiction Books*: Narrative Nonfiction

Send: Query; Synopsis; Writing sample
How to send: Online submission system

List consists of fiction and narrative nonfiction for all ages, from the innovatively literary to the unabashedly commercial, and includes multiple million-copy bestsellers and award-winners.

Associate Agent: Maria Bell (**L054**)

L666 Jessica Stewart

Literary Agent
United Kingdom

Literary Agency: Independent Talent Group Ltd (**L340**)

L667 Sam Stoloff

President; Senior Agent
United States

https://goldinlit.com/agents/

Literary Agency: Frances Goldin Literary Agency, Inc.

Fiction
Graphic Novels: Literary
Novels: Literary; Speculative

Nonfiction
Graphic Nonfiction: General
Nonfiction Books: Culture; Current Affairs; Environment; Food; History; Journalism; Legal; Memoir; Narrative Nonfiction; Philosophy; Politics; Science; Sociology; Sustainable Living; Technology

Send: Query; Writing sample
How to send: Submittable

Interested in books that advance the public conversation on crucial issues and groundbreaking work of all kinds, including literary fiction, memoir, history, accessible sociology and philosophy, cultural studies, serious journalism on contemporary and international affairs, and narrative and topical nonfiction with a progressive orientation. Among his particular interests are literary graphic fiction and nonfiction, works on environmental sustainability, books on legal affairs and the justice system, works that dissect the right wing and American imperialism, the history of race in America, the history of science and technology, and books on food culture and history. His taste in fiction ranges from the psychologically realistic, to first-rate speculative literature.

Authors: Susan Bordo; Monica Byrne; Mandy Catron; Pratap Chatterjee; David Cole; Cliff Conner; Dessa; Ray Douglas; Mark Edmundson; Shelley Fisher Fishkin; Bruce Grierson; Michael Hudson; Lynn Hunt; Margaret Jacob; Steven Jaffe; Barbara Kingsolver; Michelle Kuo; Anna Lappé; Daniel Medwed; Stephanie Mencimer; Rutu Modan; Alexandra Natapoff; Carla Peterson; Sam Polk; Janisse Ray; Gretchen Reynolds; Siva Vaidhyanathan; Mike Wallace; Helene Wecker

L668 Geoffrey Stone

Literary Agent
United States

gstone@rudyagency.com

http://rudyagency.com/

Literary Agency: The Rudy Agency (**L609**)

Nonfiction > *Nonfiction Books*
Christian Living; Cookery; History; Sport

Send: Query
How to send: Email

Looking for proposals and manuscripts on history, sports, cooking, personal stories, and Christian living, and is open to a wide range of non-fiction and fiction that align with those interests.

L669 The Stringer Literary Agency LLC

Literary Agency
PO Box 111255, Naples, FL 34108
United States

https://www.stringerlit.com
https://www.instagram.com/stringerlit/
https://www.pinterest.com/stringerlit/
https://www.facebook.com/StringerLit
https://twitter.com/MarleneStringer

Professional Bodies: Association of American Literary Agents (AALA); Mystery Writers of America (MWA); Society of Children's Book Writers and Illustrators (SCBWI); The Authors

Guild; Women's Fiction Writers Association (WFWA)

ADULT > **Fiction** > *Novels*

CHILDREN'S > **Fiction**
Middle Grade; *Picture Books*
YOUNG ADULT > **Fiction** > *Novels*

A full-service literary agency specializing in commercial fiction since 2008.

Authors: Melissa Amateis; Caroline L. Bayley; Emily Bleeker; Marta Bliese; Anna Bradley; Emily Cavanagh; Don Dixon; Charlie Donlea; Pat Esden; Alyxandra Harvey; Erica Hayes; Charlie N Holmberg; Suzanne Johnson; Kristin Kisska; Kallie Lane; Caitlin McFarland; Liane Merciel; Sophie Munday; Melanie Novak; Liz Perrine; Molly Pierce; Emily Rittel-King; Alexandra Rushe; Luanne G. Smith; Kate Pawson Studer; Andrea Thalasinos; Tessa Wegert; Bethany Wiggins; Clare Zeschky

Literary Agents: Shari Maurer (**L477**); Marlene Stringer (**L670**)

L670 Marlene Stringer

Literary Agent
United States

http://aaronline.org/Sys/PublicProfile/5108942/417813
https://querymanager.com/query/StringerLit

Literary Agency: The Stringer Literary Agency LLC (**L669**)

ADULT
Fiction > *Novels*
Book Club Fiction; Commercial; Contemporary; Crime; Fantasy; Historical Fiction; Literary; Romance; Suspense; Thrillers; Upmarket; Women's Fiction

Nonfiction > *Nonfiction Books*: Narrative Nonfiction

CHILDREN'S > **Fiction** > *Middle Grade*

YOUNG ADULT > **Fiction** > *Novels*
Contemporary; Fantasy

Does not want:

Fiction > *Novels*: High / Epic Fantasy

Send: Author bio; Query; Synopsis; Writing sample; Pitch; Market info
How to send: By referral; Conferences

L671 Catharine Strong

Associate Agent
United States

Literary Agency: Aevitas

L672 The Strothman Agency

Literary Agency
Box 255, Newcastle, ME 04553
United States

strothmanagency@gmail.com
info@strothmanagency.com

https://www.strothmanagency.com/
https://twitter.com/StrothmanAgency
https://www.facebook.com/StrothmanAgency/

Send: Query
How to send: Email; Query Manager
How not to send: Email attachment; Post

Only accepts electronic submissions. Physical query letters will be recycled unopened. Accepts referrals by email. Queries without referral must approach through Query Manager. Do not send entire manuscripts or attachments unless requested. All unrequested attachments will be deleted unread. Does not accept or respond to queries via fax or telephone.

Literary Agents: Lauren MacLeod (**L461**); Wendy Strothman (**L673**)

L673 Wendy Strothman

Literary Agent
United States

https://www.strothmanagency.com/about
https://querymanager.com/query/WStrothman
http://aaronline.org/Sys/PublicProfile/2176866/417813

Literary Agency: The Strothman Agency (**L672**)
Professional Body: Association of American Literary Agents (AALA)

Nonfiction > *Nonfiction Books*
Current Affairs; History; Narrative Journalism; Narrative Nonfiction; Nature; Science

Send: Query
Don't send: Full text
How to send: Email; Query Manager
How not to send: Email attachment; Fax; Phone

Looking for books that matter, books that change the way we think about things we take for granted, that tell stories that readers can't forget, and advance scholarship and knowledge. History, narrative nonfiction, narrative journalism, science and nature, and current affairs.

Accepts referrals by email; otherwise approach through Query Manager.

L674 Hannah Strouth

Assistant Agent
United States

https://www.janerotrosen.com/agents

Literary Agency: Jane Rotrosen Agency
Literary Agents: Andrea Cirillo; Kathy Schneider

Fiction > *Novels*
Contemporary; Historical Fiction; Literary; Romantic Comedy; Upmarket

Send: Query; Author bio; Synopsis; Writing sample
How to send: Online contact form

Helps maintain the lists of two agents, while keeping her sights set on growing her own list. She is constantly diving into historical fiction, contemporary rom-coms, and upmarket / literary fiction.

L675 Stuart Krichevsky Literary Agency, Inc.

Literary Agency
118 East 28th Street, Suite 908, New York, NY 10016
United States
Tel: +1 (212) 725-5288
Fax: +1 (212) 725-5275

query@skagency.com

http://skagency.com

ADULT
Fiction > *Novels*
Nonfiction > *Nonfiction Books*

YOUNG ADULT
Fiction > *Novels*
Nonfiction > *Nonfiction Books*

Send: Query; Writing sample
How to send: In the body of an email

Send query by email with first few pages of your manuscript (up to 10) pasted into body of the email (no attachments). See website for complete submission guidelines and appropriate submission addresses for each agent.

Authors: Roxanna Asgarian; Ahmed Badr; Emily Bloom; Katherine Blunt; Lyndsie Bourgon; Hannah Brencher; Caren Cooper; Hope Ewing; Victoria Facelli; Kathryn Finney; Kit Fox; Katie Fricas; Olivia Gatwood; Jessica Goudeau; Rose Hackman; Anita Hannig; Sarah Jaffe; Rachel McCarthy James; R. Dean Johnson; Sophie Lucido Johnson; Megan Kimble; Audrea Lim; Catherine Lo; Michael Loynd; Jennifer Lunden; José Olivarez; Madeline Ostrander; Robin Page; Soraya Palmer; Karen Pinchin; Shelley Puhak; Lydia Reeder; Victoria Reihana; Margot Lee Shetterly; David Shih; Bric Spangler; Rachel Swaby; Sofi Thanhauser; Kaitlyn Tiffany; Sarah Vogel; Kimberley Welman; Christina Wilcox; Nina Willner; Bernice Yeung; Sara Zin

Literary Agents: Melissa Danaczko (*L155*); Ross Harris; Barbara Jones (**L360**); Stuart Krichevsky; David Patterson; Aemilia Phillips; Hannah Schwartz; Laura Usselman (**L708**); Mackenzie Brady Watson (**L722**)

L676 Mandy Suhr

Literary Agent
United Kingdom

https://milesstottagency.co.uk/representatives/mandy-suhr/

Literary Agency: Miles Stott Children's Literary Agency (**L498**)

CHILDREN'S > **Fiction** > *Picture Books*

"I offer an experienced guiding hand to authors and illustrators, new and established, keen to work within this exciting genre. As well as editorial development of a style or story, I'll also help navigate through the business of publishing and that all important contract, ensuring each of my clients gets the best possible deal."

Authors: Rachel Bright; Lu Fraser

L677 Cathryn Summerhayes

Literary Agent
United Kingdom

Literary Agency: Curtis Brown

L678 Susan Schulman Literary Agency

Literary Agency
454 West 44th Street, New York, NY 10036
United States
Tel: +1 (212) 713-1633

Susan@Schulmanagency.com

https://twitter.com/SusanSchulman

Professional Body: Association of American Literary Agents (AALA)

Fiction > *Novels*
General, and in particular: Commercial; Literary; Women's Fiction

Nonfiction > *Nonfiction Books*
Creativity; Economics; Finance; Health; History; Legal; Memoir; Mind, Body, Spirit; Politics; Psychology; Social Issues; Writing

Send: Query; Synopsis; Writing sample; Author bio
How to send: Email

Handles commercial and literary fiction and non-fiction, specifically narrative memoir, politics, economics, social issues, history, urban planning, finance, law, health, psychology, body/mind/sprit, and creativity and writing.

Associate Agent: Emelie Burl (**L097**)

Literary Agent: Susan Schulman

L679 Susanna Lea Associates (UK)

Literary Agency
South Wing, Somerset House, Strand, London, WC2R 1LA
United Kingdom
Tel: +44 (0) 20 7287 7757

london@susannalea.com

https://www.susannalea.com

Professional Body: The Association of Authors' Agents (AAA)

Fiction > *Novels*

Nonfiction > *Nonfiction Books*

Send: Query; Synopsis; Writing sample
How to send: Email

Literary agency with offices in Paris, London, and New York. Always on the lookout for exciting new talent. No poetry, plays, screen plays, science fiction, educational text books, short stories or illustrated works. No queries by fax or post. Accepts queries by email only. Include cover letter, synopsis, and first three chapters or proposal. Response not guaranteed.

Literary Agent: Kerry Glencorse (**L268**)

L680 Alice Sutherland-Hawes

Literary Agent
United Kingdom

https://www.ashliterary.com/#about

Literary Agency: ASH Literary (**L033**)

Authors: Dina Al-Sabawi; HF Brownfield; Ryan Crawford; Alex Falase-Koya; Kereen Getten; Gina Gonzales; Sarah Guillory; Ravena Guron; Radiya Hafiza; Anika Hussain; Jennifer Iacopelli; Nansubuga Isdahl; Samantha Joyce; Richard Mercado; Yasmine Naghdi; Samuel Pollen; Ryan Robinson; Elizabeth Rounding; Cynthia So; Chitra Soundar; Claire Tomasi; Adelle Yeung

L681 Joanna Swainson

Literary Agent
United Kingdom

submissions@hardmanswainson.com

http://www.hardmanswainson.com/agents/joanna-swainson/
https://twitter.com/JoannaSwainson

Literary Agency: Hardman & Swainson (**L302**)

Fiction > *Novels*
Comedy / Humour; Commercial; Contemporary; Crime; Folk Horror; Ghost Stories; Historical Fiction; Horror; Literary; Speculative; Thrillers

Nonfiction > *Nonfiction Books*
Memoir; Narrative Nonfiction; Nature; Popular History; Science

Send: Synopsis; Full text
How to send: Email
How not to send: Post

Authors: Jon Bounds; Oggy Boytchev; Paul Braddon; Elizabeth Brooks; Mark Broomfield; Adrienne Chinn; Helen Cox; Jeremy Craddock; Sara Crowe; Emma Darwin; Stuart David; Caroline Davison; Carol Donaldson; Simon David Eden; Rachel Edwards; Nicola Ford; Harry Freedman; James Gould-Bourn; Tom Higham; Michael Jecks; Oskar Cox Jensen; Stuart Johnstone; Lucy Lawrie; Peter Laws; Kevin Macneil; S R Masters; Lauren Price; Philip C Quaintrell; Patrick Roberts; Nick Russell-Pavier; Catherine Simpson; Danny Smith; Hollie Starling; Eliska Tanzer; Sarah Tierney; B P Walter; Samantha Wilson

L682 Becky Sweren

Literary Agent
United States

https://aevitascreative.com/agents/#agent-7413

Literary Agency: Aevitas

Nonfiction > *Nonfiction Books*
Culture; History; Investigative Journalism; Memoir

Closed to approaches.

Authors: Jesse Ball; Mark Braude; Adin Dobkin; Beck Dorey-Stein; Renee Dudley; Penina Eilberg-Schwartz; Valerie Fridland; Nicholas Griffin; Lawrence Jackson; Mohamad Jebara; Faith Jones; Jillian Keenan; Jake Keiser; Sulaiman Khatib; Ali Kriegsman; Daniel Levin; Eric M. O'Neill; Matteson Perry; Pen Rhodeen; Mohammed Al Samawi; Laurie Segall; Shabtai Shavit; Gabourey Sidibe; Judith E. Stein; Noa Tishby; Steven Ujifusa; Jack Viertel; Lijia Zhang

L683 Jessica Sykes

Literary Agent
United Kingdom

Literary Agency: Independent Talent Group Ltd (**L340**)

L684 SYLA – Susan Yearwood Literary Agency

Literary Agency
2 Knebworth House, Londesborough Road, Stoke Newington, London, N16 8RL
United Kingdom
Tel: +44 (0) 20 7503 0954

submissions@susanyearwoodagency.com

https://susanyearwoodagency.com

Professional Body: The Association of Authors' Agents (AAA)

ADULT
Fiction > *Novels*
Nonfiction > *Nonfiction Books*

CHILDREN'S > **Fiction** > *Novels*

YOUNG ADULT > **Fiction** > *Novels*

Send: Query; Author bio; Writing sample; Synopsis
How to send: Email attachment

Send query by email, including synopsis and first thirty pages as Word or PDF attachment.

Authors: Rebecca Adams; Catherine Balavage; Lucy Basey; Katie Brewer; Angela Cairns; Fran Clark; Sarah Dobbs; Selina Flavius; Kimberley Glover; Liz Kolbeck; Prajwal Parajuly; Susan Quirke; Fil Reid; Sarupa Shah;

Jacqueline Shaw; Sarah Shoesmith; Mahalia Smith; Suzanne Snow; Sarah Stephenson; Kerry Young

Literary Agent: Susan Yearwood (**L750**)

L685 Laurel Symonds

Literary Agent
United States

http://www.thebentagency.com/laurel-symonds

Literary Agency: The Bent Agency (**L058**)

CHILDREN'S
Fiction
Chapter Books: General
Graphic Novels: General
Middle Grade: General, and in particular: Contemporary; Fantasy; Historical Fiction; Literary
Picture Books: General

Nonfiction > *Nonfiction Books*

YOUNG ADULT
Fiction
Graphic Novels: General
Novels: General, and in particular: Commercial; Contemporary; Fantasy; Historical Fiction
Nonfiction > *Nonfiction Books*

I am seeking young adult and middle grade fiction with a special interest in contemporary, historical, and genre-bending fantasy. I look for engaging voices, commercial hooks, and immersive worlds. My YA tastes are pretty commercial whereas my middle grade tastes can skew more literary and I'm especially interested in middle grade that might lend itself to illustration.

For picture books, graphic novels, and other illustrated work, I am seeking clients who are both authors and illustrators. My tastes are diverse, ranging from sophisticated to quirky to gently humorous. I am interested in art in all mediums, but especially appreciate a smart use of color and perspective.

I also represent select nonfiction for children and young adults, especially projects about STEM or history with age-appropriate hooks and series potential.

L686 Marin Takikawa

Literary Agent
United States

http://www.friedrichagency.com/about

Literary Agency: The Friedrich Agency LLC

Fiction > *Novels*
Literary; Upmarket

Closed to approaches.

I'm an eclectic reader, but my comfort zone resides with character-driven upmarket and literary fiction. In particular, I'm always driven by the need to understand people and discover the various kinks that aren't visible from the surface—what drives them? What do they desire most but can't get? Who and what do they love? I'm particularly enamored by narratives about complex family relationships and those that subvert forms of power, specifically neocolonialist ones.

L687 Emily Talbot

Associate Agent
United Kingdom

etalbot@unitedagents.co.uk

https://www.unitedagents.co.uk/etalbotunitedagentscouk

Literary Agency: United Agents (**L704**)
Literary Agent: Jodie Hodges (**L328**)

CHILDREN'S > **Fiction**
Middle Grade; *Picture Books*
TEEN > **Fiction** > *Novels*

YOUNG ADULT > **Fiction** > *Novels*

Send: Query; Synopsis; Writing sample

Represents children's illustrators and authors of picture books, middle grade, teenage and YA.

Authors: Aysha Awwad; Susanna Bailey; Abigail Balfe; Alex Barrow; Becky Baur; Gabby Dawnay; Sophie Deen; Chloe Douglass; Ed Eaves; Alison Guile; James Harris; Sam Hearn; Benjamin Hughes; James Lent; Rebecca Lewis-Oakes; Maggie Li; Roger McGough; Becka Moor; Polly Owen; Keith Robinson; Andy Sagar; Jion Sheibani; Qian Shi; Georgina Stevens; Barry Timms; Jacqueline Tucker; Kael Tudor; Lucy Unwin; Maddy Vian; Lucia Vinti

L688 Amy Tannenbaum

Literary Agent
United States

atannenbaum@janerotrosen.com

https://www.janerotrosen.com/agents
https://www.janerotrosen.com/contact-amy-tannenbaum

Literary Agency: Jane Rotrosen Agency

Fiction > *Novels*
Commercial; Contemporary Romance; Literary; Psychological Suspense; Thrillers; Women's Fiction

Nonfiction > *Nonfiction Books*: Narrative Nonfiction

Send: Query
How to send: In the body of an email
How not to send: Email attachment

Represents clients who write across a variety of genres including women's fiction, contemporary romance, thriller and psychological suspense. She is particularly interested in those categories, as well as fiction that falls into the sweet spot between literary and commercial, and works by diverse voices.

L689 Simon Targett

Literary Agent
United Kingdom

https://aevitascreative.com/agents/#agent-7409

Literary Agency: Aevitas Creative Management (ACM) UK (**L008**)

Fiction > *Novels*: Historical Fiction

Nonfiction > *Nonfiction Books*
Biography; Business; Current Affairs; Genealogy; History; Journalism; Leadership; Music; Nature; Popular Science; Sport; Travel

Send: Market info; Writing sample
How to send: Online submission system

Interested in a wide range of nonfiction, including business and leadership, history, journalism, current affairs, biography, sport, music, popular science, nature, travel, genealogy. Will also consider historical fiction. The common factor is an emphasis on big ideas, great stories, and fine writing.

L690 David Taylor

Literary Agent
United Kingdom

Literary Agency: Sheil Land Associates Ltd

Scripts
Film Scripts; *TV Scripts*; *Theatre Scripts*

L691 Trisha Telep

Associate Agent
Canada

https://www.therightsfactory.com/Agents/Trisha-Telep

Literary Agency: The Rights Factory

Closed to approaches.

L692 The Tennyson Agency

Literary Agency
109 Tennyson Avenue, New Malden, Surrey, KT3 6NA
United Kingdom
Tel: +44 (0) 20 8543 5939

agency@tenagy.co.uk

http://www.tenagy.co.uk

Types: Scripts
Formats: Film Scripts; Radio Scripts; TV Scripts; Theatre Scripts
Subjects: Drama
Markets: Adult

Closed to approaches.

Mainly deals in scripts for film, TV, theatre, and radio, along with related material on an ad-hoc basis. Handles writers in the European Union only. Send query with CV and outline of work. Prefers queries by email. No nonfiction, poetry, short stories, science fiction and fantasy or children's writing, or unsolicited MSS.

L693 Teresa Chris Literary Agency Ltd

Literary Agency
43 Musard Road, London, W6 8NR
United Kingdom
Tel: +44 (0) 20 7386 0633

teresachris@litagency.co.uk

http://www.teresachrisliteraryagency.co.uk

Professional Body: The Association of Authors' Agents (AAA)

Fiction > *Novels*
Commercial Women's Fiction; Commercial; Crime; Literary

Does not want:

Fiction > *Novels*
Fantasy; Horror; Science Fiction

Send: Query; Synopsis; Writing sample
How to send: Email

Welcomes submissions. Send submissions by email only, with first three chapters, and one-page synopsis. Specialises in crime fiction and commercial women's fiction. No poetry, short stories, fantasy, science fiction, horror, or children's fiction.

Authors: Stephanie Austin; Lily Baxter; Ginny Bell; M A Bennett; Victoria Blake; Stephen Booth; Benita Brown; Rory Clements; Julie Cohen; Dilly Court; Martin Davies; Ellie Dean; Linda Finlay; Marina Fiorato; Emily Freud; Kate Furnivall; Annie Groves; Clare Harvey; Debby Holt; Hunter; Corrie Jackson; Jim Kelly; Danuta Kot; Linscott; Tamara McKinley; Jane McMorland; Charlotte Parsons; Stuart Pawson; Caro Peacock/Gillian; Nicola Pryce; Eileen Ramsay; Kate Rhodes; Mary-Jane Riley; Caroline Scott; Marsali Taylor; Jane Wenham-Jones

L694 Paige Terlip

Associate Agent
United States

paige@andreabrownlit.com

https://www.andreabrownlit.com/agents.html
https://twitter.com/pterlip
https://www.instagram.com/pterlip/

Literary Agency: Andrea Brown Literary Agency, Inc.

ADULT
Fiction > *Novels*
Cozy Mysteries; Fantasy; High Concept; Magic; Psychological Suspense; Science Fiction; Thrillers; Upmarket

Nonfiction > *Nonfiction Books*
Mind, Body, Spirit; Narrative Nonfiction; Self Help

CHILDREN'S > **Fiction**
Chapter Books; *Middle Grade*; *Picture Books*
YOUNG ADULT > **Fiction** > *Novels*
High Concept; Magic

Send: Author bio; Query; Writing sample; Pitch; Market info
How to send: Query Manager

Represents all categories of children's books from picture books to young adult, as well as select adult fiction and nonfiction. She is also actively building her list of illustrators and is especially looking for author-illustrators and graphic novel illustrators.

L695 Jack Thomas

Literary Agent
United Kingdom

Literary Agency: Independent Talent Group Ltd (**L340**)

L696 Paul Thompson

Literary Agent
United Kingdom

Literary Agency: Bookseeker Agency (**L072**)

L697 Sydnie Thornton

Literary Agent
United States

sydnie.queries@irenegoodman.com

https://www.irenegoodman.com/sydnie-thornton

Literary Agency: Irene Goodman Literary Agency (IGLA)

ADULT > **Fiction** > *Novels*
Contemporary Fantasy; Historical Fiction

YOUNG ADULT > **Fiction** > *Novels*
General, and in particular: Contemporary; Fantasy; Historical Fiction; Literary; Upmarket Thrillers

How to send: Email

Interested in YA across all genres: fantasy, historical fiction, contemporary that leans literary, as well as thrillers with upmarket qualities and distinctive characterization. As for the adult side, she is actively looking for transportive, complex historical fiction and whimsical contemporary fantasy. Regardless of genre, she's very likely to connect with manuscripts that bridge the YA/Adult divide. She's also eager to champion any book that prominently features disability representation.

L698 Anne Tibbets

Literary Agent
United States

http://maassagency.com/anne-tibbets/
https://querymanager.com/query/AnneTibbets

Literary Agency: Donald Maass Literary Agency

ADULT > **Fiction** > *Novels*
Amateur Investigator; Cozy Mysteries; Diversity; Domestic Thriller; Feminism; Historical Fiction; Horror; LGBTQIA; Mystery; Police Procedural; Psychological Horror; Romance; Romantic Comedy; Romantic Suspense; Thrillers; Women's Fiction

YOUNG ADULT > **Fiction** > *Novels*
Diversity; Feminism; Historical Fiction; LGBTQIA; Thrillers

Send: Author bio; Query; Synopsis; Writing sample
How to send: Query Manager

Represents adult and young adult commercial genre, primarily thrillers, mysteries, science fiction, fantasy, horror, and historical women's fiction.

L699 The Tobias Literary Agency

Literary Agency
United States

https://www.thetobiasagency.com
https://twitter.com/TheTobiasAgency
https://www.facebook.com/TobiasLiteraryAgency
https://www.instagram.com/thetobiasliteraryagency/

Specializes in all Intellectual Property matters in the publishing industry, from the seed of an idea to the day a book hits the shelves. A full-service literary agency headquartered in New York City with satellite offices in Boston, Nashville, and soon-to-be Los Angeles. Represents established and debut authors.

Associate Agent: Maria Rogers (**L600**)

Literary Agent / President: Lane Heymont (**L323**)

Literary Agents: Matt Belford; Stefanie Rossitto (**L605**)

Senior Agent: Natascha Morris (**L510**)

L700 Hannah Todd

Literary Agent
United Kingdom

submissions@madeleinemilburn.com

https://madeleinemilburn.co.uk/team-member/hannah-todd/

Literary Agency: Madeleine Milburn Literary, TV & Film Agency (**L464**)

Fiction > *Novels*
Commercial; Cozy Mysteries; Crime; Historical Fiction; LGBTQIA; Police Procedural; Romance; Romantic Comedy; Saga; Thrillers; Women's Fiction; World War I; World War II

Send: Query; Pitch; Market info; Synopsis; Writing sample
How to send: Email attachment
How not to send: Post

Actively looking for: commercial fiction across all genres including women's fiction; police procedurals; clever thrillers; cosy crime; romantic comedies; accessible historical fiction focusing on WW2 and including dual timeline novels; sagas; emotional issues-led fiction. If you can make her laugh, cry or fall in love then you're onto a winner!

L701 Nick Turner

Literary Agent
United Kingdom

Literary Agency: Nick Turner Management Ltd (**L526**)

L702 The Two Piers Literary Agency

Literary Agency
Brighton
United Kingdom

hello@twopiersagency.com

https://twopiersagency.com
https://twitter.com/TwoPiersAgency
https://www.facebook.com/TwoPiersAgency
https://www.instagram.com/twopiersagency/

ADULT
Fiction > *Novels*
Nonfiction > *Nonfiction Books*

CHILDREN'S > **Fiction** > *Middle Grade*

YOUNG ADULT > **Fiction** > *Novels*

Send: Query; Synopsis; Writing sample; Author bio
How to send: Online submission system

Costs: Offers services that writers have to pay for. Sister company provides online novel-writing course.

Literary agency based in Brighton, which represents writers from all over the world and sells their work into the UK, US and international territories. An editorially focused agency that works closely with authors to produce manuscripts that are as strong as they can possibly be before submitting them to publishers.

Literary Agent: Rufus Purdy (*L577*)

L703 Union Literary

Literary Agency
30 Vandam Street, Suite 5A, New York, NY 10013
United States
Tel: +1 (212) 255-2112

queries@threeseaslit.com

https://www.unionliterary.com

Professional Body: Association of American Literary Agents (AALA)

Types: Fiction; Nonfiction
Subjects: Autobiography; Business; Cookery; History; Literary; Science; Society
Markets: Adult

Send: Query
Don't send: Full text
How to send: Email

Prefers queries by email. Include a proposal and sample chapter for nonfiction, or a synopsis and sample pages for fiction. See website for specific agent interests and contact details, and approach one agent only. Response only if interested.

Literary Agents: Christina Clifford; Taylor Curtin; Trena Keating

L704 United Agents

Literary Agency
12-26 Lexington Street, London, W1F 0LE
United Kingdom
Tel: +44 (0) 20 3214 0800
Fax: +44 (0) 20 3214 0802

info@unitedagents.co.uk

https://www.unitedagents.co.uk
https://twitter.com/UnitedAgents
https://www.instagram.com/unitedagents/

Professional Body: The Association of Authors' Agents (AAA)

Fiction > *Novels*

Nonfiction > *Nonfiction Books*

Send: Query; Pitch; Market info; Synopsis; Writing sample
How to send: Email
How not to send: Post

Do not approach the book department generally. Consult website and view details of each agent before selecting a specific agent to approach personally. Accepts submissions by email only. Submissions by post will not be returned or responded to.

Agency Assistants: Molly Jamieson; Olivia Martin

Associate Agents: Seren Adams (**L006**); Millie Hoskins (**L331**); Eli Keren (**L383**); Emily Talbot (**L687**); Kate Walsh (**L720**)

Authors: Kim Adrian; Amrou Al-Kadhi; Laura Albert; Rosie Alison; Nina Allan; Karin Altenberg; Jessica Anthony; Oana Aristide; Aysha Awwad; Susanna Bailey; Adam Baker; Joan Bakewell; Abigail Balfe; Alex Barrow; Becky Baur; Deborah Bee; Hina Belitz; Alan Bennett; Stephen Bernard; LMK Berry; Sophie Ellis Bextor; Marieke Bigg; Mark Blacklock; Quentin Blake; Stefan Merrill Block; Ezekiel Boone; Melitta Breznik; Molly Brodak; Maggie Brookes; Christopher Brookmyre; Sylvia Brownrigg; Robin Bunce; John Burnside; Sarah Burton; Jen Calleja; Emma Campbell; Robin Carhart-Harris; Brian Catling; Carl Cattermole; Jessie Cave; Alex Alvina Chamberland; Clare Chambers; Roland Chambers; Tom Chivers; Emma Cline; Amanda Coe; Sean Patrick Cooper; Wendy Cope; Marion Coutts; Leah Cowan; Al Crow; Dan Cruickshank; Lauren Aimee Curtis; Rosie Dastgir; Carys Davies; Gabby Dawnay; Jill Dawson; Tim Dee; Sophie Deen; JP Delaney; Sam Diamond; Susannah Dickey; Minoo Dinshaw; Paddy Docherty; Chloe Douglass; Miranda Doyle; Dennis Duncan; Douglas Dunn; Elanor Dymott; Ben Eastham; Ed Eaves; Christy Edwall; Lucie Elven; Chris England; Hermione Eyre; James Fenton; Toby Ferris; Rakaya Fetuga; Tim Finch; Ronan Fitzgerald; William Fowler; Amaryllis Gacioppo; Rivka Galchen; William Ghosh; Rebecca Gibb; Maria Giron; Sue Glover; Rebecca Gowers; Ysenda Maxtone Graham; Huho Greenhalgh; Charlotte Grimshaw; Camilla Grudova; Alison Guile; Tessa Hadley; Lili Hamlyn; Lynsey Hanley; Robert Hardman; James Harris; David Harsent; Jack Hartnell; Samantha Harvey; Will Hayward; Sam Hearn; Colin Heber-Percy; Sheila Heti; Ben Hinshaw; Susannah Hoffman; Michael Hofmann; Richard Holloway; Joseph Hone; Benjamin Hughes; Caoilinn Hughes; Catherine Humble; Mark Hussey; Nicholas Hytner; Alison Irvine; William Irvine; Mick Jackson; Blair James; Liza St. James; Lenka Janiurek; Annaleese Jochems; Ioan Marc Jones; Peter Stephan Jungk; Francesca Kay; I. J. Kay; Tobias Kelly; Katharine Kilalea; Ana Kinsella; Katie Kirby; Clement Knox; Sonal Kohli; Laura Kounine; Nakul Krishna; Richard Lambert; James Lasdun; David Lawrence; Paul Lay; Mike Leigh; James Lent; Louise Levene; Rebecca Lewis-Oakes; Nell Leyshon; Maggie Li; Samara Linton; Victor Lodato; Tom Lubbock; Johanna Lukate; Anna Mackmin; Caroline Maclean; Deirdre Madden; Aileen Maguire; Emily St. John Mandel; Adam Mars-Jones; Philip Marsden; Andrew Martin; Anita Mason; Laura Maw; Simon Mawer; Patrick McGinley; Roger McGough; Daisy McNally; James McNicholas; Coco Mellors; Livi Michael; David Miles; Peter Moffat; Sinéad Mooney; Becka Moor; Michelle Morgan; Jan Morris; Ottessa Moshfegh; Sarah Moss; John Mullan; Nicholas Murray; Malik Al Nasir; Anna Neima; Caleb Azumah Nelson; Anthea Nicholson; Trevor Norton; Alissa Nutting; Redmond O'Hanlon; Timothy Ogene; Nat Ogle; David Olusoga; Alice Oswald; Polly Owen; Bobby Palmer; William Palmer; Tim Parks; Ambrose Parry; Ian Pattison; Ruth Pavey; Helen Pike; Joanna Pocock; Jem Poster; Miranda Pountney; Philip Pullman; Issa Quincy; Karina Lickorish Quinn; Julya Rabinowich; Natasha Randall; Victoria Redel; Gemma Reeves; Ruth Rendell; Talulah Riley; Sam Riviere; Michael Symmons Roberts; Michèle Roberts; Laura Robertson; Keith Robinson; Juno Roche; Jane Rogers; Michael

Rosen; Olivia Rosenthall; LJ Ross; Alan Rossi; Saumya Roy; Taylor-Dior Rumble; Andy Sagar; Michael Salu; Kate Saunders; Lina Scheynius; Claire Seeber; Jenn Shapland; Jion Sheibani; Qian Shi; Mika Simmons; Tracey Slaughter; Laura Southgate; Olivia Spring; Alexander Starritt; Wendell Steavenson; Georgina Stevens; Sean Stoker; Alexander Stuart; Jordan Sullivan; Alain Claude Sulzer; David Szalay; George Szirtes; Georgina Terry; Emily Thomas; Barry Timms; Jacqueline Tucker; Kael Tudor; Peter Turnbull; Ryan Turner; Zakia Uddin; Lucy Unwin; Kenechi Uzor; Maddy Vian; James Vincent; Lucia Vinti; Francesca Wade; Lauren Wallach; Stephen Walsh; Natasha Walter; James Walvin; Eva Warrick; Gavin Weightman; Sam White; Derek Wilson; Gaby Wood; Rohullah Yakobi; An Yu; Zinovy Zinik; Tirdad Zolghadr

Literary Agents: Sarah Ballard (**L043**); Caroline Dawnay (**L166**); Ariella Feiner (**L216**); Jim Gill (**L259**); Jodie Hodges (**L328**); Robert Kirby (**L389**); Laura Macdougall (**L456**); Zoe Ross (**L604**); Sophie Scard (**L623**); Rosemary Scoular (**L629**); Charles Walker (**L716**); Anna Webber (**L725**)

L705 The Unter Agency

Literary Agency
141 Parkway Road, Suite 10, Bronxville, NY 10708
United States
Tel: +1 (212) 401-4068

Jennifer@theunteragency.com

http://www.theunteragency.com
https://twitter.com/JenniferUnter
https://www.linkedin.com/in/jennifer-unter-6b379a45/

ADULT
Fiction > *Novels*

Nonfiction > *Nonfiction Books*
General, and in particular: Adventure; Biography; Cookery; Crime; Environment; Fitness; Food; Health; Memoir; Nature; Politics; Popular Culture; Travel

CHILDREN'S > **Fiction**
Middle Grade; *Picture Books*
YOUNG ADULT > **Fiction** > *Novels*

Send: Query
How to send: Email

Interested in quality fiction and general nonfiction, particularly memoir, food/cooking, nature/environment, biography, pop culture, travel/adventure, true crime, politics and health/fitness. Also all types of children's literature (picture books, middle grade, and young adult). Send query letter by email. If no response within three months, assume rejection.

Associate Agent: Jen Nadol (**L519**)

Literary Agent: Jennifer Unter

L706 Jo Unwin

Literary Agent
United Kingdom

Literary Agency: Jo Unwin Literary Agency (**L354**)

Closed to approaches.

L707 Upstart Crow Literary

Literary Agency
594 Dean Street, Office 47, Brooklyn, NY 11238
United States

http://www.upstartcrowliterary.com

ADULT
Fiction > *Novels*
Nonfiction > *Nonfiction Books*

CHILDREN'S > **Fiction**
Middle Grade; *Novels*; *Picture Books*
YOUNG ADULT > **Fiction** > *Novels*

Send: Query
How to send: Email

Send query by email with 20 pages of your ms, in the body of an email. No attachments or hard copy submissions. See website for more details, and specific agent interests and contact details.

Literary Agents: Danielle Chiotti (**L126**); Kayla Cichello (**L131**); Susan Hawk (**L313**)

L708 Laura Usselman

Literary Agent
United States

http://skagency.com/agents/laura-usselman/

Literary Agency: Stuart Krichevsky Literary Agency, Inc. (**L675**)

Fiction > *Novels*

Nonfiction > *Nonfiction Books*
General, and in particular: Memoir

Represents adult fiction and nonfiction. Her fiction interests include character-centered fiction of all stripes, from the formally strange to the family saga. For nonfiction, she is interested in thoughtful narrative nonfiction for younger readers, restlessly curious idea books, and voice-driven memoir.

Authors: Emily Bloom; Katherine Blunt; Victoria Facelli; Sarah Jaffe; Rachel McCarthy James; Madeline Ostrander; Robin Page; Soraya Palmer; David Shih; Sofi Thanhauser; Kaitlyn Tiffany

L709 Vanessa Holt Ltd

Literary Agency
1422/4 London Road, Leigh On Sea, Essex, SS9 2UL
United Kingdom

v.holt791@btinternet.com

https://find-and-update.company-information.service.gov.uk/company/02391626

Professional Body: The Association of Authors' Agents (AAA)

Fiction > *Novels*

Nonfiction > *Nonfiction Books*

Literary Agent: Vanessa Holt (**L330**)

L710 Leslie Varney

Literary Agent; President
United States

Literary Agency: Prentis Literary (**L574**)

L711 Sarah Veecock

Literary Agent
United Kingdom

Literary Agency: The Narrow Road Company (**L520**)

L712 Veritas Literary Agency

Literary Agency
601 Van Ness Avenue, Opera Plaza Suite E, San Francisco, CA 94102
United States

submissions@veritasliterary.com

http://www.veritasliterary.com
https://www.twitter.com/verlit

Professional Body: Association of American Literary Agents (AALA)

ADULT
Fiction > *Novels*
Commercial; Fantasy; Historical Fiction; Speculative; Women's Fiction

Nonfiction > *Nonfiction Books*
Biography; Cultural History; History; Memoir; Narrative Nonfiction; Nature; Popular Culture; Popular Science; Women's Studies

CHILDREN'S > **Fiction** > *Middle Grade*

YOUNG ADULT > **Fiction** > *Novels*

Send: Query; Writing sample
How to send: In the body of an email
How not to send: Post

Send query or proposal by email only. Submit further information on request only. For fiction, include cover letter listing previously published work, one-page summary and first five pages. For nonfiction, include author bio, overview, chapter-by-chapter summary, sample chapters or text, and analysis of competing titles.

Literary Agents: Katherine Boyle (**L076**); Michael Carr (**L108**)

Literary Scout: Chiara Rosati

L713 The Vines Agency, Inc.

Literary Agency
320 7th Avenue, Suite 178, Brooklyn, NY

11215
United States
Tel: +1 (212) 777-5522
Fax: +1 (718) 228-4536

http://www.vinesagency.com

Professional Bodies: The Authors Guild; Writers Guild of America (WGA)

Fiction > *Novels*
Commercial; Historical Fiction; Literary; Mystery; Science Fiction

Nonfiction > *Nonfiction Books*: Commercial

Closed to approaches.

This agency is closed to new clients and is no longer accepting query letters or submissions.

Authors: Laura Doyle; Shawne Johnson; Bernice McFadden; Christine Moriarty; Don Winslow; Moon Unit Zappa

Literary Agent: James C. Vines (*L714*)

L714 James C. Vines

Literary Agent
United States

Literary Agency: The Vines Agency, Inc. (**L713**)

L715 The Viney Agency

Literary Agency
21, Dartmouth Park Ave, London, NW5 IJL
United Kingdom

charlie@thevineyagency.com

http://thevineyagency.com

Professional Body: The Association of Authors' Agents (AAA)

ADULT
Fiction > *Novels*

Nonfiction > *Nonfiction Books*
Biography; History; Journalism

CHILDREN'S > **Fiction** > *Novels*

Send: Query
Don't send: Full text
How not to send: Email

Handles high quality nonfiction, and adult and children's fiction. See website for examples of the kinds of books represented. Send query by first or second class post.

Literary Agents: Amberley Lowis (**L442**); Charlie Viney

L716 Charles Walker

Literary Agent
United Kingdom
Tel: +44 (0) 20 3214 0874

cwalker@unitedagents.co.uk

https://www.unitedagents.co.uk/cwalkerunitedagentscouk

Literary Agency: United Agents (**L704**)

Fiction > *Novels*
Crime; Historical Fiction; Literary; Science Fiction

Nonfiction > *Nonfiction Books*
History; Memoir

Send: Query; Synopsis; Writing sample
How to send: Email

In nonfiction deals mainly in history and memoir. In fiction, leans toward literary fiction, although it can contain historical and crime and very occasionally sci-fi. Send query by email to assistant.

Agency Assistant: Olivia Martin

Authors: Adam Baker; Alan Bennett; Wendy Cope; Dan Cruickshank; Paddy Docherty; Douglas Dunn; Chris England; Sue Glover; Robert Hardman; David Harsent; Colin Heber-Percy; Mark Hussey; Richard Lambert; David Lawrence; Paul Lay; Mike Leigh; Anita Mason; Simon Mawer; Patrick McGinley; Roger McGough; Livi Michael; Peter Moffat; Nicholas Murray; Malik Al Nasir; Redmond O'Hanlon; David Olusoga; William Palmer; Ruth Rendell; Michèle Roberts; Jane Rogers; Michael Rosen; Alexander Stuart; Peter Turnbull; James Walvin; Gavin Weightman; Derek Wilson

L717 The Wallace Literary Agency

Literary Agency
United States

contact@wallaceliteraryagency.com

http://www.wallaceliteraryagency.com

Literary Agencies: Robin Straus Agency, Inc.; Andrew Nurnberg Associates, Ltd (**L021**)

L718 Clare Wallace

Literary Agent
United Kingdom

https://www.darleyandersonchildrens.com/about-us
https://twitter.com/LitAgentClare

Literary Agencies: The Darley Anderson Agency; Darley Anderson Children's (**L159**)

ADULT > **Fiction** > *Novels*: Commercial Women's Fiction

CHILDREN'S > **Fiction**
Middle Grade; *Picture Books*
TEEN > **Fiction** > *Novels*

YOUNG ADULT > **Fiction** > *Novels*

Scouting for new authors of picture books, middle grade, teenage, YA and illustrators. Also represents a boutique list of commercial and accessible literary women's fiction but is closed to new submissions.

Assistant Agent: Chloe Davis (**L164**)

Authors: Honor Cargill-Martin; Sophie Cousens; Tom Ellen; Alex Evelyn; Kerry Fisher; Martyn Ford; Polly Ho-Yen; Nathanael Lessore; Ayaan Mohamud; Phaedra Patrick; Beth Reekles; Pat Sowa; Deirdre Sullivan; Samantha Tonge

L719 Caroline Walsh

Literary Agent
United Kingdom

https://www.davidhigham.co.uk/agents-dh/caroline-walsh/

Literary Agency: David Higham Associates Ltd (**L161**)

ADULT
Fiction > *Novels*
Nonfiction > *Nonfiction Books*

CHILDREN'S > **Fiction**
Chapter Books; *Novels*; *Picture Books*

Client list is made up predominantly of children's writers and illustrators, many of them award-winners and bestsellers. In addition she handles some adult fiction and non-fiction and is always on the look-out for original contemporary writing and talented author/illustrators.

Assistant Agent: Becca Challis (*L113*)

Authors: Kelly Andrew; Antonia Barber; Suzanne Barton; Ella Beech; Joe Berger; Tim Bowler; Theresa Breslin; Martin Brown; Mike Brownlow; Kathryn Cave; Jason Chapman; Emma Chichester Clark; Trish Cooke; Cressida Cowell; Susie Day; Kady MacDonald Denton; Lucy Dillamore; Ruth Eastham; Eve Edwards; Jonathan Emmett; Ben Faulks; Corina Fletcher; Alex Foulkes; P. M. Freestone; Jane Gardam; Susan Gates; Adèle Geras; Julia Golding; Ryan Graudin; Candida Harper; Leigh Hodgkinson; Jesse Hodgson; Dianne Hofmeyr; Anna Hoghton; Meredith Hooper; Suzanna Hubbard; Julia Jarman; Amie Kaufman; Anna Kemp; Clive King; Jay Kristoff; Fifi Kuo; Eleanor Lavender; Jo Lodge; Jan Mark; Ellie Marney; Tom McLaughlin; Gwen Millward; Myfanwy Millward; Kate Milner; Alex Milway; Tony Mitton; Laura Mucha; Jenny Nimmo; C. S. Pacat; Liz Pichon; Tamora Pierce; Madhvi Ramani; Catherine Rayner; Jacqui Rayner; Gwyneth Rees; Jasmine Richards; Fiona Roberton; Rachel Rooney; Alexander McCall Smith; Joss Stirling; Sally Symes; Vanessa Tait; Frances Thomas; Theresa Tomlinson; Ann Turnbull; Martin Waddell; Melanie Walsh; Gina Wilson; Jacqueline Wilson; David Wojtowycz

L720 Kate Walsh

Associate Agent
United Kingdom
Tel: +44 (0) 20 3214 0884

kwalsh@unitedagents.co.uk

https://www.unitedagents.co.uk/kwalshunitedagentscouk

Literary Agency: United Agents (**L704**)
Literary Agent: Robert Kirby (**L389**)

Fiction > *Novels*

Nonfiction > *Nonfiction Books*
Commercial; Current Affairs; Music; Politics

Send: Query; Synopsis; Writing sample
How to send: Email

Actively building her list. She's on the lookout mainly for commercial non-fiction, particularly with a political or current affairs slant, and anything that feels like a fresh and original way of looking at the world. She is especially drawn to 20th and 21st century affairs, and anyone willing to speculate on what comes next. Whilst working mainly with non-fiction, she is always excited to read anything, fiction or non-, with a strong and transporting sense of place and time.

Authors: Will Hayward; Rohullah Yakobi

L721 Nick Walters

Literary Agent
United Kingdom

nick@davidluxtonassociates.co.uk

https://www.davidluxtonassociates.co.uk/the-agency/

Literary Agency: David Luxton Associates (**L162**)

Nonfiction > *Nonfiction Books*
Commercial; Leadership; Lifestyle; Self Help; Sport

Send: Synopsis; Writing sample; Author bio
How to send: Email

Agent and Rights Manager. Principle interests are in the fields of sport, true crime, current affairs, lifestyle and self-help.

L722 Mackenzie Brady Watson

Literary Agent
United States

mbwquery@skagency.com

http://skagency.com/agents/mackenzie-brady-watson/

Literary Agency: Stuart Krichevsky Literary Agency, Inc. (**L675**)

ADULT > **Nonfiction** > *Nonfiction Books*
Business; Food; Investigative Journalism; Memoir; Narrative Nonfiction; Science; Sociology

YOUNG ADULT > **Fiction** > *Novels*

Focuses on narrative non-fiction for all ages and select Young Adult fiction. As a former genetics lab technician, she has a great passion for science books, especially if they are historically driven or revolutionize current theory, as well as sociology, investigative journalism, food writing, memoir, and business books. She particularly appreciates work that sheds light on marginalized experiences and helps contribute to the cultural conversation.

Authors: Roxanna Asgarian; Ahmed Badr; Lyndsie Bourgon; Hannah Brencher; Caren Cooper; Hope Ewing; Kathryn Finney; Kit Fox; Katie Fricas; Olivia Gatwood; Jessica Goudeau; Rose Hackman; Anita Hannig; Sarah Jaffe; R. Dean Johnson; Sophie Lucido Johnson; Megan Kimble; Audrea Lim; Catherine Lo; Michael Loynd; Jennifer Lunden; José Olivarez; Karen Pinchin; Shelley Puhak; Lydia Reeder; Victoria Reihana; Margot Lee Shetterly; Bric Spangler; Rachel Swaby; Sarah Vogel; Kimberley Welman; Christina Wilcox; Nina Willner; Bernice Yeung; Sara Zin

L723 Rebecca Watson

Literary Agent
United Kingdom

Literary Agency: Valerie Hoskins Associates

L724 Jessica Watterson

Literary Agent
United States

https://www.dijkstraagency.com/agent-page.php?agent_id=Watterson
https://querymanager.com/query/jessicawatterson

Literary Agency: Sandra Dijkstra Literary Agency

ADULT > **Fiction** > *Novels*
Cozy Mysteries; Romance; Women's Fiction

CHILDREN'S
Fiction > *Picture Books*

Nonfiction > *Nonfiction Books*: Popular Culture

YOUNG ADULT > **Fiction** > *Novels*
Contemporary; Romance

Send: Query; Synopsis; Writing sample
How to send: Query Manager

Most interested in all genres of romance. Also loves women's fiction and is open to select Cozy Mysteries. In Young Adult, will consider just about anything in the contemporary sphere, particularly with some romance. Will also consider author-illustrated books and nonfiction on Pop Culture by authors who have established platforms.

L725 Anna Webber

Literary Agent
United Kingdom
Tel: +44 (0) 20 3214 0876

awebber@unitedagents.co.uk

https://www.unitedagents.co.uk/awebberunitedagentscouk
https://twitter.com/acewebber

Literary Agency: United Agents (**L704**)

Fiction > *Novels*

Nonfiction > *Nonfiction Books*: Literary

Poetry > *Any Poetic Form*

Send: Synopsis; Writing sample; Proposal

Represents both fiction and non-fiction, with a special focus on literary fiction and voice-driven non-fiction. She is open for submissions, but can only take on a small number of new clients per year.

Associate Agent: Seren Adams (**L006**)

Authors: Laura Albert; Rosie Alison; Nina Allan; Karin Altenberg; Jessica Anthony; Deborah Bee; Mark Blacklock; Stefan Merrill Block; Ezekiel Boone; Melitta Breznik; Molly Brodak; Sylvia Brownrigg; John Burnside; Robin Carhart-Harris; Carl Cattermole; Roland Chambers; Emma Cline; Amanda Coe; Marion Coutts; Rosie Dastgir; Carys Davies; Tim Dee; Miranda Doyle; Dennis Duncan; Elanor Dymott; Ben Eastham; Christy Edwall; Hermione Eyre; James Fenton; Toby Ferris; William Fowler; Rivka Galchen; William Ghosh; Rebecca Gowers; Samantha Harvey; Sheila Heti; Ben Hinshaw; Michael Hofmann; Joseph Hone; Caoilinn Hughes; Nicholas Hytner; William Irvine; Mick Jackson; Peter Stephan Jungk; Francesca Kay; I. J. Kay; Katharine Kilalea; James Lasdun; Louise Levene; Nell Leyshon; Victor Lodato; Tom Lubbock; Anna Mackmin; Caroline Maclean; Deirdre Madden; Emily St. John Mandel; Adam Mars-Jones; Philip Marsden; Andrew Martin; Daisy McNally; Ottessa Moshfegh; Sarah Moss; John Mullan; Anthea Nicholson; Trevor Norton; Alissa Nutting; Nat Ogle; Alice Oswald; Tim Parks; Ian Pattison; Helen Pike; Miranda Pountney; Julya Rabinowich; Natasha Randall; Victoria Redel; Sam Riviere; Michael Symmons Roberts; Jenn Shapland; Alexander Starritt; Wendell Steavenson; Alain Claude Sulzer; David Szalay; George Szirtes; Natasha Walter; Gaby Wood; An Yu; Zinovy Zinik; Tirdad Zolghadr

L726 Frank Weimann

Literary Agent; Partner
United States
Tel: +1 (212) 400-1494

fweimann@foliolit.com

https://www.publishersmarketplace.com/members/weimann/

Literary Agency: Folio Literary Management, LLC

Nonfiction > *Nonfiction Books*
General, and in particular: African American; Biography; Business; CIA; Celebrity; Comedy / Humour; Finance; Health; History; Mafia; Memoir; Military; Narrative Nonfiction; Pets; Prescriptive Nonfiction; Religion; Science; Special Forces; Sport

Send: Query; Writing sample
How to send: In the body of an email

Authors: Kareem Abdul-Jabbar; Dan Abrams; Gregg Allman; George Anastasia; Michael Baden; Joe Bonanno; Terry Bradshaw; Charles Brandt; John "Chick" Donohue; John Douglas; Tamer Elnoury; Rickson Gracie; John Gray; Homer Hickam; Harry Markopolos; Kevin Maurer; Maria Menounos; Mark Olshaker; Joe Pistone; Laura Prepon; Bill Russell; Gina Schock

L727 Alexandra Weiss

Associate Agent
United States

http://www.azantianlitagency.com/pages/team-awe.html
https://querymanager.com/query/AlexandraWeiss

Literary Agency: Azantian Literary Agency (**L037**)

ADULT > **Nonfiction**
Gift Books: General
Nonfiction Books: Environment; Mental Health; Science; Space
CHILDREN'S
Fiction
Graphic Novels; *Picture Books*
Nonfiction
Chapter Books: General
Middle Grade: Adventure; Contemporary; Magic; Science Fiction; Time Travel
Picture Books: General

YOUNG ADULT > **Fiction**
Graphic Novels: General
Novels: Coming of Age; Contemporary; Folklore, Myths, and Legends; Low Fantasy; Magical Realism; Romantic Comedy; Soft Science Fiction

How to send: Query Manager

Represents fiction and nonfiction picture books, middle grade, young adult, graphic novels, and select adult nonfiction.

L728 Karmen Wells

Associate Agent
Canada

karmen@therightsfactory.com

https://www.therightsfactory.com/Agents/Karmen-Wells
https://twitter.com/KarmenEdits

Literary Agency: The Rights Factory

Fiction > *Novels*
Comedy / Humour; Coming of Age; Commercial; Drama; Dystopian Fiction; High Concept; Horror; LGBTQIA; Literary; Popular Culture; Science Fiction

Nonfiction > *Nonfiction Books*: Narrative Nonfiction

Send: Query; Pitch; Author bio; Writing sample
How to send: Email

Looking for published or to-be-published books to represent to producers for film or TV adaptation.

Authors: Daniel Barnett; Kelly Florence; Rhonda J. Garcia; Jessica Guess; Meg Hafdahl; Tim Meyer

L729 Wendy Schmalz Agency

Literary Agency
United States

wendy@schmalzagency.com

https://www.schmalzagency.com

CHILDREN'S
Fiction > *Middle Grade*
Nonfiction > *Middle Grade*

YOUNG ADULT
Fiction > *Novels*
Nonfiction > *Nonfiction Books*

Send: Query; Synopsis
Don't send: Full text; Writing sample
How to send: Email

Handles books for middle grade and young adults. No science fiction, fantasy, or picture books. Send query by email. No unsolicited mss or sample chapters. If no response after two weeks, assume no interest.

Literary Agent: Wendy Schmalz

L730 Katherine Wessbecher

Literary Agent
United States

https://bradfordlit.com/about/katherine-wessbecher/
https://querymanager.com/query/katherinewessbecher
https://twitter.com/KatWessbecher

Literary Agency: Bradford Literary Agency (**L077**)

ADULT
Fiction > *Novels*
Commercial; Literary; Upmarket

Nonfiction
Graphic Nonfiction: General
Nonfiction Books: Narrative Nonfiction

CHILDREN'S
Fiction
Middle Grade: Epistolary; Fantasy; Historical Fiction
Picture Books: General

Nonfiction
Graphic Nonfiction: General
Nonfiction Books: Narrative Nonfiction

YOUNG ADULT
Fiction > *Novels*
Epistolary; Fantasy; Historical Fiction

Nonfiction
Graphic Nonfiction: General
Nonfiction Books: Narrative Nonfiction

Does not want:

Fiction > *Novels*
High / Epic Fantasy; Romance; Science Fiction; Thrillers

Nonfiction > *Nonfiction Books*
Business; Memoir

Poetry > *Any Poetic Form*

Scripts
Film Scripts; *TV Scripts*

How to send: Query Manager

Looking for children's books (picture books through YA), upmarket adult fiction, and narrative nonfiction for all ages.

L731 Erin Casey Westin

Literary Agent
United States

erin@galltzacker.com

Literary Agency: Gallt & Zacker Literary Agency

CHILDREN'S > **Fiction**
Middle Grade; *Picture Books*
YOUNG ADULT
Fiction
Graphic Novels; *Novels*
Nonfiction > *Nonfiction Books*

Closed to approaches.

L732 Michaela Whatnall

Literary Agent
United States

mwhatnall@dystel.com

https://www.dystel.com/michaela-whatnall
https://querymanager.com/query/michaelawhatnall
https://twitter.com/mwhatnall

Literary Agency: Dystel, Goderich & Bourret LLC

ADULT
Fiction > *Novels*
Fantasy; Science Fiction; Speculative

Nonfiction > *Nonfiction Books*
General, and in particular: Arts; History; Lifestyle; Narrative Nonfiction

CHILDREN'S > **Fiction**
Middle Grade; *Picture Books*
YOUNG ADULT > **Fiction**
Graphic Novels; *Novels*

How to send: Query Manager

Strong interest in children's literature, from picture books up through middle grade and young adult novels and graphic novels. In the adult fiction space, they are particularly seeking character-driven speculative fiction, sci-fi/fantasy, and other genre fiction that features historically underrepresented characters. They are also interested in nonfiction for both children and adults, especially narrative nonfiction in the areas of history, the creative arts, and lifestyle.

L733 Maria Whelan

Literary Agent
United States

http://www.inkwellmanagement.com/staff/maria-whelan

Literary Agency: InkWell Management

Fiction > *Novels*
Comedy / Humour; Commercial; Culture; Literary; Magical Realism; Speculative; Upmarket Women's Fiction

Nonfiction > *Nonfiction Books*
General, and in particular: Cultural Commentary; Society

Send: Query; Writing sample
How to send: In the body of an email

Enjoys literary fiction, magical realism, upmarket women's fiction and humor, as well as non-fiction, revolving around peculiar topics especially overlooked facets of society.

L734 Alice Whitwham

Literary Agent
United States

https://www.cheneyagency.com/alice-whitwham

Literary Agency: The Cheney Agency

L735 Gary Wild

Literary Agent
United Kingdom

Literary Agency: JFL Agency (**L353**)

L736 Alice Williams

Literary Agent
United Kingdom

alice@alicewilliamsliterary.co.uk

https://twitter.com/alicelovesbooks

Literary Agency: Alice Williams Literary (**L015**)

L737 Ike Williams

Literary Agent
United States

Literary Agency: Kneerim & Williams

Closed to approaches.

L738 Sarah Williams

Literary Agent
United Kingdom

Literary Agency: Independent Talent Group Ltd (**L340**)

L739 Kathryn Willms

Associate Agent
Canada

kathryn@therightsfactory.com

https://www.therightsfactory.com/Agents/Kathryn-Willms
https://querymanager.com/query/2039

Literary Agency: The Rights Factory

Nonfiction > *Nonfiction Books*
Environment; Food and Drink; Nature; Social Justice; Sport

Closed to approaches.

Currently focused on building her non-fiction list in sports, social justice, nature/environmental topics, and food and drink. However, as a generalist who simply likes "good books," she's open to a variety of genres. She is passionate about bringing ambitious, unconventional, and joyous books into the world, would rather laugh than cry, and is ultimately a sucker for a good story compellingly told.

Authors: Chloe Ackerman; Lisa Brahin; Lynda Calvert; Meghan Chayka; Lana Hall; Alyssa Huizing; Andrew Mayeda; Michelle McIvor; Nancy Pearson; Karen Pierce; Laura Pratt; Bațuta Rubess; Zed Zha

L740 Desiree Wilson

Literary Agent
United States

https://www.thebentagency.com/desiree-wilson
https://querymanager.com/query/dwilson
https://desir.ee/submissions/
https://twitter.com/swindlesoiree

Literary Agency: The Bent Agency (**L058**)

ADULT
Fiction
Graphic Novels: Contemporary; Fantasy; Horror; Magical Realism; Science Fiction; Speculative
Novels: Contemporary; Fantasy; Horror; Magical Realism; Romantic Comedy; Science Fiction; Speculative; Thrillers; Upmarket
Short Fiction: General

Nonfiction > *Nonfiction Books*: Narrative Nonfiction

CHILDREN'S
Fiction
Graphic Novels: General
Middle Grade: Gender; Horror; Mental Health
Nonfiction > *Middle Grade*
Engineering; History; Mathematics; Science; Technology

YOUNG ADULT > **Fiction**
Graphic Novels: High Concept; Relationships
Novels: Fairy Tales; Fantasy; High Concept; Horror; LGBTQIA; Romance; Romantic Comedy; Science Fiction; Urban Fantasy

Does not want:

Fiction > *Novels*: Hard Science Fiction

Closed to approaches.

I represent upper middle grade, YA, and adult genre fiction, especially horror (and kid-horror), high-concept fantasy, speculative fiction, magical realism, and accessible or near-future science fiction. I am also looking for select middle grade nonfiction about history or STEM.

L741 Ed Wilson

Literary Agent
United Kingdom
Tel: +44 (0) 20 7251 0125

ed@johnsonandalcock.co.uk

http://www.johnsonandalcock.co.uk/ed-wilson
https://twitter.com/literarywhore

Literary Agency: Johnson & Alcock (**L356**)

ADULT
Fiction
Graphic Novels: General
Novels: Commercial; Crime; Experimental; Fantasy; High Concept; Literary; Science Fiction; Speculative; Thrillers
Nonfiction > *Nonfiction Books*
History; Nature; Politics; Popular Culture; Sport

YOUNG ADULT > **Fiction** > *Novels*

Send: Query; Synopsis; Writing sample
How to send: Email attachment

With a background studying postmodern American literature he doesn't fear the experimental, speculative, and downright weird. He is actively building a SFF list and is always on the lookout for books that transcend genre. He's open to all forms of high concept writing, intelligent crime and thrillers. He represents some YA, but only books at the older end, and with crossover potential to an adult market.

His non-fiction tastes cover a wide range: from politics and serious history, to sport, natural history and popular culture. He loves intelligent and original graphic novels and infographics, and anything quirky. He is not currently taking on any children's authors and does not represent poetry or scripts.

L742 Rebecca Winfield

Literary Agent
United Kingdom

https://www.davidluxtonassociates.co.uk/the-agency/

Literary Agency: David Luxton Associates (**L162**)

Nonfiction
Nonfiction Books: History; Memoir; Travel
Reference: Popular Reference

Send: Synopsis; Writing sample; Author bio
How to send: Email
How not to send: Post

L743 Gordon Wise

Literary Agent
United Kingdom

Literary Agency: Curtis Brown

L744 Caryn Wiseman

Executive Agent
United States

https://www.andreabrownlit.com/agents.html
https://querymanager.com/query/CarynWiseman
https://www.facebook.com/caryn.wiseman
https://twitter.com/CarynWiseman

Literary Agency: Andrea Brown Literary Agency, Inc.

CHILDREN'S
Fiction
Chapter Books: General, and in particular: Diversity; Social Justice
Graphic Novels: General, and in particular: Diversity; Social Justice
Middle Grade: General, and in particular: Diversity; Social Justice
Picture Books: General, and in particular: Diversity; Social Justice
Nonfiction
Nonfiction Books: General, and in particular: Diversity; Social Justice
Picture Books: General, and in particular: Biography; Diversity; Social Justice
YOUNG ADULT
Fiction > *Novels*
General, and in particular: Diversity; Romance; Social Justice

Nonfiction > *Nonfiction Books*
General, and in particular: Diversity; Social Justice

Send: Author bio; Query; Writing sample; Pitch; Market info
How to send: Query Manager

Drawn to contemporary YA and middle grade with a strong voice, multifaceted characters, complex relationships, beautiful writing, and a well-developed hook. Great world-building is essential, whether it's a real time and place that becomes almost a character in a book, or a light fantasy element in a unique story that's grounded in reality. Zombies, horror, and high fantasy will, most likely, never appeal. She is particularly interested in books for children and teens that explore themes of diversity and social justice. She would be thrilled to see more books by underrepresented authors that deeply explore their culture, as well as books in which the ethnicity of the character is not the issue. She adores a swoon-worthy, layered romance; a funny or poignant middle grade novel with a hook that makes it stand out from the crowd would hold great appeal; and she's partial to lyrical, non-institutional picture book biographies and character-driven, not-too-sweet picture book fiction, particularly by author-illustrators.

L745 Jade Wong-Baxter

Associate Agent
United States

jwb@goldinlit.com

https://goldinlit.com/contact/

Literary Agency: Frances Goldin Literary Agency, Inc.

Fiction > *Novels*
Literary; Magical Realism; Upmarket

Nonfiction > *Nonfiction Books*
Cultural Criticism; History; Memoir; Narrative Nonfiction; Popular Culture

Send: Query; Writing sample
How to send: Email

L746 Bryony Woods

Literary Agent
United Kingdom

http://dkwlitagency.co.uk/agents/
https://twitter.com/BryonyWoods

Literary Agency: Diamond Kahn and Woods (DKW) Literary Agency Ltd

Closed to approaches.

L747 Jessica Woollard

Literary Agent
United Kingdom

jessicawoollard@davidhigham.co.uk

https://www.davidhigham.co.uk/agents-dh/jessica-woollard/

Literary Agency: David Higham Associates Ltd (**L161**)

Fiction > *Novels*: Literary

Nonfiction > *Nonfiction Books*
Activism; Africa; Culture; Current Affairs; Environment; Gender; Japan; Memoir; Middle East; Narrative Nonfiction; Nature; Science; South-East Asia

Represents a diverse range of international literary fiction and narrative non-fiction. South East Asia, Japan, Africa and the Middle East are areas of particular interest; she lived in Mumbai for five years. She's long worked with memoir, perhaps it's the new novel, and books that explore multiple genres; science, natural history, gender, landscape, cultural and current affairs and the way these subjects impact on our daily lives, poetic, awake, activist, environmentally aware writing.

Author: Natalie Lawrence

L748 Writers' Representatives, LLC

Literary Agency
116 W. 14th St., 11th Fl., New York, NY 10011-7305
United States
Tel: +1 (212) 620-0023
Fax: +1 (212) 620-0023

transom@writersreps.com

http://www.writersreps.com

Types: Fiction; Nonfiction; Poetry
Formats: Reference
Subjects: Autobiography; Business; Comedy / Humour; Cookery; Current Affairs; Finance; History; Legal; Literary; Literary Criticism; Mystery; Personal Development; Philosophy; Politics; Science; Thrillers
Markets: Adult

Send: Full text
How to send: Email

Costs: Author covers sundry admin costs.

Send email describing your project and yourself, or send proposal, outline, CV, and sample chapters, or complete unsolicited MS, with SASE. See website for submission requirements in FAQ section. Specialises in serious and literary fiction and nonfiction. No screenplays. No science fiction or children's or young adult fiction unless it aspires to serious literature.

L749 Joanne Wyckoff

Literary Agent
United States

joanne@carolmannagency.com

https://www.carolmannagency.com/joanne-wyckoff

Literary Agency: Carol Mann Agency (**L104**)

Nonfiction > *Nonfiction Books*
General, and in particular: African American Issues; Animals; Comedy / Humour; Culture; Education; Food; Health; History; Memoir; Narrative Journalism; Narrative Nonfiction; Nature; Psychology; Religion; Science; Spirituality; Sport; Wellbeing; Women's Issues

Send: Query
How to send: Email

Represents a wide array of nonfiction. Has vast experience working with academics and experts in diverse fields, helping them develop and write books for a broad market. She also has a particular love of the memoir, narrative nonfiction, the personal narrative, and narrative journalism. She is always looking for writers with strong, original voices who explore a subject in new and surprising ways. Her list includes books in psychology, women's issues, history, education, science, health and wellness, sports, humour, food and culture, natural history and anything about animals, religion and spirituality, and African American issues.

L750 Susan Yearwood

Literary Agent
United Kingdom

submissions@susanyearwoodagency.com

https://susanyearwoodagency.com

Literary Agency: SYLA – Susan Yearwood Literary Agency (**L684**)

ADULT

Fiction > *Novels*
Book Club Fiction; Commercial; Crime; Romance; Saga; Thrillers

Nonfiction > *Nonfiction Books*
General, and in particular: Business; Cookery; Finance; Lifestyle; Self Help; Wellbeing

CHILDREN'S > **Fiction** > *Middle Grade*

TEEN > **Fiction** > *Novels*

YOUNG ADULT > **Fiction** > *Novels*

Send: Query; Author bio; Writing sample; Synopsis
How to send: Email attachment

Looks for book club fiction, commercial fiction including romance and saga, genre fiction i.e. crime/thriller, children's aged 9+ and teen/young adult novels as well as non-fiction, particularly business and finance, self-help and well-being, and lifestyle, including cookery.

Authors: Rebecca Adams; Catherine Balavage; Lucy Basey; Katie Brewer; Angela Cairns; Fran Clark; Sarah Dobbs; Selina Flavius; Kimberley Glover; Liz Kolbeck; Prajwal Parajuly; Susan Quirke; Fil Reid; Sarupa Shah; Jacqueline Shaw; Mahalia Smith; Suzanne Snow; Sarah Stephenson; Kerry Young

L751 Rachel Yeoh

Associate Agent
United Kingdom

submissions@madeleinemilburn.com

https://madeleinemilburn.co.uk/team-member/rachel-yeoh/

Literary Agency: Madeleine Milburn Literary, TV & Film Agency (**L464**)

Fiction > *Novels*
Autofiction; Book Club Fiction; Literary; Magical Realism; Nature; Philosophy; Politics; Postcolonialism; Social Commentary; Upmarket

Nonfiction > *Nonfiction Books*: Memoir

Send: Query; Pitch; Market info; Author bio
How to send: Email

Actively looking for: literary, upmarket, book club, autobiographical fiction, political perspectives, social critiques, postcolonial literature, magical realism, nature writing, philosophical themes, classical retellings, character-driven stories, topical issues, narrative memoir, global voices, diaspora.

I am looking for global voices in literary, upmarket and book club fiction that tell compelling stories reflective of the human experience, as well as autobiographical fiction and narrative non-fiction.

L752 YMU Books

Literary Agency
United Kingdom

YMUBooksEnquiries@ymugroup.com

https://www.ymugroup.com
https://books.ymugroup.com

Nonfiction > *Nonfiction Books*
Celebrity; Commercial

Closed to approaches.

A market-leading literary agency in premium brand and platform representation, working with writers and creators who excel in their genres.

L753 Claudia Young

Literary Agent
United Kingdom

http://greeneheaton.co.uk/agents/claudia-young/
https://twitter.com/ClaudiaL_Young

Literary Agency: Greene & Heaton Ltd (**L285**)

Fiction > *Novels*
Contemporary; Crime; Historical Fiction; Literary; Thrillers

Nonfiction > *Nonfiction Books*
Comedy / Humour; Cookery; Food Journalism; Travel

Interested in all types of writing, in particular cooking and food journalism, comedy and travel writing. Loves literary fiction, contemporary as well as historical novels, crime fiction and thrillers.

Authors: Sam Akbar; Anthony Anaxagorou; Ros Atkinson; Laurie Bolger; Jordan Bourke; Aine Carlin; Matt Chapple; Martha Collison; Jack Cooke; Kevan Davis; Kim Duke; Ella Frears; Francis Gimblett; Lewis Goodall; Peter Harper; Alice Hart; Wayne Holloway-Smith; Lizzie King; Vanessa King; Jenny Lee; Eleanor Maidment; Janina Matthewson; Ciara Ohartghaile; Val Payne; Alice Procter; Rejina Pyo; James Ramsden; Rosie Ramsden; Charlie Ryrie; Kat Sadler; Viviane Schwarz; Tim Sebastian; Dale Shaw; Rachel de Thample; Regina Wong

L754 Cyle Young

Literary Agent; Author
United States

cyle@hartlineliterary.com
submissions@cyleyoung.com

https://cyleyoung.com
http://hartlineagency.com/agentsandauthors/
https://www.facebook.com/cyleyoung

Literary Agencies: Hartline Literary Agency (**L311**); Cyle Young Literary Elite (**L152**)

ADULT

Fiction > *Novels*
Amish Romance; Christianity; Fantasy; Romance; Science Fiction; Speculative

Nonfiction > *Nonfiction Books*
Christianity; Leadership; Parenting; Self Help

Scripts
Film Scripts; *TV Scripts*

CHILDREN'S > **Fiction**
Chapter Books; *Early Readers*; *Middle Grade*; *Picture Books*

YOUNG ADULT > **Fiction** > *Novels*

How to send: Conferences; Online pitch events
How not to send: Email

Represents work in both the General and Christian markets.

Author / Junior Agent: Del Duduit (**L183**)

Authors: Dreama Archibald; Starr Ayers; Deborah Bailey; Marie E. Bast; Del Bates; Don Best; Lisa E. Betz; Cherrilynn Bisbano; Adam Blumer; Catherine Brakefield; Clare Campbell; George Cargill; Andy Clapp; Ray Comfort; Karen Condit; Elaine Marie Cooper; Jacy Corral; Shelley Cummings; Robin Currie; Callie Daruk; Bryan Davis; Melody Delgado; Rene Dick; Joyce K. Ellis; Diana Estell; Ryan Farr; C. Hope Flinchbaugh; Jennifer Froelich; Mary Gardner; Carla Gasser; Darlo Gemeinhardt; Annette Griffin; P.K. Hallinan; Jennifer Hallmark; Ruth Hartman; Cindy Huff; Carlton Hughes; Nancy L. Hull; Pauline Hylton; Kathy Ide; Ashley Kirby Jones; Jeff Jones; Stephanie Kehr; Marcie Keithley; Lisa Kibler; Victoria Kimble; Cary Knox; D.L. Koontz; Julie Lavender; Sarah Limardo; Beckie Lindsey; Jan Lis; Robin Luftig; Jayme Mansfield; Lori Marett; Jann Martin; Jake McCandless; Britt Mooney; Kay Mortimer; Susan Neal; Shelley Pierce; Dana Romanin; Andrew Roth; Patty Schell; Nicole Schrader; Olivia Schwab; Tim Shoemaker; Susan Holt Simpson; Donna L. H. Smith; John Snyder; Debbie Sprinkle; Kendra Stanton-Lee; Bruce A. Stewart; Melissa Stroh; Janet Surette; Rachel Swanson; Elaine Tomski; John Turney;

Bill Watkins; Molly White; Y.K. Willemse; Jean Wilund; Jean Wise

L755 Hugo Young

Literary Agent
United Kingdom

Literary Agency: Independent Talent Group Ltd (**L340**)

L756 Lane Zachary

Literary Agent
United States

lane@mmqlit.com

http://www.mmqlit.com/about/
http://www.mmqlit.com/contact/

Literary Agency: Massie & McQuilkin

Fiction > *Novels*

Nonfiction > *Nonfiction Books*

Send: Query
How to send: Email

Looking for books of nonfiction and fiction that are beautifully crafted and have the capacity to change the way in which we see and live in the world. Response only if interested. If no response within 6 weeks, assume rejection.

L757 Marietta B. Zacker

Literary Agent
United States

marietta@galltzacker.com
querymarietta@galltzacker.com

https://www.galltzacker.com/submissions.html
https://querymanager.com/query/querymarietta

Literary Agency: Gallt & Zacker Literary Agency

CHILDREN'S > **Fiction**
Middle Grade; *Picture Books*
YOUNG ADULT
Fiction
Graphic Novels; *Novels*
Nonfiction > *Nonfiction Books*

Closed to approaches.

Currently only accepting queries from illustrators and author/illustrators.

L758 Leslie Zampetti

Literary Agent
United States

https://www.dunhamlit.com/leslie-zampetti.html
http://aaronline.org/Sys/PublicProfile/46970641/417813
https://twitter.com/literarylesliez
https://www.facebook.com/LiteraryLeslieZ
https://www.instagram.com/literarylesliez/

Literary Agency: Dunham Literary, Inc. (**L184**)
Professional Bodies: Association of American Literary Agents (AALA); Society of Children's Book Writers and Illustrators (SCBWI)

ADULT
Fiction > *Novels*
Historical Fiction; Literary Mystery; Upmarket Romance

Nonfiction > *Nonfiction Books*
Crime; Literature; Memoir

CHILDREN'S
Fiction > *Middle Grade*
Baseball; Contemporary; Florida; Historical Fiction; Mystery; Romance

Nonfiction > *Picture Books*
Comedy / Humour; Diversity; Florida

Poetry > *Novels in Verse*

YOUNG ADULT > **Fiction** > *Novels*
Baseball; Contemporary; Florida; Historical Fiction; Mystery; Romance

Send: Query
Don't send: Full text
How to send: Email
How not to send: Phone; Fax; Email attachment; Post

Seeks middle grade and young adult novels, especially mysteries and contemporary fiction. Historical fiction with a specific hook to the time and place, novels in verse, and off-the-beaten-path romances are on her wish list. For picture books, she prefers nonfiction that tells a story almost too good to be true, stories that show everyday diversity to mirror under-represented readers and open windows to others (per Dr. Rudine Sims Bishop), witty wordplay, and dry, sly humor. Drawn to books about Florida, odd homes, and kids with book smarts and big hearts.

For adult fiction, she is interested in literary mysteries, upmarket romance with interfaith or marginalized couples, and historical fiction set in regions other than Europe and North America. For nonfiction, she finds narrative nonfiction that straddles the boundaries between crime, memoir, and literature especially appealing. An armchair adventurer, she enjoys experiencing wild places and extreme challenges from the comfort of her chair. Though she reads widely, she's not a fit for political thrillers, inspirational Christian fiction, memoirs about violence against women, or hard sci-fi.

L759 Zeno Agency Ltd

Literary Agency
Primrose Hill Business Centre, 110 Gloucester Avenue, London, NW1 8HX
United Kingdom
Tel: +44 (0) 20 7096 0927

louisebuckleyagent@gmail.com

http://zenoagency.com

Professional Body: The Association of Authors' Agents (AAA)

Types: Fiction; Nonfiction
Subjects: Autobiography; Commercial; Cookery; Crime; Fantasy; Health; History; Horror; Lifestyle; Literary; Nature; Science Fiction; Society; Suspense; Thrillers; Women's Interests
Markets: Adult; Children's; Young Adult

London-based literary agency specialising in Science Fiction, Fantasy, and Horror, but expanding into other areas such as crime, thrillers, women's fiction, and young adult fiction. Adult fiction must be at least 75,000 words and children's fiction should be at least 50,000 words. Send query by email with synopsis up to two pages, and first three chapters (or approximately 50 double-spaced pages) as attachments in .docx or .pdf format. No submissions by post.

Associate Agent: Kristina Perez (**L555**)

Authors: Travis Baldree; Alice Bell; Andrew Cartmel; Mário Coelho; Marina Evans; Craig Laurance Gidney; J.T. Greathouse; Jennifer Wolf Kam; Anna McNuff; Adam Oyebanji; Martin Purbrick; Farrah Riaz; Troy Tassier; Katherine Toran; Amy True / Amy Trueblood; Johanna van Veen; R.R. Virdi; Angus Watson; Gary Wigglesworth; Jasmine Wigham; Yudhanjaya Wijeratne

Literary Agents: John Berlyne (**L059**); Louise Buckley; Stevie Finegan (**L227**)

L760 Ayla Zuraw-Friedland

Literary Agent
United States

azf@goldinlit.com

https://www.goldinlit.com/ayla-zuraw-friedland
https://twitter.com/kaylasansk

Literary Agency: Frances Goldin Literary Agency, Inc.

Fiction
Graphic Novels: General
Novels: Literary

Nonfiction > *Nonfiction Books*
Arts; LGBTQIA; Social Class; Technology

Poetry > *Poetry Collections*

Send: Query; Writing sample
How to send: Email

Interested in literary fiction and nonfiction that inspect big questions about queer identity, class, community, and art and technology through a personal lens, as well as poetry and a limited number of graphic or hybrid projects.

Magazines

For the most up-to-date listings of these and hundreds of other magazines, visit https://www.firstwriter.com/magazines

To claim your free access to the site, please see the back of this book.

M001 110% Gaming

Magazine
United Kingdom

Newspaper Publisher / Magazine Publisher: DC Thomson Media

M002 The 2River View

Online Magazine
Santa Rosa, CA 95404
United States

Be1ong@2river.org

https://www.2river.org
https://2river.submittable.com/submit

Poetry > *Any Poetic Form*

Send: Full text
How to send: Submittable

Costs: A fee is charged upon submission. $2 reading fee per submission.

Considers unpublished poems only. Submit via online submission system. See website for more details.

Editor: Richard Long

M003 30 North

Magazine
United States

https://30northliterarymagazine.com

Fiction > *Short Fiction*: Literary

Nonfiction > *Short Nonfiction*: Creative Nonfiction

Poetry > *Any Poetic Form*

Send: Full text
How to send: Submittable

Publishes previously unpublished poetry, fiction, creative non-fiction, and art by undergraduate writers and artists. Submit via online submission system.

M004 32 Poems

Magazine
Washington & Jefferson College, Department of English, 60 S. Lincoln Street, Washington, PA 15301
United States

submissions@32poems.com

http://32poems.com

Nonfiction > *Reviews*: Poetry as a Subject

Poetry > *Any Poetic Form*

Send: Full text
How to send: Submittable; Duosuma

Costs: A fee is charged for online submissions. $3 fee for online submissions.

Publishes poems and reviews of recent poetry collections. Submit via online submission systems. Will re-open to postal submissions in January 2022.

Editor: George David Clark

Managing Editor: Elisabeth Clark

M005 34th Parallel

Magazine
United States

editorial@34thParallel.net

https://34thparallel.net

Fiction > *Short Fiction*: Literary

Nonfiction
Articles: Journalism
Essays: Creative Nonfiction

Poetry > *Any Poetic Form*

Send: Full text

Costs: A fee is charged upon submission. $14.50 fee includes download of latest digital edition.

Publishes fiction, creative nonfiction, essays, scripts, poetry, and artwork. Submit via online submission system.

M006 365 Tomorrows

Magazine
United States

submissions@365tomorrows.com

https://365tomorrows.com

Types: Fiction
Formats: Short Fiction
Subjects: Science Fiction
Markets: Adult

Send: Full text

Website publishing daily flash fiction up to 600 words. Accepts all kinds of science fiction. Submit via form on website.

M007 417 Magazine

Magazine
Whitaker Publishing, 2111 S. Eastgate Ave., Springfield, MO 65809
United States
Tel: +1 (417) 883-7417

https://www.417mag.com
http://facebook.com/417mag
http://instagram.com/417mag
http://twitter.com/417mag
http://pinterest.com/417magazine
https://www.linkedin.com/company/whitaker-publishing

Nonfiction > *Articles*
Food; Lifestyle; Missouri; Outdoor Activities

Publishes material of local interest to southwest Missouri only. Potential contributors are advised to study the magazine before approaching.

Editor: Gregory Holman

M008 5-7-5 Haiku Journal

Online Magazine
United Kingdom

https://575haikujournal.wordpress.com/

Book Publisher / Magazine Publisher: Atlantean Publishing (**P056**)

Poetry
Haibun; *Haiku*; *Senryu*; *Tanka*

Send: Full text
How to send: In the body of an email

Publishes Haiku (and related forms such as senryu and scifaiku). Plus, Haiku Sequences, Haibun and Tanka.

M009 AARP The Magazine

Magazine
c/o Editorial Submissions, 601 E St. NW, Washington, DC 20049
United States

pubspitches@aarp.org

https://www.aarp.org/magazine/

Nonfiction
Articles: General, and in particular: Fitness; Food; Health; Investments; Nutrition; Personal Finance; Relationships; Travel
Essays: Personal Essays

Send: Query
Don't send: Full text
How to send: Email

Magazine for those over 50. Rarely uses unsolicited ideas but will review those submitted in accordance with the guidelines on the website.

M010 About Place Journal

Magazine
PO Box 24, Black Earth, WI 53515-0424
United States

blackearthinstitute@gmail.com

https://aboutplacejournal.org

Fiction > *Short Fiction*: Literary

Nonfiction
Essays: General
Short Nonfiction: Creative Nonfiction

Poetry > *Any Poetic Form*

Closed to approaches.

Publishes poetry, fiction, and essays / creative nonfiction. Accepts submissions during specific submission windows. See website for details and for themes.

M011 The Account

Online Magazine
United States

poetryprosethought@gmail.com

https://theaccountmagazine.com
https://theaccountajournalofpoetryprosethought.submittable.com/submit
https://twitter.com/TheAccountMag
https://www.facebook.com/TheAccountAJournalOfPoetryProseAndThought

Fiction > *Short Fiction*

Nonfiction > *Short Nonfiction*: Creative Nonfiction

Poetry > *Any Poetic Form*

Send: Full text

Accepts poetry, fiction, and creative nonfiction. Send 3-5 poems, essays up to 6,000 words, or fiction between 1,000 and 6,000 words, through online submission system. Each piece of work must be accompanied by an account between 150 and 500 words, giving voice to the artist's approach.

Editors: Brianna Noll, Poetry Editor; Jennifer Hawe, Nonfiction Editor; M. Milks, Fiction Editor; Tyler Mills, Editor-in-Chief; Christina Stoddard, Managing Editor/ Publicist

M012 Accountancy Age

Magazine
United Kingdom

https://www.accountancyage.com
https://www.twitter.com/accountancyage/
https://www.linkedin.com/groups?gid=2352548

PROFESSIONAL > **Nonfiction** > *Articles*
Accounting; Business; Finance

Weekly magazine publishing articles on accountancy, business, and the financial world.

Editors: Aaran Fronda; Michael McCaw; Beth McLoughlin

M013 ACR Journal

Magazine
United Kingdom

Magazine Publisher: Warners Group Publications

M014 Ad Astra

Magazine
United States

adastra@nss.org

https://space.nss.org/ad-astra-the-magazine-of-the-national-space-society/

Nonfiction
Articles: Space
News: Space

Send: Query; Author bio; Writing sample; Full text
How to send: Email

Non-technical magazine, reporting on a broad range of space-related topics, including domestic and international space policy and programs, transportation, commercialisation, planetary science, extraterrestrial resources, colonisation, education, and space advocacy. No science fiction or UFO stories. Accepts unsolicited mss, but prefers queries from writers seeking assignments, including details of author expertise, credits, and writing samples.

Editor: Frank Sietzen Jr

M015 Africa Poetry Magazine

Online Magazine
101-5170 Dunster Road, Suite 108, Nanaimo, BC, V9T 6M4
Canada
Tel: +1 (250) 667-7748

info@waxpoetryart.com

http://waxpoetryart.com/africa/

Magazine Publisher: Wax Poetry and Art Network

Poetry > *Any Poetic Form*
General, and in particular: Africa

How to send: Email

Accepts poetry submissions from poets living in Africa. Read the Submissions page and follow the guidelines to submit.

M016 Agni

Magazine
Boston University, 236 Bay State Road, Boston, MA 02215
United States

agni@bu.edu

https://agnionline.bu.edu
https://twitter.com/AGNIMagazine
https://facebook.com/agnimag

Fiction > *Short Fiction*

Nonfiction > *Essays*

Poetry > *Any Poetic Form*

Closed to approaches.

Submit one story, one essay, or up to five poems, and wait for reply before sending more. Accepts submissions by post with SASE or via online submission system. No submissions by email. Open to submissions between September 1 and December 15; and between February 15 and May 31.

Editor: Sven Birkerts

M017 Agony Opera

Online Magazine
188 A/23 Maniktala Main Road, Parvati Residency, flat-304, Opposite Kankurgachhi post office
India
Tel: +919831778983

hiyamukherjeephysics@gmail.com

https://www.agonyopera.com

Fiction in Translation > *Short Fiction*
Contemporary; Culture; Erotic; Experimental; Fantasy; Literary; New Age; Philosophy; Politics; Social Commentary; Speculative; Surreal

Fiction > *Short Fiction*
Contemporary; Culture; Erotic; Experimental; Fantasy; Literary; New Age; Philosophy; Politics; Social Commentary; Speculative; Surreal

Poetry in Translation > *Any Poetic Form*
Experimental; Literary; Surreal

Poetry > *Any Poetic Form*
Experimental; Literary; Surreal

How to send: Email

We like things edgy, experimental (be it in language or form), surreal, magic-real, speculative, avant-garde. In short anything out of the box.

We have a soft spot for literature which makes a staunch stand on politics. And by politics, we mean the politics regarding the rights of the 99%, not the other way round. Though, we must admit socialist realism doesn't excite us that much.

M018 Agricultural History

Magazine
Kennesaw State University, Dept. of History and Philosophy, 402 Bartow Ave., Kennesaw, GA 30144
United States

aghistory@kennesaw.edu

https://www.aghistorysociety.org/the-journal
https://read.dukeupress.edu/agricultural-history/pages/Submission_Guidelines
https://mc04.manuscriptcentral.com/aghistory

ACADEMIC > **Nonfiction** > *Articles*
Agriculture; History

Send: Full text

Publishes articles on all aspects of the history of agriculture and rural life with no geographical or temporal limits. Submit via online submission system. See website for full guidelines.

Editor: Albert Way

M019 Air & Space Quarterly

Magazine
United States

https://airandspace.si.edu/air-and-space-quarterly

Magazine Publisher / Book Publisher: Smithsonian Institution (**P719**)

Nonfiction > *Articles*
Aviation; Military Aviation; Space

Magazine exploring topics in aviation and space, from the earliest moments of flight to today.

Editor: George Larson

M020 Alaska Quarterly Review

Magazine
Center for the Narrative & Lyric Arts, PO Box 140932, Anchorage, AK 99514-0932
United States

aqr@uaa.alaska.edu

https://aqreview.org
https://alaskaquarterlyreview.submittable.com/submit
https://www.facebook.com/AlaskaQuarterlyReview/
https://www.youtube.com/channel/UCvtOaG2FJ7tuEs8Vsd-rbFQ
https://twitter.com/AQReview

Fiction
Novel Excerpts: Experimental; Traditional
Novellas: Experimental; Traditional
Short Fiction: Experimental; Traditional
Nonfiction > *Short Nonfiction*
Experimental; Literary; Traditional

Poetry > *Any Poetic Form*
Experimental; Traditional

Scripts > *Theatre Scripts*
Drama; Experimental; Traditional

Closed to approaches.

The editors invite submissions of fiction, short plays, poetry, photo essays, and literary nonfiction in traditional and experimental styles.

Editor: Ronald Spatz

M021 Aleph

Magazine
The Sidney M. Edelstein Center, The Hebrew University of Jerusalem, Givat Ram, 91904 Jerusalem
Israel
Tel: +972.2.658.56
Fax: +972.2.658.67.09

edelstein.aleph@mail.huji.ac.il

https://iupress.org/journals/aleph/

ACADEMIC > **Nonfiction** > *Essays*
History; Judaism; Science

Send: Full text

Magazine devoted to the exploration of the interface between Judaism and science in history.

Editors: Resianne Fontaine; Reimund Leicht

M022 Alfred Hitchcock Mystery Magazine

Magazine
6 Prowitt Street, Norwalk, CT 06855
United States

https://www.alfredhitchcockmysterymagazine.com

Fiction > *Short Fiction*
Courtroom Dramas; Crime; Mystery; Police Procedural; Suspense

How to send: Online submission system

Interested in nearly every kind of mystery: stories of detection of the classic kind, police procedurals, private eye tales, suspense, courtroom dramas, stories of espionage, and so on. Only requirement is that the story be about a crime (or the threat or fear of one).

Editor: Linda Landrigan

M023 Alternatives Journal

Magazine
PO Box 26016 College PO, Kitchener ON N2G 0A4
Canada
Tel: +1 (519) 578-2327

https://www.alternativesjournal.ca
http://twitter.com/AlternativesJ
https://www.youtube.com/user/alternativesjournal
https://www.facebook.com/AlternativesJ

Nonfiction > *Articles*
Environment; Sustainable Living

Publishes features, articles, and news on environmental action and ideas.

Editor: Nicola Ross

M024 Ambit

Magazine
United Kingdom

contact@ambitmagazine.co.uk

https://ambitmagazine.co.uk
https://www.instagram.com/ambitmagazine/
https://www.facebook.com/ambitmagazine
https://www.youtube.com/user/Ambitmag

Fiction > *Short Fiction*

Poetry > *Any Poetic Form*

Send: Full text
How to send: Submittable

Costs: A fee is charged upon submission. £2.50 fee for a single submission, and £3.50 for up to 5 poems. Submission is free for the unwaged, entirely skint, and students.

An international magazine. Potential contributors are advised to read a copy before submitting work. Send up to 5 poems, a story up to 4,000 words, or flash fiction up to 1,000 words. Submit via online portal. Accepts submission only during specific submission windows – see website for details.

M025 America's Civil War

Magazine
United States

acw@historynet.com

http://americascivilwarmag.com
https://www.historynet.com/magazines/mag-acw

Magazine Publisher: HistoryNet LLC

Nonfiction > *Articles*: American Civil War

Publishes material on the American Civil War, including features and articles for columns on the subjects of weapons, units, eye-witness accounts, and profiles of figures involved.

M026 American Book Review

Magazine
School of Arts & Sciences, University of Houston-Victoria, 3007 N. Ben Wilson, Victoria, TX 77901
United States
Tel: +1 (361) 570-4848

americanbookreview@uhv.edu

http://americanbookreview.org

Nonfiction > *Reviews*
Cultural Criticism; Fiction as a Subject; Literary Criticism; Poetry as a Subject

Closed to approaches.

Specializes in reviews of frequently neglected works of fiction, poetry, and literary and cultural criticism from small, regional, university, ethnic, avant-garde, and women's presses. In nonfiction, reviews important books of criticism, biographies, and cultural studies. No reviews of "how-to" or "self-help" books. Would consider a review of innovative children's literature, but not usually part of the preferred content. Prefers books that have been published in the past six months, but will review books that have been published in the past year. No unsolicited reviews.

Editor: Lisa Savage

M027 American Heritage

Online Magazine
United States

https://www.americanheritage.com
https://www.facebook.com/ameriheritage/
https://twitter.com/AmeriHeritage

Nonfiction > *Articles*
American History; Culture; Travel; United States

Magazine of American history, travel, food and culture. Originally a print magazine, now an online magazine as of 2017.

Editor: Richard Snow

M028 Amethyst Review

Online Magazine
United Kingdom

editor@amethystmagazine.org
Sarah.Poet@gmail.com

https://amethystmagazine.org
https://www.facebook.com/AmethystReview/

Fiction > *Short Fiction*: Spirituality

Nonfiction > *Short Nonfiction*: Spirituality

Poetry > *Any Poetic Form*: Spirituality

Send: Full text; Author bio
How to send: Word file email attachment; In the body of an email

Publishes work that engages in some way with spirituality or the sacred. Submit up to five poems (of any length) and / or prose pieces of up to 2,000 words. Simultaneous submissions if notification of acceptance elsewhere is provided. No previously published work. Send submissions by email with author bio of around 50 words. See website for full guidelines.

Editor: Sarah Law

M029 Anaverde Magazine

Magazine
38713 Tierra Subida Avenue #128, Palmdale, CA 93551
United States
Tel: +1 (661) 200-9156

hello@anaverde-magazine.com

http://www.anaverde-magazine.com
http://www.facebook.com/anaverdemagazine
http://www.twitter.com/anaverdemagazine
https://www.instagram.com/anaverdemagazine

Fiction > *Short Fiction*

Nonfiction
Articles: Arts; Beauty; Crafts; Culture; Design; Entertainment; Fashion; Finance; Gardening; Health; Hobbies; Leisure; Lifestyle; Nature; Spirituality; Women's Interests
Interviews: General

Send: Full text
How to send: Email

First issue in June 2020. The publication is mailed directly to the residents in the Anaverde community, which is located in the Antelope Valley.

Editors: Malena Jackson; Samantha Jennings

M030 And Magazine

Magazine
India

https://andmagazine824063762.wordpress.com

Fiction > *Short Fiction*: Literary

Nonfiction > *Articles*

Poetry > *Any Poetic Form*

Send your best work poems, article, essay, paper, artwork in MS word file and images in jpeg format by email.

All the accepted accepted works will be published with ISBN No. and will available in major bookstores worldwide.

M031 Angela Poetry Magazine

Online Magazine
Wax Poetry and Art, Attn: Angela Poetry Magazine, 101-5170 Dunster Road, Suite 108, Nanaimo, BC, V9T 6M4,
Canada
Tel: +1 (250) 667-7748

info@waxpoetryart.com

http://waxpoetryart.com/angela/

Magazine Publisher: Wax Poetry and Art Network

Poetry > *Any Poetic Form*: Contemporary

How to send: Email

Accepts poetry submissions from everyone on Earth and orbiting spacecraft. Publishes poems that are curious, humorous, and generally on the lighter side of life. Read the Submissions page and follow the guidelines to submit.

M032 The Antigonish Review

Magazine
PO Box 5000, Antigonish, Nova Scotia, B2G 2W5
Canada
Tel: +1 (902) 867-3962
Fax: +1 (902) 867-5563

tar@stfx.ca

https://antigonishreview.com
https://twitter.com/antigonishrevie
https://www.facebook.com/The-Antigonish-Review-332083480162513/
https://www.linkedin.com/in/the-antigonish-review-7602052a

Fiction in Translation > *Short Fiction*: Literary

Fiction > *Short Fiction*: Literary

Nonfiction > *Essays*
Creative Nonfiction; Culture; History; Memoir; Sport; Travel

Poetry in Translation > *Any Poetic Form*

Poetry > *Any Poetic Form*

Send: Full text
How to send: Submittable
How not to send: Post; Email

Costs: A fee is charged upon submission. $5 for prose; $2 for poetry.

Submit via online portal only. Submit no more than 6-8 poems (preferably 3-4) and submit no more till a response is received. Considers poetry on any subject written from any point of view and in any form. For fiction, send only one story at a time. Also publishes poetry and prose translated into English from other languages (be sure to indicate source language). Also considers critical articles and essays that are fresh, vigorous, and free from jargon. Welcomes creative nonfiction. No email submissions, postal submissions, or simultaneous submissions.

M033 The Antioch Review

Magazine
One Morgan Place, Yellow Springs, OH 45387
United States
Tel: +1 (937) 769-1365

review@antiochcollege.edu

http://review.antiochcollege.org

Fiction > *Short Fiction*

Nonfiction
Essays: General
Reviews: Literature

Poetry > *Any Poetic Form*

Closed to approaches.

Send MS with SASE for return. Strongly encourages potential contributors to buy a sample copy and peruse the magazine before submitting. Considers fiction from September

1 to May 31 only, and accepts poetry from September 1 to April 30 only. Do not mix poetry and prose submissions in the same envelope. No email submissions or unsolicited book reviews.

Editor: Robert S. Fogarty

M034 Aquila

Magazine
United Kingdom
Tel: +44 (0) 1323 431313

submissions@aquila.co.uk

https://www.aquila.co.uk
https://www.facebook.com/AquilaChildrensMagazine
https://twitter.com/aquilamag

CHILDREN'S
Fiction > *Short Fiction*

Nonfiction > *Articles*
General, and in particular: History; Science

How to send: Email

Describes itself as the ultimate intelligent read for inquisitive kids. Full of exuberant articles and challenging puzzles that will get the whole family involved, every issue covers science, history and general knowledge.

M035 The Architectural Review

Magazine
69-77 Paul Street, London, EC2A 4NW
United Kingdom
Tel: +44 (0) 20 3953 2000

https://www.architectural-review.com

Magazine Publisher: EMAP Publishing

PROFESSIONAL > **Nonfiction** > *Articles*
Architecture; Design

Magazine of architecture and design aimed at professionals.

Editor: Paul Finch

M036 Arena Fantasy

Magazine
11 East Street, Bicester, Oxfordshire, OX26 2EY
United Kingdom
Tel: +44 (0) 7528 924361

submissions@arenafantasymagazine.co.uk

https://arenafantasymagazine.co.uk

Fiction > *Short Fiction*: Fantasy

Nonfiction > *Articles*
Creative Writing; Fantasy

Send: Query; Outline; Author bio
How to send: Email

Fantasy ezine that publishes every quarter. We specialise in fantasy stories as well as articles that help authors old and new. There are also competitions and a myriad of tools that will help you grow as an author.

Submissions – Prose and Artwork

Query via email initially. Your query should contain your Name, Pseudonym email address and contact details. Please give us a brief overview of your piece and a brief bio of anything you have published before if we like your work we will let you know and invite you to submit your piece.

Editor: Andy Hesford

M037 Areopagus Magazine

Magazine
United Kingdom

editor@areopagus.org.uk

https://www.areopagus.org.uk

Fiction > *Short Fiction*
Christianity; Evangelism

Nonfiction > *Articles*
Christianity; Evangelism

Poetry > *Any Poetic Form*
Christianity; Evangelism

Send: Full text
How to send: Email; Domestic Post

Costs: A subscription is required in order to submit. £5 for electronic subscription / £15 for print.

A Christian-based arena for creative writers. A forum for debate on contemporary issues relating to Christianity and wider issues. A chance for new writers to have their work published for the first time. We can only consider MSS which are submitted by subscribers to the magazine. Subscribers may submit by email, or by post if within the UK.

Editor: Julian Barritt

M038 The Armourer

Magazine
United Kingdom

Magazine Publisher: Warners Group Publications

M039 Art Monthly

Magazine
Peveril Garden Studios, 140 Great Dover Street, London, SE1 4GW
United Kingdom
Tel: +44 (0) 20 7240 0389

info@artmonthly.co.uk

http://www.artmonthly.co.uk
https://www.twitter.com/artmonthly
https://www.facebook.com/artmonthly
https://instagram.com/art_monthly_uk

Nonfiction
Articles: Arts
Interviews: Arts
Reviews: Arts

Magazine of contemporary visual art. Publishes in-depth features, interviews with artists, profiles on emerging artists and coverage of major trends and developments by independent critics.

Editor: Patricia Bickers

M040 Art Papers

Magazine
PO Box 5748, Atlanta, GA 31107
United States
Tel: +1 (404) 588-1837
Fax: +1 (678) 999-7002

editor@artpapers.org
info@artpapers.org

https://www.artpapers.org
https://www.facebook.com/artpapers
https://twitter.com/artpapers
https://www.instagram.com/artpapers/

Nonfiction > *Articles*
Arts; Contemporary; Culture

The independent critical voice covering contemporary art and culture in the world today.

Editor: Sylvie Fortin

M041 Art Times Journal

Online Magazine
PO Box 730, Mount Marion, NY 12456
United States
Tel: +1 (914) 246-6944
Fax: +1 (914) 246-6944

info@arttimesjournal.com

https://www.arttimesjournal.com
http://www.youtube.com/user/arttimes
https://facebook.com/ArtTimesJournal
https://twitter.com/ARTTIMESjournal
https://www.instagram.com/arttimesjournal/

Fiction > *Short Fiction*: Literary

Nonfiction > *Articles*
Arts; Culture

Poetry > *Any Poetic Form*

Send: Full text
How to send: Email

Formerly a print journal, online-only since 2016. Publishes articles on arts and culture, literary fiction, poetry, and opinion pieces relating to creativity and the arts. Send submissions by email. See website for full guidelines.

Editor: Raymond J. Steiner

M042 The Artist

Magazine
The Maltings, West Street, Bourne, Lincolnshire, PE10 9PH
United Kingdom
Tel: +44 (0) 1580 763673

https://www.painters-online.co.uk
https://www.facebook.com/paintersonline
https://twitter.com/artpublishing
https://www.instagram.com/paintersonline/
https://www.pinterest.co.uk/paintersonline/

Magazine Publisher: Warners Group Publications

Nonfiction > *Articles*: Arts

Written by artists for artists, since 1931, this magazine has inspired generations of passionate, practising artists from experienced amateur up to professionals, with practical painting and drawing articles and projects, designed to improve painting technique.

Editor: Sally Bulgin

M043 ARTmosterrific

Online Magazine
19 Ila-Orangun Street, Ketu
Nigeria
Tel: 08164187014

dhadarms@gmail.com
Prose@artmosterrific.com
Editor@artmosterrific.com
Poetry@artmosterrific.com

https://artmosterrific.com
https://facebook.com/artmosterrific
https://twitter.com/artmosterrific
https://instagram.com/_artmosterrific
https://duotrope.com/listing/31866/artmosterrific-magazine

Fiction > *Short Fiction*

Nonfiction > *Essays*
Contemporary; Personal Essays

Poetry > *Any Poetic Form*

Closed to approaches.

An online platform and community by and for African undergraduates. It runs on five sections, all different and independent from one another: Virtual residence where 3 college writers are mentored to complete a book of art; the African Prize for Undergraduates awarded every year to an African undergraduate; the Biannual Chapbook that works as an anthology, exploring thematic issues in society, the Online Issue/Mag (Prose, Poetry, Essay, Photography), and the Community (with webinars, Book Chat, Bookstore, Physical Conference, etc). Check our submission page for detailed information on each section, and feel free to subscribe to our newsletter.

Editorial Calendar

Issue Submission (January — February)

Virtual Residence (March — April)

Chapbook Submission (May — June)

Funso Oris Prize / African Prize For Undergraduates (June — July)

ISSUE SUBMISSION (August — September)

CHAPBOOK SUBMISSION (October — November)

Dates and time for community programmes, such as the book chat, webinar, undergraduate-led auditorium conference, are subject to factors.

A literary publication that features fiction, poetry, creative nonfiction, and photography for everything that makes you sleep, keeps you awake, breaks your heart and repairs it. Everything that rusts and unrusts you. Send us your flaws and strengths, awesome and bizarre, brilliant and outrageous. However, please note that while we accept all submissions, we are especially on the lookout for works by African undergraduates. Send us your terrific work anyways!

M044 Arts & Letters

Magazine
United States
Tel: +1 (478) 445-1289

https://artsandletters.gcsu.edu
https://artsandletters.submittable.com/submit
https://www.facebook.com/artslettersgc
https://twitter.com/ArtsLettersGC
https://artsandlettersjournal.tumblr.com/

Fiction > *Short Fiction*: Literary

Nonfiction > *Short Nonfiction*: Creative Nonfiction

Poetry > *Any Poetic Form*

Send: Full text
How to send: Submittable

Costs: A fee is charged upon submission. $3 submission fee.

Send between four and six poems, or up to 25 pages (typed, double-spaced) of fiction or creative nonfiction. Accepts submissions between August 1 and January 31.

Editor: Martin Lammon

M045 Asimov's Science Fiction

Magazine
United States

asimovs@dellmagazines.com

https://www.asimovs.com
http://asimovs.magazinesubmissions.com/

Magazine Publisher: Dell Magazines

Fiction > *Short Fiction*
Fantasy; Science Fiction; Slipstream; Surreal

Poetry > *Any Poetic Form*
Fantasy; Science Fiction; Slipstream; Surreal

Does not want:

Fiction > *Short Fiction*: Sword and Sorcery

How to send: Online submission system; Post

Seeks serious, character-orientated science fiction and (borderline) fantasy, slipstream, and surreal. The characters should always be the main focus, rather than the science. Humour will be considered. No simultaneous submissions, sword-and-sorcery, horror, explicit sex, or violence.

Editor: Gardner Dozois

M046 Ask

Magazine
United States

Magazine Publisher: Cricket Media, Inc.

M047 Atlanta Review

Magazine
Suite 333, 686 Cherry St. NW, Atlanta, GA 30332-0161
United States

atlantareview@gatech.edu

http://atlantareview.com
https://atlantareview.submittable.com/submit
https://twitter.com/ATLReview
https://www.facebook.com/atlantareview
https://www.instagram.com/atlantareviewpojo/

Poetry > *Any Poetic Form*

Closed to approaches.

Costs: A fee is charged for online submissions. $3. Also runs competitions for which a fee is charged.

Accepts submissions of poetry between January 1 and June 1, and between September 15 and December 1. Submit online ($3 submission fee) or by post with SASE. Also runs competitions.

M048 The Atlantic

Magazine
United States

politics@theatlantic.com
culture@theatlantic.com
science@theatlantic.com
family@theatlantic.com
education@theatlantic.com
global@theatlantic.com
ideas@theatlantic.com
fiction@theatlantic.com
poetry@theatlantic.com

https://www.theatlantic.com
https://support.theatlantic.com/hc/en-us/articles/360011374734-Submit-a-piece-for-editorial-consideration-at-The-Atlantic
https://www.facebook.com/TheAtlantic
https://www.instagram.com/theatlantic
https://www.youtube.com/user/TheAtlantic
https://twitter.com/TheAtlantic
https://www.linkedin.com/company/the-atlantic
https://flipboard.com/@theatlantic

Fiction > *Short Fiction*

Nonfiction > *Articles*
Business; Culture; Education; Family; Health; International; Literature; Politics; Science; Technology

Poetry > *Any Poetic Form*

Send: Pitch; Full text
How to send: Word file email attachment; PDF file email attachment; In the body of an email

Always interested in great nonfiction, fiction, and poetry. A general familiarity with what we have published in the past is the best guide to what we're looking for. All manuscripts should be submitted as a Word document or PDF. Succinct pitches may be submitted in the body of an email.

Editor: Cullen Murphy

M049 Auroras & Blossoms PoArtMo Anthology

Online Magazine
United Kingdom

submissions@abpositiveart.com

https://abpositiveart.com
https://www.facebook.com/abpositiveart
https://twitter.com/ab_positiveart
https://www.youtube.com/channel/UCkAh-EnwcJbd865SEXJQsEw

ADULT
Fiction > *Short Fiction*
Nonfiction > *Essays*

TEEN
Fiction > *Short Fiction*
Nonfiction > *Essays*

How to send: Online submission system

Costs: A fee is charged upon submission. $12 for up to three pieces for ages 17 and over. Free for ages 13-16. .

Annual anthology sold in ebook format.

Editors / Poets: David Ellis; Cendrine Marrouat

M050 Authentic Shorts

Online Magazine
United Kingdom

enquiries@integrity-media.co.uk

http://integrity-media.co.uk

Book Publisher: Integrity Media (**P399**)

Fiction > *Short Fiction*

Send: Query; Outline; Full text
How to send: Email

An online platform for publishing short stories. We are open minded with regard to the subject of short stories and will consider submissions across all genres.

There is no perfect length for a short story, only the author can decide, but we would expect them to be no more than 7,000 to 8,000 words. This will allow them to be adaptable for online publication, either as a serialisation or under small collections of aligned works.

M051 Aviation News

Magazine
United Kingdom

https://www.key.aero/aviationnews

Magazine Publisher: Key Publishing

Nonfiction
Articles: Aviation
News: Aviation

Publishes news and features related to aviation, including military, civil, business, historical, contemporary, aircraft, airports, and equipment.

Editors: David Baker; Jamie Ewan

M052 Awen

Magazine
Atlantean Publishing, 4 Pierrot Steps, 71 Kursaal Way, Southend-on-Sea, Essex, SS1 2UY
United Kingdom

atlanteanpublishing@hotmail.com

http://atlanteanpublishing.wikia.com/wiki/Awen
https://atlanteanpublishing.wordpress.com/guidelines/

Book Publisher / Magazine Publisher: Atlantean Publishing (**P056**)

Fiction > *Short Fiction*

Poetry > *Any Poetic Form*

How to send: Email; Post

Now normally eight A4 sides in length, it contains poetry and short prose fiction and has appeared four times a year since 2013. Submit by post or by email.

Editor: David-John Tyrer

M053 Babybug

Magazine
United States

https://cricketmedia.com
https://cricketmedia.com/babybug-submission-guidelines/
https://cricketmag.submittable.com/submit

Magazine Publisher: Cricket Media, Inc.

CHILDREN'S
Fiction > *Short Fiction*
Nonfiction > *Short Nonfiction*
Poetry > *Any Poetic Form*

Send: Full text

Publishes poetry, stories, and nonfiction (including activities and parent–child interaction) for children aged 6 months to 3 years. Stories should be up to six short sentences; poems should be rhythmic and rhyming and up to eight lines long.

Editor: Marianne Carus

M054 Backcountry Magazine

Magazine
60 Main Street, PO Box 190, Jeffersonville, VT 05464
United States
Tel: +1 (802) 644-6606

https://backcountrymagazine.com

Nonfiction > *Articles*
Skiing; Snowboarding

Send: Query
How to send: Email

Magazine of skiing and snowboarding. Send query by email.

Editor: Lucy Higgins

Managing Editor: Betsy Manero

M055 Bacopa Literary Review

Magazine
United States

https://writersalliance.org/bacopa-literary-review/

Fiction > *Short Fiction*: Literary

Nonfiction > *Short Nonfiction*: Creative Nonfiction

Poetry > *Any Poetic Form*

Closed to approaches.

Annual print journal publishing short stories, creative nonfiction, poetry, and prose poetry. Accepts submissions only through free annual contest.

M056 The Baffler

Magazine
234 5th Avenue, New York, NY 10001
United States
Tel: +1 (212) 390-1569

https://thebaffler.com
https://www.facebook.com/TheBafflerMagazine/
https://twitter.com/thebafflermag

Fiction > *Short Fiction*
Comedy / Humour; Politics; Satire

Nonfiction > *Articles*
Culture; Left Wing Politics

Poetry > *Any Poetic Form*

Send: Pitch
How to send: Online submission system

Describes itself as "America's leading voice of interesting and unexpected left-wing political criticism, cultural analysis, short stories, poems and art". Submit pitch using online form on website.

Editor: Jonathon Sturgeon

M057 Balance

Magazine
Wells Lawrence House, 126 Back Church Lane, London, E1 1FH
United Kingdom
Tel: +44 (0) 3451 232399
Fax: +44 (0) 20 7424 1001

helpline@diabetes.org.uk

https://www.diabetes.org.uk/balance

Nonfiction
Articles: Diabetes; Exercise; Health; Recipes
News: Diabetes

News articles and features of interest to people with diabetes.

Editor: Martin Cullen

M058 Banipal

Magazine
1 Gough Square, London, EC4A 3DE
United Kingdom

editor@banipal.co.uk

http://www.banipal.co.uk
https://www.facebook.com/BanipalMagazine/
https://twitter.com/banipalmagazine

Fiction in Translation > *Short Fiction*

Nonfiction
Interviews: Writing
Reviews: Books

Poetry in Translation > *Any Poetic Form*

Send: Query
How to send: Email; Post

Contemporary Arab authors in English translations. Publishes new and established writers, and diverse material including translations, poetry, short stories, novel excerpts, profiles, interviews, appreciations, book reviews, reports of literary festivals, conferences, and prizes. Welcomes submissions by post, but queries only by email. Unsolicited email submissions with attachments will be automatically deleted. Response in 3-6 months.

Editor: Margaret Obank

M059 Bard

Magazine
Atlantean Publishing, 4 Pierrot Steps, 71 Kursaal Way, Southend-on-Sea, Essex, SS1 2UY
United Kingdom

atlanteanpublishing@hotmail.com

http://atlanteanpublishing.wikia.com/wiki/Bard
https://atlanteanpublishing.wordpress.com
https://www.facebook.com/groups/169974286448031/

Book Publisher / Magazine Publisher: Atlantean Publishing (**P056**)

Poetry > *Any Poetic Form*

Send: Full text; Self-Addressed Stamped Envelope (SASE)
How to send: Post; Email

Flyer-style broadsheet of poetry released roughly monthly and available for free to subscribers of the publisher's magazines. Occasionally runs themed issues but generally open to any and all poetry. See website for full submission guidelines.

M060 Barren Magazine

Magazine
United States

info@barrenmagazine.com
poetry@barrenmagazine.com
fiction@barrenmagazine.com
flashcnf@barrenmagazine.com
creativenonfiction@barrenmagazine.com

https://barrenmagazine.com
http://twitter.com/BarrenMagazine
http://facebook.com/BarrenMagazine
http://instagram.com/barrenmagazine

Fiction > *Short Fiction*

Nonfiction > *Nonfiction Books*: Creative Nonfiction

Poetry > *Any Poetic Form*

Send: Full text
How to send: Email

An Alt.Lit Introspective.

A literary publication that features fiction, poetry, creative nonfiction, and photography for hard truths, long stares, and gritty lenses. We revel in the shadow-spaces that make up the human condition, and aim to find antitheses to that which defines us: light in darkness; beauty in ugliness; peace in disarray. We invite you to explore it with us.

Editor: Jason D. Ramsey

M061 BBC Countryfile Magazine

Magazine
Eagle House, Bristol, BS1 4ST
United Kingdom
Tel: +44 (0) 1173 147399

editor@countryfile.com

http://www.countryfile.com

Nonfiction > *Articles*
Countryside; Nature

Send: Query
Don't send: Full text

Magazine on British countryside and rural life. Send queries with ideas by email. No unsolicited mss.

Editor: Fergus Collins

M062 BBC Gardeners' World Magazine

Magazine
Immediate Media, 2nd Floor, Vineyard House, 44 Brook Green, Hammersmith, London, W6 7BT
United Kingdom
Tel: +44 (0) 20 7150 5770

magazine@gardenersworld.com

https://www.gardenersworld.com
https://www.facebook.com/GWmagazine
http://uk.pinterest.com/gwmag
https://twitter.com/gwmag
https://www.youtube.com/channel/UC8kRP4T6HbZnsheHCulB_FQ
https://www.instagram.com/gardenersworldmag/

Magazine Publisher: Immediate Media Co.

Nonfiction > *Articles*: Gardening

Publishes advice and ideas about gardening.

Editor: Adam Pasco

M063 BBC Music Magazine

Magazine
Eagle House, Colston Avenue, Bristol, BS1 4ST
United Kingdom

music@classical-music.com

https://www.classical-music.com
https://www.facebook.com/classicalmagazine
https://twitter.com/MusicMagazine
https://www.youtube.com/channel/UC0TNxfRDOfvSlieR6Zq51eg
https://www.instagram.com/musicmagazinepics/

Nonfiction > *Articles*: Classical Music

Monthly magazine covering all areas of classical music.

Editor: Oliver Condy

M064 Beano

Magazine
United Kingdom

Newspaper Publisher / Magazine Publisher: DC Thomson Media

M065 The Beano

Magazine
185 Fleet Street, London, EC4A 2HS
United Kingdom

https://www.beano.com

CHILDREN'S > **Fiction** > *Cartoons*: Comed y / Humour

Publishes comic strips for children aged 6-12.

M066 The Bear Deluxe Magazine

Magazine
820 N. River Street, Suite 112, Portland, OR 97227
United States
Tel: +1 (971) 235-2734

thebear@orlo.org
beardeluxe@orlo.org

https://orlo.org
https://www.facebook.com/pages/Bear-Deluxe-Magazine/115925931775159
https://twitter.com/orlobear

Fiction > *Short Fiction*

Nonfiction > *Articles*
Arts; Culture; Environment

Poetry > *Any Poetic Form*

Send: Full text
How to send: Email

Magazine of the arts, culture and environment. Send submissions by email.

Editor: Tom Webb

M067 Beat Scene

Magazine
United Kingdom

kevbeatscene@gmail.com

https://www.beatscene.net

Nonfiction > *Articles*: Beat Generation

A magazine about the Beat Generation, Jack Kerouac, William Burroughs, Allen Ginsberg, Lawrence Ferlinghetti, Gary Snyder, Michael McClure, Philip Whalen, Anne Waldman, Joanne Kyger, Charles Bukowski and others.

Editor: Kevin Ring

M068 Beir Bua Journal

Online Magazine
Ireland

BeirBuaJournal@Gmail.com

https://beirbuajournal.wordpress.com
https://twitter.com/beirbuajournal
https://instagram.com/beirbuajournal
https://www.youtube.com/channel/UCdlyd1MKVthfnqJ__fW99Aw
https://www.facebook.com/BeirBuaJournal/

Nonfiction > *Articles*
Arts; Creative Writing; Poetry as a Subject

Poetry
Any Poetic Form: Avant-Garde; Experimental; Ireland; Motherhood; Postmodernism; Religion; Women's Issues
Experimental Poetry: General
Visual Poetry: General

Send: Full text; Author bio
How to send: Email

Costs: Offers services that writers have to pay for. Offers expedited submissions and feedback for a fee.

Interested in conceptual poetics of new language, women's issues, motherhood, slanted unreality, polarity and plurality of time, religion, Ireland's history. Would love more Irish women experimental poets.

M069 Bella

Magazine
Academic House, 24-28 Oval Road, London, NW1 7DT
United Kingdom

Bella.Hotline@bauermedia.co.uk

https://www.bellamagazine.co.uk
https://twitter.com/#!/bellamagazineUK
http://facebook.com/bellamagazineUK
https://www.instagram.com/bellamagazineuk/

Magazine Publisher: Bauer Media Group

Nonfiction > *Articles*
Celebrity; Diet; Fashion; Real Life Stories; Travel

Send: Query
How to send: Email

Human interest magazine for women, publishing articles on celebs, diet, style, travel, and real-life stories. Send query by email.

Editor: Jayne Marsden

M070 Belmont Story Review

Magazine
United States

belmontstoryreview@gmail.com

https://belmontstoryreview.wixsite.com/website
https://belmontstoryreview.submittable.com/submit

Fiction > *Short Fiction*

Nonfiction > *Short Nonfiction*: Creative Nonfiction

Poetry > *Any Poetic Form*

Closed to approaches.

Established in 2016, the magazine aims to surprise and delight readers through an eclectic mix of storytelling which includes fiction, personal essay, poetry, songwriting, drama, graphic narrative, and photography; as well as creative reportage, including coverage of music, film, creativity and collaboration, and the intersection of faith and culture. "Faith" is not a specific religious perspective but a broad idea of faith is important for all selected publications.

We seek to publish new and established writers passionate about their craft, fearlessly encountering difficult ideas, seeking to explore human experience in all its broken blessedness.

M071 Beloit Fiction Journal

Magazine
Box 11, Beloit College, 700 College Street, Beloit, WI 53511
United States

https://www.beloit.edu/fiction-journal/
https://beloitfictionjournal.submittable.com/submit

Fiction > *Short Fiction*: Literary

Closed to approaches.

Costs: A fee is charged upon submission. $3 per submission.

Open to literary fiction on any subject or theme, up to 13,000 words. Also accepts flash fiction. Showcases new writers as well as established writers. Simultaneous submissions are accepted.

Editor: Heather Skyler

M072 Best

Magazine
United Kingdom

best@hearst.co.uk

https://www.hearst.co.uk/brands/best
https://www.facebook.com/bestmagazine/
https://twitter.com/BestMagOfficial

Magazine Publisher: Hearst Magazines UK

Nonfiction > *Articles*
Beauty; Celebrity; Diet; Fashion; Finance; Real Life Stories; Recipes; TV

Jam packed with amazing real-life stories, showbiz news, diet, recipes, fashion, beauty advice and so much more.

Editor: for fiction Pat Richardson.

M073 Better Homes and Gardens

Magazine
United States

bhgeditor@meredith.com

https://www.bhg.com
https://www.facebook.com/mybhg/
https://twitter.com/bhg/
https://www.pinterest.com/bhg/
https://www.instagram.com/betterhomesandgardens/

Magazine Publisher: Dotdash Meredith

Nonfiction > *Articles*
Cookery; Gardening; Home Improvement; Recipes

The fourth best-selling magazine in the United States. Publishes articles on gardening, home improvement, cleaning and organizing, and cooking and recipes.

Editor: Karol DeWulf Nickell

M074 Better Than Starbucks

Magazine
PO Box 673, Mayo, FL 32066
United States
Tel: +1 (561) 719-8627

betterthanstarbucks2@gmail.com

https://www.betterthanstarbucks.org

ADULT

Fiction > *Short Fiction*

Nonfiction > *Short Nonfiction*: Creative Nonfiction

Poetry in Translation > *Any Poetic Form*

Poetry
Any Poetic Form: Africa; Comedy / Humour; International
Experimental Poetry: General
Formal Poetry: General
Free Verse: General
Haiku: General
Prose Poetry: General

CHILDREN'S > **Poetry** > *Any Poetic Form*

Send: Full text; Author bio
How to send: Email

Publishes African Poetry, International Poetry, Prose Poetry, Forms as well as Formal Poetry, Poetry Translations, Experimental Poetry and poetry for children. Encourages sentiment in poetry. Also publishes Fiction, Flash Fiction, Micro Fiction and Creative Nonfiction. Submitted opinion pieces will be considered.

Editor: Vera Ignatowitsch

M075 Big Fiction

Online Magazine
Seattle University, English Dept, c/o Juan Carlos Reyes, P.O. Box 222000, Seattle, WA 98122-1090
United States

editors@bigfiction.com

https://www.bigfictionmagazine.org

Fiction > *Novelette*

Nonfiction
Essays: General
Reviews: Fiction as a Subject
Short Nonfiction: Creative Nonfiction

Closed to approaches.

Costs: A fee is charged upon submission. $5 for novelettes; $3 for essays.

Literary magazine devoted to longer short fiction, between 7,500 and 20,000 words.

M076 BIGnews

Magazine
United States

http://www.mainchance.org

Fiction > *Short Fiction*

Nonfiction
Articles: Arts; Literature
Essays: Arts; Literature
Interviews: Arts; Literature

Publishes features, interviews, personal essays, short stories, and serialised novels from the outsider's perspective. Interested in presenting the art and literature of the outsider, rather than simply drumming up sympathy for the homeless.

Editor: Ron Grunberg

M077 Bike Magazine

Magazine
United Kingdom

https://www.bikemagazine.co.uk
https://www.facebook.com/bikemagazineUK
https://twitter.com/BikeMagazine

Magazine Publisher: Bauer Media Group

Nonfiction > *Articles*: Motorbikes

Your definitive guide to the world of motorcycling. Every issue features incredible motorcycling travel stories from our team and readers with amazing adventures and epic photography. Plus there's expert opinion on all the new motorcycles available in the UK, giving you all the details you need to choose your next bike.

Editors: John Westlake; Hugo Wilson

M078 Bikers Club

Online Magazine
7B Tejal Bhuvan, N.P.Thakkar Road, Vile Parle, Mumbai 400057
India
Tel: +91 9820189969

rm@bikersclub.in

https://www.bikersclub.in
https://www.facebook.com/bikersclubapp/
https://www.instagram.com/bikersclubapp/
https://twitter.com/Bikersclubapp

Nonfiction
Articles: Biker Lifestyle; Motorbikes; Motorcycling; Motorsports; Travel
Interviews: Motorbikes; Motorcycling; Motorsports
Reviews: Motorbikes

Send: Full text
How to send: Email

Monthly digitally issued magazine dedicated to the bikers and the traveller worldwide. It includes interview, reviews of bikes and destinations, lifestyles, shout out, current affairs and travel stories.

Editor: Rahul Mehta

M079 Birds & Blooms

Magazine
1610 North 2nd Street, Suite 102, Milwaukee, WI 53212
United States

customercare@birdsandblooms.com

https://www.birdsandblooms.com
https://www.facebook.com/BirdsBlooms
https://twitter.com/birdsblooms
https://www.pinterest.com/birdsblooms/
https://www.instagram.com/birdsblooms/

Nonfiction > *Articles*
Birds; Gardening

Send: Full text
How to send: Online submission system

Magazine for backyard / bird enthusiasts, covering how to improve your garden and attract birds. Conversational tone.

M080 Black Beauty & Hair

Magazine
United Kingdom

info@blackbeautyandhair.com

http://www.blackbeautyandhair.com
https://www.facebook.com/BlackBeautyandHair
https://twitter.com/BlackBeautyMag
https://www.youtube.com/user/blackbeautymag
http://instagram.com/BlackBeautyMag
https://www.pinterest.com/blackbeautyhair/

Nonfiction > *Articles*
Beauty; Fashion; Hairstyles; Weddings

Publishes articles and features on black hair, beauty, fashion, and lifestyle. Also publishes bridal features.

Editor: Irene Shelley

M081 Black Belt

Magazine
United States

https://blackbeltmag.com
https://www.instagram.com/blackbeltmag/
https://twitter.com/black_belt_mag
https://www.facebook.com/BlackBeltMagazine/
https://www.linkedin.com/company/black-belt-magazine/

Nonfiction > *Articles*: Martial Arts

Magazine on martial arts for the experienced and inexperienced alike.

Editor-in-Chief: Robert Young

M082 Black Moon Magazine

Online Magazine
United States

blackmoonmageditors@gmail.com

http://www.blackmoonmag.com
https://www.facebook.com/BlackMoonMagazine
https://www.instagram.com/black.moon.mag/
https://twitter.com/Black_Moon_Mag

Fiction > *Short Fiction*

Nonfiction
Interviews: Literature
Reviews: Books

Poetry > *Any Poetic Form*

Send: Full text; Query; Author bio
How to send: Email attachment

Submit up to three short stories between 1,000 and 8,000 words, or up to five poems of up to five pages each. Also accepts book reviews and interviews with professionals in the writing community for online publication.

M083 Black Static

Magazine
United Kingdom

blackstatic@ttapress.com

http://ttapress.com/blackstatic/

Magazine Publisher / Book Publisher: TTA Press (**P782**)

Fiction > *Short Fiction*
Dark; Horror

Send: Full text
How to send: Email attachment

Always open to unsolicited submissions of new dark/horror stories up to a maximum of 10,000 words.

Editor: Andy Cox

M084 Black Warrior Review

Magazine
United States

blackwarriorreview@gmail.com
fiction.bwr@gmail.com
poetry.bwr@gmail.com
nonfiction.bwr@gmail.com

https://bwr.ua.edu
https://www.facebook.com/pages/Black-Warrior-Review/335215809212
https://twitter.com/BlackWarriorRev

Fiction
Cartoons: General
Short Fiction: General, and in particular: Experimental

Nonfiction
Graphic Nonfiction; *Short Nonfiction*

Poetry
Any Poetic Form; *Visual Poetry*

How to send: Submittable; Email

Costs: A fee is charged upon submission. $3. Black, indigenous, and incarcerated writers may submit by email for free.

Accepts short stories and nonfiction up to 7,000 words, or submit up to five poems up to 10 pages total. Accepts work that takes risk or is experimental, in lieu of convention and/or grammatical cleanliness. Seeks nonfiction pieces outside western traditions; pieces that defy any such categorization. Welcomes submissions of striking visual narratives (think: graphic novel or memoir in short form).

Editor: Dan Kaplan

Online Magazine: Boyfriend Village (**M091**)

M085 Blithe Spirit

Magazine
United Kingdom

ed.blithespirit@gmail.com

http://britishhaikusociety.org.uk

Poetry > *Haiku*

Send: Full text
How to send: Email

Only accepts submissions from members, however members do not enjoy an automatic right to publication – quality is key. Non-members may appear as featured writers. All work must be original. Submissions should be sent by email with a covering note.

Editor: Caroline Skanne

M086 Blue Collar Review

Magazine
PO 11417, Norfolk, VA 23517
United States

red-ink@earthlink.net

https://www.partisanpress.org

Book Publisher: Partisan Press (**P568**)

Fiction > *Short Fiction*: Working Class

Nonfiction
Essays: Culture; Working Class
Reviews: General

Poetry > *Any Poetic Form*: Working Class

Send: Full text; Self-Addressed Stamped Envelope (SASE)

Magazine that aims to "expand and promote a progressive working class vision of culture that inspires us and that moves us forward as a class". Submit up to five poems or short stories, essays, or reviews up to 1,000 words by post with SASE for response.

M087 Blue Earth Review

Magazine
230 Armstrong Hall, Minnesota State University, Mankato, Mankato, MN 56001
United States

blueearthreview@gmail.com

https://blueearthreview.mnsu.edu
https://www.facebook.com/theblueearthreview/
https://twitter.com/BlueEarthReview

Fiction > *Short Fiction*

Nonfiction
Essays: Personal Essays
Short Nonfiction: Creative Nonfiction; Memoir

Poetry > *Any Poetic Form*

Send: Full text
How to send: Submittable

Publishes fiction, creative nonfiction and poetry. Interested in creative nonfiction (memoir and personal essay) with contemporary themes. No literary criticism. Submit up to five poems at a time.

Managing Editor: Christina Olson

M088 Bluegrass Unlimited

Magazine
Owensboro, KY
United States

https://www.bluegrassunlimited.com
https://www.facebook.com/BluegrassUnlimited/
https://www.instagram.com/bluegrassunlimited/
https://twitter.com/bgunlimitedmag
https://www.youtube.com/channel/UCxNYVomNcDI-5mrOy3KgoHA

Nonfiction
Articles: Bluegrass
Interviews: Bluegrass
News: Bluegrass
Reviews: Bluegrass

A print magazine that has been dedicated to the furtherance of bluegrass music for over 50 years.

Editor: Peter V. Kuykendall

M089 Booklaunch

Magazine
12 Wellfield Avenue, London, N10 2EA, United Kingdom

book@booklaunch.london

https://www.booklaunch.london
https://www.facebook.com/booklaunch.london/
https://twitter.com/booklaunch_ldn
https://www.youtube.com/channel/UCNQfRhWa8DdObMJ9xxxvvcA/videos
https://www.instagram.com/booklaunchlondon/

Fiction > *Novel Excerpts*

Nonfiction > *Book Extracts*

Poetry > *Book Extracts*

Does not want:

Fiction > *Novel Excerpts*
Erotic; Fantasy; Gothic; Romance; Suspense; Westerns

Nonfiction > *Nonfiction Books*
Hobbies; How To; Leisure; New Age; Self Help; Spirituality

Send: Full text
How to send: PDF file email attachment

Costs: A fee is charged for publication.

Carries extracts from new and newish books. Its editorial balance is largely towards non-fiction but also accepts novels and poetry. (See past issues on website.) Tabloid format with space for approx 1,600 words per page. Does not run extracts at less than a page. Charges for inclusion. Has the largest print run of any books magazine in the UK. Page rate a fifth of that of rival publications. Uploads and archives every print edition. Helps its authors to record audio tracks to its YouTube channel. Contact by email for ratecard.

M090 The Bookseller

Magazine
47 Bermondsey Street, London, SE1 3XT
United Kingdom
Tel: +44 (0) 20 7403 1818

https://www.thebookseller.com
http://twitter.com/thebookseller
http://www.facebook.com/TheBooksellerMagazine
http://www.linkedin.com/company/the-bookseller-magazine
https://www.instagram.com/_thebookseller/
https://www.youtube.com/channel/UCF5SoBkJKDO9CXtmr1eGW9Q

Magazine Publisher: The Stage Media Company Ltd

PROFESSIONAL > **Nonfiction** > *Articles*
Book Publishing; Books

Magazine for the book business covering publishing, the book trade, retail, and libraries, publishing trade news and features.

Editor: Neill Denny

M091 Boyfriend Village

Online Magazine
United States

https://bwr.ua.edu/about-boyfriend-village/

Magazine: Black Warrior Review (**M084**)

Fiction > *Short Fiction*

Nonfiction > *Short Nonfiction*

Poetry > *Any Poetic Form*

Closed to approaches.

Costs: A fee is charged upon submission. $3.

There is one submission category for all genres. Accepts fiction, poetry, nonfiction, hybrid, visual and multimedia art, as well as sound collage, video, games, and more.

M092 Brick

Magazine
P.O. Box 609, STN P, Toronto, ON, M5S 2Y4
Canada

info@brickmag.com

https://brickmag.com/
https://twitter.com/brickMAG
https://facebook.com/brickmagazine
https://instagram.com/brickliterary

Nonfiction
Essays: Arts; City and Town Planning; Dance; Food; History; Literature; Music; Photography; Science; Sport; Travel; Writing
Interviews: Arts; Literature; Performing Arts
Reviews: Arts; Literature; Performing Arts
Short Nonfiction: Literary; Memoir

Send entire submission in first instance. Please read magazine before submitting. Accepts unsolicited nonfiction submissions on a variety of subjects between March 1 and April 30 and between September 1 and October 31 each year. No unsolicited fiction or poetry.

Editor: Vivien Leong

M093 Britain Magazine

Magazine
The Chelsea Magazine Company, Jubilee House, 2 Jubilee Place, London, SW3 3QW
United Kingdom
Tel: +44 (0) 20 7349 3700

editor@britain-magazine.co.uk

https://www.britain-magazine.com
https://www.facebook.com/BritainMagazine/
https://www.instagram.com/britain_magazine/
https://twitter.com/BritainMagazine

Magazine Publisher: The Chelsea Magazine Company

Nonfiction > *Articles*
Culture; History; Nature; Royalty; Travel; United Kingdom

Magazine of UK travel, culture, heritage and style, and the go-to publication for visitors fascinated by British history. Each issue is packed with tales of kings and queens, heroes and villains and the stories behind British castles, cathedrals, stately homes and gardens, countryside, and coastline.

Editor: Andrea Spain

M094 British Railway Modelling

Magazine
United Kingdom

Magazine Publisher: Warners Group Publications

M095 The Broons

Magazine
United Kingdom

Newspaper Publisher / Magazine Publisher: DC Thomson Media

M096 Brush Talks

Magazine
United States

editor@brushtalks.com

http://www.brushtalks.com
https://twitter.com/BrushTalks

Nonfiction > *Essays*
Arts; China; Culture; History; Memoir; Narrative Nonfiction; Science; Technology; Travel

Poetry in Translation > *Any Poetic Form*: China

Poetry > *Any Poetic Form*: China

Send: Full text
How to send: Email attachment

A journal of creative nonfiction, photography, and poetry related to China. Articles can take many forms: general essays, travel essays, profiles, memoir, and narrative nonfiction. We seek submissions about places, people, history, culture, the arts, science and technology — anything related to China that is well written, creative, and true (we do not publish fiction). Rolling submissions, no fee. Please visit our website for more information and read the guidelines before submitting.

M097 Business London

Magazine
210 Dundas St., Suite 201, London, ON N6A 5J3
Canada

https://lfpress.com/category/business-london/

Media Company: The London Free Press

PROFESSIONAL > **Nonfiction** > *Articles*: B usiness

Business magazine for southwestern Ontario.

Editor: Sarah Jones

Managing Editor: Madisyn Latham

M098 Business Traveller

Magazine
10 John Street, London, WC1N 2EB
United Kingdom
Tel: +44 (0) 20 7821 2700

editorial@businesstraveller.com
enquiries@panaceapublishing.com

https://www.businesstraveller.com
https://www.linkedin.com/groups/2136397
https://www.facebook.com/BusinessTraveller
https://www.twitter.com/BTUK

https://www.instagram.com/businesstravelleruk/

Nonfiction > *Articles*
Business; Travel

The leading magazine around the world for the frequent corporate traveller. A consumer publication, it is aimed at entertaining business travellers, saving them money and making their travelling life easier. Each edition is packed with editorial on the latest news about airlines, airports, hotels and car rental.

Editor: Tom Otley

M099 Buttered Toast

Magazine
United States

https://www.toadhalleditions.ink/buttered-toast

Book Publisher / Self Publishing Service: Toad Hall Editions (**P770**)

CHILDREN'S
Fiction > *Short Fiction*

Nonfiction
Essays: General
Short Nonfiction: Creative Nonfiction

Poetry > *Any Poetic Form*

Closed to approaches.

Annual journal publishing work by and for young people up to 18 years old.

M100 The Cafe Irreal

Magazine
United States

editors@cafeirreal.com

http://cafeirreal.alicewhittenburg.com

Types: Fiction
Formats: Short Fiction
Subjects: Literary
Markets: Adult

Send: Full text
How to send: Email

Quarterly webzine publishing fantastic fiction resembling the work of writers such as Franz Kafka and Jorge Luis Borges. Send stories up to 2,000 in the body of an email. No simultaneous submissions.

M101 Cahoodaloodaling

Magazine
United States

cahoodaloodaling@gmail.com

https://cahoodaloodaling.com
https://cahoodaloodaling.submittable.com/submit

Fiction > *Short Fiction*

Nonfiction
Articles: Publishing; Writing
Essays: Publishing; Writing
Interviews: General
Reviews: Books

Poetry > *Any Poetic Form*

Closed to approaches.

Themed triannual journal, publishing poetry, fiction, and articles and essays that are either about writing and publishing, or match the current submission call. See website for upcoming themes, and to submit via online submission system. If you would like your book reviewing, query by email with a brief sample.

Editor: Raquel Thorne

M102 Cake Craft

Magazine
United Kingdom

Magazine Publisher: Warners Group Publications

M103 Cake Craft Guides

Magazine
United Kingdom

Magazine Publisher: Warners Group Publications

M104 Cambridgeshire Pride

Magazine
United Kingdom
Tel: +44 (0) 1733 242312

info@pridepublications.co.uk

http://www.pridepublications.co.uk
https://sites.google.com/view/pridepublications/home/cambridgeshire-pride

Magazine Publisher: Pride Publications

Nonfiction
Articles: Business; Cambridgeshire; Education; Fashion; Fishing; Food; Gardening; Lifestyle; Music; Travel; Wine
News: Cambridgeshire
Reviews: Books

Interested in news and features relating to the Cambridgeshire UK area in particular.

Editor: Carol Lawless

M105 Campaign

Magazine
Bridge House, 69 London Road, Twickenham, TW1 3SP
United Kingdom

https://www.campaignlive.co.uk
https://www.facebook.com/campaignmag/
https://twitter.com/campaignmag
https://www.linkedin.com/groups/3614115/
https://www.instagram.com/campaignmagazine/
https://www.youtube.com/CampaignLiveTV

Magazine Publisher: Haymarket Media Group

PROFESSIONAL > **Nonfiction**
Articles: Advertising; Business; Marketing; Media
News: Advertising; Business; Marketing; Media

Describes itself as the world's leading business media brand serving the marketing, advertising and media communities.

Editor: Claire Beale

Editor-in-Chief: Gideon Spanier

M106 Campervan

Magazine
United Kingdom

Magazine Publisher: Warners Group Publications

M107 Camping Magazine

Magazine
United Kingdom

Magazine Publisher: Warners Group Publications

M108 Car Mechanics

Magazine
The Granary, Downs Court, Yalding Hill, Yalding, Maidstone, Kent, ME18 6AL
United Kingdom
Tel: +44 (0) 1959 543747

https://shop.kelsey.co.uk/subscription/CME

Magazine Publisher: Kelsey Media

ADULT > **Nonfiction** > *Articles*
Cars; Engineering

PROFESSIONAL > **Nonfiction** > *Articles*
Cars; Engineering

The UK's only magazine with essential advice on maintaining and repairing popular makes and models of car. If you fancy yourself as a home mechanic, then this is an invaluable motoring resource that appeals to both the DIY car enthusiast and the more experienced motor trade professional.

Editor: Peter Simpson

M109 Caravan

Magazine
United Kingdom

Magazine Publisher: Warners Group Publications

M110 The Casket of Fictional Delights

Online Magazine
United Kingdom

https://thecasket.co.uk
https://www.facebook.com/casketfiction/
https://twitter.com/casketfiction
https://uk.pinterest.com/thecasket/

Fiction > *Short Fiction*

Send: Full text
How to send: By referral

Online magazine publishing flash fiction and short stories. Submissions by invitation and recommendation only.

Editor: Joanna Sterling

M111 Cemetery Dance

Magazine
132-B Industry Lane, Unit 7, Forest Hill, MD 21050
United States
Tel: +1 (410) 588-5901
Fax: +1 (410) 588-5904

info@cemeterydance.com

https://www.cemeterydance.com/
https://www.cemeterydance.com/cemetery-dance-magazine.html

Fiction > *Short Fiction*
Dark; Horror; Mystery; Suspense

Nonfiction
Articles: Dark; Horror; Mystery; Suspense
Interviews: Dark; Horror; Mystery; Suspense
News: Dark; Horror; Mystery; Suspense
Reviews: Dark; Horror; Mystery; Suspense

Closed to approaches.

Publishes horror, dark mystery, crime, and suspense stories which are powerful, emotional, pacy, and original.

Editor: Richard Chizmar

M112 Chapman

Magazine
4 Broughton Place, Edinburgh, EH1 3RX
United Kingdom
Tel: +44 (0) 131 557 2207

chapman-pub@blueyonder.co.uk

http://www.chapman-pub.co.uk

Fiction > *Short Fiction*: Literary

Nonfiction > *Articles*: Literary Criticism

Poetry > *Any Poetic Form*

Send: Full text; Self-Addressed Stamped Envelope (SASE)
How to send: Post
How not to send: Email

Describes itself as Scotland's leading literary magazine, publishing new creative writing: poetry, fiction, discussion of cultural affairs, theatre, reviews and the arts in general, plus critical essays. It publishes international as well as Scottish writers and is a dynamic force for artistic and cultural change and development. Always open to new writers and ideas.

Fiction may be of any length, but average is around 3,000 words. Send one piece at a time. Poetry submissions should contain between four and ten poems. Single poems are not usually published.

Articles and reviews are usually commissioned and ideas should be discussed with the editor in advance.

All submissions must include an SAE or IRCs or email address for response. No submissions by email.

Editor: Joy Hendry

M113 Charleston Style and Design Magazine

Magazine
United States

https://www.charlestonstyleanddesign.com
https://www.facebook.com/Charleston-Style-Design-Magazine-108903839161607/
https://www.instagram.com/chasstyleanddesign/
https://twitter.com/CharlestonSDMa1
https://www.pinterest.com/charlestonsdmag/

Nonfiction > *Articles*
Architecture; Arts; Design; Fashion; Food; Lifestyle; Travel; Wine

Design and lifestyle magazine for the Lowcountry, covering architects, designers and builders, home projects, lifestyle trends, restaurants, wines, fashions, art galleries, and travel destinations.

Editor: Mary Love

M114 CharlottesvilleFamily

Magazine
4282 Ivy Rd, Charlottesville, VA 22901
United States
Tel: +1 (434) 984-4714

jennifer@ivylifeandstylemedia.com

http://www.charlottesvillefamily.com
https://www.facebook.com/CharlottesvilleFamily
https://twitter.com/ChvilleFamily
https://www.linkedin.com/company/ivylifeandstylemedia/

Magazine Publisher: Ivy Life & Style Media

Nonfiction > *Articles*
Albemarle; Charlottesville; Education; Health; Leisure; Lifestyle; Parenting

Send: Query

An award-winning quarterly magazine dedicated to serving families in Virginia's Charlottesville-Albemarle area with engaging feature stories on parenting, education, health and recreation as well as useful resources designed to help "Make Parenting Easier & Growing Up Fun."

M115 Chautauqua Literary Journal

Magazine
United States

chautauquajournal@gmail.com

https://chautauquajournal.wixsite.com/website
https://chautauqua.submittable.com/submit
https://www.instagram.com/chautauquajournal/
https://www.facebook.com/chautauqualiteraryjournal/
https://twitter.com/chautauqualit
http://chautauqualit.tumblr.com/

Fiction > *Short Fiction*

Nonfiction > *Short Nonfiction*: Creative Nonfiction

Poetry > *Any Poetic Form*

Closed to approaches.

Welcomes unsolicited submissions of poetry, flash, fiction, and creative nonfiction from February 15 to April 1 and from September 1 to November 1.

Editor: Richard Foerster

M116 Cholla Needles

Magazine
United States

editor@chollaneedles.com

https://www.chollaneedles.com

Poetry > *Any Poetic Form*: Literary

Send: Full text
How to send: Email

We look for poetry that reaches readers, with a special emphasis on poetry that readers desire to return to. Each issue contains 10 distinctly different poets, and we are very happy to introduce new writers to our audience in each issue. We have no restriction as to writing style or format, but do expect that the work submitted is ready for an audience. Payment in US is by contributor's copy, and outside the US is by pdf copy.

M117 Church Music Quarterly

Magazine
RSCM, 19 The Close, Salisbury, Wiltshire, SP1 2EB
United Kingdom
Tel: +44 (0) 1722 424848

cmq@rscm.com

https://www.rscm.org.uk/our-resources/magazines/church-music-quarterly/

Nonfiction > *Articles*: Church Music

Send: Full text
How to send: Email; Post

Publishes reports, press releases and letters on or related to church music.

Editor: Esther Jones

M118 The Cincinnati Review

Magazine
PO Box 210069, Cincinnati, Ohio 45221-0069
United States

editors@cincinnatireview.com

https://www.cincinnatireview.com/
https://facebook.com/CincinnatiReview
https://twitter.com/CincinnReview
https://www.youtube.com/channel/UCbDPomwAnBAddHtuKKh4HqA

Fiction in Translation > *Short Fiction*: Literary

Fiction > *Short Fiction*: Literary

Nonfiction > *Short Nonfiction*
Creative Nonfiction; Literary

Poetry in Translation > *Any Poetic Form*

Poetry > *Any Poetic Form*

Scripts
Film Scripts; *Theatre Scripts*

How to send: Online submission system

Submit up to ten pages of poetry, up to forty pages of double-spaced fiction, or up to twenty pages of double-spaced literary nonfiction during September, December, or May.. Accepts micro submissions year-round, except when accepting contest submissions.

Editors: Michael Griffith; Kristen Iversen; Rebecca Lindenberg

Fiction Editor: Brock Clarke

Managing Editor: Nicola Mason

Poetry Editor: Jim Cummins

M119 Cirque

Magazine
United States

cirquejournal@gmail.com

https://cirquejournal.com

Fiction > *Short Fiction*: North Pacific Rim

Nonfiction
Reviews: North Pacific Rim
Short Nonfiction: North Pacific Rim

Poetry > *Any Poetic Form*: North Pacific Rim

Scripts > *Theatre Scripts*: North Pacific Rim

Send: Full text
How to send: Submittable

Publishes short stories, poems, creative nonfiction, translations, and plays by writers born in, or resident for at least five years in, the North Pacific Rim (Alaska, Washington, Oregon, Idaho, Montana, Hawaii, Yukon Territory, Alberta, and British Columbia). Submit via online submission system.

Editor: Sandra Kleven

M120 Civil War Times

Magazine
United States

Magazine Publisher: HistoryNet LLC

M121 Classic & Sports Car

Magazine
United Kingdom

https://www.classicandsportscar.com
https://www.facebook.com/candscmagazine
https://twitter.com/candscmagazine?lang=en
https://www.youtube.com/user/candscmagazine
https://www.instagram.com/classicandsportscar

Magazine Publisher: Haymarket Media Group

Nonfiction > *Articles*
Classic Cars; Sports Cars

Describes itself as "the world's best-selling classic car magazine, and the undisputed authority for anyone buying, owning, selling, maintaining or even just dreaming about classic cars".

Editor: James Elliott

Editor-in-Chief: Alastair Clements

M122 Click

Magazine
United States

Magazine Publisher: Cricket Media, Inc.

M123 Climbing

Magazine
United States

https://www.climbing.com
https://www.facebook.com/climbingmagazine
https://twitter.com/climbingmag
https://www.youtube.com/user/ClimbingMagazine
https://www.instagram.com/climbingmagazine

Magazine Publisher: Outside Interactive Inc.

Nonfiction > *Articles*: Climbing

Climbing photography and writing magazine.

Editor: Jeff Achey

M124 Coal City Review

Magazine
English Department, University of Kansas, Lawrence KS, 66045
United States

https://coalcity.org
http://www.facebook.com/CoalCityReviewAndPress/
http://twitter.com/CoalCityReview
http://instagram.com/coalcityreview

Book Publisher / Magazine Publisher: Coal City Press (**P171**)

Fiction > *Short Fiction*

Poetry > *Any Poetic Form*

Send: Full text; Self-Addressed Stamped Envelope (SASE)
How to send: Post
How not to send: Email

Publishes poetry, short stories, and flash fiction. Send up to 6 poems, or one story up to 4,000 words, per year. Submissions by post only, with SASE for reply.

Editor: Brian Daldorph

M125 The Coil

Online Magazine
United States

https://medium.com/the-coil
https://twitter.com/CoilMag
https://alternatingcurrent.submittable.com/submit

Book Publisher: Alternating Current Press (**P033**)

Fiction
Novel Excerpts: General
Short Fiction: Literary

Nonfiction
Essays; *Interviews*; *Reviews*

Poetry > *Any Poetic Form*
General, and in particular: History

How to send: Submittable

Independent online literary magazine.

M126 Coin Collector

Magazine
United Kingdom

Magazine Publisher: Warners Group Publications

M127 Coin News

Magazine
8 Oaktree Place, Manaton Close, Matford Business Park, Exeter, Devon, EX2 8WA
United Kingdom
Tel: +44 (0) 1404 46972

info@tokenpublishing.com

https://www.tokenpublishing.com

Magazine Publisher: Token Publishing

Nonfiction > *Articles*: Numismatics (Coin / Currency Collecting)

Magazine covering coin collecting.

M128 Collectors Magazine

Magazine
United Kingdom

Magazine Publisher: Warners Group Publications

M129 The Comics Journal

Magazine
7563 Lake City Way NE, Seattle, WA 98115
United States

editorial@tcj.com

http://tcj.com

Book Publisher: Fantagraphics

Nonfiction > *Articles*: Comic Books

Send: Pitch
How to send: Email

Journal covering comics as an art form. Send pitch by email with subject line "Submission Inquiry".

Managing Editor: Dirk Deppey

News Editor: Michael Dean

M130 Commando

Magazine
185 Fleet Street, London, EC4A 2HS
United Kingdom

generalenquiries@commandomag.com

https://www.commandocomics.com
https://www.facebook.com/Commando-Comics-168688426504994

Newspaper Publisher / Magazine Publisher: DC Thomson Media

ADULT > **Fiction** > *Cartoons*
Adventure; Warfare

CHILDREN'S > **Fiction** > *Cartoons*
Adventure; Warfare

YOUNG ADULT > **Fiction** > *Cartoons*
Adventure; Warfare

Publishes stories of action and adventure set in times of war, told in graphic novel format. May be wars of the modern age or ancient wars, or even occasionally wars of the future.

M131 The Common Tongue Magazine

Online Magazine
United States

submissions@commontonguezine.com

https://www.commontonguezine.com
https://twitter.com/commontonguemag
https://www.facebook.com/commontonguezine/

Fiction > *Short Fiction*
Dark Fantasy; High / Epic Fantasy

Nonfiction > *Articles*
Fantasy; Writing

Poetry > *Any Poetic Form*: Dark Fantasy

Send: Full text
How to send: Online submission system

Writer's submissions must adhere to our guidelines to be considered for publication in our magazine. While we allow our writers a vast amount of room for creativity and writer's interpretation, we want to be sure that they support us in our quest for retaining that dark, dangerous tone that invokes our brand image.

We currently pay 3 cents USD per word for prose; $20 for a poem.

We invite all writers, regardless of level, to submit their short story submissions. We appreciate everyone's interest in the magazine and seek to honor that interest. While we are proud of being a leader in fantasy publications, we are also foremost writers and artists, and so we have extreme pride in supporting our contributors and those that make this all possible.

If you are interested in submitting short stories to be published in our bimonthly magazine, please review the writer guidelines to be considered on our website.

Online Magazine: The Undercommons (**M504**)

M132 Commonweal

Magazine
475 Riverside Drive, Room 405, New York, NY 10115
United States
Tel: +1 (212) 662-4200

editors@commonwealmagazine.org

https://www.commonwealmagazine.org
https://www.facebook.com/commonwealmagazine
https://twitter.com/commonwealmag

Nonfiction > *Articles*
Culture; Politics; Religion

Poetry > *Any Poetic Form*

How to send: Submittable

Journal of opinion edited by Catholic lay people. Publishes articles on religion, literature, and the arts. More interested in articles which examine the links between "worldly" concerns and religious beliefs than churchy or devotional pieces. Also publishes poetry.

Editor: Paul Baumann

M133 Computing

Magazine
New London House, 172 Drury Lane, London, WC2B 5QR
United Kingdom
Tel: +44 (0) 20 7484 9744

stuart.sumner@incisivemedia.com

https://www.computing.co.uk
https://www.youtube.com/playlist?list=PL2k5gwH-ELDedgZlV4iYGTMJKMvzSLKEA
https://twitter.com/computing_news
https://www.linkedin.com/showcase/computing--/
https://www.facebook.com/ComputingUK

Magazine Publisher: Incisive Media

PROFESSIONAL > **Nonfiction**
Articles: Computers
News: Computers

Publishes news and articles for IT professionals.

Editor: Bryan Glick

M134 Concho River Review

Magazine
United States

http://www.conchoriverreview.org
https://www.facebook.com/conchoriverreview

Fiction > *Short Fiction*

Nonfiction
Essays: General
Reviews: Books
Short Nonfiction: Creative Nonfiction

Poetry > *Any Poetic Form*

How to send: Submittable

Costs: A fee is charged upon submission. $3 per submission.

Published biannually, welcomes submissions of high-quality fiction, nonfiction, poetry, and book reviews year-round.

Accepts only original work that has not been published previously.

Accepts submissions from writers residing outside the United States, however, international contributors should provide a domestic address to which a contributor's copy can be mailed.

Editor: T.A. Dalrymple

M135 Condé Nast Traveller

Magazine
United Kingdom

https://www.cntraveller.com
https://www.facebook.com/CNTraveller/
https://twitter.com/cntraveller
https://www.instagram.com/condenasttraveller/
https://www.youtube.com/user/condenasttraveller
https://www.pinterest.co.uk/cntraveller/

Magazine Publisher: Condé Nast Britain

Nonfiction > *Articles*: Travel

A luxury travel magazine aimed at the upmarket, independent traveller.

Editor: Abigail Chisman

M136 Conjunctions

Magazine
21 East 10th St., #3E, New York, NY 10003
United States

conjunctions@bard.edu

http://www.conjunctions.com
https://conjunctions.submittable.com/submit
http://www.facebook.com/pages/Conjunctions/133404885505
https://www.instagram.com/_conjunctions/
https://twitter.com/_conjunctions

Fiction > *Short Fiction*: Literary

Nonfiction > *Short Nonfiction*: Creative Nonfiction

Poetry > *Any Poetic Form*

Send: Full text; Self-Addressed Stamped Envelope (SASE)
How to send: Post; Submittable

Publishes short and long form fiction, poetry, and creative nonfiction. No academic essays or book reviews. Do not query or send samples – submit complete ms by post with SASE (year-round) or using online submission system (during specific online submission windows in autumn and winter). See website for full guidelines.

Editor: Bradford Morrow

Online Magazine: Conjunctions Online (**M137**)

M137 Conjunctions Online

Online Magazine
21 E 10th Street, #3E, New York, NY 10003
United States

http://www.conjunctions.com/online/
https://conjunctions.submittable.com/submit
http://www.facebook.com/pages/Conjunctions/133404885505
https://www.instagram.com/_conjunctions/
https://twitter.com/_conjunctions

Magazine: Conjunctions (**M136**)

Fiction > *Short Fiction*

Nonfiction > *Short Nonfiction*: Creative Nonfiction

Poetry > *Any Poetic Form*

How to send: Post; Submittable

Weekly online magazine. No thematic restrictions. Postal submissions are accepted year-round, but online submissions are open only during specific windows.

M138 Conscience

Magazine
United States

conscience@catholicsforchoice.org

https://www.catholicsforchoice.org/conscience-magazine/about/
https://twitter.com/Catholic4Choice
https://www.facebook.com/CatholicsforChoice

Nonfiction > *Articles*
Christianity; Feminism; Gender; Politics; Sexuality; Social Issues

How to send: Email

Magazine offers in-depth, cutting-edge coverage of vital contemporary issues, including reproductive rights, sexuality and gender, feminism, the religious right, church and state issues and US politics. Send submissions by email.

M139 The Corridor of Uncertainty

Magazine
United Kingdom

clarky@corridorofuncertainty.com

https://www.corridorofuncertainty.com
https://twitter.com/clarkyfanzine
https://www.facebook.com/groups/10963081916

Nonfiction > *Articles*: Cricket

Unofficial England cricket fanzine.

Editor: James Buttler

M140 Cosmopolitan

Magazine
House of Hearst, 30 Panton Street, London, SW1Y 4AJ
United Kingdom
Tel: +44 (0) 1858 438423

cosmopolitan-UK@hearst.co.uk

https://www.cosmopolitan.com/uk
https://facebook.com/cosmopolitanuk
https://twitter.com/CosmopolitanUK
https://www.pinterest.com/cosmopolitanuk/
https://instagram.com/cosmopolitanuk
https://www.youtube.com/user/cosmopolitanuk

Magazine Publisher: Hearst Magazines UK

Nonfiction > *Articles*
Beauty; Current Affairs; Entertainment; Fashion; Health; Politics; Relationships; Sex

Magazine aimed at modern-minded women in their mid-twenties, including a range of articles, particularly on careers, relationships, and news.

Editor: Sam Baker

Features Editor: Catherine Gray

M141 Country Living

Magazine
House of Hearst, 30 Panton Street, London, SW1Y 4AJ
United Kingdom

https://www.countryliving.com
https://www.facebook.com/countrylivinguk
https://twitter.com/countrylivinguk
https://www.pinterest.com/UKcountryliving/
https://www.instagram.com/countrylivinguk/

Magazine Publisher: Hearst Magazines UK

Nonfiction > *Articles*
Country Lifestyle; Countryside; Crafts; Gardening; Houses; Nature; Recipes; Travel; Wellbeing

Magazine for people who love the country, whether they live in it or not. Includes articles on the countryside, wildlife, conservation, gardens, houses, rural life, etc.

Editor: Susy Smith

M142 Country Smallholding

Magazine
The Granary, Downs Court, Yalding Hill, Yalding, Kent, ME18 6AL
United Kingdom
Tel: +44 (0) 7725 829575

https://www.countrysmallholding.com/

Magazine Publisher: Kelsey Media

Nonfiction > *Articles*
Country Lifestyle; Countryside; Gardening; Self-Sufficiency; Smallholdings

Magazine for smallholders, small farmers and landowners, and those interested in both rural and urban self-sufficiency.

Editor: Diane Cowgill

M143 Cowboys & Indians

Magazine
Three Forest Plaza, 12221 Merit Drive, Suite 1610, Dallas, Texas 75251
United States
Tel: +1 (386) 246-0179

queries@cowboysindians.com

https://www.cowboysindians.com
https://www.facebook.com/cowboysindians/
http://pinterest.com/cowboysindians/
http://www.twitter.com/CI_Magazine
http://instagram.com/cowboysindiansmagazine#

Nonfiction > *Articles*
American West; Arts; Culture; Entertainment; Fashion; Food and Drink; Houses; Ranch Lifestyle; Ranches; Travel

Magazine focusing on the past and present of the American West, including both historical and lifestyle material.

M144 Crab Orchard Review

Magazine
United States

https://craborchardreview.siu.edu
https://craborchardreview.submittable.com/submit

Fiction > *Short Fiction*

Nonfiction > *Essays*

Poetry > *Any Poetic Form*

Closed to approaches.

Closed to submissions for the foreseeable future following the death of the editor in December 2019. Check website for current status.

Editors: Allison Joseph; Jon Tribble

Prose Editor: Carolyn Alessio

M145 Crannog Magazine

Magazine
47 Dominick, St Lower, Galway, H91 X0AP
Ireland

hello@crannogmagazine.com

http://www.crannogmagazine.com

Fiction > *Short Fiction*: Literary

Poetry > *Any Poetic Form*

Send: Full text; Author bio
How to send: Online submission system; Word file email attachment
How not to send: Post

Costs: A purchase is required. Authors who have not previously been published in the magazine must purchase the current issue before submitting.

A literary magazine publishing fiction and poetry only. No reviews or nonfiction. Published twice yearly in March and September. Accepts submissions in May and November. Authors who have been previously published in the magazine are required to purchase a copy of the current issue (or take out a subscription); for authors who have not been previously published in the magazine this is a requirement. Send up to one story or up to three poems via online submission system.

Editor: Sandra Bunting, Tony O'Dwyer, Ger Burke, Jarlath Fahy

M146 Crazyhorse

Magazine
Department of English, College of Charleston, 66 George Street, Charleston, SC 29424
United States
Tel: +1 (843) 953-4470

crazyhorse@cofc.edu

https://crazyhorse.cofc.edu
https://www.facebook.com/CrazyhorseLiteraryJournal
https://twitter.com/crazyhorselitjo

Fiction > *Short Fiction*

Nonfiction > *Short Nonfiction*: Creative Nonfiction

Poetry > *Any Poetic Form*

Closed to approaches.

Costs: A fee is charged upon submission. $3.00.

Send between 2,500 and 8,500 words of prose or 3-5 poems via online submission system. Accepts submissions between September 1 and May 31 (except for January).

Editor: Garrett Doherty

M147 Cream City Review

Magazine
Department of English, University of Wisconsin-Milwaukee, P.O. Box 413, Milwaukee, WI 53201
United States

poetry@creamcityreview.org
fiction@creamcityreview.org
nonfiction@creamcityreview.org
art@creamcityreview.org
io@creamcityreview.org

https://uwm.edu/creamcityreview/
https://www.facebook.com/creamcityreview/
https://twitter.com/creamcityreview
https://www.instagram.com/cream_city_review/

Fiction > *Short Fiction*

Nonfiction > *Short Nonfiction*: Creative Nonfiction

Poetry > *Any Poetic Form*

Closed to approaches.

Send prose up to 20 pages, or up to five poems of any length. Open to submissions January 1 to April 1 and August 1 to November 1.

M148 Creative Nonfiction

Magazine
607 College Avenue, Pittsburgh, PA 15232
United States
Tel: +1 (412) 404-2975
Fax: +1 412-345-3767

information@creativenonfiction.org

https://creativenonfiction.org
https://creativenonfiction.submittable.com/submit/
https://www.facebook.com/creativenonfiction
https://twitter.com/cnfonline
https://instagram.com/creativenonfiction/

Nonfiction > *Essays*
Creative Nonfiction; Memoir; Personal Essays

How to send: Submittable

Publishes all types of creative nonfiction, from immersion reportage to lyric essay to memoir and personal essays. See website for specific submission calls and their topics, or submit a pitch for a column year-round.

Editor: Lee Gutkind

M149 Crimewave

Magazine
United Kingdom

http://www.ttapress.com/crimewave/

Magazine Publisher / Book Publisher: TTA Press (**P782**)

Fiction > *Short Fiction*
Crime; Mystery

Closed to approaches.

Publishes crime and mystery short stories. See website for complete guidelines.

Editor: Andy Cox

M150 Critical Quarterly

Magazine
Newbury, Crediton, Devon, EX17 5HA
United Kingdom

CRIQ@wiley.com
CQpoetry@gmail.com
CQcriticism@gmail.com

http://onlinelibrary.wiley.com/journal/10.1111/(ISSN)1467-8705

Book Publisher: John Wiley & Sons, Inc.

Fiction > *Short Fiction*

Nonfiction > *Essays*
Culture; Literary Criticism

Poetry > *Any Poetic Form*

How to send: Online submission system

Internationally renowned for its unique blend of literary criticism, cultural studies, poetry and fiction. The journal addresses the whole range of cultural forms so that discussions of, for example, cinema and television can appear alongside analyses of the accepted literary canon. It is a necessary condition of debate in these areas that it should involve as many and as varied voices as possible, and the journal welcomes submissions from new researchers and writers as well as more established contributors.

Editors: Clare Bucknell; Colin MacCabe

M151 CrossStitcher

Magazine
United Kingdom

Magazine Publisher: Warners Group Publications

M152 Cruising World

Magazine
517 N. Virginia Ave, Winter Park, FL 32789
United States
Tel: +1 (407) 628-4802

https://www.cruisingworld.com
https://www.facebook.com/cruisingworld/
https://twitter.com/cruisingworld/
https://www.instagram.com/cruisingworldmag/
https://www.youtube.com/c/cruisingworld

Media Company: Bonnier Corporation

Nonfiction > *Articles*
Boats; Sailing

Send: Full text
How to send: Email

Magazine for owners of sailboats between 20 and 50 feet in length. Authors should familiarise themselves with the magazine before approaching.

Editor: Mark Pillsbury

M153 Crystal Magazine

Magazine
3 Bowness Avenue, Prenton, Birkenhead, CH43 0SD
United Kingdom
Tel: +44 (0) 1516 089736

christinecrystal@hotmail.com

http://www.christinecrystal.blogspot.com

Fiction > *Short Fiction*
Adventure; Fantasy; Horror; Mystery; Romance; Science Fiction; Suspense; Thrillers; Westerns

Nonfiction
Articles: Comedy / Humour; Literature; Nature; Travel
News: General

Poetry > *Any Poetic Form*

Send: Full text
How to send: Email

Costs: A subscription is required in order to submit. Subscription £21pa UK/£25pa overseas for six issues. Sample £2.

An A4, 40-page, spiral-bound, print only bi-monthly. Intended for subscribers. They will receive six issues a year. Non-subscribers may send in work and purchase the issue it appears in. Contents are stories, poems and articles with colour images. There are usually pages of letters. Also an opportunity to share writing achievements and anything of interest to writers. There are yearly Surprise Competitions open to all.

Editor: Christine Carr

M154 CutBank

Magazine
University of Montana, English Dept, LA 133, Missoula, MT 59812
United States

editor.cutbank@gmail.com

http://www.cutbankonline.org
https://cutbank.submittable.com/submit
https://twitter.com/cutbankonline
http://instagram.com/cutbankmag
https://www.facebook.com/cutbanklitmag/

Fiction > *Short Fiction*

Nonfiction > *Short Nonfiction*: Creative Nonfiction

Poetry > *Any Poetic Form*

Closed to approaches.

Costs: A fee is charged upon submission. $5 reading fee.

Accepts poetry, fiction, creative nonfiction, and visual art submissions. Please only submit online; paper submissions will be recycled.

M155 Cyphers

Magazine
3 Selskar Terrace, Ranelagh, Dublin 6, D06 DW66
Ireland

letters@cyphers.ie

https://www.cyphers.ie

Fiction in Translation > *Short Fiction*

Fiction > *Short Fiction*

Poetry in Translation > *Any Poetic Form*

Poetry > *Any Poetic Form*

Send: Full text
How to send: Post
How not to send: Email

Publishes poetry and fiction in English and Irish, from Ireland and around the world. Translations are welcome. No unsolicited critical articles. Submissions by post only. Attachments sent by email will be deleted. See website for full guidelines.

M156 Dalesman

Magazine
The Gatehouse, Skipton Castle, Skipton, North Yorkshire, BD23 1AL
United Kingdom
Tel: +44 (0) 1756 701381

https://www.dalesman.co.uk
https://www.facebook.com/yorkshire.dalesman
https://twitter.com/The_Dalesman
https://www.youtube.com/user/TheYorkshireDalesman
https://www.instagram.com/dalesmanmagazine/

Book Publisher / Magazine Publisher: Dalesman Publishing Co. Ltd (**P195**)

Nonfiction > *Articles*: Yorkshire

Magazine publishing material of Yorkshire interest.

Editor-in-Chief: Dan Clare

Editors: Paul Jackson; Mick Smith

M157 Dame

Magazine
United States

editorial@damemagazine.com

https://www.damemagazine.com

Types: Nonfiction
Formats: Articles; Essays; News
Subjects: Arts; Business; Culture; Finance; Health; Nature; Politics; Science; Technology; Women's Interests
Markets: Adult

Magazine of news and opinion from a female perspective.

Editor: Kera Bolonik

M158 Dancing Times

Magazine
82 St John Street, London, EC1M 4JN
United Kingdom
Tel: +44 (0) 20 3773 6557

editorial@dancing-times.co.uk

https://www.facebook.com/1dancingtimes/
https://twitter.com/dancingtimes

Nonfiction
Articles: Dance
News: Dance
Reviews: Dance

Monthly magazine of dance, publishing features, news, and review.

M159 The Dark Horse

Magazine
PO Box 8342, Kilwinning, KA13 9AL
United Kingdom

https://www.thedarkhorsemagazine.com
https://www.facebook.com/The-Dark-Horse-Magazine-184043168311270/
https://twitter.com/thedarkhorsemag

Poetry > *Any Poetic Form*

Send: Full text; Self-Addressed Stamped Envelope (SASE)
How to send: Post
How not to send: Email

International literary magazine committed to British, Irish and American poetry. Send submissions by post only, to UK or US editorial addresses. No simultaneous submissions. See website for full guidelines.

Editor: Gerry Cambridge

M160 Dark Tales

Magazine
7 Offley Street, Worcester, WR3 8BH
United Kingdom

stories@darktales.co.uk

https://www.darktales.co.uk
https://twitter.com/DarkTalesUK

Fiction > *Short Fiction*
Horror; Speculative

Send: Full text
How to send: Email; Post

Costs: A fee is charged upon submission; Offers services that writers have to pay for. £4 to submit. Also offers critiques.

Created as an outlet primarily for unpublished writers of sci-fi, dark fantasy and horror short stories. Published stories are the winners and shortlisted entries from the monthly competition (£4 entry fee). Also offers optional critiques.

Editor: Sean Jeffery

M161 Darts World

Magazine
United Kingdom

info@dartsworld.com

https://www.dartsworld.com
https://www.facebook.com/dartsworldmagazine
https://twitter.com/darts_world

Nonfiction
Articles: Darts
News: Darts

Publishes articles and news on the subject of darts only.

Editor: Tony Wood

M162 The Dawntreader

Magazine
24 Forest Houses, Halwill, Beaworthy, Devon, EX21 5UU
United Kingdom

dawnidp@indigodreams.co.uk

https://www.indigodreams.co.uk/magazines

Book Publisher: Indigo Dreams Publishing **(P396)**

Fiction > *Short Fiction*
Environment; Folklore, Myths, and Legends; Mysticism; Nature; Spirituality

Nonfiction > *Articles*
Environment; Folklore, Myths, and Legends; Mysticism; Nature; Spirituality

Poetry > *Any Poetic Form*
Environment; Folklore, Myths, and Legends; Mysticism; Nature; Spirituality

Send: Full text
How to send: Email attachment

A quarterly publication specialising in myth, legend; in the landscape, nature; spirituality and love; the mystic, the environment. Submit up to five poems, and prose, articles, and local legends up to 1,000 words.

Editor: Ronnie Goodyer

M163 Decision

Magazine
United States

https://decisionmagazine.com
https://www.facebook.com/Decisionmagazine/
https://twitter.com/DecisionNews

Nonfiction
Articles: Christianity; Evangelism; Politics
News: Christianity; Evangelism; Politics

Magazine publishing news and articles of relevance to Christians and evangelism.

Editor: Bob Paulson

M164 Deep Overstock Magazine

Magazine
United States

submissions@deepoverstock.com

https://deepoverstock.com/issues/
https://deepoverstock.com/submission-guidelines/

Book Publisher / Magazine Publisher: Deep Overstock Publishing **(P205)**

Fiction > *Short Fiction*

Nonfiction > *Essays*

Poetry > *Any Poetic Form*

Send: Full text; Author bio
How to send: In the body of an email

Accepts fiction, poetry, and essays. Issues are themed. Check website for current theme. Prefers essays and fiction to be under 3,000 words. Accepts up to seven poems per theme.

M165 Diecast Collection

Magazine
United Kingdom

Magazine Publisher: Warners Group Publications

M166 Dogs Monthly

Magazine
The Old Print House, 62 The High Street, Chobham, Surrey, GU24 8AA
United Kingdom
Tel: +44 (0) 1276 402599

https://dogsmonthly.co.uk
https://www.facebook.com/DogsMonthly
https://www.instagram.com/dogsmonthlymagazine/
https://twitter.com/dogsmonthly

Nonfiction > *Articles*: Dogs

Send: Query
How to send: Online contact form; Phone; Post

Magazine for dog enthusiasts publishing articles on breeds, topical news, and features. Contact through form on website, or by phone or post in first instance.

Editor: Caroline Davis

M167 Dolls House and Miniature Scene

Magazine
United Kingdom

Magazine Publisher: Warners Group Publications

M168 The Drake Magazine

Magazine
PO Box 11546, Denver, CO 80211
United States
Tel: +1 (303) 917-9006

info@drakemag.com

https://drakemag.com/
https://www.instagram.com/thedrakemagazine/
https://twitter.com/Drakemagazine
https://www.facebook.com/TheDrakeMagazine/
http://feeds.feedburner.com/Drakemag

Nonfiction > *Articles*: Fishing

Send: Query
Don't send: Full text
How to send: Post; Email

Fishing magazine publishing educational and entertaining fishing stories. Does not publish how-to and where-to stories, but rather pieces which tell stories in a literary way. See website for details.

Editor: Tom Bie

M169 Dream Catcher

Magazine
109 Wensley Drive, Leeds, LS7 2LU
United Kingdom

http://www.dreamcatchermagazine.co.uk

Fiction > *Short Fiction*

Nonfiction > *Interviews*

Poetry > *Any Poetic Form*

Send: Full text
How to send: Post

Send submissions by post, following guidelines on website. No electronic submissions.

Editor: Wendy Pratt

M170 E/The Environmental Magazine

Online Magazine
United States

http://www.emagazine.com
https://www.facebook.com/askearthtalk/
https://twitter.com/EEnviroMag

Nonfiction
Articles: Environment; Nature; Sustainable Living
News: Environment

Send: Query
How to send: Online contact form

Former print magazine (now online only) focusing on environmental issues, dispensing news and information and advising people on how they can make a difference. Potential contributors should query in the first instance via contact form on website.

Editor: Jim Motavalli

M171 Early American Life

Magazine
Firelands Media Group LLC, Post Office Box 221230, Shaker Heights, OH 44122-0996
United States

queries@firelandsmedia.com

https://www.ealonline.com

Magazine Publisher: Firelands Media Group LLC

Nonfiction > *Articles*
American History; Antiques; Architecture

Send: Query
How to send: Email

Magazine aimed at people with an interest in the style of the period 1600-1840 in America, and its use in their modern homes and lives. Covers architecture, antiques, etc. Will consider unsolicited mss but prefers initial queries by email.

M172 Eclipse Lit

Magazine
United States

hello@eclipselit.org

https://www.eclipselit.org
https://twitter.com/eclipse_lit
http://www.instagram.com/jlfaccend

Fiction > *Short Fiction*: Literary

Nonfiction > *Essays*

Poetry > *Any Poetic Form*

Closed to approaches.

We are a nonprofit literary magazine that focuses on sharing the work of writers and artists while benefiting a different organization through each issue. Our mission is to give an outlet for writers to heal through art while benefiting organizations dedicated to helping people with trauma.

M173 The Economist

Magazine
The Adelphi, 1-11 John Adam Street, London, WC2N 6HT
United Kingdom

https://www.economist.com
https://www.facebook.com/theeconomist
https://www.instagram.com/theeconomist
https://www.twitter.com/theeconomist
https://www.linkedin.com/company/the-economist
https://www.youtube.com/user/economistmagazine

Nonfiction
Articles: Business; Current Affairs; Finance; Politics
News: Business; Current Affairs; Finance; Politics

Magazine covering economics, business, finance, politics, and current affairs.

M174 Ecotone

Magazine
Department of Creative Writing, University of North Carolina Wilmington, 601 South College Road, Wilmington, NC 28403-5938
United States

ecotone@uncw.edu

https://ecotonemagazine.org

Fiction > *Short Fiction*

Nonfiction > *Short Nonfiction*

Poetry > *Any Poetic Form*

Send: Full text

Publishes work from a wide range of voices. Particularly interested in hearing from writers historically underrepresented in literary publishing and in place-based contexts: people of colour, Indigenous people, people with disabilities, gender-nonconforming people, LGBTQIA+, women, and others. Check website for specific reading periods and submit prose up to 30 double-spaced pages or 3-5 poems by post with SAE or using online system ($3 charge). No hard copy submissions from outside the US.

Editor: David Gessner

M175 Edinburgh Review

Magazine
United Kingdom

https://edinburgh-review.com
https://www.facebook.com/Edinburgh-Review-202034306209/
https://twitter.com/EdinburghReview

Fiction > *Short Fiction*: Literary

Nonfiction > *Essays*
Arts; Culture; Literary Criticism; Literature; Philosophy; Politics

Poetry > *Any Poetic Form*

Closed to approaches.

Publishes Scottish and international fiction and accessible essays on the relationship of philosophy to the visual and literary arts.

Editor: Brian McCabe

M176 The Ekphrastic Review

Online Magazine
Canada

theekphrasticreview@gmail.com

https://www.ekphrastic.net

Fiction > *Short Fiction*

Nonfiction
Articles: Arts
Interviews: Literature
Reviews: Literature
Short Nonfiction: General

Poetry in Translation > *Any Poetic Form*: Arts

Poetry > *Any Poetic Form*: Arts

Send: Full text
How to send: Email

Publishes poetry that responds to, explores, or is inspired by a piece of art, and fiction and nonfiction of any kind, including book interviews or profiles, and articles about ekphrastic writing. Accepts submissions during specific windows only (see website for details).

Editor: Lorette C. Luzajic

M177 El Portal

Magazine
United States

el.portal@enmu.edu

https://elportaljournal.com

Types: Fiction; Nonfiction; Poetry
Formats: Essays; Short Fiction
Subjects: Literary
Markets: Adult

Send: Full text
How to send: Email

Accepts submissions of flash fiction up to 500 words, short stories and creative nonfiction up to 4,000 words, or up to five poems, by email. See website for full guidelines.

Editor: Jennifer Baros

M178 Electrical Times

Magazine
Purple Media Solutions Ltd, The Old School House, St Stephen's Street, Tonbridge, Kent, TN9 2AD
United Kingdom
Tel: +44 (0) 1732 371579

https://www.electricaltimes.co.uk

Magazine Publisher: Purple Media Solutions

PROFESSIONAL > **Nonfiction** > *Articles*: Electrical Contracting

Magazine for electrical contractors, installers, and designers.

Editor: Louise Frampton

M179 The Elks Magazine

Magazine
425 West Diversey Parkway, Chicago, IL 60614
United States

magnews@elks.org

https://www.elks.org/elksmag/

Nonfiction > *Articles*
Americana; Finance; Health; History; Leisure; Nature; Retirement; Science; Sport; Technology

Send: Full text; Self-Addressed Stamped Envelope (SASE)
How to send: Post; Email

Publishes features of general interest. Seeks articles that are fresh, thought provoking, well researched, and well documented. Typical readership consists of individuals over 40, with some college, an above-average income, from towns of half a million or less. Send submissions by email or by post with SASE. No religious, political, or first-person articles, or poetry.

Editor: Anna L. Idol

M180 Elle

Magazine
30 Panton Street, Leicester Square, London, SW1Y 4AJ
United Kingdom
Tel: +44 (0) 1858 438796

ellefeatures@elleuk.com

https://www.elle.com/uk/
https://www.facebook.com/ELLEuk
https://twitter.com/ELLEUK
https://www.pinterest.com/ellemag/
https://www.instagram.com/elleuk/
https://www.youtube.com/user/ELLEUKTV

Magazine Publisher: Hearst Magazines UK

Nonfiction
Articles: Beauty; Culture; Fashion; Horoscopes; Lifestyle
News: Celebrity

Send: Query; Author bio
How to send: Email

For features, send query with CV by email.

Editor: Lorraine Candy

Features Editor: Anna Pursglove

M181 Empire

Magazine
United Kingdom

https://www.empireonline.com
http://facebook.com/empiremagazine
http://twitter.com/empiremagazine

Magazine Publisher: Bauer Media Group

Nonfiction
Articles: Cinemas / Movie Theaters; Film Industry; Films; Technology
News: Cinemas / Movie Theaters; Film Industry; Films; Technology
Reviews: Films; Technology

Magazine of films and film-makers, as well as some attention to supporting technologies. Publishes behind-the-scenes articles, news, and reviews.

Editor: Colin Kennedy

M182 Emrys Journal

Magazine
Emrys Foundation, P.O. Box 8813, Greenville, SC 29604
United States
Tel: +1 (864) 202-4906

info@emrys.org

https://www.emrys.org
https://www.facebook.com/EmrysFoundation
https://twitter.com/EmrysFoundation
https://www.instagram.com/emrysfoundation/
https://www.youtube.com/playlist?list=PL36cHhWtnzVMd45OyB6TspqM9xwBZfcMy

Fiction > *Short Fiction*

Nonfiction > *Short Nonfiction*: Creative Nonfiction

Poetry > *Any Poetic Form*

Closed to approaches.

Literary journal publishing fiction, poetry, and creative nonfiction. Submit via online submission system during specific submission windows.

Editor: Katherine Burgess

M183 Entrepreneur

Magazine
18061 Fitch, Irvine CA, 92614
United States

https://www.entrepreneur.com/
https://www.facebook.com/EntMagazine
https://twitter.com/entrepreneur
https://www.linkedin.com/company/entrepreneur-media
https://www.pinterest.com/entrepreneurmedia
https://www.instagram.com/entrepreneur/
https://www.youtube.com/user/EntrepreneurOnline

Nonfiction > *Articles*
Business; Entrepreneurship; Finance; How To

Magazine for people who have started and are running their own business, providing news o current trends, practical how-to articles, features on combining work and life, etc. Runs features and several regular columns, as well as an inner magazine on start-ups.

Editor: Karen Axelton

M184 Erotic Review

Online Magazine
United Kingdom

editorial@ermagazine.org

https://eroticreviewmagazine.com
https://www.facebook.com/EroticReviewMag
https://twitter.com/EroticReviewMag
https://www.instagram.com/eroticreview/

Fiction > *Short Fiction*
Erotic; Literary

Nonfiction
Articles: Lifestyle; Literature; Sex; Sexuality
Reviews: Arts; Books; Erotic

Closed to approaches.

Literary lifestyle publication about sex and sexuality aimed at sophisticated, intelligent and mature readers. Print version has been retired and is now online only. Publishes articles, short stories, and reviews. See website for full submission guidelines.

Editor / Literary Agent: Jamie Maclean (**L460**)

M185 Event

Magazine
PO Box 2503, New Westminster, BC, V3L 5B2
Canada
Tel: +1 (604) 527-5293

event@douglascollege.ca

https://www.eventmagazine.ca
https://twitter.com/EVENTmags
https://www.facebook.com/eventmagazine
http://www.youtube.com/channel/UCKuYlH5b3uRaitKO4lCk8zA?feature=watch

Fiction > *Short Fiction*

Nonfiction
Reviews: Books
Short Nonfiction: Creative Nonfiction

Poetry > *Any Poetic Form*

How to send: Submittable

One of Western Canada's longest-running literary magazines. Welcomes submissions in English from around the world during specific submission windows.

M186 Faces

Magazine
1751 Pinnacle Drive, Suite 600, McLean, VA 22102
United States

faces@cricketmedia.com

http://cricketmedia.com/Faces-travel-magazine-for-kids

Magazine Publisher: Cricket Media, Inc.

CHILDREN'S
Fiction > *Short Fiction*: Folklore, Myths, and Legends

Nonfiction
Articles: Culture; Lifestyle; Travel
Interviews: Culture; Lifestyle; Travel

Send: Query
Don't send: Full text
How to send: Email

Magazine for children aged 9-14 covering the ways in which people living in other countries and cultures live. All issues are themed so essential to check upcoming themes before querying. Send query with one-page outline of proposed article and detailed bibliography of materials. See website for full details.

Editor: Elizabeth Crooker Carpentiere

M187 Fangoria

Magazine
United States

editorial@fangoria.com

https://fangoria.com
https://www.facebook.com/FANGORIA/
https://twitter.com/fangoria
https://www.instagram.com/fangoria
https://www.youtube.com/user/fangoriamagazine

Nonfiction
Articles: Films; Horror
Reviews: Films; Horror

Send: Pitch; Writing sample
How to send: Email

Horror entertainment magazine founded in 1979. Send pitch with writing sample by email.

Editor: Anthony Timpone

M188 Farm & Ranch Living

Magazine
1610 North 2nd Street, Suite 102, Milwaukee, WI 53212
United States

feedback@farmandranchliving.com

http://www.farmandranchliving.com

PROFESSIONAL > **Nonfiction** > *Articles*: Farming

Send: Full text
How to send: Online submission system

Reader-written magazine about farming and life on a ranch, publishing personal stories and photographs. Submit via online submission system.

M189 Fashion x Film

Magazine
United States

info@fashionxfilm.com

https://fashionxfilm.com

Types: Nonfiction
Formats: Articles; Film Scripts
Subjects: Beauty; Culture; Fashion
Markets: Academic; Adult

Send: Full text
How to send: Email

Online publication dedicated to unravelling the hidden meaning of fashion in film, be it through a single work, a director's oeuvre, or some common theme. Aims for an academic, cerebral tone. Send queries or complete submissions by email. See website for full guidelines.

M190 Fate

Magazine
PO Box 774, Hendersonville, NC 28793
United States
Tel: +1 (828) 702-3032

Phyllis@fatemag.com

https://www.fatemag.com
https://www.youtube.com/channel/UCAjXG-tsjV5VJM-i-afsvqA
https://twitter.com/Fate_Magazine
https://instagram.com/fatemagazine

Nonfiction > *Articles*
Mystery; Science; Supernatural / Paranormal

How to send: Post; Email

Magazine of mysterious and unexplained phenomena.

Editor-in-Chief: Phyllis Galde

M191 Faultline

Magazine
UCI Department of English, 435 Humanities Instructional Building, Irvine, CA 92697-2650
United States
Tel: +1 (949) 824-1573

faultline@uci.edu
ucifaultline@gmail.com

https://faultline.sites.uci.edu/
https://www.facebook.com/uci.faultline
https://twitter.com/faultline_journ

Fiction in Translation > *Short Fiction*

Fiction > *Short Fiction*

Nonfiction in Translation > *Short Nonfiction*: Creative Nonfiction

Nonfiction > *Short Nonfiction*: Creative Nonfiction

Poetry in Translation > *Any Poetic Form*

Poetry > *Any Poetic Form*

Closed to approaches.

Send up to five poems or up to 20 pages of fiction or creative nonfiction, between October 15 and December 15 only.

Fiction Editor: Sara Joyce Robinson

Poetry Editor: Lisa P. Sutton

M192 Fee: Foundation for Economic Education

Online Magazine
1819 Peachtree Road NE, Suite 300, Atlanta, GA 30309
United States
Tel: +1 (404) 554-9980
Fax: +1 (404) 393-3142

submissions@fee.org

https://fee.org
https://fee.org/submissions

Nonfiction > *Articles*
Culture; History; Philosophy; Politics

Send: Query; Full text

We welcome compelling, thoughtful articles exploring trends, principles, history, and ideas underlying a free society: private property, the rule of law, voluntary exchange, individual rights, morality, personal character, cultural evolution, self-responsibility, charity, mutual aid, and limitations on power.

M193 Feminist Review

Magazine
c/o Centre for Gender Studies, SOAS University of London, Thornhaugh Street, LONDON, WC1H 0XG
United Kingdom

feministreview@soas.ac.uk

https://journals.sagepub.com/home/fer
https://twitter.com/FeministReview_

Book Publisher / Magazine Publisher: Sage Publications (**P674**)

ACADEMIC > **Nonfiction** > *Articles*: Feminism

Send: Full text
How to send: Online submission system

A peer reviewed, interdisciplinary journal contributing to new agendas for feminism. The journal invites critical reflection on the relationship between materiality and representation, theory and practice, subjectivity and communities, contemporary and historical formations.

Editor: Joanna Hoare, Assistant Editor

M194 Feminist Studies

Magazine
4137 Susquehannna Hall, 4200 Lehigh Road, University of Maryland, College Park, MD 20742
United States
Tel: +1 (301) 405-7415
Fax: +1 (301) 405-8395

info@feministstudies.org
submit@feministstudies.org
creative@feministstudies.org
art@feministstudies.org
review@feministstudies.org

http://www.feministstudies.org

ACADEMIC > **Nonfiction** > *Essays*
Cultural Criticism; Literary Criticism

ADULT
Fiction > *Short Fiction*: Feminism

Nonfiction > *Articles*
Arts; Culture; Feminism

Poetry > *Any Poetic Form*: Feminism

Send: Full text; Proposal; Writing sample; Author bio
How to send: Email

Feminist journal publishing research and criticism, creative writing, art, essays, and other forms of writing and visual expression. See website for submission guidelines and specific submission email addresses.

M195 Fenland Poetry Journal
Magazine
PO Box 1523, Peterborough, PE2 2XZ
United Kingdom

fenlandpoetryjournal@gmail.com

https://fenlandpoetryjournal.co.uk

Poetry > *Any Poetic Form*
Contemporary; Literary

Send: Full text
How to send: Email

Contemporary poetry journal accepting submissions from anywhere in the world, though particularly encouraged from Fenland. No line limits.

M196 FHM
Online Magazine
United Kingdom

editor@fhm.com

http://www.fhm.com

Nonfiction
Articles: Cars; Entertainment; Fashion; Lifestyle; Sex; Sport
Interviews: General

Formerly the world's best-selling print male lifestyle magazine, now an online magazine.

Editor: Ross Brown

M197 Fiction
Magazine
c/o Department of English, City College of New York, Convent Ave. at 138th Street, New York, NY 10031
United States

fictionmageditors@gmail.com

http://www.fictioninc.com
http://submissions.fictioninc.com/
http://instagram.com/fiction.magazine
https://twitter.com/fictionmag
https://www.facebook.com/fiction.mag/

Fiction > *Short Fiction*: Literary

Closed to approaches.

Accepts short stories, novelettes, and novellas of any length (though staying under 5,000 words is encouraged). Submit by post or using online submission system between October 15 and April 15 only.

Editor: Mark J. Mirsky

M198 The Fiddlehead
Magazine
Campus House, 11 Garland Court, University of New Brunswick, PO Box 4400, Fredericton NB, E3B 5A3
Canada
Tel: +1 (506) 453-3501

fiddlehd@unb.ca

https://thefiddlehead.ca
https://twitter.com/TheFiddlehd
http://www.facebook.com/pages/The-Fiddlehead-Atlantic-Canadas-International-Literary-Journal/174825212565312

Fiction
Novel Excerpts; *Short Fiction*
Nonfiction > *Short Nonfiction*: Creative Nonfiction

Poetry > *Any Poetic Form*

Closed to approaches.

Publishes poetry, fiction, and creative nonfiction in a variety of styles, including experimental genres. Also publishes excerpts from longer works, and reviews. Submit up to six poems (up to 12 pages total), or a piece of fiction up to 6,000 words. All submissions must be original and unpublished. Prefers submissions through online submission system (January 1 to March 31 and September 15 to November 30 only), but will accept submissions by post all year round. See website for full details.

M199 Film Review
Online Magazine
United States

https://filmreviewonline.com
https://www.facebook.com/Film-Review-Online-139186982814321

Nonfiction
Interviews: Celebrity; Entertainment; Films; TV
News: Cinemas / Movie Theaters; Film Industry; Films; TV
Reviews: Films; TV

Film and TV website publishing reviews, profiles, interviews, and news. Includes editors based in New York, Los Angeles, and London.

Editor: Neil Corry

M200 Firmament
Magazine
United States

support@sublunaryeditions.com

https://sublunaryeditions.com/firmament
https://oleada.io/publication/sublunary-editions

Book Publisher / Magazine Publisher: Sublunary Editions (**P746**)

Fiction > *Short Fiction*

Nonfiction > *Interviews*

Features new writing from around the world, along with in-depth interviews, excerpts from upcoming titles, regular columns, and more.

M201 The First Line
Magazine
PO Box 250382, Plano, Texas 75025-0382
United States

submission@thefirstline.com

http://www.thefirstline.com

Fiction > *Short Fiction*

Nonfiction > *Essays*: Literary Criticism

Poetry > *Any Poetic Form*

Send: Full text; Self-Addressed Stamped Envelope (SASE)
How to send: Word file email attachment; Post
How not to send: PDF file email attachment; Google Docs shared document

Prefers submissions by email, but will also accept submissions by post with SASE. Prefers attachments as a Word or Word Perfect file. Stories must begin with the appropriate first line for that issue, as provided on the website. Occasionally accepts poems starting with the specified first line. Also accepts essays on your favourite first line from a book.

M202 Five Points
Magazine
Georgia State University, P.O. Box 3999, Atlanta, GA 30302-3999
United States

http://fivepoints.gsu.edu

Fiction in Translation
Novel Excerpts: Literary
Short Fiction: Literary

Fiction > *Short Fiction*: Literary

Nonfiction in Translation > *Essays*

Nonfiction > *Short Nonfiction*
General, and in particular: Literary

Poetry in Translation > *Any Poetic Form*

Poetry > *Any Poetic Form*

Closed to approaches.

Costs: A fee is charged upon submission.

Welcomes unsolicited submissions of fiction, poetry, flash fiction and nonfiction, and literary nonfiction. Submit through online submission system.

Editor: Megan Sexton

M203 Flaneur
Online Magazine
United Kingdom

editor@flaneur.me.uk

http://www.flaneur.me.uk

Nonfiction > *Articles*
Arts; Films; Food and Drink; Literature; Music; Politics; Sport; TV; Theatre; Travel

Send: Full text
How to send: In the body of an email

Online magazine of arts, culture, politics, and sport.

Editor: J Powell

M204 Flash: The International Short-Short Story Magazine

Magazine
International Flash Fiction Association, Department of English, University of Chester, Parkgate Road, Chester, CH1 4BJ
United Kingdom

flash.magazine@chester.ac.uk

https://www1.chester.ac.uk/flash-magazine/submissions

Fiction > *Short Fiction*

Send: Full text
How to send: Email

Publishes flash fiction up to 360 words, including the title. Send up to four pieces per issue. Attach submissions to a single email. See website for full submission guidelines.

Editors: Dr Peter Blair; Dr Ashley Chantler

M205 Florida Living

Magazine
999 Douglas Avenue, Suite 3301, Altamonte Springs, FL 32714
United States

Publisher@FloridaMagazine.com

https://www.floridamagazine.com

Nonfiction > *Articles*
Florida; Food; History; Lifestyle; Outdoor Activities; Travel

General interest magazine covering Florida lifestyle and travel. Focuses on the state's history and heritage, outdoor activities, travel and vacations, food, dining, scenic beauty, greenways and trails, state parks, homes and gardens, and every other aspect of life and travel in Florida.

M206 Flyfishing & Tying Journal

Magazine
United States

https://ftjangler.com

Book Publisher / Magazine Publisher: Amato Books (**P035**)

Nonfiction > *Articles*: Fly Fishing

Magazine for both new and veteran anglers, covering flyfishing and fly tying. Magazine is released quarterly, and each issue is appropriate to the given season.

Editor: Dave Hughes

M207 Focus

Magazine
United Kingdom

devhotmail@yahoo.co.uk

https://bsfa.co.uk/focus

Professional Body: BSFA (British Science Fiction Association)

Nonfiction > *Articles*
Creative Writing; Science Fiction

Send: Query
How to send: Email

Writing magazine, devoted to the craft and practice of writing genre fiction. Publishes articles on writing science fiction. Query by email.

Editor: Dev Agarwal

M208 Folio

Magazine
United States

folio.editors@gmail.com

https://www.american.edu/cas/literature/folio/
https://www.facebook.com/FolioLitJournal/
https://twitter.com/FolioLitJournal
https://www.linkedin.com/in/folio-literary-journal-a235a8b4
http://folio-lit-journal.tumblr.com/

Fiction > *Short Fiction*: Literary

Nonfiction > *Essays*: Creative Nonfiction

Poetry > *Any Poetic Form*

Closed to approaches.

Accepts submissions of fiction, nonfiction, and poetry on specific themes during specific submission windows. See website for details.

M209 Fortean Times: The Journal of Strange Phenomena

Magazine
Diamond Publishing Ltd, 7th Floor, Vantage West, Great west Road, Brentford, TW8 9AG
United Kingdom

hello@metropolis.co.uk

http://subscribe.forteantimes.com
https://www.instagram.com/forteantimes/
https://www.facebook.com/ForteanTimes
https://twitter.com/forteantimes

Magazine Publisher: Diamond Publishing

Nonfiction > *Articles*: Supernatural / Paranormal

Publishes accounts of strange phenomena, experiences, curiosities, mysteries, prodigies, and portents. No fiction or poetry.

Editor: David Sutton

M210 Foundation: The International Review of Science Fiction

Magazine
28 St John's Road, Guildford, GU2 7UH
United Kingdom

sff@beccon.org

https://www.sf-foundation.org/about-the-sff-journal

Nonfiction
Articles: Science Fiction
Reviews: Books; Science Fiction

Describes itself as the essential critical review of science fiction, publishing articles up to 6,000 words and reviews up to 1,500 words.

Editor: Dr Farah Mendlesohn

M211 The Fourth River

Magazine
United States

4thriver@gmail.com

https://www.thefourthriver.com
https://twitter.com/thefourthriver
https://www.instagram.com/thefourthriver/
https://www.facebook.com/TheFourthRiver

Fiction > *Short Fiction*: Literary

Nonfiction > *Short Nonfiction*: Creative Nonfiction

Poetry > *Any Poetic Form*

Send: Full text
How to send: Submittable

Costs: A fee is charged upon submission. $3 submission fee.

Print and digital literary magazine publishing creative writing that explores the relationship between humans and their environments, whether natural or man-made. Submit 3-5 poems or prose up to 4,000 words between July 1 and September 1 for print, or December 1 and February 1 for online, via online submission system. No submissions by email.

M212 The Frogmore Papers

Magazine
21 Mildmay Road, Lewes, East Sussex, BN7 1PJ
United Kingdom

frogmorepress@gmail.com

http://www.frogmorepress.co.uk

Fiction
Novel Excerpts; *Short Fiction*
Poetry > *Any Poetic Form*

Send: Full text; Self-Addressed Stamped Envelope (SASE)
How to send: Domestic Post; International Email

Poetry and prose by new and established authors. There is no house style but the extremes of tradition and experiment are equally unlikely to find favour.

Send between four and six poems, or up to two prose pieces.

Editor: Jeremy Page

M213 Fugue

Magazine
United States

fugue@uidaho.edu

https://fuguejournal.com
https://twitter.com/FugueJournal
https://www.instagram.com/fugue_journal/
https://www.facebook.com/fuguejournal/

Fiction > *Short Fiction*

Nonfiction
Essays: General
Reviews: Books

Poetry > *Any Poetic Form*

Closed to approaches.

Costs: A fee is charged upon submission. $3.

Submit 3 to 5 poems, up to two short shorts, one story, or one essay per submission. Accepts submissions online only, between September 1 and May 1. Submission service charges $3 per submission.

Editors: Scott Dorsch; Ryan Downum; Emmy Newman; Steven Pfau; Clare Shearer; Keene Short

M214 Funny Times

Magazine
PO Box 18530, Cleveland Heights, OH 44118
United States
Tel: +1 (888) 386-6984

submissions@funnytimes.com
info@funnytimes.com

https://funnytimes.com
https://www.facebook.com/TheFunnyTimes

Fiction
Cartoons: Business; Comedy / Humour; Current Affairs; Food; Pets; Politics; Relationships; Religion; Technology
Short Fiction: Business; Comedy / Humour; Current Affairs; Food; Pets; Politics; Relationships; Religion; Technology

Send: Full text; Self-Addressed Stamped Envelope (SASE)
How to send: Email; Post

Send query with SASE and details of previous publishing history (where applicable).

Publishes funny stories and cartoons only. No fax or email submissions.

Editor: Raymond Lesser, Susan Wolpert

M215 The Future Fire

Online Magazine
United Kingdom

fiction@futurefire.net
nonfiction@futurefire.net

http://futurefire.net

Fiction in Translation > *Short Fiction*

Fiction > *Short Fiction*
Crime; Environment; Feminism; LGBTQIA; Mystery; Noir; Postcolonialism; Speculative

Nonfiction > *Reviews*
Arts; Books; Films; Magazines

Poetry in Translation > *Any Poetic Form*

Poetry > *Any Poetic Form*
Environment; Feminism; LGBTQIA; Postcolonialism; Speculative

Send: Full text
How to send: Email attachment

Magazine of social political and speculative cyber fiction. Publishes short stories generally up to 10,000 words, however may consider stories up to 17,500. Also publishes nonfiction reviews. Accepts email submissions for fiction; for reviews send query by email before submitting material. See website for full submission guidelines.

Editors: Djibril Alayad; Bruce Stenning

M216 Garden Answers

Magazine
Bauer Media, Media House, Lynch Wood, PE2 6EA
United Kingdom
Tel: +44 (0) 1733 468000

gardenanswers@bauermedia.co.uk

https://www.gardenanswersmagazine.co.uk/
https://www.facebook.com/gardenanswers
https://twitter.com/GardenAnswers

Magazine Publisher: Bauer Media Group

Nonfiction > *Articles*: Gardening

A vibrant and inspiring gardening magazine filled with ingenious design ideas and exciting plant combinations guaranteed to make your garden beautiful.

Editor: Geoff Stebbings

M217 Garden News

Magazine
United Kingdom

https://www.gardennewsmagazine.co.uk
https://www.facebook.com/GardenNewsOfficial
https://twitter.com/GardenNewsmag

Magazine Publisher: Bauer Media Group

Nonfiction > *Articles*: Gardening

Weekly gardening magazine publishing tips, reminders, and expert advice.

Editor: Neil Pope

M218 Garden Rail

Magazine
United Kingdom

Magazine Publisher: Warners Group Publications

M219 The Garden

Magazine
The Royal Horticultural Society, 80 Vincent Square, London, SW1P 2PE
United Kingdom
Tel: +44 (0) 20 3176 5800

thegarden@rhs.org.uk

https://www.rhs.org.uk/about-the-rhs/publications/the-garden

Magazine Publisher: The Royal Horticultural Society (RHS)

Nonfiction > *Articles*: Gardening

Gardening magazine publishing practical garden design ideas, plant profiles and outstanding gardens large and small. Also carries news of flower shows, special garden openings, books, etc.

Editor: Ian Hodgson

M220 Gateway

Magazine
Missouri Historical Society, PO Box 775460, St. Louis, MO 63177
United States

https://mohistory.org/publications/gateway/

Nonfiction > *Articles*
African American; Civil Rights; Culture; History; Missouri; Music; Society; Theatre

Magazine covering St. Louis's and Missouri's historical and contemporary cultural, social, and political issues. Particularly interested in articles and essays on preservation and architecture; folk culture and oral history; music and theatre traditions; civil rights and African American history, as well as original poetry, photography, and literature.

Editor: Victoria W. Monks

M221 Geochemistry: Exploration, Environment, Analysis

Magazine
United Kingdom

Book Publisher / Magazine Publisher: The Geological Society Publishing House (**P288**)

M222 The Georgia Review

Magazine
The University of Georgia, Athens, GA 30602-9009
United States
Tel: +1 (800) 542-3481

https://thegeorgiareview.com
https://thegeorgiareview.submittable.com/submit
https://www.instagram.com/georgiareview/
https://www.facebook.com/thegeorgiareview/
https://twitter.com/home

Fiction > *Short Fiction*: Literary

Nonfiction
Essays: General
Reviews: Books

Poetry > *Any Poetic Form*

Closed to approaches.

Costs: A fee is charged for online submissions. $3 for online submissions. Postal submissions are free.

Publishes literary fiction, poetry (submit 6-10 pages of poetry or one long poem), essays and book reviews. Submissions accepted between August 15 and May 15 only. Submissions received between May 15 and August 15 are returned unread.

Editor: T. R. Hummer

M223 German Life

Magazine
PO Box 3000, Denville, NJ 07834-9723
United States
Tel: +1 (866) 867-0251

comments@germanlife.com

https://germanlife.com
http://www.facebook.com/https://www.facebook.com/germanlifemag/

Magazine Publisher: Zeitgeist Publishing

Nonfiction > *Articles*
Austria; Culture; Germany; Politics; Social Commentary; Switzerland

Magazine on German history, culture, and travel, and the way in which Germany and German immigrants have helped shape America.

Editor: Mark Slider

M224 Gertrude

Online Magazine
United States

EditorGertrudePress@gmail.com

https://www.gertrudepress.org

Book Publisher: Gertrude Press (**P291**)

Fiction > *Short Fiction*
General, and in particular: LGBTQIA

Nonfiction
Essays: Creative Nonfiction; LGBTQIA
Short Nonfiction: Creative Nonfiction; LGBTQIA; Memoir

Poetry > *Any Poetic Form*
General, and in particular: LGBTQIA

Closed to approaches.

Costs: A fee is charged upon submission. £3 submission fee.

Online LGBTQA journal publishing fiction, poetry, and creative nonfiction. Subject matter need not be LGBTQA-specific, and writers from all backgrounds are welcomed. Submit fiction or creative nonfiction up to 3,000 words, or up to five poems (no line limit, but under 40 lines preferred), via online submission system. For book reviews and interviews, email editor with proposal. See website for full guidelines.

Editor: Tammy

M225 Get Creative With...

Magazine
United Kingdom

Magazine Publisher: Warners Group Publications

M226 The Gin Kin

Online Magazine
United Kingdom

https://www.theginkin.com

Newspaper Publisher / Magazine Publisher: DC Thomson Media

M227 Go World Travel Magazine

Online Magazine
United States

submissions@goworldtravel.com

https://www.goworldtravel.com
https://www.facebook.com/Go.World.Travel
https://www.instagram.com/goworldtravelmagazine/
https://pinterest.com/goworldtravel/
https://twitter.com/GoWorldMagazine
https://www.youtube.com/user/GoWorldPublishing

Nonfiction > *Articles*: Travel

How to send: Email

A digital publication for world travelers. We work with journalists around the world, and partner with destination marketing organizations and other tourism and travel businesses to promote travel.

Editor: Heike Schmidt, Senior Editor

M228 Golf Tips

Magazine
iGolf Sports Network LLC, 13800 Panama City Beach PKWY, Suite 106D, #138, Panama City Beach, FL 32407
United States
Tel: +1 (850) 588-1550

ted@igolfsportsnetwork.com

https://www.golftipsmag.com

Nonfiction > *Articles*
Golf; How To; Travel

Publishes tips, guides, and features on golf.

M229 Good Homes

Magazine
United Kingdom

https://www.goodhomesmagazine.com
https://www.facebook.com/GoodHomes
https://uk.pinterest.com/goodhomes/
https://twitter.com/GoodHomesMag
https://www.instagram.com/goodhomesmag/

Magazine Publisher: Media 10

Nonfiction > *Articles*
Decorating; Interior Design

Magazine of decorating and interior design.

Editor: Lisa Allen

M230 The Good Ski Guide

Magazine
1 Esher Place Avenue, KT10 8PU
United Kingdom
Tel: +44 (0) 1372 469874

johnh@goodholidayideas.com

https://www.goodskiguide.com/
https://www.facebook.com/goodskiguide.official
https://twitter.com/officialGSG
https://www.youtube.com/goodskiguideoffical

Nonfiction > *Articles*
Skiing; Travel

Magazine of skiing and ski resorts.

Editors: Nick Dalton; John Hill

M231 Graffiti Magazine

Magazine
United Kingdom

writersinthebrewery@yahoo.co.uk

https://www.facebook.com/pages/Graffiti-Magazine/63653000411

Fiction > *Short Fiction*

Poetry > *Any Poetic Form*

Publishes poetry and prose. Each edition has a short story competition.

Editor: Rona Laycock

M232 Granta

Magazine
12 Addison Avenue, Holland Park, London, W11 4QR

United Kingdom
Tel: +44 (0) 20 7605 1360

editorial@granta.com

https://granta.com

Fiction > *Short Fiction*

Nonfiction > *Short Nonfiction*

Poetry > *Any Poetic Form*

Closed to approaches.

Costs: A fee is charged upon submission. £3 for prose; £2 for poems.

Submit one story or essay, or up to four poems, via online submission system. £3 charge for prose submissions; £2 for poems. No specific length limits for prose, but most pieces are between 3,000 and 6,000 words. Unlikely to read anything over 10,000 words.

Editor: Sigrid Rausing

M233 The Great Outdoors (TGO)

Magazine
Kelsey Media Ltd, The Granary, Downs Court, Yalding Hil, Yalding, Kent, ME18 6AL
United Kingdom

carey.davies@kelsey.co.uk

https://www.tgomagazine.co.uk

Magazine Publisher: Kelsey Media

Nonfiction > *Articles*: Walking

Magazine publishing articles on walking and back-packing.

Editor: Carey Davies

M234 Grit

Magazine
1503 S.W. 42nd St., Topeka, KS 66609
United States
Tel: +1 (785) 274-4300
Fax: +1 (785) 274-4305

Letters@grit.com

https://www.grit.com
https://www.facebook.com/GritMagazine/
https://www.pinterest.com/gritmagazine
https://www.instagram.com/grit1882/
https://www.youtube.com/user/MotherEarthNewsMag
https://twitter.com/GritMagazine

Nonfiction > *Articles*
Farming; Gardening; Rural Living; Urban Farming

Send: Query
Don't send: Full text
How to send: Word file email attachment

Family magazine distributed across America, with a positive approach to life, providing a voice for rural lifestyle farmers. Potential contributors must be knowledgeable on rural life. Send query in first instance, preferably by email (with the word "Query" in the subject line).

Editor: K.C. Compton

Editorial Director: Oscar H. Will

M235 Gutter Magazine

Magazine
United Kingdom

contactguttermagazine@gmail.com

https://www.guttermag.co.uk/

Fiction > *Short Fiction*
International; Literary; Scotland

Nonfiction > *Essays*
Creative Nonfiction; International; Literary; Scotland

Poetry > *Any Poetic Form*
International; Scotland

Scripts > *Theatre Scripts*
International; Literary; Scotland

Send: Full text
How to send: Online submission system

Publishes poetry, short stories, and drama. Publishes work by writers born or living in Scotland alongside international writing. Send up to five poems up to 120 lines total, or prose up to 3,000 words. Submit through online submission system. See website for full guidelines.

Editors: Colin Begg; Kate MacLeary; Laura Waddell

M236 Hair

Magazine
United Kingdom

http://hairmagazine.co.uk

Magazine Publisher: Haversham Publications Ltd

Nonfiction > *Articles*: Hairstyles

Magazine on hair and beauty, publishing articles and features on trends in fashion and hair styling.

M237 Half Mystic Journal

Print Magazine
United States

hello@halfmystic.com

https://www.halfmystic.com

Book Publisher: Half Mystic Press (**P322**)

Fiction in Translation > *Short Fiction*
Experimental; Music

Fiction > *Short Fiction*
Experimental; Music

Nonfiction in Translation > *Short Nonfiction*
Creative Nonfiction; Experimental; Music

Nonfiction > *Short Nonfiction*
Creative Nonfiction; Experimental; Music

Poetry in Translation
Any Poetic Form: Music
Experimental Poetry: Music

Poetry
Any Poetic Form: Music
Experimental Poetry: Music

Closed to approaches.

Publishes all genres of poetry, prose, creative nonfiction, translations, and experimental work—as long as each piece pertains in some way to music. See website for the theme of the current issue.

M238 Hanging Loose

Magazine
PO Box 150608, Brooklyn, NY 11215
United States
Tel: +1 (857) 998-9473

https://www.hangingloosepress.com
https://www.facebook.com/hangingloosepress
https://twitter.com/HangingLooseNY

Fiction > *Short Fiction*

Poetry > *Any Poetic Form*

Send: Full text; Self-Addressed Stamped Envelope (SASE)
How to send: Post
How not to send: Email

Send up to six poems or one story at a time. Potential contributors should familiarise themselves with the magazine before submitting. Includes regular section of High School writers. Send submissions by post with SASE. Allow up to three months for a response.

M239 Harper's Magazine

Magazine
666 Broadway, 11th Floor, New York, NY 10012
United States
Tel: +1 (212) 420-5720

helpdesk@harpers.org

https://harpers.org
https://twitter.com/Harpers
https://www.facebook.com/HarpersMagazine/
https://www.instagram.com/harpersmagazine/

Fiction > *Short Fiction*

Nonfiction
Articles: Culture; Current Affairs; Environment; Journalism; Politics; Society
Essays: Culture; Current Affairs; Environment; Politics; Society

Send: Query; Full text; Self-Addressed Stamped Envelope (SASE)
How to send: Post
How not to send: Email

Current affairs magazine publishing topical essays, and fiction. Considers unsolicited fiction MSS, however no unsolicited nonfiction (query in first instance). All queries and submissions must be sent by post.

Editor: Roger D. Hodge

M240 Harpur Palate

Magazine
Binghamton University, English Department, P.O. Box 6000, Binghamton, NY 13902-6000
United States

harpur.palate@gmail.com

https://harpurpalate.binghamton.edu
https://twitter.com/harpurpalate
https://www.instagram.com/harpurpalate
https://www.facebook.com/harpurpalate
https://harpurpalate.submittable.com/submit

Fiction > *Short Fiction*

Nonfiction > *Short Nonfiction*: Creative Nonfiction

Poetry > *Any Poetic Form*

Closed to approaches.

Submit up to five poems, up to 15 pages total; prose up to 5,500 words; or three pieces of short prose up to 1,000 words each. Submit through online submission system.

M241 Harvard Magazine

Magazine
7 Ware Street, Cambridge, Mass. 02138-4037
United States
Tel: +1 (617) 495-5746
Fax: +1 (617) 495-0324

https://www.harvardmagazine.com
https://www.facebook.com/HarvardMagazine
https://twitter.com/harvardmagazine
https://www.linkedin.com/company/harvard-magazine
https://www.youtube.com/user/HarvardMagazine
https://www.instagram.com/harvardmagazine/

Nonfiction > *Articles*: Harvard

Send: Query
How to send: Email

Magazine for faculty, alumni, and students of the university. Aims to keep alumni connected to the university community, covering the work and thinking being done at the university, and raising contemporary social and political issues and reflecting upon them. Also includes alumni news. Send query to the editor by email.

Editor: John S. Rosenberg

M242 Healthy

Magazine
United Kingdom

healthy@therivergroup.co.uk

https://www.healthy-magazine.co.uk
https://www.facebook.com/HealthyMagazine
https://twitter.com/healthymag
http://instagram.com/healthymagdaily

Magazine Publisher: The River Group

Nonfiction > *Articles*
Beauty; Fitness; Food; Health; Lifestyle

Magazine of holistic health and lifestyle. Send query by email in first instance.

Editor: Heather Beresford

M243 Heat Pumps Today

Magazine
United Kingdom

Magazine Publisher: Warners Group Publications

M244 The Helix

Magazine
United States

helixmagazine@gmail.com

https://helixmagazine.org

Fiction > *Short Fiction*

Nonfiction > *Short Nonfiction*

Poetry > *Any Poetic Form*

Closed to approaches.

Publishes fiction, creative nonfiction, poetry, plays, and art. Submit prose up to 3,000 words each, or up to four poems.

Editor: Victoria-Lynn Bell

M245 Here Comes Everyone

Magazine
United Kingdom

https://hcemagazine.com
https://www.facebook.com/HCEmagazine/
https://twitter.com/herecomesevery1

Fiction > *Short Fiction*

Nonfiction > *Articles*

Poetry > *Any Poetic Form*

Closed to approaches.

Biannual literature and arts magazine publishing poetry, fiction, articles, and artwork. Each issue is themed. See website for upcoming themes and to submit.

Editors: Matthew Barton; Raef Boylan

M246 Hi-Fi News

Magazine
United Kingdom

https://www.hifinews.com
https://www.facebook.com/pages/Hi-Fi-News-Record-Review/299204350193416
https://twitter.com/hifinewsmag

Magazine Publisher: AV Tech Media Ltd

Nonfiction
News: Audio Technology
Reviews: Audio Technology

Reviews audiophile-oriented sound-reproduction and recording equipment, and includes information on new products and developments in audio.

Editor: Paul Miller

M247 Highway News

Magazine
1525 River Road, Marietta, PA 17547
United States
Tel: +1 (717) 426-9977

info@tfcglobal.org

https://tfcglobal.org/highway-news/current-issue/

Nonfiction > *Articles*
Hauliers; Religion

Religious magazine aimed at truck drivers and their families. Publishes testimonials, teachings, and human interest stories that have a foundation in Biblical/Christian values.

Editor: Jennifer Landis

M248 History Scotland

Magazine
United Kingdom

Magazine Publisher: Warners Group Publications

M249 History Today

Magazine
2nd Floor, 9 Staple Inn, London, WC1V 7QH
United Kingdom
Tel: +44 (0) 20 3219 7810

submissions@historytoday.com
admin@historytoday.com
enquiries@historytoday.com

https://www.historytoday.com

Nonfiction > *Articles*: History

Send: Query; Author bio
How to send: Email

Historical magazine publishing short articles (up to 1,000 words); mid-length articles (1,300-2,200 words) and feature articles (3,000 to 3,400 words). Send query by email with proposal and details of your career / academic background. See website for full guidelines.

M250 Homes & Antiques

Magazine
United Kingdom

https://www.homesandantiques.com
https://www.facebook.com/homesantiques
http://uk.pinterest.com/homesantiques
https://twitter.com/@homes_antiques
https://www.youtube.com/channel/UChlvNbVVoLcWle1xHnuAZlQ
https://www.instagram.com/homes_antiques

Magazine Publisher: Immediate Media Co.

Nonfiction > *Articles*
Antiques; Decorating; Interior Design

Magazine of home interest, antiques, and collectibles.

Editor: Angela Linforth

M251 Horse & Rider

Magazine
7500 Alamo Road NW, Albuquerque, NM 87120
United States
Tel: +1 (303) 253-6405

HorseandRider@equinenetwork.com

https://my.horseandrider.com
https://www.facebook.com/HorseandRider
https://www.pinterest.com/hrsrdrmag/
https://www.instagram.com/horseandridermag/
https://twitter.com/Horse_and_Rider

Magazine Publisher: Equine Network

Nonfiction > *Articles*
American West; Horses; Travel

Provides all you need for today's Western horse life. Learn from top professional trainers, clinicians, and horse-keeping experts. Experience Western life. Travel to Western destinations and scenic trails. Your resource to live today's Western horse life.

Editor: Debbie Moors, Associate Editor

M252 Horse and Rider

Magazine
DJ Murphy Publishers Ltd, Olive Studio, Grange Road, Tilford, Farnham, Surrey, GU10 2DQ
United Kingdom
Tel: +44 (0) 1428 601020

editor@djmurphy.co.uk

https://www.horseandrideruk.com

Magazine Publisher: DJ Murphy Publishers Ltd

Nonfiction > *Articles*
Equestrian; Horses

Magazine on horses, including news, instructional features, etc. Aimed mainly at horse-owners.

Editor: Louise Kittle

M253 Hotel Amerika

Magazine
C/O The Department of Creative Writing, Columbia College Chicago, 600 South Michigan Avenue, Chicago, IL 60605
United States
Tel: +1 (312) 369-8175

http://www.hotelamerika.net

Fiction > *Short Fiction*: Literary

Nonfiction > *Essays*

Poetry > *Any Poetic Form*

Closed to approaches.

Costs: A fee is charged upon submission. $3.00.

Submissions will be considered between September 1 and April 1. Materials received after April 1 and before September 1 will not be considered.

Editor: David Lazar

M254 Hoxie Gorge Review

Magazine
United States

editor@hoxiegorgereview.com

http://hoxiegorgereview.com

Types: Fiction; Nonfiction; Poetry
Subjects: Literary
Markets: Adult

Send: Full text

Online literary journal publishing poetry, fiction, and creative nonfiction. Submit via website through online submission system.

Editor: Heather Bartlett

M255 The Hudson Review

Magazine
33 West 67th Street, New York, NY 10023
United States
Tel: +1 (212) 650-0020

info@hudsonreview.com

https://hudsonreview.com
https://www.facebook.com/The-Hudson-Review-134346783271591/
https://twitter.com/TheHudsonReview

Fiction > *Short Fiction*

Nonfiction
Articles: Contemporary Culture
Essays: Arts; Dance; Films; Literary Criticism; Music; Theatre
Reviews: Books

Poetry > *Any Poetic Form*

Send: Full text; Self-Addressed Stamped Envelope (SASE)
How to send: Post; Online submission system

Publishes fiction, poetry, essays, book reviews; criticism of literature, art, theatre, dance, film and music; and articles on contemporary cultural developments.

Accepts certain material at only certain times of year: poetry between April 1 and June 30; fiction between September 1 and November 30; and nonfiction between January 1 and March 31. MSS submitted out of season are returned if adequate return postage is provided only. MSS of subscribers are read year-round.

No specialisation in any particular type of writing – literary quality is the only criteria. Read a sample copy of the magazine for a flavour of the kinds of material published.

No simultaneous submissions. Electronic submissions for fiction only.

Editor: Paula Deitz

M256 Hunger Mountain

Magazine
United States

hungermtn@vcfa.edu

https://hungermtn.org

Fiction in Translation > *Short Fiction*: Literary

Fiction > *Short Fiction*: Literary

Nonfiction in Translation > *Short Nonfiction*: Creative Nonfiction

Nonfiction > *Short Nonfiction*: Creative Nonfiction

Poetry in Translation > *Any Poetic Form*

Poetry > *Any Poetic Form*

Closed to approaches.

Costs: A fee is charged upon submission in some cases. Offers competitions for which there is an entry fee.

Submit prose up to 6,000 words, or up to three flash pieces, or up to five poems, via online submission system. Accepts general submissions between May 1 and October 15, and contest submissions between April 1 and June 15.

Editor: Caroline Mercurio

M257 I-70 Review

Magazine
913 Joseph Drive, Lawrence, KS 66044
United States

i70review@gmail.com

http://i70review.fieldinfoserv.com

Fiction > *Short Fiction*

Poetry > *Any Poetic Form*

Send: Full text; Author bio
How to send: Word file email attachment

Accepts submissions of fiction and flash fiction or 3-5 poems, by email, during the reading period that runs from July 1 to December 31. Accepts simultaneous submissions. See website for full details.

M258 Iconoclast

Magazine
1675 Amazon Road, Mohegan Lake, NY 10547-1804
United States

http://www.iconoclastliterarymagazine.com

Fiction > *Short Fiction*: Literary

Poetry > *Any Poetic Form*

Send: Full text
How to send: Post

Publishes poetry and prose from authors interested in the creation, sharing, and transmission of ideas, imaginings, and experiences. Send prose up to 3,500 words or poetry up to two pages with SASE. See website for full guidelines.

Editor: Phil Wagner

M259 Idaho Review

Magazine
Boise State University, 1910 University Drive, Boise, Idaho 83725
United States

mwieland@boisestate.edu

https://www.idahoreview.org
https://theidahoreview.submittable.com/submit
http://www.facebook.com/10213528569031037
http://twitter.com/idahoreview
http://www.instagram.com/theidahoreview

Fiction > *Short Fiction*: Literary

Nonfiction
Essays: General
Short Nonfiction: Creative Nonfiction

Poetry > *Any Poetic Form*

Closed to approaches.

Costs: A fee is charged for online submissions. $3 to submit online.

Annual literary journal publishing poetry and fiction. No specific limit for fiction, but most of the stories accepted are under 25 double-spaced pages. For poetry, submit up to five poems. Reading period runs from September to March (see website for specific dates for this year). Accepts submissions by post with SASE, but prefers submissions through online submission system ($3 fee).

M260 Ideal Home

Magazine
161 Marsh Wall, London, E14 9AP
United Kingdom

ideal_home@futurenet.com

https://www.idealhome.co.uk
https://www.facebook.com/idealhome.co.uk
https://twitter.com/idealhome
https://www.pinterest.co.uk/idealhomemag/
https://www.instagram.com/idealhomeuk/

Magazine Publisher: Future

Nonfiction > *Articles*
Gardening; Interior Design

Monthly magazine on the home, covering interior design, decoration, furnishing, home improvements, gardening, etc.

Editor: Susan Rose

M261 Identity Theory

Online Magazine
United States

fiction@identitytheory.com
essays@identitytheory.com
poetry@identitytheory.com

http://www.identitytheory.com
https://identitytheory.submittable.com/submit

Fiction > *Short Fiction*

Nonfiction
Essays: Lyric Essays; Personal Essays
Interviews: General
Short Nonfiction: Creative Nonfiction; Memoir

Poetry > *Any Poetic Form*

Send: Full text
How to send: Submittable; Email

Online literary magazine. Send fiction or essays up to 4,000 words through Submittable or through specific email address, or 3-5 unpublished poems in the body of an email.

Editor: Matt Borondy

M262 Image

Magazine
3307 Third Avenue West, Seattle, WA 98119
United States
Tel: +1 (206) 281-2988

Image@imagejournal.org

https://imagejournal.org
http://facebook.com/imagejournal
http://twitter.com/image_journal
https://www.instagram.com/image_journal

Fiction > *Short Fiction*
Culture; Literary; Religion; Spirituality

Nonfiction > *Essays*
Arts; Culture; Literature; Religion; Spirituality

Poetry > *Any Poetic Form*
Culture; Religion; Spirituality

Fosters contemporary art and writing that grapple with the mystery of being human by curating, cultivating, convening, and celebrating work that explores religious faith and faces spiritual questions. A vibrant thread in the fabric of culture, contributing to mainstream literary and artistic communities by demonstrating the vitality of contemporary art and literature invigorated by religious faith.

Editor: Gregory Wolfe

M263 Iman Collective

Online Magazine
Nigeria

imancollectivemag@gmail.com

https://imancollective.wordpress.com

Fiction > *Short Fiction*
Islam; Literary

Nonfiction > *Short Nonfiction*
Islam; Literary

Poetry > *Any Poetic Form*
Islam; Literary

Send: Query
How to send: Email

This is a quarterly magazine publishing Muslim literature in the genres of poetry, fiction, and nonfiction.

M264 Indefinite Space

Magazine
PO Box 40101, Pasadena, CA 91114
United States

indefinitespace@yahoo.com

http://www.indefinitespace.net

Poetry > *Experimental Poetry*

Send: Full text
How to send: Email

Literary journal publishing innovative, imagistic, philosophical, and experimental poetry, drawings, collage, photography and paintings. Reads year round.

M265 Indiana Review

Magazine
Indiana University, Indiana Review Journal, Department of English, Lindley 215, 150 S Woodlawn Ave, Bloomington, IN 47405-7104
United States

inreview@indiana.edu

https://indianareview.org
https://twitter.com/indianareview
https://www.facebook.com/IndianaReview

Fiction in Translation > *Short Fiction*: Literary

Fiction > *Short Fiction*: Literary

Nonfiction in Translation > *Essays*

Nonfiction > *Essays*

Poetry in Translation > *Any Poetic Form*

Poetry > *Any Poetic Form*

Send: Full text
Don't send: Query
How to send: Online submission system

Costs: A fee is charged upon submission. $3 per submission.

Send fiction or nonfiction up 6,000 words or 3-6 poems per submission, during specific submission windows only (see website for details). No submissions by post or by email – all submissions must be made through online submission manager ($3 fee). See website for full guidelines, and to submit.

Editor: Tessa Yang

Editor-in-Chief: Mariah Gese

M266 InfoWorld

Online Magazine
140 Kendrick Street, Building B, Needham, MA 02494
United States

https://www.infoworld.com
https://www.linkedin.com/company/164364
https://twitter.com/infoworld
https://www.facebook.com/InfoWorld

Magazine Publisher: Foundry

PROFESSIONAL > **Nonfiction** > *Articles*
Computers; Technology

Closed to approaches.

The leading voice in emerging enterprise technology, is the go-to resource for developers, architects, and business leaders launching next-generation initiatives on scalable cloud platforms, where such future-focused tech as AI/machine learning, big data analytics, and NoSQL databases evolve continuously. Does not publish contributed articles.

Editor: Steve Fox, Editor in Chief

M267 Ink Sweat and Tears

Online Magazine
United Kingdom

inksweatandtearssubmissions@gmail.com
inksweatandtearsinterns@gmail.com

https://inksweatandtears.co.uk
https://twitter.com/InkSweatTears
https://www.facebook.com/InkSweatandTears
https://www.instagram.com/insta.inksweatandtears/

Nonfiction > *Reviews*
Literature; Poetry as a Subject

Poetry
Any Poetic Form; *Haibun*; *Haiga*; *Haiku*; *Prose Poetry*

Send: Full text
How to send: Email

UK-based webzine publishing poetry, prose, prose-poetry, word and image pieces, and poetry reviews. Send 4-6 pieces of poetry (or 1-2 short prose/flash fiction works) by email only. Accepts unsolicited reviews of poetry and short story collections. See website for full guidelines.

Editor: Helen Ivory

M268 Inque

Magazine
United Kingdom

info@inquemag.com

https://inquemag.com
http://instagram.com/inquemag
http://twitter.com/inquemagazine

Fiction > *Short Fiction*: Literary

Nonfiction
Articles: Arts; Literature
Interviews: Arts; Literature

Annual literary magazine dedicated to extraordinary new writing. Documenting what is going to be an era-defining decade, it will run no advertising, have no web version, and only ever publish 10 issues. Contributors include Margaret Atwood, Max Porter, Joyce Carol Oates, Ocean Vuong, Tom Waits, Ben Lerner, Alexander Chee, Kae Tempest, and more.

M269 Inspiralist

Online Magazine
United Kingdom

Newspaper Publisher / Magazine Publisher: DC Thomson Media

M270 Inspire

Magazine
1 Easting Close, Worthing, BN14 8HQ
United Kingdom
Tel: +44 (0) 1903 263354

editor@inspiremagazine.org.uk

https://www.inspiremagazine.org.uk
https://twitter.com/inspirestories
https://www.facebook.com/InspireMagazineUK/

Nonfiction > *Articles*: Christianity

Christian magazine dedicated to telling the good news stories of God at work transforming individuals, churches and communities around the UK and across the world.

Editor: Russ Bravo

M271 InStyle

Magazine
United States
Tel: +1 (800) 274-6200

letters@instylemag.com

https://www.instyle.com
https://www.facebook.com/InStyle
https://twitter.com/InStyle
https://www.pinterest.com/instyle/
https://www.instagram.com/instylemagazine/

Magazine Publisher: Meredith Corporation

Nonfiction
Articles: Beauty; Celebrity; Fashion; Hairstyles; How To; Lifestyle; Politics; Popular Culture; Social Issues
News: General

Magazine providing readers with a mix of fashion and beauty advice and celebrity news and lifestyle.

Editor: Louise Chunn

M272 International Piano

Magazine
St Jude's Church, Dulwich Road, London, SE24 0PB
United Kingdom

international.piano@rhinegold.co.uk

http://www.rhinegold.co.uk
https://www.rhinegold.co.uk/rhinegold-publishing/magazines/international-piano/
https://twitter.com/IP_mag
https://www.facebook.com/internationalpiano/
https://www.instagram.com/internationalpianomagazine
https://www.youtube.com/channel/UCOKPU5skkhcvQRjXVkou10Q

Magazine Publisher: Rhinegold Publishing

ACADEMIC > **Nonfiction** > *Articles*: Piano

ADULT > **Nonfiction** > *Articles*: Piano

PROFESSIONAL > **Nonfiction** > *Articles*: Piano

Offers a rich mix of inspiration and guidance to pianists and piano fans around the world, from dedicated amateurs and students to professional pianists, teachers and aficionados.

Editor: Jeremy Siepmann

M273 The Interpreter's House

Online Magazine
United Kingdom

interpretershousesubmissions@gmail.com

https://theinterpretershouse.org

Fiction > *Short Fiction*

Nonfiction
Essays; *Interviews*; *Reviews*
Poetry > *Any Poetic Form*

Send up to five poems or up to two short stories by email during specific submission windows (see website for details).

Editor: Georgi Gill

M274 Interzone

Magazine
United Kingdom

submissions@interzone.press

https://interzone.press
https://interzone.press/submissions/

Magazine Publisher: MYY Press

Fiction > *Short Fiction*
Fantasy; Horror; Science Fiction

Send: Full text
How to send: Email

Publishes fantastika (including science fiction, fantasy, and horror) short stories up to 17,500 words. See website for full guidelines.

Editor: Andy Cox

M275 Investors Chronicle

Magazine
United Kingdom

https://www.investorschronicle.co.uk
https://www.linkedin.com/showcase/financial-times---investors-chronicle/
https://twitter.com/ichronicle
https://www.instagram.com/investorschronicle/
https://www.facebook.com/InvestorsChronicleOnline

PROFESSIONAL > **Nonfiction** > *Articles*
Business; Finance

Magazine for investors.

Editors: Rosie Carr; John Hughman

M276 The Iowa Review

Magazine
The University of Iowa, 308 English-Philosophy Building, Iowa City, IA 52242
United States
Tel: +1 (319) 335-0462
Fax: +1 (319) 335-2535

iowa-review@uiowa.edu

http://www.iowareview.org

Types: Fiction; Poetry; Translations
Formats: Essays; Reviews; Short Fiction
Subjects: Literary
Markets: Adult

Send: Full text

Publishes poetry, fiction, and nonfiction. Submit in September, October, and November only, via online submission system ($4 charge for non-subscribers) or by post with SASE. Accepts prose up to 25 pages and poetry up to 8 pages (query by email if your poem is longer). Do not mix genres in a single envelope. Work must be unpublished. Simultaneous submissions accepted if immediate notification of acceptance elsewhere is given.

Editor: Lynne Nugent

M277 Irish Pages

Magazine
129 Ormeau Road, Belfast, BT7 1SH
United Kingdom
Tel: +44 (0) 2890 434800

editor@irishpages.org
sales@irishpages.org
gaeilge@irishpages.org

https://irishpages.org
https://twitter.com/irishpages
https://www.youtube.com/channel/UC08ArKYYmKVUpP5eHfEMz0w

Fiction in Translation > *Short Fiction*

Fiction > *Short Fiction*

Nonfiction in Translation
Essays: General
Short Nonfiction: Autobiography; Creative Nonfiction; History; Literary Journalism; Memoir; Nature; Religion; Science
Nonfiction
Essays: General
Short Nonfiction: Autobiography; Creative Nonfiction; History; Literary Journalism; Memoir; Nature; Religion; Science
Poetry in Translation > *Any Poetic Form*

Poetry > *Any Poetic Form*

Send: Full text
How to send: Post
How not to send: Email

Non-partisan and non-sectarian literary journal publishing writing from the island of Ireland and elsewhere in equal measure. Publishes work in English, and in the Irish Language or Ulster Scots with English translations or glosses. Accepts submissions throughout the year by post only with stamps, coupons or cash for return postage (no self-addressed envelope is needed). See website for more details.

M278 Iron Cross

Magazine
United Kingdom

Magazine Publisher: Warners Group Publications

M279 Island

Magazine
PO Box 4703, Hobart TAS 7000
Australia
Tel: +61 (0) 3 6234 1462

admin@islandmag.com

https://islandmag.com
https://island.submittable.com/submit

Fiction > *Short Fiction*

Nonfiction
Articles; *Essays*
Poetry > *Any Poetic Form*

How to send: Submittable

Welcomes submissions of nonfiction, fiction and poetry from Australia, New Zealand and the Pacific, as well as from Australians living abroad. See website for details and to submit using online submission system.

Online Magazine: Island Online (**M280**)

M280 Island Online

Online Magazine
Australia

admin@islandmag.com
ben@islandmag.com

https://islandmag.com/online
https://island.submittable.com/submit
http://www.facebook.com/islandmagtas
http://instagram.com/islandmagtas
https://twitter.com/IslandMagTas

Magazine: Island (**M279**)

Fiction > *Short Fiction*
Arts; Culture; Environment; Experimental; Literary; Nature; Society

Nonfiction > *Essays*
Arts; Culture; Environment; Nature; Society

Closed to approaches.

Digital publishing platform operated in conjunction with longstanding print magazine.

M281 Janes Defence Weekly

Magazine
United Kingdom
Tel: +44 (0) 20 3997 6594

customer.care@janes.com

https://www.janes.com
https://www.linkedin.com/company/ihs-jane's/
https://www.youtube.com/channel/UCEC1WX1I030Ss6oNk7ynsBA
https://www.facebook.com/JanesIntelligence/

PROFESSIONAL > **Nonfiction**
Articles: Military; Secret Intelligence; Warfare; Weapons
News: Military; Secret Intelligence; Warfare; Weapons

Magazine covering defence topics of worldwide interest. No history.

Editor: Peter Felstead

M282 Jazz Journal

Online Magazine
United Kingdom

editor@jazzjournal.co.uk

https://jazzjournal.co.uk

Nonfiction
Articles: Jazz
News: Jazz
Reviews: Jazz

The oldest English-language magazine dedicated to the coverage of jazz music. Published in print for seven decades and from 2019 as a web-only publication. Provides a rolling jazz news and review service with columns and features added on an ad-hoc, roughly monthly basis. Publishes approximately 70 reviews of newly issued jazz recordings per month.

Editor: Janet Cook

M283 Jewish Chronicle

Magazine
United Kingdom

editorial@thejc.com

https://www.thejc.com
https://www.instagram.com/thejewishchronicle/
https://twitter.com/jewishchron
https://www.facebook.com/pages/The-Jewish-

Chronicle/99875692725
https://www.pinterest.co.uk/thejewishchroni/

Nonfiction
Articles: Jewish Culture; Judaism; Lifestyle
News: Jewish Culture; Judaism; Sport

Weekly paper publishing material of Jewish interest. No fiction.

M284 Journal of Apicultural Research

Magazine
United Kingdom

https://www.tandfonline.com/toc/tjar20/current

ACADEMIC > **Nonfiction** > *Articles*: Apiculture (Beekeeping)

Send: Full text
How to send: Online submission system

Publishes research articles, theoretical papers, notes, comments and authoritative reviews on scientific aspects of the biology, ecology, natural history and culture of all types of bee.

M285 Journal of the Geological Society

Magazine
United Kingdom

Book Publisher / Magazine Publisher: The Geological Society Publishing House (**P288**)

M286 Juniper

Magazine
United Kingdom

Newspaper Publisher / Magazine Publisher: DC Thomson Media

M287 Kerning

Magazine
United States

https://www.toadhalleditions.ink/kerning-a-space-for-words

Book Publisher / Self Publishing Service: Toad Hall Editions (**P770**)

Fiction > *Short Fiction*

Nonfiction
Essays: General
Short Nonfiction: Creative Nonfiction

Poetry > *Any Poetic Form*

Closed to approaches.

Costs: Invites donations. Choose to pay $7, $14, or no fee when submitting.

Publishes work by women and gender diverse people only.

M288 Kerrang!

Magazine
90 – 92 Pentonville Road, London, N1 9HS
United Kingdom

feedback@kerrang.com

https://www.kerrang.com
https://www.facebook.com/kerrangmagazine/
https://twitter.com/KerrangMagazine
https://www.instagram.com/kerrangmagazine_/
https://www.youtube.com/user/KerrangPodcast
https://www.tiktok.com/kerrangmagazine_

Magazine Publisher: Wasted Talent

Nonfiction
Articles: Heavy Metal; Music; Punk; Rock Music
News: Heavy Metal; Music; Punk; Rock Music

Weekly rock, metal, and punk magazine.

Editor: Paul Brannigan

M289 Kids Alive!

Magazine
The Salvation Army, 101 Newington Causeway, London, SE1 6BN
United Kingdom
Tel: +44 (0) 20 7367 4910

kidsalive@salvationarmy.org.uk

https://www.salvationist.org.uk/media/kidsalive

CHILDREN'S
Fiction > *Cartoons*: Christianity

Nonfiction > *Articles*: Christianity

Christian children's magazine publishing puzzles, comic strips, etc.

Editor: Justin Reeves

M290 Lancashire Life

Magazine
United Kingdom

https://www.lancashirelife.co.uk

Magazine Publisher: Archant

Nonfiction > *Articles*
Food and Drink; Lancashire; Property / Real Estate; Travel

Publishes articles, features, and pictures of Lancashire.

Editors: Roger Borrell; Paul Mackenzie

M291 Land Rover Monthly

Magazine
United Kingdom

Magazine Publisher: Warners Group Publications

M292 Leisure Painter

Magazine
The Maltings, West Street, Bourne, Lincolnshire, PE10 9PH
United Kingdom

https://www.painters-online.co.uk

Magazine Publisher: Warners Group Publications

Nonfiction > *Articles*: Painting

Magazine offering artistic inspiration, guidance, tuition and encouragement for beginners and amateur artists. Includes features and step-by-step painting and drawing demonstrations.

Editor: Ingrid Lyon

M293 Light & Life

Magazine
United States

https://lightandlife.fm
https://twitter.com/lightandlifemag
https://www.facebook.com/lightandlifemagazine
https://www.youtube.com/channel/UCr8nd1V-UnRFTBeCTSPB68A
https://vimeo.com/llcomm
https://www.linkedin.com/company/559925
https://www.flickr.com/photos/llcomm/

Nonfiction > *Articles*: Methodism

Bimonthly magazine that exists to promote thoughtful Christian discipleship from a Wesleyan-Arminian perspective.

Editor: Doug Newton

Executive Editor: Jeff Finley

M294 Lighthouse

Magazine
United Kingdom

submissions@lighthouse.gatehousepress.com
lighthouseprosesubmissions@gmail.com

https://storymachines.co.uk/portfolio/lighthouse/

Fiction > *Short Fiction*

Poetry > *Any Poetic Form*

Send: Full text
How to send: Email

A literary journal dedicated to publishing new writing and championing new writers. Aims to publish the best short fiction, poetry, and art emerging from the UK scene.

M295 Lincolnshire Life

Magazine
County House, 9 Checkpoint Court, Sadler Road, Lincoln, LN6 3PW
United Kingdom
Tel: +44 (0) 1522 689671

studio@lincolnshirelife.co.uk

https://www.lincolnshirelife.co.uk
http://www.facebook.com/lincolnshirelife
https://twitter.com/lincslife

Nonfiction > *Articles*
Business; Contemporary; Culture; Food; History; Leisure; Lifestyle; Lincolnshire

A monthly magazine devoted to the history, culture and contemporary life of Lincolnshire, England.

Editor: Judy Theobald

M296 Literary Mama

Online Magazine
United States

LMinfo@literarymama.com
LMreviews@literarymama.com
LMnonfiction@literarymama.com
LMfiction@literarymama.com
LMpoetry@literarymama.com

https://literarymama.com
http://www.facebook.com/litmama
http://twitter.com/literarymama
https://www.instagram.com/literary_mama/

Fiction > *Short Fiction*: Motherhood

Nonfiction
Reviews: Books; Motherhood
Short Nonfiction: Creative Nonfiction; Motherhood

Poetry > *Any Poetic Form*: Motherhood

Send: Full text; Query
How to send: In the body of an email

Online magazine publishing fiction, poetry, creative nonfiction, and book reviews focusing on mother writers, and the complexities and many faces of motherhood. Accepts submissions in the text of emails only – no snail mail submissions. See website for full submission guidelines.

Editor: Amy Hudock

M297 Litro Magazine

Magazine
90 York Way, London, N1 9AG
United Kingdom
Tel: +44 (0) 207 917 2887

editor@litro.co.uk
online@litro.co.uk
podcasts@litro.co.uk

https://www.litro.co.uk
https://www.facebook.com/Litromedia/
https://open.spotify.com/show/78fpfD5ejecJXXdsVHGJqb
https://www.instagram.com/litromedia/
https://twitter.com/litromagazine

Fiction > *Short Fiction*

Nonfiction > *Short Nonfiction*
Literary Journalism; Memoir; Travel

How to send: Submittable
How not to send: Email

Accepts short fiction, flash/micro fiction, nonfiction (memoir, literary journalism, travel narratives, etc), and original artwork (photographs, illustrations, paintings, etc) based on the designated monthly theme. Works translated into English are also welcome. See website for upcoming themes.

M298 Living

Magazine
United Kingdom

Newspaper Publisher / Magazine Publisher: DC Thomson Media

M299 Loaded

Online Magazine
United Kingdom

https://loaded.co.uk
https://www.facebook.com/LoadedMagazine
https://twitter.com/loadedonline
https://www.pinterest.com/loadedonline/

Nonfiction
Articles: Entertainment; Lifestyle; Sport; Women
News: General

Online men's lifestyle magazine. Originally a print publication, now online only.

Editors: Scott Manson; Andrew Woods

M300 The London Magazine

Magazine
Flat 5, 11 Queen's Gate, London, SW7 5EL
United Kingdom
Tel. +44 (0) 20 7584 5977

info@thelondonmagazine.org

http://thelondonmagazine.org

Types: Fiction; Nonfiction; Poetry
Formats: Articles; Essays; Reviews; Short Fiction
Subjects: Arts; Autobiography; Literary; Literary Criticism
Markets: Adult

Send: Full text

Send submissions through online submission system or by email. Does not normally publish science fiction or fantasy writing, or erotica. Will consider postal submissions, but prefers submissions electronically. See website for full guidelines and to access online submission system.

M301 Long Poem Magazine

Magazine
20 Spencer Rise, London, NW5 1AP
United Kingdom

longpoemmagazine@gmail.com

http://longpoemmagazine.org.uk
https://www.facebook.com/groups/longpoemmagazine/
https://twitter.com/LongPoemMag

Nonfiction
Essays: Poetry as a Subject
Reviews: Books

Poetry > *Long Form Poetry*

Closed to approaches.

Magazine dedicated to publishing long poems and sequences. Publishes unpublished poems of at least 75 lines (but no book length poems). Also publishes essays on aspects of the long poem and reviews of books featuring long poems or sequences. Send submissions by email as Word file attachments. Does not accept poems submitted in the body of emails. See website for full guidelines and submission months. Poems submitted outside submission months will be discarded.

M302 Louisiana Literature

Magazine
United States

lalit@selu.edu

http://www.louisianaliterature.org
https://twitter.com/LaLiterature
https://louisianaliterature.submittable.com/submit

Fiction > *Short Fiction*: Literary

Nonfiction > *Essays*: Creative Nonfiction

Poetry > *Any Poetic Form*

Closed to approaches.

Literary journal publishing fiction, poetry, and creative nonfiction. Submit via online system available at the website.

Editor: Dr Jack Bedell

M303 The MacGuffin

Magazine
Schoolcraft College, 18600 Haggerty Road, Livonia, MI 48152
United States
Tel: +1 (734) 462-5327

macguffin@schoolcraft.edu

https://schoolcraft.edu/macguffin

Fiction > *Short Fiction*

Nonfiction > *Short Nonfiction*: Creative Nonfiction

Poetry
Any Poetic Form; *Experimental Poetry*; *Free Verse*

Closed to approaches.

Publishes fiction, creative nonfiction, and poetry. Submit up to five poems or up to two pieces of prose via online submission system.

M304 Machine Knitting Monthly

Magazine
PO Box 1479, Maidenhead, Berkshire, SL6 8YX
United Kingdom
Tel: +44 (0) 1628 783080

mail@machineknittingmonthly.net

https://machineknittingmonthly.net

Nonfiction > *Articles*: Knitting

Editor: Anne Smith

M305 The Magazine of Fantasy & Science Fiction

Magazine
PO Box 3447, Hoboken, NJ 07030
United States

fsfmag@fandsf.com

http://fandsf.com
https://fandsf.moksha.io/publication/fsf

Fiction > *Short Fiction*
Fantasy; Science Fiction

Send: Full text; Self-Addressed Stamped Envelope (SASE)
How to send: Moksha; Post

We have no formula for fiction, but we like to be surprised by stories, either by the character insights, ideas, plots, or prose. The speculative element may be slight, but it should be present. We prefer character-oriented stories, whether it's fantasy, science fiction, horror, humor, or another genre. We encourage submissions from diverse voices and perspectives, and have published writers from all over the world. Do not query for fiction; submit the entire manuscript. We publish fiction up to 25,000 words in length. Please read the magazine before submitting. A sample copy (print edition) is available for $7.00 in the US and $17.50 elsewhere (to NJ address).

We do not accept simultaneous submissions. Please prepare your submission according to standard guidelines. If you're mailing your manuscript, put your name on each page, and enclose a self-addressed, stamped envelope. Writers are encouraged to submit their work electronically.

We prefer not to see more than one submission from a writer at a time.

Allow 8 weeks for a response.

Payment is 8-12 cents per word on acceptance. We buy first North American and foreign serial rights and an option on anthology rights. All other rights are retained by the author.

Our columns and non-fiction articles are assigned in-house. We do not accept freelance submissions in those areas.

Editor: Gordon Van Gelder

M306 Making Cards

Magazine
United Kingdom

Magazine Publisher: Warners Group Publications

M307 The Malahat Review

Magazine
University of Victoria, McPherson Library, PO Box 1800, Stn CSC, Victoria, BC V8W 3H5
Canada

malahat@uvic.ca

http://www.malahatreview.ca
https://twitter.com/malahatreview

Fiction > *Short Fiction*

Nonfiction
Essays: Personal Essays
Reviews: Books
Short Nonfiction: Biography; Creative Nonfiction; History; Memoir; Narrative Nonfiction; Social Commentary; Travel

Poetry > *Any Poetic Form*

How to send: Submittable

Publishes poetry, short fiction, and creative nonfiction by new and established writers mostly from Canada, reviews of Canadian books, and the best writing from abroad. Submissions from Canadian writers are accepted year-round. Fiction and poetry submissions from international writers only accepted during specific windows.

Editor: John Barton

M308 Manoa

Magazine
University of Hawai'i at Mānoa, Department of English, 1733 Donaghho Road, Honolulu, HI 96822
United States
Tel: +1 (808) 956-3070
Fax: +1 (808) 956-3083

mjournal-l@lists.hawaii.edu

https://manoa.hawaii.edu/manoajournal/

ACADEMIC > **Nonfiction** > *Essays*
Asia; Culture; Literature; Pacific

ADULT

Fiction in Translation > *Short Fiction*
Asia; Pacific

Fiction > *Short Fiction*
Asia; Pacific

Poetry in Translation > *Any Poetic Form*
Asia; Pacific

Poetry > *Any Poetic Form*
Asia; Pacific

Closed to approaches.

A Pacific journal, however material does not need to be related to the Pacific, or by authors from the region.

Editor: Frank Stewart

M309 marie claire

Magazine
United States

marieclairepr@futurenet.com

https://www.marieclaire.com
https://www.facebook.com/MarieClaire
https://twitter.com/marieclaire
https://www.pinterest.com/MarieClaire
https://instagram.com/marieclairemag
https://www.youtube.com/c/MarieClaire

Magazine Publisher: Future

Nonfiction > *Articles*
Beauty; Career Development; Celebrity; Culture; Fashion; Finance; Fitness; Food and Drink; Health; Horoscopes; Politics; Relationships; Sex; Travel; Women's Interests

Lifestyle magazine aimed at the younger working woman.

M310 marie claire (UK)

Magazine
Future PLC, 121 – 141 Westbourne Terrace, Paddington, London, W2 6JR
United Kingdom

https://www.marieclaire.co.uk
https://www.facebook.com/MarieClaireUK/
https://twitter.com/marieclaireuk
https://www.pinterest.co.uk/marieclaireuk/
https://www.instagram.com/marieclaireuk/

Magazine Publisher: Future

Nonfiction > *Articles*
Beauty; Celebrity; Entertainment; Fashion; Hairstyles; Health; Lifestyle; Relationships; Sex

Glossy magazine for women.

Editor: Trish Halpin

M311 Marlin

Magazine
517 N. Virginia Ave, Winter Park, FL 32789
United States

editor@marlinmag.com

https://www.marlinmag.com
https://www.facebook.com/marlinmag/
https://twitter.com/MarlinMagazine/
http://instagram.com/marlinmag/
http://www.youtube.com/MarlinMagazine/

Nonfiction > *Articles*
Boats; How To; Offshore Gamefishing; Travel

Publishes articles, features, and news items relating to offshore fishing, destinations, personalities, fishery regulations, the boating industry and related topics, including how-to and technical information.

Editor: Dave Ferrel

M312 The Massachusetts Review

Magazine
Photo Lab 309, University of Massachusetts, Amherst, MA 01003
United States
Tel: +1 (413) 545-2689
Fax: +1 (413) 577-0740

massrev@external.umass.edu

http://www.massreview.org
https://www.facebook.com/pages/The-Massachusetts-Review/40580092594
https://twitter.com/MassReview
http://instagram.com/themassachusettsreview?ref=badge
http://themassreview.tumblr.com/

Fiction in Translation > *Short Fiction*: Literary

Fiction > *Short Fiction*: Literary

Nonfiction in Translation > *Essays*
Arts; Current Affairs; Drama; Literature; Music; Philosophy; Science

Nonfiction
Articles: Arts; Current Affairs; Drama; Literature; Music; Philosophy; Science
Essays: Arts; Current Affairs; Drama; Literature; Music; Philosophy; Science
Poetry in Translation > *Any Poetic Form*

Poetry > *Any Poetic Form*

Closed to approaches.

Costs: A fee is charged for online submissions. $3.

Send one story of up to 25–30 pages or up to six poems of any length (though rarely publishes poems of more than 100 lines). White people may not submit between May 1 and September 30. Others may submit year-round, and may use email if the online submission system is closed. White people are not permitted to submit by email. Articles and essays of breadth and depth are considered, as well as discussions of leading writers; of art, music, and drama; analyses of trends in literature, science, philosophy, and public affairs. No plays, reviews of single books, or submissions by fax or email.

Editor: David Lenson

M313 Maxim

Magazine
United States

Editor@maxim.com

https://www.maxim.com
https://www.facebook.com/maximmagazine
https://twitter.com/MaximMag
https://www.youtube.com/user/videosbyMaxim
https://www.instagram.com/maximmag
https://pinterest.com/maximmag

Nonfiction > *Articles*
Cars; Entertainment; Fashion; Food and Drink; Luxury Lifestyle; Sport; Technology; Travel; Women

Glossy magazine for men publishing articles and features on entertainment, fashion, sex, sport, travel, motoring, and tech. No poetry or fiction.

Editor: Tom Loxley

M314 Mayfair Times

Magazine
United Kingdom

https://mayfairtimes.co.uk
https://www.facebook.com/mayfairtimes/
https://twitter.com/MayfairTimes
https://instagram.com/Mayfair.Times

Nonfiction
Articles: Arts; Business; Culture; Fashion; Finance; Food and Drink; Houses; Lifestyle; Local; Travel
News: Local

A monthly luxury lifestyle magazine, which has been serving the people of Mayfair, Marylebone and St James's for 35 years.

M315 Meetinghouse

Magazine
United States

submissions@meetinghousemag.org

https://www.meetinghousemag.org
https://twitter.com/meethousemag

Fiction > *Short Fiction*

Poetry > *Any Poetic Form*

Closed to approaches.

A literary magazine that provides a space for diverse voices to speak with one another. Submit up to two pieces of prose and up to five poems per submission.

M316 Metropolis Magazine

Magazine
United States
Tel: +1 (212) 934-2800

info@metropolismag.com

https://www.metropolismag.com/
https://www.facebook.com/MetropolisMag
https://metropoliseditorialaccount.submittable.com/submit
https://twitter.com/MetropolisMag
https://www.linkedin.com/company/metropolis-magazine
https://www.instagram.com/metropolismag/

Magazine Publisher: Sandow

Nonfiction > *Articles*
Architecture; Arts; City and Town Planning; Culture; Design; Interior Design; Sustainable Living; Technology

Send: Pitch
How to send: Submittable

Magazine examining contemporary life through design: architecture, interior design, product design, graphic design, crafts, planning, and preservation.

M317 mg Magazine

Magazine
6520 Platt Ave., Suite 399, West Hills, CA 91307
United States
Tel: +1 (310) 421-1860

https://mgretailer.com

Magazine Publisher: Inc Media

PROFESSIONAL > **Nonfiction**
Articles: Business; Cannabis; Current Affairs; Farming; Health; Hemp; How To; Legal; Politics; Science; Technology
Interviews: Business; Cannabis; Current Affairs; Farming; Health; Hemp; How To; Legal; Politics; Science; Technology
News: Business; Cannabis; Current Affairs; Farming; Health; Hemp; How To; Legal; Politics; Science; Technology

How to send: Email

The resource professionals in the legal cannabis industry turn to for insight and intel to help them increase revenues and scale their businesses. Each glossy monthly issue is filled with high-concept copy and photographs covering topics including retail design and merchandising; advertising; branding and marketing; law, regulations, and politics; human resources; products, technology, and finance. Issues typically include two features (3,000 words each), an executive profile (3,000 words), a business profile (1,500 words), a finance column, and a retail design feature, all of which are freelance-written. The associated websites provide freelance-written news, business tips, how-tos, data analysis, business profiles, and other material.

M318 MHQ

Magazine
United States

Magazine Publisher: HistoryNet LLC

M319 Michigan Quarterly Review

Magazine
3277 Angell Hall, 435 S. State Street, Ann Arbor, MI 48109-1003
United States
Tel: +1 (734) 764-9265

mqr@umich.edu

https://sites.lsa.umich.edu/mqr/
https://mqr.submittable.com/submit

Fiction in Translation > *Short Fiction*

Fiction > *Short Fiction*

Nonfiction
Articles; *Essays*

Poetry in Translation > *Any Poetic Form*

Poetry > *Any Poetic Form*

Closed to approaches.

An interdisciplinary and international literary journal, combining distinctive voices in poetry, fiction, and nonfiction, as well as works in translation.

Editor: Laurence Goldstein

M320 Mid-American Review

Magazine
Department of English, Bowling Green State University, Bowling Green, OH 43403
United States
Tel: +1 (419) 372-2725

mar@bgsu.edu

https://casit.bgsu.edu/midamericanreview/

Fiction in Translation > *Short Fiction*: Literary

Fiction > *Short Fiction*: Literary

Nonfiction
Essays: General
Reviews: Books

Poetry in Translation > *Any Poetic Form*

Poetry > *Any Poetic Form*

Closed to approaches.

Accepts fiction, poetry, translations, and nonfiction (including personal essays, essays on writing, and short reviews). Submit by post with SASE or through online submission system.

Editor: Michael Czyzniejewski

M321 Midway Journal

Online Magazine
United States

editors@midwayjournal.com

http://midwayjournal.com
https://www.facebook.com/midway.journal
https://twitter.com/MidwayJournal

Fiction > *Short Fiction*

Nonfiction
Essays: General
Interviews: General
Short Nonfiction: Creative Nonfiction

Poetry > *Any Poetic Form*

Send: Full text
How to send: Submittable

Costs: A fee is charged. $2.50 for expedited submissions, available year-round. Free submissions during specific windows only.

Aims to act as a bridge between aesthetics (and coasts), and create an engaging sense of place. Publishes work that aims to complicate and question the boundaries of genre, binary, and perspective. It offers surprises and ways of re-seeing, re-thinking, and re-feeling.

Fiction Editor: Ralph Pennel

Nonfiction Editor: Allie Mariano

Poetry Editors: Mariela Lemus; Paige Riehl

M322 Military History

Magazine
1919 Gallows Road, Ste 400, Vienna, VA 22182
United States

militaryhistory@historynet.com

https://www.historynet.com/magazines/mag-mh

Magazine Publisher: HistoryNet LLC

Nonfiction > *Articles*: Military History

Send: Query
Don't send: Full text
How to send: Email

Magazine of military history. No unsolicited MSS. Send one-page query with details of any previous writing experience. Potential contributors advised to familiarise themselves with the magazine before approaching.

Editor: Michael Robbins

M323 Miniature Wargames

Magazine
United Kingdom

Magazine Publisher: Warners Group Publications

M324 MiniWorld Magazine

Magazine
The Granary, Downs Court, Yalding Hill, Yalding, Kent, ME18 6AL
United Kingdom
Tel: +44 (0) 1959 543747

https://shop.kelsey.co.uk/miniworld-magazine
http://www.facebook.com/miniworldmagazine
https://twitter.com/MagMiniWorld

Magazine Publisher: Kelsey Media

Nonfiction > *Articles*: Mini Cars

Magazine devoted to the mini, including technical advice, tuning, restoration, social history, maintenance, etc.

Editor: Monty Watkins

M325 Mississippi Review

Magazine
118 College Drive #5144, Hattiesburg, Mississippi 39406-0001
United States
Tel: +1 (601) 266-4321

msreview@usm.edu

http://sites.usm.edu/mississippi-review/

Fiction > *Short Fiction*

Nonfiction > *Essays*

Poetry > *Any Poetic Form*

Costs: A fee is charged upon submission. $16 competition entry fee.

Publishes work submitted to competition only. No unsolicited MSS. See website for competition details.

Editor: Frederick Barthelme

Managing Editor: Rie Fortenberry

M326 The Missouri Review

Magazine
453 McReynolds Hall, University of Missouri, Columbia, MO 65211
United States

question@moreview.com

https://www.missourireview.com
https://www.facebook.com/themissourireview
https://twitter.com/missouri_review
https://www.instagram.com/themissourireview/

Fiction > *Short Fiction*

Nonfiction > *Essays*

Poetry > *Any Poetic Form*

Does not want:

Nonfiction > *Essays*: Literary Criticism

Send: Query; Self-Addressed Stamped Envelope (SASE); Full text
How to send: Post; Online submission system

Costs: A fee is charged for online submissions. $4 submission fee for online submissions.

Publishes poetry, fiction, and essays of general interest. No literary criticism. Submit by post with SASE, or via online system. There is a $4 charge for online submissions.

Editor: Speer Morgan

M327 Modern Poetry in Translation

Magazine
United Kingdom

editor@mptmagazine.com

http://modernpoetryintranslation.com
https://twitter.com/MPTmagazine
https://www.instagram.com/modernpoetryintranslation/

Poetry in Translation > *Any Poetic Form*

Send: Full text
How to send: Submittable

Respected poetry series originally founded by prominent poets in the sixties. New Series continues their editorial policy: translation of good poets by translators who are often themselves poets, fluent in the foreign language, and sometimes working with the original poet. Publishes translations into English only. No original English language poetry. Send submissions via online submission system.

M328 Monomyth

Magazine
Atlantean Publishing, 4 Pierrot Steps, 71 Kursaal Way, Southend-on-Sea, Essex, SS1 2UY
United Kingdom

atlanteanpublishing@hotmail.com

https://atlanteanpublishing.fandom.com/wiki/Monomyth
https://atlanteanpublishing.wordpress.com/guidelines/

Book Publisher / Magazine Publisher: Atlantean Publishing (**P056**)

Fiction > *Short Fiction*

Poetry > *Any Poetic Form*

Send: Full text; Self-Addressed Stamped Envelope (SASE)
How to send: Email; Post

Features mostly short fiction, covering a wide variety of genres but often quirky, offbeat or fantastical. Send submissions by email or by post with SAE / email address for response. See website for full guidelines.

Editor: David-John Tyrer

M329 The Moth

Magazine
Ardan Grange, Milltown, Belturbet, Co. Cavan
Ireland
Tel: 353 (0) 87 2657251

submissions@themothmagazine.com

https://www.themothmagazine.com

Fiction > *Short Fiction*: Literary

Poetry > *Any Poetic Form*

Send: Full text
How to send: Email; Post

Submit up to six poems or up to two short stories by post or by email. Accepts fiction submissions between September and April only. Poetry submissions are open all year. See website for full submission guidelines.

Editor: Rebecca O'Connor

M330 Motor Boat & Yachting

Magazine
United Kingdom

mby@futurenet.com

https://www.mby.com
https://www.youtube.com/user/ybwtv
https://www.facebook.com/motorboatandyachting
https://twitter.com/mbymagazine
https://www.instagram.com/motorboat_and_yachting/

Magazine Publisher: Future

Nonfiction > *Articles*
Motor Boats; Yachts

Magazine publishing news and features related to motor boats and motor cruising.

Editor: Hugo Andreae

M331 Motorcaravan Motorhome Monthly (MMM)

Magazine
Warners Group Publications, The Maltings, West Street, Bourne, LINCS, PE10 9PH
United Kingdom

https://www.outandaboutlive.co.uk/motorhomes

Magazine Publisher: Warners Group Publications

Nonfiction > *Articles*
Motorhomes; Travel

Publishes articles on motorhome travel.

Editor: Mike & Jane Jago

Managing Editor: Daniel Atwood

M332 Mountain Living

Magazine
United States

https://www.mountainliving.com
https://www.facebook.com/mountainlivingmag
https://www.instagram.com/mountainlivingmag/
https://www.pinterest.com/mtnlivingmag/

Nonfiction > *Articles*
Architecture; Interior Design; Luxury Lifestyle; Mountain Lifestyle

Send: Query
How to send: Email

Magazine featuring mountain residences, from luxurious high-country retreats to charming guest cabins, with styles that range from traditional to contemporary. Submit via email and include a brief description of the home with size, location and any distinctive details.

Editor: Irene Rawlings, Editor in Chief

Editor-in-Chief: Darla Worden

M333 Moving Worlds: A Journal of Transcultural Writings

Magazine
School of English, University of Leeds, Leeds, LS2 9JT
United Kingdom
Tel: +44 (0) 1133 434792
Fax: +44 (0) 1133 434774

mworlds@leeds.ac.uk

http://www.movingworlds.net
https://twitter.com/Moving_Worlds

ACADEMIC > **Nonfiction** > *Essays*
Culture; Literary Criticism; Literature; Multicultural

ADULT
Fiction in Translation > *Short Fiction*
General, and in particular: Experimental

Fiction > *Short Fiction*
General, and in particular: Experimental

Poetry in Translation > *Any Poetic Form*
General, and in particular: Experimental

Poetry > *Any Poetic Form*
General, and in particular: Experimental

Biannual international magazine for creative work as well as criticism, literary as well as visual texts, writing in scholarly as well as more personal modes, in English and translations into English. It is open to experimentation, and represents work of different kinds and from different cultural traditions. Its central concern is the transcultural.

Editors: Shirley Chew; Stuart Murray

M334 Mslexia

Magazine
PO Box 656, Newcastle upon Tyne, NE99 1PZ
United Kingdom
Tel: +44 (0) 1912 048860

postbag@mslexia.co.uk

https://mslexia.co.uk

Fiction > *Short Fiction*

Nonfiction
Articles: Creative Writing
Essays: Creative Writing; Memoir; Personal Essays
Interviews: Creative Writing

Poetry > *Any Poetic Form*

Send: Full text
How to send: Online submission system; Post

By women, for women who write, who want to write, who teach creative writing or who have an interest in women's literature and creativity. Publishes short stories, flash fiction, poetry, memoir and life writing, articles, and interviews.

M335 Muse

Magazine
United States

Magazine Publisher: Cricket Media, Inc.

M336 My Weekly

Magazine
D C Thomson & Co Ltd, My Weekly, 2 Albert Square, Dundee, DD1 1DD
United Kingdom
Tel: +44 (0) 1382 223131

sjohnstone@dctmedia.co.uk
srodger@dctmedia.co.uk
swatson@dctmedia.co.uk

https://www.myweekly.co.uk/
https://www.facebook.com/My-Weekly-199671216711852/
http://twitter.com/My_Weekly
https://www.instagram.com/my_weekly_magazine/

Newspaper Publisher / Magazine Publisher: DC Thomson Media

Fiction > *Short Fiction*

Nonfiction > *Articles*
Beauty; Cookery; Crafts; Fashion; Films; Food and Drink; Gardening; Health; Lifestyle; Personal Finance; Real Life Stories; TV; Travel; Women's Interests

Weekly women's magazine aged at the over-50s, publishing a mix of lifestyle features, true life stories, and fiction.

Editor: S. Johnstone

M337 Mystery Magazine

Magazine
United States

https://www.mysteryweekly.com
https://www.facebook.com/MysteryWeekly
https://twitter.com/MysteryWeekly
https://www.instagram.com/mystery_magazine/
https://www.linkedin.com/in/mystery-magazine-8559811 0a/

Fiction > *Short Fiction*: Mystery

Send: Full text
How to send: Online submission system

Submit mysteries between 2,500 and 7,500 words through online submission system available on website. No simultaneous or multiple submissions.

M338 Mythaxis Review

Online Magazine; Print Magazine
United States

https://mythaxis.com
https://www.youtube.com/channel/UC4LGvC_n_Fk7jLmoU-KgRag
https://twitter.com/mythaxisreview
https://www.instagram.com/mythaxisreview
https://www.facebook.com/mythaxisreview
https://www.linkedin.com/company/mythaxis-review
https://www.reddit.com/user/Mythaxis/
https://www.crunchbase.com/organization/mythaxis-review

Nonfiction
Articles: Arts; Books; Films; Music; Poetry as a Subject; Technology
Interviews: Arts; Technology

A cutting edge publication that seeks to present art and artists at the axis of curiosity and the energetic core of the creative act. Looks at books, movies, music and more.

M339 Nanoism

Online Magazine
United States

editor@nanoism.net

http://nanoism.net

Fiction > *Short Fiction*: Literary

Send: Full text
How to send: In the body of an email
How not to send: Email attachment

Twitterzine publishing short stories up to 140 characters. Also accepts serials of up to 3-7 parts, though each must be able to stand on its own. Submit no more than once per week, by email.

M340 Narrow Gauge World

Magazine
United Kingdom

Magazine Publisher: Warners Group Publications

M341 NB Magazine

Magazine
Studio 10, Glove Factory Studios, Brook Lane, Holt, Wiltshire, BA14 6RL
United Kingdom

editor@nbmagazine.co.uk

https://nbmagazine.co.uk

Nonfiction > *Articles*: Book Publishing

Magazine and online platform for book lovers, book clubs and all round bibliophiles. Publishes articles and features on books and the book trade, as well as extracts from books.

M342 Neon

Magazine
United Kingdom

subs@neonmagazine.co.uk

https://www.neonmagazine.co.uk

Fiction > *Short Fiction*
Dark; Literary; Speculative; Surreal

Poetry
Any Poetic Form: Dark; Literary; Surreal
Graphic Poems: Dark; Literary; Surreal

Send: Full text
How to send: Email

Quarterly online magazine publishing stylised poetry and prose, particularly the new, experimental, and strange. Welcomes genre fiction. Dark material preferred over humour; free verse preferred over rhyme. Send work pasted into the body of an email with a biographical note and the word "Submission" in the subject line.

Editor: Krishan Coupland

M343 Nerve Cowboy

Magazine
PO Box 4973, Austin, Texas 78765
United States

http://www.nervecowboy.com/
https://www.facebook.com/Nerve-Cowboy-240567569317649

Fiction > *Short Fiction*

Nonfiction > *Reviews*: Live Music

Poetry > *Any Poetic Form*

Send: Full text; Self-Addressed Stamped Envelope (SASE)
How to send: Post
How not to send: Email

Send poems, and stories up to five pages in length, with SASE. Contributors are encouraged to have acquired and familiarised themselves with the magazine before submitting. Not a cowboy-themed magazine. No simultaneous submissions or submissions by email.

Editors: Jerry Hagins; Joseph Shields; Elissa Yeates

M344 The New Accelerator

Online Magazine
United Kingdom

https://newaccelerator.substack.com

Fiction > *Short Fiction*: Science Fiction

Digital science fiction short story anthology. The aim of the anthology is to bring cutting-edge fiction to an eager and discerning global science fiction audience.

Editor: Andy Coughlan and David Winstanley

M345 New England Review

Magazine
Middlebury College, Middlebury, VT 05753
United States
Tel: +1 (802) 443-5075

nereview@middlebury.edu

https://www.nereview.com
https://newenglandreview.submittable.com/submit
https://www.facebook.com/NewEnglandReviewMiddlebury/
https://twitter.com/nerweb

Fiction
Novel Excerpts; *Novellas*; *Short Fiction*
Nonfiction in Translation > *Essays*

Nonfiction
Essays: Personal Essays
Short Nonfiction: Arts; Cultural Criticism; Environment; Films; Literary Criticism; Travel
Poetry > *Any Poetic Form*

Scripts > *Theatre Scripts*: Drama

How to send: Submittable; Post

Costs: A fee is charged for online submissions. $3 per submission.

Welcomes submissions in fiction, poetry, nonfiction, drama, and translation. Different submission windows for different categories of work. See website for details.

Editor: Stephen Donadio

M346 New Orleans Review

Online Magazine
United States

noreview@loyno.edu

https://www.neworleansreview.org
https://www.facebook.com/neworleans.review/
https://twitter.com/NOReview

Fiction > *Short Fiction*: Literary

Nonfiction
Reviews: Literature
Short Nonfiction: General

Poetry > *Any Poetic Form*

Send: Full text
How to send: Submittable

Costs: A fee is charged upon submission. $3 per submission.

A journal of contemporary literature and culture. Send one story or piece of nonfiction up to 5,000 words, or up to five poems via online submission system.

Editor: Christopher Chambers

M347 The New Shetlander

Magazine
United Kingdom

vas@shetland.org

https://www.shetland-communities.org.uk/subsites/vas/the-new-shetlander.htm

Fiction > *Short Fiction*
Literary; Shetland

Nonfiction > *Articles*
Arts; Culture; History; Literature; Politics; Shetland

Poetry > *Any Poetic Form*: Shetland

Send: Full text
How to send: Email

Publishes short stories, poetry, and historical articles with a Shetland interest. Contributions and enquiries may be sent by email.

Editors: Laureen Johnson; Brian Smith

M348 New Theatre Quarterly

Magazine
United Kingdom

M.Shevtsova@gold.ac.uk

https://www.cambridge.org/core/journals/new-theatre-quarterly

ACADEMIC > **Nonfiction**
Articles: Theatre
Interviews: Theatre

Send: Full text
How to send: Email

Provides a lively international forum where theatrical scholarship and practice can meet, and where prevailing assumptions can be subjected to vigorous critical questioning. The journal publishes articles, interviews with practitioners, documentation and reference materials covering all aspects of live theatre.

Editors: Maria Shevtsova; Simon Trussler

M349 New Welsh Reader

Magazine
United Kingdom

editor@newwelshreview.com

https://newwelshreview.com/new-welsh-reader

Fiction > *Short Fiction*: Literary

Nonfiction
Essays: General
Short Nonfiction: Creative Nonfiction

Poetry > *Any Poetic Form*

Send: Full text
How to send: Online submission system

Focus is on Welsh writing in English, but has an outlook which is deliberately diverse, encompassing broader UK and international contexts. For feature articles, send 300-word query by email. Submit through online submission system only. Postal submissions will be returned unopened. Full details available on website.

Editor: Gwen Davies

M350 No.1

Magazine
United Kingdom

Newspaper Publisher / Magazine Publisher: DC Thomson Media

M351 The North

Magazine
The Poetry Business, Campo House, 54 Campo Lane, Sheffield, S1 2EG
United Kingdom
Tel: +44 (0) 1144 384074

office@poetrybusiness.co.uk

https://poetrybusiness.co.uk

Poetry > *Any Poetic Form*: Contemporary

Closed to approaches.

Send up to 6 poems with SASE / return postage. We publish the best of contemporary poetry. No "genre" or derivative poetry. Submitters should be aware of, should preferably have read, the magazine before submitting. See our website for notes on submitting poems. No submissions by email. Overseas submissions may be made through online submission system.

Editors: Ann Sansom; Peter Sansom

M352 Nursery World

Magazine
MA Education, St Jude's Church, Dulwich Road, London, SE24 0PB
United Kingdom

https://www.nurseryworld.co.uk

PROFESSIONAL > **Nonfiction** > *Articles*
Childcare; Preschool

Magazine aimed at professionals dealing with the care of children in nurseries, primary schools, childcare, etc.; nannies and foster parents; and those involved with caring for expectant mothers, babies, and young children.

Editor: Karen Faux

Editor-in-Chief: Liz Roberts

M353 The Oakland Arts Review

Magazine
United States

ouartsreview@oakland.edu

https://oar.submittable.com/submit
http://www.facebook.com/oarjournal
https://twitter.com/OARjournal
http://www.instagram.com/oaklandartsreview/

Fiction
Cartoons: Literary
Graphic Novels: Literary
Short Fiction: Literary

Nonfiction
Graphic Nonfiction: Memoir
Short Nonfiction: Creative Nonfiction

Poetry
Experimental Poetry; *Formal Poetry*; *Free Verse*

Scripts
Film Scripts; *Radio Scripts*; *TV Scripts*; *Theatre Scripts*

Send: Full text
How to send: Submittable

Literary journal publishing work by undergraduates around the world. Publishes fiction between 10 and 15 double spaced pages; creative nonfiction between 7 and 10 double spaced pages; comics of high literary quality; screenwriting; and both free verse and formal poetry (submit 3-5 poems). Submit through online submission system via website.

M354 Obsidian: Literature in the African Diaspora

Magazine
Illinois State University, Williams Hall Annex,

Normal, IL 61790
United States

https://obsidianlit.org
https://obsidian.submittable.com/submit

Fiction > *Short Fiction*: African Diaspora

Poetry > *Any Poetic Form*: African Diaspora

Scripts > *Theatre Scripts*: African Diaspora

Send: Full text
How to send: Submittable

Publishes scripts, fiction, and poetry focused on Africa and her Diaspora. See website for submission guidelines and to submit via online submission system.

M355 The Official Jacqueline Wilson Mag

Magazine
United Kingdom

Newspaper Publisher / Magazine Publisher: DC Thomson Media

M356 OK! Magazine

Magazine
One Canada Square, Canary Wharf, London, E14 5AB
United Kingdom
Tel: +44 (0) 20 8612 7000

https://www.ok.co.uk

Magazine Publisher: Reach Magazines Publishing

Nonfiction
Articles: Lifestyle; Women's Interests
Interviews: Celebrity
News: Celebrity

Celebrity magazine, welcoming ideas for features and interviews/pictures of celebrities.

Editor: Charlotte Seligman

Editors-in-Chief: Karen Cross; Caroline Waterston

M357 Old Glory

Magazine
United Kingdom

https://heritagemachines.com
https://www.facebook.com/OldGloryMag/
https://www.kelsey.co.uk/brand/transport-machinery/old-glory/

Magazine Publisher: Kelsey Media

Nonfiction > *Articles*
History; Steam Engines; Steam Power

Publishes articles, features, and news covering industrial and transport heritage in the United Kingdom and overseas, particularly vintage vehicles and the preservation and restoration of steam engines.

Editor: Colin Tyson

M358 On Spec

Magazine
Canada

onspecmag@gmail.com

https://www.onspec.ca

Fiction > *Short Fiction*
Fantasy; Horror; Science Fiction; Speculative

Poetry > *Any Poetic Form*
Fantasy; Horror; Science Fiction; Speculative

Closed to approaches.

Publishes speculative writing of all kinds, but nothing derivative. Try to avoid what you think are trends.

Fiction Editor: Diane L. Walton

Poetry Editor: Barry Hammond

M359 Oor Wullie

Magazine
United Kingdom

Newspaper Publisher / Magazine Publisher: DC Thomson Media

M360 Orbis International Literary Journal

Magazine
17 Greenhow Avenue, West Kirby, Wirral, CH48 5EL
United Kingdom

carolebaldock@hotmail.com

http://www.orbisjournal.com

Fiction in Translation > *Short Fiction*

Fiction > *Short Fiction*

Nonfiction > *Articles*

Poetry in Translation
Any Poetic Form; *Prose Poetry*
Poetry
Any Poetic Form; *Prose Poetry*

Send: Query; Full text; Author bio; Self-Addressed Stamped Envelope (SASE)
How to send: Post; International Email
How not to send: Domestic Email; Email attachment

Send four poems or prose up to 1,000 words by post with SASE. No submissions by email, unless from overseas, in which case two submissions maximum and no attachments.

Editor: Carole Baldock

M361 The Orchid Review

Magazine
United Kingdom

Magazine Publisher: The Royal Horticultural Society (RHS)

M362 Outside

Magazine
United States

https://www.outsideonline.com
https://www.facebook.com/outsidemagazine
https://twitter.com/outsidemagazine
https://www.instagram.com/outsidemagazine

Magazine Publisher: Outside Interactive Inc.

Nonfiction > *Articles*
Environment; Fitness; Outdoor Activities; Sport; Travel

Magazine of the outdoors. Covers travel, sports, gear, and fitness, as well as the personalities, the environment, and the style and culture of the outdoors.

M363 Oxford Poetry

Magazine
c/o Partus Press, Suite 270, 266 Banbury Road, Oxford, OX2 7DL
United Kingdom

editors@oxfordpoetry.co.uk

http://www.oxfordpoetry.co.uk

Book Publisher / Magazine Publisher: Partus Press

Nonfiction
Articles: Literature
Essays: Literature
Interviews: Literature
Reviews: Literature

Poetry in Translation > *Any Poetic Form*

Poetry > *Any Poetic Form*

Closed to approaches.

Costs: A fee is charged upon submission. £3 submission fee.

Publishes poems, interviews, reviews, and essays. Accepts unpublished poems on any theme and of any length during specific biannual submission windows, which are announced on the website. Send up to four poems by email. See website for full details.

M364 Oyez Review

Magazine
United States

oyezreview@gmail.com

https://medium.com/oyez-review/
https://www.facebook.com/OyezReview

Fiction > *Short Fiction*: Literary

Nonfiction > *Short Nonfiction*: Creative Nonfiction

Poetry > *Any Poetic Form*

An award-winning literary magazine published annually. There are no restrictions on style, theme, or subject matter. Though we consider it part of our mission to publish undiscovered writers, we also have a strong tradition of publishing some of today's best writers, including Charles Bukowski, James McManus, Carla Panciera, Sandra Kohler, and Saul Bennett.

Editor: Janet Wondra

M365 The Paddock Review

Magazine
United States

https://paddockreview.com

Types: Poetry
Subjects: Literary
Markets: Adult

Send: Full text

Submit 1-3 poems through online submission system. Accepts previously published poems and simultaneous submissions. Include short bio.

M366 Pain

Magazine
United Kingdom

pain@partuspress.com

https://www.painpoetry.co.uk
https://partus.submittable.com/submit

Book Publisher / Magazine Publisher: Partus Press

Nonfiction
Articles: Literature
Essays: Creative Nonfiction

Poetry > *Any Poetic Form*

Closed to approaches.

Costs: A fee is charged upon submission. £3.00 fee per submission.

Publishes unpublished poems as well as short essays and articles with a literary focus.

M367 Parchment Craft

Magazine
United Kingdom

Magazine Publisher: Warners Group Publications

M368 The Paris Review

Magazine
544 West 27th Street, Floor 3, New York, NY 10001
United States
Tel: +1 (212) 343-1333

queries@theparisreview.org

https://www.theparisreview.org
https://www.facebook.com/parisreview
https://twitter.com/parisreview
http://theparisreview.tumblr.com/

Fiction > *Short Fiction*: Literary

Nonfiction
Interviews; *Short Nonfiction*

Poetry > *Any Poetic Form*

Closed to approaches.

Send submissions through online submission system or by post. All submissions must be in English and previously unpublished, though translations are acceptable if accompanied by copy of the original text. Simultaneous submissions accepted as long as immediate notification is given of acceptance elsewhere.

Executive Editor: Brigid Hughes

M369 Park & Holiday Home Inspiration

Magazine
United Kingdom

Magazine Publisher: Warners Group Publications

M370 Park Home and Holiday Living

Magazine
The Granary, Downs Court, Yalding Hill, Yalding, Kent, ME18 6AL
United Kingdom
Tel: +44 (0) 1959 541444

phhc.ed@kelsey.co.uk

https://www.parkhomemagazine.co.uk

Magazine Publisher: Kelsey Media

Nonfiction > *Articles*
Caravans; Holiday Homes; Lifestyle

Magazine for those owning holiday caravans or living in residential park homes.

Editor: Alex Melvin

M371 Peace and Freedom

Magazine
United Kingdom

p_rance@yahoo.co.uk

http://pandf.booksmusicfilmstv.com/

Fiction > *Short Fiction*
Environment; Social Issues

Nonfiction
Articles: Environment; Social Issues
Essays: Environment; Social Issues

Poetry > *Any Poetic Form*
Environment; Social Issues

Magazine publishing poetry, fiction, and articles, with an emphasis on social, humanitarian and environmental issues. Also publishes interviews of animal welfare/environmental/human rights campaigners, writers, poets, artists, film, music and TV personalities, up to 1,000 words. Reviews of books / records / events etc. up to 50 words also considered. Email submissions accepted for reviews, short stories, and interviews ONLY.

Editor: Paul Rance

M372 Pensacola Magazine

Magazine
21 E. Garden St., Ste. 205, Pensacola, FL 32502
United States
Tel: +1 (850) 433-1166
Fax: +1 (850) 435-9174

info@ballingerpublishing.com

http://www.pensacolamagazine.com
https://www.facebook.com/pensacolamagazine
https://www.instagram.com/pensacola_magazine/

Magazine Publisher: Ballinger Publishing

Nonfiction > *Articles*
Business; Culture; Entertainment; Fashion; Health; Lifestyle; Pensacola

Publishes articles and stories on business, entertainment, culture, fashion, healthcare, lifestyle and other topics important to the Northwest Florida community.

Editor: Shannon Lord

M373 People's Friend Pocket Novels

Magazine
DC Thomson & Co. Ltd, 2 Albert Square, Dundee, DD1 9QJ
United Kingdom

tsteel@dctmedia.co.uk

https://www.thepeoplesfriend.co.uk

Magazine: The People's Friend (**M374**)

Fiction > *Novellas*
Family Saga; Romance

Send: Query; Synopsis; Writing sample
How to send: Email; Post

Publishes romance and family fiction between 37,000 and 39,000 words, aimed at adults aged over 30. Send query by post or by email (preferred) with synopsis and first two chapters in first instance. See website for more information.

Editor: Tracey Steel

M374 The People's Friend

Magazine
DC Thomson & Co. Ltd., 2 Albert Square, Dundee, DD1 9QJ
United Kingdom

peoplesfriend@dcthomson.co.uk

http://www.thepeoplesfriend.co.uk

Newspaper Publisher / Magazine Publisher: DC Thomson Media

Fiction > *Short Fiction*: Women's Fiction

Nonfiction > *Nonfiction Books*
Cookery; Crafts; Lifestyle; Women's Interests

Publishes complete short stories (1,200-3,000 words (4,000 for specials)) and serials, focusing on character development rather than complex plots, plus 10,000-word crime thrillers. Also considers nonfiction from nature to nostalgia and from holidays to hobbies, and poetry. Guidelines available on website.

Magazine: People's Friend Pocket Novels (**M373**)

M375 Petroleum Geoscience

Magazine
United Kingdom

Book Publisher / Magazine Publisher: The Geological Society Publishing House (**P288**)

M376 The Philosopher

Online Magazine
United Kingdom

http://www.the-philosopher.co.uk

Nonfiction > *Articles*: Philosophy

Publishes philosophical articles up to 3,000 words. Articles are considered without discrimination as to subject matter or author. The only criterion is that it must be philosophical in method. See website for submission guidelines.

Editor: Martin Cohen

M377 The Photographer

Magazine
The British Institute of Professional Photography, The Artistry House, 16 Winckley Square, Preston, PR1 3JJ
United Kingdom
Tel: +44 (0) 1772 367968

admin@bipp.com

https://www.bipp.com

PROFESSIONAL > **Nonfiction** > *Articles*: P hotography

Photography magazine for professional photographers.

M378 Pianist

Magazine
United Kingdom

Magazine Publisher: Warners Group Publications

M379 Pilot

Magazine
United Kingdom

https://www.pilotweb.aero

Magazine Publisher: Kelsey Media

ADULT > **Nonfiction** > *Articles*
Air Travel; Piloting

PROFESSIONAL > **Nonfiction** > *Articles*
Air Travel; Piloting

Send: Full text
How to send: Email

Aimed at private, commercial and would-be flyers, including enthusiasts.

Editors: Nick Bloom; Philip Whiteman

M380 Planet

Magazine
PO Box 44, Aberystwyth, Ceredigion, SY23 3ZZ
United Kingdom
Tel: +44 (0) 1970 611255

submissions@planetmagazine.org.uk

http://www.planetmagazine.org.uk

Types: Fiction; Nonfiction; Poetry
Formats: Articles; Reviews; Short Fiction; Theatre Scripts
Subjects: Arts; Current Affairs; Literary; Literature; Music; Politics
Markets: Adult

Closed to approaches.

Publishes mostly commissioned material, but will accept ideas for articles and reviews, and unsolicited submissions of fiction and poetry. Submit one piece of short fiction between 1,500 and 2,500 words, or 4-6 poems at a time. A range of styles and themes are accepted, but postal submissions will not be considered unless adequate return postage is provided. If you have an idea for a relevant article send a query with brief synopsis.

Editor: Emily Trahair

M381 The Plant Review

Magazine
United Kingdom

Magazine Publisher: The Royal Horticultural Society (RHS)

M382 Platinum Magazine

Magazine
United Kingdom

Newspaper Publisher / Magazine Publisher: DC Thomson Media

M383 Pleiades

Magazine
Department of English, Martin 336, University of Central Missouri, 415 E. Clark St., Warrensburg, MO 64093
United States
Tel: +1 (660) 543-4268

pleiadespoetryeditor@gmail.com
pleiadesfictioninquiries@gmail.com
pleiadescnf@gmail.com
pleiadesreviews@gmail.com

https://pleiadesmag.com
https://twitter.com/pleiadesmag
https://www.facebook.com/UCMPleiades
http://websta.me/n/pleiades_magazine
https://www.pinterest.com/pleiadesUCM/

Fiction > *Short Fiction*

Nonfiction
Reviews: Books
Short Nonfiction: Creative Nonfiction

Poetry > *Any Poetic Form*

Send submissions through online submission system during specific windows only.

Editor: Kevin Prufer

M384 Ploughshares

Magazine
Emerson College, 120 Boylston St., Boston, MA 02116-4624
United States

https://www.pshares.org
http://facebook.com/ploughshares
http://www.pinterest.com/pshares
http://twitter.com/pshares
https://instagram.com/psharesjournal/

Fiction > *Short Fiction*

Nonfiction > *Short Nonfiction*

Poetry > *Any Poetic Form*

Send: Self-Addressed Stamped Envelope (SASE); Full text
How to send: Online submission system; Post

Costs: A fee is charged for online submissions. $3 fee for online submissions, except for subscribers, who may submit for free.

Welcomes unsolicited submissions of fiction, poetry, and nonfiction during the regular reading period, which runs from June 1 to January 15. The literary journal is published four times a year: mixed issues of poetry and prose in the Spring and Winter, a prose issue in the summer, and a longform prose issue in the Fall, with two of the four issues per year guest-edited by a different writer of prominence.

Editor: Don Lee

M385 Poetry Ireland Review

Magazine
11 Parnell Square East, Dublin 1, D01 ND60
Ireland
Tel: +353 (0)1 6789815
Fax: +353 (0)1 6789782

pir@poetryireland.ie
info@poetryireland.ie

https://www.poetryireland.ie

Nonfiction
Articles: Poetry as a Subject
Reviews: Poetry as a Subject

Poetry > *Any Poetic Form*

Send: Full text; Proposal
How to send: Post; Submittable

Send up to four poems through online submission system, or by post. Poetry is accepted from around the world, but must be previously unpublished. No sexism or racism. Articles and reviews are generally commissioned, however proposals are welcome. No unsolicited reviews or articles.

Editor: Colette Bryce

M386 The Poetry Review

Magazine
The Poetry Society, 22 Betterton Street, London, WC2H 9BX
United Kingdom
Tel: +44 (0) 20 7420 9880

poetryreview@poetrysociety.org.uk

https://poetrysociety.org.uk/
https://thepoetrysociety.submittable.com/submit

Nonfiction
Essays: Poetry as a Subject
Reviews: Poetry as a Subject

Poetry in Translation > *Any Poetic Form*

Poetry > *Any Poetic Form*

Send: Full text
How to send: Submittable

Costs: A fee is charged upon submission in some cases. Non-members pay £2 to submit.

Describes itself as "one of the liveliest and most influential literary magazines in the world", and has been associated with the rise of the New Generation of British poets – Carol Ann Duffy, Simon Armitage, Glyn Maxwell, Don Paterson... though its scope extends beyond the UK, with special issues focusing on poetries from around the world. Send up to 6 unpublished poems, or literary translations of poems, through online submission system.

M387 Poetry Wales

Magazine
Suite 6, 4 Derwen Road, Bridgend, CF31 1LH
United Kingdom
Tel: +44 (0) 1656 663018

poetrywalessubmissions@gmail.com
info@poetrywales.co.uk
editor@poetrywales.co.uk

https://poetrywales.co.uk
https://poetrywales.submittable.com/submit
http://twitter.com/poetrywales
http://facebook.com/poetrywales
http://instagram.com/poetrywales

Nonfiction
Articles: Poetry as a Subject
Reviews: Books; Poetry as a Subject
Poetry > *Any Poetic Form*

Send: Full text
How to send: Submittable; Post; Email

Publishes poetry, features, and reviews from Wales and beyond. Submit via online submission system, or by post. If online form is not working, use email. Also runs competitions.

Editor: Nia Davies

M388 The Political Quarterly

Magazine
12 Hempland Avenue, York, YO31 1DE
United Kingdom

submissions@politicalquarterly.org.uk

http://www.politicalquarterly.org.uk

Nonfiction > *Articles*: Politics

Send: Full text
How to send: Email

Magazine covering national and international politics. Accepts unsolicited articles.

M389 Popshot Quarterly

Magazine
United Kingdom

submit@popshotpopshot.com

https://www.popshotpopshot.com

Fiction > *Short Fiction*: Literary

Poetry > *Any Poetic Form*

Send: Full text
How to send: Email

Publishes flash fiction, short stories, and poetry on the theme of the current issue (see website). Submit by email.

M390 Prac Crit

Magazine
United Kingdom

editors@praccrit.com

http://www.praccrit.com

Types: Nonfiction
Formats: Essays; Interviews
Subjects: Contemporary; Literary; Literary Criticism
Markets: Adult

Send: Query
Don't send: Full text
How to send: Email

Publishes close analysis of poems; essays; interviews; and reflections from poets. Most articles are commissioned, but will accept proposals for essays or interviews. No direct submissions of poetry.

M391 Practical Boat Owner Magazine

Magazine
United Kingdom
Tel: +44 (0) 3303 906467

pbo@futurenet.com

https://www.pbo.co.uk

Magazine Publisher: Future

Nonfiction > *Articles*: Boats

Cruising boats magazine covering both power and sail. Publishes technical articles on maintenance, restoration, modifications, etc.

M392 Practical Fishkeeping

Magazine
The Maltings, West Street, Bourne, Lincolnshire, PE10 9PH
United Kingdom
Tel: +44 (0) 1778 391194

editorial@practicalfishkeeping.co.uk

https://www.practicalfishkeeping.co.uk
https://www.facebook.com/PFKmag/
https://www.twitter.com/PFKmagazine
https://www.instagram.com/pfkmag/
https://www.youtube.com/channel/UC--fz-Y9Zn6cZ-XKcIBjeGw

Magazine Publisher: Warners Group Publications

Nonfiction > *Articles*: Pet Fish

Publishes practical articles on all aspects of keeping fish.

Editor: Karen Youngs

M393 The Practising Midwife

Magazine
Saturn House, Mercury Rise, Altham Industrial Park, Altham, Lancashire, BB5 5BY
United Kingdom

info@all4maternity.com

https://www.all4maternity.com
https://twitter.com/all4maternity
https://www.facebook.com/all4maternity/

PROFESSIONAL > **Nonfiction**
Articles: Midwifery
News: Midwifery

Publishes accessible, authoritative and readable information for midwives, students and other professionals in the maternity services.

Editor-in-Chief: Alys Einion

Editors: Claire Feeley; Laura Yeates

M394 The Practitioner

Magazine
United Kingdom

editor@thepractitioner.co.uk

https://www.thepractitioner.co.uk

PROFESSIONAL > **Nonfiction**
Articles: Health; Medicine
News: Health; Medicine

Send: Query; Full text
How to send: Email

Monthly magazine for General Practitioners, covering latest clinical issues. Considers ideas for articles and submissions of case reports.

Editor: Corinne Short

M395 Preservation Magazine

Magazine
2600 Virginia Avenue NW, Suite 1100,
Washington, DC 20037
United States
Tel: +1 (202) 588-6013

preservation@savingplaces.org

https://savingplaces.org/preservation-magazine

Nonfiction > *Articles*
History; Travel

Send: Query
How to send: Phone; Email

Magazine publishing material on the preservation of historic buildings and neighbourhoods in the United States.

Editor: Arnold Berke

M396 Pride

Magazine
1 Garrat Lane, London, SW18 4AQ
United Kingdom
Tel: +44 (0) 20 8870 3755

editor@pridemagazine.com

http://pridemagazine.com
http://www.facebook.com/PrideMagazine
http://www.instagram.com/pridemaguk

Nonfiction
Articles: Beauty; Career Development; Entertainment; Fashion; Hairstyles; Health; Lifestyle
News: Ethnic Groups; Social Issues

Magazine aimed at black women. Publishes news, and articles and features on entertainment, hair, beauty, and fashion.

Editor: CJ Cushnie

M397 Proceedings of the Yorkshire Geological Society

Magazine
United Kingdom

Book Publisher / Magazine Publisher: The Geological Society Publishing House (**P288**)

M398 Prole

Magazine
United Kingdom

submissionspoetry@prolebooks.co.uk
submissionsprose@prolebooks.co.uk

https://prolebooks.co.uk
https://facebook.com/Prole-236155444300
https://twitter.com/Prolebooks

Fiction > *Short Fiction*: Literary

Nonfiction > *Short Nonfiction*: Creative Nonfiction

Poetry > *Any Poetic Form*

Send: Full text
How to send: In the body of an email

Publishes accessible literature of high quality, including poetry, short fiction, and creative nonfiction. Seeks to appeal to a wide audience and avoid literary elitism (obscure references and highly stylised structures and forms are unlikely to find favour). No previously published material or simultaneous submissions. Submit one piece of prose or up to five poems (or three longer poems) in the body of an email, with your name, contact details, word count and third person author bio up to 100 words. See website for appropriate email addresses for prose and poetry submissions, and full submission guidelines. No attachments.

M399 Psychic News

Magazine
Unit 2, Griggs Business Centre, West Street,
Coggeshall, Essex, CO6 1NT
United Kingdom
Tel: +44 (0) 1376 563091

pneditorials@gmail.com

https://www.psychicnews.org.uk
https://www.facebook.com/psychicnews/
https://twitter.com/psychicnewsmag

Nonfiction > *Articles*: Spirituality

Magazine of the paranormal, covering ghosts, spiritual healing, psychic research, etc.

Editor: Tony Ortzen

M400 Pushing Out the Boat

Magazine
United Kingdom

info@pushingouttheboat.co.uk

https://www.pushingouttheboat.co.uk

Fiction > *Short Fiction*: Literary

Poetry > *Any Poetic Form*

Scripts > *Theatre Scripts*

How to send: Online submission system

Magazine of prose, poetry and visual arts, based in North-East Scotland. Welcomes work in English, Doric or Scots. Submit via online submission system during open reading periods. See website for details.

M401 Qu Literary Magazine

Magazine
United States

qulitmag@queens.edu

http://www.qulitmag.com

Fiction > *Short Fiction*: Literary

Nonfiction > *Essays*

Poetry > *Any Poetic Form*

Scripts
Film Scripts; *TV Scripts*; *Theatre Scripts*

Send: Full text
How to send: Submittable

Submit prose or poems via online submission system. $2 fee. Does not accept international submissions.

M402 Quail Bell

Magazine
United States

submissions@quailbellmagazine.com

http://www.quailbellmagazine.com

Fiction > *Short Fiction*
Intersectional Feminism; Literary

Nonfiction > *Articles*: Intersectional Feminism

Poetry > *Any Poetic Form*: Intersectional Feminism

Send: Full text
How to send: Email

An intersectional feminist magazine. Send submissions by email. See website for full guidelines.

M403 Quarter After Eight

Magazine
United States

editor@quarterafter eight.org

http://www.quarteraftereight.org

Types: Fiction; Nonfiction; Poetry; Scripts; Translations
Formats: Interviews; Reviews
Subjects: Drama; Experimental
Markets: Adult

Send: Full text

Publishes fiction, poetry, and nonfiction. Submit one story or essay or up to three flash prose pieces or four poems via online submission system. Accepts online submissions between October 15 and April 15 only.

M404 Quarterly Journal of Engineering Geology and Hydrogeology

Magazine
United Kingdom

Book Publisher / Magazine Publisher: The Geological Society Publishing House (**P288**)

M405 Rabble Review

Online Magazine
United States

rabblereview420@gmail.com

https://rabblereview.com
https://www.instagram.com/rabble_review/
https://twitter.com/rabble_review

Fiction > *Short Fiction*

Nonfiction > *Essays*
Creative Nonfiction; Cultural Criticism; Current Affairs; Literature; Politics

Poetry > *Any Poetic Form*

How to send: Online submission system

Unapologetically leftist in politics, we recognize the complete abolition of capitalism, coerced labor, and the State as absolute pre-conditions for human and artistic liberation. We want to capture the working class in its full spectrum, that is, we're committed to solidarity among workers of all races, genders, sexual orientations, abilities, and their intersections. By spreading accessible leftist thought, encouraging direct action, and providing a space for revolutionary aesthetics to develop we hope to do our part in the radicalization and ultimate liberation of the working class.

M406 Rabid Oak

Online Magazine
United States

rabidoak@gmail.com

https://rabidoak.com

Fiction > *Short Fiction*

Nonfiction > *Short Nonfiction*

Poetry > *Any Poetic Form*

Send: Full text; Author bio
How to send: Email

Online literary journal. Send up to five poems or two pieces of fiction or nonfiction (up to 1,000 words) in a Word document attachment.

M407 Race & Class

Magazine
United Kingdom

raceandclass@irr.org.uk

https://journals.sagepub.com/home/rac

Types: Nonfiction
Formats: Articles; Essays
Subjects: Sociology
Markets: Academic

Refereed, ISI-ranked journal on racism and imperialism in the world today.

Editors: Jenny Bourne; Hazel Waters

M408 Racecar Engineering

Magazine
The Chelsea Magazine Company, Jubilee House, 2 Jubilee Place, London, SW3 3TQ
United Kingdom
Tel: +44 (0) 20 7349 3700

editorial@racecarengineering.com

https://www.racecar-engineering.com
https://www.facebook.com/RacecarEngineering/
https://twitter.com/RacecarEngineer

Magazine Publisher: The Chelsea Magazine Company

Nonfiction
Articles: Engineering; Racecars
News: Engineering; Racecars

Publishes news articles and in-depth features on racing cars and related products and technology. No material on road cars or racing drivers.

Editor: Charles Armstrong-Wilson

M409 Racing Post

Magazine
Floor 7, Vivo Building, South Bank Central, 30 Stamford Street, London, SE1 9LS
United Kingdom

help@racingpost.com

https://www.racingpost.com

Nonfiction
Articles: Horse Racing
News: Horse Racing

Daily paper of horse racing, plus some general sport.

M410 The Racket

Magazine
United States

theracketreadingseries@gmail.com

https://theracketsf.com

Fiction > *Short Fiction*

Poetry > *Any Poetic Form*

Send: Full text
How to send: Email

Considers submissions that contain work(s) of poetry and/or prose with a total combined word count of 2,000 words or fewer. See website for full guidelines.

M411 Radar Poetry

Magazine
United States

radarpoetry@gmail.com

https://www.radarpoetry.com

Poetry > *Any Poetic Form*

Closed to approaches.

Costs: A fee is charged upon submission. $3.

Electronic journal, published quarterly. Submit 3-5 original, previously unpublished poems through online submission system. Accepts submissions November 1 to January 1 (free), and March 1 to May 1 ($3) annually.

Editors: Rachel Marie Patterson; Dara-Lyn Shrager

M412 Radio User

Magazine
United Kingdom

https://www.radioenthusiast.co.uk/
https://www.facebook.com/radioenthusiasts/
https://twitter.com/renthusiasts

Magazine Publisher: Warners Group Publications

Nonfiction > *Articles*: Radio Technology

Magazine relating to receiving and listening to radio signals, aimed at radio enthusiasts.

Editors: Elaine Richards; Georg Wiessala

M413 Ramsay's

Magazine
United Kingdom

Magazine Publisher: Warners Group Publications

M414 Reach

Magazine
24 Forest Houses, Halwill, Beaworthy, Devon, EX21 5UU
United Kingdom

publishing@indigodreams.co.uk

https://www.indigodreams.co.uk/magazines

Book Publisher: Indigo Dreams Publishing (**P396**)

Poetry > *Any Poetic Form*: Literary

Send: Full text
How to send: Email

Costs: A subscription is required in order to submit.

Currently accepting submissions from subscribers only.

Publishes quality poetry from both experienced and new poets. Formal or free verse, haiku... everything is considered. Submit up to two poems by email. No simultaneous submissions.

Editor: Ronnie Goodyer

M415 The Reader

Magazine
The Mansion House, Calderstones Park, Liverpool, L18 3JB
United Kingdom
Tel: + 44 (0) 1517 292200

https://www.thereader.org.uk
https://www.thereader.org.uk/what-we-do/the-reader-magazine/
https://twitter.com/thereaderorg
https://www.facebook.com/thereaderorg
https://www.instagram.com/thereaderorg/

Nonfiction > *Articles*: Literature

Magazine of charity promoting shared reading through reading aloud groups. No longer publishes original fiction and poetry.

M416 Relevant

Magazine
United States

submissions@relevantmediagroup.com

https://relevantmagazine.com

Types: Nonfiction
Formats: Articles
Subjects: Culture; Lifestyle; Religion
Markets: Adult

Send: Full text
How to send: Email

Christian lifestyle magazine aimed at adults in their 20s and 30s, covering faith, culture, and "intentional living".

M417 Resurgence & Ecologist

Magazine
The Resurgence Centre, Fore Street, Hartland, Bideford, Devon, EX39 6AB
United Kingdom

brendan@theecologist.org

https://theecologist.org

Nonfiction
Articles: Environment
News: Environment

Aims to foster a greater connection to nature in order to enhance personal wellbeing, support resilient communities and inform social change towards regenerative societies that enrich rather than deplete our natural environment.

Editor: Zac Goldsmith

M418 Right Start Online

Online Magazine
United Kingdom

info@rightstartonline.co.uk

https://www.rightstartonline.co.uk

Nonfiction > *Articles*: Parenting

Magazine covering pre-school children's health, lifestyle, development, education, etc. Contact the editor by email to discuss editorial opportunities.

Editor: Lynette Lowthian

M419 Riptide

Magazine
The Department of English, The University of Exeter, Queen's Building, Queen's Drive, Exeter, EX4 6QH
United Kingdom

editors@riptidejournal.co.uk

http://www.riptidejournal.co.uk
http://twitter.com/#!/RiptideJournal
http://www.facebook.com/pages/Riptide-Journal/161555683865263

Fiction > *Short Fiction*: Literary

Poetry > *Any Poetic Form*

Closed to approaches.

Bi-annual anthology of new short fiction and poetry by both established and emerging writers. Send one unpublished original story up to 5,000 words or up to five poems up to 40 lines each, by post or as a Word file email attachment.

M420 Rising Innovator

Online Magazine
United States

editorial@risinginnovator.com

https://www.risinginnovator.com
https://docs.google.com/document/d/1_YIzJeFywByFcqOfNEod86dNiAR1MnTQbtSUXERqDn4/edit
https://facebook.com/risinginnovator/
https://www.linkedin.com/company/rising-innovator
https://www.instagram.com/risinginnovator/
https://twitter.com/risinginnovate
https://pinterest.com/risinginnovator

ADULT > **Nonfiction** > *Articles*
Business; Entrepreneurship

CHILDREN'S > **Nonfiction** > *Articles*
Business; Entrepreneurship

PROFESSIONAL > **Nonfiction** > *Articles*
Business; Education; Entrepreneurship

Send: Pitch
How to send: Email; Online contact form

A web-only publication to support entrepreneurship in children. We have three basic targets: children aged 8 to 18, their parents, and any school staff that teach entrepreneurship. We offer news, profiles, guides, advice, and any articles of interest to our audience. We also offer a few free online tools as well, such as a quiz that helps children select a business idea.

Because of our different targets, sometimes we solicit the same content to be written for two different audiences. We keep content differentiated on our website. If you have further questions then please refer to the guidelines above or email us.

M421 River Styx

Magazine
3301 Washington Ave, Suite 2C, St. Louis, MO 63103
United States

ManagingEditor@riverstyx.org

http://www.riverstyx.org
https://twitter.com/riverstyxmag/
https://www.facebook.com/RiverStyxLiteraryMagazine/
https://www.linkedin.com/company/river-styx/
https://www.instagram.com/riverstyxmag/

Fiction > *Short Fiction*

Nonfiction > *Essays*

Poetry > *Any Poetic Form*

Scripts > *Theatre Scripts*

How to send: Submittable; Post
How not to send: Email

Costs: A fee is charged for online submissions; Offers services that writers have to pay for. $3 submission fee for online submissions. Offers critiquing services.

A multicultural magazine of poetry, short fiction, essays, short plays, and art. Seeks to publish work that is striking in its originality, energy, and craft, from both new and established writers.

Editor: Richard Newman

M422 Riverbed Review

Online Magazine
Ireland

riverbedreview@gmail.com

https://riverbedreview.wordpress.com
https://www.instagram.com/riverbedreview/
https://twitter.com/RiverbedReview

Fiction > *Short Fiction*
Literary; Rivers

Poetry > *Any Poetic Form*: Rivers

Closed to approaches.

Publishes original and unpublished stories and poems that are set around (or are about) a river — fictional or otherwise. Submissions are accepted from March 16 to May 16; and October 16 to December 16.

M423 Rugby World

Magazine
Unit 415, Winnersh Triangle, Eskdale Road, Winnersh, RG41 5TU
United Kingdom
Tel: +44 (0) 330 390 6479

sarah.mockford@futurenet.com

https://www.rugbyworld.com
https://www.facebook.com/rugbyworldmagazine
https://www.youtube.com/user/rugbyworld08
https://twitter.com/rugbyworldmag

Magazine Publisher: Future

Nonfiction
Articles: Rugby
News: Rugby

Send: Query; Author bio; Synopsis

Magazine publishing news and articles related to rugby. Send idea with coverline, headline, and 50-word synopsis, along with brief resume of your experience.

Editor: Sarah Mockford

M424 Rural Builder

Magazine
Shield Wall Media LLC, PO Box 255, Iola, WI

54945
United States

https://ruralbuildermagazine.com

PROFESSIONAL > **Nonfiction**
Articles: Architecture; Building / Construction; Design; How To
News: Architecture; Building / Construction; Design; How To

Magazine for builders and suppliers of primarily low-rise agricultural and small retail and municipal structures in cities with populations under 250,000.

Editor: Karen Knapstein

M425 Sable

Online Magazine
SAKS Publications, PO Box 33504, London, E9 7YE
United Kingdom

editorial@sablelitmag.org
micro@sablelitmag.org

http://www.sablelitmag.org
https://www.facebook.com/SABLELitmag.org
https://twitter.com/SABLELitMag

Fiction > *Short Fiction*

Nonfiction > *Reviews*

Send: Full text
How to send: Email

A showcase of new creative work by writers of colour. Publishes reviews and flash fiction up to 600 words.

M426 Saddlebag Dispatches

Magazine
United States

submissions@saddlebagdispatches.com

https://saddlebagdispatches.com

Types: Fiction; Nonfiction; Poetry
Formats: Articles; Short Fiction
Subjects: Westerns
Markets: Adult

Send: Full text
How to send: Email

Publishes fiction, nonfiction, and poetry about the American West. Looks for themes of open country, unforgiving nature, struggles to survive and settle the land, freedom from authority, cooperation with fellow adventurers, and other experiences that human beings encounter on the frontier. Send submissions by email. See website for full guidelines.

M427 SAIL Magazine

Magazine
23a Glendale Street, Salem, MA 01970
United States
Tel: +1 (860) 767-3200
Fax: +1 (860) 767-1048

sailmail@sailmagazine.com

https://www.sailmagazine.com

Types: Nonfiction
Formats: Articles
Subjects: Leisure; Sport; Travel
Markets: Adult

Sailing magazine covering boats, DIY, cruising, racing, equipment, etc.

Editor: Adam Cort

M428 Sailing Today

Magazine
The Chelsea Magazine Company, Jubilee House, 2 Jubilee Place, London, SW3 3QW
United Kingdom
Tel: +44 (0) 20 7349 3700

editor@sailingtoday.co.uk

https://www.sailingtoday.co.uk
https://www.facebook.com/sailingtoday/
https://twitter.com/SailingTodayMag
https://www.youtube.com/channel/UCah1Wlfp86HD0tpbhW1LP1Q

Nonfiction > *Articles*: Sailing

Practical magazine for cruising sailors. Offers a wealth of practical advice and a dynamic mix of in-depth boat, gear and equipment news.

Editor: Rodger Witt

M429 Sainsbury's Magazine

Magazine
United Kingdom

feedback@sainsburysmagazine.co.uk
editor@seven.co.uk

https://www.sainsburysmagazine.co.uk
https://www.instagram.com/sainsburysmag/
https://www.pinterest.com/sainsburysmag/
https://twitter.com/sainsburysmag
https://www.facebook.com/sainsburys/

Magazine Publisher: Seven Publishing

Nonfiction > *Articles*
Cookery; Food; Lifestyle; Recipes

Focuses mainly on food and cookery.

Editor: Sue Robinson

M430 Sarasvati

Magazine
24 Forest Houses, Halwill, Beaworthy, Devon, EX21 5UU
United Kingdom

dawnidp@indigodreams.co.uk

https://www.indigodreams.co.uk/magazines

Book Publisher: Indigo Dreams Publishing (**P396**)

Fiction > *Short Fiction*

Poetry > *Any Poetic Form*

How to send: Email

Showcases poetry and prose. Each contributor will have three to four A5 pages available to their work. Submit up to four poems, or prose up to 1,000 words.

Editor: Dawn Bauling

M431 Scintilla

Magazine
United Kingdom

poetry@vaughanassociation.org

http://www.vaughanassociation.org

Fiction > *Short Fiction*
Contemporary; Metaphysical

Nonfiction > *Essays*
17th Century; Literature; Metaphysical

Poetry > *Any Poetic Form*
Contemporary; Metaphysical

Send: Full text
How to send: Email attachment

An international, peer-reviewed journal of literary criticism, prose, and new poetry in the metaphysical tradition.

Editor: Dr. Kevin Mills

General Editor: Joseph Sterrett

Poetry Editor: Damian Walford Davies

Prose Editor: Erik Ankerberg

M432 Scottish Caravans & Motorhomes

Magazine
United Kingdom

Newspaper Publisher / Magazine Publisher: DC Thomson Media

M433 The Scottish Farmer

Magazine
200 Renfield St, Glasgow, G2 3QB
United Kingdom

https://www.thescottishfarmer.co.uk
https://www.facebook.com/scottishfarmer
https://twitter.com/scottishfarmer
https://www.instagram.com/scottishfarmernewspaper/
https://www.linkedin.com/company/17949188

Magazine Publisher: Newsquest Media Group

PROFESSIONAL > **Nonfiction**
Articles: Farming; Scotland
News: Farming; Scotland

Agricultural magazine publishing news and features on political, personal, and technological developments in farming, as well as rural and craft items. Approach with ideas by email or fax.

Editors: Alasdair Fletcher; Deputy Editor: Ken Fletcher

M434 Scottish Field

Magazine
Fettes Park, 496 Ferry Road, Edinburgh, EH5 2DL
United Kingdom
Tel: +44 (0) 1315 511000
Fax: +44 (0) 1315 517901

editor@scottishfield.co.uk

https://www.scottishfield.co.uk
https://www.facebook.com/scottishfield
http://www.twitter.com/scottishfield

Nonfiction > *Articles*
Beauty; Culture; Fashion; Food and Drink; Gardening; Interior Design; Lifestyle; Outdoor Activities; Scotland; Travel

Lifestyle magazine publishing articles and features of general Scottish interest.

Editors: Richard Bath; Claire Grant

M435 Scottish Journal of Geology

Magazine
United Kingdom

Book Publisher / Magazine Publisher: The Geological Society Publishing House (**P288**)

M436 Scottish Wedding

Magazine
United Kingdom

Newspaper Publisher / Magazine Publisher: DC Thomson Media

M437 Scout Life

Magazine
1325 West Walnut Hill Lane, PO Box 152079, Irving, TX 75015-2079
United States
Tel: +1 (866) 584-6589

https://scoutlife.org
https://facebook.com/scoutlifemag
https://twitter.com/scoutlifemag
https://www.instagram.com/boyslifemagazine/
https://www.youtube.com/c/boyslife
https://www.pinterest.com/ScoutLifeMag/

CHILDREN'S > **Nonfiction** > *Articles*
Comedy / Humour; Games; Hobbies; Leisure; Outdoor Activities

Magazine aimed at young people aged between 6 and 18. Includes games, jokes, contests, giveaways, and articles on hobbies and outdoor activities.

M438 Screen International

Magazine
Zetland House, 5-25 Scrutton Street, London, EC2A 4HJ
United Kingdom
Tel: +44 (0) 20 8102 0900

info@mbi.london

https://www.screendaily.com
https://www.facebook.com/ScreenDaily/
https://twitter.com/screendaily
https://www.linkedin.com/company-beta/2298039/
https://www.youtube.com/channel/UCKV7nCATTd4LFbD93ScBUoA
https://www.instagram.com/screendaily/?hl=en

Magazine Publisher: Media Business Insights (MBI)

PROFESSIONAL > **Nonfiction** > *Articles*
Cinemas / Movie Theaters; Film Industry; Films; TV

International trade paper for the film and television industries.

Editors: Leo Barraclough; Matt Mueller

M439 Scribble

Magazine
14 The Park, Stow on the Wold, Cheltenham, Glos., GL54 1DX
United Kingdom
Tel: +44 (0) 1451 831053

enquiries@parkpublications.co.uk

http://www.parkpublications.co.uk/scribble.html

Magazine Publisher: Park Publications

Fiction > *Short Fiction*

Send: Full text
How to send: Email; Post

Costs: A fee is charged upon submission. £3. Free for subscribers.

Accepts short stories on any subject from new and experienced writers. Each quarter prizes of £75, £25, and £15 will be awarded for the best three stories in the edition. These competitions are free to annual subscribers, who also have the option to submit by email. See website for further details.

Editor: David Howarth

M440 Scribbler Arts and Literary Magazine

Magazine
United States

bookwormpublishinghouse@gmail.com

http://www.scribblerliterarymagazine.com

CHILDREN'S
Fiction > *Short Fiction*
Nonfiction > *Essays*
Poetry > *Any Poetic Form*
Scripts > *Theatre Scripts*

YOUNG ADULT
Fiction > *Short Fiction*
Nonfiction > *Essays*
Poetry > *Any Poetic Form*
Scripts > *Theatre Scripts*

Send: Full text
How to send: Online submission system; Email

Magazine aimed at children and young adults, publishing original work by children aged 7-13. Submit up to 5 poems or up to 3,000 words of prose.

M441 The Scribbler

Magazine
11 Northgate, Peebles, EH45 8RX
United Kingdom
Tel: +44 (0) 7522 934770

greyladiesOCB@gmail.com

http://www.thescribblerreview.co.uk

Fiction > *Short Fiction*

Nonfiction > *Reviews*: Literature

Each issue contains reviews of much-loved and less well-known fiction for women and children, and a short story.

M442 Sea Breezes

Magazine
The Office, Strenaby Farm, Lonan Church Road, Laxey, Isle of Man, IM4 7JX
United Kingdom
Tel: +44 (1624) 863672

sb.enquiries@seabreezes.co.im

https://seabreezes.co.im
https://twitter.com/seabreezesmag
https://www.facebook.com/seabreezesmagazine/

PROFESSIONAL > **Nonfiction** > *Articles*: Shipping

Monthly magazine devoted to the worldwide shipping industry.

Editor: Captain Andrew C. Douglas

M443 Second Factory

Print Magazine
United States

https://uglyducklingpresse.org/about/submissions/
https://udp.submittable.com/submit

Book Publisher: Ugly Duckling Presse (**P788**)

Fiction > *Short Fiction*
General, and in particular: Experimental

Nonfiction > *Short Nonfiction*
General, and in particular: Experimental

Poetry > *Any Poetic Form*

Closed to approaches.

Publishes mainly poetry. Fiction and nonfiction will have a better chance if it is fairly short (more than 4 pages per contributor are not usually published) and if it has a fairly experimental and/or playful nature. 'Traditional' fiction and prose submissions are not as likely to be accepted, but open to surprises.

M444 Seen and Heard

Magazine
United Kingdom

nagalro@nagalro.com

http://www.nagalro.com/seen-and-heard-journal/seen-and-heard.aspx

Types: Nonfiction
Formats: Articles; News
Subjects: Legal
Markets: Academic; Professional

Association magazine for children's guardians, family court advisers and independent social workers who work with children and parents in family court proceedings. Provided free to members. See website for submission guidelines.

Editor: Rodney Noon

M445 Sentinel Literary Quarterly

Magazine
120 Warland Road, London, SE18 2ET
United Kingdom
Tel: +44 (0) 7812 755751

editor@sentinelquarterly.com

https://sentinelquarterly.com
http://www.facebook.com/pages/Sentinel-Literary-Quarterly/99050249348
http://twitter.com/sentinelpoetry

Fiction
Novel Excerpts; *Short Fiction*
Nonfiction
Essays; *Interviews*; *Reviews*
Poetry > *Any Poetic Form*

Scripts > *Theatre Scripts*

Send: Full text
How to send: Email

Magazine publishing poetry on any subject, short stories and excerpts from novels on any theme, academic essays, reviews, and interviews. Submit by email only; send 6 poems up to 60 lines each, or one long poem up to 200 lines with two shorter poems, or one piece of prose. Turnaround in 6 weeks. No simultaneous submissions.

M446 Ships Monthly Magazine

Magazine
Kelsey Media, The Granary, Downs Court, Yalding Hil, Yalding, Kent, ME18 6AL
United Kingdom
Tel: +44 (0) 1959 543747

https://shipsmonthly.com

Magazine Publisher: Kelsey Media

ADULT > **Nonfiction** > *Articles*: Ships

PROFESSIONAL > **Nonfiction** > *Articles*
Shipping; Ships

Magazine aimed at ship enthusiasts and maritime professionals. Publishes news and illustrated articles related to all kinds of ships, including reports on the ferry, cruise, new building and cargo ship scene as well as navies across the world.

Editor: Nicholas Leach

M447 Shooter Literary Magazine

Magazine
United Kingdom

submissions.shooterlitmag@gmail.com

https://shooterlitmag.com

Fiction > *Short Fiction*

Nonfiction
Essays: General
Short Nonfiction: Memoir

Poetry > *Any Poetic Form*

Send: Full text; Author bio
How to send: Email

Publishes literary fiction, poetry, creative nonfiction and memoir relating to specific themes for each issue. See website for current theme and full submission guidelines.

M448 Shoreline of Infinity

Magazine
United Kingdom

editor@shorelineofinfinity.com

https://www.shorelineofinfinity.com
https://shorelineofinfinity.submittable.com/submit
https://www.facebook.com/ShorelineOfInfinity/
https://twitter.com/shoreinf
https://www.youtube.com/channel/UCm2N3L9V2rvnkS5dCRzttCg
https://www.instagram.com/shoreinf/

Fiction > *Short Fiction*
Fantasy; Science Fiction

Poetry > *Any Poetic Form*: Science Fiction

How to send: Submittable

Science Fiction magazine from Scotland. We want stories that explore our unknown future. We want to play around with the big ideas and the little ones. We want writers to tell us stories to inspire us, give us hope, provide some laughs. Or to scare the stuffing out of us. We want good stories: we want to be entertained. We want to read how people cope in our exotic new world, we want to be in their minds, in their bodies, in their souls.

Editor: Noel Chidwick

M449 Shout

Magazine
United Kingdom

Newspaper Publisher / Magazine Publisher: DC Thomson Media

M450 Slime Factory

Magazine
United Kingdom

Newspaper Publisher / Magazine Publisher: DC Thomson Media

M451 Smart Retailer

Magazine
PO Box 5000, N7528 Aanstad Road, Iola, WI 54945-5000
United States
Tel: +1 (715) 445-5000
Fax: +1 (715) 445-4053

danb@jonespublishing.com

http://smart-retailer.com

Types: Nonfiction
Formats: Articles; Interviews; News
Subjects: Business; Finance; How To; Legal
Markets: Professional

Send: Full text
How to send: Email

Trade magazine for independent gift retailers. Send complete ms by email with CV and published clips.

Editor: Dan Brownell

M452 Smithsonian Magazine

Magazine
Capital Gallery, Suite 6001, MRC 513, PO Box 37012, Washington, DC 20013
United States
Tel: +1 (202) 275-2000

smithsonianmagazine@si.edu

http://www.smithsonianmag.com

Magazine Publisher / Book Publisher: Smithsonian Institution (**P719**)

Types: Nonfiction
Formats: Articles
Subjects: Anthropology; Archaeology; Arts; Culture; History; Lifestyle; Nature; Science; Technology
Markets: Adult

Send: Query
Don't send: Full text

Publishes articles on archaeology, arts, different lifestyles, cultures and peoples, nature, science and technology. Submit proposal through online form on website.

M453 Smoke

Magazine
1-27 Bridport Street, Liverpool, L3 5QF
United Kingdom
Tel: +44 (0) 7710 644325

windowsproject@btinternet.com

https://smokemagazine.wordpress.com

Writing Group: The Windows Project

Poetry > *Any Poetic Form*

Send: Full text; Self-Addressed Stamped Envelope (SASE)
How to send: Post

New writing, poetry and graphics by some of the best established names alongside new work from Merseyside, from all over the country and the world.

M454 Sonder Magazine

Print Magazine
Dublin
Ireland

sonderlit@gmail.com

https://sonderlit.com
https://www.instagram.com/sonder_lit/
https://twitter.com/MagazineSonder
https://www.facebook.com/sonderlit
https://www.linkedin.com/company/sonder-magazine/
https://www.youtube.com/channel/UCm3GnFrr2QXkz14LeOe7IHA

Fiction > *Short Fiction*

Nonfiction > *Short Nonfiction*: Creative Nonfiction

Poetry > *Any Poetic Form*

Closed to approaches.

A Dublin-based print journal, focused on the idea of sonder, the self, and others: that existential feeling you get when you're walking down the street or sitting in the pub and are overcome by the realization that everyone you pass is just out there doing their own thing, thinking their own thoughts and living their own lives. Publishes short stories, flash fiction, creative non-fiction and poetry, all based around the individual and how we interact with each other.

M455 South Carolina Review

Magazine
314 Strode Tower, Clemson, SC 29634
United States
Tel: +1 (864) 656-3151

km@clemson.edu

https://www.clemson.edu/caah/sites/south-carolina-review
https://thesouthcarolinareview.submittable.com/submit

Fiction > *Short Fiction*

Nonfiction
Essays: General
Reviews: Books
Short Nonfiction: Creative Nonfiction

Poetry > *Any Poetic Form*

Send: Full text
How to send: Submittable
How not to send: Email

Publishes fiction and poetry primarily, but will also consider creative nonfiction, scholarly essays, and book reviews.

Editor: Wayne Chapman

M456 Southern Humanities Review

Magazine
9088 Haley Center, Auburn University, Auburn, AL 36849
United States
Tel: +1 (334) 844-9088

shr@auburn.edu

http://www.southernhumanitiesreview.com
https://www.facebook.com/southernhumanitiesreview
https://twitter.com/SouthernHReview
https://www.instagram.com/southernhumanitiesreview/
https://www.youtube.com/channel/UCnywOlZbBtEX7OFYMUMSQsg

Fiction > *Short Fiction*

Nonfiction > *Essays*
Creative Nonfiction; Literary Journalism; Literary; Lyric Essays; Memoir; Personal Essays; Travel

Poetry > *Any Poetic Form*

Closed to approaches.

Submissions for all fiction and nonfiction are open from August 24 until November 1 in the fall and from January 15 until March 14 in the spring. Poetry submissions are open from August 24 until September 7 in the fall and from January 15 until March 14 in the spring. Nonfiction submissions are open year-round.

Editors: Anton DiSclafani; Virginia M. Kouidis; Dan Latimer; Rose McLarney

M457 The Southern Review

Magazine
338 Johnston Hall, Louisiana State University, Baton Rouge, LA 70803
United States
Tel: +1 (225) 578-6467
Fax: +1 (225) 578-6461

southernreview@lsu.edu

https://thesouthernreview.org
https://www.facebook.com/lsusouthernreview
https://twitter.com/southern_review
https://soundcloud.com/lsupress_and_tsr

Fiction in Translation > *Short Fiction*

Fiction > *Short Fiction*

Nonfiction in Translation > *Essays*

Nonfiction > *Essays*

Poetry in Translation > *Any Poetic Form*

Poetry > *Any Poetic Form*

Closed to approaches.

Costs: A fee is charged upon submission. $3 per submission.

Strives to discover and promote a diverse array of engaging, relevant, and challenging literature—including fiction, nonfiction, poetry, and translation from literary luminaries as well as the best established and emerging writers.

M458 Southword Journal

Magazine
Frank O'Connor House, 84 Douglas Street, Cork
Ireland
Tel: +353 (0) 21 4322396

info@munsterlit.ie

http://www.munsterlit.ie/Southword%20Journal.html
https://www.facebook.com/Southword.Journal/
https://southword.submittable.com/submit/

Fiction > *Short Fiction*

Poetry > *Any Poetic Form*

Closed to approaches.

Accepts submissions during specific submission windows only. See website for details.

M459 The Sow's Ear

Magazine
United States

sowsearsubmit@gmail.com

http://www.sowsearpoetry.org
https://www.facebook.com/SowsEarPoetryReview?ref=hl
https://twitter.com/SowsEarPR

Poetry > *Any Poetic Form*

Send: Full text
How to send: Post; Email

Submissions of fine poetry in any style and length. Wants work that is carefully crafted, keenly felt, and freshly perceived. Like poems with voice, specificity, delight in language, and a meaning that unfolds.

Art Editor: Kristin Zimet

Editor: Janet Harrison

M460 Spelt Magazine

Magazine
United Kingdom

Speltmagazine@gmail.com

https://speltmagazine.com

Nonfiction > *Short Nonfiction*
Creative Nonfiction; Farming; Rural Living

Poetry > *Any Poetic Form*
Farming; Rural Living

How to send: In the body of an email

Publishes poetry and creative non-fiction that has something to say about the rural experience. Send up to six poems or up to two pieces of creative nonfiction (up to 1,500 words each) in the body of an email.

M461 Square Mile Magazine

Magazine
United Kingdom

https://squaremile.com
https://twitter.com/squaremile_com
https://www.facebook.com/squaremileuk/
https://instagram.com/squaremile_com

Magazine Publisher: Threadneedle Media

Nonfiction > *Articles*
Arts; Books; Boxing; Cars; Comedy / Humour; Culture; Films; Fitness; Food and Drink; Formula One; Golf; Investments; London; Motorbikes; Music; Property / Real Estate; Pubs; Sport; TV; Technology; Travel; Whisky; Wine; Yachts

Luxury lifestyle magazine targeting wealthy men working in London's financial districts.

Editor: Martin Deeson

M462 Stamp Collector

Magazine
United Kingdom

Magazine Publisher: Warners Group Publications

M463 Stand Magazine

Magazine
School of English, Leeds University, Leeds, LS2 9JT
United Kingdom
Tel: +44 (0) 113 233 4794

engstand@leeds.ac.uk
enquiries@standmagazine.org

https://standmagazine.org
https://www.facebook.com/pages/Stand-Magazine/270598523017007
https://twitter.com/Stand_poetry

Fiction > *Short Fiction*: Literary

Poetry > *Any Poetic Form*

Send: Full text
How to send: Email

A well established magazine of poetry and literary fiction. Has previously published the work of, among others, Samuel Beckett, Angela Carter, Seamus Heaney, Geoffrey Hill, and Andrew Motion.

M464 Stickman Review

Online Magazine
United States

fiction@stickmanreview.com
nonfiction@stickmanreview.com
poetry@stickmanreview.com

http://www.stickmanreview.com

Fiction > *Short Fiction*: Literary

Nonfiction > *Essays*: Literary

Poetry > *Any Poetic Form*

Send: Full text
How to send: Email

Publishes literary fiction, poetry, and literary nonfiction. Accepts submissions February to April and August to October.

M465 The Stinging Fly

Magazine
PO Box 6016, Dublin 1
Ireland

stingingfly@gmail.com
submissions.stingingfly@gmail.com

https://stingingfly.org
https://www.facebook.com/StingingFly
http://twitter.com/stingingfly

Fiction in Translation > *Short Fiction*

Fiction > *Short Fiction*

Nonfiction
Essays: General
Interviews: Books; Creative Writing
Poetry in Translation > *Any Poetic Form*

Poetry > *Any Poetic Form*

Closed to approaches.

A literary magazine, a book publisher, an education provider, and an online platform. Independent and not for profit. Aims to seek out, nurture, publish and promote the very best new Irish and international writing.

Publisher: Declan Meade

M466 Stitch

Magazine
United Kingdom

Magazine Publisher: Warners Group Publications

M467 Strand Magazine

Magazine
33228 West 12 Mile Rd. #285, Farmington Hills, MI 48334
United States
Tel: +1 (800) 300-6652

strandmag@strandmag.com

https://strandmag.com
https://www.facebook.com/strandmagazine/
https://twitter.com/StrandMag
https://www.instagram.com/strandmag/?hl=en
https://www.pinterest.com/strandmag/

Fiction > *Short Fiction*: Mystery

Nonfiction
Articles: Creative Writing; Mystery
Interviews: Mystery
Reviews: Mystery; Thrillers

Originally founded in 1891 in England, but closed due to economic difficulties in the 1950s. Publishes mystery stories, and articles, interviews, and reviews related to the genre.

Editor: A.F. Gulli

M468 Strange Horizons

Online Magazine
United States

management@strangehorizons.com

http://strangehorizons.com
https://strangehorizons.moksha.io/publication/strange-horizons/guidelines
https://www.facebook.com/groups/strangehorizons/
https://twitter.com/strangehorizons
https://www.patreon.com/strangehorizons

Fiction > *Short Fiction*
Fantasy; Science Fiction; Slipstream; Speculative

Nonfiction
Articles: Fantasy; Science Fiction; Slipstream; Speculative
Essays: Fantasy; Science Fiction; Slipstream; Speculative
Interviews: Fantasy; Science Fiction; Slipstream; Speculative
Reviews: Fantasy; Science Fiction; Slipstream; Speculative
Poetry > *Any Poetic Form*
Fantasy; Science Fiction; Slipstream; Speculative

Send: Full text
How to send: Moksha
How not to send: Email

Weekly online magazine of speculative fiction, poetry, and nonfiction on related topics. Submit via online submission system only.

Editor-in-Chief: Susan Marie Groppi

M469 Subtropics

Magazine
PO Box 112075, 4008 Turlington Hall, University of Florida, Gainesville, FL 32611-2075
United States

subtropics@english.ufl.edu

http://subtropics.english.ufl.edu
http://www.facebook.com/subtropicsmag/
https://twitter.com/subtropicsmag/

Fiction > *Short Fiction*: Literary

Nonfiction > *Essays*

Poetry > *Any Poetic Form*

Closed to approaches.

Costs: A fee is charged upon submission. $3.00 for each submission.

Publishes literary fiction, essays, and poetry, of any length. Submit via online submission system during open windows. $3 charge per submission.

Editor: David Leavitt

Managing Editor: Mark Mitchell

Poetry Editors: Ange Mlinko; Sidney Wade

M470 Sunshine Artist

Magazine
N7528 Aanstad Rd., Iola, WI 54945
United States
Tel: +1 (800) 597-2573

https://sunshineartist.com

Magazine Publisher: JP Media LLC

PROFESSIONAL > **Nonfiction** > *Reviews*
Arts; Crafts

Publishes reviews of fine art fairs, festivals, events, and small craft shows around the country, for professionals making a living through art shows.

Editor: Joyce Greenholdt

Managing Editor: Melissa Jones

M471 Sunspot Literary Journal

Print Magazine; Online Magazine
Durham, NC
United States
Tel: +1 (919) 928-2245

Sunspotlit@gmail.com

https://sunspotlit.com
https://sunspotlit.submittable.com/submit

Fiction in Translation > *Short Fiction*

Fiction > *Short Fiction*

Nonfiction > *Essays*

Poetry in Translation > *Any Poetic Form*

Poetry > *Any Poetic Form*

Scripts
Film Scripts; *Theatre Scripts*

How to send: Submittable

Costs: Offers services that writers have to pay for; A fee is charged upon submission in some cases. Offers a poetry feedback service and competitions for which there is an entry fee.

Since launching in January of 2019, this journal has amplified diverse multinational voices. New works have been published in their original language side-by-side with English translations. Boundaries that exclude meaningful and important works have been broken by accepting extremely long-form pieces, a rarity in publishing today.

M472 The Supplement

Magazine
Atlantean Publishing, 4 Pierrot Steps, 71 Kursaal Way, Southend-on-Sea, Essex, SS1 2UY
United Kingdom

atlanteanpublishing@hotmail.com

https://atlanteanpublishing.wordpress.com/
https://atlanteanpublishing.fandom.com/wiki/The_Supplement

Book Publisher / Magazine Publisher: Atlantean Publishing (**P056**)

Fiction > *Short Fiction*

Nonfiction
Articles: General
News: Small Press
Reviews: Books; Films

Poetry > *Any Poetic Form*

Send: Full text; Self-Addressed Stamped Envelope (SASE)
How to send: Email; Post

Publishes small-press news and advertisements, reviews covering new publications from small presses, independent and mainstream books, films and much more beside, and various articles on an equally wide variety of topics — as well as the occasional poem or very short piece of fiction, often related to the non-fiction content.

Editor: David-John Tyrer

M473 Surface

Magazine
3921 Alton Road, Suite 413, Miami Beach, FL 33140
United States
Tel: +1 (212) 229-1500

editorial@surfacemag.com

https://www.surfacemag.com
https://twitter.com/SurfaceMag
https://www.instagram.com/surfacemag/
https://www.facebook.com/surfacemag
https://www.pinterest.com/surfacemag/
https://www.youtube.com/surfacemedia/videos

Magazine Publisher: Future Media Group

Nonfiction > *Articles*
Architecture; Arts; Contemporary Culture; Design; Fashion; Travel

American magazine of global contemporary design. Covers architecture, art, design, fashion, and travel, with a focus on how these fields shape and are shaped by contemporary culture.

M474 Sweet Princess Magic

Magazine
United Kingdom

Newspaper Publisher / Magazine Publisher: DC Thomson Media

M475 Tabletop Gaming

Magazine
United Kingdom

Magazine Publisher: Warners Group Publications

M476 Tahoma Literary Review

Magazine
United States

poetry@tahomaliteraryreview.com
fiction@tahomaliteraryreview.com
nonfiction@tahomaliteraryreview.com

https://tahomaliteraryreview.com

Fiction > *Short Fiction*
Experimental; Literary

Nonfiction
Essays: General, and in particular: Experimental; Lyric Essays
Short Nonfiction: Narrative Nonfiction

Poetry
Formal Poetry; *Free Verse*; *Long Form Poetry*

Closed to approaches.

Costs: A fee is charged upon submission; Offers services that writers have to pay for. $4 for poetry and flash prose; $5 for longer prose. Critiques available for an additional fee.

Publishes poetry, fiction, and nonfiction. Charges $4 submission fee for short works; $5 submission fee for long works. Submit online through online submission system.

M477 Takahe

Magazine
New Zealand

essays@takahe.org.nz
fiction@takahe.org.nz
poetry@takahe.org.nz
reviews@takahe.org.nz

https://www.takahe.org.nz
https://twitter.com/takahemagazine

Fiction > *Short Fiction*: Literary

Nonfiction
Essays: Cultural Criticism; New Zealand; South Pacific
Reviews: Books

Poetry > *Any Poetic Form*

Send: Full text; Author bio
How to send: Email attachment

Exists to foster and promote art and literature that represents the diverse voices of Aotearoa New Zealand within the global context. It does this by publishing innovative prose, poetry, art, and critique by emerging and established writers and artists.

Art Editor: Andrew Paul Wood

Essays Editor: Alie Benge

Fiction Editor: Zoë Meager

Poetry Editors: Jeni Curtis; Gail Ingram; Erik Kennedy

Reviews Editors: Michelle Elvy; Sile Mannion

M478 Take a Break

Magazine
United Kingdom

feedback@takeabreak.co.uk

https://takeabreak.co.uk
http://www.facebook.com/takeabreakmag
http://instagram.com/takeabreak.mag
https://twitter.com/takeabreakmag
https://www.youtube.com/channel/UCWNCQhPiJ5WXsMi0Fnpmuag

Magazine Publisher: Bauer Media Group

Nonfiction > *Articles*
Beauty; Cookery; Fashion; Health; Pets; Real Life Stories; Travel

Weekly magazine publishing compelling true-life stories, the latest health, fashion and beauty tips, plus cookery and travel.

Editor: John Dale

M479 Tammy Journal

Print Magazine
United States

thetjournal@gmail.com

https://www.tammyjournal.com

Book Publisher / Magazine Publisher: Tammy Chapbooks

Fiction > *Short Fiction*: Literary

Poetry > *Any Poetic Form*

Closed to approaches.

Costs: A fee is charged upon submission. $3 per submission. $15 to submit and receive a copy of the journal. $20 for expedited response.

Submit poetry up to to 10 pages, or fiction up to 20 pages.

M480 Tampa Review

Magazine
University of Tampa Press, The University of Tampa, 401 West Kennedy Blvd., Tampa, FL 33606-1490, Box 19F
United States
Tel: (813) 253-6266
Fax: (813) 253-6266

utpress@ut.edu

https://tampareview.ut.edu

Types: Fiction; Nonfiction; Poetry; Translations
Formats: Essays; Interviews; Short Fiction
Subjects: Commercial; Culture; Experimental; Fantasy; History; Literary
Markets: Adult

Closed to approaches.

Submit 3-6 poems or one piece of prose up to 5,000 words with SASE between September and December only. Submissions received prior to August are returned unread. No submissions by email or simultaneous submissions.

Editor: Richard Mathews

Fiction Editor: Lisa Birnbaum and Kathleen Ochshorn

Nonfiction Editor: Elizabeth Winston

Poetry Editor: Donald Morrill and Martha Serpas

M481 Tate Etc.

Magazine
Tate, Millbank, London, SW1P 4RG
United Kingdom
Tel: +44 (0) 20 7887 8606

https://www.tate.org.uk/tate-etc

Types: Nonfiction
Formats: Articles
Subjects: Arts; Contemporary; History
Markets: Adult

Magazine of the visual arts, aiming to blend the historic with the contemporary.

Deputy Editor: Enrico Tassi

Editor: Aaron Juneau, Assistant Editor

M482 Tears in the Fence

Magazine
Flats, Durweston Mill, Mill Lane, Durweston, Blandford Forum, Dorset, DT11 0QD
United Kingdom
Tel: +44 (0) 7824 618708

tearsinthefence@gmail.com

https://tearsinthefence.com

Fiction > *Short Fiction*

Nonfiction
Essays: General
Interviews: General
Reviews: General
Short Nonfiction: Creative Nonfiction

Poetry
Any Poetic Form; *Prose Poetry*

Send: Full text
How to send: Email attachment; In the body of an email

International literary magazine publishing poetry, fiction, prose poems, essays, translations, interviews and reviews. Publishes fiction as short as 100 words or as long as 3,500. Maximum 6 poems per poet per issue. No simultaneous submissions or previously published material. Send submissions by email as both an attachment and in the body of the email.

Editor: David Caddy

M483 Teen Breathe

Magazine
GMC Publications Ltd, 86 High Street, Lewes, BN7 1XU
United Kingdom
Tel: +44 (0) 1273 477374

hello@breathemagazine.com

https://www.teenbreathe.co.uk

YOUNG ADULT > **Nonfiction** > *Articles*
Health; Lifestyle

Send: Full text

Magazine for young people who want to find time for themselves. Focuses on Wellbeing, Mindfulness, Creativity and Escaping. Experienced writers should send ideas with examples of previous work. New writers should submit complete articles. Submit using forms on website.

M484 The Temz Review

Online Magazine
London, ON
Canada

thetemzreview@gmail.com

https://www.thetemzreview.com

Fiction > *Short Fiction*: Literary

Nonfiction > *Reviews*: Literature

Poetry > *Any Poetic Form*

Send: Full text
How to send: Moksha

Quarterly online magazine. Submit one piece of fiction or creative nonfiction (or more than one if under 1,000 words) or 1-8 poems via online submission system. For reviews, send query by email.

M485 That's Life!

Magazine
FREEPOST LON12043, H Bauer Publishing, London, NW1 1YU
United Kingdom

stories@thatslife.co.uk

http://www.thatslife.co.uk

Types: Nonfiction
Formats: Articles; News
Subjects: Lifestyle
Markets: Adult

Publishes nonfiction true life stories. See website for details.

M486 the6ress

Print Magazine
United Kingdom

the6ress@gmail.com

https://the6ress.com
https://www.instagram.com/the6ress/
https://twitter.com/the6ress/

Poetry
Any Poetic Form; *Visual Poetry*

Publishes poetry, art, and word art. See website for submission windows and issue themes.

M487 Thema

Magazine
Box 8747, Metairie, LA 70011-8747
United States

thema@cox.net

http://themaliterarysociety.com

Fiction > *Short Fiction*

Poetry > *Any Poetic Form*

How to send: Post; International Email
How not to send: Domestic Email

All issues are themed, so imperative to check website for upcoming themes before submitting. Material need not have specified theme as central to the plot, but must not be incidental.

See website for detailed submission guidelines.

Editor: Virginia Howard

Poetry Editor: Gail Howard

M488 Thin Air Magazine

Magazine
United States

https://thinairmagazine.org
https://www.instagram.com/thinairmagazine/
https://twitter.com/thinairmagazine
https://www.facebook.com/thinairmagazine/

Fiction > *Short Fiction*: Literary

Nonfiction > *Short Nonfiction*

Poetry > *Any Poetic Form*

Send: Full text
How to send: Submittable

Costs: A fee is charged upon submission. $3 per submission.

A non-profit, graduate-student-run, literary magazine. Submit up to three poems, or prose up to 3,000 words.

Editor: Bobby Carlson

M489 Third Coast

Magazine
United States

editors@thirdcoastmagazine.com

http://thirdcoastmagazine.com
https://thirdcoastmagazine.submittable.com/submit
http://facebook.com/thirdcoastmagazine
http://twitter.com/thirdcoastmag
http://instagram.com/thirdcoastmag

Fiction > *Short Fiction*

Nonfiction > *Short Nonfiction*: Creative Nonfiction

Poetry > *Any Poetic Form*

Closed to approaches.

All submissions should be sent via Submittable, through the portals of their respective genres. All attachments sent by email will be deleted, and any submissions sent via postal mail or social media will not be read. Accepts simultaneous submissions, but not multiple submissions; please submit no more than one manuscript at a time. No previously published works.

Editor: Glenn Deutsch

M490 This Is

Magazine
United Kingdom

Newspaper Publisher / Magazine Publisher: DC Thomson Media

M491 This Is Little Baby Bum

Magazine
United Kingdom

Newspaper Publisher / Magazine Publisher: DC Thomson Media

M492 The Threepenny Review

Magazine
PO Box 9131, Berkeley, CA 94709
United States

wlesser@threepennyreview.com

http://www.threepennyreview.com

Fiction > *Short Fiction*: Literary

Nonfiction > *Articles*
Arts; Culture; Literature

Poetry > *Any Poetic Form*

Closed to approaches.

National literary magazine with coverage of the visual and performing arts. Send complete MS by post with SASE or via online submission system. No previously published material, simultaneous submissions, or submissions from May to December. Prospective contributors are advised to read the magazine before submitting.

Editor: Wendy Lesser

M493 Tocher

Magazine
School of Scottish Studies Archives, University of Edinburgh, 29 George Square, Edinburgh, EH8 9LD
United Kingdom

scottish.studies.arhives@ed.ac.uk

https://www.ed.ac.uk/literatures-languages-cultures/celtic-scottish-studies/research/publications/in-house/tocher

ACADEMIC > **Nonfiction** > *Articles*
Culture; Folklore, Myths, and Legends; Music; Scotland

ADULT
Fiction in Translation > *Short Fiction*: Scotland
Fiction > *Short Fiction*: Scotland

The journal contains traditional Scottish songs, stories, music, customs, beliefs, local history, rhymes and riddles transcribed from tapes held in the sound archive.

M494 Tolka

Magazine
Ireland

https://www.tolkajournal.org
https://www.instagram.com/tolkajournal/
https://twitter.com/tolkajournal

Fiction > *Short Fiction*: Autofiction

Nonfiction
Essays: Personal Essays
Short Nonfiction: Memoir; Travel

Closed to approaches.

Biannual literary journal of non-fiction: publishing essays, reportage, travel writing, auto-fiction, individual stories and the writing that flows in between.

M495 Total Film

Magazine
11 West 42nd Street, 15th Floor, New York, NY 10036
United States

https://www.gamesradar.com/uk/totalfilm/

Magazine Publisher: Future US

Nonfiction
Articles: Film Industry; Films
News: Film Industry; Films

A cheeky, irreverent, but always passionate and authoritative look at every part of the film world. From all the latest blockbusters, comic-book tent poles and sci-fi extravaganzas to the very best Oscar-baiters, arthouse masterpieces, hidden gems and festival hits.

M496 Total Film (UK Edition)

Magazine
Quay House, The Ambury, Bath, BA1 1UA
United Kingdom

https://www.gamesradar.com/uk/totalfilm/

Magazine Publisher: Future

Nonfiction
Articles: Film Industry; Films
News: Film Industry; Films

"A cheeky, irreverent but always passionate and authoritative look at every part of the film world".

M497 Toy Collectors Price Guide

Magazine
United Kingdom

Magazine Publisher: Warners Group Publications

M498 Traction

Magazine
United Kingdom

Magazine Publisher: Warners Group Publications

M499 The Tusculum Review

Magazine
60 Shiloh Road, Greeneville, TN 37745
United States

review@tusculum.edu

https://ttr.tusculum.edu

Fiction > *Short Fiction*: Literary

Nonfiction > *Essays*

Poetry > *Any Poetic Form*

Scripts > *Theatre Scripts*: Drama

Send: Full text
How to send: Submittable

Costs: A fee is charged upon submission. $2.

We seek well-crafted writing that takes risks. We publish work in and between all genres: poetry, fiction, essays, and plays--we appreciate work in experimental and traditional modes. We accept prose submissions of less than 6,000 words (24 double-spaced pages) and poetry submissions under 10 pages. We publish scripts in the 10-minute format (10 pages).

M500 TV Times

Magazine
United Kingdom

https://www.futureplc.com/brand/tv-times/

Magazine Publisher: Future

Nonfiction > *Articles*
Entertainment; TV

Magazine publishing television news, listings, and articles.

M501 Ulster Business

Magazine
Belfast Telegraph House, 33 Clarendon Road, Clarendon Dock, Belfast, BT1 3BG
United Kingdom
Tel: +44 (0) 28 9026 4000

https://www.ulsterbusiness.com
https://www.belfasttelegraph.co.uk/business/ulsterbusiness/

Newspaper: Belfast Telegraph

PROFESSIONAL > **Nonfiction**
Articles: Business
Interviews: Business
News: Business

Business magazine for Ulster, publishing news, articles, features, and interviews with local businessmen.

Editor: David Cullen

M502 Ulster Tatler

Magazine
39 Boucher Road, Belfast, BT12 6UT
United Kingdom
Tel: +44 (0) 28 9066 3311

edit@ulstertatler.com
info@ulstertatler.com

https://www.ulstertatler.com
https://www.facebook.com/ulstertatlermag/
https://twitter.com/ulstertatlermag
https://www.youtube.com/channel/UCHH_sMGsPuy8i0VUj5L0_kA
https://www.instagram.com/ulstertatler/

Nonfiction > *Articles*
Fashion; High Society; Lifestyle

Lifestyle and society magazine based in Northern Ireland, covering Northern Ireland social events and local fashions.

Editor: Chris Sherry

Features Editor: James Sherry

Fiction Editor: Richard Sherry

M503 Umbrella Factory

Magazine
United States

https://umbrellafactorymagazine.com

Types: Fiction; Nonfiction; Poetry
Formats: Short Fiction
Subjects: Literary
Markets: Adult

Send: Full text

Submit fiction between 1,000 and 5,000 words, three poems, or a piece of nonfiction. Submit through online submission system. See website for full guidelines.

Editors: Anthony ILacqua; Sharyce Winters

M504 The Undercommons

Online Magazine
United States

https://www.commontonguezine.com

Online Magazine: The Common Tongue Magazine (**M131**)

Fiction
Novellas: Dark Fantasy
Short Fiction: Dark Fantasy

Poetry > *Any Poetic Form*: Dark Fantasy

How to send: Online submission system

Dark fantasy magazine. Each issue includes one novella, one short story, and one poem.

M505 Understorey Magazine

Magazine
Alexa McDonough Institute for Women, Gender and Social Justice, Mount Saint Vincent University, 166 Bedford Highway, Halifax, NS, B3M 2J6
Canada

editor@understoreymagazine.ca

https://understoreymagazine.ca

Fiction > *Short Fiction*
Feminism; Women's Issues; Women

Nonfiction > *Short Nonfiction*
Creative Nonfiction; Feminism; Women's Issues; Women

Poetry > *Any Poetic Form*
Feminism; Women's Issues; Women

Closed to approaches.

Publishes fiction, poetry, and creative nonfiction by Canadian women. Send prose up to 1,500 words or up to five poems by email. See website for full guidelines.

M506 Unfit Magazine

Magazine
Eugene, OR 97401
United States

contact@unfitmag.com

http://unfitmag.com

Magazine Publisher: Longshot Press

Fiction > *Short Fiction*
Adventure; Alien Invasion; Alternative History; Cyberpunk; Genetics; Military; Post-Apocalyptic; Science Fiction; Space Opera; Time Travel

Closed to approaches.

This magazine is about fiction that isn't fit for "them". What do I mean by "them"? Who in particular are "they"? They are the government. They are your parents. They are your teachers. They are everywhere.

Editor: Daniel Scott White

M507 Unicorn Universe

Magazine
United Kingdom

Newspaper Publisher / Magazine Publisher: DC Thomson Media

M508 Unreal Magazine

Magazine
United States

contact@unrealmag.com

https://unrealmag.com

Magazine Publisher: Longshot Press

Fiction > *Short Fiction*
Adventure; Alternative History; Comedy / Humour; Experimental; Fairy Tales; Fantasy; Folklore, Myths, and Legends; Gaslamp Fantasy; High / Epic Fantasy; Historical Fiction; Magical Realism; Military;

Superhero Fantasy; Sword and Sorcery

Nonfiction > *Articles*
Fantasy; Magical Realism

Closed to approaches.

We want stories that are well written, intelligent, and enjoyable to read. We are looking for stories with metaphors and emotional ambience and imaginative descriptive writing.

M509 Unthology

Magazine
Unthank Submissions (Unthology), PO Box 3506, Norwich, NR7 7QP
United Kingdom

unthology@unthankbooks.com

http://www.unthankbooks.com

Types: Fiction; Nonfiction
Formats: Essays; Short Fiction
Subjects: Experimental; Literary; Traditional
Markets: Adult

Closed to approaches.

Publishes the work of new or established writers and can include short stories of any length, reportage, essays or novel extracts from anywhere in the world. Allows space for stories of different styles and subjects to rub up against each other, featuring classic slice-of-life alongside the experimental, the shocking and strange. Submit by post with SAE and personal contact details, or by email.

M510 Urthona

Magazine
Old Abbey House, Abbey Road, Cambridge, CB5 8HQ
United Kingdom
Tel: +44 (0) 7443 499384

urthonamag@gmail.com

https://urthona.com

Nonfiction > *Essays*
Arts; Buddhism; Contemporary; Culture

Poetry > *Any Poetic Form*

How to send: Email

Magazine of Buddhism and the Arts, linking Buddhism and Western culture.

M511 US Equestrian Magazine

Magazine
United States Equestrian Federation (USEF), 4047 Iron Works Parkway, Lexington, KY 40511
United States
Tel: +1 (859) 258-2472
Fax: +1 (859) 231-6662

goakford@usef.org

http://www.usef.org
https://www.usef.org/media/equestrian-magazine

Nonfiction > *Articles*
Equestrian; Horses

Send: Query
How to send: Email

Magazine publishing articles, features, and interviews about horses and people related to them.

Editors: Glenye Oakford; Brian Sosby

M512 Vagabond City

Online Magazine
United States

vagabondcitypoetry@gmail.com
vagabondcityfiction@gmail.com
vagabondcitynonfic@gmail.com
vagabondcityliterary@gmail.com
vagabondcityinterviews@gmail.com

https://vagabondcitylit.com

Fiction > *Short Fiction*

Nonfiction
Essays: Creative Nonfiction
Interviews: General
Reviews: Books

Poetry > *Any Poetic Form*

Send: Full text
How to send: Email

Electronic magazine featuring poetry, fiction, art, creative nonfiction and essays by marginalised creators. Also publishes book reviews and interviews. Submit up to five pieces at a time in the body of an email or as a Word file attachment. See website for full guidelines.

M513 Vallum

Magazine
5038 Sherbrooke West, P.O. Box 23077 CP Vendome Station, Montreal, Quebec, H4A 1T0
Canada
Tel: +1 (514) 937-8946
Fax: +1 (514) 937-8946

editors@vallummag.com

https://vallummag.com
https://www.facebook.com/VallumMagazine
https://twitter.com/vallummag
https://www.instagram.com/vallummag/
https://soundcloud.com/vallum-magazine
https://www.youtube.com/channel/UCARH_nOH0vXwmpXSxzpgQZg

Nonfiction
Essays; *Interviews*; *Reviews*
Poetry > *Any Poetic Form*: Contemporary

Closed to approaches.

Send 4-7 poems, essays of 4-6 pages, interviews of 3-5 pages, reviews of 1-3 pages, through online submission system only. No fiction, plays, movie scripts, memoir, or creative nonfiction. Check website for submission windows and themes.

M514 Veggie

Magazine
United Kingdom

https://www.vegetarianrecipesmag.com

Nonfiction > *Articles*
Health; Vegetarian Cooking; Vegetarian Food; Vegetarianism

Magazine of vegetarian food, wellness, and lifestyle.

Editors: Sian Bunney; Rachael Perrett

M515 Verbicide

Magazine
United States

info@scissorpress.com

https://www.verbicidemagazine.com

Types: Fiction; Nonfiction
Formats: Articles; Interviews; Reviews; Short Fiction
Subjects: Entertainment; Music
Markets: Adult

Send: Full text
How to send: Email

Entertainment periodical, online-only since 2009. Accepts short stories between 500 and 3,000 words. For features or music reviews contact by email in advance. See website for specific email addresses and full submission guidelines.

M516 Vestal Review

Online Magazine
United States

info@vestalreview.org

https://www.vestalreview.net
https://vestalreview.submittable.com/submit
https://www.facebook.com/VestalReview/
https://www.instagram.com/vestalreview/
https://twitter.com/VestalReview

Fiction > *Short Fiction*

Nonfiction
Interviews; *Reviews*

Send: Full text
How to send: Submittable

Publishes flash fiction up to 500 words. Accepts submissions between February 1 and May 31, and between August 1 and November 30. Also accepts proposals for interviews and reviews.

Editor: Mark Budman

M517 Vietnam

Magazine
United States

Magazine Publisher: HistoryNet LLC

M518 View From Atlantis

Online Magazine
United Kingdom

atlanteanpublishing@hotmail.com

https://viewfromatlantis.wordpress.com

Book Publisher / Magazine Publisher: Atlantean Publishing (**P056**)

Fiction > *Short Fiction*
General, and in particular: Fantasy; Horror; Science Fiction; Speculative; Supernatural / Paranormal

Poetry
Any Poetic Form: General, and in particular: Fantasy; Horror; Science Fiction; Speculative; Supernatural / Paranormal
Prose Poetry: General, and in particular: Fantasy; Horror; Science Fiction; Speculative; Supernatural / Paranormal

How to send: In the body of an email

Primarily interested in speculative poetry (fantasy, science fiction, supernatural horror, etc), but literary poems and poetry from other genres will be considered as long as they fit the issue theme. Prose poems and flash fiction will also be considered. Please check the website for themes and submission periods. Submissions sent outside of submission periods will be deleted unread.

M519 The Virginia Quarterly Review

Magazine
5 Boar's Head Lane, PO Box 400223, Charlottesville, VA 22904
United States
Tel: +1 (434) 924-3675
Fax: +1 (434) 924-1397

editors@vqronline.org

https://www.vqronline.org
https://www.facebook.com/vqreview
https://twitter.com/vqr

Fiction > *Short Fiction*

Nonfiction > *Short Nonfiction*
Arts; Creative Nonfiction; Cultural Criticism; History; Literary Criticism; Politics

Poetry > *Any Poetic Form*

Does not want:

Fiction > *Short Fiction*
Fantasy; Romance; Science Fiction

Closed to approaches.

Strives to publish the best writing they can find. Has a long history of publishing accomplished and award-winning authors, but they also seek and support emerging writers.

Editor: Ted Genoways

M520 Viz

Magazine
United Kingdom

hello@metropolis.co.uk

https://viz.co.uk
https://www.facebook.com/VizComic/
https://twitter.com/vizcomic

Magazine Publisher: Diamond Publishing

Fiction > *Cartoons*: Comedy / Humour

Nonfiction > *Articles*
Comedy / Humour; Satire

Magazine of adult humour, including cartoons, spoof articles, etc.

M521 Waccamaw

Online Magazine
United States

http://waccamawjournal.com
https://www.facebook.com/Waccamaw-A-Journal-of-Contemporary-Literature-164290950299653/
https://twitter.com/waccamawjournal
https://www.instagram.com/waccamawjournal/

Book Publisher: Athenaeum Press (**P054**)

Fiction > *Short Fiction*: Literary

Nonfiction > *Essays*

Poetry > *Any Poetic Form*

Closed to approaches.

Online literary journal publishing poems, stories, and essays. Submit prose up to 6,000 words or 3-5 poems between August 1 and September 8 annually. Submit via online submission system only.

M522 Walk Magazine

Magazine
United Kingdom

https://www.ramblers.org.uk/walkmag
https://twitter.com/walkmagazine

Nonfiction > *Articles*: Walking

Rambling magazine publishing features on any aspect of walking in Britain. No general travel articles.

Editor: Dominic Bates

M523 The Wallace Stevens Journal

Magazine
University of Antwerp, Prinsstraat 13, 2000 Antwerp
Belgium

https://www.press.jhu.edu/journals/wallace-stevens-journal

ACADEMIC > **Nonfiction**
Articles: Biography; Literary Criticism; Poetry as a Subject
Essays: Biography; Literary Criticism; Poetry as a Subject
News: Literature
Reviews: Books

ADULT > **Poetry** > *Any Poetic Form*

Send: Full text
How to send: Email attachment

Publishes articles and essays on all aspects of Wallace Stevens' poetry and life. Also accepts poetry inspired by the poet. See website for full submission guidelines.

Editor: Bart Eeckhout

M524 Walloon Writers Review

Magazine
United States

https://walloonwriters.com

Types: Fiction; Nonfiction; Poetry
Formats: Essays
Subjects: Literary
Markets: Adult

Publishes stories, poetry, and creative writing inspired by or about Northern Michigan and the Upper Peninsula.

M525 Wasafiri

Magazine
c/o School of English and Drama, Queen Mary, University of London, Mile End Road, London, E1 4NS
United Kingdom
Tel: +44 (0) 20 7882 2686

wasafiri@qmul.ac.uk

https://www.wasafiri.org
https://www.facebook.com/wasafiri.magazine
https://twitter.com/Wasafirimag
https://www.youtube.com/channel/UC4J-lxAIL8iBiaRR2AOpGFg
https://www.linkedin.com/groups/8343914/profile

Fiction > *Short Fiction*: Literary

Nonfiction
Articles: Culture; Literature
Essays: Culture; Literature

Poetry > *Any Poetic Form*

Closed to approaches.

The indispensable journal of contemporary African, Asian Black British, Caribbean and transnational literatures.

In over fifteen years of publishing, this magazine has changed the face of contemporary writing in Britain. As a literary magazine primarily concerned with new and postcolonial writers, it continues to stress the diversity and range of black and diasporic writers world-wide. It remains committed to its original aims: to create a definitive forum for the voices of new writers and to open up lively spaces for serious critical discussion not available elsewhere. It is Britain's only international magazine for Black British, African, Asian and Caribbean literatures. Get the whole picture, get the magazine at the core of contemporary international literature today.

Submit via online submissions portal only (see website).

Editor: Malachi McIntosh

M526 Weber—The Contemporary West

Magazine
Weber State University, 1395 Edvalson Street, Dept. 1405, Ogden, Utah 84408-1405
United States

weberjournal@weber.edu

https://www.weber.edu/weberjournal
https://www.facebook.com/weberjournal
https://twitter.com/WeberJournal

Fiction > *Short Fiction*
American West; Culture; Environment

Nonfiction
Essays: Personal Essays
Short Nonfiction: Commentary; Creative Nonfiction
Poetry > *Any Poetic Form*
American West; Culture; Environment

Send: Full text
How to send: Email

Invites submissions in the genres of personal narrative, critical commentary, fiction, creative non-fiction, and poetry that offer insight into the environment and culture (both broadly defined) of the contemporary western United States.

Editor: Brad L. Roghaar

M527 Welsh Country

Magazine
Aberbanc, Llandysul, Ceredigion, SA44 5NP
United Kingdom
Tel: +44 (0) 1559 372010

info@welshcountry.co.uk

http://www.welshcountry.co.uk

Nonfiction
Articles: Arts; Business; Crafts; Culture; Fishing; Gardening; History; Nature; Wales; Walking
News: Wales

Magazine covering Welsh villages, history, wildlife, walking, gardening, fishing, business news, places to stay, local artisan Welsh food producers, and the Welsh arts and crafts scene.

Editor: Kath Rhodes

M528 West Branch

Magazine
Stadler Center, Bucknell University, 1 Dent Drive, Lewisburg, PA 17837
United States

westbranch@bucknell.edu

https://westbranch.blogs.bucknell.edu

Fiction > *Short Fiction*

Nonfiction
Essays; *Reviews*
Poetry > *Any Poetic Form*

Closed to approaches.

Send all submissions via online submission system, between August 1 and April 1 annually.

Editor: Paula Closson Buck

Fiction Editor: Ron Mohring

M529 Western Humanities Review

Magazine
Department of English, Languages & Communication BLDG, 255 S Central Campus Drive, Room 3500, SLC, UT 84112-0494
United States
Tel: +1 (801) 581-6168
Fax: +1 (801) 585-5167

managingeditor.whr@gmail.com

http://www.westernhumanitiesreview.com
https://www.facebook.com/WHReview/
https://whr.submittable.com/submit

Fiction > *Short Fiction*

Nonfiction
Essays: General
Reviews: Books

Poetry > *Any Poetic Form*

Send: Full text
How to send: Submittable

Costs: A fee is charged upon submission. $2 for poetry and prose submissions.

Send one story or essay, or up to five poems, via online submission system. Also accepts book reviews.

M530 What Motorhome

Magazine
United Kingdom

Magazine Publisher: Warners Group Publications

M531 The White Review

Magazine
A.103 Fuel Tank, 8-12 Creekside, London, SE8 3DX
United Kingdom

editors@thewhitereview.org

https://www.thewhitereview.org
http://www.facebook.com/thewhitereview
http://www.twitter.com/thewhitereview
http://www.instagram.com/thewhitereview

Fiction in Translation > *Short Fiction*: Literary

Fiction > *Short Fiction*: Literary

Nonfiction
Essays: Arts; Literature
Interviews: Arts; Literature
Poetry in Translation > *Any Poetic Form*

Poetry > *Any Poetic Form*

Send: Pitch; Author bio
How to send: Email

Print and online arts and literature magazine. Publishes cultural analysis, reviews, and new fiction and poetry. Accepts submissions only in specific submission windows. Prose submissions should be a minimum of 1,500 words. See website for guidelines and submit by email.

M532 WI Life

Magazine
104 New Kings Road, London, SW6 4LY
United Kingdom
Tel: +44 (0) 20 7731 5777 ext 217

wilife@nfwi.org.uk

https://www.thewi.org.uk/wie-and-wi-life

Types: Nonfiction
Formats: Articles
Subjects: Cookery; Crafts; Gardening; Nature; Women's Interests
Markets: Adult

Magazine for Women's Institute membership. Welcomes contributions from WI members.

M533 Willow Springs

Magazine
United States

willowspringsewu@gmail.com

http://willowspringsmagazine.org
https://willowsprings.submittable.com/submit

Fiction > *Short Fiction*

Nonfiction
Essays; *Interviews*
Poetry > *Any Poetic Form*

How to send: Submittable

Costs: A fee is charged upon submission. $3 reading fee per submission. Writers who cannot afford the reading fee should contact by email to have the fee waived.

Publishes each spring and fall. Accepts fiction and poetry submissions between September 1 and May 31. Nonfiction is open year-round. Submit one packet of work at a time and wait to receive a response before submitting again.

Editor: Samuel Ligon

Managing Editor: Adam O'Connor Rodriguez

M534 Wine & Country Life

Magazine
United States

Concierge@ivypublications.com
editor@ivylifeandstylemedia.com

https://wineandcountrylife.com
https://www.facebook.com/WineAndCountryLife/
https://www.instagram.com/wineandcountrylife/
https://www.pinterest.com/wclifeva/

Magazine Publisher: Ivy Life & Style Media

Nonfiction > *Articles*
Architecture; Arts; Beer Making; Country Lifestyle; Entertainment; Gardening; Interior Design; Literature; Music; Virginia; Wine

Send: Query
How to send: Email

Celebrates elevated living in the heart of Virginia wine country. Each issue of our luxury print magazine highlights Virginia wine, farm-to-table food, architecture, gardens & décor, hunt country, the arts and elegant entertaining, as well as Virginia craft spirits, beer And ciders.

M535 Wine & Country Weddings

Magazine
4282 Ivy Road, Charlottesville, VA 22903
United States
Tel: +1 (434) 984-4713

Concierge@ivypublications.com

https://wineandcountryweddings.com

Magazine Publisher: Ivy Life & Style Media

Nonfiction > *Articles*
Lifestyle; Virginia; Weddings

Send: Query
How not to send: Email

A uniquely curated magazine for creating the elegant country wedding in Jefferson's Virginia, one that will inspire couples as well as top event planners across the nation from New York City to Beverly Hills.

M536 Woman & Home

Magazine
121-141 Westbourne Terrace, London, W2 6JR
United Kingdom
Tel: +44 (0) 20 3148 5000

https://www.womanandhome.com

Magazine Publisher: Future

Nonfiction > *Articles*
Beauty; Fashion; Food; Health; Lifestyle; Travel; Wellbeing; Women's Interests

Our mission is to keep 40+ women informed on the subjects that matter to them, so they can live smarter, healthier and happier lives. We publish celebrity news for grown-ups, as well as informative, no-nonsense health and wellbeing features about subjects like the menopause. We speak to internationally renown experts to give up-to-date advice on dieting and weight-loss plans. We aim to delight you with delicious – and healthy – recipes. And to inspire your next holiday destinations with travel recommendations both near and far. We filter through the latest fashion and beauty noise to offer you advice on the trends you'll want to try, because they're flattering as well as stylish.

Editor: Catherine Westwood

M537 Woman's Weekly

Magazine
161 Marsh Wall, London, E14 9AP
United Kingdom

womansweeklypostbag@futurenet.com

https://www.womansweekly.com
https://www.facebook.com/WomansWeekly
https://twitter.com/Womans_Weekly
http://uk.pinterest.com/womansweekly/

Magazine Publisher: Future

Fiction > *Short Fiction*

Nonfiction > *Articles*
Crafts; Gardening; Knitting; Lifestyle; Recipes

How to send: Post
How not to send: Email

Publishes features of interest to women over forty, plus fiction between 1,000 and 2,000 words and serials in four or five parts of 3,400 words each. Only uses experienced journalists for nonfiction. No submissions by email. Submit by post with SAE.

Editor: Diane Kenwood

Features Editor: Sue Pilkington

Fiction Editor: Gaynor Davies

M538 Woman's Weekly Fiction Special

Magazine
161 Marsh Wall, London, E14 9AP
United Kingdom

womansweeklypostbag@futurenet.com

https://www.womansweekly.com
https://www.facebook.com/WomansWeekly
https://twitter.com/Womans_Weekly
http://uk.pinterest.com/womansweekly/

Magazine Publisher: Future

Fiction > *Short Fiction*

Send: Full text
How to send: Post
How not to send: Email

Publishes short stories for women between 1,000 and 8,000 words. Send stories by post with SAE – no correspondence by email.

Editor: Gaynor Davies

M539 Yachting Monthly

Magazine
United Kingdom

yachtingmonthly@futurenet.com

https://www.yachtingmonthly.com
http://www.youtube.com/user/YachtingMonthly
http://www.facebook.com/yachtingmonthlymag
http://twitter.com/yachtingmonthly

Magazine Publisher: Future

Nonfiction > *Articles*
Sailing; Yachts

Magazine publishing articles and features on yachting and cruising.

Editor: Paul Gelder

M540 Yachting World

Magazine
United Kingdom

yachting.world@timeinc.com

https://www.yachtingworld.com

Types: Nonfiction
Formats: Articles; News
Subjects: Leisure; Sport
Markets: Adult

Publishes news and features relating to yacht racing, yachting events, and cruising.

Editor: Elaine Bunting

M541 The Yale Review

Magazine
United States

theyalereview@yale.edu

https://yalereview.yale.edu
https://www.facebook.com/YaleReview/
https://www.instagram.com/yalereview/
https://twitter.com/YaleReview

Fiction > *Short Fiction*: Literary

Nonfiction > *Essays*
Arts; Cultural Criticism; Films; History; Literary Criticism; Memoir; Music; Politics; TV

Poetry > *Any Poetic Form*

Closed to approaches.

Open for submissions of poetry, nonfiction, and fiction from October 5 to November 3, 2020.

Editor: Meghan O'Rourke

M542 Yemassee

Magazine
Department of English, University of South Carolina, Columbia, SC 29208
United States

questions@yemasseejournal.com

http://yemasseejournal.com
https://www.facebook.com/Yemassee
https://www.instagram.com/yemassee.journal
https://twitter.com/YemasseeJournal

Fiction > *Short Fiction*: Literary

Poetry > *Any Poetic Form*

Closed to approaches.

Costs: A fee is charged upon submission. $3 submission fee.

Publishes poetry, fiction, and nonfiction. Submit 3-5 poems or pieces of flash fiction up to 1,000 words, or a longer short story up to 8,000 words (1,000 words to 5,000 words preferred), via online submission system. See website for full guidelines. $3 submission fee.

Editors: Cody Hosek; Dylan Nutter; Victoria Romero

M543 Yes Poetry Magazine

Online Magazine
United States

editor@yespoetry.com

https://www.yespoetry.com
https://twitter.com/yespoetry
https://yespoetry.tumblr.com/

Fiction > *Short Fiction*

Nonfiction
Essays; *Interviews*; *Reviews*
Poetry > *Any Poetic Form*

Closed to approaches.

A lifestyle art publication that encourages deep analysis and thought, pushing for progressive change and identification.

Book Publisher: Yes Poetry Chapbooks (**P880**)

M544 Your Best Ever Christmas

Magazine
United Kingdom

Newspaper Publisher / Magazine Publisher: DC Thomson Media

M545 Your Cat

Magazine
United Kingdom

https://www.yourcat.co.uk
https://www.facebook.com/yourcatmagazine
https://www.twitter.com/yourcatmagazine
https://www.instagram.com/yourcatmagazine
https://www.youtube.com/YourCatYourDog

Magazine Publisher: Warners Group Publications

Nonfiction > *Articles*: Cats

Practical magazine covering the care of cats and kittens.

Editor:

M546 Your Dog

Magazine
The Maltings, West Street, Bourne, Lincolnshire, PE10 9PH
United Kingdom
Tel: +44 (0) 1778 395070

editorial@yourdog.co.uk

https://www.yourdog.co.uk

Magazine Publisher: Warners Group Publications

Nonfiction
Articles: Dogs
News: Dogs

Publishes news and articles aimed at dog owners, offering practical advice and some personal experience pieces.

Editor: Sarah Wright

M547 Yours

Magazine
Media House, Peterborough Business Park, Peterborough, PE2 6EA
United Kingdom

yours@bauermedia.co.uk

https://www.yours.co.uk
https://www.facebook.com/Yoursmagazine
https://twitter.com/yoursmagazine
https://www.pinterest.com/yoursmagazine/

Magazine Publisher: Bauer Media Group

Nonfiction
Articles: Beauty; Fashion; Finance; Health; Recipes; Travel; Women's Interests
Interviews: Celebrity

Magazine for women over 50. Publishes tips and expert advice on a range of topics from travel to financial guidance as well as discovering the latest fashion trends, beauty, and health tips. Also exclusive celebrity interviews and recipes for healthy meals or hearty treats.

Editor: Sharon Reid

M548 Zone 3

Magazine
APSU Box 4565, Clarksville, TN 37044
United States
Tel: +1 (931) 221-7031

https://www.zone3press.com

Book Publisher / Magazine Publisher: Zone 3 Press

Fiction > *Short Fiction*
Contemporary; Literary

Nonfiction > *Short Nonfiction*
Contemporary; Creative Nonfiction; Literary

Poetry > *Any Poetic Form*

Closed to approaches.

Costs: A fee is charged upon submission. $3.

Publishes fiction, poetry, and creative nonfiction. Accepts submissions through online submission system between August 1 and April 1 annually. $3 submission fee.

Editor: Susan Wallace

Book Publishers

For the most up-to-date listings of these and hundreds of other book publishers, visit https://www.firstwriter.com/publishers

To claim your free access to the site, please see the back of this book.

P001 1517 Media

Book Publisher
United States

https://1517.media

Publishing Imprint: Fortress Press (**P275**)

P002 23 House Publishing

Book Publisher
United States
Fax: +1 (214) 367-4343

editor@23house.com

http://www.23house.com

Nonfiction > *Nonfiction Books*
Ghosts; Regional

Currently looking for nonfiction, regional ghost story manuscripts. A prospective book should contain both the history and ghost stories of the specific region. The maximum word count is 65,000, and the minimum is 40,000 – photos, maps, and other visual aids are a major plus.

P003 4 Color Books

Publishing Imprint
United States

http://www.randomhousebooks.com/imprints/

Book Publisher: Random House (**P640**)

Nonfiction > *Nonfiction Books*
Arts; Contemporary Politics; Cookery; Health; Sustainable Living

Collaborates with the most forward-thinking and groundbreaking BIPOC chefs, writers, artists, activists, and innovators to craft visually stunning nonfiction books that inspire readers and give rise to a more healthy, just, and sustainable world for all.

P004 4RV Biblical Based

Publishing Imprint
United States

Book Publisher: 4RV Publishing (**P008**)

Fiction > *Novels*: Christianity

Nonfiction > *Nonfiction Books*: Christianity

Publishes fiction and nonfiction based on the Bible, including Christian works.

P005 4RV Children's Corner

Publishing Imprint
United States

Book Publisher: 4RV Publishing (**P008**)

CHILDREN'S > **Fiction**
Chapter Books; *Early Readers*; *Picture Books*

Closed to approaches.

Publishes books for any aged reader below 5th grade.

P006 4RV Fiction

Publishing Imprint
United States

Book Publisher: 4RV Publishing (**P008**)

ADULT > **Fiction** > *Novels*
General, and in particular: Fantasy; Romance; Science Fiction

NEW ADULT > **Fiction** > *Novels*

Does not want:

Fiction > *Novels*: Erotic

Publishes novels for adults or young people with high reading abilities.

P007 4RV Nonfiction

Publishing Imprint
United States

Book Publisher: 4RV Publishing (**P008**)

Nonfiction > *Nonfiction Books*

Publishes nonfiction works above Young Adult.

P008 4RV Publishing

Book Publisher
35427 State Highway 58, Hydro, OK 73048
United States
Tel: +1 (405) 820-9640

Administrator@4rvpublishingllc.com

https://www.4rvpublishing.com
https://www.facebook.com/4RV-Publishing-LLC-20479523692/
https://twitter.com/4RV
https://www.youtube.com/user/4RVPublishingLLC

ADULT

Fiction > *Novels*
General, and in particular: Christianity; Fantasy; Romance; Science Fiction

Nonfiction > *Nonfiction Books*

Poetry > *Poetry Collections*

CHILDREN'S > **Fiction**
Chapter Books; *Early Readers*; *Middle Grade*; *Picture Books*
TEEN > **Fiction** > *Novels*

YOUNG ADULT > **Fiction** > *Novels*

Does not want:

Fiction > *Novels*: Erotic

Send: Query; Synopsis; Writing sample
How to send: Email attachment

Accepts most genres of fiction and nonfiction books for all ages, including nonfiction, mystery, romance, mainstream, western, Christian, and science-fiction, as well as children's books, middle grade and young adult novels. No poetry or graphic sex or violence. Language should not be overly profane or vulgar. Accepts submissions by email from the US, UK, and Australia. Not accepting children's books as at May 2022. See website for current status and full guidelines.

Publishing Imprints: 4RV Biblical Based (**P004**); 4RV Children's Corner (**P005**); 4RV Fiction (**P006**); 4RV Nonfiction (**P007**); 4RV Tweens & Teens (**P009**); 4RV Young Adult (**P010**)

P009 4RV Tweens & Teens

Publishing Imprint
United States

Book Publisher: 4RV Publishing (**P008**)

CHILDREN'S > **Fiction** > *Middle Grade*

TEEN > **Fiction** > *Novels*

Publishes books for teens / tweens grades 5-8.

P010 4RV Young Adult

Publishing Imprint
United States

Book Publisher: 4RV Publishing (**P008**)

YOUNG ADULT > **Fiction** > *Novels*

Publishes books for young adults aged 14-18.

P011 4th Estate

Publishing Imprint
The News Building, 1 London Bridge Street, London, SE1 9GF
United Kingdom
Tel: +44 (0) 20 8741 7070

4thestate.marketing@harpercollins.co.uk

http://www.4thestate.co.uk

Book Publisher: HarperCollins UK (**P347**)

Types: Fiction; Nonfiction
Formats: Reference
Subjects: Biography; Comedy / Humour; Current Affairs; Literary; Science; Travel
Markets: Adult

Closed to approaches.

Strong reputation for Literary and nonfiction. No unsolicited mss.

P012 A-R Editions

Book Publisher
1600 Aspen Cmns, Suite 100, Middleton WI 53562
United States
Tel: +1 (608) 836-9000

info@areditions.com

https://www.areditions.com
https://www.facebook.com/areditions

Nonfiction > *Nonfiction Books*: Music

Send: Query; Proposal
How to send: Email; File sharing service

Publisher of modern critical editions of music based on current musicological research, aimed at scholars and performers. See website for submission guidelines.

Managing Editor: Paul L. Ranzini

Publishing Imprint: Greenway Music Press (**P309**)

P013 Aardwolf Press

Book Publisher
United States

aardwolfpress@aol.com

http://www.aardwolfpress.com

Fiction > *Novels*
Fantasy; Horror; Science Fiction; Speculative

Does not want:

Fiction > *Novels*
Hard Science Fiction; Space Opera

Send: Query; Outline; Writing sample
How to send: Email
How not to send: Email attachment

Small publisher of speculative fiction between 50,000 and 100,000 words. Send query by email with first five pages in the body of the text. No attachments, poetry, previously published books (including online in any form), children's, stories set mainly off the Earth or earlier than the 20th century, books about elves, dragons, wizards, quests for rings/jewels/swords etc. space opera or hard science fiction.

P014 ABC-CLIO

Book Publisher
147 Castilian Drive, Santa Barbara, CA 93117
United States
Tel: +1 (800) 368-6868
Fax: +1 (805) 968-1911

CustomerService@abc-clio.com

https://www.abc-clio.com/
https://www.facebook.com/ABCCLIO
https://twitter.com/ABC_CLIO
https://www.youtube.com/user/ABCCLIOLive
https://www.linkedin.com/company/abc-clio/

ACADEMIC > **Nonfiction** > *Reference*
General, and in particular: History; Sociology

Publishes academic reference works and periodicals primarily on topics such as history and social sciences for educational and public library settings.

Publishing Imprints: ABC-CLIO / Greenwood; Libraries Unlimited (*P440*); Praeger (*P619*)

P015 Abdo Publishing Co

Book Publisher
1920 Lookout Drive, North Mankato MN 56003
United States
Tel: +1 (800) 800-1312
Fax: +1 (800) 862-3480

fiction@abdobooks.com

http://abdopublishing.com

Types: Fiction; Nonfiction
Subjects: Anthropology; Arts; Biography; Cookery; Crafts; Culture; Current Affairs; Design; Entertainment; History; Hobbies; Medicine; Politics; Religion; Science; Sociology; Sport; Technology; Travel; Warfare
Markets: Children's

Closed to approaches.

Publishes nonfiction, educational material for children up to the 12th grade, plus fiction series for children. Not accepting nonfiction submissions as at May 2017 (see website for current situation). Writers with a concept for a fiction series should send samples of manuscripts by email.

Editor: Paul Abdo

P016 Absolute Press

Publishing Imprint
United Kingdom

office@absolutepress.co.uk

http://www.absolutepress.co.uk
http://instagram.com/absolute_cooks
http://twitter.com/absolute_cooks

Book Publisher: Bloomsbury Publishing Plc (**P107**)

Nonfiction > *Nonfiction Books*
Cookery; Food and Drink

One of the UK's leading food and drink book lists.

Managing Director: Jon Croft

P017 Abson Books London

Book Publisher
5 Sidney Square, London, E1 2EY
United Kingdom
Tel: +44 (0) 20 7790 4737
Fax: +44 (0) 20 7790 7346

book.sales@absonbooks.co.uk

http://www.absonbooks.co.uk

Nonfiction > *Nonfiction Books*
Dialects; Slang

Publisher of pocket-size books on dialect and slang.

Publisher: M.J. Ellison

P018 Abuzz Press

Book Publisher
United States

https://www.abuzzpress.com

Fiction > *Novels*
General, and in particular: Adventure; Christianity

Nonfiction
Colouring Books: General
Nonfiction Books: Adventure; Christianity; How To

How to send: Online submission system

Publishes nonfiction, adult colouring books, how-to, new age, and exceptional fiction. No poetry, short story collections, books with colour interiors, or illegal material. Send submissions via form on website.

P019 Acair Ltd

Book Publisher
An Tosgan, 54 Seaforth Road, Stornoway, Isle of Lewis, HS1 2SD

United Kingdom
Tel: +44 (0) 1851 703020

info@acairbooks.com

https://www.acairbooks.com
https://www.facebook.com/acairbooks
https://twitter.com/AcairBooks
https://www.pinterest.co.uk/acairbooks/

ADULT
Fiction in Translation > *Novels*: Gaelic

Nonfiction in Translation > *Nonfiction Books*: Gaelic

Nonfiction > *Nonfiction Books*

Poetry in Translation > *Any Poetic Form*: Gaelic

CHILDREN'S > **Fiction in Translation**
Novels: Gaelic
Picture Books: Gaelic

Publishes a wide range of Gaelic, English and Bilingual books, including children's fiction. 75% of children's books published are exclusively Gaelic.

P020 Adams Media

Publishing Imprint

Book Publisher: Simon & Schuster Adult Publishing (**P711**)

P021 Addison Wesley

Publishing Imprint
United States

Book Publisher: Pearson

ACADEMIC > **Nonfiction** > *Nonfiction Books*
Computer Science; Finance; Mathematics; Statistics

Publishes academic textbooks, learning programs, and multimedia in the areas of computer science, economics, finance, mathematics and statistics.

P022 Adlard Coles

Publishing Imprint
United Kingdom

adlardcoles@bloomsbury.com

https://www.bloomsbury.com/uk/connect/contact-us/writing-for-bloomsbury/

Book Publisher: Bloomsbury Publishing Plc (**P107**)

Nonfiction > *Nonfiction Books*: Nautical

Send: Query; Synopsis; Writing sample; Outline; Market info; Author bio
How to send: Email

Nautical imprint of large international publisher. Happy to accept unsolicited submissions, but response only if interested. Send all submissions by email with the word "submission" in the subject line.

P023 Adonis and Abbey Publishing

Book Publisher
Adonis & Abbey Publishers Ltd, P.O. Box 43418, London, SE11 4XZ, United Kingdom
United Kingdom
Tel: +44 (0) 20 7793 8893

editor@adonis-abbey.com

http://www.adonisandabbey.com

Types: Nonfiction
Formats: Reference
Subjects: Anthropology; Culture; Current Affairs; History; Lifestyle; Literary; Traditional
Markets: Academic; Adult

Send: Full text

This press is actively seeking personal material from an experiential point of view while employing a vocabulary that will educate the reader with a real sense of presence. They are also seeking highly academic books on current events and history. Manuscripts with an African or African American view point are also sought. Query first.

P024 AdventureKEEN

Book Publisher
United States
Tel: +1 (800) 678-7006
Fax: +1 (877) 374-9016

info@adventurewithkeen.com

https://adventurewithkeen.com
https://www.instagram.com/adventurewithkeen/
https://twitter.com/adventurekeen
https://www.facebook.com/adventurekeen/
https://www.pinterest.com/adventurekeen/
https://www.linkedin.com/company/adventurekeen

Nonfiction > *Nonfiction Books*
Adventure; Local History; Nature; Outdoor Activities; Sport; Travel

A nonfiction publisher of books on a wide range of subjects, including adventure, outdoors, travel, nature, local history, sports, and more.

Publishing Imprint: Menasha Ridge Press (**P488**)

P025 AFK

Publishing Imprint

Book Publisher: Scholastic (**P688**)

P026 Agora Books

Book Publisher
55 New Oxford Street, London, WC1A 1BS
United Kingdom
Tel: +44 (0) 20 7344 1000

submissions@agorabooks.co

https://www.agorabooks.co

Literary Agency: Peters Fraser + Dunlop (**L560**)

Types: Fiction
Subjects: Crime; History; Mystery; Suspense; Women's Interests
Markets: Adult

Send: Query
Don't send: Full text

Send synopsis and first three chapters (or 50 pages) as Word document attachments by email. See website for full guidelines.

P027 Aladdin

Publishing Imprint

Book Publisher: Simon & Schuster Children's Publishing (**P713**)

P028 Alfred A. Knopf

Publishing Imprint
United States

Book Publisher: Knopf Doubleday Publishing Group (**P426**)

P029 Algonquin Books

Publishing Imprint
PO Box 2225, Chapel Hill, NC 27515-2225
United States
Tel: +1 (919) 967-0108
Fax: +1 (919) 933-0272

inquiry@algonquin.com

https://www.algonquin.com
http://twitter.com/algonquinbooks
http://facebook.com/AlgonquinBooks
http://instagram.com/algonquinbooks

Book Publisher: Workman Publishing Company

Fiction > *Novels*

Nonfiction
Illustrated Books: General
Nonfiction Books: Agriculture; Animals; Arts; Biography; Business; Comedy / Humour; Cookery; Crafts; Family; Farming; Food and Drink; Gardening; Health; History; How To; Memoir; Nature; Parenting; Pets; Recreation; Relationships; Science; Self Help; Sport; Travel; Wellbeing
Reference: General

Poetry > *Poetry Collections*

Closed to approaches.

Publishes both fiction and nonfiction. Does not accept unsolicited submissions.

P030 Allen & Unwin

Book Publisher
SYDNEY:, 83 Alexander St, Crows Nest, NSW 2065, MELBOURNE:, 406 Albert Street, East Melbourne, Vic 3002

Australia
Tel: +61 (0) 2 8425 0100

fridaypitch@allenandunwin.com

https://www.allenandunwin.com
https://www.allenandunwin.com/about/submission-guidelines/the-friday-pitch
https://www.facebook.com/AllenandUnwinBooks
https://twitter.com/AllenAndUnwin
http://instagram.com/allenandunwin

ADULT
Fiction > *Novels*
Nonfiction > *Nonfiction Books*

CHILDREN'S > **Fiction**
Board Books; *Chapter Books*; *Early Readers*; *Middle Grade*; *Picture Books*
YOUNG ADULT > **Fiction** > *Novels*

Send: Query; Synopsis; Writing sample
How to send: Email

Publisher with offices in Australia, New Zealand, and the UK. Accepts queries by email. See website for detailed instructions.

P031 Allison & Busby Ltd

Book Publisher
11 Wardour Mews, London, W1F 8AN
United Kingdom
Tel: +44 (0) 20 3950 7834

susie@allisonandbusby.com

https://www.allisonandbusby.com
http://www.facebook.com/pages/Allison-Busby-Books/51600359534
https://twitter.com/allisonandbusby
https://www.youtube.com/channel/UCrYAc6ndJZWJWAONHCn8-Qw
https://www.tiktok.com/@allisonandbusby
https://www.instagram.com/allisonandbusby/

Fiction > *Novels*
Contemporary; Crime; Fantasy; Historical Fiction; Mystery; Romance; Saga; Thrillers

Nonfiction
Gift Books: General
Nonfiction Books: Biography; Comedy / Humour; Crime; Memoir

How to send: Through a literary agent

Accepts approaches via a literary agent only. No unsolicited MSS or queries from authors.

Publishing Director: Susie Dunlop

P032 Alma Books Ltd

Book Publisher
Thornton House, Thornton Road, Wimbledon, London, SW19 4NG
United Kingdom

info@almabooks.com

https://www.almabooks.com
https://www.facebook.com/AlmaPublishing/
https://twitter.com/almabooks
https://www.pinterest.co.uk/almabooks/
https://www.instagram.com/almapublishing/

Fiction in Translation > *Novels*

Fiction > *Novels*

Nonfiction in Translation > *Nonfiction Books*

Nonfiction > *Nonfiction Books*

Send: Query
How to send: Email

Closed to submissions of contemporary fiction. Accepts proposals for translations of classic literature, and welcomes proposals and ideas for the Classics list.

Publishing Imprints: Alma Classics; Calder Publications Ltd (**P135**)

P033 Alternating Current Press

Book Publisher
PO Box 270921, Louisville, CO 80027
United States

alt.current@gmail.com

http://www.alternatingcurrentarts.com

ADULT
Fiction > *Novels*
Nonfiction > *Nonfiction Books*

CHILDREN'S > **Fiction** > *Chapter Books*

Indie press dedicated to publishing and promoting incredible literature that challenges readers and has an innate sense of self, timelessness, and atmosphere:

Online Magazine: The Coil (**M125**)

P034 AMACOM Books

Book Publisher
United States
Tel: +1 (800) 250-5308

harpercollinsleadershipcc@harpercollins.com

https://www.harpercollinsleadership.com/amacombooks/

Book Publisher: HarperCollins Leadership (**P346**)

PROFESSIONAL > **Nonfiction** > *Nonfiction Books*
Business; Finance; Leadership; Management

Publishes business books only, covering such topics as finance, management, sales, marketing, human resources, customer services, quality control, career growth, etc.

P035 Amato Books

Book Publisher; Magazine Publisher
United States
Tel: +1 (800) 541-9498

customerservice@amatobooks.com

https://amatobooks.com

Nonfiction > *Nonfiction Books*
Alaska; Fishing; Fly Fishing; History; How To; Hunting; Offshore Gamefishing; Walking

Magazine: Flyfishing & Tying Journal (**M206**)

P036 American Catholic Press

Book Publisher
16565 S. State Street, South Holland, Illinois 60473
United States
Tel: +1 (708) 331-5485
Fax: +1 (708) 331-5484

acp@acpress.org

http://www.americancatholicpress.org

Nonfiction > *Nonfiction Books*
Christianity; Church Music

Publishes books on the Roman Catholic liturgy, including new music for use in church services. No religious poetry.

Editorial Director: Rev. Michael Gilligan PhD

P037 Amistad

Publishing Imprint

Book Publisher: HarperCollins

P038 Anchor Books

Publishing Imprint
United States

Book Publisher: Knopf Doubleday Publishing Group (**P426**)

P039 Andersen Press Ltd

Book Publisher
20 Vauxhall Bridge Road, London, SW1V 2SA
United Kingdom

anderseneditorial@penguinrandomhouse.co.uk

https://www.andersenpress.co.uk
https://twitter.com/andersenpresshttps://twitter.com/andersenpress
https://www.facebook.com/andersenpress

CHILDREN'S > **Fiction** > *Picture Books*

How to send: Through a literary agent

Publishes rhyming stories, but no poetry, adult fiction, fiction for older children, nonfiction, or short story collections. Accepts submissions through literary agents only.

P040 Angry Robot

Publishing Imprint
Unit 11, Shepperton House, 89 Shepperton Road, London, N1 3DF
United Kingdom
Tel: +44 (0) 20 3813 6940

incoming@angryrobotbooks.com

https://www.angryrobotbooks.com
https://twitter.com/#!/angryrobotbooks

https://www.instagram.com/angryrobotbooks
http://www.facebook.com/angryrobotbooks
https://www.youtube.com/channel/UC_2x8RXR5uL-_psvMmeBwNg
https://www.tiktok.com/@angryrobotbooks?lang=en

Book Publisher: Watkins Media

Fiction > *Novels*
Cyberpunk; Fantasy; Hard Science Fiction; Horror; Science Fiction; Space Opera; Time Travel

How to send: Through a literary agent; Email

Publisher of science fiction and fantasy. Accepts submissions through literary agents only, apart from a specific open door period held each year. See the company's social media for updates.

Black writers can submit directly. All other races must approach through a literary agent.

P041 Anthony Bourdain Books

Publishing Imprint

Book Publisher: HarperCollins

P042 Anvil Press Publishers

Book Publisher
P.O. Box 3008, MPO, Vancouver, B.C., V6B 3X5
Canada
Tel: +1 (604) 876-8710

info@anvilpress.com

https://www.anvilpress.com
https://www.facebook.com/Anvil-Press-115437275199047/
https://www.twitter.com/anvilpress
https://www.instagram.com/anvilpress_publishers/

Fiction > *Novels*

Nonfiction > *Nonfiction Books*
Arts; Photography

Poetry > *Poetry Collections*

Scripts > *Theatre Scripts*: Drama

Closed to approaches.

Publisher designed to discover and nurture Canadian literary talent. Considers work from Canadian authors only.

Editor: Brian Kaufman

P043 Apex Publishing Ltd

Book Publisher
307 Holland Road, Holland on Sea, Essex, CO15 6PD
United Kingdom
Tel: +44 (0) 1255 812555

mail@apexpublishing.co.uk

http://www.apexpublishing.co.uk

Fiction > *Novels*: Contemporary

Nonfiction > *Nonfiction Books*
Biography; Entertainment; Lifestyle; Memoir; Real Life Stories; Sport

Send: Submission Form
How to send: Post

Will consider publishing a wide range of high-quality non-fiction and also well-written works of contemporary fiction. Has a particular interest in real-life stories, biographies, memoirs, entertainment and lifestyle and sport.

Editor: Chris Cowlin

P044 Applause

Publishing Imprint
United States

Book Publisher: The Globe Pequot Press (**P296**)

P045 Arc Music

Publishing Imprint

Book Publisher: Arc Publications (**P046**)

P046 Arc Publications

Book Publisher
Nanholme Mill, Shaw Wood Road, Todmorden, Lancs, OL14 6DA
United Kingdom
Tel: +44 (0) 1706 812338

info@arcpublications.co.uk

https://www.arcpublications.co.uk

Types: Poetry; Translations
Subjects: Contemporary; Music
Markets: Adult

Send: Full text

Send 16-24 poems by email as a Word / PDF attachment, maximum one poem per page, during December only. Submissions from outside the UK and Ireland should be sent to specific address for international submissions, available on website. Cover letter should include short bio and details of the contemporary poets you read. See website for full guidelines.

Publishing Imprint: Arc Music (*P045*)

P047 Arcadia Books

Publishing Imprint
United Kingdom

https://www.quercusbooks.co.uk/landing-page/arcadia-books/

Publishing Imprint: MacLehose Press (**P467**)

Fiction in Translation > *Novels*

Fiction > *Novels*
Crime; Literary

Publisher of translated fiction, literary fiction and crime.

P048 Arcana

Publishing Imprint

Book Publisher: Aurelia Leo (**P060**)

P049 Arcturus Publishing Ltd

Book Publisher
26/27 Bickels Yard, 151-153 Bermondsey Street, London, SE1 3HA
United Kingdom
Tel: +44 (0) 20 7407 9400
Fax: +44 (0) 20 7407 9444

info@arcturuspublishing.com

https://arcturuspublishing.com
https://www.facebook.com/ArcturusPublishing/
https://twitter.com/arcturusbooks
https://www.instagram.com/arcturusbooks/

ADULT > **Nonfiction**
Nonfiction Books: Classics / Ancient World; New Age; Practical Art
Puzzle Books: General
Reference: General

CHILDREN'S > **Nonfiction** > *Nonfiction Books*

Non-fiction ranges cover reference, practical art, new age, classics, puzzles and children's books.

P050 Arsenal Pulp Press

Book Publisher
202-211 East Georgia Street, Vancouver, BC, V6A 1Z6
Canada
Tel: +1 (604) 687-4233
Fax: +1 (604) 687-4283

info@arsenalpulp.com

https://arsenalpulp.com

ADULT
Fiction > *Novels*
LGBTQIA; Literary

Nonfiction > *Nonfiction Books*
British Columbia; Culture; LGBTQIA; Literary; Politics; Regional; Sociology; Youth Culture

CHILDREN'S
Fiction > *Novels*
Diversity; LGBTQIA

Nonfiction > *Nonfiction Books*
Diversity; LGBTQIA

YOUNG ADULT
Fiction > *Novels*: LGBTQIA

Nonfiction > *Nonfiction Books*: LGBTQIA

Send: Synopsis; Outline; Writing sample; Market info; Self-Addressed Stamped Envelope (SASE)
How to send: Post
How not to send: Fax; Email; Phone

Publishes Cultural studies, Political/sociological studies, Regional studies and guides, in particular for British Columbia, Cookbooks, Gay and lesbian fiction and nonfiction (including young adult and children's), Visual art, Multicultural fiction and nonfiction, Literary fiction and nonfiction (no genre fiction, such as mysteries, thriller, or romance), Youth culture, Health, and books for children (especially those that emphasise diversity). Send query with synopsis, chapter by chapter outline for nonfiction, writing credentials, 50-page excerpt, and marketing analysis. Include self-addressed envelope and appropriate return postage (either Canadian postage or IRCs), or email address for response. See website for full details. No submissions by fax or email, or queries by phone.

P051 Arte Publico Press

Book Publisher
University of Houston, 4902 Gulf Fwy, Bldg. 19, Room 100, Houston, TX 77204-2004
United States
Fax: +1 (713) 743-2847

submapp@uh.edu

https://artepublicopress.com
https://www.facebook.com/artepublico/
https://twitter.com/artepublico
https://www.instagram.com/artepublico/
https://www.pinterest.com/artepublico/
http://artepublicopress.tumblr.com/

Fiction > *Novels*
Central America; Culture; History; Politics; South America

Nonfiction > *Nonfiction Books*
Central America; Culture; History; Politics; South America

Send: Writing sample
How to send: Online submission system
How not to send: Post

Publisher of contemporary and recovered literature by US Hispanic authors.

Editor: Nicolas Kanellos

Publishing Imprint: Pinata Books (**P607**)

P052 Ascend Books, LLC

Book Publisher
11722 West 91st Street, Overland Park, Kansas 66214
United States
Tel: +1 (913) 948-5500

bsnodgrass@ascendbooks.com

http://ascendbooks.com
http://www.twitter.com/Ascend_Books

ADULT > **Nonfiction** > *Nonfiction Books*
Entertainment; Sport

CHILDREN'S > **Fiction**
Board Books; *Picture Books*

Send: Query; Self-Addressed Stamped Envelope (SASE)
How to send: Post
How not to send: Email

Highly specialised publishing company with a burgeoning presence in sports, entertainment and commemoration events. Send query by email.

Editor: Bob Snodgrass

P053 Ashley Drake Publishing Ltd

Book Publisher
PO Box 733, Cardiff, CF14 7ZY
United Kingdom

post@ashleydrake.com

http://www.ashleydrake.com

ACADEMIC > **Nonfiction** > *Nonfiction Books*
Education; History; Medieval Literature; Politics; Scandinavia

ADULT > **Nonfiction**
Nonfiction Books: Leisure; Sport
Reference: Popular

Send: Proposal

Publishes English and Welsh language trade and academic books. Welcomes proposals. Forms for proposals can be found on the website.

Publishing Imprints: Gwasg Addysgol Cymru; Morgan Publishing; Scandinavian Academic Press; St David's Press; Welsh Academic Press; YDdraig Fach

P054 Athenaeum Press

Book Publisher
United States

https://theathenaeumpress.com
https://www.facebook.com/theathenaeumpress/
https://www.instagram.com/athenaeumpress/
https://twitter.com/athenaeum_press
http://www.amazon.com/shops/athenaeumpress

Closed to approaches.

Online Magazine: Waccamaw (**M521**)

P055 Atheneum

Publishing Imprint

Book Publisher: Simon & Schuster Children's Publishing (**P713**)

P056 Atlantean Publishing

Book Publisher; Magazine Publisher
4 Pierrot Steps, 71 Kursaal Way, Southend-on-Sea, Essex, SS1 2UY
United Kingdom

atlanteanpublishing@hotmail.com

https://atlanteanpublishing.fandom.com/wiki/Atlantean_Publishing
https://atlanteanpublishing.wordpress.com/
https://www.facebook.com/Atlantean.Publishing

Fiction > *Short Fiction*

Poetry > *Any Poetic Form*

Non-profit-making small press. Produces several serial publications and numerous one-off releases, specialising in poetry and short fiction, both 'general' and 'genre'.

Editor: David-John Tyrer

Magazines: Awen (**M052**); Bard (**M059**); Monomyth (**M328**); The Supplement (**M472**)

Online Magazines: 5-7-5 Haiku Journal (**M008**); View From Atlantis (**M518**)

P057 Atlantic Books

Book Publisher
Ormond House, 26-27 Boswell Street, London, WC1N 3JZ
United Kingdom
Tel: +44 (0) 20 7269 1610
Fax: +44 (0) 20 7430 0916

enquiries@atlantic-books.co.uk

https://atlantic-books.co.uk

Types: Fiction; Nonfiction
Subjects: Autobiography; Current Affairs; History; Literary; Politics
Markets: Adult

Send: Query
Don't send: Full text

Open to submissions of complete novels, extensive partials, or short stories, within the literary genre. Send submissions with a one line pitch and a one paragraph pitch, outlining the submission.

P058 Atlantic Monthly Press

Publishing Imprint
United States

Book Publisher: Grove Atlantic Inc. (**P312**)

P059 Atria

Publishing Imprint

Book Publisher: Simon & Schuster Adult Publishing (**P711**)

P060 Aurelia Leo

Book Publisher
4212 Algonquin Parkway, Louisville, KY 40211-2402
United States

hello@pridebookcafe.com

https://pridebookcafe.com/aurelia-leo/

Fiction > *Short Fiction*
Erotic Romance; Fantasy; LGBTQIA; Science Fiction

Closed to approaches.

Currently looking for lesbian, gay, bisexual, and transgender erotic romance with elements of sci-fi and fantasy for a themed anthology. 1,000 to 17,500 words.

Editor: Zelda Knight

Publishing Imprint: Arcana (*P048*)

P061 Aurora Metro Press

Book Publisher
67 Grove Avenue, Twickenham, TW1 4HX
United Kingdom
Tel: +44 (0) 20 3261 0000

submissions@aurorametro.com

https://aurorametro.com

ADULT
Fiction
Novels; *Short Fiction*
Nonfiction > *Nonfiction Books*
Arts; Biography; History; Popular Culture; Travel; Wellbeing
Scripts
Film Scripts; *Theatre Scripts*
YOUNG ADULT > **Fiction** > *Novels*

Send: Query; Synopsis; Author bio; Writing sample

Publishes adult fiction, YA fiction, drama, and non-fiction biography and books about the arts and popular culture.

P062 Authentic Ideas

Publishing Imprint
85 Great Portland Street, First Floor, London, W1W 7LT
United Kingdom
Tel: +44 (0) 20 3745 0658

enquiries@integrity-media.co.uk

http://www.integrity-media.co.uk

Book Publisher: Integrity Media (**P399**)

Fiction > *Novels*
Comedy / Humour; Crime; Drama; Fantasy; Horror; Literary; Mystery; Science Fiction; Thrillers

Send: Query; Synopsis; Writing sample
How to send: Email

Seeks to help up and coming authors to find their voice, display their creativity and deliver a novel of which they can be proud. It is our desire, that through this imprint our authors find their written voice and peace from their past. And through this imprint, a road for the future.

P063 Authentic Life

Publishing Imprint
85 Great Portland Street, First Floor, London, W1W 7LT
United Kingdom
Tel: +44 (0) 20 3745 0658

enquiries@integrity-media.co.uk

http://www.integrity-media.co.uk

Book Publisher: Integrity Media (**P399**)

Nonfiction > *Nonfiction Books*
Autobiography; Biography; Health; Mental Health; Philosophy; Psychology; Self Help; Spirituality

Send: Query; Synopsis; Writing sample
How to send: Email

Focuses on relaying stories that cut to the heart of the society we all share. These are stories of normal individuals. Tales of hardship, suffering, injustice, endurance, strength, tenacity, resilience, faith and hope, that convey a picture of the world most of us witness and experience.

P064 Autumn Publishing Ltd

Book Publisher
Cottage Farm, Mears Ashby Road, Sywell, Northants, NN6 0BJ
United Kingdom
Tel: +44 (0) 1604 741116
Fax: +44 (0) 1604 670495

customerservice@igloobooks.com

https://autumnpublishing.co.uk

Book Publisher: Bonnier Books (UK) (**P117**)

CHILDREN'S > **Nonfiction**
Activity Books: General
Nonfiction Books: English; Health; Mathematics; Nature; Science

Deals in books for babies and toddlers, activity books, early learning books, and sticker books. Publisher's philosophy is that children should enjoy learning with books, and to this end combines activity and learning by turning simple workbooks into activity books, allowing children to learn whilst they play.

Editorial Director: Lyn Coutts

Publishing Imprint: Byeway Books

P065 Avalon Travel

Publishing Imprint
United States

https://www.avalontravelbooks.com

Book Publisher: Perseus Books (**P594**)

Nonfiction > *Nonfiction Books*: Travel

How to send: Through a literary agent

Publishes independent travel guides.

P066 Avery

Publishing Imprint

Book Publisher: Penguin Publishing Group (**P585**)

P067 Avid Reader Press

Publishing Imprint

Book Publisher: Simon & Schuster Adult Publishing (**P711**)

P068 Avon

Publishing Imprint
United Kingdom

Book Publisher: HarperCollins UK (**P347**)

P069 Avon Books

Publishing Imprint
United States

https://www.harpercollins.com
https://www.harpercollins.com/pages/avonromance
https://twitter.com/avonbooks
https://www.instagram.com/avonbooks/
https://www.facebook.com/avonromance

Book Publisher: HarperCollins

Fiction > *Novels*
Contemporary Romance; Historical Romance; Romance; Romantic Comedy; Supernatural / Paranormal Romance

Publishing award-winning romance since 1941. Recognized for having pioneered the historical romance category and continues to publish in wide variety of other genres, including paranormal, urban fantasy, contemporary and regency.

P070 Backbeat

Publishing Imprint
United States

Book Publisher: The Globe Pequot Press (**P296**)

P071 Bad Press Ink

Book Publisher
United Kingdom

enquiries@badpress.ink

https://badpress.ink
https://www.facebook.com/BADPRESS.iNKPublishing
https://twitter.com/badpressink
https://www.youtube.com/user/iainparkebadpress

Fiction > *Novels*

Publishes alternative books and niche lifestyle fiction. Complete online submission process on website.

Editors: Pat Blayney; Iain Parke

P072 Badger Learning

Book Publisher
Unit 55 Oldmedow Road, Hardwick Industrial Estate, King's Lynn, Norfolk, PE30 4JJ
United Kingdom
Tel: +44 (0) 1553 816082
Fax: +44 (0) 1553 768646

info@badger-publishing.co.uk

https://www.badgerlearning.co.uk
https://twitter.com/@BadgerLearning
https://en-gb.facebook.com/badger.learning

ACADEMIC > **Nonfiction** > *Nonfiction Books*
English; History; Mathematics; Science

CHILDREN'S
Fiction
Chapter Books; *Early Readers*; *Middle Grade*
Nonfiction > *Nonfiction Books*

TEEN
Fiction > *Novels*
Nonfiction > *Nonfiction Books*

YOUNG ADULT
Fiction > *Novels*
Nonfiction > *Nonfiction Books*

Publishes books for UK schools, particularly books to engage reluctant and struggling readers.

P073 Baker Publishing Group

Book Publisher
6030 East Fulton Road, Ada, MI 49301
United States
Tel: +1 (616) 676-9185
Fax: +1 (616) 676-9573

http://bakerpublishinggroup.com

Fiction > *Novels*: Christianity

Nonfiction > *Nonfiction Books*: Christianity

Publishes high-quality writings that represent historic Christianity and serve the diverse interests and concerns of evangelical readers.

Book Publishers: Baker Academic; Baker Books; Brazos Press; Chosen Books; Fleming H. Revell

P074 Ballantine

Publishing Imprint

Book Publisher: Random House (**P640**)

P075 Balzer + Bray

Publishing Imprint

Book Publisher: HarperCollins

P076 Bantam

Publishing Imprint
United States

http://www.randomhousebooks.com/imprints/

Book Publisher: Random House (**P640**)

Fiction > *Novels*

Nonfiction > *Nonfiction Books*

How to send: Through a literary agent

Publishes original works of fiction and nonfiction in all formats.

Magazine: island

P077 Baobab Press

Book Publisher
121 California Avenue, Reno, NV 89503
United States
Tel: +1 (775) 786-1188

info@baobabpress.com

https://baobabpress.com

ADULT
Fiction
Graphic Novels: General
Novels: Contemporary; Literary
Short Fiction: Contemporary; Literary
Nonfiction
Essays: General
Short Nonfiction: Memoir

Poetry > *Poetry Collections*

CHILDREN'S > **Fiction**
Board Books; *Picture Books*

How to send: Submittable

Constantly strives to discover, cultivate, and nurture authors working in all genres. Publishes Creative Nonfiction, Short-Story, Novel, and Comic/Visual Narrative manuscripts (Comic/Visual Narrative manuscripts will not be considered without artwork). Also publishes children's picture and board books (send text with or without artwork). Submit via online submission system.

P078 Barbour Publishing

Book Publisher
United States
Tel: +1 (800) 852-8010

submissions@barbourbooks.com

https://www.barbourbooks.com
https://www.facebook.com/BarbourPublishing/
https://twitter.com/barbourbuzz
https://www.youtube.com/user/BarbourPublishing1
https://www.instagram.com/barbourbooks/

ADULT
Fiction > *Novels*
Amish; Contemporary; Historical Fiction; Romance; Suspense

Nonfiction
Nonfiction Books: Bible Studies; Bibles; Christian Living; Christianity; Evangelism; Inspirational
Puzzle Books: General

CHILDREN'S > **Nonfiction**
Activity Books: General
Nonfiction Books: Bible Stories; Bible Studies; Bibles
Puzzle Books: General

How to send: Through a literary agent

Publishes a range of fiction and nonfiction, but all must demonstrate a conservative, evangelical Christian world view, and speak to broad segments of the evangelical Christian market.

Fiction Editor: Rebecca Germany

Nonfiction Editor: Paul Muckley

Publishing Imprint: Heartsong Presents

P079 Barefoot Books

Book Publisher
United States
Tel: +1 (866) 417-2369

help@barefootbooks.com
submission@barefootbooks.com

https://www.barefootbooks.com
https://www.facebook.com/barefootbooks
https://twitter.com/BarefootBooks
http://www.pinterest.com/BarefootBooks/
http://instagram.com/barefootbooks/
https://www.youtube.com/user/barefootbooks
https://www.tiktok.com/@barefootbooks

CHILDREN'S > **Fiction**
Board Books; *Picture Books*

How to send: Through a literary agent

An independent children's book publisher focusing on diverse, inclusive, beautifully illustrated board books and picture books for ages 0–12.

P080 Barricade Books

Book Publisher
2005 Palmer Ave, Ste 800, Larchmont, NY 10538
United States

Info@barricadebooks.com

http://www.barricadebooks.com

Nonfiction > *Nonfiction Books*

Editor: Carole Stuart

P081 Barrington Stoke

Book Publisher
18 Walker Street, Edinburgh, EH3 7LP
United Kingdom
Tel: +44 (0) 131 225 4113

info@barringtonstoke.co.uk

https://www.barringtonstoke.co.uk

Types: Fiction; Nonfiction
Formats: Reference
Markets: Children's; Professional

Closed to approaches.

Commissions books via literary agents only. No unsolicited material. Publishes books for "reluctant, dyslexic, disenchanted and under-confident" readers and their teachers.

P082 BatCat Press

Book Publisher
c/o Lincoln Park Performing Arts Charter School, One Lincoln Park, Midland, PA 15059
United States

batcatpress@gmail.com

https://batcatpress.com

Fiction > *Short Fiction*

Nonfiction > *Nonfiction Books*: Creative Nonfiction

Poetry > *Any Poetic Form*

Closed to approaches.

Publishes literary fiction, poetry, and creative nonfiction. Submit via online submission system.

P083 Batsford

Publishing Imprint

Book Publisher: Pavilion Books (**P572**)

P084 BBC Books

Publishing Imprint
United Kingdom

https://www.penguin.co.uk/company/publishers/ebury/bbc-books.html

Book Publisher: Ebury (**P226**)

Nonfiction > *Nonfiction Books*
General, and in particular: Entertainment; Food and Drink; Nature; Popular Culture; TV

Specialises in TV and radio tie-ins, as well as food and drink, nature, and history, etc.

Editor: Stuart Biles

P085 BCS (British Computer Society)

Book Publisher
United Kingdom
Tel: +44 (0) 1793 417417

publishing@bcs.uk

https://www.bcs.org/

PROFESSIONAL > **Nonfiction** > *Nonfiction Books*
Business; Cyber Security; Data and Information Systems; Finance; Leadership; Legal; Management; Procurement; Project Management; Service Management; Software Development

Publishes books for business and technology professionals.

Editor: Matthew Flynn

P086 Beach Lane Books

Publishing Imprint

Book Publisher: Simon & Schuster Children's Publishing (**P713**)

P087 becker&mayer! books

Publishing Imprint
11120 NE 33rd Place Suite 101, Bellevue, WA 98004
United States
Tel: +1 (425) 827-7120
Fax: +1 (425) 828-9659

mike.oprins@quarto.com

https://www.quartoknows.com/brand/2113/becker-mayer/

Book Publisher: The Quarto Group, Inc. (**P633**)

Types: Nonfiction
Markets: Adult; Children's

Publishes illustrated nonfiction for adults and children.

Editor: Mike Oprins

P088 becker&mayer! kids

Publishing Imprint

Book Publisher: The Quarto Group, Inc. (**P633**)

P089 Berghahn Books Ltd

Book Publisher
3 Newtec Place, Magdalen Rd, Oxford, OX4 1RE
United Kingdom
Tel: +44 (0) 1865 250011
Fax: +44 (0) 1865 250056

editorial@berghahnbooks.com

https://www.berghahnbooks.com
https://www.facebook.com/BerghahnBooks
https://twitter.com/berghahnbooks
https://www.youtube.com/channel/UCuh-JFDwm_HfzX1zJ92tzcw
https://www.instagram.com/berghahnbooks/

ACADEMIC > **Nonfiction** > *Nonfiction Books*
Anthropology; Archaeology; Culture; Education; Environment; Films; Gender; History; Politics; Sociology; TV; Warfare

Send: Query; Submission Form; Outline
How to send: Email attachment

Academic publisher of books and journals covering the social sciences. Download New Book Outline form from website, complete, and submit by email with an outline and/or chapter summary.

Editor: Marion Berghahn

P090 Berkley

Publishing Imprint

Book Publisher: Penguin Publishing Group (**P585**)

P091 Berrett-Koehler Publishers

Book Publisher
1333 Broadway, Suite 1000, Oakland, CA 94612
United States
Tel: +1 (510) 817-2277
Fax: +1 (510) 817-2278

bkpub@bkpub.com

https://www.bkconnection.com
https://www.facebook.com/BerrettKoehler
https://twitter.com/Bkpub
https://www.linkedin.com/company/berrett-koehler-publishers/
https://www.pinterest.com/berrettkoehler/
https://www.youtube.com/berrettkoehler

Nonfiction > *Nonfiction Books*
Business; Career Development; Communication; Creativity; Economics; Equality; Leadership; Management

Send: Proposal; Outline; Writing sample; Market info
How to send: PDF file email attachment

Connecting people and ideas to create a world that works for all. Publishes titles that promote positive change at personal, organizational, and societal levels.

Senior Editor: Jeevan Sivasubramaniam

P092 Bess Press

Book Publisher
3565 Harding Avenue, Honolulu, HI 96816
United States
Tel: +1 (808) 734-7159
Fax: +1 (808) 732-3627

submission@besspress.com

https://www.besspress.com

ACADEMIC > **Nonfiction** > *Nonfiction Books*
Hawai'i; Pacific

ADULT
Fiction > *Novels*
Hawai'i; Pacific

Nonfiction > *Nonfiction Books*
Biography; Hawai'i; Memoir; Pacific

CHILDREN'S > **Fiction**
Activity Books: Hawai'i; Pacific
Board Books: Hawai'i; Pacific
Picture Books: Hawai'i; Pacific

Send: Query
How to send: Email

Publishes books about Hawai'i and the Pacific. All submissions should be sent by email. See website for full guidelines.

P093 Between the Lines

Book Publisher
401 Richmond Street West, Studio 281, Toronto, Ontario M5V 3A8
Canada
Tel: +1 (416) 535-9914

info@btlbooks.com
submissions@btlbooks.com

https://btlbooks.com
http://twitter.com/readBTLbooks
http://facebook.com/BTLbooks
https://www.instagram.com/btlbooks

Nonfiction > *Nonfiction Books*
Politics; Social Issues

How to send: Email

We publish nonfiction books that expose and challenge oppression in our society. We aim to amplify the struggles of Black, Indigenous, and racialized communities; migrants; women; queer folks; and working-class people. We are proudly left-wing and the books we publish reflect our activist roots and our commitment to social justice struggles. Our authors are academics, journalists, artists, and activists—all our authors hope their books will spark political and social change.

Acquisitions Editor: Paul Eprile

P094 BFI Publishing

Book Publisher
United Kingdom

https://www.bfi.org.uk
https://www.bfi.org.uk/bfi-book-releases-trade-sales
https://www.bloomsbury.com/uk/discover/bloomsbury-academic/authors/contacts-for-authors/

Book Publisher: Bloomsbury Academic (**P105**)

ACADEMIC > **Nonfiction** > *Nonfiction Books*
Film Industry; Films

Publishes film and television-related books and resources, both for schools and academic readerships, and more generally.

P095 Birlinn Ltd

Book Publisher
West Newington House, 10 Newington Road, Edinburgh, EH9 1QS
United Kingdom
Tel: +44 (0) 1316 684371

info@birlinn.co.uk

http://birlinn.co.uk
https://www.facebook.com/birlinnbooks/
https://twitter.com/BirlinnBooks
https://www.youtube.com/channel/UChVAhFnMniUb_3XiVmXPT7Q
https://www.instagram.com/birlinnbooks/

Fiction
Novels: Comedy / Humour; Crime; Historical Fiction; Thrillers
Short Fiction Collections: General

Nonfiction > *Nonfiction Books*
Art History; Arts; Biography; Business; Comedy / Humour; Crime; Current Affairs; Folklore, Myths, and Legends; Food; Gaelic; Gardening; Geology; Local History; Memoir; Nature; Photography; Politics; Scotland; Sport; Traditional Music; Travel

Send: Query; Synopsis; Writing sample
How to send: Email
How not to send: Post

Focuses on Scottish material: local, military, and Highland history; humour, adventure; reference, guidebooks, and folklore. No longer accepting submissions for fiction, poetry, or children's books. Submissions for these areas must be made through a literary agent. Continues to accept direct submissions for nonfiction.

P096 Bitter Lemon Press

Book Publisher
47 Wilmington Square, London, WC1X 0ET
United Kingdom
Tel: +44 (0) 20 7278 3738

books@bitterlemonpress.com

http://www.bitterlemonpress.com

Types: Fiction
Subjects: Crime; Literary; Thrillers
Markets: Adult

How to send: Through a literary agent

Accepts submissions in the literary crime and thriller genres. Submissions may be sent by email and must come through a literary agent.

P097 Black & White Publishing Ltd

Book Publisher
Nautical House, 104 Commercial Street, Edinburgh, EH6 6NF
United Kingdom
Tel: +44 (0) 1316 254500
Fax: +44 (0) 1316 254501

submissions@blackandwhitepublishing.com
mail@blackandwhitepublishing.com

https://blackandwhitepublishing.com
https://twitter.com/bwpublishing
https://www.facebook.com/blackandwhitepublishing/
https://www.instagram.com/bwpublishing/
https://www.youtube.com/user/blackandwhitePub

Fiction > *Novels*

Nonfiction > *Nonfiction Books*
Celebrity Memoir; Comedy / Humour; Food and Drink; Ireland; Lifestyle; Nature; Scotland; Sport

Send: Query; Proposal
How to send: Email; Through a literary agent

Publisher of general fiction and nonfiction. See website for an idea of the kind of books normally published. Accepts fiction submissions during specific submission windows only, or through a literary agent year-round. Check website for details and to submit via online submission system. No poetry, short stories, or work in languages other than English.

Editors: Campbell Brown; Alison McBride

Publishing Imprints: Ink Road; Itchy Coo

P098 Black Cat

Publishing Imprint
United States

Book Publisher: Grove Atlantic Inc. (**P312**)

P099 Black Dog & Leventhal

Publishing Imprint
United States

Book Publisher: Perseus Books (**P594**)

P100 Black Heron Press

Book Publisher
PO Box 614, Anacortes, WA 98221
United States

https://blackheronpress.com

Fiction > *Novels*: Literary

Send: Query; Writing sample; Self-Addressed Stamped Envelope (SASE)
How to send: Post

Publisher of literary fiction. No submissions or queries by email. Send query with first 30-40 pages by post with SASE.

Publisher: Jerry Gold

P101 Black Lizard

Publishing Imprint
United States

Book Publisher: Knopf Doubleday Publishing Group (**P426**)

P102 Black Velvet Seductions

Book Publisher
United States

https://blackvelvetseductions.com
https://www.facebook.com/blackvelvetseductions/
https://twitter.com/BVSBooks
https://www.instagram.com/bvsbooks/
https://www.pinterest.com/BVSPublishing/

Fiction > *Novels*
Adventure; Contemporary; Erotic; Fantasy; Historical Fiction; Supernatural / Paranormal; Thrillers; Westerns

Send: Full text; Synopsis
How to send: Online submission system

We are looking for a marriage of the romance genre (think Harlequin, Silhouette, MIRA) with a much higher degree of eroticism. We want all of the emotional impact, all the angst, all the character development, and all the conflict you would find in any traditional romance novel. But we want it to go several steps beyond the normal romance when it comes to sexual content and eroticism.

Stories may include any of the tried and true plot elements that have worked in romance novels for years. For example, authors can use secret baby, forced marriage, marriage of convenience, revenge, etc. as elements of their stories.

While we want a higher level of eroticism and a greater diversity of sexual activity in our books we do not want books that sacrifice the romance's story line in an effort to force a quick sexual pace. We believe the specific story and the make-up of the characters should decide the placement and frequency of sex scenes and we give authors wide latitude.

There are very few taboos in our line but the following are very firm. We do not want to see material containing bestiality, necrophilia or paedophilia.

Editor: Laurie Sanders

P103 Blackstaff Press

Book Publisher
Jubilee Business Park, 21 Jubilee Road, Newtownards, BT23 4YH
United Kingdom
Tel: +44 (0) 28 9182 0505

sales@colourpoint.co.uk

https://blackstaffpress.com
https://facebook.com/Blackstaffpressni
https://twitter.com/BlackstaffNI

Book Publisher: Colourpoint Educational **(P174)**

Fiction > *Novels*

Nonfiction > *Nonfiction Books*
General, and in particular: Biography; History; Ireland; Memoir; Northern Ireland; Politics; Sport

Closed to approaches.

Focuses on subjects of interest to the Irish market, both north and south. However, will consider other proposals if they are strong enough to generate interest from farther afield and specially if there is a connection to Ireland.

Editor: Patsy Horton

Publishing Imprint: Beeline

P104 Bloodaxe Books Ltd

Book Publisher
Eastburn, South Park, Hexham, Northumberland, NE46 1BS
United Kingdom
Tel: +44 (0) 01434 611581

editor@bloodaxebooks.com
submissions@bloodaxebooks.com

https://www.bloodaxebooks.com

Poetry > *Poetry Collections*

Send: Writing sample; Self-Addressed Stamped Envelope (SASE)
How to send: Post
How not to send: Email

Submit poetry only if you have a track record of publication in magazines. If so, send sample of up to a dozen poems with SAE. No submissions by email or on disk. Poems from the UK sent without return postage will be recycled unread; submissions by email will be deleted unread. No longer accepting poets who have already published a full-length collection with another publisher. Considers poets from beyond the UK and Ireland by invitation or recommendation only. See website for full details.

Editorial Director: Neil Astley

P105 Bloomsbury Academic

Book Publisher
50 Bedford Square, London, WC1B 3DP
United Kingdom
Tel: +44 (0) 20 7631 5600

contact@bloomsbury.com

http://www.bloomsburyacademic.com

Book Publisher: Bloomsbury Publishing Plc **(P107)**

ACADEMIC > **Nonfiction** > *Nonfiction Books*
Africa; Archaeology; Architecture; Arts; Asia; Business; Classics / Ancient World; Computer Science; Crime; Design; Drama; Economics; Education; Engineering; Fashion; Films; Food; Gender; Health; History; Interior Design; Language; Legal; Literature; Management; Mathematics; Media; Middle East; Music; Nursing; Philosophy; Politics; Psychology; Psychotherapy; Religion; Science; Sexuality; Society; Sociology; South America; Sport; Visual Culture

Publishes books for students, researchers, and independent thinkers.

Book Publisher: BFI Publishing **(P094)**

P106 Bloomsbury Professional

Book Publisher
50 Bedford Square, London, WC1B 3DP
United Kingdom
Tel: +44 (0) 20 7631 5600

contact@bloomsbury.com

https://www.bloomsburyprofessional.com
https://twitter.com/BloomsburyPro
https://www.linkedin.com/company/bloomsbury-professional

Book Publisher: Bloomsbury Publishing Plc **(P107)**

PROFESSIONAL > **Nonfiction** > *Nonfiction Books*
Accounting; Legal; Taxation

Publishes high quality books and digital products for lawyers, tax practitioners, accountants and business professionals.

Editor: Martin Casimir

P107 Bloomsbury Publishing Plc

Book Publisher
50 Bedford Square, London, WC1B 3DP
United Kingdom

https://www.bloomsbury.com
https://www.facebook.com/BloomsburyPublishing/
https://www.instagram.com/bloomsburypublishing/
https://twitter.com/BloomsburyBooks
https://www.youtube.com/bloomsburypublishing

ACADEMIC > **Nonfiction** > *Nonfiction Books*

ADULT
Fiction > *Novels*
Nonfiction > *Nonfiction Books*

CHILDREN'S > **Fiction** > *Novels*

PROFESSIONAL > **Nonfiction** > *Nonfiction Books*

YOUNG ADULT > **Fiction** > *Novels*

Publishes books for the adult, academic, professional, children's, and young adult markets.

Book Publishers: A & C Black Publishers Limited; Bloomsbury Academic **(P105)**; Bloomsbury Professional **(P106)**; Bloomsbury Spark; Walker & Company

Publishing Imprints: Absolute Press **(P016)**; Adlard Coles **(P022)**

P108 Blue Guides

Publishing Imprint
Unit 2, Old Brewery Road, Wiveliscombe, Somerset, TA4 2PW
United Kingdom

editorial@blueguides.com

https://www.blueguides.com

Book Publisher: Somerset Books **(P724)**

Nonfiction > *Nonfiction Books*: Travel

Send: Query
How to send: Email; Online contact form

Publishes travel guides. Always on the lookout for new authors. Contact by email in first instance, giving an indication of your areas of interest.

P109 Blue Jeans Books

Publishing Imprint
United Kingdom

submissions@sunpenny.com

https://www.sunpenny.com/imprints/

Book Publisher: Sunpenny Publishing **(P748)**

Fiction > *Novels*: Romance

Does not want:

Fiction > *Novels*: Christian Romance

Romance genre imprint, non-Christian based.

P110 Blue Lamp Books

Publishing Imprint
United Kingdom

https://mangobooks.co.uk/pages/about-mango-books

Book Publisher: Mango Books (**P478**)

Nonfiction > *Nonfiction Books*: Police History

Publishes nonfiction books on police history.

P111 Blue Rider Press

Publishing Imprint
United States

Book Publisher: Penguin Publishing Group (**P585**)

P112 Blue Star Press

Book Publisher
Bend, OR
United States

brenna@bluestarpress.com
contact@bluestarpress.com

https://www.bluestarpress.com

Nonfiction > *Nonfiction Books*
Arts; Comedy / Humour; Creativity; Wellbeing

Send: Submission Form
How to send: Email

Focuses on the arts, creative processes, wellness, and witty non-fiction.

P113 Bluemoose Books Ltd

Book Publisher
25 Sackville Street, Hebden Bridge, HX7 7DJ
United Kingdom

kevin@bluemoosebooks.com

http://www.bluemoosebooks.com

Types: Fiction
Markets: Adult

Send: Query
Don't send: Full text

Send query with synopsis and first three chapters by email. No unsolicited MSS, children's books, or young adult.

Editors: Hetha Duffy; Kevin Duffy

P114 BOA Editions, Ltd

Book Publisher
250 North Goodman Street, Suite 306, Rochester, NY 14607
United States
Tel: +1 (585) 546-3410

contact@boaeditions.org

https://www.boaeditions.org

Fiction > *Short Fiction Collections*: Literary

Nonfiction > *Nonfiction Books*
Literature; Poetry as a Subject

Poetry in Translation > *Poetry Collections*

Poetry > *Poetry Collections*

Closed to approaches.

Publisher of literary fiction, poetry, and prose about poetry and poetics. Specific reading periods (see website). Also runs annual poetry and fiction competitions. See website for more details.

Editors: Peter Conners; Nora A. Jones; Thom Ward

P115 Boathooks Books

Publishing Imprint
United Kingdom

submissions@sunpenny.com

https://www.sunpenny.com/imprints/

Book Publisher: Sunpenny Publishing (**P748**)

Nonfiction > *Nonfiction Books*
Boats; Sailing

Send: Query; Author bio; Marketing Plan; Synopsis; Full text
How to send: Email
How not to send: Post

Publishes books on boating of all kinds.

P116 The Bodley Head

Publishing Imprint
United Kingdom

Book Publisher: Vintage (**P827**)

P117 Bonnier Books (UK)

Book Publisher
4th Floor, Victoria House, Bloomsbury Square, London, WC1B 4DA
United Kingdom
Tel: +44 (0) 20 3770 8888

hello@bonnierbooks.co.uk

https://www.bonnierbooks.co.uk

ADULT
Fiction > *Novels*
Nonfiction > *Nonfiction Books*

CHILDREN'S
Fiction
Chapter Books; *Early Readers*; *Picture Books*
Nonfiction > *Nonfiction Books*

How to send: Through a literary agent

Publishes adult fiction and nonfiction, and children's books. Accepts approaches through a literary agent only.

Book Publishers: Autumn Publishing Ltd (**P064**); Hot Key Books (**P380**)

Publishing Imprint: Templar Books (**P760**)

P118 Book Sales

Publishing Imprint

Book Publisher: The Quarto Group, Inc. (**P633**)

P119 Bookouture

Book Publisher
United Kingdom

http://www.bookouture.com
https://twitter.com/bookouture

Book Publisher: Hachette UK (**P321**)

Fiction > *Novels*
Book Club Fiction; Chick Lit; Commercial; Contemporary Romance; Cozy Mysteries; Crime; Domestic Suspense; Historical Fiction; Multicultural; Police Procedural; Psychological Thrillers; Romantic Comedy; Thrillers; Women's Fiction

Nonfiction > *Nonfiction Books*

Send: Full text
How to send: Online submission system

Publishes commercial fiction and some text-lead nonfiction.

For most authors outside the bestseller lists, traditional publishers simply aren't adding enough value to justify low royalty rates. And because authors aren't all experts in editing, design, or marketing, self-publishing doesn't get the most out of their books or time. Digital publishing offers incredible opportunities to connect with readers all over the world – but finding the help you need to make the most of them can be tricky.

That's why we bring both big publisher experience and small team creativity. We genuinely understand and invest in brands – developing long-term strategies, marketing plans and websites for each of our authors.

And we work with the most brilliant editorial, design and marketing professionals in the business to make sure that everything we do is perfectly tailored to you and ridiculously good.

Combine all of that with an incredible 45% royalty rate we think we're simply the perfect combination of high returns and inspirational publishing.

P120 The Borough Press

Publishing Imprint
United Kingdom

Book Publisher: HarperCollins UK (**P347**)

P121 Boxtree

Publishing Imprint
United Kingdom

Book Publisher: Pan Macmillan (**P564**)

P122 Brave Books

Book Publisher
United States

https://www.bravebooks.us
https://www.facebook.com/BraveBooksUS/
https://www.instagram.com/bravebooks.us/
https://twitter.com/bravebooksus

CHILDREN'S > **Fiction** > *Picture Books*: Conservative

Publishes conservative children's books set in a single world with its own map and set of characters. Partners with conservative figures to create stories that take place in this world, and teaches children either a topical or foundational conservative lesson.

P123 Breedon Books

Publishing Imprint
United Kingdom

Book Publisher: Brewin Books Ltd (**P124**)

P124 Brewin Books Ltd

Book Publisher
19 Enfield Ind. Estate, Redditch, Worcestershire, B97 6BY
United Kingdom
Tel: +44 (0) 1527 854228
Fax: +44 (0) 1527 60451

admin@brewinbooks.com

https://www.brewinbooks.com
http://www.facebook.com/brewinbooks
http://www.twitter.com/brewinbooks

ADULT
- **Fiction** > *Novels*
  Contemporary; Ghost Stories
- **Nonfiction** > *Nonfiction Books*
  Arts; Biography; Comedy / Humour; Creativity; Family; Health; History; Memoir; Military History; Military; Music; Police; Social History; Sport; The Midlands; Transport; Wellbeing

CHILDREN'S
- **Fiction**
  Novels; *Picture Books*
- **Nonfiction** > *Nonfiction Books*

Send: Query; Synopsis; Author bio
How to send: Email; Post

Publishes regional books on Midland history in the areas of the police, hospitals, the military, family, social and biographies. Also publishes contemporary fiction and books for children. Welcomes submissions from aspiring authors.

Authors: Rob Blakeman; Carl Chinn; Alton Douglas; Brian Drew; Audrey Duggan; Jean Field; Jill Fraser; Gwen Freeman; Patrick Hayes; Nick Owen; Shirley Thompson

Publishing Imprints: Breedon Books (*P123*); Brewin Books; History into Print; Hunt End Books (*P387*); Richards Publishing (*P652*)

P125 Bridge House Publishing LLP

Book Publisher
United Kingdom

editor@bridgehousepublishing.co.uk

http://www.bridgehousepublishing.co.uk

Fiction > *Short Fiction*

An independent publishing house that specialises in fiction which is a little bit different. We focus mainly on short story collections. Run by writers for writers we do it all for love but we like to give new writers a voice.

Editor: Debz Hobbs-Wyatt

P126 Bright Press

Publishing Imprint

Book Publisher: The Quarto Group, Inc. (**P633**)

P127 Bristol University Press

Book Publisher
1-9 Old Park Hill, Bristol, BS2 8BB
United Kingdom
Tel: +44 (0) 1173 746645

bup-info@bristol.ac.uk

http://bristoluniversitypress.co.uk
http://www.facebook.com/BristolUniversityPress
http://twitter.com/BrisUniPress
https://www.youtube.com/ThePolicyPress
http://www.linkedin.com/company/bristol-university-press
http://www.instagram.com/bristoluniversitypress

ACADEMIC > **Nonfiction** > *Nonfiction Books*
  Business; Crime; Economics; Environment; Geography; International; Legal; Management; Politics; Science; Society; Sociology; Sustainable Living; Technology

Send: Query; Proposal; Outline; Author bio; Writing sample

Publishes scholarship in the social sciences and aligned disciplines.

Publishing Imprint: Policy Press (*P614*)

P128 The British Academy

Book Publisher
10–11 Carlton House Terrace, London, SW1Y 5AH
United Kingdom
Tel: +44 (0) 20 7969 5200

pubs@thebritishacademy.ac.uk

https://www.thebritishacademy.ac.uk
https://www.thebritishacademy.ac.uk/publishing/

ACADEMIC > **Nonfiction** > *Nonfiction Books*
  Archaeology; Culture; History; Philosophy; Society

Registered charity publishing not for profit. Publishes humanities and social sciences, particularly history, philosophy, and archaeology.

P129 Broadside Books

Publishing Imprint

Book Publisher: HarperCollins

P130 Bromley House Editions

Publishing Imprint

Book Publisher: Five Leaves Publications (**P269**)

P131 Burgess Lea Press

Publishing Imprint

Book Publisher: The Quarto Group, Inc. (**P633**)

P132 Burning Chair

Book Publisher
United Kingdom

info@burningchairpublishing.com

https://burningchairpublishing.com

Fiction > *Novels*
  Adventure; Commercial; Crime; Historical Fiction; Horror; Mystery; Supernatural / Paranormal; Suspense; Thrillers

Closed to approaches.

We promise to always put our authors and their books first with: an open, supportive and collaborative approach; fair royalties; tailored, cutting edge production, marketing and promotion.

P133 C&T Publishing

Book Publisher
1651 Challenge Drive, Concord, CA 94520-5206
United States

ctinfo@ctpub.com

https://www.ctpub.com

Nonfiction > *Nonfiction Books*
  Embroidery; Quilting; Sewing

Publishes books on sewing and related crafts.

Publishing Imprints: Crosley-Griffith (*P188*); FunStitch Studio (*P282*); Kansas City Star Quilts; Stash Books (*P741*)

P134 Caitlin Press Inc.

Book Publisher; Ebook Publisher
3375 Ponderosa Way, Qualicum Beach, BC, V9K 2J8
Canada
Tel: +1 (604) 741-4200

vici@caitlin-press.com

https://caitlin-press.com
http://facebook.com/caitlinbooks
http://twitter.com/caitlinpress
http://instagram.com/caitlinpress.daggereditions

ADULT
Fiction
Novels: General, and in particular: Adventure
Short Fiction Collections: General

Nonfiction
Essays: General
Nonfiction Books: General, and in particular: Arts; Biography; British Columbia; Comedy / Humour; Cookery; History; Memoir; Nature; Outdoor Activities; Photography; Politics; Sport; Travel; Women's Issues; Women's Studies
Poetry > *Poetry Collections*

CHILDREN'S > **Fiction** > *Novels*

Send: Query; Outline; Author bio; Writing sample
Don't send: Full text
How to send: Post
How not to send: Email

Publishes books on topics concerning or by writers from the British Columbia Interior and stories about and by British Columbia women. No submissions by email. See website for full guidelines.

Editors: Sarah Corsie; Vici Johnstone; Holly Vestad

P135 Calder Publications Ltd

Publishing Imprint
3 Castle Yard, Richmond TW10 6TF
United Kingdom
Tel: +44 (0) 20 8940 6917

info@almabooks.com

https://almabooks.com/product-category/calder-collection/?imprint=4

Book Publisher: Alma Books Ltd (**P032**)

Types: Fiction; Nonfiction; Poetry; Scripts
Formats: Theatre Scripts
Subjects: Autobiography; Drama; Fantasy; Literary; Literary Criticism; Music; Politics; Sociology
Markets: Adult

Closed to approaches.

Publishes a wide range of material, with a reputation for being controversial. Not accepting any new material.

P136 Cambridge University Press

Book Publisher
Shaftesbury Road, Cambridge, CB2 8EA
United Kingdom
Tel: +44 (0) 1223 553311

directcs@cambridge.org

https://www.cambridge.org
https://www.facebook.com/CambridgeUniversityPress
https://twitter.com/CambridgeUP
https://www.youtube.com/CambridgeUP
https://www.linkedin.com/company/cambridge-university-press
https://instagram.com/cambridgeuniversitypress

ACADEMIC > **Nonfiction** > *Nonfiction Books*
Animals; Anthropology; Archaeology; Arts; Astronomy; Biology; Chemistry; Classics / Ancient World; Computer Science; Culture; Economics; Education; Engineering; Environment; Geography; History; Language; Legal; Literature; Management; Mathematics; Medicine; Music; Philosophy; Physics; Politics; Psychology; Religion; Science; Sociology; Statistics; Theatre

World's oldest publisher, with offices around the world. Publishes nonfiction, reference, academic textbooks, educational material, and academic journals. No fiction or poetry.

P137 Campbell Books

Publishing Imprint
United Kingdom

Book Publisher: Pan Macmillan (**P564**)

P138 Candy Jar Books

Book Publisher
Mackintosh House, 136 Newport Road, Cardiff, CF24 1DJ
United Kingdom
Tel: +44 (0) 29 2115 7202

shaun@candyjarbooks.co.uk

http://www.candyjarbooks.co.uk

Types: Fiction; Nonfiction
Markets: Adult; Young Adult

Send: Full text

Award-winning independent book publisher, publishing a wide variety of books, from nonfiction, general fiction and children's, through to a range of cult TV books. Submit by post or using online submission form. No children's picture books. See website for full guidelines.

Publishing Director: Shaun Russell

P139 Canongate Books

Book Publisher
14 High Street, Edinburgh, EH1 1TE
United Kingdom
Tel: +44 (0) 1315 575111

info@canongate.co.uk

https://canongate.co.uk

Types: Fiction; Nonfiction; Translations
Subjects: Autobiography; Comedy / Humour; Culture; History; Literary; Politics; Science; Travel
Markets: Adult

How to send: Through a literary agent

Publisher of a wide range of literary fiction and nonfiction, with a traditionally Scottish slant but becoming increasingly international. Publishes fiction in translation under its international imprint. No children's books, poetry, or drama. Accepts submissions through literary agents only.

Publishing Imprints: Canongate Classics (*P140*); Canongate International (*P141*)

P140 Canongate Classics

Publishing Imprint

Book Publisher: Canongate Books (**P139**)

P141 Canongate International

Publishing Imprint

Book Publisher: Canongate Books (**P139**)

P142 Canopus Publishing Ltd

Book Publisher
United Kingdom

robin@canopusbooks.com

http://www.canopusbooks.com

Types: Nonfiction
Subjects: Arts; Science; Technology
Markets: Academic; Adult

Publishes books spanning the arts and sciences, including physics, astronomy, and engineering.

Editor: Robin Rees

P143 Canterbury Press

Publishing Imprint
Hymns Ancient and Modern Ltd, 3rd Floor, Invicta House, 108-114 Golden Lane, London, EC1Y 0TG
United Kingdom
Tel: +44 (0) 20 7776 7540
Fax: +44 (0) 20 7776 7556

https://canterburypress.hymnsam.co.uk
https://twitter.com/canterburypress
https://www.facebook.com/Canterbury-Press-176777199005586/

Book Publisher: Hymns Ancient & Modern Ltd

Nonfiction > *Nonfiction Books*
Biography; Christianity; Comedy / Humour; Spirituality; Travel

Supplier of popular religious books. Publishes a wide range of titles, covering liturgy, worship, mission, ministry, spirituality, biography, travel and even humour.

Publishing Imprint: RMEP

P144 Carina Press

Publishing Imprint
United States

submissions@carinapress.com
CustomerService@Harlequin.com

https://www.carinapress.com
https://www.writeforharlequin.com/carina-press-submission-guidelines/
https://www.facebook.com/CarinaPress
https://carinapress.submittable.com/submit

Book Publisher: Harlequin Enterprises (**P326**)

Fiction > *Novels*
Contemporary Romance; Erotic Romance; Fantasy Romance; Historical Romance; Mystery; Romantic Suspense; Science Fiction; Supernatural / Paranormal Romance; Urban Fantasy

Send: Query; Full text; Synopsis
How to send: Submittable
How not to send: Email

Digital-first adult fiction imprint. See website for details submission guidelines and to submit via online submission system.

Editors: Kerri Buckley; Stephanie Doig

P145 Carolrhoda Lab

Publishing Imprint

Book Publisher: Lerner Publishing Group (**P438**)

P146 Cartwheel Books

Publishing Imprint

Book Publisher: Scholastic (**P688**)

P147 Castle Point Books

Publishing Imprint

Publishing Imprint: St Martin's Press (**P733**)

P148 The Catholic University of America Press

Book Publisher
620 Michigan Ave NE, 240 Leahy Hall, Washington, DC 20064
United States

https://www.cuapress.org
https://www.facebook.com/CUAPR/
https://twitter.com/CUAPress

ACADEMIC > **Nonfiction** > *Nonfiction Books*
Christianity; History; Language; Literature; Medieval; Philosophy; Politics; Religion

ADULT > **Nonfiction** > *Nonfiction Books*
Christianity; History; Language; Literature; Medieval; Philosophy; Politics; Religion

Send: Query; Proposal; Table of Contents; Author bio; Market info; Self-Addressed Stamped Envelope (SASE)
How to send: Post; Email

Publishes books disseminating scholarship in the areas of theology, philosophy, church history, and medieval studies. Send query with outline, CV, sample chapter, and publishing history.

Acquisitions Editor: John Martino

Editorial Director: Trevor Lipscombe

P149 Catnip Publishing Ltd

Book Publisher
Hathaway House, Popes Drive, London, N3 1QF
United Kingdom

http://www.catnippublishing.co.uk
https://www.facebook.com/catnipbooks/

CHILDREN'S > **Fiction**
Novels; *Picture Books*
TEEN > **Fiction** > *Novels*

YOUNG ADULT > **Fiction** > *Novels*

Publishes fiction for children of all ages, from picture books to teen.

Editor: Non Pratt

Publishing Imprints: Happy Cat; Happy Cat First Readers

P150 Caxton Press

Book Publisher
312 Main Street, Caldwell, Idaho 83605
United States
Tel: +1 (800) 657-6465

orders@caxtonpress.com

https://www.caxtonpress.com
https://www.facebook.com/pages/Caxton-Press/201137615839
https://twitter.com/CaxtonPrint?lang=en

Fiction > *Novels*
Historical Fiction; Westerns

Nonfiction > *Nonfiction Books*
General, and in particular: American West; Cookery; History; Travel

Send: Query; Proposal; Market info; Outline; Table of Contents; Writing sample; Self-Addressed Stamped Envelope (SASE)
How to send: Post

Publishes nonfiction trade books for general audiences. May consider a manuscript on any subject, but prefers nonfiction with a theme such as western or frontier history, travel, pictorials, narratives or western themed cookbooks. Will consider historical fiction if it deals with the West. No poetry.

Editor: Wayne Cornell

P151 CF4K

Publishing Imprint
United Kingdom

https://www.christianfocus.com

Book Publisher: Christian Focus Publications (**P163**)

CHILDREN'S
Fiction
Board Books: Christianity; Evangelism
Chapter Books: Christianity; Evangelism
Early Readers: Christianity; Evangelism
Middle Grade: Christianity; Evangelism
Picture Books: Christianity; Evangelism
Nonfiction > *Nonfiction Books*
Christianity; Evangelism

Books for children, including Sunday school and Home school titles.

P152 Chambers

Publishing Imprint
United Kingdom

enquiries@chambers.co.uk

https://chambers.co.uk
https://www.facebook.com/wordlovers/
https://twitter.com/chamberswords

Book Publisher: John Murray (Publishers) Ltd

Nonfiction
Puzzle Books: General
Reference: Language

Publishes dictionaries, thesauruses, and puzzle books, including crosswords.

P153 Charisma House

Book Publisher
600 Rinehart Rd, Lake Mary, FL 32746
United States
Tel: +1 (407) 333-0600

info@charismamedia.com

https://charismahouse.com
https://www.facebook.com/CharismaHouse/
https://twitter.com/charismahouse
https://www.instagram.com/charismahousebooks/

Media Company: Charisma Media

Fiction > *Novels*: Christianity

Nonfiction > *Nonfiction Books*
Christian Living; Christianity; Politics

Through the power of the Holy Spirit we inspire people to radically change their world. Providing Spirit-Filled Christians globally with resources to empower them to change their world through the power of the Holy Spirit.

Publishing Imprints: CharismaKids; Creation House Press; Siloam.

P154 Charles River Press

Book Publisher
United States
Tel: +1 (508) 364-9851

info@charlesriverpress.com

http://www.charlesriverpress.com
https://www.facebook.com/charles.r.press/
https://twitter.com/CharlesRiverLLC
https://www.youtube.com/user/CharlesRiverPress/

ADULT
Fiction > *Novels*: Erotic

Nonfiction > *Nonfiction Books*: Sport

YOUNG ADULT > **Fiction** > *Novels*

Send: Author bio; Market info; Synopsis; Full text

Costs: Offers services that writers have to pay for. Also offers editing and design services.

Currently accepting young adult, sports, and erotica manuscripts.

Authors: Richard Herrick; John McMullen; Mike Ryan; Tony Schiavone; Jonathan Womack; Rowena Womack

Editor: Jonathan Womack

P155 Charlesbridge Publishing

Book Publisher
9 Galen Street, Watertown, MA 02472
United States
Tel: +1 (617) 926-0329

tradeeditorial@charlesbridge.com

https://www.charlesbridge.com
https://twitter.com/charlesbridge
https://www.facebook.com/CharlesbridgePublishingInc
https://www.pinterest.com/charlesbridge/
https://www.instagram.com/charlesbridgepublishing/
https://charlesbridgebooks.tumblr.com/
https://www.youtube.com/user/Charlesbridge1

CHILDREN'S
Fiction
Board Books; *Early Readers*; *Middle Grade*; *Picture Books*
Nonfiction
Board Books: General
Early Readers: General
Middle Grade: Arts; Biography; History; Mathematics; Nature; Science; Social Issues
Picture Books: General

Send: Full text
How to send: Word file email attachment; PDF file email attachment
How not to send: In the body of an email

Publishes books for children, with teen and adult imprints.

Publishing Imprints: Charlesbridge Teen (**P156**); Imagine Publishing (**P391**)

P156 Charlesbridge Teen

Publishing Imprint
9 Galen Street, Watertown, MA 02472
United States
Tel: +1 (800) 225-3214

ya.submissions@charlesbridge.com

https://charlesbridgeteen.com
https://twitter.com/CharlesbridgeYA
https://www.facebook.com/CharlesbridgePublishingInc/
https://www.pinterest.com/charlesbridge/
https://www.instagram.com/charlesbridgeteen/
http://charlesbridgebooks.tumblr.com/

Book Publisher: Charlesbridge Publishing (**P155**)

YOUNG ADULT
Fiction > *Novels*
Nonfiction > *Nonfiction Books*

Send: Query; Synopsis; Writing sample; Proposal; Outline
How to send: Email attachment

Features storytelling that presents new ideas and an evolving world. Our carefully curated stories give voice to unforgettable characters with unique perspectives. We publish books that inspire teens to cheer or sigh, laugh or reflect, reread or share with a friend, and ultimately, pick up another book. Our mission – to make reading irresistible!

P157 Chatto & Windus

Publishing Imprint
United Kingdom

Book Publisher: Vintage (**P827**)

P158 Chequered Flag Publishing

Book Publisher
3 Sparkham Close, Shrewsbury, Shropshire, SY3 6BX
United Kingdom

mail@chequeredflagpublishing.co.uk

http://www.chequeredflagpublishing.co.uk
http://www.twitter.com/cheqflagpub
http://www.facebook.com/cheqflagpub

Nonfiction > *Nonfiction Books*: Sport

Closed to approaches.

An independent publisher dedicated to making available innovative and exciting sports books that are overlooked by other publishers.

Browse the sport shelves of your local bookshop and you'll see spine after spine of humdrum autobiographies of sport 'personalities'. These books, most of which are ghost written, purport to tell the life story of yet another footballer or cricketer, some of whom are barely out of their teens!

We want to break out of the restrictive mould that has been set by the commercial and financial brains in the offices of mainstream publishers. We want to tell the stories behind less well-known sports. We want to bring to life the characters behind the headlines. We want to inspire and excite, to make you stop and think.

Above all, we want to publish the kind of books that will take pride of place on your bookshelf.

Editor: Scott Reeves

P159 Child's Play (International) Ltd

Book Publisher
United Kingdom

office@childs-play.com

http://www.childs-play.com
https://www.facebook.com/ChildsPlayBooks/
https://twitter.com/ChildsPlayBooks
http://pinterest.com/childsplaybooks/
http://www.instagram.com/childsplaybooks/
https://www.youtube.com/channel/UCik8Eew5rGc2LfpggFgX4Qg

CHILDREN'S
Fiction
Activity Books; *Board Books*; *Picture Books*
Poetry > *Picture Books*

Closed to approaches.

Specialises in publishing books that allow children to learn through play. No novels.

Editor: Sue Baker

P160 Childswork / ChildsPLAY, LLC

Book Publisher
40 Aero Road, Unit #2, Bohemia, NY 11716
United States
Tel: +1 (800) 962-1141

https://childswork.com
https://www.facebook.com/childsworkchildsplay/
https://twitter.com/childswork
https://www.pinterest.com/childswork/
https://www.instagram.com/childsworkchildsplay/
https://www.youtube.com/childsworkchildsplay
https://www.linkedin.com/company/child%27s-work

PROFESSIONAL > **Nonfiction** > *Nonfiction Books*
Child Psychotherapy; Education; Psychology

How not to send: Post

A leading provider in child therapy resources, focusing on therapeutic tools used by counselors, teachers and therapists.

P161 Choc Lit

Book Publisher
Penrose House, Camberley, Surrey, GU15 2AB
United Kingdom
Tel: +44 (0) 1276 586367

info@choc-lit.com
submissions@choc-lit.com

https://www.choc-lit.com
https://twitter.com/choclituk
https://www.facebook.com/Choc-Lit-30680012481/
https://www.instagram.com/choclituk/
https://www.youtube.com/channel/UCLZBZ2qcR5gtOyDoqEjMbQw

Fiction > *Novels*
Contemporary Romance; Fantasy Romance; Historical Romance; Romance; Romantic Suspense; Timeslip Romance

Send: Query; Synopsis
How to send: Online submission system

Publishes romance suitable for an adult audience, between 60,000 and 100,000 words in length.

Author: Juliet Archer

Publishing Imprint: Ruby Fiction (**P666**)

P162 Chris Andrews Publications

Book Publisher
15 Curtis Yard, North Hinksey Lane, Oxford, OX2 0LX
United Kingdom
Tel: +44 (0) 1865 723404
Fax: +44 (0) 1865 244243

enquiries@cap-ox.com

https://cap-ox.com
https://www.facebook.com/ChrisAndrewsPublications/
https://twitter.com/capoxford
https://www.instagram.com/capoxford/

Nonfiction > *Coffee Table Books*
Photography; Travel

Publishes souvenir books with photography of various locations.

Book Publisher: Oxford Picture Library

Publisher: Chris Andrews

P163 Christian Focus Publications

Book Publisher
Geanies House, Fearn by Tain, Ross-shire, IV20 1TW
United Kingdom
Tel: +44 (0) 1862 871011

info@christianfocus.com

https://www.christianfocus.com
https://twitter.com/christian_focus
https://www.facebook.com/christianfocus
https://www.linkedin.com/company/christian%E2%80%93focus%E2%80%93publications-limited

Nonfiction > *Nonfiction Books*: Evangelism

Send: Synopsis; Table of Contents; Writing sample; Author bio; Submission Form
How to send: Email; Post

A conservative, evangelical publishing house.

Publishing Imprints: CF4K (**P151**); Christian Focus; Christian Heritage; Mentor

P164 ChristLight Books

Publishing Imprint
United Kingdom

https://www.sunpenny.com/imprints/

Book Publisher: Sunpenny Publishing (**P748**)

Fiction > *Novels*: Christianity

Nonfiction > *Nonfiction Books*: Christianity

Send: Query; Author bio; Marketing Plan; Synopsis; Full text
How to send: Email

Publishes Christian fiction and nonfiction books.

P165 Chronicle Books LLC

Book Publisher
680 Second Street, San Francisco, California 94107
United States
Tel: +1 (415) 537 4200

submissions@chroniclebooks.com

https://www.chroniclebooks.com
https://facebook.com/ChronicleBooks
https://twitter.com/ChronicleBooks
https://pinterest.com/ChronicleBooks
https://instagram.com/ChronicleBooks

ADULT > **Nonfiction** > *Nonfiction Books*
Arts; Beauty; Cookery; Design; Fashion; Interior Design; Photography; Popular Culture; Relationships

CHILDREN'S
Fiction
Activity Books; *Board Books*; *Chapter Books*; *Early Readers*; *Middle Grade*; *Picture Books*
Nonfiction
Activity Books; *Board Books*; *Chapter Books*; *Early Readers*; *Middle Grade*; *Picture Books*

Send: Query; Outline; Writing sample; Market info; Author bio
How to send: Word file email attachment; PDF file email attachment

Publishes nonfiction for adults, and fiction and nonfiction for children. See website for full guidelines.

P166 Cinnamon Press

Book Publisher
Office 49019, PO Box 15113, Birmingham, B2 2NJ
United Kingdom

jan@cinnamonpress.com

https://www.cinnamonpress.com

Fiction > *Novels*

Nonfiction > *Nonfiction Books*

Poetry > *Poetry Collections*

Closed to approaches.

Small-press publisher of full length poetry collections, unique and imaginative novels, and practical and informative nonfiction with wide appeal. Willing to consider most genres as long as writing is thought-provoking, enjoyable, and accessible; but does not publish genre fiction (romantic, erotica, horror or crime), biography, autobiography, academic, technical or how-to. No unsolicited MSS. See website for submission details.

Editor: Jan Fortune

P167 Clairview Books

Book Publisher
Russet, Sandy Lane, West Hoathly, West Sussex, RH19 4QQ
United Kingdom

office@clairviewbooks.com

https://www.clairviewbooks.com
https://www.facebook.com/Clairview-Books-190962737588974/

Nonfiction > *Nonfiction Books*
Arts; Current Affairs; History; Politics; Science; Spirituality

Send: Query; Proposal; Table of Contents; Writing sample
Don't send: Full text
How to send: Email; Post

Publishes nonfiction books which challenge conventional thinking. Send query by post or by email, with outline of around 200 words, list of chapters, and a sample chapter. No unsolicited MSS.

Authors: Wendy Cook; Howard Storm; Gore Vidal

Managing Director: Mr S. Gulbekian

P168 Clarion Books

Publishing Imprint
United States

https://www.hmhbooks.com/imprints/clarion

Book Publisher: Houghton Mifflin Harcourt Books for Young Readers Division (**P381**)

CHILDREN'S
Fiction
Chapter Books; *Middle Grade*; *Picture Books*

Nonfiction > *Nonfiction Books*

Publishes fiction for children (including picture books) and nonfiction for all ages. Began publishing children's fiction and picture books in 1965 and has published many award-winning titles throughout the years. Its distinguished author list includes National Book Award winners, Caldecott, Newbery, Printz, and Sibert Medal and Honor recipients.

Authors: Eve Bunting; Eileen Christelow; Russell Freedman; Mary Downing Hahn; Kate Milford; Linda Sue Park; Catherine Reef; Marilyn Singer

P169 Clarkson Potter

Publishing Imprint
1745 Broadway, New York, NY 10019
United States
Tel: +1 (212) 782-9000

http://crownpublishing.com/archives/imprint/clarkson-potter

Book Publisher: Random House (**P640**)

Types: Nonfiction
Subjects: Arts; Commercial; Cookery; Design; Lifestyle; Literary
Markets: Adult

How to send: Through a literary agent

Imprint dedicated to lifestyle, publishing books by chefs, cooks, designers, artists, and writers. Accepts approaches via literary agents only.

P170 Cleis Press

Book Publisher
221 River St, 9th Fl, Hoboken, NJ 07030
United States
Tel: +1 (212) 431-5455

cleis@cleispress.com
acquisitions@cleispress.com

https://cleispress.com
https://instagram.com/cleis_press
https://twitter.com/cleispress
https://www.facebook.com/CleisPress.Page
https://www.pinterest.com/cleispress/
https://cleispress.tumblr.com/

Fiction > *Novels*
Erotic Romance; Erotic

Nonfiction > *Nonfiction Books*
Feminism; Health; LGBTQIA; Memoir; Relationships; Self Help; Sex; Sexuality; Women's Studies

Send: Query; Author bio; Writing sample
How to send: Email

The largest independent sexuality publishing company in the United States. With a focus on LGBTQ, BDSM, romance, and erotic writing for all sexual preferences.

P171 Coal City Press

Book Publisher; Magazine Publisher
English Department, University of Kansas, Lawrence KS, 66045
United States

https://coalcity.org
http://www.facebook.com/CoalCityReviewAndPress/
http://twitter.com/CoalCityReview
http://instagram.com/coalcityreview

Poetry > *Poetry Collections*

Closed to approaches.

Submissions by invitation only.

Magazine: Coal City Review (**M124**)

P172 College Press Publishing

Book Publisher
1307 W 20th Street, Joplin, MO 64804
United States
Tel: +1 (417) 623-6280

collpressbooks@gmail.com
collpressjoplin@gmail.com

https://collegepress.com
https://www.facebook.com/collpresspublishing/

Nonfiction > *Nonfiction Books*
Bible Studies; Biography; Christianity; Evangelism; History

Send: Query; Proposal
How to send: Post; Email

Publishes Bible studies, topical studies (biblically based), apologetic studies, historical biographies of Christians, Sunday/Bible School curriculum (adult electives). No poetry, game or puzzle books, books on prophecy from a premillennial or dispensational viewpoint, or any books that do not contain a Christian message.

Publishing Imprint: HeartSpring Publishing (*P364*)

P173 Collins

Publishing Imprint
United Kingdom

Book Publisher: HarperCollins UK (**P347**)

P174 Colourpoint Educational

Book Publisher
Colourpoint House, Jubilee Business Park, 21 Jubilee Road, Newtownards, Northern Ireland, BT23 4YH
United Kingdom
Tel: +44 (0) 28 9182 0505

sales@colourpoint.co.uk

https://colourpointeducational.com
https://twitter.com/ColourpointEdu

ACADEMIC > **Nonfiction** > *Nonfiction Books*
Biology; Business; Chemistry; Design; Digital Technology; English; French; Gaelic; Geography; Health; History; Home Economics / Domestic Science; Legal; Lifestyle; Mathematics; Physical Edication; Physics; Politics; Religion; Technology

Send: Query
How to send: Email

Provides textbooks, ebooks and digital resources for Northern Ireland students at Key Stage 3 level, and the CCEA revised specification at GCSE and AS/A2/A-level.

Book Publisher: Blackstaff Press (**P103**)

Editor: Wesley Johnston

P175 Columbia University Press

Book Publisher
61 West 62nd Street, New York, NY 10023
United States
Tel: +1 (212) 459 0600

https://cup.columbia.edu
https://www.facebook.com/ColumbiaUniversityPress
https://twitter.com/Columbiaup
http://www.pinterest.com/columbiaup
http://www.cupblog.org/

ACADEMIC > **Nonfiction** > *Nonfiction Books*
African American; African Diaspora; Animals; Arts; Biography; Business; Climate Science; Economics; Films; Finance; Food; Gender; History; Journalism; Language; Literature; Media; Memoir; Middle East; New York City; Philosophy; Politics; Psychology; Religion; Science; Sexuality; Sociology

Send: Proposal; Table of Contents; Market info; Author bio
How to send: Email

American scholarly publisher based in New York.

Editorial Director: Jennifer Crewe

Publishing Imprint: Wallflower Press

P176 Concord Theatricals

Literary Agency; Book Publisher
250 W. 57th Street, 6th Floor, New York, NY 10107-0102
United States
Tel: +1 (866) 979-0447

info@concordtheatricals.com

https://www.concordtheatricals.com/

Scripts > *Theatre Scripts*

Closed to approaches.

Publishes plays and represents writers of plays. Deals in well-known plays from Broadway and London's West End.

P177 Concord Theatricals Ltd

Book Publisher
Aldwych House, 71 – 91 Aldwych, London, WC2B 4HN

United Kingdom
Tel: +44 (0) 20 7054 7298

acquisitions@concordtheatricals.co.uk

https://www.concordtheatricals.co.uk

Scripts > *Theatre Scripts*
Drama; Musicals

Closed to approaches.

Publishes plays only. Send submissions by email only, following the guidelines on the website.

P178 Convergent Books

Publishing Imprint

Book Publisher: Random House (**P640**)

P179 Cool Springs Press

Publishing Imprint

Book Publisher: The Quarto Group, Inc. (**P633**)

P180 Corazon Books

Book Publisher
Wyndham Media Ltd, 27 Old Gloucester Street, London, WC1N 3AX
United Kingdom

readers@greatstorieswithheart.com
b2b@greatstorieswithheart.com
pr@greatstorieswithheart.com

https://greatstorieswithheart.com

Fiction > *Novels*
Crime; Family Saga; Historical Fiction; Medicine; Romance

Nonfiction > *Nonfiction Books*: Biography

Closed to approaches.

Publishes bestselling stories, specialising in romantic fiction, historical fiction, family sagas, medical fiction, biography and crime.

P181 Cornerstone

Book Publisher

Book Publisher: Penguin Random House UK (**P587**)

P182 Coyote Arts

Book Publisher
PO Box 6690, Albuquerque, NM 87197-6690
United States

sales@coyote-arts.com

https://coyote-arts.com
https://www.facebook.com/coyoteartsllc/
https://twitter.com/coyoteartsllc
https://instagram.com/coyoteartsllc
https://www.pinterest.com/coyoteartsllc/

Fiction > *Novels*
Arts; Literary

Nonfiction > *Nonfiction Books*: Arts

Poetry > *Any Poetic Form*

A literary arts publisher dedicated to the power of words and images to transform human lives and the environment we inhabit. Publishes works in the genres of poetry, fiction, non-fiction, and drama that engage the sense of wonder and possibility.

P183 Crabtree Publishing

Book Publisher
347 Fifth Ave, Suite 1402-145, New York, NY 10016
United States
Tel: +1 (212) 496-5040
Fax: +1 (800) 355-7166

http://www.crabtreebooks.com

Types: Nonfiction
Subjects: History; Science; Sociology
Markets: Academic; Children's

Closed to approaches.

Publishes educational books for children. No unsolicited mss -- all material is generated in-house.

P184 Creative Essentials

Publishing Imprint
United Kingdom

Book Publisher: Oldcastle Books Group (**P544**)

P185 Crime & Mystery Club

Publishing Imprint
United Kingdom

Book Publisher: Oldcastle Books Group (**P544**)

P186 Crime Express

Publishing Imprint

Book Publisher: Five Leaves Publications (**P269**)

P187 Croner-i Limited

Book Publisher
240 Blackfriars Road, London, SE1 8NW
United Kingdom
Tel: +44 (0) 800 231 5199

https://www.croneri.co.uk

PROFESSIONAL > **Nonfiction** > *Nonfiction Books*
Accounting; Business; Taxation

Publishes books and resources for business professionals covering tax and accounting, human resources, health and safety, and compliance.

P188 Crosley-Griffith

Publishing Imprint
United States

Book Publisher: C&T Publishing (**P133**)

P189 Crown Archetype

Publishing Imprint

Book Publisher: Random House (**P640**)

P190 Crown Forum

Publishing Imprint

Book Publisher: Random House (**P640**)

P191 The Crowood Press

Book Publisher
The Stable Block, Crowood Lane, Ramsbury, Marlborough, Wiltshire, SN8 2HR
United Kingdom
Tel: +44 (0) 1672 520320

enquiries@crowood.com
submissions@crowood.com

https://www.crowood.com
https://twitter.com/crowoodpress
http://www.facebook.com/TheCrowoodPress
https://www.instagram.com/thecrowoodpress/

Nonfiction > *Nonfiction Books*
Architecture; Arts; Aviation; Cars; Crafts; Crocheting; Cycling; Dance; Dogs; Embroidery; Engineering; Equestrian; Films; Gardening; Home Improvement; Knitting; Lacemaking; Martial Arts; Military History; Model Making; Nature; Performing Arts; Photography; Railways; Sport; Theatre; Transport; Walking

Send: Query; Synopsis; Writing sample; Author bio
Don't send: Full text
How to send: Email; Post

Publishes high-quality books packed with detailed information on specialist interests. Send proposals by post or by email.

Book Publisher: Robert Hale Publishers

Publishing Imprint: J.A. Allen

P192 Currock Press

Book Publisher
United Kingdom

john.i.clarke@btinternet.com

https://www.currockpress.com

Poetry > *Poetry Collections*

Closed to approaches.

No current plans for any further publications.

Editor: John Clarke

P193 Custom House

Publishing Imprint

Book Publisher: HarperCollins

P194 D&B Publishing

Book Publisher
80 Walsingham Road, Hove, BN3 4FF
United Kingdom
Tel: +44 (0) 1273 711443

info@dandbpublishing.com

http://www.dandbpublishing.com

Nonfiction
Nonfiction Books: Fitness; Health; Mind, Body, Spirit; Running
Puzzle Books: General

Publishes books related to the body and mind – with books on the Alexander Technique, running and also a highly successful range of puzzle books and bridge books.

Editors: Dan Addelman; Byron Jacobs

P195 Dalesman Publishing Co. Ltd

Book Publisher; Magazine Publisher
The Gatehouse, Skipton Castle, Skipton, North Yorkshire, BD23 1AL
United Kingdom
Tel: +44 (0) 1756 693479

jon@dalesman.co.uk

https://www.dalesman.co.uk

Types: Nonfiction
Subjects: Comedy / Humour; Crafts; History; Hobbies; Travel

Publishes regional books covering Yorkshire, and the Lake and Peak districts. Considers unsolicited MSS on relevant topics.

Editor: Jon Stokoe

Magazine: Dalesman (**M156**)

P196 Dalkey Archive Press

Book Publisher
3000 Commerce Street, Dallas, Texas 75226
United States

toberead@deepvellum.org

https://www.dalkeyarchive.com
https://www.facebook.com/pages/Dalkey-Archive-Press/128046170932
https://twitter.com/Dalkey_Archive

Fiction > *Novels*
Avant-Garde; Experimental; Literary

Nonfiction > *Nonfiction Books*: Literary Criticism

Poetry > *Any Poetic Form*

Send: Query
How to send: Email

Publishes primarily literary fiction, with an emphasis on fiction that belongs to the experimental tradition of Sterne, Joyce, Rabelais, Flann O'Brien, Beckett, Gertrude Stein, and Djuna Barnes. Occasionally publishes poetry or nonfiction. Send submissions by email. See website for full guidelines.

P197 Dancing Girl Press

Book Publisher
United States

dancinggirlpress@yahoo.com

http://www.dancinggirlpress.com

Poetry > *Chapbook*

Send: Full text

Publishes chapbooks by female poets between 12 and 32 pages. No payment, but free 10 copies and 40% discount on further copies.

P198 Dancing Star Press

Book Publisher
United States

submissions@dancingstarpress.com

https://www.dancingstarpress.com

Types: Fiction
Subjects: Fantasy; Science Fiction
Markets: Adult

Send: Full text

Publishes speculative fiction novellas between 17,500 and 40,000 words in length. Accepts manuscripts by email between April 1 and June 30, and between October 1 and December 31.

P199 Darby Creek

Publishing Imprint
United States

https://lernerbooks.com/pages/our-imprints

Book Publisher: Lerner Publishing Group (**P438**)

CHILDREN'S > **Fiction**
Chapter Books; *Middle Grade*
YOUNG ADULT > **Fiction** > *Novels*

How to send: Through a literary agent; By referral

Publishes series fiction for emerging, striving, and reluctant readers ages 8 to 18 (grades 4–12). From chapter books to page-turning YA novels, aims to engage readers with strong characters, exciting premises, and accessible formats. Makes reading an adventure instead of a challenge or a chore.

P200 DAW

Publishing Imprint
United States

daw@penguinrandomhouse.com

https://www.dawbooks.com
https://submit.dawbooks.com/submit
https://twitter.com/dawbooks
https://www.facebook.com/dawbooks
https://www.instagram.com/dawbooks/

Book Publisher: Penguin Publishing Group (**P585**)

Fiction > *Novels*
Fantasy; Science Fiction

Closed to approaches.

The first publishing company ever devoted exclusively to science fiction and fantasy. Accepts unsolicited submissions of science fiction and fantasy novels. Does not consider short stories, short story collections, novellas, or poetry. The average length of the novels published varies, but is almost never fewer than 80,000 words.

A literary agent is not required for submission. Will not consider manuscripts that are currently on submission to another publisher unless prior arrangements have been made with a literary agent. It may require three months or more for the editors to review a manuscript. If longer than three months an exclusive submission is no longer required.

P201 Dawn Publications

Publishing Imprint
United States

https://www.sourcebooks.com/dawn-publications.html

Book Publisher: Sourcebooks (**P726**)

CHILDREN'S > **Nonfiction** > *Nonfiction Books*: Nature

Publishes creative nonfiction manuscripts for children that relate to nature and science.

P202 dbS Productions

Book Publisher
PO Box 94, Charlottesville, VA 22902-0094
United States
Tel: +1 (800) 745-1581
Fax: +1 (434) 293-5502

info@dbs-sar.com

http://www.dbs-sar.com

PROFESSIONAL > **Nonfiction** > *Nonfiction Books*: Search and Rescue

Describes itself as the leader in research and education in behavioral profiles of lost subjects. Always looking for new and interesting publications related to the field of search and rescue. Authors are encouraged to make contact early in the development of their projects.

Editor: Bob Adams

P203 DC Thomson

Book Publisher
2 Albert Square, Dundee, DD1 9QJ
United Kingdom

innovation@dcthomson.co.uk

http://www.dcthomson.co.uk

Types: Fiction; Nonfiction
Markets: Adult; Children's

Publisher of newspapers, magazines, comics, and books, with offices in Dundee, Aberdeen, Glasgow, and London. For fiction guidelines send large SAE marked for the attention of the Central Fiction Department.

P204 Dead End Street

Book Publisher
320 North Carson Street, Carson City, Nevada 89701
United States

https://www.deadendstreet.com

Fiction > *Novels*

Nonfiction > *Nonfiction Books*

Formed in 1997 by three lifelong friends to pioneer the still-nascent field of electronic publishing. Through fits and starts and ups and downs, the company continues to successfully publish compelling reads long after its original competitors folded.

Editor: John P. Rutledge

P205 Deep Overstock Publishing

Book Publisher; Magazine Publisher
Portland, OR
United States

dop@deepoverstock.com
submissions@deepoverstock.com
editors@deepoverstock.com

https://deepoverstock.com
https://www.facebook.com/deepoverstock
https://www.instagram.com/deepoverstock
https://www.twitter.com/deepoverstock

Fiction > *Novels*

Nonfiction > *Nonfiction Books*

Poetry > *Poetry Collections*

Send: Pitch; Author bio
How to send: In the body of an email

Publishes full-length novels and longer works by booksellers and book industry workers.

Magazine: Deep Overstock Magazine (**M164**)

P206 Del Rey

Publishing Imprint
United Kingdom

Book Publishers: Ebury (**P226**); Random House (**P640**)

P207 Del Rey/LucasBooks

Publishing Imprint

Book Publisher: Random House (**P640**)

P208 Denene Millner Books

Publishing Imprint

Book Publisher: Simon & Schuster Children's Publishing (**P713**)

CHILDREN'S > **Fiction** > *Picture Books*

P209 DeVorss & Company

Book Publisher
PO Box 1389, Camarillo, CA 93011-1389
United States

editorial@devorss.com

https://www.devorss.com

Nonfiction > *Nonfiction Books*
Alternative Health; Inspirational; Lifestyle; Mind, Body, Spirit; Religion; Self Help; Spirituality

Send: Query; Outline; Table of Contents; Market info; Author bio; Self-Addressed Stamped Envelope (SASE)
How to send: Email; Post

A book publisher and distributor of Metaphysical, Inspirational, Spiritual, Self-Help, and New Thought titles.

P210 Dewi Lewis Publishing

Book Publisher
8 Broomfield Road, Heaton Moor, Stockport, SK4 4ND
United Kingdom
Tel: +44 (0) 1614 429450
Fax: +44 (0) 1614 429450

mail@dewilewispublishing.com
dewi.lewis@btconnect.com

https://www.dewilewis.com

Nonfiction > *Illustrated Books*: Photography

Closed to approaches.

Publishes books of photography.

Editors: Dewi Lewis; Caroline Warhurst

P211 Dey Street Books

Publishing Imprint

Book Publisher: HarperCollins

P212 Dial Books for Young Readers

Publishing Imprint
United States

Book Publisher: Penguin Young Readers Group (**P591**)

CHILDREN'S
Fiction
Chapter Books; *Early Readers*; *Middle Grade*; *Picture Books*
Nonfiction
Chapter Books; *Early Readers*; *Middle Grade*; *Picture Books*
YOUNG ADULT
Fiction > *Novels*
Nonfiction > *Nonfiction Books*

Closed to approaches.

Publishes books for children, from beginner readers and picture books, to fiction and nonfiction for middle-grade and young adults. No unsolicited MSS.

Publishing Imprint: Dial Easy-to-Read

P213 The Dial Press

Publishing Imprint

Book Publisher: Random House (**P640**)

P214 Diversion Books

Book Publisher
United States
Tel: +1 (212) 961-6390

info@diversionbooks.com
submit@diversionbooks.com

http://www.diversionbooks.com

Nonfiction > *Nonfiction Books*
Business; Crime; Current Affairs; History; Music; Sport

How to send: Through a literary agent

Currently accepting submissions through literary agents only.

Editors: Melanie Madden; Keith Wallman; Mark Weinstein

P215 DK (Dorling Kindersley Ltd)

Book Publisher
One Embassy Gardens, 8 Viaduct Gardens, London, SW11 7BW
United Kingdom
Tel: +44 (0) 1206 255678

adulteditorial@uk.dk.com
childreneditorial@uk.dk.com
travelguides@uk.dk.com

https://www.dk.com
https://www.facebook.com/dkbooks.uk
https://twitter.com/DKBooks
https://www.instagram.com/DKbooks/
https://www.youtube.com/user/DKinVideo
https://www.pinterest.co.uk/dkpublishing/

Book Publisher: Penguin Random House

ADULT > **Nonfiction**
Nonfiction Books: Arts; Beauty; Business; Career Development; Comic Books; Crafts; Culture; Education; Films; Fitness; Food and Drink; Gardening; Health; History; Hobbies; Language; Medicine; Nature; Parenting; Photography; Pregnancy; Relationships; Religion; Science; Sport; TV; Transport; Travel
Reference: General

CHILDREN'S > **Nonfiction** > *Nonfiction Books*

How to send: Through a literary agent

Publishes illustrated adult nonfiction and nonfiction for children. No unsolicited MSS. Approach via a literary agent only.

Book Publisher: DK Publishing

Publishing Imprints: Eyewitness Guides; Eyewitness Travel Guides; Funfax

P216 Dodo Ink

Book Publisher
United Kingdom

dodopublishingco@gmail.com

http://www.dodoink.com

Types: Fiction
Subjects: Literary
Markets: Adult

Closed to approaches.

Independent UK publisher aiming to publish three novels per year, in paperback and digital formats. Publishes risk-taking, imaginative novels, that don't fall into easy marketing categories. Closed to submissions as at June 2017.

Editor: Sam Mills

P217 DogHorn Publishing

Book Publisher
United Kingdom

https://www.doghornpublishing.com

Fiction > *Novels*

Nonfiction > *Nonfiction Books*

Poetry > *Poetry Collections*

Scripts > *Theatre Scripts*: Drama

A boutique publisher of challenging and exciting fiction, nonfiction, drama and poetry.

Publishing Imprints: Fruit Bruise Press (*P281*); Superbia Books (*P749*)

P218 Doubleday

Publishing Imprint
United States

Book Publisher: Knopf Doubleday Publishing Group (**P426**)

P219 Down East Books

Publishing Imprint
United States

Book Publisher: The Globe Pequot Press (**P296**)

P220 Dreamspinner Press

Book Publisher
5032 Capital Circle SW, Ste 2 PMB 279, Tallahassee, FL 32305-7886
United States
Tel: +1 (800) 970-3759
Fax: +1 (888) 308-3739

contact@dreamspinnerpress.com
submissions@dreamspinnerpress.com

https://www.dreamspinnerpress.com
https://www.facebook.com/dreamspinnerpress/
https://twitter.com/dreamspinners
https://www.instagram.com/dreamspinner_press/

Fiction > *Novels*
Gay; Romance

Send: Synopsis; Full text
How to send: Email

Publishes gay male romance in all genres. While works do not need to be graphic, they must contain a primary or strong secondary romance plotline and focus on the interaction between two or more male characters. The main characters of the story must end in a gay or gay polyamorous relationship. Other relationships (heterosexual, lesbian, mixed gender polyamory) are acceptable in secondary pairings or as part of the development of a main character.

Authors: M. Jules Aedin; Rhianne Aile; Maria Albert; Eric Arvin; Mickie B. Ashling; Connie Bailey; Alix Bekins; Nicki Bennett; Sienna Bishop; Scarlett Blackwell; S. Blaise; Steven Blue-Williams; Anne Brooke; Bethany Brown; Janey Chapel; J. M. Colail; Jaymz Connelly; Lisa Marie Davis; Remmy Duchene; Giselle Ellis; Catt Ford; Lacey-Anne Frye; Reve Garrison; Andrew Grey; Felicitas Ivey; Ashlyn Kane; Sean Kennedy; V.B. Kildaire; Shay Kincaid; Marguerite Labbe; Clare London; Dar Mavison; Anais Morten; Chrissy Munder; Zahra Owens; D. G. Parker; Michael Powers; Angela Romano; Abigail Roux; Isabella Rowan; Steve Sampson; Ian Sentelik; Jane Seville; John Simpson; Jenna Hilary Sinclair; Dan Skinner; Sasha Skye; Sonja Spencer; Jaxx Steele; Jaclyn Storm; Rowena Sudbury; Fae Sutherland; Ariel Tachna; Madeleine Urban; G.S. Wiley

Publishing Imprints: DSP Publications (**P221**); Harmony Ink Press (**P329**)

P221 DSP Publications

Publishing Imprint
5032 Capital Circle SW, Ste 2 PMB 279, Tallahassee, FL 32305-7886
United States
Tel: +1 (800) 970-3759
Fax: +1 (888) 308-3739

contact@dsppublications.com

https://www.dsppublications.com
https://twitter.com/DSPPublications
https://www.facebook.com/dsppublications/

Book Publisher: Dreamspinner Press (**P220**)

Fiction > *Novels*
Fantasy; Historical Fiction; Horror; Mystery; Science Fiction; Spirituality; Supernatural / Paranormal

We are a boutique imprint producing quality fiction that pushes the envelope to present immersive, unique, and unforgettable reading experiences. We choose stories that beg to be told, tales that depart from mainstream concepts to create fantastic and compelling journeys of the mind.

P222 Duncan Petersen Publishing Limited

Book Publisher
Studio 6 82, Silverthorne Road, London SW8 3HE
United Kingdom
Tel: +44 (0) 20 0147 8220

duncan.petersen@zen.co.uk

http://duncanpetersen.blogspot.com/

Types: Nonfiction
Subjects: Antiques; Travel

Travel publishing house based in London.Publishes Hotel Guides, along with a variety of walking and cycling guides for Britain.

P223 Dutton

Publishing Imprint
United States

Book Publisher: Penguin Publishing Group (**P585**)

P224 Dutton Children's Books

Publishing Imprint
United States

Book Publisher: Penguin Young Readers Group (**P591**)

P225 Dynasty Press

Book Publisher
19 New Road, Brighton, BN1 1UF
United Kingdom
Tel: +44 (0) 7970 066894

admin@dynastypress.co.uk

http://www.dynastypress.co.uk
https://www.facebook.com/dynastypress

Nonfiction > *Nonfiction Books*
Biography; History; Royalty

Publishes books connected to royalty, dynasties and people of influence.

P226 Ebury

Book Publisher
United Kingdom

Book Publisher: Penguin Random House UK (**P587**)

Publishing Imprints: BBC Books (**P084**); Del Rey (*P206*); Ebury Enterprises (*P227*); Ebury Press (*P228*); Pop Press (*P615*); Rider Books (*P653*); Vermilion (*P821*); Virgin Books (*P832*); WH Allen (*P857*)

P227 Ebury Enterprises

Publishing Imprint
United Kingdom

Book Publisher: Ebury (**P226**)

P228 Ebury Press

Publishing Imprint
United Kingdom

Book Publisher: Ebury (**P226**)

P229 Ecco

Publishing Imprint

Book Publisher: HarperCollins

P230 Ediciones Lerner

Publishing Imprint

Book Publisher: Lerner Publishing Group (**P438**)

P231 Eerdmans Books for Young Readers

Publishing Imprint
4035 Park East Court SE, Grand Rapids, Michigan 49546
United States
Tel: +1 (616) 459-4591

info@eerdmans.com

https://www.eerdmans.com/youngreaders/

Book Publisher: William B. Eerdmans Publishing Co.

CHILDREN'S > **Fiction**
Middle Grade; *Picture Books*
YOUNG ADULT
Fiction > *Novels*
Nonfiction > *Nonfiction Books*

Send: Query; Synopsis; Writing sample; Full text
Don't send: Self-Addressed Stamped Envelope (SASE)
How to send: Post

Publishes picture books, middle reader and young adult fiction and nonfiction. Seeks manuscripts that are honest, wise, and hopeful; but also publishes stories that simply delight with their storyline, characters, or good humor. Stories that celebrate diversity, stories of historical significance, and stories that relate to contemporary social issues are of special interest at this time. Currently publishes 12 to 18 books a year. Submit by post only but do not include SASE. No return of materials or response unless interested.

P232 Electio Publishing

Book Publisher
United States

info@electiopublishing.com

http://www.electiopublishing.com

Types: Fiction
Subjects: Adventure; Autobiography; Fantasy; History; Horror; Literary; Mystery; Religion; Romance; Science Fiction
Markets: Academic; Adult

Closed to approaches.

First and foremost a faith-based publisher, but will consider anything that is marketable to a wide audience, whether it is fiction or nonfiction.

P233 Eleusinian Press

Book Publisher
United Kingdom

shop@eleusinianpress.co.uk

http://www.eleusinianpress.co.uk
https://www.facebook.com/eleusinianpress

Nonfiction > *Nonfiction Books*
Music; Politics

A small publisher specialising in madness, music and radical politics.

Authors: Tristam Vivian Adams; Liz Albl; Graham Askey; Michael Burnett; Thomas D'Angelo; Zenon Gradkowski; Esther Leslie; Andrew Roberts; Richard Shrubb; Daniel Spicer; Jan Tchamani; Ben Watson; Kit Withnail; Dave Wood

Editor: Alastair Kemp

P234 Elliott & Thompson

Book Publisher
2 John Street, London, WC1N 2ES
United Kingdom
Tel: +44 (0) 7973 956107

info@eandtbooks.com

http://www.eandtbooks.com
https://twitter.com/eandtbooks
https://www.instagram.com/elliottandthompson/

Fiction > *Novels*

Nonfiction
Gift Books: General
Nonfiction Books: Arts; Biography; Business; Comedy / Humour; Economics; History; Language; Music; Nature; Politics; Science; Sport

Publishes original and bestselling nonfiction and carefully selected fiction.

P235 Emily Bestler Books

Publishing Imprint

Book Publisher: Simon & Schuster Adult Publishing (**P711**)

P236 Emperor's New Clothes Press

Book Publisher; Consultancy
United States

http://www.encpress.com
https://www.facebook.com/ENCPress/

Fiction > *Novels*

Closed to approaches.

Costs: Offers services that writers have to pay for.

Submissions on hold, but continue to act as consultants to those wishing to self-publish.

Editor: Olga Gardner Galvin

P237 ENC Press

Book Publisher
United States

sales@encpress.com

http://www.encpress.com
https://www.facebook.com/ENCPress/

Fiction > *Novels*: Comedy / Humour

Closed to approaches.

Publishes novels that blow up boundaries of genres and formulas and keep you guessing and turning pages until the end you didn't see coming. Funny novels. Sometimes bittersweet, but always with a chuckle.

Editor: Olga Gardner Galvin

P238 Encyclopedia Britannica (UK) Ltd

Book Publisher
2nd Floor, Unity Wharf, Mill Street, London, SE1 2BH
United Kingdom
Tel: +44 (0) 20 7500 7800
Fax: +44 (0) 20 7500 7878

enqbol@britannica.co.uk

https://britannica.co.uk

ACADEMIC > **Nonfiction** > *Reference*

ADULT > **Nonfiction** > *Reference*

Global digital educational publisher, publishing information and instructional products used in schools, universities, homes, libraries and workplaces throughout the world.

P239 Engram Books

Publishing Imprint
United Kingdom

submissions@sunpenny.com

https://www.sunpenny.com/imprints/

Book Publisher: Sunpenny Publishing (**P748**)

Nonfiction > *Nonfiction Books*
Autobiography; Biography; Disabilities; Memoir

Send: Author bio; Marketing Plan; Synopsis; Full text
How to send: Email
How not to send: Post

Imprint to focus on memoirs, auto-biographies, and biographies – including books about the challenges of disabilities. Especially interested in books that will be uplifting for the disabled community; that will reach out to others and let them know they are not alone, that others have gone through similar issues; how to deal with those issues; where to find help – and similar.

P240 Enliven

Publishing Imprint

Book Publisher: Simon & Schuster Adult Publishing **(P711)**

P241 Entrepreneur Press

Book Publisher
United States

books@entrepreneur.com

https://www.entrepreneur.com/press

PROFESSIONAL > **Nonfiction** > *Nonfiction Books*
Business; Entrepreneurship; Finance

Send: Outline; Table of Contents; Writing sample; Market info; Author bio
How to send: Online submission system

An independent publishing company that publishes titles focusing on starting and growing a business, personal finance, real estate and careers. Submit proposals online via online submission system.

Publisher: Justin Koenigsberger

P242 Epic Ink

Publishing Imprint

Book Publisher: The Quarto Group, Inc. **(P633)**

P243 EPTA Books

Publishing Imprint
United Kingdom

submissions@sunpenny.com

https://www.sunpenny.com/imprints/

Book Publisher: Sunpenny Publishing **(P748)**

Nonfiction > *Coffee Table Books*

Send: Query; Author bio; Marketing Plan; Synopsis; Full text
How to send: Email
How not to send: Post

Imprint for non-fiction books and coffee-table beauties.

P244 Ertel Publishing

Book Publisher
PO Box 838, Yellow Springs, OH 45387
United States
Tel: +1 (800) 767-5828

orders@ertelpublishing.com

https://ertelgiftshop.com

Nonfiction > *Nonfiction Books*
Cars; Farm Equipment; Military Vehicles; Railways; Recreational Vehicles

Publishes books for transportation enthusiasts.

P245 Essence Press

Book Publisher
United Kingdom

essencepress@btinternet.com

https://www.juliejohnstone.com/essence-press/

Poetry > *Poetry Collections*

Publishes the work of the editor, and occasionally the work of other poets and artists, usually working in collaboration to create handbound poem-objects or artists' books.

Editor: Julie Johnstone

P246 Essex Publications

Publishing Imprint
United Kingdom

http://www.uhpress.co.uk/subject-areas/essex-publications

Book Publisher: University of Hertfordshire Press **(P802)**

ACADEMIC > **Nonfiction** > *Nonfiction Books*: Local History

This series aims to publish important scholarly studies on the historic county of Essex in attractive and well-illustrated volumes.

P247 Evan-Moor Educational Publishers

Book Publisher
18 Lower Ragsdale Drive, Monterey, CA 93940-5746
United States
Tel: +1 (800) 777-4362
Fax: +1 (800) 777-4332

customerservice@evan-moor.com

http://www.evan-moor.com
http://www.facebook.com/evanmoorcorp
https://twitter.com/evanmoor
https://www.youtube.com/channel/UCW1uyTjhrULw-vnU8PRwk0A
https://www.instagram.com/evanmoor_publisher/?hl=en

CHILDREN'S > **Nonfiction** > *Nonfiction Books*: Education

PROFESSIONAL > **Nonfiction** > *Nonfiction Books*: Education

Publishes practical, creative, and engaging PreK-8 educational materials.

P248 Everyman Chess

Publishing Imprint
United Kingdom

info@everymanchess.com

https://everymanchess.com
https://www.facebook.com/everymanchess
https://www.twitter.com/everymanchess
https://www.youtube.com/user/EverymanChessChannel
https://vimeo.com/everymanchess

Book Publisher: Gloucester Publishers **(P297)**

Nonfiction > *Nonfiction Books*: Chess

Describes itself as the world's preeminent chess book publisher.

P249 Everyman's Library

Publishing Imprint
United States

Book Publisher: Knopf Doubleday Publishing Group **(P426)**

P250 Everything With Words

Book Publisher
United Kingdom

info@everythingwithwords.com

http://www.everythingwithwords.com

ADULT > **Fiction** > *Novels*: Literary

CHILDREN'S > **Fiction** > *Novels*

How to send: Email

Publishes fiction for adults and children, including short story anthologies. No picture books or stories in rhyme for young children. Looks for good stories rather than didactic tales. No crime or fantasy.

P251 F. Warne & Co.

Publishing Imprint
United States

Book Publisher: Penguin Young Readers Group **(P591)**

P252 Facet Publishing

Book Publisher
7 Ridgmount Street, London, WC1E 7AE
United Kingdom
Tel: +44 (0) 20 4513 2831

info@facetpublishing.co.uk

https://www.facetpublishing.co.uk
https://www.facebook.com/facetpublishing
https://twitter.com/facetpublishing
https://www.youtube.com/user/facetpublishing
https://www.linkedin.com/company/facet-publishing

PROFESSIONAL > **Nonfiction** > *Nonfiction Books*
Data and Information Systems; Information Science

Describes itself as the leading publisher of books for library, information and heritage professionals worldwide.

: Sarah Busby

Publishing Imprints: Clive Bingley Books; Library Association Publishing.

P253 Fair Winds Press

Publishing Imprint

Book Publisher: The Quarto Group, Inc. **(P633)**

P254 Falstaff Books

Book Publisher
United States

info@falstaffbooks.com

http://falstaffbooks.com

Types: Fiction
Subjects: Fantasy; Horror; Romance; Science Fiction
Markets: Adult

Closed to approaches.

Publishes novels and novellas in the following genres: Fantasy, Urban Fantasy, Science Fiction, Horror, Romance, Weird West, and misfit toys.

P255 Familius

Book Publisher
United States

bookideas@familius.com

https://www.familius.com
https://www.facebook.com/familiustalk
https://www.instagram.com/familiustalk/?hl=en
https://twitter.com/familiustalk
https://www.pinterest.com/familius/
https://www.youtube.com/channel/UCe0DyumvESLsKkVQ86xQfAg?feature=emb_ch_name_ex

ADULT > **Nonfiction** > *Nonfiction Books*
Cookery; Education; Family; Health; Parenting; Relationships; Self Help; Wellbeing

CHILDREN'S > **Fiction**
Board Books: Family
Picture Books: Family

YOUNG ADULT > **Nonfiction** > *Nonfiction Books*
Health; Wellbeing

Send: Query; Outline; Writing sample; Market info; Author bio
Don't send: Full text
How to send: Email

Publishes nonfiction for adults, young adults, and children, focused on family as the fundamental unit of society. Submit by email or if necessary by post.

P256 Family Tree Books

Publishing Imprint
United States

Book Publisher: Penguin Publishing Group (**P585**)

P257 Fand Music Press

Book Publisher
Glenelg , 10 Avon Close , Petersfield , Hampshire , GU31 4LG
United Kingdom
Tel: +44 (0) 1730 267341

contact@fandmusic.com

https://fandmusic.com

Fiction > *Short Fiction*: Music

Nonfiction > *Nonfiction Books*: Music

Poetry > *Any Poetic Form*: Music

Publisher of sheet music, now also publishing books about music, CD recordings, and poetry and short stories.

Managing Editor: Peter Thompson

P258 Farrar, Straus & Giroux, Inc.

Book Publisher
120 Broadway, New York, NY 10271
United States
Tel: +1 (212) 741-6900

sales@fsgbooks.com

https://us.macmillan.com/fsg

Types: Fiction; Nonfiction; Poetry
Markets: Adult; Children's; Young Adult

Closed to approaches.

Not accepting submissions.

Publishing Imprint: Hill and Wang

P259 Farshore Books

Publishing Imprint
United Kingdom

https://www.farshore.co.uk
https://www.facebook.com/FarshoreBooks
https://www.instagram.com/farshorebooks/
https://twitter.com/FarshoreBooks

Book Publisher: HarperCollins UK (**P347**)

CHILDREN'S > **Fiction**
Chapter Books; *Early Readers*; *Middle Grade*; *Picture Books*

Aims to make every child a proud reader. This mission underpins every acquisition in their broad and inclusive portfolio of child-friendly picture books, fiction, non-fiction and brands, which offers children multiple ways into reading for pleasure.

P260 Fathom Books

Book Publisher
United States

editor@fathombooks.org

http://fathombooks.org
https://sharkpackpoetry.com/fathom-books/
https://spr.submittable.com/submit

Fiction > *Novels*
Experimental; LGBTQIA; Literary; Philosophy; Women

Poetry > *Any Poetic Form*

Closed to approaches.

Costs: Offers services that writers have to pay for. Free to submit, but fee for expedited response.

Independent small press publishing volumes of poetry, very experimental fiction, hybrids, poetics, speculation, etc. Primary interest is text by women and queers. Accepts submissions via online submission system during specific windows only.

P261 Favorite World Press

Book Publisher
United States

info@favoriteworldpress.com

https://www.favoriteworldpress.com

ADULT
Fiction > *Novels*
Animals; Environment; Nature; Sustainable Living

Nonfiction > *Nonfiction Books*
Animals; Environment; Nature; Sustainable Living

Poetry > *Any Poetic Form*
Animals; Environment; Nature; Sustainable Living

CHILDREN'S
Fiction
Middle Grade: Nature
Picture Books: Nature

Nonfiction > *Nonfiction Books*: Nature

YOUNG ADULT
Fiction > *Novels*
Animals; Environment; Nature; Sustainable Living

Nonfiction > *Nonfiction Books*
Animals; Environment; Nature; Sustainable Living

Send: Query; Author bio; Synopsis; Writing sample
How to send: Online contact form

An independent publisher based in New York City. We believe that one of the best ways to help change the world is to start small. Our primary mission is to educate, entertain, and inspire young readers with books that focus on nature, wildlife, green living, and compassionate action. Our titles are specifically chosen to encourage creativity, critical thinking, and the confidence to show caring. By fostering an appreciation for the wild and the wondrous and an understanding of the importance of being kind towards both people and the planet, we aim to help shape the next generation of brave, big-hearted, planetary stewards. We help shape them – they help shape the world!

We also focus on young adult and adult fiction and nonfiction books for a general audience that illuminate and celebrate the splendor of nature, demystify the functioning of the environment, and promote biodiversity conservation and sustainable living.

We globally distribute high-quality hardcover, paperback, and electronic books through all major outlets, including Amazon, Barnes & Noble, WHSmith, and Booktopia.

For a complete list of genres and submission guidelines please see our website.

P262 The Feminist Press

Book Publisher
365 Fifth Avenue, Suite 5406, New York, NY 10016
United States

editor@feministpress.org

https://www.feministpress.org
https://www.facebook.com/FeministPress/
http://thefeministpress.tumblr.com/
https://www.youtube.com/channel/UCClCd_SsorK5JGKCE7rD7vw
https://twitter.com/FeministPress
https://www.instagram.com/feministpress/

ADULT
Fiction
Graphic Novels: Feminism
Novels: Contemporary; Fantasy; Feminism; Mystery; Science Fiction
Nonfiction > *Nonfiction Books*
Activism; Africa; African American; Arts; Asia; Asian American; Biography; Education; Feminism; Films; Health; History; Italian American; Italy; Journalism; Judaism; LGBTQIA; Legal; Media; Medicine; Memoir; Middle East; Popular Culture; Postcolonialism; Science; Sexuality; South America

Poetry > *Poetry Collections*: Feminism

CHILDREN'S > **Fiction** > *Novels*: Feminism

Closed to approaches.

Feminist publisher, publishing an array of genres including cutting-edge fiction, activist nonfiction, literature in translation, hybrid memoirs, children's books, and more.

Editor: Florence Howe

P263 Fidra Books

Book Publisher
United Kingdom

info@fidrabooks.co.uk

http://www.fidrabooks.co.uk

Types: Fiction
Markets: Children's

Ssmall independent publisher specialising in reprinting children's books that have been unfairly neglected and deserve to be back in print. Books range from 1930s adventure stories to iconic 1960s fantasy novels and from pony books by Carnegie medal winning authors to contemporary boarding school stories.

Editors: Malcolm Robertson; Vanessa Robertson

P264 Fircone Books Ltd

Publishing Imprint
The Holme, Church Road, Eardisley, Herefordshire, HR3 6NJ
United Kingdom
Tel: +44 (0) 1544 327182

info@logastonpress.co.uk

https://logastonpress.co.uk/product-category/firconebooks/

Book Publisher: Logaston Press

Nonfiction > *Nonfiction Books*
Church Architecture; Church Art

Publishes books on church art and architecture, and children's illustrated books.

P265 Firebird

Publishing Imprint
United States

Book Publisher: Penguin Young Readers Group (**P591**)

P266 Firefly

Book Publisher
D.20, Cardiff Metropolitan University, Cyncoed Road, Cyncoed, Cardiff, CF23 6XD
United Kingdom

submissions@fireflypress.co.uk
hello@fireflypress.co.uk

https://fireflypress.co.uk
https://www.facebook.com/FireflyPress/
https://twitter.com/FireflyPress
https://www.instagram.com/fireflypress/
https://www.youtube.com/channel/UCqzaLmXCoGJEQuaooZcnb4Q

CHILDREN'S > **Fiction**
Early Readers; *Middle Grade*
TEEN > **Fiction** > *Novels*

YOUNG ADULT > **Fiction** > *Novels*

Closed to approaches.

Publishes fiction and nonfiction for children and young adults aged 5-19. Not currently accepting nonfiction submissions. Fiction submissions through agents only. Not currently publishing any picture books or colour illustrated book for any age group.

Editor: Janet Thomas

P267 Fiscal Publications

Book Publisher
Granta Lodge, 71 Graham Road, Malvern, Worcestershire, WR14 2JS
United Kingdom
Tel: +44 (0) 800 678 5934

info@fiscalpublications.com

https://www.fiscalpublications.com

ACADEMIC > **Nonfiction** > *Nonfiction Books*
Economics; Finance; Taxation

PROFESSIONAL > **Nonfiction** > *Nonfiction Books*
Economics; Finance; Taxation

Send: Query
How to send: Email

Publishes academic and professional books specialising in taxation, public finance and public economics. Materials are relevant worldwide to policy-makers, administrators, lecturers and students of the economics, politics, law and practice of taxation.

Editor: Andy Lymer

P268 Five Leaves Bookshop

Publishing Imprint

Book Publisher: Five Leaves Publications (**P269**)

P269 Five Leaves Publications

Book Publisher
14a Long Row, Nottingham, NG1 2DH
United Kingdom
Tel: +44 (0) 1158 373097

info@fiveleaves.co.uk

https://fiveleaves.co.uk/

Types: Fiction; Nonfiction; Poetry; Scripts
Formats: Short Fiction
Subjects: Arts; Biography; Crime; History; Literature; Politics; Religion; Sociology
Markets: Adult; Young Adult

Closed to approaches.

Small publisher with interests including social history, Jewish culture, politics, poetry, and fiction. Publishes both commercial and non-commercial work. No unsolicited mss.

Editor: Ross Bradshaw

Publishing Imprints: Bromley House Editions (*P130*); Crime Express (*P186*); Five Leaves Bookshop (*P268*); More Shoots More Leaves (*P506*); New London Editions (*P530*); Richard Hollis (*P651*)

P270 Flame Of The Forest Publishing Pte Ltd

Book Publisher
Blk 5 Ang Mo Kio Industrial Park 2A, #07-22/23, AMK Tech II, 567760
Singapore
Tel: (65) 6484 8887

editor@flameoftheforest.com

https://www.flameoftheforest.com

ADULT
Fiction > *Novels*
Nonfiction > *Nonfiction Books*

CHILDREN'S > **Fiction** > *Early Readers*

Send: Query; Synopsis; Writing sample
How to send: Email; Post

Submit a synopsis with a couple of sample chapters by email or by post. Submissions by post will not be returned.

Publishing Imprints: Angsana Books; Bamboo Books; Chiku Books

P271 Floris Books

Book Publisher
Canal Court, 40 Craiglockhart Avenue, Edinburgh, EH14 1LT
United Kingdom
Tel: +44 (0) 1313 372372

editorial@florisbooks.co.uk
floris@florisbooks.co.uk

https://www.florisbooks.co.uk
http://www.facebook.com/FlorisBooks
https://twitter.com/FlorisBooks
http://www.youtube.com/user/FlorisBooks
http://pinterest.com/florisbooks/

ADULT > **Nonfiction** > *Nonfiction Books*
Arts; Astrology; Health; Holistic Health; Literature; Mind, Body, Spirit; Parenting; Philosophy; Religion; Space; Spirituality

CHILDREN'S
Fiction
Board Books; *Early Readers*; *Middle Grade*; *Novels*; *Picture Books*; *Short Fiction*
Nonfiction > *Nonfiction Books*
Activities; Crafts

Send: Synopsis; Writing sample; Table of Contents; Author bio
How to send: Online submission system
How not to send: Post

Publishes a wide range of books including adult nonfiction, picture books and children's novels. No poetry or verse, fiction for people over the age of 14, or autobiography, unless it specifically relates to a relevant nonfiction subject area. No submissions by email. Send via online form. See website for full details of areas covered and submission guidelines.

Publishing Imprint: Kelpies (**P422**)

P272 Folger Shakespeare Library

Publishing Imprint

Book Publisher: Simon & Schuster Adult Publishing (**P711**)

P273 Forge

Publishing Imprint
United States

https://us.macmillan.com/tomdohertyassociates/
https://www.torforgeblog.com/
https://www.facebook.com/forgereads/

Book Publisher: Tom Doherty Associates (**P771**)

Fiction > *Novels*
Mystery; Thrillers; Westerns

Closed to approaches.

Publisher of Fiction, Thrillers, Mysteries, Westerns, and more. Open submission policy currently suspended due to COVID-19.

P274 Fort Publishing

Book Publisher
Old Belmont House, 12 Robsland Avenue, Ayr, KA7 2RW
United Kingdom
Tel: +44 (0) 1292 880693
Fax: +44 (0) 1292 270134

fortpublishing@aol.com

http://www.fortpublishing.co.uk

Nonfiction > *Nonfiction Books*
History; Scotland; Sport

One of Scotland's leading independent publishers, specialising in sport, history and local interest.

Editor: James McCarroll

P275 Fortress Press

Publishing Imprint
411 Washington Ave N, 3rd Floor, Minneapolis, MN 55401
United States
Tel: +1 (844) 993-3812
Fax: +1 (800) 722-7766

https://www.fortresspress.com
https://www.facebook.com/fortresspress/
https://twitter.com/fortresspress
https://www.youtube.com/user/FortressPress

Book Publisher: 1517 Media (**P001**)

ACADEMIC > **Nonfiction** > *Nonfiction Books*
Christianity; History

PROFESSIONAL > **Nonfiction** > *Nonfiction Books*: Christianity

Publisher of compelling theological, biblical, and ethical engagements for the church and the world in which it lives.

P276 The Foundry Publishing Company

Book Publisher
PO Box 419527, Kansas City, MO 64141-6527
United States
Tel: +1 (816) 931-1900
Fax: +1 (816) 531-0923

rmcfarland@thefoundrypublishing.com

https://www.thefoundrypublishing.com
https://www.facebook.com/TheFoundryPublishing/
https://twitter.com/WeAreTheFoundry
https://www.youtube.com/c/TheFoundryPublishing
https://www.instagram.com/thefoundrycommunity/

Nonfiction > *Nonfiction Books*
Christianity; Evangelism

Poetry > *Any Poetic Form*: Christianity

Send: Table of Contents; Synopsis; Writing sample
How to send: Word file email attachment

Publishes Christian books that reflect an evangelical Wesleyan stance in accord with the Church of the Nazarene. Also poems and anecdotes. Send submissions by email.

P277 Frances Lincoln Children's Books

Publishing Imprint
74-77 White Lion Street, London, N1 9PF
United Kingdom
Tel: +44 (0) 20 7284 9300
Fax: +44 (0) 20 7485 0490

QuartoKidsSubmissions@Quarto.com

http://www.quartoknows.com/Frances-Lincoln-Childrens-Books

Book Publisher: The Quarto Group, Inc. (**P633**)

Types: Fiction; Nonfiction; Poetry
Subjects: Culture
Markets: Children's

Publishes picture books, multicultural books, poetry, picture books and information books. Submit by email. See website for full guidelines.

Editor: Katie Cotton

Publishers: Janetta Otter-Barry; Rachel Williams

P278 Free Press

Publishing Imprint

Book Publisher: Simon & Schuster Adult Publishing (**P711**)

P279 Friends United Press

Book Publisher
101 Quaker Hill Drive, Richmond, IN 47374
United States
Tel: +1 (765) 962-7573

info@fum.org

https://bookstore.friendsunitedmeeting.org/collections/friends-united-press
https://www.facebook.com/friendsunitedmeeting/
https://www.instagram.com/friendsunitedmeeting/

Nonfiction > *Nonfiction Books*: Quakerism

Publishes books by Quakers on Quaker history, spirituality, and doctrine.

P280 Frontline Books

Publishing Imprint
47 Church Street, Barnsley, South Yorkshire, S70 2AS
United Kingdom
Tel: +44 (0) 1226 734555
Fax: +44 (0) 1226 734438

info@frontline-books.com

https://www.frontline-books.com
https://twitter.com/frontline_books

Book Publisher: Pen & Sword Books Ltd **(P578)**

Nonfiction > *Nonfiction Books*
History; Warfare

Send: Query

Military history publisher. Publishes on a wide range of military history topics and periods, from Ancient Greece and Rome to the present day. Welcomes submissions.

P281 Fruit Bruise Press

Publishing Imprint
United Kingdom

Book Publisher: DogHorn Publishing **(P217)**

P282 FunStitch Studio

Publishing Imprint
United States

Book Publisher: C&T Publishing **(P133)**

P283 G.P. Putnam's Sons

Publishing Imprint
United States

Book Publisher: Penguin Publishing Group **(P585)**

P284 G.P. Putnam's Sons Books for Young Readers

Publishing Imprint
United States

consumerservices@penguinrandomhouse.com

https://www.penguin.com/publishers/gpputnamssonsbooksforyoungread/

Book Publisher: Penguin Young Readers Group **(P591)**

CHILDREN'S > **Fiction**
Novels; *Picture Books*

How to send: Through a literary agent

Publishes approximately fifty trade hardcover books a year for children, including lively, accessible picture books and some of today's strongest voices in fiction.

P285 Gale

Book Publisher
27555 Executive Dr. Ste 350, Farmington Hills, MI 48331
United States
Tel: +1 (800) 877-4253
Fax: +1 (877) 363-4253

gale.customerservice@cengage.com

https://www.gale.com
https://www.facebook.com/GaleCengage/
https://www.linkedin.com/company/gale
https://twitter.com/galecengage
https://www.youtube.com/user/GaleCengage

Book Publisher: Cengage

ACADEMIC > **Nonfiction**
Nonfiction Books: Business; Chemistry; Computer Science; Earth Science; Economics; Education; Finance; Health; History; Legal; Literature; Mathematics; Medicine; Physics; Science; Sociology; Technology
Reference: General

ADULT > **Nonfiction**
Nonfiction Books: Agriculture; Antiques; Arts; Astronomy; Business; Chemistry; Crafts; Earth Science; Economics; Education; Finance; Gardening; Health; History; Hobbies; Legal; Literature; Medicine; Science; Sport; Technology
Reference: General

PROFESSIONAL > **Nonfiction**
Nonfiction Books: Business; Economics; Education; Finance; Health; Legal; Medicine; Science; Sociology; Technology
Reference: General

Supplies businesses, schools, and libraries with books and electronic reference materials.

Book Publisher: KidHaven Press

Publishing Imprints: The Taft Group; Blackbird Press; Charles Scribner & Sons; Five Star; G.K. Hall & Co.; Graham & Whiteside Ltd; Greenhaven Publishing; KG Saur Verlag GmbH & Co. KG; Lucent Books; Macmillan Reference USA; Primary Source Media; Schirmer Reference; St James Press; Thorndike Press; Twayne Publishers; UXL; Wheeler Publishing

P286 Gallery

Publishing Imprint

Book Publisher: Simon & Schuster Adult Publishing **(P711)**

P287 Galore Park Publishing

Book Publisher
United Kingdom

https://www.galorepark.co.uk
https://twitter.com/Galore_Park
https://www.facebook.com/Galore1Park/

Publishing Imprint: Hodder Education Group

ACADEMIC > **Nonfiction** > *Nonfiction Books*: Education

How to send: Online submission system

Specialises in preparation for 11+, pre-test and 13+ Common Entrance exams and leads the market in textbooks for pupils studying at independent schools.

P288 The Geological Society Publishing House

Book Publisher; Magazine Publisher
Unit 7, Brassmill Enterprise Centre, Brassmill Lane, Bath, BA1 3JN
United Kingdom

https://www.geolsoc.org.uk/publications

ACADEMIC > **Nonfiction**
Articles: Earth Science; Geology
Nonfiction Books: Earth Science; Geology; Memoir

Publishes postgraduate books and journals on the earth sciences.

: Angharad Hills

Magazines: Geochemistry: Exploration, Environment, Analysis (*M221*); Journal of the Geological Society (*M285*); Petroleum Geoscience (*M375*); Proceedings of the Yorkshire Geological Society (*M397*); Quarterly Journal of Engineering Geology and Hydrogeology (*M404*); Scottish Journal of Geology (*M435*)

P289 George Braziller, Inc.

Book Publisher
90 Broad Street, Suite 2100, New York, NY 10007
United States
Tel: +1 (212) 260-9256
Fax: +1 (212) 267-3165

http://www.georgebraziller.com

Fiction > *Novels*

Nonfiction > *Nonfiction Books*
Architecture; Arts; Biography

Poetry > *Poetry Collections*

Closed to approaches.

Prefers online approaches, but will accept paper submissions by post. Include SASE if return of material is required. Does not respond to email queries unless interested.

P290 George Ronald Publisher

Book Publisher
United Kingdom

sales@grbooks.com

http://grbooks.com
http://www.facebook.com/pages/George-Ronald-Books/25850856123

Nonfiction > *Nonfiction Books*: Religion

Religious publisher, concentrating solely on books of interest to Baha'is.

P291 Gertrude Press

Book Publisher
United States

editor@gertrudepress.org

https://www.gertrudepress.org

Types: Fiction; Nonfiction; Poetry
Formats: Short Fiction
Subjects: Literary
Markets: Adult

Closed to approaches.

Publishes work by writers identifying as LGBTQ, both in online journal form and as chapbooks. Considers work for chapbook publication through its annual contests only. See website for details.

Online Magazine: Gertrude (**M224**)

P292 Ghostwoods Books

Book Publisher
United Kingdom

ghostwoodsbooks@gmail.com

http://gwdbooks.com
https://www.facebook.com/GhostwoodsBooks/

Fiction > *Short Fiction*

Closed to approaches.

A small, fair-trade publishing company. Publishes collections of short stories. Accepts submissions to specific calls only.

Editors: Tim Dedopulos; Salome Jones

P293 Gill Books

Book Publisher
Hume Avenue, Park West, Dublin, D12 YV96
Ireland
Tel: +353 (01) 500 9500

https://www.gillbooks.ie
http://www.facebook.com/GillBooks
http://www.twitter.com/Gill_Books
http://www.instagram.com/GillBooks

ADULT > **Nonfiction**
Gift Books: Ireland
Nonfiction Books: Biography; Comedy / Humour; Crafts; Crime; Current Affairs; Food and Drink; History; Hobbies; Ireland; Lifestyle; Mind, Body, Spirit; Nature; Parenting; Politics; Sport
Reference: General, and in particular: Ireland
CHILDREN'S
Fiction > *Novels*
Nonfiction > *Nonfiction Books*

Send: Query; Outline; Synopsis; Table of Contents; Writing sample; Author bio
How to send: Online submission system; Post

Publishes adult nonfiction and children's fiction and nonfiction. No adult fiction, poetry, short stories or plays. In general, focuses on books of Irish interest. Prefers proposals through online submission system, but will also accept proposals by post. See website for full submission guidelines.

Editor: Deborah Marsh

P294 GL Assessment

Book Publisher
1st Floor Vantage London, Great West Road, Brentford, TW8 9AG
United Kingdom
Tel: +44 (0) 3301 235375

info@gl-assessment.co.uk

https://www.gl-assessment.co.uk

ACADEMIC > **Nonfiction** > *Nonfiction Books*

Publishes educational testing and assessment material.

P295 Glass Poetry Press

Book Publisher
United States

editor@glass-poetry.com

http://www.glass-poetry.com/submissions.html

Types: Poetry
Markets: Adult

Closed to approaches.

Publishes poetry manuscripts between 15 and 25 pages. Currently closed to submissions.

P296 The Globe Pequot Press

Book Publisher
246 Goose Lane, 2nd Floor, Guilford, CT 06437
United States

GPSubmissions@rowman.com

http://www.globepequot.com
https://rowman.com/Page/GlobePequot
https://www.facebook.com/globepequot/
https://twitter.com/globepequot

Book Publisher: Rowman & Littlefield Publishing Group

Nonfiction > *Nonfiction Books*
Biography; Business; Cookery; Gardening; History; Mind, Body, Spirit; Nature; Travel

Send: Outline; Table of Contents; Writing sample; Author bio; Market info
How to send: Email; Post

Publishes books about iconic brands and people, regional interest, history, lifestyle, cooking and food culture, and folklore – books that hit the intersection of a reader's interest in a specific place and their passion for a specific topic.

Publishing Imprints: Applause (*P044*); Astragal Press; Backbeat (*P070*); Down East Books (*P219*); FalconGuides; Lyons Press (*P464*); Mcbooks Press (*P485*); Muddy Boots (*P510*); Pineapple Press (**P608**); Prometheus (*P622*); Skip Jack Press (*P715*); Stackpole Books (**P736**); TwoDot (*P786*); Union Park Press (*P793*)

P297 Gloucester Publishers

Book Publisher
36 Chapel Road, London, SE27 0TY
United Kingdom

https://find-and-update.company-information.service.gov.uk/company/04680814

Publishing Imprint: Everyman Chess (**P248**)

P298 Gnome On Pig Productions Incorporated

Book Publisher
Canada

booksubmissions@gnomeonpigproductions.com

https://www.gnomeonpigproductions.com

Types: Fiction; Nonfiction
Subjects: Drama; Erotic; Fantasy; Horror; Science Fiction
Markets: Adult; Children's; Young Adult

Closed to approaches.

Publishes fiction for children, teens, new adults, and adults. Also occasional nonfiction. Closed to submissions as at February 2020. Check website for current status.

P299 Godstow Press

Book Publisher
60 Godstow Road, Wolvercote, Oxford, OX2 8NY
United Kingdom
Tel: +44 (0) 1865 556215

info@godstowpress.co.uk

http://www.godstowpress.co.uk

Fiction > *Novels*
Historical Fiction; Philosophy; Spirituality

Poetry > *Any Poetic Form*
Philosophy; Spirituality

Small publisher of creative work with a spiritual / philosophical content, particularly historical fiction.

Editors: David Smith; Linda Smith

P300 GoldScriptCo

Book Publisher
United States

https://www.goldscriptco.com

Poetry > *Poetry Collections*

Co-founded by two writers as a means to share their own works as well as to support other writers and artists in their creative journeys.

P301 Goldsmiths Press

Book Publisher
Room 108, Deptford Town Hall, Lewisham

Way, New Cross, London, SE14 6NW
United Kingdom

goldsmithspress@gold.ac.uk

https://www.gold.ac.uk/goldsmiths-press

ACADEMIC > **Nonfiction** > *Nonfiction Books*

Send: Query
Don't send: Full text

University press aiming to cut across disciplinary boundaries and blur the distinctions between theory, practice, fiction and non-fiction. See website for proposal forms and submit by email.

Editors: Adrian Driscoll; Sarah Kember; Ellen Parnavelas; Guy Sewell

P302 Goose Lane Editions

Book Publisher
Suite 330, 500 Beaverbrook Court,
Fredericton, NB, E3B 5X4
Canada
Tel: +1 (506) 450-4251
Fax: +1 (888) 926-8377

info@gooselane.com

https://gooselane.com
https://www.twitter.com/goose_lane
https://www.facebook.com/GooseLaneEditions/
https://www.instagram.com/goose_lane

Fiction > *Novels*: Literary

Nonfiction > *Nonfiction Books*
Arts; Biography; Creative Nonfiction; History; Nature; Politics; Popular Culture; Travel

Poetry > *Any Poetic Form*

Send: Query; Author bio; Synopsis; Writing sample
How to send: Word file email attachment
How not to send: Post

Publishes literary fiction, nonfiction, and poetry by established and up-and-coming Canadian authors. Submissions will only be considered from outside Canada if the author is Canadian and the book is of extraordinary interest to Canadian readers. No unsolicited MSS, children's, or young adult. See website for full submission details.

Editor: Angela Williams

P303 Grant Books

Book Publisher
Pershore, Worcestershire
United Kingdom
Tel: +44 (0) 1386 803803

golf@grantbooks.co.uk

https://www.grantbooks.co.uk

Nonfiction > *Nonfiction Books*: Golf

Publishes golf-related books covering history, biography, course architecture, etc. No fiction, humour, or instructional.

Editor: H.R.J. Grant

P304 Granta Books

Book Publisher
12 Addison Avenue, London, W11 4QR
United Kingdom
Tel: +44 (0) 20 7605 1360

info@granta.com

https://granta.com/books/
https://www.facebook.com/grantamag/
https://twitter.com/GrantaMag/
https://www.instagram.com/granta_magazine/

Fiction > *Novels*: Literary

Nonfiction > *Nonfiction Books*
Autobiography; Culture; History; Literary Criticism; Nature; Politics; Social Issues; Travel

Closed to approaches.

Publishes around 70% nonfiction / 30% fiction. In nonfiction publishes serious cultural, political and social history, narrative history, or memoir. Rarely publishes straightforward biographies. No genre fiction. Not accepting unsolicited submissions.

P305 Graphic Universe

Publishing Imprint

Book Publisher: Lerner Publishing Group **(P438)**

P306 Graphix

Publishing Imprint

Book Publisher: Scholastic **(P688)**

P307 Graywolf Press

Book Publisher
212 Third Avenue North, Suite 485,
Minneapolis, MN 55401
United States
Tel: +1 (651) 641-0077
Fax: +1 (651) 641-0036

wolves@graywolfpress.org

https://www.graywolfpress.org
https://graywolfpress.submittable.com/submit
https://www.facebook.com/GraywolfPress/
https://twitter.com/GraywolfPress
https://www.instagram.com/graywolfpress/

Fiction
Novels: Literary
Short Fiction Collections: Literary

Nonfiction
Essays: Creative Writing; Cultural Criticism; Literary Criticism; Literary
Nonfiction Books: Creative Writing; Cultural Criticism; Literary Criticism; Memoir

Poetry > *Poetry Collections*

Closed to approaches.

Publishes about 30 books annually, mostly poetry, memoirs, essays, novels, and short stories. Accepts submissions through literary agents, or via competitions during specific windows.

Editor: Fiona McCrae

P308 Green Books

Book Publisher
UIT Cambridge Ltd, PO Box 145, Cambridge, CB4 1GQ
United Kingdom

proposals@greenbooks.co.uk

https://www.greenbooks.co.uk
http://www.facebook.com/pages/Green-Books/128608410501418
http://twitter.com/Green_Books
http://www.youtube.com/greenbookspublishing

Nonfiction > *Nonfiction Books*
Agriculture; Arts; Business; Climate Science; Culture; Economics; Environment; Food; Gardening; Health; Literature; Nature; Science; Sustainable Living; Transport; West Country

Closed to approaches.

Set up in 1986 with the aim of spreading awareness of ecological issues and providing practical advice for those interested in living a green lifestyle.

P309 Greenway Music Press

Publishing Imprint
United States

https://www.areditions.com/gmp/shop.html

Book Publisher: A-R Editions **(P012)**

Nonfiction > *Nonfiction Books*: Music

Brings important but under-appreciated compositions to a larger audience. Focuses on music for standard chamber ensembles, solo instruments and voices, and keyboard.

P310 Greenwillow Books

Publishing Imprint

Book Publisher: HarperCollins

P311 Griffin

Publishing Imprint

Publishing Imprint: St Martin's Press **(P733)**

P312 Grove Atlantic Inc.

Book Publisher
154 West 14th Street, 12th Floor, New York, NY 10011
United States
Tel: +1 (212) 614-7850
Fax: +1 (212) 614-7886

info@groveatlantic.com

https://groveatlantic.com

Fiction > *Novels*

Nonfiction > *Nonfiction Books*

How to send: Through a literary agent

Approach through an agent only. Publishes general fiction and nonfiction.

Publishing Imprints: Atlantic Monthly Press (*P058*); Black Cat (*P098*); Grove Press (*P313*); The Mysterious Press (*P516*)

P313 Grove Press

Publishing Imprint
United States

Book Publisher: Grove Atlantic Inc. (**P312**)

P314 Gryphon House, Inc.

Book Publisher
PO Box 10, 6848 Leons Way, Lewisville, NC 27023
United States
Tel: +1 (336) 712-3490
Fax: +1 (877) 638-7576

info@ghbooks.com

https://www.gryphonhouse.com

ADULT > **Nonfiction** > *Nonfiction Books*: Parenting

PROFESSIONAL > **Nonfiction** > *Nonfiction Books*: Education

Send: Query; Market info; Table of Contents; Writing sample; Author bio

Publishes books intended to help teachers and parents enrich the lives of children from birth to age eight. See website for proposal submission guidelines.

P315 Gwasg Carreg Gwalch

Book Publisher
12 Iard yr Orsaf, Llanrwst, Conwy, LL26 0EH
United Kingdom
Tel: +44 (0) 1492 642031

llanrwst@carreg-gwalch.cymru

https://carreg-gwalch.cymru

ADULT > **Nonfiction** > *Nonfiction Books*
Folklore, Myths, and Legends; History; Travel; Wales; Walking Guides

CHILDREN'S
Fiction
Novels: Wales
Picture Books: Wales

Nonfiction > *Nonfiction Books*
History; Wales

Publishes Welsh language books, and books in English of Welsh interest, such as history and folklore. Also publishes Welsh guides and walks.

P316 Hachette Book Group

Book Publisher
United States

https://www.hachettebookgroup.com

Book Publisher: Hachette Livre (**P320**)

Types: Fiction; Nonfiction
Subjects: Contemporary; Literary
Markets: Adult

Includes 24 imprints covering the entire array of contemporary fiction and nonfiction, from the most popular to the most literary.

Book Publishers: Grand Central Publishing; Little, Brown and Company; Perseus Books (**P594**)

P317 Hachette Books

Publishing Imprint
United States

Book Publisher: Perseus Books (**P594**)

P318 Hachette Children's Group

Book Publisher
3rd Floor, Carmelite House, 50 Victoria Embankment, London, EC4Y 0DZ
United Kingdom

editorial@hachettechildrens.co.uk

https://www.hachettechildrens.co.uk
https://www.facebook.com/hachettekids/
https://twitter.com/hachettekids
https://www.instagram.com/hachettekids/

Book Publisher: Hachette UK (**P321**)

CHILDREN'S
Fiction
Board Books; *Chapter Books*; *Early Readers*; *Gift Books*; *Middle Grade*; *Picture Books*
Nonfiction
Board Books; *Gift Books*; *Nonfiction Books*

How to send: Through a literary agent

Aims to cater for every child, with baby and pre-school books, picture books, gift, fiction, non-fiction, series fiction, books for the school and library market and licensed publishing.

Publishing Imprints: Franklin Watts; Hodder Children's Books (*P374*); Little, Brown Books for Young Readers (*P450*); Orchard Books; Orion Children's Books (*P554*); Pat-a-Cake (*P569*); Quercus Children's Books (*P635*); Wayland Books (*P846*); Wren & Rook (*P875*)

P319 Hachette Go!

Publishing Imprint
United States

Book Publisher: Perseus Books (**P594**)

P320 Hachette Livre

Book Publisher
France

https://www.hachette.com

Types: Fiction; Nonfiction
Markets: Academic; Adult; Children's

International publishing group with operations in all English speaking markets.

Book Publishers: Hachette Book Group (**P316**); Hachette UK (**P321**); Quercus Books

Publishing Imprint: Headline Publishing Group

P321 Hachette UK

Book Publisher
Carmelite House, 50 Victoria Embankment, London, EC4Y 0DZ
United Kingdom
Tel: +44 (0) 20 3122 6000

enquiries@hachette.co.uk

https://www.hachette.co.uk
https://www.facebook.com/HachetteBooksUK/
https://twitter.com/hachetteuk
https://www.instagram.com/hachetteuk/

Book Publisher: Hachette Livre (**P320**)

Fiction > *Novels*

Nonfiction > *Nonfiction Books*

How to send: Through a literary agent

Publishing group made up of ten autonomous publishing divisions and over fifty imprints with a rich and diverse history. Accepts submissions via literary agents only.

Book Publishers: Bookouture (**P119**); Hachette Children's Group (**P318**); Laurence King Publishing Ltd (**P433**)

Publishing Imprints: Headline Publishing Group; Hodder & Stoughton; Hodder Education Group; John Murray; Little, Brown Book Group; Octopus Publishing Group; Orion Publishing Group

P322 Half Mystic Press

Book Publisher
United States

hello@halfmystic.com

https://www.halfmystic.com
https://halfmystic.submittable.com/submit

Fiction
Novellas; *Novels*; *Short Fiction Collections*
Nonfiction > *Nonfiction Books*
Memoir; Music

Poetry > *Poetry Collections*

How to send: Submittable

Publishes poetry, essay, and short story collections; drama; memoirs; novellas; full-length novels; experimental work. See website for full submission guidelines.

Print Magazine: Half Mystic Journal (**M237**)

P323 Halsgrove

Book Publisher
Halsgrove House, Ryelands Business Park, Bagley Road, Wellington, Somerset, TA21 9PZ
United Kingdom
Tel: +44 (0) 1823 653777

sales@halsgrove.com

https://halsgrove.com
https://www.facebook.com/daa.halsgrove.1
https://www.instagram.com/halsgrove_publishing/

Nonfiction > *Nonfiction Books*
Art History; Arts; Aviation; Leisure; Military; Nature; Political History; Politics; Regional; Transport

Send: Query; Synopsis
How to send: Email; Post

Publishes regional material covering various regions in the areas of contemporary art, art history, transport, aviation, politics, political history, natural history, exploration, military and leisure. Prefers approaches by email, but if contacting by post include email address for response.

P324 Hammersmith Books

Book Publisher
4/4A Bloomsbury Square, London, WC1A 2RP
United Kingdom

info@hammersmithbooks.co.uk

https://www.hammersmithbooks.co.uk
https://www.facebook.com/HammersmithHealthBooks
http://twitter.com/HHealthBooks
https://www.pinterest.com/hhealthbooks/

ACADEMIC > **Nonfiction** > *Nonfiction Books*
Diet; Health; Medicine; Mental Health; Nutrition; Wellbeing

ADULT > **Nonfiction** > *Nonfiction Books*
Diet; Health; Medicine; Mental Health; Nutrition; Wellbeing

PROFESSIONAL > **Nonfiction** > *Nonfiction Books*
Diet; Health; Medicine; Mental Health; Nutrition; Wellbeing

Publisher of health, medicine, and nutrition books for the general public, health professionals, and academic markets.

Editor: Georgina Bentliff

P325 HappenStance Press

Book Publisher
21 Hatton Green, Glenrothes, Fife, KY7 4SD
United Kingdom

https://www.happenstancepress.com
https://twitter.com/Nell_Nelson
https://www.facebook.com/HappenStance-Press-114680661902101/

Poetry > *Any Poetic Form*

Closed to approaches.

Small publisher of poetry chapbooks by both new and established poets. Unlikely to publish poets with no track record.

Editor: Helena Nelson

P326 Harlequin Enterprises

Book Publisher
Bay Adelaide Centre, East Tower, 22 Adelaide Street West, 41st Floor, Toronto, ON M5H 4E3
Canada
Tel: +1 (888) 432-4879

https://www.harlequin.com
https://harlequin.submittable.com/submit
https://www.facebook.com/HarlequinBooks
https://twitter.com/HarlequinBooks
https://www.pinterest.com/harlequinbooks/
https://www.youtube.com/user/harlequinbooks
https://www.instagram.com/harlequinbooks/

Book Publisher: HarperCollins

ADULT > **Fiction** > *Novels*: Romance

YOUNG ADULT > **Fiction** > *Novels*: Romance

How to send: Submittable

International publisher of romance fiction. See website for current needs, and appropriate imprints or series to submit to. Also offers manuscript critiquing service.

Book Publisher: Harlequin American Romance

Publishing Imprints: Carina Press (**P144**); HQN Books; Harlequin Books; Harlequin Dare; Luna; MIRA; Mills & Boon; Red Dress Ink; Silhouette; Steeple Hill Books;

P327 Harlequin Mills & Boon Ltd

Book Publisher
Harlequin, 1 London Bridge Street, London, SE1 9GF
United Kingdom

info@millsandboon.co.uk

https://www.millsandboon.co.uk
https://www.instagram.com/millsandboonuk/
https://www.facebook.com/millsandboon/
https://twitter.com/MillsandBoon
https://harlequin.submittable.com/submit

Fiction > *Novels*: Romance

How to send: Submittable

Major publisher with extensive romance list and various romance imprints. Submit via online submission system.

Publishing Imprints: Carina UK; Harlequin MIRA; Mills & Boon Historical; Mills & Boon Medical; Mills & Boon Modern Romance; Mills & Boon Riva; Mills and Boon Cherish

P328 Harmony Books

Publishing Imprint

Book Publishers: The Crown Publishing Group; Random House (**P640**)

P329 Harmony Ink Press

Publishing Imprint
5032 Capital Circle SW, Ste 2 PMB 279, Tallahassee, FL 32305-7886
United States
Tel: +1 (800) 970-3759
Fax: +1 (888) 308-3739

submissions@harmonyinkpress.com

https://www.harmonyinkpress.com

Book Publisher: Dreamspinner Press (**P220**)

NEW ADULT > **Fiction** > *Novels*
Fantasy; LGBTQIA; Mystery; Romance; Science Fiction; Supernatural / Paranormal

TEEN > **Fiction** > *Novels*
Fantasy; LGBTQIA; Mystery; Romance; Science Fiction; Supernatural / Paranormal

Closed to approaches.

Publishes Teen and New Adult fiction featuring significant personal growth of unforgettable characters across the LGBTQ+ spectrum.

P330 Harper Audio (UK)

Publishing Imprint
United Kingdom

Book Publisher: HarperCollins UK (**P347**)

P331 Harper Books

Publishing Imprint

Book Publisher: HarperCollins

P332 Harper Design

Publishing Imprint

Book Publisher: HarperCollins

P333 Harper Inspire

Publishing Imprint
United Kingdom

Book Publisher: HarperCollins UK (**P347**)

P334 Harper Luxe

Publishing Imprint

Book Publisher: HarperCollins

P335 Harper North

Publishing Imprint
United Kingdom

Book Publisher: HarperCollins UK (**P347**)

P336 Harper Perennial

Publishing Imprint

Book Publisher: HarperCollins

P337 Harper Voyager

Publishing Imprint
United Kingdom

Book Publishers: HarperCollins; HarperCollins UK (**P347**)

P338 Harper Wave

Publishing Imprint

Book Publisher: HarperCollins

P339 Harper360

Publishing Imprint
United Kingdom

Book Publisher: HarperCollins UK (**P347**)

P340 HarperAudio

Publishing Imprint

Book Publisher: HarperCollins

P341 HarperChildren's Audio

Publishing Imprint

Book Publisher: HarperCollins

P342 HarperCollins 360

Publishing Imprint

Book Publisher: HarperCollins

P343 HarperCollins Children's Books

Publishing Imprint
United Kingdom

Book Publishers: HarperCollins; HarperCollins UK (**P347**)

P344 HarperCollins Focus

Book Publisher

focuscc@harpercollins.com

https://www.harpercollinsfocus.com

Book Publisher: HarperCollins

Book Publisher: HarperCollins Leadership (**P346**)

P345 HarperCollins Ireland

Publishing Imprint
United Kingdom

Book Publisher: HarperCollins UK (**P347**)

P346 HarperCollins Leadership

Book Publisher

hcleadership@harpercollins.com

https://www.harpercollinsleadership.com
https://www.facebook.com/harpercollinsleadership/
https://twitter.com/hcleadership
https://www.instagram.com/hcleadership/

Book Publisher: HarperCollins Focus (**P344**)

PROFESSIONAL > **Nonfiction** > *Nonfiction Books*: Leadership

Feeds your inner drive to grow as a leader with integrated, values-based development experiences that give you the inspiration and insights you need to thrive in your current role—and your next.

Book Publisher: AMACOM Books (**P034**)

P347 HarperCollins UK

Book Publisher
The News Building, 1 London Bridge Street, London, SE1 9GF, GLASGOW OFFICE:, 103 Westerhill Road, Bishopbriggs, Glasgow, G64 2QT
United Kingdom
Tel: +44 (0) 20 8741 7070
Fax: +44 (0) 20 8307 4440

enquiries@harpercollins.co.uk

https://www.harpercollins.co.uk

Book Publisher: HarperCollins

Types: Fiction; Nonfiction
Formats: Film Scripts; Reference
Subjects: Autobiography; Cookery; Crafts; Crime; Entertainment; Fantasy; Gardening; Health; History; Leisure; Lifestyle; Literary; Media; Science; Science Fiction; Sport; Thrillers; Warfare
Markets: Adult; Children's

How to send: Through a literary agent

One of the UK's three largest publishers, with one of the broadest ranges of material published. All approaches must come through an agent. No unsolicited MSS.

Authors: Cecelia Ahern; Agatha Christie; Patricia Cornwell; Lindsey Kelk; Derek Landy

Book Publishers: HarperPress; Pavilion Books (**P572**)

Publishing Imprints: 4th Estate (**P011**); Avon (*P068*); The Borough Press (*P120*); Collins (*P173*); Farshore Books (**P259**); HQ (*P384*); HQ Digital (*P385*); Harper Audio (UK) (*P330*); Harper Inspire (*P333*); Harper North (*P335*); Harper Voyager (*P337*); Harper360 (*P339*); HarperCollins Children's Books (*P343*); HarperCollins Ireland (*P345*); HarperFiction (*P349*); HarperNonFiction (*P350*); Mills & Boon; Mudlark (*P512*); One More Chapter (*P547*); Times Books (*P768*); William Collins (*P865*)

P348 HarperFestival

Publishing Imprint

Book Publisher: HarperCollins

P349 HarperFiction

Publishing Imprint
United Kingdom

Book Publisher: HarperCollins UK (**P347**)

P350 HarperNonFiction

Publishing Imprint
United Kingdom

Book Publisher: HarperCollins UK (**P347**)

P351 HarperOne

Publishing Imprint

Book Publisher: HarperCollins

P352 HarperTeen

Publishing Imprint

Book Publisher: HarperCollins

P353 HarperTeen Impulse

Publishing Imprint

Book Publisher: HarperCollins

P354 HarperVia

Publishing Imprint

Book Publisher: HarperCollins

P355 Harriman House Ltd

Book Publisher
3 Viceroy Court, Bedford Road, Petersfield, Hampshire, GU32 3LJ
United Kingdom
Tel: +44 (0) 1730 233870

harriman@harriman-house.com

https://www.harriman-house.com

ADULT > **Nonfiction** > *Nonfiction Books*
Business; Economics; Finance; Lifestyle; Personal Finance; Trade

PROFESSIONAL > **Nonfiction** > *Nonfiction Books*
Business; Finance

UK-based, but globally focussed independent publisher operating in the business and finance sector. Publishes books across a broad spectrum of topics ranging from personal finance and creative marketing titles through to professional-level technical guides.

P356 Harvard Business Publishing

Book Publisher
United States
Tel: +1 (800) 545-7685
Fax: +1 (617) 783-7666

custserv@hbsp.harvard.edu

https://hbsp.harvard.edu
https://www.facebook.com/HarvardBizEdu/
https://twitter.com/HarvardBizEdu
https://www.linkedin.com/company/

harvardbizedu
https://www.youtube.com/channel/UCRp-04NDMZh_61j-HszFbSg

ACADEMIC > **Nonfiction** > *Nonfiction Books*
Business; Management

PROFESSIONAL > **Nonfiction** > *Nonfiction Books*
Business; Management

Publishes business books for the professional and academic markets.

Editor: Astrid Sandoval

P357 Harvard Common Press

Publishing Imprint
100 Cummings Center, Suite 253C, Beverly, MA 01915
United States
Tel: +1 (978) 282-9590
Fax: +1 (978) 282-7765

dan.rosenberg@quarto.com

http://www.harvardcommonpress.com

Book Publisher: The Quarto Group, Inc. (**P633**)

Types: Nonfiction
Subjects: Cookery; Lifestyle
Markets: Adult

Send: Query
Don't send: Full text

Publishes books on cookery and parenting. See website for full guidelines.

Editorial Director: Dan Rosenberg

Publishing Imprint: Gambit Books

P358 Harvard Square Editions (HSE)

Book Publisher
2152 Beachwood Terrace, Hollywood, CA 90068
United States

submissions@harvardsquareeditions.org

https://harvardsquareeditions.org
http://www.youtube.com/watch?v=EevUEEJH3GQ
https://twitter.com/harvardsquareed
https://www.facebook.com/HarvardSquareEditions

Fiction > *Novels*
Dystopian Fiction; Environment; Fantasy; International; Literary; Politics; Science Fiction; Social Commentary; Spirituality; Utopian Fiction

Send: Query; Synopsis; Writing sample
How to send: Online submission system

Looking for literary fiction of social, spiritual and environmental value. Its mission is to publish fiction that transcends national boundaries, especially manuscripts that are international, spiritual, political, literary, sci-fi, fantasy, utopia and dystopia.

P359 Harvard University Press

Book Publisher
79 Garden Street, Cambridge, MA 02138
United States
Tel: +1 (617) 495-2600

contact_hup@harvard.edu

https://www.hup.harvard.edu
https://www.facebook.com/HarvardPress
https://twitter.com/Harvard_Press
https://www.instagram.com/harvardpress/
https://www.linkedin.com/company/harvard-university-press-hup/
https://medium.com/@hup

ACADEMIC > **Nonfiction**
Nonfiction Books: Africa; American History; Anthropology; Archaeology; Architecture; Arts; Astronomy; Biography; Biology; Black People; Business; Classics / Ancient World; Earth Science; Economics; Engineering; Environment; Ethnic Groups; Ethnic; Evolution; Gender; Health; History; Language; Legal; Literary Criticism; Literature; Mathematics; Media; Medicine; Music; Nature; Philosophy; Physics; Politics; Popular Culture; Psychology; Religion; Science; Social Issues; Sociology; Technology; Travel
Reference: General

Publishes humanities, sciences, social sciences, etc. Academic nonfiction only. See website for manuscript guidelines and appropriate editorial contacts.

Publishing Imprint: Belknap Press

P360 Harvill Secker

Publishing Imprint
United Kingdom

Book Publisher: Vintage (**P827**)

P361 Haus Publishing

Book Publisher
4 Cinnamon Row, Plantation Wharf, London, SW11 3TW
United Kingdom
Tel: +44 (0) 20 3637 9729

submissions@hauspublishing.com
haus@hauspublishing.com

https://www.hauspublishing.com
https://www.facebook.com/hauspublishing
https://www.twitter.com/hauspublishing
https://www.instagram.com/hauspublishing/
https://www.youtube.com/channel/UCDSWSrh_wI5t_rflbyI3O7w

Fiction in Translation > *Novels*: Literary

Fiction > *Novels*

Nonfiction > *Nonfiction Books*
Arts; Biography; Current Affairs; History; Memoir; Politics; Travel

Send: Query; Proposal; Synopsis; Writing sample; Author bio
How to send: Email; Through a literary agent

Accepts fiction submissions through literary agents only. Nonfiction submissions may be submitted direct by authors.

Book Publisher: The Armchair Traveller at the bookHaus

Editor: Emma Henderson

Publishing Imprints: Arabia Books; Armchair Traveller; Haus Fiction; HausBooks; Life&Times

P362 Hawthorn Press

Book Publisher
1 Lansdown Lane, Stroud, Gloucestershire, GL5 1BJ
United Kingdom
Tel: +44 (0) 1453 757040

info@hawthornpress.com

http://www.hawthornpress.com

Nonfiction > *Nonfiction Books*
Lifestyle; Self Help

Send: Query; Table of Contents; Author bio; Self-Addressed Stamped Envelope (SASE); Submission Form
How to send: Post

Publisher aiming to contribute to a more creative, peaceful and sustainable world through its publishing. Publishes mainly commissioned work, but will consider approaches. Send first two chapters with introduction, full table of contents/book plan, brief author biography and/or CV. Allow at least 2-4 months for response.

P363 Hawthorne Books

Book Publisher
2201 NE 23rd Avenue Third Floor, Portland, OR 97212
United States
Tel: +1 (503) 327-8849

rhughes@hawthornebooks.com

http://www.hawthornebooks.com
https://www.facebook.com/HawthorneBooks
http://twitter.com//hawthornebooks
http://pinterest.com/hawthornebooks/

Fiction > *Novels*: Literary

Nonfiction > *Nonfiction Books*
Memoir; Narrative Essays

How to send: Through a literary agent

An independent literary press based in Portland, Oregon, with a national scope and deep regional roots. Focuses on literary fiction and nonfiction with innovative and varied approaches to the relationships between essay, memoir, and narrative.

Associate Editor: Adam O'Connor Rodriguez

Authors: Kassten Alonso; Poe Ballantine; Peter Donahue; Monica Drake; D'Arcy Fallon; Peter Fogtdal; Jeff Meyers; Mark Mordue; Scott Nadelson; Toby Olson; Gin Phillips; Lynne Sharon Schwartz; Tom Spanbauer; Michael Strelow; Richard Wiley

P364 HeartSpring Publishing

Publishing Imprint

Book Publisher: College Press Publishing (**P172**)

P365 Helter Skelter Publishing

Book Publisher
United Kingdom

sales@helterskelterpublishing.com

http://www.helterskelterpublishing.com

Nonfiction > *Nonfiction Books*: Music

Publishes books on music.

Editor: Sean Body

Publishing Imprint: Firefly Publishing

P366 Henry Holt Books for Young Readers

Publishing Imprint
United States

press.inquiries@macmillan.com

https://us.macmillan.com/mackids/

Book Publisher: Macmillan Children's Publishing Group (**P470**)

CHILDREN'S > **Fiction**
Chapter Books; *Novels*; *Picture Books*

Publishes quality picture books, chapter books, and novels for preschoolers through young adults.

P367 Heritage House

Book Publisher
103 – 1075 Pendergast Street, Victoria, BC, V8V 0A1
Canada

books@heritagehouse.ca
info@heritagehouse.ca

http://www.heritagehouse.ca
https://www.facebook.com/HeritageHouseBooks/
https://twitter.com/HHPublishing
https://www.instagram.com/heritagehousepublishing/

ADULT > **Nonfiction** > *Nonfiction Books*
Animals; Arts; Biography; British Columbia; Comedy / Humour; Crime; History; Legal; Leisure; Memoir; Military; Nature; Nautical; Outdoor Activities; Photography; Politics; Sport; Travel; Yukon

CHILDREN'S
Fiction
Board Books; *Early Readers*; *Picture Books*
Nonfiction > *Nonfiction Books*
Nature; Science

YOUNG ADULT > **Fiction** > *Novels*

Send: Synopsis; Author bio; Market info; Outline; Writing sample
How to send: Email
How not to send: Post

Committed to amplifying the stories and voices of the extraordinary people who have helped shape the diverse cultural landscape of Western Canada. Also publishes humour, contemporary art and photography, Indigenous studies, politics and contemporary issues, nature guides, and children's books.

P368 Heroic Books

Book Publisher; Editorial Service
United Kingdom

info@heroicbooks.com

http://www.heroicbooks.com
https://www.facebook.com/HeroicBooks/
https://twitter.com/HeroicBooks
https://www.instagram.com/heroicbooks/

ADULT > **Fiction** > *Novels*
Fantasy; Science Fiction

YOUNG ADULT > **Fiction** > *Novels*
Fantasy; Science Fiction

How to send: Online submission system

Costs: Offers services that writers have to pay for.

We are an innovative publisher across the fantasy and science fiction genre. We are committed to finding the most exciting authors and publishing their work to the highest possible quality. Experienced in media and business beyond the traditional, we are committed to breaking new ground for our authors. Working with illustrators, narrators, and other creatives, we aim to make sure every novel reaches its full potential. So, if you are an author, an artist, a narrator, a reader – please join us.

Author: Davis Ashura

Book: A Testament of Steel

Editor: Zoe George

P369 Hertfordshire Publications

Publishing Imprint
United Kingdom

http://www.uhpress.co.uk/subject-areas/hertfordshire-publications

Book Publisher: University of Hertfordshire Press (**P802**)

ACADEMIC > **Nonfiction** > *Nonfiction Books*: Local History

P370 High Stakes Publishing

Publishing Imprint
18 Coleswood Road, Harpenden, Herts., AL5 1EQ
United Kingdom
Tel: +44 (0) 1582 766348

https://highstakespublishing.co.uk

Book Publisher: Oldcastle Books Group (**P544**)

Nonfiction > *Nonfiction Books*: Gambling

Imprint publishing books on gambling.

P371 High Tide Press

Book Publisher
101 Hempstead Place Suite 1A, Joliet, Il 60433
United States
Tel: +1 (779) 702-5540

Submissions@HighTidePress.org
Greetings@HighTidePress.org

https://hightidepress.org
https://www.facebook.com/HighTidePress/
https://twitter.com/hightidepress

Nonfiction > *Nonfiction Books*
Leadership; Management; Mental Disorders; Personal Development; Psychology; Wellbeing

Send: Query; Outline; Market info; Author bio
Don't send: Full text
How to send: In the body of an email; Post
How not to send: Email attachment

Publishes titles on Person-Centered Planning; Behavioral Health; Intellectual and developmental disabilities; Positive Psychology; Nonprofit management; Leadership and management.

P372 Hippocrene Books, Inc.

Book Publisher
171 Madison Avenue, Suite 1400, New York, NY 10016
United States

editorial@hippocrenebooks.com
info@hippocrenebooks.com

https://www.hippocrenebooks.com
https://www.facebook.com/pages/Hippocrene-Books-Inc/129993534671
https://twitter.com/hippocrenebooks
https://pinterest.com/hippocrenebooks

Nonfiction
Nonfiction Books: Cookery; Ethnic
Reference: Language

How to send: Email

Publishes general nonfiction, particularly foreign language reference books and ethnic cookbooks. No fiction. Send submissions by email.

P373 The History Press

Book Publisher
97 St George's Place, Cheltenham, Gloucestershire, GL50 3QB
United Kingdom
Tel: +44 (0) 1242 895310

web@thehistorypress.co.uk

https://www.thehistorypress.co.uk
https://www.facebook.com/thehistorypressuk/
https://twitter.com/TheHistoryPress/
https://www.pinterest.com/thehistorypress/

Nonfiction > *Nonfiction Books*: History

Send: Query; Synopsis; Author bio; Market info; Proposal
Don't send: Full text
How to send: Email

Publishes books on history, from local to international. Welcomes submissions from both new and established authors. Send query by email. No unsolicited mss. See website for full guidelines.

Publishing Imprint: Phillimore (**P601**)

P374 Hodder Children's Books

Publishing Imprint

Book Publisher: Hachette Children's Group (**P318**)

P375 Hogarth

Publishing Imprint

Book Publisher: Random House (**P640**)

P376 Hogarth Press

Publishing Imprint
United Kingdom

Book Publisher: Vintage (**P827**)

P377 Hogs Back Books

Book Publisher
34 Long Street, Devizes, Wiltshire, SN10 1NT
United Kingdom

enquiries@hogsbackbooks.com
submissions@hogsbackbooks.com

http://www.hogsbackbooks.com

CHILDREN'S
Fiction
Early Readers; *Picture Books*
Nonfiction > *Nonfiction Books*

TEEN > **Fiction** > *Novels*

YOUNG ADULT
Fiction > *Novels*
Nonfiction > *Nonfiction Books*

Send: Full text; Synopsis; Writing sample
How to send: Email; Post

Publishes picture books and nonfiction for children up to 10, early readers for children up to 14, teenage fiction and young adult fiction and nonfiction. Send submissions by email or by post to an address in France (see website for details). All responses are by email.

P378 Holtzbrinck Publishing Group

Book Publisher
Germany

Book Publishers: Henry Holt & Company Inc.; The Macmillan Group (**P473**)

P379 Honest Publishing

Book Publisher
United Kingdom

info@honestpublishing.com

https://www.honestpublishing.com
https://www.facebook.com/HonestPublishing
https://twitter.com/HonestPublisher

Fiction
Novels; *Short Fiction*
Poetry > *Poetry Collections*

Closed to approaches.

A British independent book publisher of both fiction and nonfiction. Founded by three friends in 2010, the company strives to publish alternative, original voices, and to provide an audience for unique writers neglected by the mainstream.

Author: Bogdan Tiganov

P380 Hot Key Books

Book Publisher
4th Floor, Victoria House, Bloomsbury Square, London, WC1B 4DA
United Kingdom
Tel: +44 (0) 20 3770 8883

hello@bonnierbooks.co.uk

http://hotkeybooks.com
https://twitter.com/HotKeyBooks
https://instagram.com/hotkeybooks/
https://www.facebook.com/HotKeyBooks

Book Publisher: Bonnier Books (UK) (**P117**)

TEEN > **Fiction** > *Novels*

YOUNG ADULT > **Fiction** > *Novels*

How to send: Through a literary agent

Publishes fiction and nonfiction for teens and young adults. Accepts approaches through literary agents only.

P381 Houghton Mifflin Harcourt Books for Young Readers Division

Book Publisher

Book Publisher: Houghton Mifflin Harcourt

Publishing Imprint: Clarion Books (**P168**)

P382 How to Books Ltd

Publishing Imprint
Carmelite House, 50 Victoria Embankment, London, EC4Y 0DZ
United Kingdom
Tel: +44 (0) 20 3122 7000

howtobooks@littlebrown.co.uk

https://www.howto.co.uk
https://www.facebook.com/lbhowtouk/
http://www.twitter.com/LittleBrownUK/
https://www.instagram.com/howto.uk/

Publishing Imprint: Little, Brown Book Group

Nonfiction > *Nonfiction Books*
Business; Food; How To; Lifestyle; Parenting; Personal Finance; Relationships; Wellbeing

How to send: Through a literary agent

Publishes books that inspire you to make positive changes in your life, whether you're looking to advance your career, improve your relationships, boost your business, revitalise your health or develop your mind.

Editor: Nikki Read

P383 Howard

Publishing Imprint

Book Publisher: Simon & Schuster Adult Publishing (**P711**)

P384 HQ

Publishing Imprint
United Kingdom

Book Publisher: HarperCollins UK (**P347**)

P385 HQ Digital

Publishing Imprint
United Kingdom

Book Publisher: HarperCollins UK (**P347**)

P386 Human Kinetics

Book Publisher
1607 N Market Street, Champaign, Illinois 61825
United States
Tel: +1 (800) 747-4457
Fax: +1 (217) 351-1549

acquisitions@hkusa.com

https://us.humankinetics.com
https://www.facebook.com/HumanKinetics

ACADEMIC > **Nonfiction** > *Nonfiction Books*
Fitness; Health; Nutrition; Sport

ADULT > **Nonfiction** > *Nonfiction Books*
Fitness; Health; Nutrition; Sport

PROFESSIONAL > **Nonfiction** > *Nonfiction Books*
Fitness; Health; Nutrition; Sport

Send: Query; Table of Contents
How to send: Post; Email

Publishes books on health, fitness, and sport, aimed at the academic market, professionals in the field, and the general public. Send query by post or email.

P387 Hunt End Books

Publishing Imprint
United Kingdom

Book Publisher: Brewin Books Ltd (**P124**)

P388 Idyll Arbor

Book Publisher
2432 39th Street, Bedford, IN 47421
United States
Tel: +1 (812) 675-6623

sales@idyllarbor.com

https://www.idyllarbor.com

ADULT > **Nonfiction** > *Nonfiction Books*: Health

PROFESSIONAL > **Nonfiction** > *Nonfiction Books*
Health; Medicine

Send: Query; Author bio; Outline; Writing sample

Publishes books that provide practical information on the current state and art of health care practice. Currently emphasizes books for recreational therapists, for activity directors working with the elderly, and for social services professionals. The books must be useful for the health practitioner who meets face to face with patients or for instructors of undergraduate and graduate level classes.

Another line of books is aimed at health care consumers. These books are intended to provide information about a single health topic (e.g., sickle cell anemia). The level of information should include enough information for a patient to be on an equal footing with a primary care physician.

P389 Ig Publishing

Book Publisher
PO Box 2547, New York, NY 10163
United States
Tel: +1 (718) 797-0676

robert@igpub.com

http://igpub.com
https://twitter.com/Igpublishing
https://www.facebook.com/pages/Ig-Publishing/176428769078839
https://www.pinterest.com/igpublishing/
https://www.instagram.com/igpublishing/

Fiction > *Novels*: Literary

Nonfiction > *Nonfiction Books*
Culture; Politics

Send: Query
How to send: Email

A New York-based award-winning independent press dedicated to publishing original literary fiction and political and cultural nonfiction. Send query by email only.

Editor-in-Chief: Robert Lasner

P390 Image Books

Publishing Imprint

Book Publisher: Random House (**P640**)

P391 Imagine Publishing

Publishing Imprint
United States

adult.submissions@charlesbridge.com

https://www.imaginebooks.net
https://twitter.com/Imagine_CB
https://www.facebook.com/ImaginePress/
https://www.pinterest.com/charlesbridge/adult-books-from-imagine-publishing/
https://www.instagram.com/imagine_cb/

Book Publisher: Charlesbridge Publishing (**P155**)

Nonfiction
Coffee Table Books: General
Nonfiction Books: Arts; Comedy / Humour; Cookery; History; Nature; Politics; Women's Studies
Puzzle Books: General

Send: Full text; Writing sample
How to send: Email

Publishes 8-10 titles a year, primarily focused on history, politics, women's studies, and nature.

P392 Imagine That Publishing

Book Publisher
Marine House, Tide Mill Way, Woodbridge, Suffolk, IP12 1AP
United Kingdom
Tel: +44 (0) 1394 386651

customerservice@topthatpublishing.com

https://www.imaginethat.com
https://www.facebook.com/ImagineThatPublishing/
https://twitter.com/imaginethatbook
https://www.instagram.com/imaginethatbook/

CHILDREN'S
Fiction > *Novels*
Nonfiction > *Nonfiction Books*

Closed to approaches.

Publishes Activity Books, Board Books, Fiction, Magnetic Books, Novelty Books, Picture Storybooks, Press Out & Play, and Sticker Books. Does not currently publish "regular" children's or adults fiction. See online book catalogue for the kinds of books published. If suitable for the list, send submissions by email (preferred), ideally under 1MB, or by post (mss not returned). See website for full guidelines. Responds within 8 weeks if interested. No simultaneous submissions.

Editors: Dan Graham; Josh Simpkin-Betts

P393 Immanion Press

Book Publisher
United Kingdom

editorial@immanion-press.com

https://www.immanion-press.com/

Types: Fiction; Nonfiction
Subjects: Comedy / Humour; Fantasy; Horror; Literary; Science Fiction; Spirituality
Markets: Adult

Send: Query
Don't send: Full text

Closed to fiction submissions as at April 2020. Publishes innovative and intelligent dark fantasy, literary fantasy, science fiction, horror, slipstream, magic realism, and black comedies. Also publishes nonfiction on magic, qabala, Tarot and associated thematic subjects. No derivative or "twee" high fantasy, overly technical, non-character driven science fiction, or visceral gore horror. Send synopsis with first 30 pages and author bio by post or by email as Word, PDF, or plain text attachment. Full submission details on website.

P394 Impact

Publishing Imprint
United States

http://www.impact-books.com

Book Publisher: Penguin Publishing Group (**P585**)

Types: Nonfiction
Formats: Reference
Subjects: Arts; How To
Markets: Adult

Publishes books to assist artists drawing comics, superheroes, Japanese-style manga, fantasy, creatures, action, caricature, anime, etc.

Acquisitions Editor: Pamela Wissman

P395 Indiana University Press

Book Publisher
IU Office of Scholarly Publishing, Herman B Wells Library E350, 1320 E 10th Street E4, Bloomington, IN 47405-3907
United States
Tel: +1 (812) 855-8817

iuporder@indiana.edu

https://iupress.org
https://www.facebook.com/iupress
https://twitter.com/iupress
https://www.instagram.com/iu.press/

https://www.youtube.com/c/IndianaUniversityPress/videos

ACADEMIC > **Nonfiction** > *Nonfiction Books*
Africa; American Civil War; American Midwest; Eastern Europe; Films; Folklore, Myths, and Legends; Gender; International; Ireland; Jewish Holocaust; Judaism; Media; Middle East; Military History; Music; Paleontology; Performing Arts; Philosophy; Railways; Refugees; Regional; Religion; Russia; Sexuality; Transport

Send: Proposal; Outline; Table of Contents; Writing sample; Author bio
How to send: Online submission system

Submit proposals via online proposal submission form.

P396 Indigo Dreams Publishing

Book Publisher
24 Forest Houses, Halwill, Beaworthy, Devon, EX21 5UU
United Kingdom

publishing@indigodreams.co.uk

https://www.indigodreams.co.uk
https://twitter.com/IndigoDreamsPub

Poetry > *Poetry Collections*

Closed to approaches.

Publishes poetry collections up to 60/70 pages and poetry pamphlets up to 36 pages. See website for submission guidelines.

Authors: Roselle Angwin; Frances Galleymore; Paula Rae Gibson; Seema Gill; Charlie Hill; James Lawless; Robert Leach; Dennis Loccoriere; Angela Locke; Char March; Ann Pilling; Cyril Tawney

Editor: Ronnie Goodyer

Magazines: The Dawntreader (**M162**); Reach (**M414**); Sarasvati (**M430**)

P397 Influx Press

Book Publisher
United Kingdom

https://www.influxpress.com
http://instagram.com/influxpress
http://twitter.com/influxpress

Fiction > *Novels*: Gender

Nonfiction > *Nonfiction Books*: Creative Nonfiction

How to send: Through a literary agent

Publishes innovative and challenging fiction, poetry and creative non-fiction from across the UK and beyond.

P398 The Innovation Press

Book Publisher
United States

submissions@theinnovationpress.com
info@theinnovationpress.com

https://www.theinnovationpress.com
http://www.facebook.com/theinnovationpress
https://twitter.com/InnovationPress
http://instagram.com/theinnovationpress

CHILDREN'S
Fiction
Chapter Books; *Graphic Novels*; *Middle Grade*; *Picture Books*
Nonfiction
Activity Books; *Chapter Books*; *Middle Grade*; *Picture Books*

Send: Synopsis; Writing sample; Author bio
How to send: Email

Publishes memorable children's books that inspire learning, enliven creative thinking, and spark imaginations. From innovative activity books to clever fiction.

P399 Integrity Media

Book Publisher
85 Great Portland Street, First Floor, London, W1W 7LT
United Kingdom
Tel: +44 (0) 20 3745 0658

enquiries@integrity-media.co.uk

http://www.integrity-media.co.uk

A publishing company with a unique objective. We aim to provide a platform and portal for those suffering poor mental health, to find release, acceptance and growth through literature. Whether they wish to write an autobiographical work or simple write creatively.

While the above is our primary motivation, we accept submissions from all authors who fit within our areas of interest.

Online Magazine: Authentic Shorts (**M050**)

Publishing Imprints: Authentic Ideas (**P062**); Authentic Life (**P063**)

P400 International Publishers

Book Publisher
235 W 23rd Street, New York, NY 10011-2302
United States
Tel: +1 (212) 366-9816
Fax: +1 (212) 366-9820

service@intpubnyc.com

https://www.intpubnyc.com

Nonfiction > *Nonfiction Books*
Culture; Gender Issues; History; Marxism; Philosophy; Politics; Social Issues

Marxist publishers of books on labour rights, race and gender issues, Marxist science, etc.

P401 International Society for Technology in Education (ISTE)

Book Publisher
2111 Wilson Boulevard, Suite 300, Arlington, VA 22201, 621 SW Morrison Street, Suite 800, Portland, OR 97205
United States
Tel: +1 (503) 342-2848
Fax: +1 (541) 302-3778

iste@iste.org

https://www.iste.org
https://www.iste.org/professional-development/books
https://twitter.com/iste
https://www.instagram.com/isteconnects/
https://www.facebook.com/ISTEconnects
https://www.iste.org/youtube

ACADEMIC > **Nonfiction** > *Nonfiction Books*
Computer Programming; Digital Technology

PROFESSIONAL > **Nonfiction** > *Nonfiction Books*
Computer Programming; Digital Technology; Education

Publishes books and resources focused on technology in education.

Editor: Scott Harter

P402 InterVarsity Press (IVP)

Book Publisher
36 Causton Street, London, SW1P 4ST
United Kingdom
Tel: +44 (0) 20 7592 3900

submissions@ivpbooks.com

https://ivpbooks.com
https://www.facebook.com/ivpbooks
https://www.instagram.com/ivpbooks/
https://twitter.com/IVPbookcentre

ACADEMIC > **Nonfiction** > *Nonfiction Books*: Religion

ADULT > **Nonfiction** > *Nonfiction Books*
Biography; Christian Living; Church History; Contemporary Culture; Religion

Send: Query
How to send: Online contact form

Aims to produce quality, Evangelical books for the digital age. Send query through form on website.

P403 Interweave

Publishing Imprint
United States

Book Publisher: Penguin Publishing Group (**P585**)

Types: Nonfiction
Subjects: Crafts; Hobbies
Markets: Adult

Editor: Kerry Bogert

P404 Iqon Editions

Publishing Imprint

Book Publisher: The Quarto Group, Inc. **(P633)**

P405 Iron Press

Book Publisher
5 Marden Terrace, Cullercoats, North Shields, Northumberland, NE30 4PD
United Kingdom
Tel: +44 (0) 191 253 1901

peter@ironpress.co.uk

https://www.ironpress.co.uk

Fiction
Short Fiction Collections; *Short Fiction*
Poetry
Any Poetic Form; *Poetry Collections*

Closed to approaches.

Poetry and fiction publisher championing quality new writing since 1973. Publishes poetry, (including haiku), collections of short stories, and anthologies of verse and prose. No novels or unsolicited mss. Send query by email in first instance.

Editor: Peter Mortimer

P406 Ivy Kids

Publishing Imprint

Book Publisher: The Quarto Group, Inc. **(P633)**

P407 Ivy Press

Publishing Imprint

Book Publisher: The Quarto Group, Inc. **(P633)**

P408 Jacaranda Books Art Music Ltd

Book Publisher
27 Old Gloucester Street, London, WC1N 3AX
United Kingdom

office@jacarandabooksartmusic.co.uk

https://www.jacarandabooksartmusic.co.uk

Types: Fiction
Subjects: Arts; Autobiography; Beauty; Commercial; Crime; Fashion; History; Literary; Music; Photography; Science Fiction; Women's Interests
Markets: Adult

Closed to approaches.

Publishes adult fiction and nonfiction, including crime, romance, illustrated books, biography, memoir, and autobiography. Particularly interested in books where the central character or theme relates to minority groups and/or has strong female protagonists. Also interested in original works from or about African, African-American, Caribbean and black British artists working in the fields of photography, fine art, fashion, and contemporary and modern art, and artists of calibre from the soul, blues, R&B and reggae traditions. Send query with writer CV, detailed synopsis, and 20-30 pages of consecutive text. See website for full submission guidelines.

Publisher: Valerie Brandes

P409 Jessica Kingsley Publishers

Book Publisher
Carmelite House, 50 Victoria Embankment, London, EC4Y 0DZ
United Kingdom
Tel: +44 (0) 20 3122 6000

hello@jkp.com

https://www.jkp.com
https://jkp.submittable.com/submit
https://www.facebook.com/jessicakingsleypublishers
https://twitter.com/JKPBooks
http://www.pinterest.com/jkpbooks
http://instagram.com/JKPbooks

Book Publisher: John Murray (Publishers) Ltd

ACADEMIC > **Nonfiction** > *Nonfiction Books*
Autism; Culture; Gender Issues; Health; Mental Health; Parenting; Religion; Social Issues

PROFESSIONAL > **Nonfiction** > *Nonfiction Books*
Autism; Culture; Gender Issues; Health; Mental Health; Parenting; Religion; Social Issues

Send: Proposal
How to send: Submittable

Publishes books on autism, social work and arts therapies.

Editor: Jessica Kingsley

P410 Jeter Publishing

Publishing Imprint

Book Publisher: Simon & Schuster Adult Publishing **(P711)**

P411 Jo Fletcher Books

Publishing Imprint
United Kingdom

info@jofletcherbooks.co.uk
submissions@jofletcherbooks.co.uk

https://www.jofletcherbooks.com
https://www.facebook.com/jofletcherbooks
https://twitter.com/JoFletcherBooks
https://www.youtube.com/channel/UCU2vJMMmmWwI-B5cHwKKSFQ

Book Publisher: Quercus Books

Fiction > *Novels*
Fantasy; Horror; Science Fiction

Send: Query; Synopsis; Writing sample
How to send: Word file email attachment

Specialist science fiction, fantasy and horror imprint. Send query by email with synopsis and first three chapters or first 10,000 words.

Editor: Nicola Budd

P412 Joffe Books

Book Publisher
United Kingdom

submissions@joffebooks.com

https://www.joffebooks.com
https://www.facebook.com/joffebooks
https://twitter.com/joffebooks
https://www.instagram.com/joffebooks

Fiction > *Novels*
Cozy Mysteries; Crime; Domestic Noir; Historical Fiction; Mystery; Police Procedural; Psychological Thrillers; Romance; Saga; Suspense; Women's Fiction; World War II

Send: Full text; Synopsis; Author bio
How to send: Email

Publishes crime fiction, mysteries, psychological thrillers, cosy crime, police procedurals, chillers, suspense and domestic noir. Will also consider women's fiction, historical fiction and romance novels, including WWII romances and sagas. Send query by email with complete ms as an attachment, a synopsis in the body of the email, and 100 words about yourself. Include "submission" in the subject line. Reply not guaranteed unless interested. See website for full guidelines.

Editor: Jasper Joffe

P413 The Johns Hopkins University Press

Book Publisher
2715 North Charles Street, Baltimore, Maryland 21218-4363
United States
Tel: +1 (410) 516-6900

https://www.press.jhu.edu
https://twitter.com/JHUPress
https://www.facebook.com/JohnsHopkinsUniversityPress
https://www.youtube.com/user/JHUPJournals
https://www.pinterest.com/jhupress/

ACADEMIC > **Nonfiction** > *Nonfiction Books*
Architecture; Arts; Business; Classics / Ancient World; Economics; Education; Health; History; Language; Legal; Literature; Mathematics; Medicine; Music; Politics; Recreation; Religion; Science; Sociology; Sport

Publishes titles in history, science, higher education, health and wellness, humanities, classics, and public health. Provides authors with a reputable forum for evidence-based discourse and exposure to a worldwide audience.

Editor-in-Chief: Trevor Lipscombe

P414 Jolly Learning

Book Publisher
Tailours House, High Road, Chigwell, Essex, IG7 6DL
United Kingdom
Tel: +44 (0) 20 8501 0405
Fax: +44 (0) 20 8500 1696

info@jollylearning.co.uk

https://www.jollylearning.co.uk
https://www.facebook.com/Jolly-Learning-195770143786043/
http://www.twitter.com/jollylearning
https://www.youtube.com/user/jollylearning/videos

CHILDREN'S
Fiction > *Early Readers*
Nonfiction > *Early Readers*

PROFESSIONAL > **Nonfiction** > *Nonfiction Books*: Education

Publishes books for children to help with reading, using the synthetic phonics method of teaching the letter sounds in a way that aims to be fun and multi-sensory.

P415 Jonathan Cape

Publishing Imprint
United Kingdom

https://www.penguin.co.uk/company/publishers/vintage/jonathan-cape.html

Book Publisher: Vintage (**P827**)

Types: Fiction; Nonfiction; Poetry
Markets: Adult

Send: Query
Don't send: Full text

Renowned for its prizewinning fiction, nonfiction, poetry and graphic novels.

P416 JournalStone Publishing

Book Publisher
United States

journalstone.submissions@gmail.com

https://journalstone.com

Fiction > *Novels*
Gothic; Horror; Psychological Horror

Publishes horror in all its forms – from literary to weird, Gothic to psychological, and (almost) everything in between.

P417 Kamera Books

Publishing Imprint
United Kingdom

Book Publisher: Oldcastle Books Group (**P544**)

P418 Karnak House

Book Publisher
United Kingdom

karnakhouse@aol.com

https://www.karnakhouse.co.uk

Types: Fiction; Nonfiction; Poetry
Subjects: Anthropology; Culture; History; Literary Criticism; Music; Philosophy; Politics; Religion; Science; Women's Interests
Markets: Adult; Children's

Publisher of books on the culture and history of African civilisations and cultures worldwide.

P419 The Kates Hill Press

Book Publisher
39 Cowley Drive, Dudley, West Midlands, DY1 2SS
United Kingdom
Tel: +44 (0) 1384 254719

kateshillpress1992@gmail.com

https://kateshillpress.com

Types: Fiction; Nonfiction; Poetry
Formats: Short Fiction
Subjects: Autobiography; Comedy / Humour; Crime; History; Sociology; Sport
Markets: Adult

Small independent publisher producing short runs of fiction and social history books with a west midlands theme or by a west midlands writer. Also publishes booklets of poetry and dialect verse by Black Country/West Midlands poets.

P420 Katherine Tegen Books

Publishing Imprint

Book Publisher: HarperCollins

P421 Kathy Dawson Books

Publishing Imprint
Penguin Group, 375 Hudson Street, New York, NY 10014
United States

http://kathydawsonbooks.tumblr.com

Book Publishers: Penguin Group (USA); Penguin Young Readers Group (**P591**)

Types: Fiction
Markets: Children's; Young Adult

Send: Query
Don't send: Full text

Publishes middle grade and young adult fiction. Submit query by post only, with first 10 pages and details of any relevant publishing history. Do not include SASE – all submissions are recycled. Response only if interested.

P422 Kelpies

Publishing Imprint
United Kingdom

floris@florisbooks.co.uk

https://discoverkelpies.co.uk
https://www.facebook.com/DiscoverKelpies/
https://twitter.com/DiscoverKelpies

Book Publisher: Floris Books (**P271**)

CHILDREN'S
Fiction
Novels: Adventure; Comedy / Humour; Fantasy; Ghost Stories; Magic; Romance; Science Fiction; Scotland; Thrillers; Traditional
Picture Books: General, and in particular: Scotland
Nonfiction
Nonfiction Books: Education; History; Scotland; Sport
Picture Books: General, and in particular: Animals; Scotland

Publishes Scottish books for children everywhere. Does not accept unsolicited submissions direct from authors, unless they are from under-represented communities. Welcomes submissions from literary agents.

P423 Kenilworth Press

Publishing Imprint
Quiller Publishing, Wykey House, Wykey, Shrewsbury, Shropshire, SY4 1JA
United Kingdom
Tel: +44 (0) 1939 261616

info@quillerbooks.com

https://www.quillerpublishing.com/product-category/equestrian-kenilworth-press

Book Publisher: Quiller Publishing Ltd (**P636**)

Nonfiction > *Nonfiction Books*
Equestrian; Horses

Send: Synopsis; Writing sample; Market info; Author bio; Self-Addressed Stamped Envelope (SASE)
How to send: Email; Post

Equestrian publisher publishing nonfiction. Not accepting poetry or novels.

Editor: John Beaton

P424 Klutz

Publishing Imprint

Book Publisher: Scholastic (**P688**)

P425 Kluwer Law International

Book Publisher
25 Canada Square, Canary Wharf, London, E14 5LQ
United Kingdom

https://kluwerlawonline.com

Book Publisher: Wolters Kluwer (**P871**)

PROFESSIONAL > **Nonfiction** > *Nonfiction Books*: Legal

Send: Query
Don't send: Full text

Publisher of international law titles, including looseleafs and journals. Welcomes unsolicited synopses and ideas on relevant topics.

P426 Knopf Doubleday Publishing Group

Book Publisher
United States

http://knopfdoubleday.com

Book Publisher: Penguin Random House

Fiction > *Novels*

Nonfiction > *Nonfiction Books*

Publishing Imprints: Alfred A. Knopf (*P028*); Anchor Books (*P038*); Black Lizard (*P101*); Doubleday (*P218*); Everyman's Library (*P249*); Nan A. Talese (**P517**); Pantheon (*P565*); Schocken Books (*P687*); Vintage Books (*P828*)

P427 Kokila

Publishing Imprint
United States

Book Publisher: Penguin Young Readers Group (**P591**)

P428 Kore Press

Book Publisher
PO Box 42315, Tucson, AZ 85733
United States

https://korepress.org

Types: Fiction; Nonfiction; Poetry
Subjects: Autobiography; Culture; Literary; Literary Criticism
Markets: Adult

Closed to approaches.

Publishes fiction, poetry, nonfiction, hybrid, and cultural criticism. Accepts submissions both through open submission windows and competitions.

Managing Editor: Ann Dernier

P429 Krause Publications

Publishing Imprint
United States

Book Publisher: Penguin Publishing Group (**P585**)

Types: Nonfiction
Formats: Reference
Subjects: Antiques; Hobbies; How To; Sport
Markets: Adult

Largest publisher of material on hobbies and collectibles in the world. Send query with outline, sample chapter, and description of how your book will make a unique contribution.

P430 Kube Publishing

Book Publisher
MCC, Ratby Lane, Markfield, Leicestershire, LE67 9SY
United Kingdom
Tel: +44 (0) 1530 249230

info@kubepublishing.com

https://www.kubepublishing.com
https://kubepublishing.submittable.com/submit
https://www.facebook.com/kubepublishing
https://twitter.com/Kube_Publishing
http://pinterest.com/kubepub/
https://www.instagram.com/kubepublishing/
http://www.youtube.com/user/KubeVideos/feed
https://www.tiktok.com/@kubepublishing?lang=en

ACADEMIC > **Nonfiction** > *Nonfiction Books*: Islam

ADULT > **Nonfiction** > *Nonfiction Books*
Biography; Creativity; Culture; Current Affairs; History; Islam; Memoir; Politics; Spirituality

CHILDREN'S
Fiction
Board Books: Islam
Chapter Books: Islam
Early Readers: Islam
Middle Grade: Islam
Picture Books: Islam

Nonfiction
Activity Books: Islam
Nonfiction Books: Islam
Picture Books: Islam

Poetry > *Any Poetic Form*: Islam

Send: Query
How to send: Submittable

Independent publisher of general interest, academic, and children's books on Islam and the Muslim experience. Publishes nonfiction for children, young people, and adults, but fiction and poetry for children. See website for full guidelines.

P431 Langmarc Publishing

Book Publisher
PO Box 90488, Austin, Texas 78709-0488
United States
Tel: +1 (512) 394-0989

langmarc@booksails.com

https://www.langmarc.com

Fiction > *Novels*

Nonfiction > *Nonfiction Books*

Closed to approaches.

Started primarily as a publishing house for church resources and inspirational/motivational books. Now publishes novels and nonfiction.

Publishing Imprints: Harbor Lights Series; North Sea Press

P432 Lantana Publishing

Book Publisher
Clavier House, 21 Fifth Road, Newbury, RG14 6DN
United Kingdom

submissions@lantanapublishing.com

https://www.lantanapublishing.com
https://www.instagram.com/lantana_publishing/
https://www.facebook.com/lantanapublishing
https://twitter.com/lantanapub
https://www.youtube.com/channel/UC_edBCMh3Y2wDID2X9qMSkA

CHILDREN'S
Fiction
Chapter Books; *Early Readers*; *Graphic Novels*; *Middle Grade*; *Picture Books*
Poetry > *Any Poetic Form*

Send: Full text
How to send: Email

We are looking for manuscripts and book dummies by authors and illustrators from under-represented groups. We particularly love stories that make us laugh, cry or move us in some way.

P433 Laurence King Publishing Ltd

Book Publisher
Carmelite House, 50 Victoria Embankment, London, EC4Y 0DZ
United Kingdom
Tel: +44 (0)20 3122 6444

commissioning@laurenceking.com

https://www.laurenceking.com
https://twitter.com/LaurenceKingPub
https://www.instagram.com/LaurenceKingPub/
https://www.facebook.com/LaurenceKingPublishing
https://www.pinterest.co.uk/LaurenceKingPub/
https://vimeo.com/laurencekingpublishing
https://www.youtube.com/user/laurencekingpub

Book Publisher: Hachette UK (**P321**)

ACADEMIC > **Nonfiction** > *Nonfiction Books*
Architecture; Arts; Beauty; Design; Fashion; Films; Music; Nature; Photography; Popular Culture; Popular Science

ADULT > **Nonfiction** > *Nonfiction Books*
Architecture; Arts; Beauty; Design; Fashion; Films; Music; Nature; Photography; Popular Culture; Popular Science

CHILDREN'S > **Nonfiction** > *Illustrated Books*

Send: Query; Synopsis; Market info; Author bio
How to send: Email

Publisher of books on the creative arts. Send proposal by email.

P434 Leapfrog Press

Book Publisher
PO Box 1293, Dunkirk, NY 14048
United States

leapfrog@leapfrogpress.com

https://leapfrogpress.com
https://www.facebook.com/Leapfrogpress
https://twitter.com/leapfrogpress1
https://instagram.com/leapfrogpress

ADULT
Fiction > *Novels*
Nonfiction > *Nonfiction Books*
Poetry > *Poetry Collections*

CHILDREN'S > **Fiction** > *Middle Grade*

YOUNG ADULT > **Fiction** > *Novels*

Publisher with an eclectic list of fiction, poetry, and nonfiction, including paperback originals of adult, young adult and middle-grade fiction, and nonfiction.

P435 Leaping Hare Press

Publishing Imprint

Book Publisher: The Quarto Group, Inc. (**P633**)

P436 Leo Cooper

Publishing Imprint

Book Publisher: Pen & Sword Books Ltd (**P578**)

P437 Lerner Digital

Publishing Imprint

Book Publisher: Lerner Publishing Group (**P438**)

P438 Lerner Publishing Group

Book Publisher
241 First Avenue North, Minneapolis, MN 55401-1607
United States
Tel: +1 (800) 328-4929
Fax: +1 (800) 332-1132

custserve@lernerbooks.com

https://lernerbooks.com
https://www.facebook.com/lernerbooks
https://twitter.com/lernerbooks

CHILDREN'S
Fiction
Audiobooks; *Ebooks*; *Graphic Novels*; *Middle Grade*; *Novels*; *Picture Books*
Nonfiction
Audiobooks; *Ebooks*; *Nonfiction Books*
YOUNG ADULT
Fiction
Audiobooks; *Ebooks*; *Novels*
Nonfiction
Audiobooks; *Ebooks*; *Nonfiction Books*

How to send: Through a literary agent; By referral

Publishes fiction and nonfiction for children and young adults. No submissions or queries from unagented or unreferred authors.

: Zelda Wagner

Publishing Imprints: Carolrhoda Books; Carolrhoda Lab (*P145*); Darby Creek (**P199**); Ediciones Lerner (*P230*); First Avenue Editions; Graphic Universe (*P305*); Kar-Ben Publishing; Lerner Digital (*P437*); Lerner Publications; LernerClassroom (*P439*); Millbrook Press (*P497*); Twenty-First Century Books (*P785*); Zest Books (*P883*)

P439 LernerClassroom

Publishing Imprint

Book Publisher: Lerner Publishing Group (**P438**)

P440 Libraries Unlimited

Publishing Imprint
United States

Book Publisher: ABC-CLIO (**P014**)

P441 Lighthouse Trails Publishing

Book Publisher
PO Box 307, Roseburg, OR 97470
United States
Tel: +1 (541) 391-7699

editors@lighthousetrails.com
david@lighthousetrails.com

https://www.lighthousetrails.com
https://www.facebook.com/LighthouseTrailsResearch
http://www.twitter.com/LTrails
http://www.youtube.com/joiful77

ADULT
Fiction > *Novels*: Christianity

Nonfiction > *Nonfiction Books*: Christianity

CHILDREN'S > **Nonfiction**
Activity Books: Christianity
Nonfiction Books: Christianity
Picture Books: Christianity
Puzzle Books: Christianity

Publishes Christian books that promote Jesus Christ.

Acquisitions Editor: David Dombrowski

P442 Lillenas Music

Book Publisher
PO Box 419527, Kansas City, MO 64141-6527
United States
Tel: +1 (800) 363-2122
Fax: +1 (800) 849-9827

customercare@lillenas.com

https://lillenas.com

ADULT > **Nonfiction** > *Nonfiction Books*
Choral Music; Church Music; Hymnals

CHILDREN'S > **Nonfiction** > *Nonfiction Books*
Choral Music; Church Music; Hymnals

YOUNG ADULT > **Nonfiction** > *Nonfiction Books*
Choral Music; Church Music; Hymnals

Closed to approaches.

Publishes religious music books.

P443 The Lilliput Press

Book Publisher
62-63 Sitric Road, Arbour Hill, Dublin 7
Ireland

editorial@lilliputpress.ie
contact@lilliputpress.ie

https://www.lilliputpress.ie

Fiction > *Novels*: Ireland

Nonfiction
Nonfiction Books: Architecture; Arts; Biography; Cultural Criticism; Environment; Food; Genealogy; History; Ireland; Literary Criticism; Literature; Local History; Memoir; Mind, Body, Spirit; Music; Nature; Philosophy; Photography; Travel
Reference: Ireland

Poetry > *Any Poetic Form*: Ireland

Send: Query; Synopsis; Writing sample
How to send: Email
How not to send: Post

Publishes books broadly focused on Irish themes. Send query by email with one-page synopsis and three sample chapters. See website for full guidelines.

P444 Limitless Publishing

Book Publisher
United States

submissions@limitlesspublishing.com

http://www.limitlesspublishing.net
https://www.facebook.com/LimitlessPublishing
http://instagram.com/limitlessbooks/
https://twitter.com/limitlessbooks

Fiction > *Novels*
Dystopian Fiction; Fantasy; Romance; Science Fiction; Supernatural / Paranormal; Suspense; Thrillers

Nonfiction > *Nonfiction Books*
Mind, Body, Spirit; Psychic Abilities; Spirituality

Send: Query; Writing sample; Author bio; Outline
How to send: Word file email attachment

Send submissions by email with brief bio, writing background and publishing history, social networks used, description of your book, and the first four chapters as a Microsoft Word attachment.

P445 Lincoln First Editions

Publishing Imprint

Book Publisher: The Quarto Group, Inc. (**P633**)

P446 Lion Hudson

Book Publisher
John Eccles House, Science Park, Robert Robinson Ave, Littlemore, Oxford, OX4 4GP
United Kingdom
Tel: +44 (0) 1865 302750

https://www.lionhudson.com
https://www.facebook.com/LionFamilyLife/
https://twitter.com/lionhudson
https://www.instagram.com/lionhudson/
https://www.youtube.com/channel/UCvPbjM3qMkihe8ujlC8Eliw

Book Publisher: Society for Promoting Christian Knowledge (SPCK) (**P721**)

ADULT
Fiction > *Novels*: Christianity

Nonfiction
Colouring Books: Christianity
Nonfiction Books: Arts; Autobiography; Bible Studies; Biography; Christian Living; Christianity; Evangelism; Health; History; Memoir; Science; Wellbeing

CHILDREN'S
Fiction
Board Books: Christianity
Novels: Christianity
Picture Books: Christianity

Nonfiction
Activity Books: Christianity
Board Books: Christianity
Nonfiction Books: Christianity
Picture Books: Christianity

How to send: Online submission system
How not to send: Post

Publishes books that reflect Christian values or are inspired by a Christian world view, including fiction and nonfiction for adults and children.

Publishing Imprints: Candle; Lion Adult; Lion Children's Books; Monarch Books (**P504**)

P447 Liquid Light Press

Book Publisher
United States

editor@liquidlightpress.com

http://www.liquidlightpress.com

Types: Poetry
Subjects: Literary
Markets: Adult

Publishes poetry chapbooks. Send submissions by email. $25 reading fee per submission.

Editor: Markiah Friedman

P448 Little Bigfoot

Publishing Imprint
United States

Book Publisher: Sasquatch Books (**P683**)

CHILDREN'S
Fiction > *Picture Books*
General, and in particular: American West; Nature; Pacific Northwest

Nonfiction > *Nonfiction Books*
General, and in particular: American West; Nature; Pacific Northwest

P449 Little Wing

Publishing Imprint
United Kingdom

https://mangobooks.co.uk/pages/about-mango-books

Book Publisher: Mango Books (**P478**)

Nonfiction > *Nonfiction Books*: Entertainment

Publishes titles in the entertainment genre.

P450 Little, Brown Books for Young Readers

Publishing Imprint

Book Publisher: Hachette Children's Group (**P318**)

P451 Llewellyn Worldwide Ltd

Book Publisher
Acquisitions Department, 2143 Wooddale Drive, Woodbury, MN 55125
United States
Tel: +1 (612) 291-1970
Fax: +1 (612) 291-1908

submissions@llewellyn.com

http://www.llewellyn.com

Nonfiction > *Nonfiction Books*
Alternative Health; Angels; Astral Projection; Astrology; Chakras; Cryptozoology; Ghost Hunting; Kabbalah; Meditation; Mind, Body, Spirit; Paganism; Psychic Abilities; Reiki; Reincarnation; Shamanism; Spirit Guides; Spirituality; Tarot; UFOs; Wicca; Witchcraft; Yoga

Send: Query; Proposal; Full text; Outline; Table of Contents; Market info; Author bio
How to send: Word file email attachment; Post

As the world's oldest and largest independent publisher of books for body, mind, and spirit, we are dedicated to bringing our readers the very best in metaphysical books and resources. Since 1901, we've been at the forefront of holistic and metaphysical publishing and thought. We've been a source of illumination, instruction, and new perspectives on a wealth of topics, including astrology, tarot, wellness, earth-based spirituality, magic, and the paranormal.

P452 LMBPN Publishing

Book Publisher
United States

https://lmbpn.com
https://www.facebook.com/LMBPNPublishing/
https://twitter.com/lmbpn
https://www.instagram.com/lmbpn_publishing

Fiction > *Novels*
Fantasy; Mystery; Science Fiction; Thrillers; Urban Fantasy

P453 Lonely Planet

Book Publisher
Australia

https://www.lonelyplanet.com
https://www.facebook.com/lonelyplanet
https://twitter.com/lonelyplanet
https://www.pinterest.com.au/lonelyplanet/

Nonfiction > *Nonfiction Books*: Travel

Book Publishers: Lonely Planet China (**P454**); Lonely Planet India (**P455**); Lonely Planet UK (**P456**); Lonely Planet USA (**P457**)

P454 Lonely Planet China

Book Publisher
OB5A, Office Tower B, East Gate Plaza, No. 29 Dongzhong Street, Dongcheng District, Beijing 100027
China

https://www.lonelyplanet.com

Book Publisher: Lonely Planet (**P453**)

Nonfiction > *Nonfiction Books*: Travel

P455 Lonely Planet India

Book Publisher
302 DLF City Court, Sikanderpur|Gurgaon 122002
India

https://www.lonelyplanet.com

Book Publisher: Lonely Planet (**P453**)

Nonfiction > *Nonfiction Books*: Travel

Publishes travel guides.

P456 Lonely Planet UK

Book Publisher
United Kingdom

Book Publisher: Lonely Planet (**P453**)

Nonfiction > *Nonfiction Books*: Travel

P457 Lonely Planet USA

Book Publisher
1101 Red Ventures Drive, Fort Mill, SC 29707
United States

https://www.lonelyplanet.com

Book Publisher: Lonely Planet (**P453**)

Nonfiction > *Nonfiction Books*: Travel

P458 Lorena Jones Books

Publishing Imprint

Book Publisher: Random House (**P640**)

P459 Lost Lake Folk Art

Publishing Imprint

Book Publisher: Shipwreckt Books Publishing Company (**P705**)

P460 Louisiana State University Press

Book Publisher
338 Johnston Hall, Louisiana State University, Baton Rouge, LA 7080
United States

https://lsupress.org
https://blog.lsupress.org/
https://www.facebook.com/pages/LSU-Press/38236386996
https://twitter.com/lsupress
https://soundcloud.com/lsupress_and_tsr

ACADEMIC > **Nonfiction** > *Nonfiction Books*
African American; American Civil War; American History; Archaeology; Architecture; Caribbean History; Culture; Environment; History; Literature; Louisiana; Media; Poetry as a Subject; Roots Music; Social Justice; US Southern States; World War II

ADULT
Nonfiction > *Nonfiction Books*
Louisiana; US Southern States

Poetry > *Any Poetic Form*

Send: Query; Writing sample; Outline; Author bio; Table of Contents; Market info
How to send: Email attachment

Publishes scholarly monographs and general interest books about Louisiana and the South.

Poetry proposals should include a cover letter, a one-page summary of the work, few sample poems from the work, and a current resume or curriculum vitae.

Proposals for everything except poetry should include a cover letter, working title, table of contents, sample chapters, information about competitive titles, and a resume or curriculum vitae.

P461 Loyola Press

Book Publisher
8770 W Bryn Mawr Ave, Suite 1125, Chicago, IL 60631
United States
Tel: +1 (773) 281-1818
Fax: +1 (773) 281-0152

submissions@loyolapress.com

https://www.loyolapress.com
https://www.facebook.com/LoyolaPress
https://twitter.com/loyolapress
https://instagram.com/loyolapress/
https://www.youtube.com/user/LoyolaPress

Nonfiction > *Nonfiction Books*
Catholicism; Ignation Spirituality

Send: Query
How to send: Email; Post

Provides resources for readers of all ages interested in Ignatian spirituality and prayer, and supports parish ministry leaders and catechists especially in their roles of fostering and passing on a living faith.

Publishing Imprint: Loyola Classics

P462 Lund Humphries Limited

Publishing Imprint
The Alphabeta Building, 18 Finsbury Square, London, EC2A 1AH
United Kingdom
Tel: +44 (0) 20 7440 7530

info@lundhumphries.com

https://www.lundhumphries.com
http://facebook.com/LHArtBooks
https://www.twitter.com/LHArtBooks
https://instagram.com/lhartbooks
https://www.youtube.com/channel/UCt-2V5NDuUGTzJOxNGSqR7w

Book Publisher: Ashgate Publishing Ltd

ACADEMIC > **Nonfiction** > *Nonfiction Books*
Architecture; Arts; Design

ADULT > **Nonfiction** > *Nonfiction Books*
Architecture; Arts; Design

PROFESSIONAL > **Nonfiction** > *Nonfiction Books*
Architecture; Arts; Design

Send: Query; Proposal
How to send: Email

Publishes books on art, art history, and design. See website for guidelines on submitting a proposal.

Editor: Lucy Clark

P463 The Lutterworth Press

Publishing Imprint
PO Box 60, Cambridge, CB1 2NT
United Kingdom
Tel: +44 (0) 1223 350865
Fax: +44 (0) 1223 366951

publishing@lutterworth.com

https://www.lutterworth.com
https://lutterworthpress.wordpress.com
https://twitter.com/LuttPress
https://www.facebook.com/JamesClarkeandCo
https://www.instagram.com/lutterworthpress

Book Publisher: James Clarke & Co.

ADULT > **Nonfiction** > *Nonfiction Books*
Antiques; Archaeology; Architecture; Arts; Biography; Crafts; Education; Environment; Games; History; Leisure; Literature; Nature; Philosophy; Religion; Science; Sport; Technology

CHILDREN'S
Fiction > *Novels*

Nonfiction > *Nonfiction Books*: Religion

Send: Submission Form
How to send: Post; Fax; Email

Publisher of religious books. Handles nonfiction for adults, and fiction and nonfiction for children. No adult fiction, cookery books, or drama or poetry.

Not currently accepting children's books.

P464 Lyons Press

Publishing Imprint
United States

Book Publisher: The Globe Pequot Press (**P296**)

P465 M. Evans & Company

Publishing Imprint
United States

https://rowman.com/action/search/cop/m.%20evans%20&%20company

Book Publisher: Rowman & Littlefield Publishing Group

Nonfiction > *Nonfiction Books*
General, and in particular: Health; Psychology

Publishes general nonfiction, but best known for popular psychology and health books.

P466 Mabecron Books Ltd

Book Publisher
3 Briston Orchard, St Mellion, Saltash, Cornwall, PL12 6RQ
United Kingdom

sales@mabecronbooks.co.uk

https://mabecronbooks.co.uk

Types: Fiction; Nonfiction
Subjects: Cookery
Markets: Adult; Children's

Send: Full text

Welcomes submissions of books with quality, style, and saleability. Favours books with a Cornish theme. Absence of a Cornish theme will not mean a book is necessarily rejected, but makes the decision more difficult. Particularly interested in children's picture books, cookery, and children's fiction. Send submissions by post only, with SAE.

P467 MacLehose Press

Publishing Imprint
United Kingdom

Book Publisher: Quercus Books

Publishing Imprint: Arcadia Books (**P047**)

P468 Macmillan

Publishing Imprint
United Kingdom

Book Publisher: Pan Macmillan **(P564)**

P469 Macmillan Children's Books

Publishing Imprint
United Kingdom

Book Publisher: Pan Macmillan **(P564)**

P470 Macmillan Children's Publishing Group

Book Publisher

Publishing Imprint: Henry Holt Books for Young Readers **(P366)**

P471 Macmillan Digital Audio

Publishing Imprint
United Kingdom

Book Publisher: Pan Macmillan **(P564)**

P472 Macmillan Education

Book Publisher
United Kingdom

https://www.springernature.com/gp/macmillaneducation

Book Publisher: Springer Nature **(P729)**

ACADEMIC > **Nonfiction** > *Nonfiction Books*: Education

Publishes a wide range of educational materials for the international market.

P473 The Macmillan Group

Book Publisher
United States

https://macmillan.com

Book Publisher: Holtzbrinck Publishing Group **(P378)**

Book Publisher: Macmillan Publishers **(P475)**

P474 Macmillan New Writing

Publishing Imprint
United Kingdom

Book Publisher: Pan Macmillan **(P564)**

P475 Macmillan Publishers

Book Publisher
175 Fifth Avenue, New York, NY 10010
United States

press.inquiries@macmillan.com

https://us.macmillan.com

Book Publisher: The Macmillan Group **(P473)**

Types: Fiction; Nonfiction
Markets: Adult; Children's; Young Adult

How to send: Through a literary agent

US office of international publisher of hardcover, trade paperback, and paperback books for adults, children, and teens.

Book Publishers: Macmillan New Writing; Macmillan Publishers International **(P476)**; Tom Doherty Associates **(P771)**

Publishing Imprint: St Martin's Press **(P733)**

P476 Macmillan Publishers International

Book Publisher
Cromwell Place, Hampshire International Business Park, Lime Tree Way, Basingstoke, Hampshire, RG24 8YJ
United Kingdom

Book Publisher: Macmillan Publishers **(P475)**

Book Publisher: Pan Macmillan **(P564)**

P477 Mad Gleam Press

Book Publisher
482 Alvarado St, Monterey, CA 93940
United States

madgleampress@gmail.com

https://www.madgleampress.com

Types: Fiction; Poetry
Subjects: Literary
Markets: Adult

Closed to approaches.

Closed to submissions as at June 2019. Check website for current status. Publishes fiction and poetry collections. Particularly interested in collaborative / transmedia pieces. Send submissions by email with author bio / resume.

P478 Mango Books

Book Publisher
United Kingdom

https://mangobooks.co.uk

Nonfiction > *Nonfiction Books*
Crime; Mystery

How to send: Email

Publishes nonfiction on crime, detection, and mystery. Welcomes submissions.

Publishing Imprints: Blue Lamp Books **(P110)**; Little Wing **(P449)**

P479 Mango Publishing Group

Book Publisher
2850 Douglas Road, 2nd Floor, Coral Gables, FL 33134
United States
Tel: +1 (305) 428-2299

support@mangopublishinggroup.com

https://mangopublishinggroup.com
https://www.facebook.com/mangopublishing
https://twitter.com/MangoPublishing
https://www.instagram.com/mangopublishing/
https://www.pinterest.com/mangomediainc/
https://www.linkedin.com/company/mangopublishing/

ADULT
Fiction > *Novels*

Nonfiction
Nonfiction Books: Adventure; Business; Cookery; Crafts; Entertainment; Environment; Feminism; Films; Finance; Health; Hobbies; LGBTQIA; Science; Self Help; Spirituality; Technology; Veganism
Reference: General

Poetry > *Poetry Collections*

CHILDREN'S > **Nonfiction** > *Nonfiction Books*

YOUNG ADULT > **Nonfiction** > *Nonfiction Books*

An innovative independent publisher based in Miami. Publishes books from the freshest, most distinctive voices of our time, and seeks to stretch the boundaries of our online culture, social media and ideas.

P480 Margaret K. McElderry

Publishing Imprint

Book Publisher: Simon & Schuster Children's Publishing **(P713)**

P481 Marion Boyars Publishers

Book Publisher
26 Parke Road, London, SW13 9NG
United Kingdom

catheryn@marionboyars.com

http://www.marionboyars.co.uk

Types: Fiction; Nonfiction
Formats: Film Scripts; Theatre Scripts
Subjects: Anthropology; Autobiography; Culture; Drama; Literary Criticism; Music; Philosophy; Psychology; Sociology; Women's Interests
Markets: Adult; Children's

Not accepting new submissions as at March 2020. Check website for current status.

Editor: Catheryn Kilgarriff

P482 Marsh Hawk Press

Book Publisher
PO Box 206, East Rockway, NY 11518-0206
United States

https://marshhawkpress.org

Types: Poetry
Subjects: Literary
Markets: Adult

Send: Full text

Publishes poetry chapbooks submitted through its three national poetry prizes (submission fees apply).

P483 Marvel Comics

Book Publisher
1290 Avenue of the Americas, New York, NY 10104
United States
Tel: +1 (212) 576-4000

https://www.marvel.com

Types: Fiction
Subjects: Adventure; Comedy / Humour; Fantasy; Horror; Science Fiction
Markets: Adult; Children's; Young Adult

Publisher of action comics.

P484 Maryland Historical Society Press

Book Publisher
Maryland Center for History and Culture, 610 Park Ave., Baltimore, MD 21201
United States

mkado@mdhistory.org

https://www.mdhistory.org/publications/book-publishing/

Nonfiction > *Nonfiction Books*
History; Maryland

Send: Query
How to send: Post; Email

Publishes books on the history and people of Maryland. Send query by post or by email. See website for full guidelines.

Editors: Patricia Dockman Anderson; Robert Cottom

P485 Mcbooks Press

Publishing Imprint
United States

Book Publisher: The Globe Pequot Press (**P296**)

P486 McGraw Hill EMEA

Book Publisher
Unit 4, Foundation Park, Roxborough Way, Maidenhead, SL6 3UD
United Kingdom
Tel: +44 (0) 1628 502500

emea_uk_ireland@mheducation.com
emea_me@mheducation.com
emea_europe@mheducation.com

https://www.mheducation.co.uk
https://www.facebook.com/mheducationemea
https://twitter.com/mhe_emea
https://www.linkedin.com/showcase/27094331/admin/
https://www.youtube.com/channel/UCmbIrRJdSlo0J99kFa5uYfA

Book Publisher: McGraw-Hill Education

ACADEMIC > **Nonfiction** > *Nonfiction Books*: Education

PROFESSIONAL > **Nonfiction** > *Nonfiction Books*
Engineering; Health; Medicine; Science

Publisher of books for the professional and academic markets, particularly healthcare, medical, engineering, and science.

P487 Media Lab Books

Publishing Imprint

https://us.macmillan.com/publishers/media-lab-books

P488 Menasha Ridge Press

Publishing Imprint
United States

https://adventurewithkeen.com/menasha-ridge-press-submissions-form/

Book Publisher: AdventureKEEN (**P024**)

Nonfiction > *Nonfiction Books*
Cookery; Food; History; Outdoor Activities; Travel; Wilderness Sports; Wildlife

Send: Query; Pitch; Outline
How to send: Online submission system

Independent publisher covering the outdoors, wilderness sports, wildlife, cooking, history, dining, and travel worldwide.

P489 Mentor Books

Book Publisher
43 Furze Road, Sandyford Industrial Estate, Dublin 18
Ireland
Tel: 01 2952112
Fax: 01 295 2114

admin@mentorbooks.ie

http://www.mentorbooks.ie

Types: Nonfiction
Subjects: Biography; Business; Comedy / Humour; Crime; History; Politics; Science; Sport
Markets: Academic; Adult

Publishes educational books and general nonfiction of Irish interest.

P490 Menus and Music

Book Publisher
1462 66th Street, Emeryville, CA 94608
United States
Tel: +1 (510) 658-9100

info@menusandmusic.com

https://www.menusandmusic.com
https://www.facebook.com/menusandmusic
https://twitter.com/menusandmusic
https://www.pinterest.com/menusandmusic/
https://www.instagram.com/menusandmusic/

Nonfiction > *Nonfiction Books*
Arts; Food; Music; Travel

Publishes books combining inspiring food, music, art and travel.

Editor: Sharon O'Connor

P491 Merriam Press

Book Publisher; Ebook Publisher
489 South Street, Hoosick Falls NY 12090
United States
Tel: +1 (866) 357-7377

merriampress@gmail.com

https://www.merriam-press.com
https://www.facebook.com/MerriamPress

Nonfiction > *Nonfiction Books*
Military History; World War II

Closed to approaches.

Military history publisher, focusing on World War II.

P492 Messianic Jewish Publishers

Book Publisher
6120 Day Long Lane, Clarksville, MD 21029
United States
Tel: +1 (410) 531-6644

Lisa@MessianicJewish.net

http://www.messianicjewish.net

Types: Fiction; Nonfiction
Subjects: Religion
Markets: Adult

Send: Query
Don't send: Full text

Publishes books which address Jewish evangelism; the Jewish roots of Christianity; Messianic Judaism; Israel; the Jewish People. Publishes mainly nonfiction, but some fiction. See website for full submission guidelines.

P493 Methuen Publishing Ltd

Book Publisher
Orchard House, Railway Street, Slingsby, York, YO62 4AN
United Kingdom
Tel: +44 (0) 1653 628152
Fax: +44 (0) 1653 628195

editorial@methuen.co.uk

http://www.methuen.co.uk
https://twitter.com/MethuenandCo

Fiction > *Novels*

Nonfiction
Essays: General
Nonfiction Books: Autobiography; Biography; Classics / Ancient World; Literature; Politics; Sport; Theatre; Travel; World War II

Send: Query
How to send: Email
How not to send: Phone

No unsolicited submissions. Send query by email only, stating the subject area of your manuscript. No phone calls regarding submissions.

P494 Metro Publications Ltd

Book Publisher
United Kingdom
Tel: +44 (0) 20 8533 7777

info@metropublications.com

https://metropublications.com
https://twitter.com/metrolondon
https://www.instagram.com/metropublications/
https://www.linkedin.com/company/metro-publications-limited

Nonfiction > *Nonfiction Books*
Arts; Culture; Food; London; Walking Guides

Publisher of guide books on many aspects of London life.

P495 Michael Joseph

Book Publisher
80 Strand, London, WC2R 0RL
United Kingdom
Tel: +44 (0) 20 7139 3000

https://www.penguin.co.uk/company/publishers/michael-joseph.html

Book Publishers: Penguin Random House; Penguin Random House UK (**P587**)

Types: Fiction; Nonfiction
Subjects: Autobiography; Commercial; Cookery; Crime; Lifestyle; Thrillers; Women's Interests
Markets: Adult

How to send: Through a literary agent

Publishes women's fiction, crime, thrillers, cookery, memoirs and lifestyle books. Accepts submissions through literary agents only.

P496 Milkweed Editions

Book Publisher
1011 Washington Avenue South, Open Book, Suite 300, Minneapolis, MN 55415
United States
Tel: +1 (612) 332-3192

orders@milkweed.org

https://milkweed.org
http://www.facebook.com/milkweed.books
http://twitter.com/#!/Milkweed_Books
https://www.instagram.com/milkweed_books/
http://www.youtube.com/MilkweedEditions
https://www.pinterest.com/Milkfolk/

Fiction > *Novels*

Nonfiction > *Nonfiction Books*

Poetry > *Poetry Collections*

Closed to approaches.

An independent publisher of fiction, nonfiction, and poetry.

P497 Millbrook Press

Publishing Imprint

Book Publisher: Lerner Publishing Group (**P438**)

P498 Minnesota Historical Society Press

Book Publisher
345 Kellogg Blvd. West, Saint Paul, MN 55102-1906
United States
Tel: +1 (651) 259-3205
Fax: +1 (651) 297-1345

https://www.mnhs.org/mnhspress
https://www.facebook.com/Mnhspress
https://twitter.com/MNHSPress
https://www.youtube.com/playlist?list=PLRrmlN6cO7LvpRkbuLYO6paOGLjrKCoXP

Nonfiction > *Nonfiction Books*
American Midwest; Culture; History; Minnesota

Send: Query; Market info; Author bio; Table of Contents; Outline; Writing sample
How to send: Email; Post

Publishes books on the history and culture of America's Upper Midwest. Submit proposal by post including author info, working title, description of the book, table of contents/outline, intended readership, outline of the market and potential competition, the book's length, your schedule for completing it, and 15-25 sample pages. See website for detailed guidelines.

Editor: Ann Regan

Publishing Imprint: Borealis Books

P499 Minotaur

Publishing Imprint

Publishing Imprint: St Martin's Press (**P733**)

P500 Mirror Books

Book Publisher
One Canada Square, Canary Wharf, London, E14 5AP
United Kingdom

submissions@mirrorbooks.co.uk

https://mirrorbooks.co.uk

Nonfiction > *Nonfiction Books*
Celebrity; Crime; Memoir; Nostalgia

Send: Query; Outline; Synopsis; Table of Contents; Writing sample; Author bio; Marketing Plan
How to send: Email

Currently accepting submissions with a focus on nonfiction real-life (memoir, crime, nostalgia, personalities and celebrities). Send submissions by email.

P501 The MIT Press

Book Publisher
One Broadway, 12th Floor, Cambridge, MA 02142
United States
Tel: +1 (617) 253-5646

https://mitpress.mit.edu
https://www.facebook.com/mitpress
https://twitter.com/mitpress
https://www.linkedin.com/company/11587565/
https://www.pinterest.com/mitpress/
https://www.instagram.com/mitpress/
https://www.youtube.com/c/TheMITPress

ACADEMIC > **Nonfiction** > *Nonfiction Books*
Arts; Design; Science; Sociology; Technology

University press publishing books and journals at the intersection of science, technology, art, social science, and design.

Acquisitions Editors: Matthew Browne; Susan Buckley; Beth Clevenger; Katie Helke; Victoria Hindley; Justin Kehoe; Philip Laughlin; Marc Lowenthal; Gita Manaktala; Jermey Matthews; Robert Prior; Elizabeth Swayze; Emily Taber; Thomas Weaver

Publishing Imprint: Bradford Books

P502 Modern Library

Publishing Imprint

Book Publisher: Random House (**P640**)

P503 The Monacelli Press

Publishing Imprint
Attn: Acquisitions, 65 Bleecker Street, 8th Floor, New York, New York 10012
United States

submissions@themonacellipress.com

https://www.phaidon.com/store/the-monacelli-press/

Book Publisher: Phaidon Press (**P600**)

Nonfiction > *Nonfiction Books*
Architecture; Arts; Gardening; Interior Design; Photography

How to send: Post; Email

Will review book proposals in the fields of architecture and landscape architecture, fine and decorative arts, design, and photography.

P504 Monarch Books

Publishing Imprint
Lion Hudson, Part of the SPCK Group, John Eccles House, Science Park, Robert Robinson Ave, Littlemore, Oxford, OX4 4GP
United Kingdom
Tel: +44 (0) 1865 302750

https://www.lionhudson.com/monarch-books/

Book Publisher: Lion Hudson (**P446**)

Nonfiction > *Nonfiction Books*
Biography; Christianity; Education; Leadership

Send: Proposal; Writing sample; Outline
How to send: Online submission system

Co-Publishing Christian Books and Teaching Resources with Christian Organisations. Mission and confessional biographies, devotionals, Christian apologetics, as well as discipleship and leadership resources for Christians.

P505 Monday Books

Book Publisher
Festival House, Jessop Avenue, Cheltenham, GL50 3SH
United Kingdom
Tel: +44 (0) 1242 633717

info@mondaybooks.com

http://www.mondaybooks.com

Nonfiction > *Nonfiction Books*

Closed to approaches.

Independent publisher of strongly written nonfiction covering a range of subjects.

P506 More Shoots More Leaves

Publishing Imprint

Book Publisher: Five Leaves Publications (**P269**)

P507 Morrow Gift

Publishing Imprint

Book Publisher: HarperCollins

P508 Motorbooks

Publishing Imprint

Book Publisher: The Quarto Group, Inc. (**P633**)

P509 Mud Pie Books

Book Publisher
Oxford, OX2 6HY
United Kingdom
Tel: +44 (0) 7985 935320

info@mudpiebooks.com

https://mudpiebooks.com

Fiction > *Novels*: Buddhism

Nonfiction > *Nonfiction Books*: Buddhism

Poetry > *Poetry Collections*: Buddhism

Publishes books about Buddhism, and books for Buddhists.

P510 Muddy Boots

Publishing Imprint
United States

Book Publisher: The Globe Pequot Press (**P296**)

P511 Mudfog Press

Book Publisher
C/o Arts and Events, Culture and Tourism, P.O Box 99A, Civic Centre, Middlesbrough, TS1 2QQ
United Kingdom

paulinepoethughes@gmail.com

https://www.mudfog.co.uk

Fiction > *Short Fiction Collections*

Poetry > *Poetry Collections*

Send: Writing sample; Synopsis
How to send: Post; Email

Publishes poetry and short fiction by writers in the Tees Valley area. Send query with 15-20 poems or 2-3 stories, or a sample of 10-15 pages for other genres, with synopsis.

P512 Mudlark

Publishing Imprint
United Kingdom

Book Publisher: HarperCollins UK (**P347**)

P513 Murdoch Books UK Ltd

Book Publisher
United Kingdom
Tel: +44 (0) 20 8785 5995
Fax: +44 (0) 20 8785 5985

http://www.murdochbooks.co.uk

Book Publisher: Murdoch Books Pty Limited Australia

Types: Nonfiction
Subjects: Cookery; Crafts; Design; Gardening; Lifestyle
Markets: Adult

Publishers of full-colour nonfiction.

P514 Myriad Editions

Book Publisher
United Kingdom

submissions@myriadeditions.com

https://myriadeditions.com

Types: Fiction; Nonfiction
Subjects: Autobiography; Contemporary; Crime; History; Literary; Medicine; Politics; Thrillers
Markets: Adult

Closed to approaches.

Publishes literary fiction: contemporary and historical; crime fiction: psychological and political thrillers with strong female characters; graphic novels: documentary comics, graphic reportage, fiction, memoir and life writing, graphic medicine; and literary or political nonfiction: feminist, literary nonfiction, memoir. No young adult fiction, children's books, horror, science fiction, fantasy, plays or poetry, or books that have been previously published or self-published (in print or as ebooks) unless you are a graphic novelist. Do not send proposals – send complete manuscript by email. See website for full guidelines.

P515 Myrmidon Books Ltd

Book Publisher
Rotterdam House, 116 Quayside, Newcastle upon Tyne, NE1 3DY
United Kingdom
Tel: +44 (0) 1912 064005
Fax: +44 (0) 1912 064001

ed@myrmidonbooks.com

http://www.myrmidonbooks.com

Fiction > *Novels*
Commercial; Literary

Send: Query; Writing sample; Author bio
How to send: Post
How not to send: Email; Fax

Submit your initial three chapters and a one-page covering letter providing information about yourself and your work. A synopsis or structure plan may be useful for a non-fiction proposal, but a synopsis is not required for fiction submissions and will not be read.

P516 The Mysterious Press

Publishing Imprint
United States

Book Publisher: Grove Atlantic Inc. (**P312**)

P517 Nan A. Talese

Publishing Imprint
1745 Broadway, 22nd floor, New York, NY 10019
United States
Tel: +1 (212) 782-8918
Fax: +1 (212) 782-8448

ntalese@randomhouse.com

http://www.randomhouse.com/nanatalese

Book Publisher: Knopf Doubleday Publishing Group (**P426**)

Types: Fiction; Nonfiction
Subjects: Culture; History; Literary; Philosophy; Sociology
Markets: Adult

How to send: Through a literary agent

Publishes nonfiction and literary fiction with a compelling storyline, good characterisation and use of language. Accepts approaches via a literary agent only.

Editorial Director / Publisher: Nan Talese

P518 Nancy Paulsen Books

Publishing Imprint
United States

Book Publisher: Penguin Young Readers Group (**P591**)

P519 National Museums Scotland Enterprises

Book Publisher
National Museums of Scotland, Chambers Street, Edinburgh, EH1 1JF
United Kingdom
Tel: +44 (0) 1312 474026
Fax: +44 (0) 1312 474012

publishing@nms.ac.uk

https://www.nms.ac.uk/about-us/our-organisation/nms-enterprises/

Types: Nonfiction
Subjects: Archaeology; Arts; Culture; History; Literature; Nature
Markets: Academic; Adult; Children's

Publishes books reflecting the range and international importance of the museum's collections., from catalogues to children's books, academic monographs, biographies, and souvenir booklets.

P520 National Trust

Publishing Imprint

Book Publisher: Pavilion Books (**P572**)

P521 Natural History Museum Publishing

Book Publisher
The Natural History Museum, Cromwell Road, London, SW7 5BD
United Kingdom
Tel: +44 (0) 20 7942 5336

publishing@nhm.ac.uk

http://www.nhm.ac.uk/business-services/publishing.html

Types: Nonfiction
Subjects: Arts; Nature; Science
Markets: Adult

Publishes accessible, fully illustrated books about the natural world.

P522 Naturegraph & Keven Brown Publications

Book Publisher
United States

naturegraph@gmail.com

http://www.naturegraph.com

Nonfiction in Translation > *Nonfiction Books*: Islamic Philosophy

Nonfiction > *Nonfiction Books*
California; Native Americans; Nature

Publishes mainly books on nature, Native American subjects, and translations of Islamic philosophy.

Editors: Barbara Brown; Keven Brown

P523 NBM Publishing

Book Publisher
160 Broadway, Suite 700 East Wing, New York, NY 10038
United States

tnantier@nbmpub.com

http://nbmpub.com

Types: Fiction
Subjects: Comedy / Humour; Fantasy; Horror; Mystery; Satire; Science Fiction
Markets: Adult; Young Adult

Send: Query
Don't send: Full text

Publisher of graphic novels, interested in general fiction, humour, satire of fantasy and horror, and mystery. No superheroes. Accepting approaches from previously published authors only (including those with proven success in online comics). No submissions from authors outside North America. See website for full submission guidelines.

Editor: Terry Nantier

P524 Negative Capability Press

Book Publisher
United States

swalker@negativecapabilitypress.org

http://www.negativecapabilitypress.org

Types: Fiction; Nonfiction; Poetry
Subjects: Literary
Markets: Adult

Send: Full text

Publishes books of literary fiction, nonfiction, and poetry. Accepts submissions through competitions and open submissions ($25 submission fee) via online submission system.

P525 Nell James Publishers

Book Publisher
United Kingdom

info@nelljames.co.uk

https://nelljames.co.uk
https://twitter.com/NJamesPublisher

Nonfiction > *Nonfiction Books*
Contemporary; Social Issues

Send: Outline; Synopsis; Pitch; Market info; Author bio; Submission Form
How to send: Email

An independent publisher of nonfiction books, bringing awareness to issues in modern society. Download submission form from website and return by email.

P526 Nelson Books

Publishing Imprint

Book Publisher: HarperCollins

P527 New American Press

Book Publisher
PO Box 1094, Grafton, WI 53024
United States

https://newamericanpress.com
https://www.facebook.com/New-American-Press-110522495698111/
https://www.instagram.com/newamericanpress/
https://twitter.com/newamerpress

Fiction in Translation > *Novels*: Literary

Fiction > *Novels*: Literary

Nonfiction in Translation > *Nonfiction Books*

Nonfiction > *Nonfiction Books*

Poetry in Translation > *Any Poetic Form*

Poetry > *Any Poetic Form*

Send: Query
Don't send: Full text
How to send: Online contact form

An independent nonprofit literary press that publishes fiction, poetry, nonfiction, and works in translation. Does not regularly accept unsolicited manuscripts, but queries are welcome.

P528 New Harbinger Publications

Book Publisher
5674 Shattuck Avenue, Oakland, CA 94609
United States

proposals@newharbinger.com

https://www.newharbinger.com
https://www.facebook.com/NewHarbinger
https://www.instagram.com/newharbinger/
https://twitter.com/NewHarbinger
https://www.linkedin.com/company/new-harbinger-publications/
https://www.youtube.com/newharbinger

ADULT > **Nonfiction** > *Nonfiction Books*
Health; Mental Health; Psychology; Self Help

PROFESSIONAL > **Nonfiction** > *Nonfiction Books*
Health; Mental Health; Psychology

Send: Query; Proposal; Market info; Author bio; Writing sample
How to send: Email

Publishes psychology and health self-help books that must be simple and easy to understand, but also complete and authoritative. Most authors for this publisher are therapists or other helping professionals. See website for extensive author guidelines.

P529 New Holland Publishers Australia

Book Publisher
Level 1, 178 Fox Valley Road, Wahroonga, NSW, 2076

Australia
Tel: +61 2 8986 4700

orders@newholland.com.au

http://au.newhollandpublishers.com

Nonfiction > *Nonfiction Books*
General, and in particular: Arts; Autobiography; Biography; Cookery; Crafts; Drinks; Gardening; Health; Memoir; Military; Nature; Pets; Sport

Send: Query; Author bio; Market info; Synopsis; Writing sample; Full text
How to send: Post

Publisher with offices in Australia and New Zealand. Welcomes all manuscript submissions from authors wishing to be published. However, primarily deals with non-fiction categories.

P530 New London Editions

Publishing Imprint

Book Publisher: Five Leaves Publications (**P269**)

P531 New Walk Editions

Book Publisher
c/o Nick Everett, School of English, Leicester University, University Road, Leicester, LE1 7RH
United Kingdom

newwalkmagazine@gmail.com

https://newwalkmagazine.com

Poetry > *Poetry Collections*

Send: Full text; Author bio
How to send: Word file email attachment; Post

A small press specialising in extremely high quality poetry pamphlets. Interested in poetic plurality: equally interested in established and new poets, and a broad church stylistically and thematically. Send 12-20 pages of poems by email or by post.

Editor: Nick Everett

P532 No Starch Press, Inc.

Book Publisher
245 8th Street, San Francisco, CA 94103
United States
Tel: +1 (415) 863-9900
Fax: +1 (415) 863-9950

editors@nostarch.com
support@nostarch.com

https://nostarch.com

ADULT > **Nonfiction** > *Nonfiction Books*
Arts; Computer Programming; Computer Science; Computers; Design

CHILDREN'S > **Nonfiction** > *Nonfiction Books*
Arts; Computer Programming; Computer Science; Computers; Design

Send: Query; Outline; Synopsis; Market info; Author bio
How to send: Email

Publishes unique books on computer programming, security, hacking, alternative operating systems, STEM, and LEGO.

P533 North Light Books

Publishing Imprint
United States

Book Publisher: Penguin Publishing Group (**P585**)

P534 Northern Eye Books

Book Publisher
22 Crosland Terrace, Helsby, Frodsham, Cheshire, WA6 9LY
United Kingdom
Tel: +44 (0) 1829 770309

tony@northerneyebooks.com

https://www.northerneyebooks.co.uk
https://www.facebook.com/NorthernEyeBooks/
https://twitter.com/northerneyeboo
https://www.pinterest.co.uk/tony9709/

Nonfiction > *Nonfiction Books*: Walking Guides

Send: Query

Publishes walking books for the Lake District, Peak District, Yorkshire Dales, other UK National Parks, the Wales Coast Path, South West Coast Path, Wales and Cheshire. Most books are commissioned, but willing to consider ideas or a sample chapter.

Authors: Jen Darling; Roger Redfern; Carl Rogers

Editor: Tony Bowerman

Publishing Imprint: Marabooks

P535 Northern Illinois University Press

Publishing Imprint
Sage House, 512 East State Street, Ithaca, NY 14850
United States
Tel: +1 (607)253-2338

cupressinfo@cornell.edu

https://www.cornellpress.cornell.edu/imprints/northern-illinois-university-press/

Book Publisher: Cornell University Press

ACADEMIC > **Nonfiction** > *Nonfiction Books*
American Midwest; Christianity; Culture; European History; History; Philosophy; Politics; Religion; Russia; South-East Asia

ADULT > **Nonfiction** > *Nonfiction Books*
American Midwest; Christianity; Culture; European History; History; Philosophy; Politics; Religion; Russia; South-East Asia

Publishes scholarly and trade books in the humanities and social sciences for both specialists and general readers. The Press has long published major works in Russian and Eurasian studies and has additional series in Orthodox Christianity and Southeast Asian studies. Also publishes books on politics, philosophy, religion, European history, and American Midwest history and culture.

Acquisitions Editor: Melody Herr

Editorial Director: Mary Lincoln

P536 NorthSouth Books

Book Publisher
600 Third Avenue, 2nd Floor, NY, NY 10016
United States
Tel: +1 (917) 699-2079

info@northsouth.com
submissionsnsb@gmail.com

https://northsouth.com

CHILDREN'S > **Fiction**
Board Books; *Picture Books*

Closed to approaches.

Publishes picture books for children up to 1,000 words. Seeks fresh, original fiction on universal themes that would appeal to children aged 3-8. Generally does not acquire rhyming texts, as must also be translated into German. Send submissions by email as Word document or pasted directly into the body of the email. Authors do not need to include illustrations, but if the author is also an illustrator sample sketches can be included in PDF or JPEG form.

P537 Nosy Crow

Book Publisher
The Crow's Nest, 14 Baden Place, Crosby Row, London, SE1 1YW
United Kingdom
Tel: +44 (0) 20 7089 7575

hello@nosycrow.com

https://nosycrow.com
https://www.facebook.com/NosyCrow
https://www.instagram.com/nosycrow/
https://twitter.com/nosycrow
https://www.youtube.com/user/NosyCrow

CHILDREN'S
Fiction
Board Books; *Chapter Books*; *Middle Grade*; *Picture Books*
Nonfiction > *Nonfiction Books*

Closed to approaches.

Publishes child-focused, parent-friendly children's books for ages 0-12. No submissions from white people.

Editor: Adrian Soar

P538 Oak Tree Press

Book Publisher
33 Rochestown Rise, Rochestown, Cork
Ireland
Tel: +353 86 244 1633
Fax: +353 86 330 7694

info@oaktreepress.com

https://oaktreepress.eu

Types: Nonfiction
Subjects: Business; Finance; Legal
Markets: Professional

Publishes books on business, particularly for small business owners and managers.

P539 Oghma Creative Media

Book Publisher
United States

submissions@oghmacreative.net

https://oghmacreative.com

ADULT
Fiction > *Novels*
Contemporary Romance; Contemporary; Crime; Diversity; Environment; Fantasy; High / Epic Fantasy; Historical Fiction; Historical Romance; Horror; LGBTQIA; Mainstream; Military; Mystery; Nautical; Police Procedural; Romance; Romantic Comedy; Romantic Thrillers; Science Fiction; Secret Intelligence; Space Opera; Supernatural / Paranormal; Thrillers; Traditional; Westerns

Nonfiction > *Nonfiction Books*
Biography; Entertainment; History; Military; Mind, Body, Spirit; Music; TV

CHILDREN'S > **Fiction**
Chapter Books; *Middle Grade*; *Picture Books*
NEW
ADULT > **Fiction** > *Novels*: Contemporary Romance

YOUNG ADULT > **Fiction** > *Novels*

Send: Query; Synopsis; Full text
How to send: Email; Through a literary agent

A traditional publisher reaching out to authors who don't want to take the self-publishing route. Provides a team of editors, designers, and marketers to help bring your work to its finished form. Aims to develop long-term relationships with authors and artists. Closed to submissions between November 1 and April 1.

Currently only accepting submissions from agents and authors who have already published with them.

P540 The Ohio State University Press

Book Publisher
United States
Tel: +1 (773) 702-7000
Fax: +1 (614) 292-2065

OSUPInfo@osu.edu

https://ohiostatepress.org

ACADEMIC > **Nonfiction** > *Nonfiction Books*
19th Century; Central America; Classics / Ancient World; Comic Books; Communication; Creative Nonfiction; Culture; Disabilities; Ethnic Groups; Films; Gender; History; Language; Literature; Media; Medieval; Ohio; Politics; Sexuality; South America; United States

ADULT
Fiction > *Novels*
Poetry > *Poetry Collections*

Send: Query; Outline; Table of Contents; Writing sample; Market info; Author bio
How to send: Email attachment

Publishes mainly academic nonfiction, but also has imprints for regional books that are of interest to the citizens of the state of Ohio, primarily about their history, environment, and culture; and creative works, including the winners of the poetry and prose prizes.

Acquisitions Editor: Ana Maria Jimenez-Moreno

Acquisitions Editor / Managing Editor: Tara Cyphers

Associate Editor: Becca Bostock

Editor-in-Chief: Kristen Elias Rowley

Publishing Director: Tony Sanfilippo

P541 Ohio University Press

Book Publisher
30 Park Place, Suite 101, Athens, OH 45701-2909
United States

huard@ohio.edu

https://www.ohioswallow.com

ACADEMIC > **Nonfiction** > *Nonfiction Books*
Africa; American History; American Midwest; Anthropology; Appalachia; Art History; Arts; Asia; Central America; Environment; Europe; Films; Food; Gender; Health; History; Journalism; Legal; Literature; Media; North America; Ohio; Performing Arts; Philosophy; Politics; Religion; South America; Sport; TV; Women

Send: Query; Table of Contents; Writing sample; Author bio
Don't send: Full text

Publishes primarily nonfiction. See website for full guidelines.

Editor: Ricky S. Huard

Publishing Imprint: Swallow Press (*P751*)

P542 Old Street Publishing Ltd

Book Publisher
8 Hurlingham Business Park, Sulivan Road, London, SW6 3DU
United Kingdom
Tel: +44 (0) 20 8787 5812

info@oldstreetpublishing.co.uk

http://www.oldstreetpublishing.co.uk
https://twitter.com/oldstpublishing

Fiction > *Novels*

Nonfiction > *Nonfiction Books*

Send: Query; Outline
Don't send: Full text
How to send: Email

Independent British publisher of fiction and nonfiction.

Chair: David Reynolds

Managing Director: Ben Yarde-Buller

P543 Oldcastle Books

Publishing Imprint
United Kingdom

Book Publisher: Oldcastle Books Group (**P544**)

P544 Oldcastle Books Group

Book Publisher
18 Coleswood Road, Harpenden, Hertfordshire, AL5 1EQ
United Kingdom
Tel: +44 (0) 1582 766348

publicity@oldcastlebooks.com

http://www.oldcastlebooks.co.uk

Fiction > *Novels*

Nonfiction > *Nonfiction Books*

How to send: Through a literary agent

Accepts submissions through literary agents only.

Managing Director: Ion S. Mills

Publishing Imprints: Creative Essentials (*P184*); Crime & Mystery Club (*P185*); High Stakes Publishing (**P370**); Kamera Books (*P417*); No Exit Press; Oldcastle Books (*P543*); Pocketessentials; Pulp! The Classics (*P627*)

P545 Oleander Press

Book Publisher
16 Orchard Street, Cambridge, CB1 1JT
United Kingdom

editor@oleanderpress.com

http://www.oleanderpress.com

Types: Fiction; Nonfiction; Poetry
Formats: Reference
Subjects: Biography; History; Horror;

Literature; Travel
Markets: Adult; Children's

Closed to approaches.

Closed to submissions as at June 2020.

Publishes biography, Cambridge / local, children's, classic horror, language and literature, fiction, games and pastimes, modern poets, Arabia, and Libya. Looking for nonfiction – in particular children's nonfiction. Send submissions by email or by post.

Editor: Jon Gifford

P546 Omnibus Press

Book Publisher
14/15 Berners Street, London, W1T 3LJ
United Kingdom
Tel: +44 (0) 20 7612 7400

omniinfo@wisemusic.com

https://omnibuspress.com

Book Publisher: Wise Music Group (**P868**)

Types: Nonfiction
Subjects: Biography; Music
Markets: Adult

Publisher of music books, including song sheets and rock and pop biographies.

P547 One More Chapter

Publishing Imprint
United Kingdom

Book Publisher: HarperCollins UK (**P347**)

P548 One Signal

Publishing Imprint

Book Publisher: Simon & Schuster Adult Publishing (**P711**)

P549 One World

Publishing Imprint

Book Publisher: Random House (**P640**)

P550 Oneworld Publications

Book Publisher
10 Bloomsbury Street, London, WC1B 3SR
United Kingdom
Tel: +44 (0) 20 7307 8900

submissions@oneworld-publications.com

https://oneworld-publications.com
https://www.facebook.com/oneworldpublications
https://twitter.com/OneworldNews
https://www.instagram.com/oneworldpublications/
https://www.youtube.com/user/oneworldpublications

ADULT
Fiction in Translation > *Novels*

Fiction > *Novels*
General, and in particular: Crime; Thrillers

Nonfiction
Gift Books: General
Nonfiction Books: Anthropology; Arts; Baha'i; Biography; Buddhism; Business; Christianity; Comedy / Humour; Current Affairs; Economics; Feminism; Gender; Health; Hinduism; History; Islam; Judaism; Literature; Memoir; Middle East; Nature; Philosophy; Politics; Popular Psychology; Popular Science; Psychology; Religion; Science; Self Help; Spirituality
CHILDREN'S > **Fiction** > *Novels*

Send: Query; Submission Form
How to send: Email

Not accepting fiction submissions as at May 2022. Hopes this will change in the near future, but has been hoping this since at least 2018. Check website for current status.

Nonfiction authors must be academics and/or experts in their field. Approaches for fiction must provide a clear and concise synopsis, outlining the novel's main themes. See website for full submission guidelines, and forms for fiction and nonfiction, which should be submitted by email.

P551 Ooligan Press

Book Publisher
PO Box 751, Portland, OR 97207
United States
Tel: +1 (503) 725-9748
Fax: +1 (503) 725-3561

https://ooligan.pdx.edu

Types: Fiction; Nonfiction; Poetry
Subjects: Autobiography; History; Literary; Sociology
Markets: Adult; Young Adult

Send: Query
Don't send: Full text

Publishes works of historical and social value, or significance to the Pacific Northwest region (Northern California, Oregon, Idaho, Washington, British Columbia, and Alaska). Accepts queries by email and proposals via online submission system. See website for full details.

P552 Open University Press

Book Publisher
United Kingdom

Laura.Pacey@mheducation.com

https://www.mheducation.co.uk/professionals/open-university-press

Book Publisher: McGraw-Hill Education

Types: Nonfiction
Subjects: Health; Psychology; Sociology
Markets: Academic; Professional

Publishes books on social sciences only.

P553 Orchard Books

Publishing Imprint
United States

Book Publisher: Scholastic (**P688**)

P554 Orion Children's Books

Publishing Imprint

Book Publisher: Hachette Children's Group (**P318**)

P555 Ouen Press

Book Publisher
United Kingdom

submissions@ouenpress.com

http://www.ouenpress.com
https://www.facebook.com/ouenpress
https://twitter.com/ouenp

Fiction > *Novels*: Contemporary

Nonfiction > *Nonfiction Books*
Biography; Travel

Send: Query; Outline; Author bio; Writing sample
How to send: Email
How not to send: Post; Email attachment

Seeking to publish well written Contemporary Fiction, Travel Literature, and Biography if edgy! No genre, no children's books, no poetry, no single short stories, no guide books, no recipe books. Response only if interested. If no response after 60 days, assume rejection.

P556 Our Sunday Visitor

Book Publisher
200 Noll Plaza, Huntington, IN 46750
United States
Tel: +1 (260) 356-8400

https://www.osv.com

Nonfiction > *Nonfiction Books*: Catholicism

Non-profit Catholic publisher particularly interested in Apologetics and Catechetics, reference and prayer, heritage and saints, the family, and the parish.

P557 Oxbow Books

Book Publisher
The Old Music Hall, 106-108 Cowley Road, OX4 1JE
United Kingdom
Tel: +44 (0) 1865 241249
Fax: +44 (0) 1865 794449

orders@oxbowbooks.com

https://www.oxbowbooks.com
https://www.facebook.com/oxbowbooks
https://www.twitter.com/oxbowbooks
https://www.linkedin.com/company/oxbow-books

ACADEMIC > **Nonfiction** > *Nonfiction Books*: Archaeology

Publisher of academic books on archaeology.

Editor: Richard Purslow

Publishing Imprint: Aris & Phillips

P558 Oxford University Press

Book Publisher
Great Clarendon Street, Oxford, OX2 6DP
United Kingdom
Tel: +44 (0) 1865 556767
Fax: +44 (0) 1865 556646

onlinequeries.uk@oup.com

https://global.oup.com

Types: Fiction; Nonfiction
Formats: Reference
Subjects: Current Affairs; Drama; Finance; History; Legal; Literature; Medicine; Music; Philosophy; Politics; Religion; Science; Sociology
Markets: Academic; Adult; Children's; Professional

Publishes academic works including journals, schoolbooks, dictionaries, reference works, classics, and children's fiction, and nonfiction.

Book Publisher: Nelson Thornes Limited

P559 P8tech

Book Publisher
6 Woodside, Churnet View Road, Oakamoor, Staffordshire, ST10 3AE
United Kingdom

info@P8tech.com

https://www.p8tech.com

Types: Nonfiction
Subjects: Technology
Markets: Professional

Publishes IT books and ebooks for technology professionals. Current emphasis on Java and Oracle technologies. Books are heavy on the practical and full of code and screenshots.

P560 Pace Press

Book Publisher
2006 S Mary St, Fresno, CA 93721
United States
Tel: +1 (800) 345-4447

kent@lindenpub.com

https://quilldriverbooks.com/pace-press/

Types: Fiction
Subjects: Fantasy; History; Horror; Mystery; Romance; Science Fiction; Thrillers; Westerns
Markets: Adult

Closed to approaches.

Closed to submissions as at January 2020. Check website for current status. Send query by post or email with synopsis, author bio, and first three or four chapters / 50 pages of your manuscript. See website for full guidelines.

P561 Pale Fire Press

Book Publisher
United States
Tel: +1 (520) 282-1442

http://palefirepress.com

Fiction > *Novels*: Literary

Closed to approaches.

Closed to submissions as at January 2020. Check website for current status.

P562 Palgrave Macmillan

Book Publisher
United Kingdom

https://www.palgrave.com

Book Publisher: Springer Nature (**P729**)

ACADEMIC > **Nonfiction**
Nonfiction Books: Business; Culture; Economics; Environment; Films; Geography; Health; History; International; Journalism; Language; Literature; Media; Neuroscience; Philosophy; Politics; Psychology; Sociology; TV; Theatre
Reference: Business; Philosophy
PROFESSIONAL > **Nonfiction** > *Nonfiction Books*
Business; Management

Send: Query; Submission Form; Author bio; Writing sample
How to send: Online submission system

Submit via online submission system.

P563 Pan

Publishing Imprint
United Kingdom

Book Publisher: Pan Macmillan (**P564**)

P564 Pan Macmillan

Book Publisher
Cromwell Place, Hampshire International Business Park, Lime Tree Way, Basingstoke, Hampshire, RG24 8YJ
United Kingdom

webqueries@macmillan.co.uk
TorUKSubmissions@macmillan.com

https://www.panmacmillan.com
https://www.facebook.com/pages/Pan-Macmillan/246973468695197
https://twitter.com/panmacmillan
https://www.instagram.com/panmacmillan

Book Publisher: Macmillan Publishers International (**P476**)

ADULT
Fiction > *Novels*
Crime; Fantasy; Historical Fiction; Literary; Romance; Science Fiction; Thrillers

Nonfiction > *Nonfiction Books*
Biography; Crime; History; Nature; Politics; Science; Self Help; Wellbeing

Poetry > *Any Poetic Form*
CHILDREN'S
Fiction
Board Books; *Chapter Books*; *Middle Grade*; *Picture Books*
Poetry > *Any Poetic Form*

YOUNG ADULT > **Fiction** > *Novels*
Dystopian Fiction; Fantasy; Friends; Romance; Science Fiction

How to send: Through a literary agent; Email

Accepts submissions for science fiction and fantasy direct from authors. Submissions in all other areas must come via a literary agent.

Book Publisher: Pan Macmillan Australia

Publishing Imprints: Bello; Bluebird; Boxtree (*P121*); Campbell; Campbell Books (*P137*); Kingfisher; Macmillan (*P468*); Macmillan Children's Books (*P469*); Macmillan Digital Audio (*P471*); Macmillan New Writing (*P474*); Mantle; Pan (*P563*); Picador; Sidgwick & Jackson (*P707*); Tor; Two Hoots

P565 Pantheon

Publishing Imprint
United States

Book Publisher: Knopf Doubleday Publishing Group (**P426**)

P566 Paradise Cay Publications

Book Publisher
120 Monda Way, Blue Lake, CA 95525
United States
Tel: +1 (707) 822-9063
Fax: +1 (707) 822-9163

info@paracay.com

http://www.paracay.com

ADULT > **Nonfiction**
Gift Books: General, and in particular: Bigfoot
Nonfiction Books: Outdoor Activities; Pacific Northwest; Sailing; Travel
CHILDREN'S
Fiction > *Picture Books*
Nonfiction > *Picture Books*

Publishes specialty book titles as well as an ever expanding selection of field guides, travel maps, and children's books.

Editors: Jim Morehouse; Matt Morehouse

Publishing Imprint: Pardey Books

P567 Parthian Books

Book Publisher
The Old Surgery, Napier Street, Cardigan, SA43 1ED
United Kingdom
Tel: +44 (0) 7890 968246

info@parthianbooks.com

https://www.parthianbooks.com

Fiction
Novels: Literary
Short Fiction: Literary

Nonfiction > *Nonfiction Books*

Poetry > *Poetry Collections*

Closed to approaches.

Publisher of poetry, fiction, and creative nonfiction, of Welsh origin, in the English language. Also publishes English language translations of Welsh language work. Send query with SAE, and (for fiction) a one-page synopsis and first 30 pages, or (for poetry) a sample of 15-20 poems. No email submissions, genre fiction of any kind, or children's / teenage fiction. See website for full submission guidelines.

Author: Richard Owain Roberts

P568 Partisan Press

Book Publisher
PO 11417, Norfolk, VA 23517
United States

red-ink@earthlink.net

https://www.partisanpress.org
https://www.angelfire.com/va/bcr/ptsn.html

Poetry > *Poetry Collections*: Working Class

Not for profit publisher of working class poetry. Aims to create an awareness of and involvement in working class culture as well as to promote a progressive vision that will move our class and our society forward toward a more just and peaceful future.

Magazine: Blue Collar Review (**M086**)

P569 Pat-a-Cake

Publishing Imprint

Book Publisher: Hachette Children's Group (**P318**)

P570 Patrician Press

Book Publisher
United Kingdom
Tel: +44 (0) 7968 288651

patricia@patricianpress.com

https://patricianpress.com

Types: Fiction; Nonfiction; Poetry
Formats: Short Fiction
Markets: Adult; Children's

Closed to approaches.

Small and independent non-profit press, with the aim of encouraging and promoting writers of high quality fiction and poetry. Imprint publishes books for children. Contact by email only.

Publishing Imprint: Pudding Press

P571 Paula Wiseman Books

Publishing Imprint

Book Publisher: Simon & Schuster Children's Publishing (**P713**)

P572 Pavilion Books

Book Publisher
The News Building, 1 London Bridge St, London, SE1 9GF
United Kingdom
Tel: +44 (0) 20 8741 7070

https://www.pavilionbooks.com
https://www.instagram.com/pavilionbooks/
https://twitter.com/PavilionBooks
https://uk.pinterest.com/pavilionbook

Book Publisher: HarperCollins UK (**P347**)

ADULT > **Nonfiction** > *Illustrated Books*
Arts; Comedy / Humour; Crafts; Design; Fashion; Food and Drink; Games; Gardening; History; Lifestyle; Popular Culture

CHILDREN'S
Fiction
Board Books; *Early Readers*; *Picture Books*
Nonfiction
Activity Books; *Colouring Books*

Closed to approaches.

A London-based publisher specialising in illustrated books for the UK and international markets. At the core of the business are specialist lists such as craft, cookery and children's.

Publishing Imprints: Batsford (*P083*); Collins & Brown; National Trust (*P520*); Pavilion; Pavilion Children's (*P573*); Portico (*P618*)

P573 Pavilion Children's

Publishing Imprint

Book Publisher: Pavilion Books (**P572**)

P574 Pavilion Publishing

Book Publisher
Blue Sky Offices Shoreham, 25 Cecil Pashley Way, Shoreham-by-Sea, West Sussex, BN43 5FF
United Kingdom
Tel: +44 (0) 1273 434943

info@pavpub.com

http://www.pavpub.com

Types: Nonfiction
Formats: Reference
Subjects: Health; Sociology
Markets: Professional

Publishes books and resources for public, private and voluntary workers in the health, social care, education and community safety sectors. Welcomes submissions from both new and established authors, and organisations that are developing training materials.

P575 Peepal Tree Press

Book Publisher
17 King's Avenue, Leeds, LS6 1QS
United Kingdom
Tel: +44 (0) 113 245 1703

contact@peepaltreepress.com

https://www.peepaltreepress.com

Fiction > *Short Fiction Collections*
Black People; Caribbean Diaspora; Caribbean

Nonfiction > *Nonfiction Books*
Arts; Black People; Caribbean Diaspora; Caribbean; Cultural Criticism; Literary Criticism; Memoir

Poetry > *Poetry Collections*
Black People; Caribbean Diaspora; Caribbean

Publishes international Caribbean, Black British, and south Asian writing. Submit through online submission system.

P576 Pelican Publishing Company

Book Publisher
990 N. Corporate Drive, Suite 100, New Orleans, LA 70123
United States

editorial@pelicanpub.com

https://www.pelicanpub.com

Book Publisher: Arcadia Publishing

ADULT > **Nonfiction** > *Nonfiction Books*
Comedy / Humour; Music; Sport

CHILDREN'S
Fiction
Middle Grade: Adventure
Picture Books: Adventure; Holidays
Nonfiction
Middle Grade: Biography; Cookery; Regional History
Picture Books: Biography; Holidays; Regional History

YOUNG ADULT
Fiction > *Novels*: Adventure

Nonfiction > *Nonfiction Books*
Biography; Regional History

Send: Query; Author bio; Synopsis; Table of Contents; Writing sample
How to send: Email

Publishes nonfiction for all ages and fiction for children and young adults only. No adult fiction. Send query by email. See website for full guidelines.

Editor: Nina Kooij

P577 Pen & Sword Aviation

Publishing Imprint

Book Publisher: Pen & Sword Books Ltd (**P578**)

P578 Pen & Sword Books Ltd

Book Publisher
47 Church Street, Barnsley, South Yorkshire, S70 2AS
United Kingdom
Tel: +44 (0) 1226 734222
Fax: +44 (0) 1226 734438

editorialoffice@pen-and-sword.co.uk

https://www.pen-and-sword.co.uk

Types: Nonfiction
Subjects: Antiques; Archaeology; Arts; Autobiography; Crafts; Crime; Gardening; Health; History; Lifestyle; Nature; Photography; Science; Sociology; Sport; Travel; Warfare
Markets: Adult

Send: Query
Don't send: Full text

Publishes across a number of areas including military history, naval and maritime history, aviation, local history, family history, transport, discovery and exploration, collectables and antiques, nostalgia and true crime. In 2017, launched a new lifestyle imprint which publishes books on areas such as health and diet, hobbies and sport, gardening and wildlife and space. Submit proposal using form on website.

Editor: Lisa Hooson

Publishing Imprints: Frontline Books (**P280**); Leo Cooper (*P436*); Pen & Sword Aviation (*P577*); Pen & Sword Maritime (*P579*); Remember When (**P649**); Wharncliffe Books (**P858**); White Owl (*P860*)

P579 Pen & Sword Maritime

Publishing Imprint

Book Publisher: Pen & Sword Books Ltd (**P578**)

P580 Penguin Books

Publishing Imprint
United States

Book Publisher: Penguin Publishing Group (**P585**)

P581 Penguin Classics

Publishing Imprint
United States

Book Publisher: Penguin Publishing Group (**P585**)

P582 Penguin General

Book Publisher

Book Publisher: Penguin Random House UK (**P587**)

P583 Penguin Press

Book Publisher

Book Publisher: Penguin Random House UK (**P587**)

P584 The Penguin Press

Publishing Imprint
United States

Book Publisher: Penguin Publishing Group (**P585**)

P585 Penguin Publishing Group

Book Publisher
United States

Book Publisher: Penguin Group (USA)

Publishing Imprints: Avery (*P066*); Berkley (*P090*); Blue Rider Press (*P111*); DAW (**P200**); Dutton (*P223*); Family Tree Books (*P256*); G.P. Putnam's Sons (*P283*); Impact (**P394**); Interweave (**P403**); Krause Publications (**P429**); North Light Books (*P533*); Penguin Books (*P580*); Penguin Classics (*P581*); The Penguin Press (*P584*); Plume (*P612*); Popular Woodworking Books (**P616**); Portfolio Penguin (*P617*); Riverhead Books (**P655**); Sentinel (*P698*); TarcherPerigee (*P756*); Viking (*P822*); Writer's Digest Books (*P876*)

P586 Penguin Random House Children's

Book Publisher

Book Publisher: Penguin Random House UK (**P587**)

Book Publisher: Puffin (UK) (**P626**)

P587 Penguin Random House UK

Book Publisher
One Embassy Gardens, 8 Viaduct Gardens, London, SW11 7BW, 20 Vauxhall Bridge Road, London, SW1V 2SA
United Kingdom
Tel: +44 (0) 20 7010 3000

https://www.penguin.co.uk
https://www.facebook.com/penguinbooks
https://www.instagram.com/penguinukbooks/
https://twitter.com/PenguinUKBooks
https://www.youtube.com/user/penguinbooks

Book Publisher: Penguin Random House

ADULT
- **Fiction** > *Novels*
- **Nonfiction** > *Nonfiction Books*

CHILDREN'S
- **Fiction**
  - *Chapter Books*; *Early Readers*; *Middle Grade*; *Novels*; *Picture Books*
- **Nonfiction** > *Nonfiction Books*

How to send: Through a literary agent

Publishes a wide range of fiction, nonfiction, poetry, and reference, for children and adults. No queries or unsolicited MSS, other than through a literary agent.

Audio Book Publisher: Penguin Random House UK Audio

Book Publishers: Cornerstone (*P181*); Ebury (**P226**); Michael Joseph (**P495**); Penguin General (*P582*); Penguin Press (*P583*); Penguin Random House Children's (**P586**); Transworld Publishers (**P778**); Vintage (**P827**)

P588 Penguin Random House Verlagsgruppe

Book Publisher
Germany

https://www.penguinrandomhouse.de

Book Publisher: Penguin Random House

Book Publisher: Prestel Publishing Ltd (**P621**)

P589 Penguin Workshop

Publishing Imprint
United States

Book Publisher: Penguin Young Readers Group (**P591**)

P590 Penguin Young Readers

Publishing Imprint
United States

Book Publisher: Penguin Young Readers Group (**P591**)

P591 Penguin Young Readers Group

Book Publisher
United States

https://www.penguin.com/publishers/penguin-young-readers-group/

Book Publisher: Penguin Group (USA)

Publishing Imprints: Dial Books for Young Readers (**P212**); Dutton Children's Books (*P224*); F. Warne & Co. (*P251*); Firebird (*P265*); G.P. Putnam's Sons Books for Young Readers (**P284**); Kathy Dawson Books (**P421**); Kokila (*P427*); Nancy Paulsen Books (*P518*); Penguin Workshop (*P589*); Penguin Young Readers (*P590*); Penguin Young Readers Licenses (*P592*); Philomel (*P602*); Puffin (*P625*); Razorbill (**P645**); Speak (*P727*); Viking Children's Books (*P823*)

P592 Penguin Young Readers Licenses

Publishing Imprint
United States

Book Publisher: Penguin Young Readers Group (**P591**)

P593 Persephone Books

Book Publisher
8 Edgar Buildings, Bath, BA1 2EE

United Kingdom
Tel: +44 (0) 1225 425050

info@persephonebooks.co.uk

https://persephonebooks.co.uk
http://instagram.com/persephonebooks
https://twitter.com/PersephoneBooks

Fiction > *Novels*

Nonfiction > *Nonfiction Books*

Closed to approaches.

Publisher of neglected fiction and nonfiction by mid-twentieth century (mostly) women writers, all in elegant matching grey editions.

P594 Perseus Books

Book Publisher
United States

https://www.perseusbooks.com
https://www.facebook.com/pages/Perseus-Books-Group/108204045874204
https://twitter.com/PerseusBooks
https://www.instagram.com/perseus_books/

Book Publisher: Hachette Book Group (**P316**)

Nonfiction > *Nonfiction Books*

How to send: Through a literary agent

Independent publishing division acquired in 2016.

Publishing Imprints: Avalon Travel (**P065**); Basic Books; Black Dog & Leventhal (*P099*); Counterpoint Press; Da Capo Press; Hachette Books (*P317*); Hachette Go! (*P319*); PublicAffairs (*P624*); Running Press (*P667*); Westview Press

P595 Peter Lang

Book Publisher
John Eccles House, Science Park, Robert Robinson Avenue, Littlemore, OX4 4GP
United Kingdom

Publishing@peterlang.com
info@peterlang.com

https://www.peterlang.com
https://www.facebook.com/pages/Peter-Lang-Oxford/260315267419469
https://twitter.com/peterlangoxford
http://peterlangoxford.wordpress.com/

Book Publisher: Peter Lang Group (**P596**)

ACADEMIC > **Nonfiction** > *Nonfiction Books*
Arts; Communication; Culture; Economics; Education; English; France; Germany; History; Italy; Language; Legal; Management; Media; Philosophy; Politics; Religion; Romania; Science; Slavs; Society; Spain

Send: Query
How to send: Email

Select appropriate editor from website and query by email.

Editor: Na Li

Publishing Director: Lucy Melville

Senior Editors: Tony Mason; Dr Laurel Plapp

P596 Peter Lang Group

Book Publisher
Place de la Gare 12, 1003 Lausanne
Switzerland

https://www.peterlang.com

Book Publisher: Peter Lang (**P595**)

P597 Peter Lang Publishing

Book Publisher
80 Broad St, Fl 5, New York, NY 10004-4145
United States
Tel: +1 (844) 882-0928

editorial@peterlang.com

https://www.peterlang.com
https://www.facebook.com/PeterLangPublishingUSA
https://twitter.com/PeterLangUSA
https://www.instagram.com/peterlangpublishing

ACADEMIC > **Nonfiction** > *Nonfiction Books*
Arts; Communication; Culture; Economics; Education; English; France; Germany; History; Italy; Language; Legal; Management; Media; Philosophy; Politics; Religion; Romania; Science; Slavs; Society; Spain

Send: Query
How to send: Online submission system

International academic publisher. Submit query via web form.

P598 Peter Owen Publishers

Book Publisher
Beech Lawn House, 10 South Entrance, Saxmundham, Suffolk, IP17 1DQ
United Kingdom

info@peterowen.com

https://www.peterowen.com
https://twitter.com/PeterOwenPubs
https://www.facebook.com/peter.owen.publishers
https://www.instagram.com/peterowenpublishing

Fiction > *Novels*
International; Literary

Nonfiction > *Nonfiction Books*

Does not want:

Nonfiction > *Nonfiction Books*
Memoir; Self Help; Spirituality; Sport

Closed to approaches.

Publishes general nonfiction and international literary fiction. No first novels, short stories, poetry, plays, sport, spirituality, self-help, or children's or genre fiction. Accepts query by email only, including cover letter, synopsis, and one or two sample chapters. No submissions by post. Prefers fiction to come from an agent or translator as appropriate.

Editorial Director: Antonia Owen

P599 Peter Pauper Press

Book Publisher
202 Mamaroneck Avenue, White Plains, NY 10601-5376
United States
Tel: +1 (914) 681-0144
Fax: +1 (914) 681-0389

customerservice@peterpauper.com
orders@peterpauper.com

https://www.peterpauper.com
https://www.facebook.com/pages/Peter-Pauper-Press-Inc/137389080124
https://twitter.com/PeterPauperPres
https://pinterest.com/peterpauperpres/

ADULT > **Nonfiction** > *Gift Books*

CHILDREN'S > **Nonfiction** > *Activity Books*

Closed to approaches.

Described as a preeminent gift and stationery publisher.

Editor: Barbara Paulding

P600 Phaidon Press

Book Publisher
United Kingdom

submissions@phaidon.com

https://www.phaidon.com
https://www.instagram.com/phaidonsnaps/
https://twitter.com/Phaidon
https://www.facebook.com/phaidoncom/
https://youtube.com/phaidonpress
https://linkedin.com/company/phaidon-press

ADULT > **Nonfiction** > *Nonfiction Books*
Architecture; Arts; Contemporary; Cookery; Cultural History; Culture; Design; Fashion; Films; Food; Interior Design; Music; Performing Arts; Photography; Travel

CHILDREN'S > **Nonfiction** > *Nonfiction Books*

Send: Outline; Author bio
How to send: Email

Publishes books in the areas of art, architecture, design, photography, film, fashion, contemporary culture, decorative arts, interior design, music, performing arts, cultural history, food, and cookery, travel, and books for children. No fiction or approaches by post. Send query by email only, with CV and short description of the project. Response only if interested.

Publishing Imprint: The Monacelli Press (**P503**)

P601 Phillimore

Publishing Imprint
United Kingdom

https://www.thehistorypress.co.uk

Book Publisher: The History Press (**P373**)

Types: Nonfiction
Subjects: History
Markets: Adult

P602 Philomel

Publishing Imprint
United States

Book Publisher: Penguin Young Readers Group (**P591**)

P603 Piatkus Books

Publishing Imprint
50 Victoria Embankment, London, EC4Y 0DZ
United Kingdom
Tel: +44 (0) 20 3122 7000

enquiries@hachette.co.uk

https://www.littlebrown.co.uk/imprint/piatkus/page/lbbg-imprint-piatkus/
https://business.facebook.com/piatkusfiction/?business_id=873802706096561
https://twitter.com/PiatkusBooks

Publishing Imprint: Little, Brown Book Group

Fiction > *Novels*
Fantasy; Historical Fiction; Popular; Romance; Supernatural / Paranormal; Suspense

Nonfiction > *Nonfiction Books*
Business; Health; Mind, Body, Spirit; Parenting; Personal Development; Popular Psychology; Self Help

How to send: Through a literary agent

No longer accepts unsolicited submissions. Accepts material through a literary agent only.

Fiction Editor: Emma Beswetherick

Nonfiction Editor: Gill Bailey

P604 Piccadilly Press

Book Publisher
80-81 Wimpole Street, London, W1G 9RE
United Kingdom
Tel: +44 (0) 20 7490 3875

hello@bonnierbooks.co.uk

http://www.piccadillypress.co.uk

Types: Fiction; Nonfiction
Subjects: Comedy / Humour; Contemporary
Markets: Children's; Young Adult

How to send: Through a literary agent

No longer accepts unsolicited submissions. Approach through a literary agent.

P605 Pimpernel Press

Book Publisher
22 Marylands Road, London, W9 2DY
United Kingdom
Tel: +44 (0) 7976 047767

info@pimpernelpress.com

http://www.pimpernelpress.com
https://www.facebook.com/pimpernelpress/
https://twitter.com/pimpernelpress
https://www.pinterest.co.uk/pimpernelpress/

Nonfiction > *Nonfiction Books*
Arts; Design; Gardening; Houses

Publishes books on art, design, houses, and gardens.

P606 Pimsleur

Publishing Imprint

Audio Book Publisher: Simon & Schuster Audio Publishing

P607 Pinata Books

Publishing Imprint
Arte Publico Press, University of Houston, 4902 Gulf Fwy, Bldg 19, Rm100, Houston, TX 77204-2004
United States
Fax: +1 (713) 743-2847

submapp@uh.edu

https://artepublicopress.com/pinata-books/

Book Publisher: Arte Publico Press (**P051**)

CHILDREN'S > **Fiction** > *Novels*
Central America; Culture; South America

YOUNG ADULT > **Fiction** > *Novels*
Central America; Culture; South America

Send: Query; Synopsis; Writing sample
How to send: Online submission system

Publishes children's and young adult literature that authentically and realistically portrays themes, characters, and customs unique to US Hispanic culture. Submit via form on website.

P608 Pineapple Press

Publishing Imprint
246 Goose Lane, 2nd Floor, Guilford, CT 06437
United States

http://pineapplepress.com
https://www.facebook.com/PineapplePress/

Book Publisher: The Globe Pequot Press (**P296**)

ADULT
Fiction > *Novels*
Florida; Folklore, Myths, and Legends

Nonfiction
Nonfiction Books: Animals; Arts; Florida; Gardening; History; Nature; Travel
Reference: Florida

CHILDREN'S
Fiction > *Novels*: Florida

Nonfiction > *Nonfiction Books*: Florida

Send: Query; Outline; Table of Contents; Writing sample; Author bio; Market info
How to send: Email; Post

Publishes quality books that educate and entertain while making the real Florida accessible to readers nationwide. Topics include gardening, nature, art, folklore, history, travel, and children's books and fiction that feature the sunshine state.

Editor: June Cussen

P609 Platypus Media

Book Publisher
725 8th Street, SE, Washington DC 20003
United States
Tel: +1 (202) 546-1674

info@platypusmedia.com
submissions@platypusmedia.com

https://www.platypusmedia.com
https://www.facebook.com/PlatypusMedia/
https://twitter.com/PlatypusMedia

ADULT > **Nonfiction** > *Nonfiction Books*
Family; Parenting

CHILDREN'S > **Nonfiction** > *Nonfiction Books*
Animals; Family

PROFESSIONAL > **Nonfiction** > *Nonfiction Books*
Education; Family

Send: Query; Author bio; Writing sample; Full text; Market info; Self-Addressed Stamped Envelope (SASE)
How to send: Post
How not to send: Email

Publishes books focusing on the family and child development, including fiction and nonfiction for children, and parenting guides for adults. Send material with SASE for response.

P610 Plexus Publishing Limited

Book Publisher
26 Dafforne Road, London, SW17 8TZ
United Kingdom

plexus@plexusuk.demon.co.uk

http://www.plexusbooks.com

Types: Nonfiction
Formats: Film Scripts
Subjects: Biography; Culture; Music
Markets: Adult

Publishes illustrated nonfiction books specialising in biography, popular culture, movies and music.

P611 Plexus Publishing, Inc.

Book Publisher
143 Old Marlton Pike, Medford, NJ 08055
United States
Tel: +1 (609) 654-6500, ext. 330
Fax: +1 (609) 654-6760

info@plexuspublishing.com
rcolding@plexuspublishing.com

https://www.plexuspublishing.com

ACADEMIC > **Nonfiction** > *Nonfiction Books*
Biology; Environment; Medicine

ADULT
Fiction > *Novels*: New Jersey

Nonfiction > *Nonfiction Books*
Biology; Environment; History; Medicine; Nature; New Jersey; Travel

Send: Query; Synopsis; Table of Contents; Market info; Marketing Plan; Author bio; Writing sample; Proposal
How to send: Post

In addition to being a regional book publisher, publishes practical, popular, and scholarly titles in the fields of biology, ecology, and clinical research. New Jersey regional book program encompasses numerous topics and genres including history, nature and the environment, and travel/tourism. Publishes a limited amount of fiction, including original novels and new editions of worthy out-of-print works with regional appeal.

Editor-in-Chief: John Bryans

P612 Plume

Publishing Imprint
United States

Book Publisher: Penguin Publishing Group **(P585)**

P613 Pocket Mountains

Book Publisher
The Old Church, Annanside, Moffat, DG10 9HB
United Kingdom
Tel: +44 (0) 1683 221641

robbie@pocketmountains.com

https://pocketmountains.com
https://www.facebook.com/Pocket-Mountains-Ltd-107054847745288/
https://twitter.com/pocketmountains
https://www.instagram.com/pocketmountainsltd/

Nonfiction > *Nonfiction Books*
Adventure; Cycling; Nature; Running; Walking Guides

Publishes accessible and inspiring pocket-sized guidebooks for anyone who likes a bit of an adventure, including cycling, easy walking, wildlife and running guides to various parts of Scotland, England and Wales.

Editors: Robbie Porteous; April Simmons

P614 Policy Press

Publishing Imprint

Book Publisher: Bristol University Press **(P127)**

P615 Pop Press

Publishing Imprint
United Kingdom

Book Publisher: Ebury **(P226)**

P616 Popular Woodworking Books

Publishing Imprint
United States

Book Publisher: Penguin Publishing Group **(P585)**

Types: Nonfiction
Subjects: Crafts; Hobbies
Markets: Adult

Publishes books for woodwork enthusiasts.

P617 Portfolio Penguin

Publishing Imprint
United States

Book Publisher: Penguin Publishing Group **(P585)**

P618 Portico

Publishing Imprint

Book Publisher: Pavilion Books **(P572)**

P619 Praeger

Publishing Imprint
United States

Book Publisher: ABC-CLIO **(P014)**

P620 Press 53

Book Publisher
560 N. Trade Street, Suite 103, Winston-Salem, NC 27101
United States
Tel: +1 (336) 770-5353

editor@press53.com

https://www.press53.com

Fiction > *Short Fiction Collections*

Poetry > *Poetry Collections*

Publishes collections of poetry and short stories by US-based authors. No novels or book length fiction. Finds authors through its competitions, and through writers being active in the literary community and literary magazines.

Editor: Kevin Morgan Watson

P621 Prestel Publishing Ltd

Book Publisher
16-18 Berners Street, London, W1T 3LN
United Kingdom
Tel: +44 (0) 20 7323 5004

sales@prestel-uk.co.uk

https://prestelpublishing.penguinrandomhouse.de

Book Publisher: Penguin Random House Verlagsgruppe **(P588)**

Nonfiction > *Nonfiction Books*
Architecture; Arts; Design; Photography

Send: Proposal
How to send: Email

One of the world's leading publishers in the fields of art, architecture, photography and design. The company has its headquarters in Munich, offices in New York and London, and an international sales network.

P622 Prometheus

Publishing Imprint
United States

Book Publisher: The Globe Pequot Press **(P296)**

P623 Prufrock Press

Publishing Imprint
United States

https://www.routledge.com/go/prufrock-press

Book Publisher: Routledge **(P665)**

ACADEMIC > **Nonfiction** > *Nonfiction Books*
Arts; Language; Mathematics; Science; Society

CHILDREN'S > **Nonfiction** > *Nonfiction Books*

PROFESSIONAL > **Nonfiction** > *Nonfiction Books*
Arts; Education; Language; Mathematics; Science; Society

Publisher of professional learning resources, gifted child identification instruments, and curricula designed for gifted students, advanced learners, and twice-exceptional children. Comprehensive line of more than 500 titles across the areas of Language Arts, Math, Science, Social Studies, Children's Nonfiction, and more, Offers teachers and parents exciting, research-based resources for helping gifted, advanced, and special needs learners succeed.

Acquisitions Editors: Larry Elwood; Jennifer Robins

Editor: Misha Kydd

Publisher: Joel McIntosh

P624 PublicAffairs

Publishing Imprint
United States

Book Publisher: Perseus Books (**P594**)

P625 Puffin

Publishing Imprint
United States

Book Publisher: Penguin Young Readers Group (**P591**)

P626 Puffin (UK)

Book Publisher
United Kingdom

https://www.penguin.co.uk/brands/puffin.html

Book Publisher: Penguin Random House Children's (**P586**)

CHILDREN'S
Fiction
Chapter Books; *Middle Grade*; *Novels*; *Picture Books*
Nonfiction > *Nonfiction Books*

Publishing Imprint: Tamarind Books (**P754**)

P627 Pulp! The Classics

Publishing Imprint
United Kingdom

Book Publisher: Oldcastle Books Group (**P544**)

P628 Purdue University Press

Book Publisher
504 West State Street, West Lafayette, IN 47907-2058
United States

pupress@purdue.edu

http://www.thepress.purdue.edu

ACADEMIC > **Nonfiction** > *Nonfiction Books*
Agriculture; Anthropology; Business; Education; Engineering; Health; History; Indiana; Judaism; Language; Leadership; Literature; Philosophy; Politics; Science; Technology

PROFESSIONAL > **Nonfiction** > *Nonfiction Books*
Agriculture; Business; Education; Engineering; Health; Leadership; Science; Technology

Send: Query; Author bio; Table of Contents; Proposal; Writing sample

Publishes scholarly and professional information. Welcomes proposals in its core subjects, which should be emailed to the Director.

Editorial Director: Justine Race

Managing Editor: Margaret Hunt

Publishing Imprint: PuP

P629 PUSH

Publishing Imprint

Book Publisher: Scholastic (**P688**)

P630 QED Publishing

Publishing Imprint
The Old Brewery, 6 Blundell Street, London, N7 9BH
United Kingdom
Tel: +44 (0) 20 7812 8633

QuartoHomesSubmissions@Quarto.com

https://www.quartoknows.com/QED-Publishing

Book Publisher: The Quarto Group, Inc. (**P633**)

CHILDREN'S
Fiction > *Picture Books*
Nonfiction > *Illustrated Books*

Send: Query; Proposal
How to send: Email

Publishes fresh, informative, high-quality books that will appeal to children, parents and teachers alike, from entertaining, innovative facts for the classroom to beautifully illustrated fiction that kids will want to take home. Always on the lookout for authors and artists with creative ideas that enhance and broaden their publishing list of children's books.

Publisher: Steve Evans

P631 Quarry

Publishing Imprint

Book Publisher: The Quarto Group, Inc. (**P633**)

P632 Quarto Children's Books

Publishing Imprint

Book Publisher: The Quarto Group, Inc. (**P633**)

P633 The Quarto Group, Inc.

Book Publisher
The Old Brewery, 6 Blundell Street, London, N7 9BH
United Kingdom
Tel: +44 (0) 20 7700 6700
Fax: +44 (0) 20 7700 8066

http://www.quarto.com

ADULT > **Nonfiction** > *Nonfiction Books*

CHILDREN'S > **Nonfiction** > *Nonfiction Books*

Publisher of illustrated nonfiction books for adults and children.

Publishing Imprints: Apple Press; Aurum Press; Book Sales (*P118*); Bright Press (*P126*); Burgess Lea Press (*P131*); Cool Springs Press (*P179*); Epic Ink (*P242*); Fair Winds Press (*P253*); Frances Lincoln; Frances Lincoln Children's Books (**P277**); Harvard Common Press (**P357**); Iqon Editions (*P404*); Ivy Kids (*P406*); Ivy Press (*P407*); Jacqui Small; Leaping Hare Press (*P435*); Lincoln First Editions (*P445*); Motorbooks (*P508*); QED Publishing (**P630**); Quarry (*P631*); Quarto Children's Books (*P632*); Quarto Publishing (*P634*); Race Point Publishing (*P638*); Rock Point Gift & Stationery (*P657*); Rockport Publishing (*P659*); SmartLab Toys (*P717*); Union Books; Voyageur Press (**P834**); Walter Foster Jr. (*P838*); Walter Foster Publishing (**P839**); Wellfleet Press (*P852*); White Lion Publishing (*P859*); Wide-Eyed Editions; Words & Pictures (**P873**); becker&mayer! books (**P087**); becker&mayer! kids (*P088*); small world creations (*P716*)

P634 Quarto Publishing

Publishing Imprint

Book Publisher: The Quarto Group, Inc. (**P633**)

P635 Quercus Children's Books

Publishing Imprint

Book Publisher: Hachette Children's Group (**P318**)

P636 Quiller Publishing Ltd

Book Publisher
The Hill, Merrywalks, Stroud, GL5 4EP
United Kingdom
Tel: +44 (0) 1939 261616

info@quillerbooks.com

https://www.quillerpublishing.com
https://www.facebook.com/QuillerPublishing
https://twitter.com/QuillerBooks
https://www.pinterest.co.uk/QuillerPublishing/
https://instagram.com/quillerpublishing/

Nonfiction > *Nonfiction Books*
Archery; Arts; Biography; Canoeing; Climbing; Country Lifestyle; Crafts; Deer; Dogs; Environment; Equestrian; Falconry; Farming; Fishing; Food and Drink; History; Shooting

Send: Proposal; Synopsis; Writing sample; Table of Contents; Market info; Author bio; Self-Addressed Stamped Envelope (SASE)
How to send: Email; Post

Publishes books for all lovers of fishing, shooting, equestrian and country pursuits. Accepts unsolicited MSS from authors. Send submissions as hard copy only, with email address for reply or SAE if return of ms is required. Proposals may be sent by email.

Editor: Andrew Johnston

Publishing Imprints: The Sportsman's Press; Kenilworth Press (**P423**); Quiller Press; Swan Hill Press

P637 R D Publishers

Book Publisher
Robert D. Reed Publishers, POB 1992, Bandon, OR 97411,
United States
Tel: +1 (541) 347-9882
Fax: +1 (531) 347-9883

4bobreed@msn.com

https://rdrpublishers.com

Types: Fiction; Nonfiction; Scripts
Formats: Film Scripts; TV Scripts
Subjects: Arts; Comedy / Humour; Commercial; Drama; Entertainment; Fantasy; Lifestyle; Media; Psychology; Romance; Science; Science Fiction
Markets: Adult; Children's; Young Adult

Closed to approaches.

This company is looking for developing authors with a drive and the talent to submit ready manuscripts in for film, television, and print publication. They have a proven track record of success and are willing to work with the right author who has the right ideas for a saleable market.

Authors: Arun Gandhi; Daniel Quinn; Bernie Siegel

P638 Race Point Publishing

Publishing Imprint

Book Publisher: The Quarto Group, Inc. (**P633**)

P639 Rand McNally

Book Publisher
United States
Tel: +1 (877) 446-4863

tndsupport@randmcnally.com

https://www.randmcnally.com
https://www.randmcnally.com/publishing

ADULT > **Nonfiction**
Activity Books: Travel
Reference: Road Atlases; Travel
CHILDREN'S > **Nonfiction** > *Activity Books*: Travel

Publishes road atlases and activity books for adults and children, focusing on travel.

P640 Random House

Book Publisher
United States

http://www.randomhousebooks.com

Book Publisher: Penguin Random House

Fiction > *Novels*

Nonfiction > *Nonfiction Books*

How to send: Through a literary agent

Accepts queries through agents only – does not deal direct with aspiring writers.

Book Publishers: Bantam Doubleday Dell Books for Young Readers; Knopf Publishing Group

Publishing Imprints: 4 Color Books (**P003**); Alibi; Ballantine (*P074*); Bantam (**P076**); Broadway Books; Clarkson Potter (**P169**); Convergent Books (*P178*); Crown; Crown Archetype (*P189*); Crown Forum (*P190*); Currency; Del Rey (*P206*); Del Rey/LucasBooks (*P207*); Delacorte Press; The Dial Press (*P213*); Harmony Books (*P328*); Hogarth (*P375*); Image Books (*P390*); Lorena Jones Books (*P458*); Loveswept; Modern Library (*P502*); One World (*P549*); Random House (Imprint) (*P641*); Rodale Books (*P661*); Three Rivers Press; Tim Duggan Books; WaterBrook Multnomah (*P841*); Watson-Guptill (*P842*)

P641 Random House (Imprint)

Publishing Imprint

Book Publisher: Random House (**P640**)

P642 Ransom Note Press

Book Publisher
United States

editorial@ransomnotepress.com

http://www.ransomnotepress.com

Fiction > *Novels*
Mystery; Suspense

Send: Query; Synopsis; Author bio; Writing sample
Don't send: Full text
How to send: In the body of an email
How not to send: Email attachment; Post

Publishes mystery and suspense novels only. Accepts approaches via email only. See website for full submission guidelines.

P643 Ransom Publishing Ltd

Book Publisher
Unit 7, Brocklands Farm, West Meon, Hampshire, GU32 1JN
United Kingdom
Tel: +44 (0) 1730 829091

steve@ransom.co.uk

http://www.ransom.co.uk

Types: Fiction; Nonfiction
Markets: Adult; Children's; Professional; Young Adult

Closed to approaches.

An independent specialist publisher of high quality, inspirational books that encourage and help children, young adults, and adults to develop their reading skills. Books are intended to have content which is age appropriate and engaging, but reading levels that would normally be appropriate for younger readers. Also publishes resources for both the library and classroom. No picture books or early years books. Will consider unsolicited mss. Email with synopsis and sample (up to three chapters) in first instance, or full ms if under thousand words.

Editor: Steve Rickard

P644 Ravenstone

Publishing Imprint
Canada

info@turnstonepress.com

https://www.turnstonepress.com/books/ravenstone.html
https://www.facebook.com/turnstone.press.3
https://twitter.com/turnstonepress
http://www.pinterest.com/turnstonepress/
https://www.instagram.com/turnstone_press/
https://www.youtube.com/user/TurnstonePress
http://www.goodreads.com/user/show/16275125-turnstone-press

Book Publisher: Turnstone Press (**P783**)

Fiction > *Novels*
Mystery; Noir; Thrillers

Send: Full text
How to send: Online submission system

Publishes literary mysteries, thrillers, noir, speculative fiction, and urban fantasy.

P645 Razorbill

Publishing Imprint
345 Hudson Street, New York, NY 10014
United States

http://www.razorbillbooks.com

Book Publisher: Penguin Young Readers Group (**P591**)

Types: Fiction; Nonfiction
Subjects: Adventure; Comedy / Humour; Contemporary; Culture; Fantasy; Literary; Romance; Science Fiction; Suspense
Markets: Children's; Young Adult

Send: Query
Don't send: Full text

Publishes mainly fiction for middle grade and young adult. Send query with SASE, outline, target group, publishing credits (if any), and up to 30 pages. No picture books. Response only if interested.

P646 REaDLips Press

Book Publisher
United States

readlipspress@gmail.com

https://readlipspress.com

Types: Fiction
Subjects: Literary
Markets: Adult

Send: Query
Don't send: Full text

Publishes literary fiction novellas between 20,000 and 60,000 words. Send blurb, bio, and summary by email. See website for full guidelines.

P647 Red Squirrel Publishing

Book Publisher
Suite 235, 15 Ingestre Place, London, W1F 0DU
United Kingdom

https://www.redsquirrelbooks.com

Nonfiction > *Nonfiction Books*
Culture; Society; United Kingdom

Publishes books aimed at helping people pass the British Citizenship test. No fiction, poetry, or children's.

Managing Director: Henry Dillon

P648 Regency House Publishing Limited

Book Publisher
The Manor House, High Street, Buntingford, Hertfordshire, SG9 9AB
United Kingdom

https://beta.companieshouse.gov.uk/company/02673368

Nonfiction > *Nonfiction Books*

Publishes and packages mass-market nonfiction. Does not accept fiction or unsolicited MSS.

Chair: Brian Trodd

Managing Director: Nicolette Trodd

P649 Remember When

Publishing Imprint
47 Church Street, Barnsley, South Yorkshire, S70 2AS
United Kingdom
Tel: +44 (0) 1226 734222
Fax: +44 (0) 1226 734438

editorialoffice@pen-and-sword.co.uk
enquiries@pen-and-sword.co.uk

https://www.pen-and-sword.co.uk
https://www.pen-and-sword.co.uk/Remember-When/i/6

Book Publisher: Pen & Sword Books Ltd (**P578**)

Nonfiction > *Nonfiction Books*
Antiques; History; Nostalgia

Send: Synopsis; Market info; Author bio
How to send: Online submission system

Publishes books on nostalgia and antique collecting. Submit proposals via online submission system. See website.

Editor: Fiona Shoop

P650 RFF Press

Book Publisher
1616 P St. NW, Suite 600, Washington, DC 20036
United States
Tel: +1 (202) 328-5000
Fax: +1 (202) 939-3460

info@rff.org

https://www.rff.org

ACADEMIC > **Nonfiction** > *Nonfiction Books*: Environment

ADULT > **Nonfiction** > *Nonfiction Books*: Environment

PROFESSIONAL > **Nonfiction** > *Nonfiction Books*: Environment

Publishes books about important issues in environmental and natural resource policy.

P651 Richard Hollis

Publishing Imprint

Book Publisher: Five Leaves Publications (**P269**)

P652 Richards Publishing

Publishing Imprint
United Kingdom

Book Publisher: Brewin Books Ltd (**P124**)

P653 Rider Books

Publishing Imprint
United Kingdom

Book Publisher: Ebury (**P226**)

P654 Rising Stars

Book Publisher
Carmelite House, 50 Victoria Embankment, London, EC4Y 0DZ
United Kingdom
Tel: +44 (0) 20 3122 6000

primary@hachette.co.uk

https://www.risingstars-uk.com
https://www.youtube.com/channel/UCTO7hZc1TrfzBKFEo4i8qkQ
https://twitter.com/risingstarsedu
https://www.facebook.com/Rising-Stars-547479242046479/timeline/
https://www.instagram.com/risingstarsedu

Book Publisher: Hodder Education

ACADEMIC > **Nonfiction** > *Nonfiction Books*: Education

Send: Query
How to send: Online submission system

Publisher of educational books and software for children aged 3-18. Always looking for people bursting with ideas and imagination and a view of primary education. Complete survey online in first instance.

Publishing Director: Ben Barton

P655 Riverhead Books

Publishing Imprint
United States

Book Publisher: Penguin Publishing Group (**P585**)

Types: Fiction; Nonfiction
Subjects: Commercial; Contemporary; Literary
Markets: Adult

Publisher of bestselling literary fiction and quality nonfiction.

Editor: Megan Lynch

P656 Robert D. Reed Publishers

Book Publisher
POB 1992, Bandon, OR 97411
United States
Tel: +1 (541) 347-9882

cleonelreed@gmail.com

https://rdrpublishers.com

Nonfiction > *Nonfiction Books*
Autism; Business; Children; Comedy / Humour; Education; Finance; Fitness; Health; History; Leadership; Memoir; Parenting; Poetry as a Subject; Psychology; Self Help; Spirituality

Closed to approaches.

Publishes nonfiction by authors with a platform to sell their books. Manuscripts must have been professionally edited. Send query through contact form on website. No longer publishes fiction.

P657 Rock Point Gift & Stationery

Publishing Imprint

Book Publisher: The Quarto Group, Inc. (**P633**)

P658 Rocket Science Press

Publishing Imprint

Book Publisher: Shipwreckt Books Publishing Company (**P705**)

P659 Rockport Publishing

Publishing Imprint

Book Publisher: The Quarto Group, Inc. (**P633**)

P660 Rocky Nook

Book Publisher
1010 B Street, Ste 350, San Rafael, CA 94901
United States

editorial@rockynook.com
info@rockynook.com

https://rockynook.com
https://www.facebook.com/rockynookinc/
https://rockynook.com/wp-content/uploads/

2017/05/tw-rn.png
https://www.instagram.com/rocky_nook/

Nonfiction > *Nonfiction Books*
Crafts; Drawing; Graphic Design; Painting; Photography

Send: Author bio; Query; Outline; Writing sample; Market info
How to send: Email

A small, independent publishing company with the goal of helping photographers of all levels improve their skills in capturing those moments that matter. Creates books that help you master the technology, find inspiration, and hone your craft in order to create better pictures. Also now publishing books on drawing, painting, graphic design, crafts, and much more.

P661 Rodale Books

Publishing Imprint

Book Publisher: Random House (**P640**)

P662 Romance Publications

Book Publisher
United States

romancepublications@gmail.com

https://www.facebook.com/romance.publications/

Fiction
Novelette: Romance
Novellas: Romance
Novels: Romance
Short Fiction: Romance

How to send: Email

Publishes romantic stories that include a central love story and emotionally satisfying and optimistic ending. In addition to novels, we publish novellas, novelettes, and short stories. We are currently accepting short stores (450-550) words to be published in our monthly newsletters and anthologies of short stories. Anthologies will be sold for a profit, and the authors will receive a portion of the royalties that is typically given to a single author, which is 25%.

P663 Rose and Crown Books

Publishing Imprint
United Kingdom

submissions@sunpenny.com

https://www.sunpenny.com/imprints

Book Publisher: Sunpenny Publishing (**P748**)

Fiction > *Novels*
Christian Romance; Inspirational

Send: Author bio; Marketing Plan; Synopsis; Full text
How to send: Email
How not to send: Post

We were the first publishers in the UK to start publishing Christian / Inspirational Romance as a genre. Later, others followed, but we were proud to be the first.

P664 Round Hall

Publishing Imprint; Magazine Publisher
12/13 Exchange Place, International Financial Services Centre, Dublin 1
Ireland

https://www.sweetandmaxwell.co.uk/roundhall/

Book Publisher: Thomson Reuters

PROFESSIONAL > **Nonfiction**
Articles: Legal
Nonfiction Books: Legal

Send: Query
How to send: Email

Publishes information on Irish law in the form of books, journals, periodicals, looseleaf services, CD-ROMs and online services. Contact by email.

Company Director: Martin McCann

Editors: Pamela Moran

P665 Routledge

Book Publisher
United Kingdom

https://www.routledge.com

Book Publisher: Taylor & Francis Group (**P757**)

Types: Nonfiction
Subjects: Anthropology; Archaeology; Architecture; Business; Crime; Finance; Health; Legal; Nature; Politics; Psychology; Science; Technology
Markets: Academic; Adult; Professional

Send: Query
Don't send: Full text

International academic imprint. Send proposal with sample chapters and author CV (see website for detailed guidelines). No fiction, poetry, travel, or astrology.

Book Publisher: David Fulton (Publishers) Ltd

Editor: Misha Kydd

Publishing Imprint: Prufrock Press (**P623**)

P666 Ruby Fiction

Publishing Imprint
Penrose House, Crawley Drive, Camberley, Surrey, GU15 2AB
United Kingdom

info@rubyfiction.com
submissions@rubyfiction.com

https://www.rubyfiction.com
https://twitter.com/rubyfiction
https://www.facebook.com/pages/RubyFiction

Book Publisher: Choc Lit (**P161**)

Fiction > *Novels*
Romance; Thrillers; Women's Fiction

Send: Author bio; Synopsis
How to send: Online submission system

Publishes thrillers, women's fiction and romances without the hero's point of view, between 60,000 and 100,000 words, suitable for a female adult audience.

P667 Running Press

Publishing Imprint
United States

Book Publisher: Perseus Books (**P594**)

P668 Rutgers University Press

Book Publisher
106 Somerset St., 3rd Floor, New Brunswick, NJ 08901
United States

https://www.rutgersuniversitypress.org
https://www.pinterest.com/rutgersuniv0180/
http://www.facebook.com/pages/Rutgers-University-Press/212072346925
https://www.instagram.com/RutgersUPress/
https://twitter.com/RutgersUPress
https://www.youtube.com/user/RutgersUPress

ACADEMIC > **Nonfiction**
Nonfiction Books: General, and in particular: 18th Century; African American; Anthropology; Architecture; Arts; Asia; Asian American; Biography; Business; Caribbean; Comic Books; Crime; Culture; Environment; Ethnic Groups; Films; Food; Gardening; Gender; Health; History; Judaism; LGBTQIA; Leadership; Legal; Leisure; Literature; Management; Media; Medicine; Memoir; Middle East; Military History; Music; Nature; New Jersey; New York City; New York State; Philosophy; Politics; Regional; Religion; Science; Social Issues; Sociology; South America; Sport; Travel; United States; Urban; Women's Studies
Reference: General

Send: Outline; Table of Contents; Writing sample; Market info; Author bio
How to send: Post; Email

Publishes scholarly books, regional, social sciences and humanities. No original fiction or poetry. See website for full submission guidelines and individual editor contacts.

P669 RYA (Royal Yachting Association)

Book Publisher
RYA House, Ensign Way, Hamble, Southampton, Hampshire, SO31 4YA
United Kingdom
Tel: +44 (0) 23 8060 4100

reception@rya.org.uk

https://www.rya.org.uk/

Nonfiction > *Nonfiction Books*
Boats; Sailing; Yachts

Publisher of books on boating and sailing.

Editor: Phil Williams-Ellis

P670 Ryland Peters & Small and CICO Books

Book Publisher
United Kingdom

enquiries@rps.co.uk

https://rylandpeters.com
https://www.facebook.com/RylandPetersandSmall
https://twitter.com/rylandpeters
https://www.pinterest.co.uk/rpscicobooks/
https://www.instagram.com/rylandpetersandsmall/
https://www.youtube.com/channel/UC-zcYDB1m8QxPJhWhRmytjA

ADULT > **Nonfiction** > *Illustrated Books*
Comedy / Humour; Crafts; Food and Drink; Health; Interior Design; Mind, Body, Spirit; Popular Culture

CHILDREN'S > **Nonfiction** > *Illustrated Books*
Crafts; Gardening; Science

Send: Query; Synopsis; Table of Contents; Author bio; Writing sample
How to send: Email

Independent, illustrated publisher creating books in the areas of interior design, food and drink, craft, mindfulness and spirituality, health, humour and pop culture. Also produces gifts and stationery, as well as books for kids.

Book Publisher: Cico Books

Managing Director: David Peters

Publishing Director: Alison Starling

P671 Safari Press

Book Publisher
15621 Chemical Lane, Huntington Beach, CA 92649
United States

info@safaripress.com

https://www.safaripress.com
https://www.facebook.com/SafariPress

Nonfiction > *Nonfiction Books*
Firearms; Hunting

Publisher of big-game hunting, wingshooting, and sporting-firearms books.

Editor: Jacqueline Neufeld

P672 Safer Society Press

Book Publisher
PO Box 340, Brandon, VT 05733-0340
United States
Tel: +1 (802) 247-3132
Fax: +1 (802) 247-4233

davidprescott@safersociety.org

https://safersocietypress.org
http://twitter.com/@SaferSocietyFI
https://www.facebook.com/safersocietyfoundation/timeline
https://www.pinterest.com/safersociety/

PROFESSIONAL > **Nonfiction** > *Nonfiction Books*
Health; Mental Health; Psychiatry

Send: Query; Outline; Author bio; Market info
Don't send: Full text
How to send: Email

Publishes books and other resources for professionals who treat, educate, supervise, and provide social services to children and adolescents whose life circumstances place them at risk of poor social, emotional, and physical health, cognitive difficulties, and problematic behaviors throughout their lives.

Editorial Director: Gaen Murphree

P673 Saga Press

Publishing Imprint

Book Publisher: Simon & Schuster Children's Publishing (**P713**)

P674 Sage Publications

Book Publisher; Magazine Publisher
1 Oliver's Yard, 55 City Road, London, EC1Y 1SP
United Kingdom
Tel: +44 (0) 20 7324 8500
Fax: +44 (0) 20 7324 8600

info@sagepub.co.uk

https://uk.sagepub.com

Types: Nonfiction
Subjects: Anthropology; Archaeology; Arts; Business; Crime; Finance; Health; History; Media; Medicine; Politics; Psychology; Religion; Science; Sociology; Technology
Markets: Academic; Professional

Publishes academic books and journals. See website for guides for authors and making submissions, etc.

Book Publisher: CQ Press

Magazine: Feminist Review (**M193**)

P675 Saint Andrew Press

Publishing Imprint
Norwich Books and Music, 13a Hellesdon Park Road, Norwich, NR6 5DR
United Kingdom
Tel: +44 (0) 1603 785925
Fax: +44 (0) 1603 785915

admin@norwichbooksandmusic.co.uk

https://standrewpress.hymnsam.co.uk

Book Publisher: Hymns Ancient & Modern Ltd

Types: Nonfiction
Formats: Reference
Subjects: Religion
Markets: Adult; Children's

Send: Query
Don't send: Full text

Publisher of religious books for the UK and international Christian retail and trade markets, including general reference and children's books. See website for full submission guidelines.

P676 Salaam Reads

Publishing Imprint

Book Publisher: Simon & Schuster Children's Publishing (**P713**)

P677 Salo Press

Book Publisher
United Kingdom

editorsalopress@gmail.com

https://salopress.weebly.com

Types: Poetry
Subjects: Experimental; Literary
Markets: Adult

An independent micro publisher focusing on poetry of an experimental / weird / surreal / cerebral nature. See website for current submission opportunities.

Editor: Sophie Essex

P678 Salt Publishing

Book Publisher
12 Norwich Road, CROMER, Norfolk, NR27 0AX
United Kingdom

submissions@saltpublishing.com

https://www.saltpublishing.com
https://twitter.com/saltpublishing
https://www.facebook.com/SaltPublishing
https://instagram.com/saltpublishing/

Fiction
Novels: Contemporary
Short Fiction Collections: General

Poetry > *Poetry Collections*

How to send: Word file email attachment

Publishes contemporary novels and collections of poetry and short stories, by British and Irish authors. Prefers to work with writers living in the British Isles. See website for full guidelines.

P679 Samosir Books

Book Publisher
United Kingdom

https://samosirbooksltd.blogspot.com

Types: Nonfiction
Subjects: Adventure; Comedy / Humour;

Culture; Travel
Markets: Adult

Dedicated to publishing and distributing travel related literature worldwide.

Authors: Chris Raven; Simon Raven

P680 Sandstone Press Ltd

Book Publisher
Suite 1, Willow House, Stoneyfield Business Park, Inverness, IV2 7PA
United Kingdom
Tel: +44 (0) 1349 865484

submissions@sandstonepress.com
info@sandstonepress.com

https://sandstonepress.com
https://www.youtube.com/channel/UC_36jtKtY2dy8roy5jQMQHg
https://www.facebook.com/SandstonePress
https://twitter.com/sandstonepress

Fiction > *Novels*

Nonfiction > *Nonfiction Books*

Send: Query; Submission Form; Synopsis; Writing sample
How to send: Word file email attachment; Through a literary agent

Accepts submissions of nonfiction from agents and authors all year. Accepts submissions of fiction from agents all year, but accepts submissions of fiction from authors during specific windows only. Check website for status regarding fiction submissions from authors. Accepts approaches via email only. See website for full guidelines.

P681 Saqi Books

Book Publisher
26 Westbourne Grove, London, W2 5RH
United Kingdom
Tel: +44 (0) 20 7221 9347
Fax: +44 (0) 20 7229 7492

submissions@saqibooks.com

https://saqibooks.com
http://www.twitter.com/SaqiBooks
https://www.facebook.com/SaqiBooks/
https://www.youtube.com/channel/UCqvwvEp1N5rHauJEmmXq16g
http://instagram.com/saqibooks

ACADEMIC > **Nonfiction** > *Nonfiction Books*
Middle East; North Africa

ADULT > **Nonfiction** > *Nonfiction Books*
Middle East; North Africa

Send: Query; Synopsis; Table of Contents; Writing sample; Author bio; Market info
How to send: Email

Publisher of books related to the Arab world and the Middle East. See website for full submission guidelines.

Publishing Imprint: Telegram Books (**P759**)

P682 SAS Press

Book Publisher
SAS Campus Drive, Cary, NC 27513-2414
United States
Tel: +1 (919) 677-8000
Fax: +1 (919) 677-4444

https://support.sas.com/en/books/publish.html

ACADEMIC > **Nonfiction** > *Nonfiction Books*
Data and Information Systems; Leadership; Software

ADULT > **Nonfiction** > *Nonfiction Books*
Data and Information Systems; Leadership; Software

PROFESSIONAL > **Nonfiction** > *Nonfiction Books*
Data and Information Systems; Leadership; Software

How to send: Online submission system

Publishes books on the use of and programming for the software of the parent company only, and its application in solving real-world, business, and academic challenges.

Editor-in-Chief: Julie M. Platt

P683 Sasquatch Books

Book Publisher
1904 Third Avenue, Suite 710, Seattle, Washington 98101
United States

custserve@sasquatchbooks.com

https://sasquatchbooks.com
https://www.facebook.com/SasquatchBooksSeattle/
https://twitter.com/sasquatchbooks
https://www.instagram.com/sasquatchbooks/

Nonfiction > *Nonfiction Books*
Arts; Business; Family; Food; Gardening; Literature; Nature; Politics; Wine

Closed to approaches.

Publishes books by the most gifted writers, artists, chefs, naturalists, and thought leaders in the Pacific Northwest and on the West Coast, and brings their talents to a national audience.

Publishing Imprints: Little Bigfoot (**P448**); Spruce Books (*P730*)

P684 Schiffer Kids

Publishing Imprint
4880 Lower Valley Road, Atglen, PA 19310
United States
Tel: +1 (610) 593-1777
Fax: +1 (610) 593-2002

proposals@schifferbooks.com

https://www.schiffer-kids.com
https://www.facebook.com/schifferkids/
https://twitter.com/schifferkids
https://www.instagram.com/schifferkids/

Book Publisher: Schiffer Publishing (**P686**)

CHILDREN'S
Fiction
Activity Books; *Board Books*; *Early Readers*; *Graphic Novels*; *Middle Grade*; *Picture Books*
Nonfiction
Activity Books; *Board Books*; *Early Readers*; *Middle Grade*; *Picture Books*

Send: Query; Outline; Pitch; Author bio; Table of Contents; Writing sample; Market info
How to send: Email

Our mission is to build the knowledge base for SEED and STEAM learning through content that promotes critical thinking, opens up conversations, and ultimately inspires young minds. Our award-winning titles explore concepts such as managing emotions, forming positive relationships, and making informed behavioral decisions. As a platform for the leading voices in social and emotional education, we support the SEED learning process by elevating their voices.

P685 Schiffer Military

Publishing Imprint
United States

proposals@schifferbooks.com

https://www.schiffermilitary.com
https://schifferbooks.com/pages/schiffer-imprints

Book Publisher: Schiffer Publishing (**P686**)

Nonfiction > *Nonfiction Books*
Aviation; History; Military

Send: Query; Outline; Pitch; Author bio; Table of Contents; Writing sample; Market info
How to send: Email

Dedicated to publishing definitive books on military and aviation history by the world's leading historians.

P686 Schiffer Publishing

Book Publisher
4880 Lower Valley Road, Atglen, PA 19310
United States
Tel: +1 (610) 593-1777
Fax: +1 (610) 593-2002

proposals@schifferbooks.com

https://schifferbooks.com
https://www.facebook.com/schifferpublishing
https://twitter.com/Schifferbooks
https://www.instagram.com/SchifferPublishing/
https://www.youtube.com/user/SchifferPublishing1
https://schifferpublishing.tumblr.com/
https://pinterest.com/schifferbooks/

Nonfiction > *Nonfiction Books*
Antiques; Architecture; Arts; Fashion; Health; Lifestyle; Popular Culture; Regional; Transport

Send: Query; Outline; Pitch; Author bio; Table of Contents; Writing sample; Market info
How to send: Email

Focused on creating publications that inspire, educate, and inform inquisitive readers seeking trusted content to enrich their lives and passions.

Editor: Tina Skinner

Publishing Imprints: Schiffer Kids (**P684**); Schiffer Military (**P685**)

P687 Schocken Books

Publishing Imprint
United States

Book Publisher: Knopf Doubleday Publishing Group (**P426**)

P688 Scholastic

Book Publisher
557 Broadway, New York, NY 10012
United States

TeachingResources@Scholastic.com

https://www.scholastic.com
https://scholastic.force.com/scholasticfaqs/s/article/How-do-I-submit-a-manuscript-for-teaching-ideas

CHILDREN'S
Fiction
Chapter Books; *Early Readers*; *Middle Grade*; *Novels*; *Picture Books*
Nonfiction
Chapter Books; *Early Readers*; *Illustrated Books*; *Middle Grade*
PROFESSIONAL > **Nonfiction** > *Nonfiction Books*: Education

Send: Query; Table of Contents; Writing sample

The world's largest publisher and distributor of children's books. Provides professional services, classroom magazines, and produces educational and popular children's media.

Book Publishers: Arthur A. Levine Books; Chicken House Publishing; Scholastic UK

Publishing Imprints: AFK (*P025*); Cartwheel Books (*P146*); Graphix (*P306*); Klutz (*P424*); Orchard Books (*P553*); PUSH (*P629*); Scholastic Audio (*P689*); Scholastic Focus (*P690*); Scholastic Inc. (*P691*); Scholastic Press (*P692*); Scholastic Reference (*P693*)

P689 Scholastic Audio

Publishing Imprint

Book Publisher: Scholastic (**P688**)

P690 Scholastic Focus

Publishing Imprint

Book Publisher: Scholastic (**P688**)

P691 Scholastic Inc.

Publishing Imprint

Book Publisher: Scholastic (**P688**)

P692 Scholastic Press

Publishing Imprint

Book Publisher: Scholastic (**P688**)

P693 Scholastic Reference

Publishing Imprint

Book Publisher: Scholastic (**P688**)

P694 SCM Press

Publishing Imprint
United Kingdom

https://scmpress.hymnsam.co.uk

Book Publisher: Hymns Ancient & Modern Ltd

Nonfiction > *Nonfiction Books*: Christianity

Publishes books which engage academic theology with the wider church and with society. We release around 40 new books a year across biblical studies, practical theology, ecclesiology and ethics.

P695 Scout Press

Publishing Imprint

Book Publisher: Simon & Schuster Adult Publishing (**P711**)

P696 Seal Press

Publishing Imprint
1290 Avenue of the Americas, New York, NY 10104
United States

Seal.Press@hbgusa.com

https://www.sealpress.com
https://www.facebook.com/sealpress
https://twitter.com/sealpress
https://www.instagram.com/sealpress/

Publishing Imprint: Da Capo Press

Nonfiction > *Nonfiction Books*: Feminism

Founded in 1976 and stands as one of the most enduring feminist publishing houses to emerge from the women's press movement of the 1970s. Publishes radical and groundbreaking books that inspire and challenge readers, that humanize urgent issues, that build much-needed bridges in divisive times, and help us see the world in a new light.

P697 Seaworthy Publications

Book Publisher
6300 N Wickham Road, Unit #130-416, Melbourne, FL 32940
United States
Tel: +1 (321) 610-3634

queries@seaworthy.com

http://www.seaworthy.com

Nonfiction > *Articles*
Boats; Sailing

Send: Full text

Nautical book publisher specialising in recreational boating. Send query by email outlining your work and attaching sample table of contents and two or three sample chapters. See website for full submission guidelines.

P698 Sentinel

Publishing Imprint
United States

Book Publisher: Penguin Publishing Group (**P585**)

P699 September Publishing

Book Publisher
United Kingdom
Tel: +44 (0) 20 3637 0116

info@septemberpublishing.org
submissions@septemberpublishing.org

https://www.septemberpublishing.org

Nonfiction > *Nonfiction Books*
Adventure; Arts; Creativity; Current Affairs; Folklore, Myths, and Legends; Memoir; Nature; Personal Development; Photography; Politics; Trains; Travel

Send: Synopsis; Writing sample
How to send: Email

Currently accepting nonfiction submissions for a general, adult readership. Send a synopsis and three sample chapters by email.

P700 Seren Books

Book Publisher
Suite 6, 4 Derwen Road, Bridgend, CF31 1LH
United Kingdom
Tel: +44 (0) 1656 663018

Seren@SerenBooks.com

https://www.serenbooks.com
https://www.facebook.com/SerenBooks
http://www.twitter.com/SerenBooks
http://www.pinterest.com/SerenBooks

Fiction
Novels: Literary
Short Fiction: Literary

Nonfiction > *Nonfiction Books*
Arts; Biography; Current Affairs; Drama; History; Literary Criticism; Memoir; Music; Photography; Sport; Travel

Poetry > *Poetry Collections*

Send: Full text

Publishes fiction, nonfiction, and poetry. Specialises in English-language writing from Wales and aims to bring Welsh culture, art, literature, and politics to a wider audience. Accepts nonfiction submissions by post or by email. Accepts poetry submissions by post only. Accepts fiction only from authors with whom there is an existing publishing relationship.

Poetry Editor: Amy Wack

Publisher: Mick Felton

P701 Severn House Publishers

Book Publisher
Eardley House, 4 Uxbridge Street, London, W8 7SY
United Kingdom
Tel: +44 (0) 20 7467 0840

info@severnhouse.com

https://severnhouse.com
https://www.facebook.com/severnhouse/
https://twitter.com/severnhouse
https://www.instagram.com/severnhouseimprint/

Fiction > *Novels*
Cozy Mysteries; Historical Fiction; Horror; Police Procedural; Romance; Science Fiction; Thrillers

Dedicated to publishing unputdownable genre fiction: from gritty procedurals to cosy mysteries and tense thrillers, as well as sci-fi, horror, romance, historical fiction, and more.

P702 Shambhala Publications

Book Publisher
2129 13th Street, Boulder, CO 80302
United States

submissions@shambhala.com
editors@shambhala.com

https://www.shambhala.com
http://www.facebook.com/ShambhalaPublications
http://www.instagram.com/shambhala_publications/

Fiction > *Novels*: Adventure

Nonfiction > *Nonfiction Books*
Activities; Arts; Buddhism; Christianity; Crafts; Creativity; Hinduism; Judaism; Martial Arts; Meditation; Memoir; Parenting; Philosophy; Psychology; Religion; Sufism; Taoism; Theravada Buddhism; Yoga; Zen

Poetry > *Poetry Collections*
Classics / Ancient World; Contemporary; Inspirational; Spirituality

Send: Proposal
How to send: Email
How not to send: Post

Specialises in books that present creative and conscious ways of transforming individuals, society, and the planet. Focuses mainly on religion and philosophy, but covers a wide range of subjects including sciences, arts, Buddhism, Christianity, literature, poetry, psychology, etc. See website for full range of books published.

P703 Shearsman Books

Book Publisher
PO Box 4239, Swindon, SN3 9FN
United Kingdom
Tel: +44 (0) 1179 572957

editor@shearsman.com

https://www.shearsman.com

Types: Nonfiction; Poetry; Translations
Subjects: Autobiography; Literary Criticism
Markets: Adult

Send: Query
Don't send: Full text

Publishes poetry books of at least 60 A5 pages. Publishes mainly poetry by British, Irish, North American and Australian/New Zealand poets, plus poetry in translation from any language – although particular interest in German, Spanish and Latin American poetry. Submit only if MS is of appropriate length and most of it has already appeared in UK or US magazines of some repute. Send selection of 6-10 pages by post with SASE or by email with material embedded in the text or as PDF attachment. No other kind of attachments accepted. Also sometimes publishes literary criticism on poetry, and essays or memoirs by poets.

Editor: Tony Frazer

P704 Shelf Stuff

Publishing Imprint

Book Publisher: HarperCollins

P705 Shipwreckt Books Publishing Company

Book Publisher
Ruchford, MN
United States

contact@shipwrecktbooks.com

http://www.shipwrecktbooks.com

Types: Fiction; Nonfiction; Poetry
Subjects: Autobiography; Comedy / Humour; Culture; Current Affairs; Fantasy; Gardening; Health; History; Legal; Leisure; Lifestyle; Literary; Medicine; Mystery; Nature; Politics; Science Fiction; Spirituality; Sport; Suspense; Warfare; Women's Interests
Markets: Adult; Children's; Young Adult

Closed to approaches.

Not accepting submissions as at May 2020. Publishes books and literary magazine. Submit brief bio, synopsis, and first ten pages (or a couple of poems) using form on website.

Publishing Imprints: Lost Lake Folk Art (*P459*); Rocket Science Press (*P658*); Up On Big Rock Poetry (*P819*)

P706 Short Books

Book Publisher
Unit 316, ScreenWorks, 22 Highbury Grove, London, N5 2EF
United Kingdom
Tel: +44 (0) 20 7833 9429

info@shortbooks.co.uk

https://shortbooks.co.uk
https://twitter.com/shortbooksUK
https://www.facebook.com/#!/pages/Short-Books/138762006187086
https://www.instagram.com/shortbooks_uk_

Nonfiction > *Nonfiction Books*
Food; Health; Mental Health; Nature; Politics; Popular; Psychology; Sociology

How to send: Through a literary agent

A publisher of first-class, popular non-fiction with a focus on health, diet, nature, psychology and social sciences.

P707 Sidgwick & Jackson

Publishing Imprint
United Kingdom

Book Publisher: Pan Macmillan (**P564**)

P708 Silvertail Books

Book Publisher
United Kingdom

editor@silvertailbooks.com

http://www.silvertailbooks.com

Types: Fiction; Nonfiction
Subjects: Commercial
Markets: Adult

Welcomes submissions for commercial fiction and nonfiction, either through an agent or direct from authors. Submit by email only. No postal submissions. Response not guaranteed.

Author / Literary Agent / Publisher: Humfrey Hunter (**L337**)

P709 Simon & Schuster

Book Publisher
United States

https://www.simonandschuster.com
https://www.facebook.com/simonandschuster
https://twitter.com/SimonSchuster
https://www.youtube.com/user/SimonSchusterVideos
https://instagram.com/simonandschuster

Fiction > *Novels*

Nonfiction > *Nonfiction Books*

How to send: Through a literary agent

Large publishing house covering a wide range of fiction and nonfiction.

Audio Book Publisher: Simon & Schuster Audio Publishing

Book Publishers: Simon & Schuster Adult Publishing (**P711**); Simon & Schuster Children's Publishing (**P713**)

Publishing Imprint: The Free Press

P710 Simon & Schuster (Imprint)

Publishing Imprint

Book Publisher: Simon & Schuster Adult Publishing (**P711**)

P711 Simon & Schuster Adult Publishing

Book Publisher
United States

Book Publisher: Simon & Schuster (**P709**)

How to send: Through a literary agent

Publishing Imprints: Adams Media (*P020*); Atria (*P059*); Avid Reader Press (*P067*); Emily Bestler Books (*P235*); Enliven (*P240*); Folger Shakespeare Library (*P272*); Free Press (*P278*); Gallery (*P286*); Howard (*P383*); Jeter Publishing (*P410*); One Signal (*P548*); Scout Press (*P695*); Scribner; Simon & Schuster (Imprint) (*P710*); Simon Element (**P714**); Threshold (*P766*); Tiller Press; Touchstone (*P776*)

P712 Simon & Schuster Audio

Publishing Imprint

Audio Book Publisher: Simon & Schuster Audio Publishing

P713 Simon & Schuster Children's Publishing

Book Publisher
United States

https://www.simonandschuster.com/kids
https://www.facebook.com/simonandschuster
https://twitter.com/SimonSchuster
https://www.youtube.com/user/SimonSchusterVideos
https://instagram.com/simonandschuster

Book Publisher: Simon & Schuster (**P709**)

CHILDREN'S
- **Fiction**
  - *Board Books*; *Chapter Books*; *Early Readers*; *Middle Grade*; *Picture Books*
- **Nonfiction**
  - *Board Books*; *Middle Grade*; *Picture Books*

YOUNG ADULT > **Fiction** > *Novels*

Closed to approaches.

Does not review, retain or return unsolicited materials or artwork.

Publishing Imprints: Aladdin (*P027*); Atheneum (*P055*); Beach Lane Books (*P086*); Denene Millner Books (**P208**); Little Simon; Margaret K. McElderry (*P480*); Paula Wiseman Books (*P571*); Saga Press (*P673*); Salaam Reads (*P676*); Simon & Schuster Books for Young Readers; Simon Pulse; Simon Spotlight

P714 Simon Element

Publishing Imprint
United States

https://www.simonelement.com

Book Publisher: Simon & Schuster Adult Publishing (**P711**)

Nonfiction > *Nonfiction Books*
Business; Cookery; Design; Diet; Domestic; Drinks; Fitness; Food; Health; How To; Inspirational; Lifestyle; Memoir; Narrative Nonfiction; Parenting; Personal Development; Popular Culture; Relationships; Science; Self Help; Spirituality; Wellbeing; Wine

Publishes books addressing topics that are foundational to how we live—from the meals we eat to the relationships we nurture, the households we manage, and the personal and professional goals we set and strive to achieve.

P715 Skip Jack Press

Publishing Imprint
United States

Book Publisher: The Globe Pequot Press (**P296**)

P716 small world creations

Publishing Imprint

Book Publisher: The Quarto Group, Inc. (**P633**)

P717 SmartLab Toys

Publishing Imprint

Book Publisher: The Quarto Group, Inc. (**P633**)

P718 Smith/Doorstop Books

Book Publisher
The Poetry Business, Campo House, 54 Campo Lane, Sheffield, S1 2EG
United Kingdom
Tel: +44 (0) 1484 434840
Fax: +44 (0) 1484 426566

office@poetrybusiness.co.uk

https://poetrybusiness.co.uk

Types: Nonfiction; Poetry
Subjects: Arts; Autobiography; Crime; Culture; Literary; Literary Criticism
Markets: Adult; Children's

Resolves to discover new and exciting poetry to showcase and publish. Accepts unsolicited mss only during open calls for submissions to guest-edited anthologies. See website for upcoming anthology publication opportunities. Also publishes winners of annual competitions.

P719 Smithsonian Institution

Magazine Publisher; Book Publisher
PO Box 37012, MRC 513, Washington, DC 20013-7012
United States

info@si.edu

https://www.si.edu
https://www.facebook.com/Smithsonian
https://instagram.com/smithsonian
https://www.pinterest.com/smithsonian/
https://smithsonian.tumblr.com/
https://twitter.com/smithsonian
https://www.youtube.com/c/smithsonian

Magazines: Air & Space Quarterly (**M019**); Smithsonian Magazine (**M452**)

P720 Snowbooks

Book Publisher
55 North Street, Thame, OXON, OX9 3BH
United Kingdom

submissions@snowbooks.com

http://www.snowbooks.com

Types: Fiction; Nonfiction
Subjects: Crafts; Crime; Fantasy; History; Horror; Leisure; Science Fiction; Sport; Thrillers
Markets: Adult

Send: Full text

Open to submissions of horror, science fiction, and fantasy novels over 70,000 words. Named joint Small Publisher of the Year at the 2006 British book Trade Awards. Friendly attitude towards authors and unsolicited approaches. See website for guidelines. Approach via email only – postal submissions will neither be read nor returned, even if sent through an agent.

Managing Director: Emma Barnes

P721 Society for Promoting Christian Knowledge (SPCK)

Book Publisher
36 Causton Street, London, SW1P 4ST
United Kingdom

contact@spck.org.uk

https://spckpublishing.co.uk
https://www.facebook.com/pages/SPCK-Publishing/205059496214486
https://www.instagram.com/spck_publishing/
https://twitter.com/SPCKPublishing

ADULT
- **Fiction** > *Novels*: Christianity
- **Nonfiction** > *Nonfiction Books*
  Arts; Bible Studies; Biography; Christian Living; Christianity; Culture; Family; Health; History; Meditation; Personal Development; Relationships; Society; Spirituality

CHILDREN'S > **Fiction** > *Picture Books*: Christianity

Send: Query; Table of Contents; Outline; Market info
How to send: Online submission system

A recognised market-leader in the areas of Theology and Christian Spirituality. Nearly all books are commissioned so rarely accepts unsolicited projects for publication.

Book Publisher: Lion Hudson (**P446**)

P722 Society of Genealogists

Book Publisher
356 Holloway Road, London, N7 6PA
United Kingdom
Tel: +44 (0) 20 7251 8799

hello@sog.org.uk

https://www.sog.org.uk
https://facebook.com/societyofgenealogists
https://twitter.com/soggenealogist
https://www.pinterest.co.uk/societyofgeneal/

Nonfiction > *Nonfiction Books*
Genealogy; History

Publishes a wide variety of family history and genealogy publications.

P723 Soho Press

Book Publisher
United States
Tel: +1 (212) 260-1900

soho@sohopress.com

https://sohopress.com

Types: Fiction
Subjects: Crime; Literary
Markets: Adult; Young Adult

Publishes bold literary voices, award-winning international crime fiction, and groundbreaking young adult fiction.

P724 Somerset Books

Book Publisher
United Kingdom

https://www.somersetbooks.com

Nonfiction > *Nonfiction Books*: Travel

Publishing Imprint: Blue Guides (**P108**)

P725 Somerville Press

Book Publisher
Dromore, Bantry, Co. Cork
Ireland
Tel: 353 (0) 28 32873

somervillepress@gmail.com

http://www.somervillepress.com
https://somervillepress.company.site

Fiction > *Novels*

Nonfiction > *Nonfiction Books*

Publishes fiction and nonfiction, mainly of Irish interest.

P726 Sourcebooks

Book Publisher
1935 Brookdale Rd, Suite 139, Naperville, IL 60563
United States
Tel: +1 (800) 432-7444
Fax: +1 (630) 961-2168

info@sourcebooks.com
editorialsubmissions@sourcebooks.com

https://www.sourcebooks.com
https://linkedin.com/company/50434/
https://twitter.com/sourcebooks
https://facebook.com/sourcebooks
https://www.pinterest.com/sbjabberwockykids/
https://www.instagram.com/sourcebooks/
https://www.sourcebooks.com/contact-us.html

ADULT
Fiction > *Novels*
General, and in particular: Mystery; Romance

Nonfiction
Gift Books: General
Nonfiction Books: General, and in particular: Beauty; Biography; Business; Education; Entertainment; Health; History; Memoir; Parenting; Psychology; Relationships; Self Help; Women's Issues
Reference: General, and in particular: Education

CHILDREN'S > **Nonfiction** > *Nonfiction Books*

YOUNG ADULT > **Fiction** > *Novels*

Send: Query; Synopsis; Author bio; Table of Contents; Writing sample; Market info
Don't send: Full text
How to send: Email
How not to send: Post

We are interested in books that will establish a unique standard in their subject area. We look for books with a well-defined, strong target market. Our list includes most nonfiction categories, including memoir, history, college reference and study aids, entertainment, general self-help/psychology, business, parenting and special needs parenting, health and beauty, reference, education, biography, love and relationships, gift books and women's issues.

Publishing Imprints: Dawn Publications (**P201**); Sourcebooks Casablanca; Sourcebooks Hysteria; Sourcebooks Landmark; Sourcebooks MediaFusion; Sphinx Publishing

P727 Speak

Publishing Imprint
United States

Book Publisher: Penguin Young Readers Group (**P591**)

P728 Special Interest Model Books Ltd

Book Publisher
50a Willis Way, Poole, Dorset, BH15 3SY
United Kingdom
Tel: +44 (0) 1202 649930
Fax: +44 (0) 1202 649950

orders@specialinterestmodelbooks.co.uk

https://www.specialinterestmodelbooks.co.uk

Nonfiction > *Nonfiction Books*
Amateur Radio; Amateur Winemaking; Hobbies; Model Aircraft; Model Making; Model Ships and Boats; Radio Control

Publishes practical manuals for hobbyists in the fields of model engineering, scale modelling, radio-controlled models and home winemaking and brewing.

Editor: Chris Lloyd

P729 Springer Nature

Book Publisher

Book Publishers: Macmillan Education (**P472**); Palgrave Macmillan (**P562**); Springer-Verlag London Ltd

P730 Spruce Books

Publishing Imprint
United States

Book Publisher: Sasquatch Books (**P683**)

P731 Square Peg

Publishing Imprint
United Kingdom

Book Publisher: Vintage (**P827**)

P732 St Martin's Paperbacks

Publishing Imprint

Publishing Imprint: St Martin's Press (**P733**)

P733 St Martin's Press

Publishing Imprint
United States

publicity@stmartins.com

https://us.macmillan.com/smp

Book Publisher: Macmillan Publishers (**P475**)

Types: Fiction; Nonfiction
Formats: Reference
Subjects: Biography; Crime; History; Mystery; Politics; Self Help; Travel
Markets: Academic; Adult

How to send: Through a literary agent

Approach via literary agent only. Began by importing UK authors to the States and continues to buy heavily in the United Kingdom. No unsolicited MSS or unagented queries.

Publishing Imprints: Castle Point Books (*P147*); Griffin (*P311*); Minotaur (*P499*); St Martin's Paperbacks (*P732*); Thomas Dunne Books; Wednesday Books (*P849*)

P734 St Pauls

Book Publisher
2187 Victory Boulevard, Staten Island, NY 10314
United States
Tel: +1 (800) 343-2522
Fax: +1 (718) 698-8390

sales@stpauls.us

http://www.stpaulsusa.com

Types: Nonfiction
Subjects: Biography; Religion; Self Help
Markets: Adult

Send: Full text

Publishes books for a Roman Catholic readership.

P735 Stacey International

Book Publisher
14 Great College Street, London, SW1P 3RX
United Kingdom

editorial@stacey-international.co.uk

http://www.stacey-international.co.uk

Fiction > *Novels*

Nonfiction > *Nonfiction Books*
Archaeology; Biography; Cookery; Geology; History; Language; Middle East; Nature; Photography; Travel

Poetry > *Poetry Collections*

Send: Full text; Proposal; Self-Addressed Stamped Envelope (SASE)
How to send: Email; Post

Publishes nonfiction, fiction, and poetry. Submit manuscripts and proposals by email or by post with SASE. See website for more information.

P736 Stackpole Books

Publishing Imprint
United States

http://www.stackpolebooks.com

Book Publisher: The Globe Pequot Press (**P296**)

Nonfiction
Nonfiction Books: American Civil War; Crafts; Fly Fishing; Hobbies; Military History; Nature; Outdoor Activities; World War II
Reference: Military

Publishes titles in the categories of Outdoors, Crafts and Military History. Strong in Fly Fishing, Nature Guides, Civil War and World War II History, Military Reference and Specialty Crafts and Hobbies.

Editors: Candi Derr; Jay Nichols; Dave Reisch

Publisher: Judith Schnell

P737 Stairwell Books

Book Publisher
161 Lowther Street, York, YO31 7LZ
United Kingdom

rose@stairwellbooks.com

https://www.stairwellbooks.co.uk
https://twitter.com/StairwellBooks

ADULT
Fiction
Novels: Crime; Environment; Fantasy; Historical Fiction; Science Fiction
Short Fiction: General

Nonfiction > *Nonfiction Books*
Climate Science; Memoir

Poetry > *Any Poetic Form*

Scripts > *Theatre Scripts*

CHILDREN'S > **Fiction** > *Novels*

YOUNG ADULT > **Fiction** > *Novels*

Send: Query
How to send: Email

Small press publisher specialising in poetry anthologies, short stories, and novels from new writers. Send query by email. See website for full details.

Editor: Rose Drew

P738 Stanford University Press

Book Publisher
485 Broadway, First Floor, Redwood City CA 94063-8460
United States
Tel: +1 (650) 723-9434
Fax: +1 (650) 725-3457

https://www.sup.org
http://www.facebook.com/stanforduniversitypress
http://www.twitter.com/stanfordpress
https://www.youtube.com/channel/UCmd8xj7yu0WGeLRqL39UjLA
http://instagram.com/stanfordupress

ACADEMIC > **Nonfiction** > *Nonfiction Books*
Anthropology; Asia; Business; Economics; Finance; History; Judaism; Legal; Literature; Middle East; Philosophy; Politics; Religion; Sociology; South America

Send: Query; Proposal; Author bio; Table of Contents
How to send: Email; Post

Submit proposals by post, or see website for list of editors and submit proposal to the appropriate editor by email.

P739 Stanley Gibbons

Book Publisher; Magazine Publisher
United Kingdom

support@stanleygibbons.com

https://www.stanleygibbons.com
https://www.stanleygibbons.com/publishing/publishing-house
https://www.facebook.com/stanleygibbonsgroup
https://twitter.com/StanleyGibbons
https://www.instagram.com/stanleygibbons/

Nonfiction > *Reference*: Stamp Collecting

Publishes handbooks and reference guides on stamps and stamp collecting.

P740 Star Bright Books

Book Publisher
13 Landsdowne Street, Cambridge, MA 02139
United States
Tel: +1 (617) 354-1300
Fax: +1 (617) 354-1399

info@starbrightbooks.com

https://starbrightbooks.org

CHILDREN'S
Fiction
Chapter Books; *Picture Books*
Nonfiction
Chapter Books: General
Picture Books: General, and in particular: Biography; Diversity

How to send: Post
How not to send: Email

Publishes books that are entertaining, meaningful and sensitive to the needs of all children. Welcomes submissions for picture books and longer works, both fiction and nonfiction. See website for full submission guidelines.

P741 Stash Books

Publishing Imprint
United States

Book Publisher: C&T Publishing (**P133**)

P742 Steerforth Press

Book Publisher
31 Hanover Street, Suite 1, Lebanon, NH 03766
United States
Tel: +1 (603) 643-4787

submissions@steerforth.com
info@steerforth.com

https://steerforth.com
https://twitter.com/SteerforthPress
https://www.instagram.com/steerforthpress/
https://www.facebook.com/steerforthpress

Nonfiction > *Nonfiction Books*
Crime; History; Investigative Journalism; Literary Journalism; Narrative Nonfiction

Send: Query; Proposal
Don't send: Full text
How to send: Email

Exclusively considering works of narrative nonfiction, such as investigative or literary journalism, true crime and history for a general audience.

Fiction Editor / Poetry Editor: Roland Pease

Publishing Imprints: For Beginners; Playboy Press; Zoland Books; Zoland Poetry

P743 The Stinging Fly Press

Book Publisher; Magazine Publisher
Ireland

submissions.stingingfly@gmail.com
editor@stingingfly.org
info@stingingfly.org

https://stingingfly.org
https://www.facebook.com/StingingFly
http://twitter.com/stingingfly

Fiction > *Short Fiction Collections*

Closed to approaches.

Publishes single-author short-story collections and multiple-author anthologies.

Publisher: Declan Meade

P744 Stone Bridge Press

Book Publisher
1393 Solano Avenue, Suite C, Albany, CA 94706
United States
Tel: +1 (510) 524-8732

sbpedit@stonebridge.com

https://www.stonebridge.com

Types: Fiction; Nonfiction; Poetry; Translations
Formats: Film Scripts; Reference
Subjects: Arts; Business; Crafts; Culture; Design; Lifestyle; Literature; Spirituality; Travel
Markets: Adult; Children's

Send: Query
Don't send: Full text

Publishes books about Asia and in particular Japan and China. Send brief query by email in the first instance.

P745 Strata Publishing, Inc.

Book Publisher
PO 1303, State College, PA 16804-1303
United States
Tel: +1 (814) 234-8545

stratapub@stratapub.com

http://www.stratapub.com

ACADEMIC > **Nonfiction** > *Nonfiction Books*
Communication; Journalism

PROFESSIONAL > **Nonfiction** > *Nonfiction Books*
Communication; Journalism

Send: Query; Outline; Market info; Table of Contents; Author bio
How to send: Post
How not to send: Email attachment

An independent publishing house producing books for college students, scholars, and professionals in communication and journalism. Send query letter giving the working title, the course(s) for which the book is intended, brief description of your general approach, major competitors, and how your book is different from them.

Editor: Kathleen Domenig

P746 Sublunary Editions

Book Publisher; Magazine Publisher
Seattle
United States

support@sublunaryeditions.com

https://sublunaryeditions.com
https://oleada.io/publication/sublunary-editions
https://twitter.com/sublunaryeds
https://instagram.com/sublunaryeditions

Fiction
Novellas: Experimental; Literary
Short Fiction: Experimental; Literary
Nonfiction > *Essays*
Experimental; Literary

Poetry
Any Poetic Form; *Experimental Poetry*

Started as a small-scale, DIY project in early 2019. For the first several months, the press's sole output as a regular envelope of new writing mailed (the old fashioned way) to subscribers. Since then, the press has expanded to publish 8-10 brief books every year, and, as of early 2021, a quarterly magazine

Magazine: Firmament **(M200)**

P747 Sunberry Books

Publishing Imprint
United Kingdom

submissions@sunpenny.com

https://www.sunpenny.com/imprints/

Book Publisher: Sunpenny Publishing **(P748)**

CHILDREN'S > **Fiction** > *Novels*

YOUNG ADULT > **Fiction** > *Novels*

Send: Author bio; Marketing Plan; Synopsis; Full text
How to send: Email
How not to send: Post

Imprint set up for children's books and YA (Young Adults).

P748 Sunpenny Publishing

Book Publisher
United Kingdom

submissions@sunpenny.com

https://www.sunpenny.com

ADULT
Fiction > *Novels*
General, and in particular: Christian Romance; Christianity; Inspirational; Romance

Nonfiction > *Nonfiction Books*
General, and in particular: Boats; Christianity

CHILDREN'S > **Fiction** > *Novels*

TEEN > **Fiction** > *Novels*

Send: Author bio; Marketing Plan; Synopsis; Full text
How to send: Email
How not to send: Post

An independent small publishing house focusing particularly on encouraging and developing new talent in writing – in fiction and non-fiction, and in Christian and romantic works.

We have a soft spot for travel, sailing, adventure, crime/detective, courage and overcoming, self-help, gift books and coffee-table books. We enjoy wit and humour, entertainment, upliftment. Sunpenny promotes beauty and excellence in publishing. Books do not have to be Christian in either topic or nature, but they do have to keep to acceptable value standards.

What we won't even consider: Unless it is suitably within an overall context of "overcoming", we do not accept depressive or self-contemplative styles, 'black comedy', racism, gratuitous sex or violence or foul language, or anything else that does not conform to good mainstream family values (and we get to be the judge!) ... our taste also does not run to the gothic – vampires, werewolves, and the like, or horror generally; nor do we enjoy the crass and the crude, no matter how witty. If it's seedy or seamy, please don't even try. And let's not even go into the futuristic games-type wild fantasy adventure "I have the power!" stuff. Intelligent sci-fi, yes. Silliness, no. Aliens, probably not. And if you have a book that expounds theories/religions such as The Big Bang, Evolution and suchlike – why even waste your time sending it to a Christian publisher? Save yourself the money. :-)

Please visit our web site and read ALL our guidelines carefully before querying.

Authors: Cheryl Cain; Rowland Evans; JS Holloway; Lucy McCarraher; Julie McGowan; Terri Tiffany

Editor: Jo Holloway

Publishing Imprints: Blue Jeans Books (**P109**); Boathooks Books (**P115**); ChristLight Books (**P164**); EPTA Books (**P243**); Engram Books (**P239**); Rose and Crown Books (**P663**); Sunberry Books (**P747**)

P749 Superbia Books

Publishing Imprint
United Kingdom

Book Publisher: DogHorn Publishing (**P217**)

P750 Sussex Academic Press

Book Publisher
United Kingdom

edit@sussex-academic.com

http://www.sussex-academic.com

ACADEMIC > **Nonfiction** > *Nonfiction Books*
Archaeology; Art History; Biography; Culture; Drama; Economics; Education; Environment; Films; Geography; History; Judaism; Literary Criticism; Management; Media; Middle East; Music; Philosophy; Politics; Psychology; Psychotherapy; Religion; Society; South America; Theatre; Women's Studies

ADULT > **Nonfiction** > *Nonfiction Books*
Archaeology; Art History; Biography; Culture; Drama; Economics; Education; Environment; Films; Geography; History; Judaism; Literary Criticism; Management; Media; Middle East; Music; Philosophy; Politics; Psychology; Psychotherapy; Religion; Society; South America; Theatre; Women's Studies

Send: Submission Form
How to send: Email attachment

Commissions and acquires works of scholarly and general non-fiction that fit in with its publishing programme. The Press seeks well-written and accessible works that expand the body of knowledge about a given subject or contribute to public debate. The Press has a particularly strong track record in monograph studies across a range of disciplines.

Editorial Director: Anthony V. P. Grahame

Publishing Imprints: Alpha Press; Sussex Academic

P751 Swallow Press

Publishing Imprint

Book Publisher: Ohio University Press (**P541**)

P752 Sweet Cherry Publishing

Book Publisher
Unit 4U18, The Book Brothers Business Park, Tolwell Road, Leicester, LE4 1BR
United Kingdom
Tel: +44 (0) 1162 536796

submissions@sweetcherrypublishing.com

https://www.sweetcherrypublishing.com
http://www.facebook.com/sweetcherrypublishing
https://twitter.com/sweetcherrypub
https://www.instagram.com/sweetcherrypublishing/

CHILDREN'S > **Fiction**
Board Books; *Chapter Books*; *Middle Grade*; *Picture Books*
YOUNG ADULT > **Fiction** > *Novels*

Send: Query; Writing sample; Synopsis; Author bio
How to send: Email

Publishes picture and board books, chapter books, middle-grade fiction, and young adult fiction. Specialises in sets and series, so unlikely to take on a stand-alone title. Send submissions by email. See website for full submission guidelines.

Editor: Abdul Thadha

P753 Sweetgum Press

Book Publisher
PO Box 472, Warrensburg, MO 64093
United States

sweetgumpresseditors@gmail.com

https://sweetgumpress.com

Fiction > *Short Fiction Collections*
American Midwest; Historical Fiction; Missouri

Poetry > *Poetry Collections*
American Midwest; History; Missouri

Closed to approaches.

Publishes book-length works (70-250 pages) by writers from the Midwest, particularly Missouri. The editors look for manuscripts that are unlikely to attract mainstream publishers but are worthy of publication because of one or more qualities, among them originality, authenticity, beauty, regional or historical appeal.

Editors: Baird Brock; RM Kinder

P754 Tamarind Books

Publishing Imprint
United Kingdom

puffin@penguinrandomhouse.co.uk

https://www.penguin.co.uk/puffin/tamarind.html

Book Publisher: Puffin (UK) (**P626**)

CHILDREN'S
Fiction
Chapter Books: Diversity
Middle Grade: Diversity
Novels: Diversity

Nonfiction > *Nonfiction Books*: Diversity

Publishes children's books and picture books with black, Asian, or mixed race children as the main protagonists.

Editor: Verna Wilkins

P755 TANSTAAFL Press

Book Publisher
United States

submissions@tanstaaflpress.com

https://tanstaaflpress.com

Types: Fiction
Formats: Short Fiction
Subjects: Fantasy; Science Fiction
Markets: Adult

Send: Query
Don't send: Full text

Publishes science fiction, cyberpunk, alternative histories, post apocalyptic and fantasy of novel length. Will consider exceptional works in other genres of fiction, or short story compilations of the above topics. Send query by email with 300-500 word summary and first 1,000 words as a text attachment. See website for full guidelines.

P756 TarcherPerigee

Publishing Imprint
United States

Book Publisher: Penguin Publishing Group (**P585**)

P757 Taylor & Francis Group

Book Publisher
2&4 Park Square, Milton Park, Abingdon, OX14 4RN
United Kingdom
Tel: +44 (0) 20 8052 0500

enquiries@taylorandfrancis.com

https://taylorandfrancis.com
https://www.facebook.com/TaylorandFrancisGroup
https://twitter.com/tandfonline
https://www.linkedin.com/company/taylor-&-francis-group/
https://www.instagram.com/tandfscience/

Book Publisher: Informa PLC

ACADEMIC > **Nonfiction** > *Nonfiction Books*
Agriculture; Arts; Biomedical Science; Business; Chemistry; Computer Science; Earth Science; Economics; Education; Engineering; Environment; Finance; Geography; Health; History; Information Science; Language; Legal; Literature; Management; Mathematics; Medicine; Nursing; Philosophy; Physics; Politics; Psychiatry; Psychology; Religion; Science; Sociology; Statistics; Sustainable Living; Technology

PROFESSIONAL > **Nonfiction** > *Nonfiction Books*
Agriculture; Biomedical Science; Business; Chemistry; Computer Science; Earth Science; Economics; Education; Engineering; Environment; Finance; Geography; Health; History; Information Science; Language; Legal; Literature; Management; Mathematics; Medicine; Nursing; Philosophy; Physics; Politics; Psychiatry; Psychology; Religion; Science; Sociology; Statistics; Sustainable Living; Technology

One of the leading research publishers in the world, serving academia and professionals in industry and government.

Book Publishers: Ashgate Publishing Limited; Focal Press; Routledge (**P665**)

Publishing Imprint: Psychology Press

P758 TCK Publishing

Book Publisher; Ebook Publisher; Audio Book Publisher
16641 Brick Road, Granger, IN 46530
United States

info@tckpublishing.com
submissions@tckpublishing.com

https://www.tckpublishing.com

ADULT
Fiction > *Novels*
General, and in particular: Adventure; Fantasy; Historical Fiction; Horror; Mystery; Romance; Science Fiction; Suspense; Thrillers

Nonfiction > *Nonfiction Books*
General, and in particular: Business; Finance; Gardening; Health; How To; Nature; Personal Development; Relationships; Self Help; Spirituality; Wellbeing

CHILDREN'S > **Fiction** > *Middle Grade*

NEW ADULT > **Fiction** > *Novels*

YOUNG ADULT > **Fiction** > *Novels*

Send: Full text
How to send: Online submission system

A traditional book publisher that pays 50% gross royalties. We love to publish meaningful and inspirational fiction and nonfiction books that inspire and educate readers.

P759 Telegram Books

Publishing Imprint
26 Westbourne Grove, London, W2 5RH
United Kingdom
Tel: +44 (0) 20 7221 9347
Fax: +44 (0) 20 7229 7492

elizabeth@saqibooks.com

https://saqibooks.com/imprint/telegram/

Book Publisher: Saqi Books (**P681**)

Fiction > *Novels*

Closed to approaches.

Publishes fiction from around the world. Not accepting submissions as at November 2020.

P760 Templar Books

Publishing Imprint
United Kingdom
Tel: +44 (0) 20 3770 8888

hello@templarco.co.uk

https://www.bonnierbooks.co.uk/childrens-imprints/templar-books/

Book Publisher: Bonnier Books (UK) (**P117**)

CHILDREN'S
Fiction > *Picture Books*

Nonfiction
Board Books; *Gift Books*; *Illustrated Books*

How to send: Through a literary agent

Publishes children's fiction and picture and novelty books. Encourage anybody who wishes to have their work considered by one of their imprints to seek representation by an agent. No unsolicited mss or proposals.

P761 Temple Lodge Publishing

Book Publisher
Hillside House, The Square, Forest Row, RH18 5ES
United Kingdom

office@templelodge.com

https://www.templelodge.com

Types: Nonfiction
Subjects: Science; Spirituality
Markets: Adult

Send: Query
Don't send: Full text

Originally founded to develop the work of Rudolf Steiner. Publishes nonfiction from a a spiritual-scientific perspective. Send a summary with list of chapters and sample chapters by email or by post with SAE.

P762 Ten Speed Press

Book Publisher
United States

https://crownpublishing.com/archives/imprint/ten-speed-press

Book Publisher: The Crown Publishing Group

Nonfiction > *Illustrated Books*
Design; Food and Drink; Gardening; Health; Popular Culture

Known for creating beautiful illustrated books with innovative design and award-winning content. Actively seeks out new and established authors who are authorities and tastemakers in the world of food, drink, pop culture, graphic novels, illustration, design, reference, gardening, and health.

Editorial Director: Aaron Wehmer

President: Phil Wood

Publishers: Jo Ann Deck; Lorena Jones

Publishing Imprints: Celestial Arts; Crossing Press; Tricycle Press

P763 Thames & Hudson Inc.

Book Publisher
500 Fifth Avenue, New York, NY 10110
United States
Tel: +1 (212) 354-3763
Fax: +1 (212) 398-1252

bookinfo@thames.wwnorton.com

https://www.thamesandhudsonusa.com
https://www.instagram.com/thamesandhudsonusa
https://twitter.com/ThamesHudsonUSA
https://www.facebook.com/ThamesandHudsonUSA

Book Publisher: Thames and Hudson Ltd

ADULT
Fiction > *Novels*

Nonfiction
Nonfiction Books: Animals; Anthropology; Antiques; Archaeology; Architecture; Arts; Biography; Business; Classics / Ancient World; Comedy / Humour; Comic Books; Crafts; Design; Evolution; Fashion; Films; Fitness; Folklore, Myths, and Legends; Food; Games; Gardening; Health; History; Houses; Interior Design; Literary Criticism; Medicine; Military History; Music; Nature; Philosophy; Photography; Religion; Science; Spirituality; Sport; TV; Theatre; Travel
Reference: General

Poetry > *Poetry Collections*

CHILDREN'S
Fiction
Chapter Books; *Early Readers*; *Picture Books*
Nonfiction
Activity Books; *Nonfiction Books*; *Picture Books*

Send: Query
Don't send: Full text
How to send: In the body of an email
How not to send: Email attachment

Send proposals up to six pages by email. No attachments or unsolicited mss.

P764 Thistle Publishing

Book Publisher
London
United Kingdom

info@thistlepublishing.co.uk

http://www.thistlepublishing.co.uk
http://twitter.com/ThistleBooks
https://www.facebook.com/ThistlePublishing/

Fiction > *Novels*

Nonfiction > *Nonfiction Books*

Send: Query; Synopsis; Author bio; Writing sample; Outline
How to send: Email

London-based publisher of quality fiction and nonfiction. Welcomes submissions. For nonfiction, send synopsis, author profile, sample chapter, and brief chapter summaries; for fiction, send synopsis and three sample chapters.

P765 Thomas Nelson

Publishing Imprint

Book Publisher: HarperCollins

P766 Threshold

Publishing Imprint

Book Publisher: Simon & Schuster Adult Publishing (**P711**)

P767 Tiger of the Stripe

Book Publisher
50 Albert Road, Richmond, Surrey, TW10 6DP
United Kingdom
Tel: +44 (0) 20 8940 8087

https://tigerofthestripe.co.uk

Fiction > *Novels*

Nonfiction > *Nonfiction Books*
Architecture; Books; Food; History; Language; Medieval; Music

Eclectic but with an emphasis on well-researched academic or semi-academic works. Also interested in biographies, history, language textbooks, cookbooks, typography. Not currently accepting new fiction.

Authors: Gerrish Gray; Jay Landesman; Julia Scott

Editor: Peter Danckwerts

P768 Times Books

Publishing Imprint
United Kingdom

Book Publisher: HarperCollins UK (**P347**)

P769 Tiny Owl

Book Publisher
6 Hatfield Road, Chiswick, London, W4 1AF
United Kingdom

info@tinyowl.co.uk

https://tinyowl.co.uk
https://www.facebook.com/tinyowlpublishing/
https://twitter.com/tinyowl_books
https://www.youtube.com/channel/UCJkMec_cxEVzTf2iUGvk2Pg
https://www.instagram.com/tiny_owl_publishing/

CHILDREN'S > **Fiction** > *Picture Books*

Closed to approaches.

Publisher of picture books for children.

P770 Toad Hall Editions

Book Publisher; Self Publishing Service
United States

hello@toadhalleditions.ink

https://www.toadhalleditions.ink
https://www.instagram.com/toadhalleditions/

Fiction
Novels; *Short Fiction Collections*
Nonfiction > *Nonfiction Books*
Creative Nonfiction; Memoir; Personal Essays

Poetry > *Poetry Collections*

Does not want:

> **Fiction** > *Novels*
> Fantasy; Historical Fiction; Horror; Mystery; Romance; Science Fiction; Thrillers
>
> **Nonfiction** > *Nonfiction Books*
> Finance; Motivational Self-Help

Send: Query; Synopsis; Author bio; Pitch
How to send: Email
How not to send: Email attachment

Costs: Offers services that writers have to pay for.

Small press publisher that also provides self-publishing services. Publishes 1-3 per year, written by women or gender-diverse people.

Magazines: Buttered Toast (**M099**); Kerning (**M287**)

P771 Tom Doherty Associates

Book Publisher
120 Broadway, New York, NY 10271
United States

https://us.macmillan.com/tomdohertyassociates/
https://www.facebook.com/torbooks
https://twitter.com/torbooks
https://www.youtube.com/user/torforge

Book Publisher: Macmillan Publishers (**P475**)

ADULT > **Fiction** > *Novels*
Fantasy; Horror; Mystery; Science Fiction; Thrillers

TEEN > **Fiction** > *Novels*
Fantasy; Science Fiction; Speculative

Publisher of Science Fiction, Fantasy, Horror, Mystery, Thriller and Suspense, and Other Speculative Fiction.

Publishing Imprints: Forge (**P273**); Tor (**P774**)

P772 Tommy Nelson

Publishing Imprint

Book Publisher: HarperCollins

P773 Top Publications, Ltd

Book Publisher
3100 Independence Parkway, Suite 311-359, Plano, TX 75075
United States
Tel: +1 (972) 490-9686
Fax: +1 (972) 233-0713

submissions@toppub.com

http://www.toppub.com

Types: Fiction
Formats: Short Fiction
Subjects: Adventure; Commercial; Contemporary; History; Horror; Mystery; Romance; Science Fiction; Suspense; Warfare
Markets: Adult; Young Adult

Send: Query
Don't send: Full text

Small press publisher of mainstream fiction. Authors should be willing to invest large amounts of time promoting their book and attending book-signings, etc. Send query letter by email only, giving information about yourself, your book, and your marketing ideas for it. No queries or submissions by post. Email approaches only. Any queries or submissions sent through the post will not be responded to.

Editor: Victoria Lam

P774 Tor

Publishing Imprint
United States

https://us.macmillan.com/tomdohertyassociates/
https://www.torforgeblog.com/

Book Publisher: Tom Doherty Associates (**P771**)

Fiction > *Novels*
Fantasy; Science Fiction

Closed to approaches.

Particular emphasis on science fiction and fantasy. Open submission policy currently suspended due to COVID-19.

Publishing Imprints: Orb; Tor; Tor Teen/Starscape; Tor/Seven Seas

P775 Torrey House Press, LLC

Book Publisher
150 S. State St. Suite 100, Salt Lake City, UT 84111
United States
Tel: +1 (801) 209-1657

mail@torreyhouse.com

http://torreyhouse.com

Types: Fiction; Nonfiction
Subjects: Culture; History; Literary; Nature
Markets: Adult

Closed to approaches.

Publishes narrative nonfiction and literary fiction with a natural history, environmental, or a natural landscape theme, or about the politics and practice of sustainable living. Submit using online submission manager on website.

Editors: Kirsten Johanna Allen; Mark Bailey

P776 Touchstone

Publishing Imprint

Book Publisher: Simon & Schuster Adult Publishing (**P711**)

P777 TouchWood Editions

Book Publisher
Canada

submissions@touchwoodeditions.com

https://www.touchwoodeditions.com

Fiction
Novels: Contemporary; Historical Fiction; Mystery; Supernatural / Paranormal
Short Fiction Collections: General

Nonfiction
Essays: General
Nonfiction Books: Alberta; Arctic; Arts; Beer; Biography; British Columbia; Contemporary; Cookery; Food; Gardening; History; Memoir; Nature; Painting; Pets; Photography; Travel; Vancouver Island; Wine; Women

Send: Query; Outline; Proposal; Synopsis; Marketing Plan; Author bio; Writing sample
How to send: PDF file email attachment

Accepts submissions by email only. Response only if interested. Publishes Canadian authors only. See website for full guidelines.

P778 Transworld Publishers

Book Publisher
61-63 Uxbridge Road, Ealing, London, W5 5SA
United Kingdom
Tel: +44 (0) 20 8579 2652

info@transworld-publishers.co.uk

https://www.penguin.co.uk/company/publishers/transworld.html

Book Publisher: Penguin Random House UK (**P587**)

Types: Fiction; Nonfiction
Subjects: Biography; Comedy / Humour; Cookery; Crime; Fantasy; Health; History; Literary; Literature; Music; Romance; Science; Science Fiction; Spirituality; Sport; Thrillers; Travel
Markets: Adult; Children's

How to send: Through a literary agent

Large publisher publishing a wide range of fiction and nonfiction for children and adults. No unsolicited MSS. Approach via a literary agent only.

Publishing Imprints: Bantam Books; Bantam Press; Black Swan; Corgi; Transworld Ireland

P779 Travelers' Tales / Solas House

Book Publisher
2320 Bowdoin Street, Palo Alto CA 94306
United States
Tel: +1 (650) 462-2110
Fax: +1 (650) 462-6305

ttales@travelerstales.com

https://travelerstales.com
https://www.facebook.com/Travelers-Tales-197098590465058/
https://twitter.com/travelerstales

Nonfiction
Nonfiction Books: Travel
Short Nonfiction: Travel

How to send: Online submission system
How not to send: Post; Email

Publishes books and anthologies of true travel tales, whether funny, adventurous, frightening, or grim. No fiction. Submit through online submission system only. No submissions by post or email. Response only if interested.

P780 Troika Books

Book Publisher
United Kingdom
Tel: +44 (0) 7710 412830

kidglovesbooks@gmail.com

https://www.troikabooks.com
https://twitter.com/TroikaBooks
https://youtube.com/channel/UCmc3CUxge0slDJwLs57WLJw

CHILDREN'S
Fiction
Novels; *Picture Books*
Poetry > *Any Poetic Form*

Closed to approaches.

Publishes picture books, fiction, and poetry for children.

Editor: Martin West

P781 Trotman Publishing

Book Publisher
21d Charles Street, Bath, BA1 1HX
United Kingdom
Tel: +44 (0) 3330 501023

info@trotman.co.uk

https://trotman.co.uk
https://twitter.com/TrotmanEd

ADULT > **Nonfiction** > *Nonfiction Books*
Career Development; Education; Walking Guides

PROFESSIONAL > **Nonfiction** > *Nonfiction Books*
Career Development; Education

Publishes books that help students get the career they want, and aid careers education professionals giving careers guidance. Also publishes walking guides.

Editor: David Lester

Publishing Imprint: White Ladder Press

P782 TTA Press

Magazine Publisher; Book Publisher
United Kingdom

http://www.ttapress.com

Magazines: Black Static (**M083**); Crimewave (**M149**)

P783 Turnstone Press

Book Publisher
Artspace Building, 206-100 Arthur Street, Winnipeg, Manitoba, Canada R3B 1H3
Canada
Tel: +1 (204) 947-1555
Fax: +1 (204) 947-1556

editor@turnstonepress.com

http://www.turnstonepress.com

Types: Fiction; Nonfiction; Poetry
Formats: Short Fiction
Subjects: Fantasy; Literary; Literary Criticism; Mystery; Thrillers
Markets: Adult

Literary publisher publishing the work of Canadian authors or landed immigrants only. Publishes literary fiction, literary non-fiction – including literary criticism – and poetry. Publishes literary mysteries, thrillers, noir, speculative fiction, and fantasy under imprint. No contact by email. All submissions must be by post with SASE. Mss without SASE will be recycled without response, as will submissions requesting response by email. See website for full guidelines.

Publishing Imprint: Ravenstone (**P644**)

P784 Turtle Books

Book Publisher
866 United Nations Plaza, Suite #525, New York, NY 10017
United States
Tel: +1 (212) 644-2020
Fax: +1 (212) 223-4387

http://www.turtlebooks.com

Types: Fiction; Nonfiction; Poetry
Subjects: Adventure; Culture; Fantasy; History; Literature; Nature; Sociology; Sport; Westerns
Markets: Children's

Send: Full text

Publishes children's illustrated books, often in both English and Spanish. Submit complete MS rather than sending a query.

Editor: John Whitman

P785 Twenty-First Century Books

Publishing Imprint

Book Publisher: Lerner Publishing Group **(P438)**

P786 TwoDot

Publishing Imprint
United States

Book Publisher: The Globe Pequot Press **(P296)**

P787 Tyndale House Publishers, Inc.

Book Publisher
351 Executive Drive, Carol Stream, IL 60188
United States
Tel: +1 (855) 277-9400
Fax: +1 (866) 622-9474

https://www.tyndale.com
https://facebook.com/TyndaleHouse
https://twitter.com/TyndaleHouse
https://pinterest.com/TyndaleHouse/
https://instagram.com/tyndalehouse/
https://youtube.com/user/TyndaleHP/

ADULT
Fiction > *Novels*
Allegory; Christianity; Contemporary Romance; Contemporary; Historical Fiction; Mystery; Romantic Suspense; Suspense; Thrillers; Westerns

Nonfiction
Nonfiction Books: Archaeology; Arts; Autobiography; Biography; Business; Christian Living; Christianity; Comedy / Humour; Culture; Current Affairs; Education; Finance; Health; History; Judaism; Leadership; Leisure; Memoir; Mental Health; Personal Development; Politics; Psychology; Sport; Travel
Reference: Christianity

CHILDREN'S
Fiction
Chapbook: Christianity
Picture Books: Christianity

Nonfiction > *Nonfiction Books*
Christian Living; Christianity

TEEN
Fiction > *Novels:* Christianity

Nonfiction > *Nonfiction Books*
Christian Living; Christianity; Relationships; Sex

How to send: Through a literary agent

Christian publisher, publishing bibles, nonfiction, fiction, and books for kids and teens.

P788 Ugly Duckling Presse

Book Publisher
The Old American Can Factory, 232 Third Street, #E303 (corner Third Avenue), Brooklyn, NY 11215
United States
Tel: +1 (347) 948-5170

office@uglyducklingpresse.org

https://uglyducklingpresse.org

Nonfiction > *Nonfiction Books:* Experimental

Poetry in Translation > *Poetry Collections*

Poetry > *Poetry Collections*

Closed to approaches.

Nonprofit publisher of poetry, translation, experimental nonfiction, performance texts, and books by artists. Check website for specific calls for submissions.

Print Magazine: Second Factory **(M443)**

P789 UKA Press

Book Publisher
United Kingdom

andrea@ukapress.com

http://www.ukapress.com

Fiction > *Novels*

Nonfiction > *Nonfiction Books*

Poetry > *Poetry Collections*

Send: Query
How to send: Through a literary agent

This publisher was created to publish fresh, exciting work by talented writers from around the world.

We're looking for originality, sparkle and the promise of something unexpected. Genre and style aren't important; quality is.

Accepts submissions through literary agents only.

P790 Ulverscroft Ltd

Book Publisher
The Green, Bradgate Road, Anstey, Leicester, LE7 7FU
United Kingdom
Tel: +44 (0) 116 236 4325

customersupport@ulverscroft.co.uk

https://www.ulverscroft.com
https://www.facebook.com/Ulverscroft
https://www.instagram.com/ulverscroftltd

Fiction > *Novels*

Nonfiction > *Nonfiction Books*

Publishes a wide variety of large print titles in hard and soft cover formats, as well as abridged and unabridged audio books. Many titles are written by the world's favourite authors.

Book Publisher: F.A. Thorpe (Publishing)

Editor: Mark Merrill

P791 Ulysses Press

Book Publisher
32 Court Street, Suite #2109, Brooklyn, New York 11201
United States

acquisitions@ulyssespress.com
ulysses@ulyssespress.com

https://ulyssespress.com
https://www.instagram.com/ulyssespress/
https://www.facebook.com/ulyssespress
https://twitter.com/UlyssesPress

ADULT
Fiction > *Novels*

Nonfiction > *Nonfiction Books*
Comedy / Humour; Cookery; Crime; Education; Fitness; Health; Home Improvement; Popular Culture; Self Help

CHILDREN'S
Fiction > *Picture Books*
Nonfiction > *Nonfiction Books*

YOUNG ADULT
Fiction > *Novels*
Nonfiction > *Nonfiction Books*

Send: Query; Synopsis; Table of Contents; Author bio; Market info; Writing sample
How to send: Email

Our publishing program seeks to move along the cultural cutting edge. We stay ahead of the competition by publishing books at the forefront of emerging trends and by finding unique angles on established topics unexplored by other publishers.

When it comes to finding new books, we are especially interested in titles that fill demonstrated niches in the trade book market. We seek books that take a specific and unique focus, a focus that can differentiate a book and make it stand out in a crowd.

P792 Unbound Press

Book Publisher
20 St Thomas Street, London, SE1 9RS
United Kingdom
Tel: +44 (0) 20 3997 6790

support@unbound.com

https://unbound.com
https://facebook.com/unbound
https://twitter.com/unbounders
https://instagram.com/unbounders

Fiction > *Novels*

Nonfiction > *Nonfiction Books*

Send: Full text

Crowdfunding publisher. Submit manuscripts via form on website.

P793 Union Park Press

Publishing Imprint
United States

Book Publisher: The Globe Pequot Press (**P296**)

P794 Unity

Book Publisher
1901 NW Blue Parkway, Unity Village, MO 64065--0001
United States
Tel: +1 (816) 524-3550

unitycustomerservice@unityonline.org

https://www.unity.org

Nonfiction > *Nonfiction Books*
Health; Lifestyle; Philosophy; Relationships; Self Help; Spirituality

Publisher of books on Spirituality, New Thought, personal growth, spiritual leadership, mind-body-spirit, and spiritual self-help.

P795 The University of Akron Press

Book Publisher
120 E. Mill Street, Suite 415, Akron, OH 44308
United States

uapress@uakron.edu

https://www.uakron.edu/uapress/
https://theuniversityofakronpress.submittable.com/submit

ACADEMIC > **Nonfiction** > *Nonfiction Books*
Culture; History; Ohio; Poetry as a Subject; Politics; Psychology

ADULT
Nonfiction > *Nonfiction Books*
Cookery; Culture; Food; History; Ohio; Sport

Poetry > *Poetry Collections*

Send: Query; Submission Form
Don't send: Full text
How to send: Submittable; Post; Email

For nonfiction, download and complete form on website, or submit through online submission system. Also publishes books of poetry, mainly through its annual competition.

P796 University of Alaska Press

Book Publisher
Editorial Department, University of Alaska Press, PO Box 756240, 104 Eielson Building, Fairbanks, AK 99775-6240
United States
Tel: +1 (720) 406-8849
Fax: +1 (720) 406-3443

https://upcolorado.com/university-of-alaska-press

ACADEMIC > **Nonfiction** > *Nonfiction Books*
Alaska; Biography; Culture; History; Language; Memoir; Nature; Politics; Science

ADULT
Fiction > *Short Fiction Collections*: Alaska

Poetry > *Poetry Collections*: Alaska

Send: Query; Proposal
How to send: Online submission system

Publishing books on politics and history, Native languages and cultures, science and natural history, biography and memoir, poetry, fiction and anthologies, and original translations, all with an emphasis on the state of Alaska.

P797 University of Arizona Press

Book Publisher
1510 E. University Blvd., P.O. Box 210055, Tucson, AZ 85721-0055
United States

https://uapress.arizona.edu
http://www.facebook.com/AZPress
http://www.twitter.com/AZPress

ACADEMIC > **Nonfiction** > *Nonfiction Books*
Anthropology; Archaeology; Arizona; Environment; Ethnic Groups; Gender; History; Native Americans; South America; Southwestern United States; Space

ADULT > **Poetry** > *Any Poetic Form*

Publishes the work of leading scholars from around the globe. Invites proposals from authors of appropriate works.

Acquisitions Editors: Allyson Carter; Patti Hartmann

P798 University of Arkansas Press

Book Publisher
McIlroy House, 105 N. McIlroy Avenue, Fayetteville, AR 72701
United States
Tel: +1 (479) 575-7544

mbieker@uark.edu

https://www.uapress.com

Types: Nonfiction; Poetry
Markets: Academic; Adult

Accepts unsolicited proposals for scholarly books in the social sciences and humanities as well as nonfiction works of local or regional interest. Also publishes poetry books through its poetry competitions, for which there is a standard entry fee. Submit via online submission system.

Editors: Mike Bieker; David Scott Cunningham

P799 University of California Press

Book Publisher
United States

krobinson@ucpress.edu

https://www.ucpress.edu
https://twitter.com/ucpress
https://www.facebook.com/ucpress
https://www.instagram.com/uc_press/
https://www.youtube.com/channel/UCX5V8BHO32jgshduh7nbR8Q
https://www.linkedin.com/company/university-of-california-press

ACADEMIC > **Nonfiction** > *Nonfiction Books*
Africa; Anthropology; Arts; Asia; Classics / Ancient World; Crime; Economics; Environment; Films; Food; Gender; Health; History; Language; Legal; Literature; Media; Middle East; Music; Philosophy; Politics; Psychology; Religion; Science; Sexuality; Sociology; South America; Technology; United States; Wine

Scholarly publisher based in California.

Acquisitions Editor: Maura Roessner

Editorial Director: Kim Robinson

P800 University of Exeter Press

Book Publisher
Reed Hall, Streatham Drive, Exeter, EX4 4QR
United Kingdom
Tel: +44 (0) 1392 263066
Fax: +44 (0) 1392 263064

n.massen@exeterpress.co.uk

http://www.exeterpress.co.uk

Types: Nonfiction
Formats: Film Scripts; Reference
Subjects: Archaeology; Culture; History; Literature; Philosophy; Religion; Sociology
Markets: Academic

Send: Query
Don't send: Full text

Publisher of academic books. See website for guidelines on submitting a proposal.

Editors: Anna Henderson; Hetty Marx; Nigel Massen

P801 University of Hawai'i Press

Book Publisher
2840 Kolowalu Street, Honolulu, HI 96822
United States

Tel: +1 (808) 956-8255
Fax: +1 (800) 650-7811

uhpbooks@hawaii.edu

https://uhpress.hawaii.edu
https://www.facebook.com/UniversityofHawaiiPress/
https://www.instagram.com/uhpress/
https://twitter.com/uhpressnews?lang=en

ACADEMIC > **Nonfiction** > *Nonfiction Books*
Anthropology; Architecture; Arts; Asia; Buddhism; Environment; Hawai'i; History; Language; Literature; Pacific; Popular Culture; Religion; South-East Asia

Send: Query; Outline; Market info; Author bio; Table of Contents; Writing sample
How to send: Email; Post

Focuses on books in the humanities, social sciences, and natural sciences in areas that include history, religion, anthropology, literature, art and architecture, the environment, and languages. Also publishes or distributes more than 25 scholarly journals that reflect the university's regional and international focus in the aforementioned subjects.

Publishing Imprints: Kolowalu Books; Latitude 20

P802 University of Hertfordshire Press

Book Publisher
College Lane, Hatfield, Hertfordshire, AL10 9AB
United Kingdom
Tel: +44 (0) 1707 284681

uhpress@herts.ac.uk

http://www.herts.ac.uk/UHPress

ACADEMIC > **Nonfiction** > *Nonfiction Books*
History; Literature; Local History; Mathematics; Psychology; Theatre

Send: Query; Submission Form
How to send: Email

Publisher of academic books on local history, including imprints for Essex, West Midlands, and Hertfordshire.

Editor: Jane Housham

Publishing Imprints: Essex Publications (**P246**); Hertfordshire Publications (**P369**); West Midlands Publications (**P855**)

P803 University of Illinois Press

Book Publisher; Magazine Publisher
1325 South Oak Street, Champaign, IL 61820-6903
United States
Tel: +1 (217) 333-0950

uipress@uillinois.edu

https://www.press.uillinois.edu
https://www.facebook.com/UniversityofIllinoisPress/
https://www.youtube.com/user/univofillinoispress
https://www.instagram.com/illinoispress/
https://open.spotify.com/user/462orqowlbwnk44jrfkk16tcb
https://twitter.com/illinoispress
https://soundcloud.com/user-511256562

ACADEMIC > **Nonfiction** > *Nonfiction Books*
18th Century; Africa; African American; Agriculture; American History; American Midwest; Animal Rights; Animals; Anthropology; Appalachia; Archaeology; Architecture; Asia; Asian American; Biography; Biology; Business; Caribbean; Chicago; Children; Classics / Ancient World; Comedy / Humour; Communication; Computers; Crime; Culture; Dance; Economics; Education; Engineering; Environment; European History; Films; Folklore, Myths, and Legends; Food; France; Geography; Germany; Illinois; Information Science; International; Ireland; Italy; Jewish Holocaust; Judaism; Language; Legal; Literature; Marxism; Mathematics; Media; Medicine; Medieval; Middle East; Military History; Mormonism; Music; Native Americans; Nature; Philosophy; Photography; Poetry as a Subject; Politics; Popular Culture; Psychology; Renaissance; Science Fiction; Science; Sexuality; Sociology; South America; Sport; Travel; Urban

ADULT > **Fiction** > *Novels*

Supports the mission of the university through the worldwide dissemination of significant scholarship, striving to enhance and extend the reputation of the university.

P804 University of Iowa Press

Book Publisher
119 West Park Road, 100 Kuhl House, Iowa City IA 52242-1000
United States
Tel: +1 (319) 335-2000
Fax: +1 (319) 335-2055

uipress@uiowa.edu

https://www.uipress.uiowa.edu

ACADEMIC > **Nonfiction** > *Nonfiction Books*
American Midwest; Archaeology; Books; Culture; Food; History; Literature; Nature; Theatre

ADULT
Fiction > *Short Fiction*
Poetry > *Any Poetic Form*

How to send: Email; Through a contest

Send proposals for nonfiction by email. Accepts fiction and poetry through annual competitions only.

P805 University of Maine Press

Book Publisher
5729 Fogler Library, Orono, ME 04469-5729
United States
Tel: +1 (207) 581-1652

alpert@maine.edu

https://umaine.edu/umpress/

ACADEMIC > **Nonfiction** > *Nonfiction Books*
Arts; Maine; Science

ADULT > **Fiction** > *Novels*: Maine

Send: Query; Synopsis; Writing sample; Self-Addressed Stamped Envelope (SASE)
Don't send: Full text
How to send: Post; Email

Publishes scholarly books and original writing in science, the arts and the humanities, focusing on the intellectual concerns of the Maine region. Occasionally publishes regional fiction. Send query by email or by post with SASE between September 1 and October 31.

P806 University of Massachusetts Press

Book Publisher
New Africa House, 180 Infirmary Way, 4th Floor, Amherst, MA 01003-9289
United States
Fax: +1 (413) 545-1226

cdougan@umpress.umass.edu

http://www.umass.edu/umpress

Types: Fiction; Nonfiction; Poetry
Subjects: Culture; History; Nature; Politics
Markets: Academic; Adult

Focuses primarily on books in the field of American studies, including books that explore the history, politics, literature, culture, and environment of the United States – as well as works with a transnational perspective. In addition to publishing works of scholarship, the Press produces books of more general interest for a wider readership. Also publishes poetry and fiction via its annual competitions only.

Editor-in-Chief: Matt Becker

P807 University of Missouri Press

Book Publisher
113 Heinkel Building, 201 S 7th Street, Columbia, MO 65211
United States
Tel: +1 (573) 882-7641
Fax: +1 (573) 884-4498

upress@missouri.edu

https://upress.missouri.edu

Types: Nonfiction
Subjects: History; Literary Criticism; Politics; Warfare
Markets: Academic

Send: Query
Don't send: Full text

Scholarly publisher of a range of subject lists, with a focus on American History (esp. US Military, African American, Political), Journalism, Political Science, Missouri History and Regional Studies, and Literary Criticism (gen. American and British). Also happy to consider enquiries regarding work in any area of the humanities or natural history. No fiction or poetry. See website for full guidelines.

Editor-in-Chief: Andrew J. Davidson

P808 University of Nevada Press

Book Publisher
University of Nevada Press, Morrill Hall Mail Stop 0166, Reno NV 89557-0166
United States
Tel: +1 (775) 784-6573

jbanducci@unpress.nevada.edu

https://www.unpress.nevada.edu

Types: Fiction; Nonfiction
Subjects: Anthropology; Arts; Culture; Current Affairs; Finance; History; Literature; Nature; Politics; Science; Sociology
Markets: Academic; Adult

Send: Query
Don't send: Full text

Publishes scholarly books in the humanities and social sciences in the fields of environmental studies, public health, mining studies, Native American studies, urban studies, Basque studies, gambling and commercial gaming, and select fiction. Will also publish books on any topic which contribute to our understanding of Nevada, the Great Basin, and American West. See website for full submission guidelines and submit proposals by email.

Editor: JoAnne Banducci

P809 University of North Texas Press

Book Publisher
1155 Union Circle #311336, Denton, TX 76203-5017
United States
Tel: +1 (940) 565-2142
Fax: +1 (940) 369-8760

https://untpress.unt.edu
https://www.facebook.com/UniversityOfNorthTexasPress/
https://twitter.com/untpress/
https://www.pinterest.com/untpress0263/

ACADEMIC > **Nonfiction** > *Nonfiction Books*
Crime; Culture; Environment; Folklore, Myths, and Legends; Food History; History; Legal; Military History; Multicultural; Music; Nature; Texas; Women's Studies

ADULT
Fiction > *Short Fiction*
Poetry > *Any Poetic Form*

Send: Query
How to send: Post; Email
How not to send: Phone

Publishes in the humanities and social sciences, with an emphasis on Texas. Also publishes fiction and poetry through its annual competitions. See website for more details.

P810 University of Oklahoma Press

Book Publisher
2800 Venture Drive, Norman, OK 73069-8216
United States

https://www.oupress.com

ACADEMIC > **Nonfiction** > *Nonfiction Books*
Arts; Autobiography; Biography; Business; Comedy / Humour; Cookery; Crafts; Drama; Economics; Education; Engineering; Family; Fitness; Health; History; Hobbies; Language; Legal; Literature; Music; Nature; Performing Arts; Pets; Philosophy; Photography; Politics; Psychology; Relationships; Religion; Science; Self Help; Sociology; Sport; Technology; Transport; Travel

How to send: Online submission system

Publishes scholarly books of significance to the state, region, nation, and world, both to convey the results of current research to other scholars and to offer broader presentations for the general public.

P811 University of Pennsylvania Press

Book Publisher
3905 Spruce Street, Philadelphia, PA 19104-4112
United States
Tel: +1 (215) 898-6261
Fax: +1 (215) 898-0404

custserv@pobox.upenn.edu

https://www.upenn.edu/pennpress

ACADEMIC > **Nonfiction** > *Nonfiction Books*
African Diaspora; Atlantic; Culture; History; Intellectual History; Judaism; Literary Criticism; Medieval; North America; Political History; Renaissance; South America

Send: Query
How to send: Email

Send query by email to appropriate editor.

Associate Editor: Jenny Tan

Company Director: Eric Halpern

Editor-in-Chief: Walter Biggins

Senior Editors: Robert Lockhart; Jerome Singerman

P812 University of Pittsburgh Press

Book Publisher
7500 Thomas Boulevard, Pittsburgh, PA 15260
United States

https://upittpress.org

ACADEMIC > **Nonfiction** > *Nonfiction Books*
Architecture; Arts; Asia; Biography; Eastern Europe; Environment; History; Literature; Medicine; Pennsylvania; Photography; Pittsburgh; Russia; Science; South America; Technology; Travel; Urban

ADULT > **Poetry** > *Any Poetic Form*

Send: Query
Don't send: Full text

Publishes books on Latin American studies, Russian and East European studies, Central Asian studies, composition and literacy studies, environmental studies, urban studies, the history of architecture and the built environment, and the history and philosophy of science, technology, and medicine. Describes its poetry series as representing many of the finest poets active today.

Acquisitions Editor: Joshua Shanholtzer

Editorial Directors: Abby Collier; Sandy Crooms

P813 University of Tennessee Press

Book Publisher
110 Conference Center, Knoxville, TN 37996-4108
United States
Tel: +1 (865) 974-3321
Fax: +1 (865) 974-3724

utpress@utk.edu

https://utpress.org
https://www.facebook.com/utennpress/
https://twitter.com/utennpress

ACADEMIC > **Nonfiction** > *Nonfiction Books*
American Civil War; American History; Anthropology; Folklore, Myths, and Legends; Literature; Music; Popular Culture; Religion; Sport

Send: Query; Table of Contents; Writing sample; Author bio

The press is committed to preserving knowledge about Tennessee and the region and, by expanding its unique publishing program, it promotes a broad base of cultural understanding and, ultimately, improves life in the state.

Acquisitions Editor: Scot Danforth

P814 University of Texas Press

Book Publisher
3001 Lake Austin Blvd, 2.200, Stop E4800, Austin, TX 78703-4206
United States

https://utpress.utexas.edu

ACADEMIC > **Nonfiction** > *Nonfiction Books*
Anthropology; Archaeology; Architecture; Arts; Biography; Classics / Ancient World; Cookery; Environment; Films; Food; History; Judaism; Media; Middle East; Music; Nature; Photography; Sexuality; South America; Southwestern United States; Texas; United States

ADULT > **Nonfiction** > *Nonfiction Books*
Art History; Arts; Culture; Current Affairs; Food; History; Music; Nature; Texas

Send: Query; Proposal; Table of Contents; Writing sample; Author bio; Submission Form
How to send: Email

Send query with proposal, table of contents, sample chapter, and CV. Publishes scholarly books and some general readership nonfiction. See website for full details.

P815 University of Virginia Press

Book Publisher
P.O. Box 400318, Charlottesville, VA 22904-4318
United States
Tel: +1 (434) 924-3468
Fax: +1 (434) 982-2655

vapress@virginia.edu

https://www.upress.virginia.edu/

ACADEMIC > **Nonfiction** > *Nonfiction Books*
18th Century; Africa; African American; American Civil War; American History; Anthropology; Archaeology; Architecture; Arts; Autobiography; Biography; Business; Caribbean; Cookery; Culture; Current Affairs; Education; Environment; European History; Food; Geography; History; Legal; Literary Criticism; Literature; Memoir; Nature; Philosophy; Photography; Politics; Publishing; Religion; Science; Sociology; Technology; Virginia; Women's Studies

ADULT
Nonfiction > *Nonfiction Books*: Virginia

Poetry > *Any Poetic Form*

Send: Submission Form

Has a reputation for publishing quality scholarship in American history and government, eighteenth-century and Victorian literature, Afro-Caribbean studies, cultural religion, architectural and environmental history, and trade books of regional interest.

P816 The University of Wisconsin Press

Book Publisher
728 State Street, Suite 443, Madison, WI 53706
United States
Tel: +1 (608) 263-1110
Fax: +1 (608) 263-1173

uwiscpress@uwpress.wisc.edu

https://uwpress.wisc.edu
https://www.facebook.com/universityofwisconsinpress
https://twitter.com/UWiscPress
https://www.instagram.com/uwiscpress
https://www.goodreads.com/user/show/24113667-university-of-wisconsin-press
https://uwpress.wisc.edu/blog.html

ACADEMIC > **Nonfiction** > *Nonfiction Books*
Africa; African American; American Civil War; American Midwest; Anthropology; Asia; Autobiography; Brazil; Caribbean; Cinemas / Movie Theaters; Classics / Ancient World; Dance; Earth Science; Eastern Europe; Environment; Ethnography; Folklore, Myths, and Legends; Germany; History; Ireland; Judaism; LGBTQIA; Media; Native Americans; Outdoor Activities; Politics; Popular Culture; Russia; Scandinavia; South America; Travel; Wisconsin

ADULT
Fiction > *Novels*
General, and in particular: Mystery

Poetry > *Any Poetic Form*

Publishes scholarly, general interest nonfiction books and books featuring the American mid-west, along with a limited number of novels and short story and poetry collections.

P817 University Press of Mississippi

Book Publisher
United States

https://www.upress.state.ms.us

ACADEMIC > **Nonfiction** > *Nonfiction Books*
African American; Caribbean; Comic Books; Culture; Films; Folklore, Myths, and Legends; History; Literature; Media; Music; Popular Culture; US Southern States

How to send: Email

Publishes books that interpret the South and its culture to the nation and the world, scholarly books of the highest distinction, and books vital to readers in African American studies, Caribbean studies, comics studies, film and media studies, folklore, history, literary studies, music, and popular culture.

P818 Unthank Books

Book Publisher
United Kingdom

information@unthankbooks.com

https://www.unthankbooks.com
https://www.facebook.com/UnthankBooks/
https://twitter.com/@unthankbooks

Fiction
Novels: Literary
Short Fiction Collections: Literary

An independent publisher nurturing distinct and vibrant literature, both in the novel and short form.

Editorial Director: Ashley Stokes

Publisher: Robin Jones

P819 Up On Big Rock Poetry

Publishing Imprint

Book Publisher: Shipwreckt Books Publishing Company (**P705**)

P820 VanderWyk & Burnham

Book Publisher
1610 Long Leaf Circle, St. Louis, MO 63146
United States
Tel: +1 (314) 432-3435
Fax: +1 (314) 993-4485

quickpublishing@sbcglobal.net

http://www.vandb.com

Types: Nonfiction
Subjects: Lifestyle; Psychology; Self Help
Markets: Adult

Closed to approaches.

Not accepting unsolicited proposals or submissions as at May 2020.

P821 Vermilion

Publishing Imprint
United Kingdom

Book Publisher: Ebury (**P226**)

P822 Viking

Publishing Imprint
United States

Book Publisher: Penguin Publishing Group (**P585**)

P823 Viking Children's Books

Publishing Imprint
United States

Book Publisher: Penguin Young Readers Group (**P591**)

P824 Viking Dog

Book Publisher
United States

contact@viking-dog.com

https://www.viking-dog.com
https://www.instagram.com/vikingdogent/
https://www.facebook.com/vikingdogent/
http://twitter.com/vikingdogent
https://www.youtube.com/channel/UCmZtTxwsFYEKNa-eBrtHxhg?view_as=subscriber
https://vimeo.com/user70568100

Fiction > *Novels*
Adventure; Fantasy; Science Fiction; Thrillers; Westerns

Scripts
Film Scripts: Adventure; Fantasy; Science Fiction; Thrillers; Westerns
TV Scripts: Adventure; Fantasy; Science Fiction; Thrillers; Westerns

Send: Query
How to send: Email

A content company based in Los Angeles that creates, publishes and distributes film and book projects.

P825 Vine Leaves Press

Book Publisher
Australia

submissions@vineleavespress.com

https://www.vineleavespress.com

Types: Fiction; Nonfiction
Formats: Reference; Short Fiction
Subjects: Autobiography; Literary
Markets: Adult

Send: Query
Don't send: Full text

Publishes novels (all genres accepted, but with a literary bent), memoirs / biographies / autobiographies, creative nonfiction, and writing / publishing reference books, and short story collections. Send query by email with first ten pages and author bio.

P826 Vinspire Publishing

Book Publisher
PO Box 1165, Ladson, SC 29456-1165
United States
Tel: +1 (843) 695-7530

vinspirepublishingeic@gmail.com

https://www.vinspirepublishing.com

ADULT
Fiction > *Novels*
African American; Contemporary Romance; Historical Fiction; Historical Romance; Inspirational; Literary; Mystery; Romance; Supernatural / Paranormal Romance

Nonfiction > *Nonfiction Books*

CHILDREN'S > **Fiction**
Middle Grade; *Picture Books*
YOUNG ADULT > **Fiction** > *Novels*

Send: Query; Author bio; Outline; Synopsis
How to send: In the body of an email

Now open to the following limited submissions that do not require an agent: Young Adult; and African-American Contemporary Romance.

P827 Vintage

Book Publisher
United Kingdom

Book Publisher: Penguin Random House UK (**P587**)

Publishing Imprints: The Bodley Head (*P116*); Chatto & Windus (*P157*); Harvill Secker (*P360*); Hogarth Press (*P376*); Jonathan Cape (**P415**); Square Peg (*P731*); Vintage Classics (*P829*); Vintage Paperbacks (*P830*); Yellow Jersey (*P879*)

P828 Vintage Books

Publishing Imprint
United States

Book Publisher: Knopf Doubleday Publishing Group (**P426**)

P829 Vintage Classics

Publishing Imprint
United Kingdom

Book Publisher: Vintage (**P827**)

P830 Vintage Paperbacks

Publishing Imprint
United Kingdom

Book Publisher: Vintage (**P827**)

P831 Virago Books

Publishing Imprint
50 Victoria Embankment, London, EC4Y 0DZ
United Kingdom
Tel: +44 (0) 20 3122 7000

https://www.virago.co.uk
https://www.facebook.com/ViragoPress
https://twitter.com/viragobooks
https://www.instagram.com/viragopress/

Publishing Imprint: Little, Brown Book Group

Fiction
Graphic Novels: Women
Novels: Women's Fiction; Women's Issues; Women

Nonfiction > *Nonfiction Books*
Feminism; Women's Issues; Women's Studies; Women

How to send: Through a literary agent

Publishes books by women. Founded in 1973 to put women centre stage; to explore the untold stories of their lives; above all to champion women's talent. Publishes award-winning fiction, agenda-setting non-fiction, a rich list of rediscovered classics – and most recently a boutique list of graphic novels.

Authors: Maya Angelou; Margaret Atwood; Jennifer Belle; Waris Dirie; Sarah Dunant; Germaine Greer; Daphne du Maurier; Michele Roberts; Gillian Slovo; Talitha Stevenson; Natasha Walter; Sarah Waters; Edith Wharton

Publishing Imprints: Virago Modern Classics; Virago.

P832 Virgin Books

Publishing Imprint
United Kingdom

Book Publisher: Ebury (**P226**)

P833 Vision Paperbacks

Book Publisher
United Kingdom

https://www.visionpaperbacks.co.uk

Nonfiction > *Nonfiction Books*
General, and in particular: Alternative Lifestyles; Autobiography; Biography; Current Affairs; Environment; Investigative Journalism; Media; Science; Sexuality; Society

Send: Synopsis; Full text; Writing sample; Market info
How to send: Online contact form

Accepts approaches from published and first-time authors for books that fit with their list. Submit material through online submission form.

Editor: Charlotte Cole

Publishing Imprint: Fusion Press

P834 Voyageur Press

Publishing Imprint
Book Proposals, Voyageur Press, Quayside Publishing Group, 400 First Avenue North, Suite 300, Minneapolis, MN 55401
United States
Tel: +1 (800) 458-0454
Fax: +1 (612) 344-8691

customerservice@quaysidepub.com

http://www.voyageurpress.com

Book Publisher: The Quarto Group, Inc. (**P633**)

Types: Nonfiction
Subjects: Culture; History; Lifestyle; Music;

Nature; Photography; Travel
Markets: Adult

Send: Query
Don't send: Full text

Publishes books on nature and the environment; country living and farming heritage; regional and cultural history; music; travel and photography. See website for full submission guidelines.

P835 W Publishing Group

Publishing Imprint

Book Publisher: HarperCollins

P836 W.W. Norton & Company Ltd

Book Publisher
15 Carlisle Street, London, W1D 3BS
United Kingdom
Tel: +44 (0) 20 7323 1579

crussell1@wwnorton.com

https://wwnorton.co.uk
https://twitter.com/wwnortonUK
https://www.instagram.com/wwnortonuk/
https://medium.com/@W.W.NortonUK
https://www.pinterest.com/wwnortonuk/

ACADEMIC > **Nonfiction** > *Nonfiction Books*
African American; Anthropology; Astronomy; Biology; Chemistry; Classics / Ancient World; Computer Science; Films; Geology; History; Immunology; Literature; Music; Philosophy; Physics; Politics; Psychology; Religion; Sociology; Statistics

ADULT
Fiction
Graphic Novels; *Novels*
Nonfiction
Essays: General
Nonfiction Books: Adventure; African American; Archaeology; Architecture; Arts; Astronomy; Biography; Business; Classics / Ancient World; Comedy / Humour; Crafts; Crime; Culture; Current Affairs; Design; Drama; Economics; Education; Environment; Films; Folklore, Myths, and Legends; Food and Drink; Games; Gardening; Health; History; Hobbies; Houses; LGBTQIA; Legal; Literature; Medicine; Memoir; Music; Nature; Parenting; Pets; Philosophy; Photography; Politics; Popular Science; Psychology; Psychotherapy; Religion; Self Help; Sociology; Sport; Statistics; Technology; Transport; Travel; Women's Studies; Writing
Poetry > *Poetry Collections*

CHILDREN'S
Fiction
Chapter Books; *Early Readers*; *Picture Books*
Nonfiction > *Nonfiction Books*

PROFESSIONAL > **Nonfiction** > *Nonfiction Books*
Addiction; Anxiety Disorders; Architecture; Autism; Child Psychotherapy; Coaching; Couple Therapy; Depression; Design; Eating Disorders; Education; Family Therapy; Genetics; Geriatrics; Health; Hypnosis; Juvenile Psychotherapy; Medicine; Neurobiology; Neuropsychology; Neuroscience; Post Traumatic Stress Disorder; Psychiatry; Psychoanalysis; Psychological Trauma; Psychotherapy; Self Help; Sexuality

UK branch of a US publisher. No editorial office in the UK – contact the main office in New York (see separate listing).

P837 Walden Pond Press

Publishing Imprint

Book Publisher: HarperCollins

P838 Walter Foster Jr.

Publishing Imprint

Book Publisher: The Quarto Group, Inc. **(P633)**

P839 Walter Foster Publishing

Publishing Imprint
Suite A, Irvine, CA 92618
United States
Tel: +1 (800) 426-0099
Fax: +1 (949) 380-7575

info@walterfoster.com

http://www.walterfoster.com

Book Publisher: The Quarto Group, Inc. **(P633)**

Types: Nonfiction
Subjects: Crafts; How To
Markets: Adult; Children's; Young Adult

Publishes how-to craft books and kits for children and adults.

P840 Washington State University Press

Book Publisher
Cooper Publications Building, PO Box 645910, Pullman, WA 99164-5910
United States
Tel: +1 (509) 335-8821
Fax: +1 (509) 335-8568

wsupress@wsu.edu

https://wsupress.wsu.edu

Types: Nonfiction
Subjects: Biography; Cookery; Culture; History; Nature; Politics; Westerns
Markets: Academic; Adult

Send: Query
Don't send: Full text

Send query by post or by email (preferred) with author CV, summary of proposed work, sample bio, and one or two sample chapters. Specialises in the American West, particularly the prehistory, history, environment, politics, and culture of the greater Northwest region. No fiction, poetry, or literary criticism. See website for full guidelines.

Editor-in-Chief: Linda Bathgate

P841 WaterBrook Multnomah

Publishing Imprint

Book Publisher: Random House **(P640)**

P842 Watson-Guptill

Publishing Imprint

Book Publisher: Random House **(P640)**

P843 Watson-Guptill Publications

Publishing Imprint
United States

http://crownpublishing.com/archives/imprint/watson-guptill

Book Publisher: The Crown Publishing Group

Types: Nonfiction
Formats: Reference; Theatre Scripts
Subjects: Architecture; Arts; Crafts; Culture; Design; How To; Lifestyle; Music; Photography
Markets: Adult; Children's

Send: Query
Don't send: Full text

Publishes art and art instruction books.

P844 Wave Books

Book Publisher
1938 Fairview Avenue East, Suite 201, Seattle, WA 98102
United States
Tel: +1 (206) 676-5337

info@wavepoetry.com

https://www.wavepoetry.com
http://twitter.com/WavePoetry
http://www.facebook.com/pages/Wave-Books/325354873993
http://wavepoetry.tumblr.com/

Poetry > *Poetry Collections*: Contemporary

Closed to approaches.

Independent poetry press based in Seattle. Accepts submissions only in response to specific calls for submissions posted on the website (see the submissions page).

Publisher: Charlie Wright

P845 Waverley Books

Publishing Imprint
Unit 31, Six Harmony Row, Glasgow

G51 3BA
United Kingdom
Tel: +44 (0) 1413 751996

https://www.waverley-books.co.uk
https://www.facebook.com/pages/WAVERLEY-BOOKS/110565462291036
https://twitter.com/WaverleyBooks

Book Publisher: Gresham Books Ltd

ADULT
Fiction
Graphic Novels: Scotland
Novels: General, and in particular: Romantic Comedy; Scotland
Nonfiction > *Nonfiction Books*
Comedy / Humour; Food and Drink; History; Scotland; Travel

CHILDREN'S
Fiction
Novels: General, and in particular: Scotland
Picture Books: General, and in particular: Scotland
Nonfiction > *Nonfiction Books*
History; Scotland

Publishes history, fiction, nostalgia, food and drink, humour, children's, graphic novels, and Scottish interest.

P846 Wayland Books

Publishing Imprint

Book Publisher: Hachette Children's Group (**P318**)

P847 Wayne State University Press

Book Publisher
4809 Woodward Avenue, Detroit, Michigan 48201-1309
United States

https://www.wsupress.wayne.edu

ACADEMIC > **Nonfiction** > *Nonfiction Books*
African American; Detroit; Fairy Tales; Films; Health; Judaism; Media; Michigan; Regional; TV

ADULT
Fiction > *Short Fiction Collections*

Nonfiction > *Nonfiction Books*: Creative Nonfiction

Poetry > *Poetry Collections*

Send: Query; Proposal; Author bio; Writing sample
Don't send: Full text
How to send: Email

Actively acquiring books in African American studies, media studies, fairy-tale studies, Jewish studies, citizenship studies, and regional studies: books about the state of Michigan, the city of Detroit, and the Great Lakes region. Send query to appropriate acquisitions editor (see website for details and individual contact details).

P848 Weasel Press

Book Publisher
United States

thedude@weaselpress.com

https://www.weaselpress.com

Types: Fiction; Nonfiction; Poetry
Formats: Short Fiction
Subjects: Experimental; Literary
Markets: Adult

Closed to approaches.

From autumn 2020 will only accept work from authors of colour, or who identify as LGBTQ+, or who are disabled. Submit through online submission system.

P849 Wednesday Books

Publishing Imprint

Publishing Imprint: St Martin's Press (**P733**)

P850 Weidenfeld & Nicolson

Book Publisher
United Kingdom

https://www.weidenfeldandnicolson.co.uk
https://twitter.com/wnbooks/
https://www.facebook.com/WeidenfeldandNicolson/
https://www.instagram.com/orionbooks/?hl=en

Book Publisher: The Orion Publishing Group Limited

Fiction > *Novels*: Literary

Nonfiction > *Nonfiction Books*

Describes itself as one of the most prestigious and dynamic literary imprints in British and international publishing, home to a wide range of literary fiction and non-fiction, modern classics, prizewinning debuts and worldwide bestsellers.

P851 Welbeck Publishing Group

Book Publisher
20 Mortimer Street, London, W1T 3JW
United Kingdom
Tel: +44 (0) 20 7612 0400
Fax: +44 (0) 20 7612 0401

submissions@welbeckpublishing.com

https://www.welbeckpublishing.com
https://www.facebook.com/welbeckpublish/
https://www.instagram.com/welbeckpublish/
https://twitter.com/welbeckpublish
https://www.youtube.com/welbeckpublishinggroup
https://www.linkedin.com/company/welbeckpublishinggroup/

ADULT
Fiction > *Novels*
Commercial; Popular

Nonfiction
Illustrated Books: Comedy / Humour; Entertainment; Fashion; History; Lifestyle; Sport
Nonfiction Books: Biography; Business; Crime; History; Memoir; Military; Narrative Nonfiction; Popular Culture; Popular Science; Psychology; Self Help; Sport
Puzzle Books: General

CHILDREN'S
Fiction > *Middle Grade*

Nonfiction
Illustrated Books: Environment; History; Hobbies; Mental Health; Nature
Nonfiction Books: General
Picture Books: General

Send: Query
Don't send: Full text

Publishes illustrated reference, sport, entertainment, commercial fiction and children's nonfiction. Synopses and ideas for suitable books are welcomed, but no unsolicited MSS, academic, or poetry. Send query by email only with short synopsis, author bio, market info, and up to two chapters up to a maximum of 20 pages. See website for full guidelines.

P852 Wellfleet Press

Publishing Imprint

Book Publisher: The Quarto Group, Inc. (**P633**)

P853 Wells College Press

Book Publisher
170 Main St, Aurora, NY 13026
United States
Tel: +1 (315) 364-3420

bookartscenter@wells.edu

https://wellsbookartscenter.org/wells-college-press/

Types: Nonfiction; Poetry
Subjects: Arts; Design
Markets: Adult

Publishes poetry chapbooks and books on art, design, and typography.

P854 Wesleyan University Press

Book Publisher
215 Long Lane, Middletown, CT 06459
United States
Tel: +1 (860) 685-7727
Fax: +1 (860) 685-7712

stamminen@wesleyan.edu

https://www.weslpress.org

ACADEMIC > **Nonfiction** > *Nonfiction Books*
Dance; Music

Send: Query; Proposal
Don't send: Full text
How to send: Email

Accepting proposals in the areas of dance and music. See website for submission guidelines.

P855 West Midlands Publications

Publishing Imprint
United Kingdom

http://www.uhpress.co.uk/subject-areas/west-midlands-publications

Book Publisher: University of Hertfordshire Press (**P802**)

ACADEMIC > **Nonfiction** > *Nonfiction Books*: Local History

This series aims to publish scholarly, attractive, well-illustrated and accessible studies on the history of the English West Midlands, a region which broadly encompasses the historic counties of Derbyshire, Herefordshire, Shropshire, Staffordshire, Warwickshire and Worcestershire.

P856 WestBow Press

Publishing Imprint

Book Publisher: HarperCollins

P857 WH Allen

Publishing Imprint
United Kingdom

Book Publisher: Ebury (**P226**)

P858 Wharncliffe Books

Publishing Imprint
United Kingdom

https://www.pen-and-sword.co.uk/Wharncliffe-Books/i/8

Book Publisher: Pen & Sword Books Ltd (**P578**)

Nonfiction > *Nonfiction Books*
History; Regional

Send: Query; Synopsis
How to send: Online submission system

Publishes local history books covering areas across the UK.

Editor: Rupert Harding

P859 White Lion Publishing

Publishing Imprint

Book Publisher: The Quarto Group, Inc. (**P633**)

P860 White Owl

Publishing Imprint

Book Publisher: Pen & Sword Books Ltd (**P578**)

P861 Whitecap Books Ltd

Book Publisher
Suite 209, 314 West Cordova Street,
Vancouver, BC, V6B 1E8
Canada

hdoll@whitecap.ca

https://www.whitecap.ca
http://www.pinterest.com/whitecapbooks/
https://twitter.com/whitecapbooks
https://www.facebook.com/whitecapbooks

Nonfiction > *Nonfiction Books*
Food; Health; Regional History; Wellbeing; Wine

Closed to approaches.

Publishes visually appealing books on food, wine, health and well-being, regional history, and regional guidebooks.

P862 Wild Goose Publications

Book Publisher
The Iona Community, Suite 9, Fairfield, 1048 Govan Road, Glasgow, G51 4XS
United Kingdom
Tel: +44 (0) 1414 297281

admin@ionabooks.com

https://www.ionabooks.com

Nonfiction > *Nonfiction Books*: Christianity

Publisher of an ecumenical community of people from different walks of life and different traditions in the Christian church.

P863 Wilderness Press

Book Publisher
c/o Keen Communications, 2204 First Avenue South, Suite 102, Birmingham, AL 35233
United States
Tel: +1 (800) 678-7006

info@adventurewithkeen.com

https://shop.adventurewithkeen.com

Nonfiction > *Nonfiction Books*
Nature; Outdoor Activities; Travel; Walking Guides

Publisher of books on the outdoors, travel, and outdoor activities.

P864 Wiley-Blackwell

Publishing Imprint
9600 Garsington Road, Oxford, OX4 2DQ
United Kingdom
Tel: +44 (0) 1865 776868
Fax: +44 (0) 1865 714591

https://www.wiley.com/WileyCDA/Brand/id-35.html

Book Publisher: John Wiley & Sons, Inc.

PROFESSIONAL > **Nonfiction**
Nonfiction Books; *Reference*

A global provider of content-enabled solutions to improve outcomes in research, education and professional practice with online tools, journals, books, databases, reference works and laboratory protocols. Has strengths in every major academic, scientific and professional field. Partners with over 800 prestigious societies representing two million members.

P865 William Collins

Publishing Imprint
United Kingdom

Book Publisher: HarperCollins UK (**P347**)

P866 William Morrow

Publishing Imprint

Book Publisher: HarperCollins

P867 Windhorse Publications Ltd

Book Publisher
38 Newmarket Road, Cambridge, CB5 8DT
United Kingdom

info@windhorsepublications.com
dhammamegha@windhorsepublications.com

https://www.windhorsepublications.com
https://www.facebook.com/windhorse.publications/
https://twitter.com/WindhorsePubs
https://www.instagram.com/windhorsepubs/
https://issuu.com/windhorsepublications
https://vimeo.com/windhorsepublications
https://soundcloud.com/windhorsepublications
https://thebuddhistcentre.com/windhorsepublications?display=latest

Nonfiction > *Nonfiction Books*: Buddhism

Send: Query
Don't send: Proposal; Full text
How to send: Email

Publishes books exploring Buddhist ideas and practices, mainly by authors connected to the Triratna Buddhist Order and Community, but also relevant and accessible works by other authors. Send initial query by email before sending proposals or manuscripts.

P868 Wise Music Group

Book Publisher

Book Publisher: Omnibus Press (**P546**)

P869 Witness

Publishing Imprint

Book Publisher: HarperCollins

P870 Wolfpack Publishing

Book Publisher
5130 S. Fort Apache Rd. 215-380, Las Vegas, NV 89148
United States

submissions@wolfpackpublishing.com

https://wolfpackpublishing.com
https://www.goodreads.com/group/show/138635-wolfpack-publishing
https://www.facebook.com/WolfpackPub/
https://twitter.com/wolfpackpub

Fiction > *Novels*
Adventure; Crime; Historical Fiction; Thrillers; Westerns

How to send: Through a literary agent

An award winning indie publisher that began life as a small Western Fiction publishing company, but which now publishes across a variety of genres.

P871 Wolters Kluwer

Book Publisher
PO Box 1030, 2400 BA, Alphen aan den Rijn
Netherlands

Book Publishers: Kluwer Law International (**P425**); Wolters Kluwer (UK) Ltd

P872 WordFarm

Book Publisher
140 Lakeside Ave, Suite A-303, Seattle, WA 98122-6538
United States
Tel: +1 (312) 281-8806

info@wordfarm.net

http://www.wordfarm.net

Fiction > *Novels*: Literary

Nonfiction > *Nonfiction Books*: Literary

Poetry > *Any Poetic Form*

Closed to approaches.

Publishes collections of poetry, short fiction, essays, and single works of fiction or literary nonfiction.

Authors: Stacy Barton; Ruth Goring; Erin Keane; Jack Leax; Lynda Rutledge; Luci Shaw; Paul Willis

Editor: Andrew Craft

P873 Words & Pictures

Publishing Imprint
The Old Brewery, 6 Blundell Street, London, N7 9BH
United Kingdom
Tel: +44 (0) 20 770 6700

QuartoHomesSubmissions@Quarto.com

https://www.quartoknows.com/words-pictures

Book Publisher: The Quarto Group, Inc. (**P633**)

CHILDREN'S > **Fiction** > *Picture Books*

How to send: Email

Always on the lookout for authors and artists with creative ideas to enhance and broaden their list of children's books. See website for submission guidelines.

Editor: Maxime Boucknooghe

Publisher: Rhiannon Findlay

P874 Wordsworth Editions

Book Publisher
PO Box 13147, Stansted, CM21 1BT
United Kingdom
Tel: +44 (0) 1920 465167

enquiries@wordsworth-editions.com

http://www.wordsworth-editions.com
https://twitter.com/WordsworthEd
https://en-gb.facebook.com/wordsworth.editions/

ADULT
Fiction > *Novels*
Poetry > *Poetry Collections*

CHILDREN'S > **Fiction** > *Novels*

Closed to approaches.

Publishes out-of-copyright titles. No submissions of new material.

Managing Director: Helen Trayler

P875 Wren & Rook

Publishing Imprint

Book Publisher: Hachette Children's Group (**P318**)

P876 Writer's Digest Books

Publishing Imprint
United States

Book Publisher: Penguin Publishing Group (**P585**)

P877 Wyldblood Press

Book Publisher; Magazine Publisher; Online Publisher
Thicket View, Bakers Row, Bakers Lane, Maidenhead, SL6 6PX
United Kingdom
Tel: +44 (0) 7961 323023

admin@wyldblood.com

https://wyldblood.com
https://www.facebook.com/Wyldblood-Press-115385210261475/

ADULT > **Fiction**
Novels: Fantasy; Science Fiction
Short Fiction: Fantasy; Science Fiction
YOUNG ADULT > **Fiction**
Novels: Fantasy; Science Fiction
Short Fiction: Fantasy; Science Fiction

Send: Query; Synopsis; Full text
How to send: Email attachment
How not to send: PDF file email attachment

We're a publisher of speculative and literary fiction. We're based in England but sell all over the world both online and in print. We believe there's always room for high quality writing and never enough spaces to find it, so we're working hard to create a new home for inspiring new work. By speculative we mean science fiction and fantasy but that reflects our tastes and not our limits. Good writing breaks through boundaries and knows no genre limits.

We will be publishing novels, anthology collections, a bimonthly magazine (from Jan 2021) (ebook and print) and flash fiction (online only).

P878 Yale University Press (London)

Book Publisher
47 Bedford Square, London, WC1B 3DP
United Kingdom
Tel: +44 (0) 20 7079 4900

trade@yaleup.co.uk

https://www.yalebooks.co.uk

ADULT > **Nonfiction**
Nonfiction Books: Architecture; Arts; Biography; Business; Computers; Current Affairs; Economics; Fashion; Health; History; Language; Legal; Literature; Mathematics; Medicine; Memoir; Music; Philosophy; Politics; Religion; Science; Society; Sociology; Technology; Wellbeing
Reference: General

CHILDREN'S > **Nonfiction** > *Nonfiction Books*: Education

Send: Query; Author bio; Market info; Table of Contents; Writing sample
How to send: Post; Email

Publishes world class scholarship for a broad readership.

Editors: Mark Eastment; Joanna Godfrey; Julian Loose; Heather McCallum; Sophie Neve

P879 Yellow Jersey

Publishing Imprint
United Kingdom

Book Publisher: Vintage (**P827**)

P880 Yes Poetry Chapbooks

Book Publisher
United States

editor@yespoetry.com

https://www.yespoetry.com

Online Magazine: Yes Poetry Magazine (**M543**)

Poetry > *Chapbook*

Closed to approaches.

Has published a poetry magazine since 2010, and since 2016 has also published poetry chapbooks. Closed to chapbook submissions as at October 2019. Check website for current status.

P881 YesYes Books

Book Publisher
1631 Broadway St #121, Portland, OR 97232-1425
United States
Tel: +1 (503) 446-3851

info@yesyesbooks.com

https://www.yesyesbooks.com
https://www.facebook.com/yesyesbooks/
https://twitter.com/YesYesBooks
https://www.instagram.com/yesyesbooks

Fiction
Novellas; *Novels*; *Short Fiction Collections*
Poetry > *Poetry Collections*

Closed to approaches.

Accepts submissions of fiction and poetry between April 1 and May 15, and via its two contests in autumn.

P882 ZED Press

Book Publisher
Canada

zedpresschapbook@gmail.com

https://zedpresswindsor.wordpress.com

Types: Poetry
Subjects: Experimental; Literary
Markets: Adult

Closed to approaches.

Publishes poetry chapbooks. Looks for experimental work and seeks to highlight voices that are underrepresented in literature.

Accepts manuscripts up to 32 pages in length, by email. See website for full guidelines.

P883 Zest Books

Publishing Imprint

Book Publisher: Lerner Publishing Group (**P438**)

P884 Zibby Books

Book Publisher
United States

info@zibbybooks.com

https://zibbyowens.com
https://zibbyowens.com/zibby-books
https://www.instagram.com/zibbybooks

Fiction > *Novels*

Nonfiction > *Nonfiction Books*: Memoir

How to send: Online contact form

A publishing home for fiction and memoir.

P885 Zonderkidz

Publishing Imprint
United States

Book Publishers: HarperCollins; Zondervan (**P886**)

P886 Zondervan

Book Publisher
United States

submissions@zondervan.com

https://www.zondervan.com

Book Publisher: HarperCollins

Nonfiction > *Nonfiction Books*: Christianity

Send: Proposal; Table of Contents; Market info; Author bio
How to send: Email

A world leading Bible publisher and provider of Christian communications.

Publishing Imprints: Zonderkidz (*P885*); Zondervan Academic (*P887*); Zondervan Books (*P888*); Zondervan Fiction (*P889*); Zondervan Gift (*P890*); Zondervan Reflective (*P891*)

P887 Zondervan Academic

Publishing Imprint
United States

Book Publishers: HarperCollins; Zondervan (**P886**)

P888 Zondervan Books

Publishing Imprint
United States

Book Publisher: Zondervan (**P886**)

P889 Zondervan Fiction

Publishing Imprint
United States

Book Publisher: Zondervan (**P886**)

P890 Zondervan Gift

Publishing Imprint
United States

Book Publisher: Zondervan (**P886**)

P891 Zondervan Reflective

Publishing Imprint
United States

Book Publisher: Zondervan (**P886**)

Index

Literary Criticism

Nonfiction Books

Get Free Access to the firstwriter.com Website

To claim your free access to the firstwriter.com website simply go to the website at https://www.firstwriter.com/subscribe and begin the subscription process as normal. On the second page, enter the required details (such as your name and address, etc.) then for "Voucher / coupon number" enter the following promotional code:

- **V92K-QKS7**

This will reduce the cost of creating a subscription by up to \$15 / £10 / €15, making it free to create a monthly, quarterly, or combination subscription. Alternatively, you can use the discount to take out an annual or life subscription at a reduced rate.

Continue the process until your account is created. Please note that you will need to provide your payment details, even if there is no up-front payment. This is in case you choose to leave your subscription running after the free initial period, but there is no obligation for you to do so.

When you use this code to take out a free subscription you are under no obligation to make any payments whatsoever and you are free to cancel your account before you make any payments if you wish.

If you need any assistance, please email support@firstwriter.com.

If you have found this book useful, please consider leaving a review on the website where you bought it.

What you get

Once you have set up access to the site you will be able to benefit from all the following features:

Databases

All our databases are updated almost every day, and include powerful search facilities to help you find exactly what you need. Searches that used to take you hours or even days in print books or on search engines can now be done in seconds, and produce more accurate and up-to-date information. Our agents database also includes independent reports from at least three separate sources, showing you which are the top agencies and helping you avoid the scams that are all over the internet. You can try out any of our databases before you subscribe:

- Search dozens of **current competitions**.
- Search **over 2,400 literary agents and agencies.**
- Search **2,300 magazines**.
- Search **over 2,700 book publishers** that **don't** charge fees.

Plus advanced features to help you with your search:

- Save searches and save time – set multiple search parameters specific to your work, save them, and then access the search results with a single click whenever you log in. You can even save multiple different searches if you have different types of work you are looking to place.
- Add personal notes to listings, visible only to you and fully searchable – helping you to organise your actions.
- Set reminders on listings to notify you when to submit your work, when to follow up, when to expect a reply, or any other custom action.
- Track which listings you've viewed and when, to help you organise your search – any listings which have changed since you last viewed them will be highlighted for your attention!

Daily email updates

As a subscriber you will be able to take advantage of our email alert service, meaning you can specify your particular interests and we'll send you automatic email updates when we change or add a listing that matches them. So if you're interested in agents dealing in romantic fiction in the United States you can have us send you emails with the latest updates about them – keeping you up to date without even having to log in.

User feedback

Our agent, publisher, and magazine databases all include a user feedback feature that allows our subscribers to leave feedback on each listing – giving you not only the chance to have your say about the markets you contact, but giving a unique authors' perspective on the listings.

Save on copyright protection fees

If you're sending your work away to publishers, competitions, or literary agents, it's vital that you first protect your copyright. As a subscriber to firstwriter.com you can do this through our site and save 10% on the copyright registration fees normally payable for protecting your work internationally through the Intellectual Property Rights Office.

Monthly newsletter

When you subscribe to firstwriter.com you also receive our monthly email newsletter – described by one publishing company as "the best in the business" – including articles, news, and interviews for writers. And the best part is that you can continue to receive the newsletter even after you stop your paid subscription – at no cost!

Terms and conditions

The promotional code contained in this publication may be used by the owner of the book only to create one subscription to firstwriter.com at a reduced cost, or for free. It may not be used by or disseminated to third parties. Should the code be misused then the owner of the book will be liable for any costs incurred, including but not limited to payment in full at the standard rate for the subscription in question. The code may be used at any time until the end of the calendar year named in the title of the publication, after which time it will become invalid. The code may be redeemed against the creation of a new account only – it cannot be redeemed against the ongoing costs of keeping a subscription open. In order to create a subscription a method of payment must be provided, but there is no obligation to make any payment. Subscriptions may be cancelled at any time, and if an account is cancelled before any payment becomes due then no payment will be made. Once a subscription has been created, the normal schedule of payments will begin on a monthly, quarterly, or annual basis, unless a life Subscription is selected, or the subscription is cancelled prior to the first payment becoming due. Subscriptions may be cancelled at any time, but if they are left open beyond the date at which the first payment becomes due and is processed then payments will not be refundable.

Printed in Great Britain
by Amazon